Lecture Notes in Computer Science 7232

Commenced Publication in 1973
Founding and Former Series Editors:
Gerhard Goos, Juris Hartmanis, and Jan van Leeuwen

Mark D. Ryan   Ben Smyth   Guilin Wang (Eds.)

Information Security Practice and Experience

8th International Conference, ISPEC 2012
Hangzhou, China, April 9-12, 2012
Proceedings

 Springer

Volume Editors

Mark D. Ryan
University of Birmingham
School of Computer Science
Birmingham B15 2TT, UK
E-mail: mdr@cs.bham.ac.uk

Ben Smyth
Toshiba Corporation
1, Komukai-Toshiba-Cho, Saiwai-ku
Kawasaki 212-8582, Japan
E-mail: toshiba@bensmyth.com

Guilin Wang
University of Wollongong
School of Computer Science and Software Engineering
Wollongong NSW 2522, Australia
E-mail: guilin@uow.edu.au

ISSN 0302-9743   e-ISSN 1611-3349
ISBN 978-3-642-29100-5   e-ISBN 978-3-642-29101-2
DOI 10.1007/978-3-642-29101-2
Springer Heidelberg Dordrecht London New York

Library of Congress Control Number: Applied for

CR Subject Classification (1998): E.3, D.4.6, C.2.0, H.2.0, K.6.5, K.4.4, J.1

LNCS Sublibrary: SL 4 – Security and Cryptology

Typesetting: Camera-ready by author, data conversion by Scientific Publishing Services, Chennai, India

Printed on acid-free paper

Springer is part of Springer Science+Business Media (www.springer.com)

Preface

The 8th International Conference on Information Security Practice and Experience (ISPEC 2012) was hosted by Hangzhou Normal University in Hangzhou, China, between 9–12 April 2012.

The ISPEC conference series is an established forum that brings together researchers and practitioners to provide a confluence of new information security technologies, including their applications and their integration with IT systems in various vertical sectors. In previous years, ISPEC has taken place in Singapore (2005), Hangzhou, China (2006), Hong Kong, China (2007), Sydney, Australia (2008), Xi'an, China (2009), Seoul, Korea (2010), and Guangzhou, China (2011). For all sessions, as this one, the conference proceedings were published by Springer in the *Lecture Notes in Computer Science* series.

In total, 109 papers from 20 countries were submitted to ISPEC 2012, and 27 were selected for inclusion in the proceedings (acceptance rate 25%), including 20 full papers and 7 works-in-progress. The accepted papers cover multiple topics of information security and applied cryptography. Each submission was anonymously reviewed by at least three reviewers and the majority of papers were reviewed by four reviewers. We are grateful to the Program Committee, which was composed of more than 53 well-known security experts from 16 countries; we heartily thank them as well as all external reviewers for their time and valued contributions to the tough and time-consuming reviewing process. In addition to the paper presentations, the program also featured three invited talks and we are grateful to each speaker for accepting our invitation to participate in the conference.

There are many people who contributed to the success of ISPEC 2012. We sincerely thank the Honorary Chair, Xiuyuan Yu, and the General Chairs, Robert H. Deng and Qi Xie, for their strong support. We also thank the Organizing Committee – namely, Xiumei Li, Wenhao Liu, Shengbao Wang, Xianqin Xiang, Mingrui Yu, and Zhenming Yuan – for dealing with local issues. We are grateful to the authors from around the world for submitting and presenting their papers. We are also deeply grateful to the Program Committee members for their fair review. It would have been impossible to organize ISPEC 2012 without the hard work of all our chairs and committees. Finally, we would like to thank all the participants for their contribution to ISPEC 2012.

April 2012

Mark D. Ryan
Ben Smyth
Guilin Wang

ISPEC 2012

8th International Conference on Information Security Practice and Experience

Hangzhou, China
April 9–12, 2012

Hosted by

Hangzhou Normal University, China

Honorary Chair

Xiuyuan Yu — Hangzhou Normal University, China

General Chairs

Robert H. Deng — Singapore Management University, Singapore
Qi Xie — Hangzhou Normal University, China

Program Chairs

Mark D. Ryan — University of Birmingham, UK
Guilin Wang — University of Wollongong, Australia

Program Committee

Moritz Becker	Microsoft, Cambridge, UK
Sergiu Bursuc	University of Birmingham, UK
Rohit Chadha	ENS Cachan, France
David Chadwick	University of Kent, UK
Kostas Chatzikokolakis	École Polytechnique, France
Kefei Chen	Shanghai Jiaotong University, China
Tom Chothia	University of Birmingham, UK
Sherman S.M. Chow	University of Waterloo, Canada
Richard Clayton	University of Cambridge, UK
Jason Crampton	Royal Holloway, University of London, UK
Cas Cremers	ETH Zürich, Switzerland
Stéphanie Delaune	ENS Cachan, France
Xuhua Ding	Singapore Management University, Singapore
Pooya Farshim	TU Darmstadt, Germany
Flavio D. Garcia	Radboud University Nijmegen, The Netherlands

Organizing Committee

Xiumei Li	Hangzhou Normal University, China
Wenhao Liu	Hangzhou Normal University, China
Shengbao Wang	Hangzhou Normal University, China
Xianqin Xiang	Hangzhou Normal University, China
Mingrui Yu	Hangzhou Normal University, China
Zhenming Yuan	Hangzhou Normal University, China

External Reviewers

Shweta Agrawal
Toru Akishita
Man Ho Au
Matteo Avalle
Joonsang Baek
Subhadeep Banik
Gilles Barthe
Rana Barua
Joseph Bonneau
Sébastien Canard
Silvio Cesare
Shan Chen
Yu Chen
Kai-Yuen Cheong
Céline Chevalier
Cheng-Kang Chu
Ozgur Dagdelen
George Danezis
Prem Laxman Das
Angelo De Caro
Gerhard De Koning Gans
Ning Ding
Ehab Elsalamouny
Jia Fan
Daniel Fett
Pierre-Alain Fouque
Steven Galbraith
David Galindo
Sugata Gangopadhyay
Wei Gao
Thomas Gross
Haihua Gu
Hauhua Gu
Fuchun Guo

Satoshi Hada
Jinguang Han
Feng Hao
Julio Cesar Hernandez-Castro
Dennis Hofheinz
Xinyi Huang
Sorina Ionica
Vincenzo Iovino
Mahavir Jhawar
Dingding Jia
Jonathan Katz
Wei Ming Khoo
Markulf Kohlweiss
Yuichi Komano
Fabien Laguillaumie
Junzuo Lai
Jean Lancrenon
Fagen Li
Juanru Li
Zhenqi Li
Hongliang Liang
Kaitai Liang
Changlu Lin
Hsi-Chung Lin
Joseph Liu
Yamin Liu
Zhen Liu
Zhiqiang Liu
Zongbin Liu
Yu Long
Haining Lu
Jiqiang Lu
Xianhui Lu
Jiqiang Lv

Sergio Maffeis
Hamid Mala
Xianping Mao
Takahiro Matsuda
Murat Moran
Steven Murdoch
Sean Murphy
David Naccache
Takashi Nishide
Kazumasa Omote
Goutam Paul
Baodong Qin
Elizabeth A. Quaglia
Mohammad Reza Reyhanitabar
Alfredo Rial
Somitra Sanadhya
Santanu Sarkar
Patrick Schweitzer
Michael Scott
Sourav Sen Gupta
Taizo Shirai
Masaaki Shirase
Riccardo Sisto
Efstathios Stathakidis
Graham Steel
Koutarou Suzuki
Katsuyuki Takashima
Xiao Tan
Qiang Tang
Stefan Tillich
Jheng-Hong Tu

Max Tuengerthal
Joop Van De Pol
Roel Verdult
Andreas Vogt
Daoshun Wang
Jun Wang
Liangliang Wang
Yu Wang
Gaven J. Watson
Robert Watson
Lingbo Wei
Yongzhuang Wei
Sheng Wen
Gaoyao Xiao
Zhi Xin
Xi Xiong
Yanjiang Yang
Rehana Yasmin
Tomoko Yonemura
Ching-Hua Yu
S. Yu
Tsz Hon Yuen
Greg Zaverucha
Hailong Zhang
Jun Zhang
Shengzhi Zhang
Wei Zhang
Xusheng Zhang
Zongyang Zhang
Mingyi Zhao
Bin Zhu

Table of Contents

Digital Signatures

Public Key Cryptography

Cryptanalysis I: Differential Attacks

Applications I.i: Oblivious Transfer

Applications I.ii: Internet Security (Works-in-Progress)

Key Management

Applied Cryptography

Applications II.i: PINs

Applications II.ii: Fundamentals (Works-in-Progress)

Cryptanalysis II: Fault Attacks and Key Recovery

Cryptanalysis III: Key Recovery (Works-in-Progress)

A Pre-computable Signature Scheme with Efficient Verification for RFID

Fuchun Guo[1], Yi Mu[1], Willy Susilo[1], and Vijay Varadharajan[2]

[1] Centre for Computer and Information Security Research
School of Computer Science and Software Engineering
University of Wollongong, Wollongong, Australia
{fg278,ymu,wsusilo}@uow.edu.au
[2] Information and Networked Systems Security Research
Department of Computing, Faculty of Science
Macquarie University, Sydney, Australia
vijay.varadharajan@mq.edu.au

Abstract. Passive RFID tags have limited rewritable memory for data storage and limited computation power, which pose difficulties to implement security protection on RFID tags. It has been shown that strong security and privacy protections for RFID require utilizing public-key cryptography. Unfortunately, the implementation of public key cryptography is infeasible in low-cost passive tags. With this issue in mind, in this work, we propose a pre-computable signature scheme with a very efficient signature verification algorithm for RFID applications. Our signature scheme is provably secure under the DDH assumption and a variant of q-SDH assumption. With pre-computations, no exponentiation is required in our signature verification. Our research shows that it is feasible for low-cost RFID tags to verify signatures with the basic modular multiplication only (if they have a small amount of writable memory).

Keywords: RFID, Low-cost RFID tags, Signature verification, Modular multiplication.

1 Introduction

Radio-frequency identification (RFID) is a technique that can be used to replace barcodes. In an RFID system, an RFID tag, which contains a unique identification code, can be identified by an RFID reader through radio waves without requiring any physical contact. Using this technique, large-scale objects can be identified and managed easily. RFID exhibits many applications. For example, RFID has been found applicable in supply chain management for goods tracking [2], healthcare for tracking disabled people [17] and warehouses for distribution and inventory [7].

RFID technique introduces new security challenges. A strong security and privacy protection [26,22] requires public-key cryptography, which needs to perform exponentiations. However, passive RFID tags have limited rewritable memory

M.D. Ryan, B. Smyth, and G. Wang (Eds.): ISPEC 2012, LNCS 7232, pp. 1–16, 2012.

and lightweight logic circuits [27]. According to [14], it requires at least 11,904 gates to implement the point multiplication (i.e., exponentiation) of elliptic curve cryptography and higher for others. Circuits for implementing exponentiation are costly for low-cost RFID tags.

In this work, we explore new signature schemes with efficient signature verification for low-cost tags. We believe that the tag's ability to authenticate RFID readers is a significant issue, which should be looked at. A secure authentication between tags and readers can be simply done by utilizing a symmetric cryptography (e.g. a pseudo random function) with a shared secret [22]. However, to enhance the RFID security to a satisfactory level, we must adopt digital signatures. It not only provides secure reader-to-tag authentication, but also a proof so that readers cannot deny communications with tags. We found that all traditional signature schemes must involve exponentiations in signature verification. To be able to verify signatures, RFID tags must add a costly exponentiation circuit. To find a signature scheme without exponentiations in signature verification therefore becomes interesting and challenging.

Currently, there exist the following three related approaches that could potentially improve the efficiency of signature verification.

Divisible Online/Offline Signatures. Online/offline signatures were proposed to improve the efficiency of signature generation. The notion of divisible online/offline signatures [12] is a variant of online/offline signatures [9], where the offline signature token can be sent to the verifier prior to signature generation. However, most of divisible online/offline signature schemes shown in [12] do not meet the requirement of pre-verification and require exponentiation computations in the online phase. The exception is the generic scheme presented in [9] based on the one-time signature scheme [16]. With an interaction between signer and verifier in the offline phase, the verifier performs hashing operations only in the online phase. This scheme requires the verifier to interact with the signer prior to signature generation and the signer to store all one-time signing keys.

Server (Signer)-Aided Signature Verification. Server (signer)-aided signature verification enables the verifier to delegate a substantial part of verification workload to a powerful server like [13,8] (or singer like [18]). With pre-computations, the best efficient server-aided verification protocols can speed up signature verification but still requiring a small exponentiation computation. The server-aided verification technique indeed improves the verification efficiency. However, the circuit implementation of this algorithm is not reduced. The small exponentiation based on an elliptic group still requires the point doubling and point addition like normal exponentiations. This scheme improves verification efficiency, but it is not suitable for low-cost RFID tags.

Batch Verification. Batch verification of digital signatures was studied in [11,1,25,10]. Roughly speaking, with this verification approach, the cost of verifying n signatures together is significantly less than the sum of cost one by one in a separated way. Batch verification is useful in reducing the pairing computation of pairing-based signatures and the time of verifying batch signatures, since the pairing computation generally more expensive than exponentiations. This technique improves the verification efficiency on average, but it gives a more complicated algorithm in signature verification compared to traditional signature schemes. It is therefore not suitable for RFID tags to simplify verification algorithm.

In this paper, we propose a pre-computable signature scheme in which signature verification is very efficient without need of exponentiation computations. Intuitively, when the signer generates a signature of any message for the verifier, the verifier with a pre-computation token will interact with the signer in order to avoid exponentiation computations in signature verification. The rest of computation for the verifier is a modular multiplication (a 160-bit modulus) and bitwise comparisons. We prove the security of our signature scheme under the DDH assumption held in the pairing group and a new assumption called the oracle q-SDH assumption. In Section 4.2, we compare our scheme to the divisible online/offline signature scheme and the server (signer)-aided signature verification. It shows that ours is the most computationally efficient for the verifier.

To apply our signature verification in low-cost RFID tags without exponentiation computations, we assume that pre-computation tokens for tags are generated outside (e.g. generated by the trusted backend server) with a powerful device. When verifying signatures, tags only need the computational capability of modular multiplication and bitwise comparisons. In Section 4.1, we show that the logic gate requirement of our verification algorithm for tags is significantly less compared to the point multiplication according to the implementation in [14,20]. As an additional note, we notice that pre-computation consumes about 2KB memory for each signature verification, and each pre-computation token is one-time in use. The tradeoff of memory and computing capability for RFID is none-trivial and has been studied in [15] for identification. Our scheme indicates that for those low-cost tags with at least 2KB writable memory, to add the capability of signature verification, we only need to add the circuit of modular multiplication instead of point multiplication.

Paper Organization. We organize the rest of this paper as follows. In Section 2, we introduce some preliminaries and definitions of our pre-computable signature scheme. The detail of our signature construction is proposed in Section 3. In Section 4, we discuss the hardware requirement for RFID application and give the comparison. In Section 5, we show how to further improve signature verification when messages to be signed are partially known. We conclude this paper in Section 6.

2   Preliminaries and Definitions

2.1   Definition of Our Signature

A pre-computable signature scheme with efficient verification consists of the following four algorithms.

Setup: Taking as input a security parameter 1^λ, the signer generates a key pair (pk, sk), where pk is the public key and sk is the signing key.

Pre-Com: Taking as input the public key pk, the signature recipient (verifier) generates the one-time pre-computable token PC without interacting with the signer.

Sign-Verify: Taking as input the message m, the token PC provided by the recipient and the signing key sk provided by the signer, the signature generation protocol returns a valid signature σ_m of m or outputs 0 (reject). This is an interactive protocol between the signature recipient and the signer.

Re-verify: Taking as input the signed message (m, σ_m) and the public key pk, return 1 if σ_m is a valid signature on m signed by sk, or 0 for invalid. This algorithm allows anyone to verify the signature.

The completeness of the above signature scheme requires that for all (pk, sk), tokens PC and messages m, a signature σ_m of m accepted by the recipient in the Sign-Verify algorithm must be also accepted by a verifier in the Re-verify algorithm.

Each pre-computable token PC is one-time for the recipient during running the Sign-Verify algorithm. To be able to verify k signatures, the signature recipient should pre-compute $PC_1, PC_2, \cdots, PC_k$. This is similar to the structure of online/offline signatures [9,24] for efficient signing in which each pre-computation token is one-time in use.

Our signature definition is different from traditional signatures. In traditional signature schemes, there is only one verification algorithm for all verifiers. In our definition, the signature recipient and other verifiers run different verification algorithms. We define the Pre-Com and Sign-Verify algorithms for those signature recipient who will receive signatures from signers, and the Re-verify algorithm for others. Our pre-computable signature scheme speeds up verification for the verifiers of signature recipient.

Applying the signature scheme in RFID systems, readers are the signers and tags are the signature recipients. The tag owner runs the Pre-Com algorithms for tags, and the tags run the Sign-Verify algorithm for receiving and verifying signatures. Signatures are re-verified through the Re-verify algorithm. Here, the tag owner can be the trusted backend server of RFID system, and we assume that the tag owner can securely upload pre-computation tokens to tags through a secure channel, which is guaranteed by a basic authentication ability of RFID tags described in [26,22].

The signature scheme should be secure against chosen-message attacks. The model modified from the standard model is defined as follows:

Setup: The challenger runs the algorithm Setup to obtain a pair of public key and signing key (pk, sk). The public key pk is forwarded to the adversary.

Query: The adversary adaptively makes a signature query on m_i. To query the signature, the adversary computes PC and takes as input (m, PC) into the Sign-Verify algorithm. The challenger responds by following the Sign-Verify algorithm. Let q_s be the number of signature queries made by the adversary in this phase.

Forgery: The adversary outputs a signed message pair (m^*, σ_{m^*}) and wins the game if no signature query on m^* and Re-Verify$[\sigma_{m^*}, m, pk] = 1$.

Definition 1. *A pre-computable signature scheme is (t, q_s, ϵ)-secure against cho-sen-message attacks defined above, if no adversary who makes q_s signature queries can forge a valid signature with probability ϵ in t polynomial time.*

2.2 Bilinear Groups

Our signature scheme is built from a bilinear pairing or Tate pairing denoted by $\mathbb{BP} = (g_1, g_2, \mathbb{G}_1, \mathbb{G}_2, \mathbb{G}_T, p, e)$. Here, g_1 is a generator of $\mathbb{G}_1$, g_2 is a generator of $\mathbb{G}_2$, p is the group order of all $\mathbb{G}_1, \mathbb{G}_2, \mathbb{G}_T$, and the bilinear map $e : \mathbb{G}_1 \times \mathbb{G}_2 \to \mathbb{G}_T$ satisfies that

- For all $g_1 \in \mathbb{G}_1, g_2 \in \mathbb{G}_2$ and $a_1, a_2 \in \mathbb{Z}_p$, we have $e(g_1^{a_1}, g_2^{a_2}) = e(g_1, g_2)^{a_1 a_2}$.
- If g_1, g_2 are generators of $\mathbb{G}_1, \mathbb{G}_2$ respectively, we have $e(g_1, g_2)$ is a generator of $\mathbb{G}_T$.

If $\mathbb{G}_1 \neq \mathbb{G}_2$, we also name $\mathbb{BP}$ as asymmetric pairing; otherwise, we call it symmetric pairing. Many cryptosystems (e.g. [3]) based on bilinear groups can be instantiated with an asymmetric pairing or a symmetric pairing. An asymmetric pairing is used to reduce the presentation of groups elements. Following the same notations in [3,4], the elements from $\mathbb{G}_1$ can be half size of that from $\mathbb{G}_2$. However, some of them (e.g. [5]) must use the asymmetric pairing, and require the decisional Diffie-Hellman (DDH) assumption holds in the group $\mathbb{G}_1$ (even although the DDH assumption in $\mathbb{G}_2$ is easy). Our scheme requires the hardness of DDH problem in the group $\mathbb{G}_1$, but does not require an efficiently computable group homomorphism $\psi : \mathbb{G}_2 \to \mathbb{G}_1$.

2.3 Complexity Assumptions

The complexity assumptions we resort to in our scheme are the DDH assumption in $\mathbb{G}_1$ and a variant of the q-Strong Diffie-Hellman assumption [3], associated with an oracle. We name the variant q-SDH assumption as the Oracle q-Strong Diffie-Hellman assumption (Oracle q-SDH, in short).

Decisional Diffie-Hellman Assumption:
    Instance: $(g_1,\ g_1^{x_1},\ g_1^{r_1 x_1},\ g_1^{x_2},\ g_1^{r_2 x_2}) \in \mathbb{G}_1$.
    Intractable: check $r_1 \overset{?}{=} r_2$.

Definition 2. *The DDH assumption is (t, ϵ)-hard in $\mathbb{G}_1$ if no adversary can check whether r_1 is equal to r_2 in running time t with probability ϵ at least.*

Given an instance of DDH problem $(g_1^{x_1}, g_1^{r_1 x_1}, g_1^{x_2}, g_1^{r_2 x_2})$ under the base g_1, it is actually composed of two instances of the DL problem $(g_1^{x_1}, g_1^{r_1 x_1})$ and $(g_1^{x_2}, g_1^{r_2 x_2})$ under different bases. When the DDH assumption holds, we have it is hard to decide whether the solutions of two DL instances under different bases are the same or not. We shall adopt this property to construct our signature scheme secure against malicious signers.

Before defining the oracle q-SDH assumption, we firstly revisit the q-SDH assumption and the modified q-SDH assumption [6].

q-Strong Diffie-Hellman Assumption:

Instance: $(g_1, g_1^a, g_1^{a^2}, \cdots, g_1^{a^q}) \in \mathbb{G}_1$ and $(g_2, g_2^a) \in \mathbb{G}_2$.

Intractable: find any pair $\left(c, g_1^{\frac{1}{a+c}}\right) \in \mathbb{Z}_p \times \mathbb{G}_1$.

Modified q-Strong Diffie-Hellman Assumption:

Instance: $(g_1, g_1^a) \in \mathbb{G}_1, (g_2, g_2^a) \in \mathbb{G}_2$ and q pairs $\left(c_i, g_1^{\frac{1}{a+c_i}}\right) \in \mathbb{Z}_p \times \mathbb{G}_1$.

Intractable: find any pair $\left(c, g_1^{\frac{1}{a+c}}\right) \in \mathbb{Z}_p \times \mathbb{G}_1$ for $c \notin \{c_1, c_2, \cdots, c_q\}$.

Oracle q-Strong Diffie-Hellman Assumption:

Instance: $(g_1, g_1^a) \in \mathbb{G}_1, (g_2, g_2^a) \in \mathbb{G}_2$ and $O_a(\cdot)$.

Oracle: On input $(c_i, h_i) \in \mathbb{Z}_p \times \mathbb{G}_1$,

the oracle computes $O_a(c_i, h_i) = h_i^{\frac{1}{a+c_i}}$.

Intractable: find any pair $\left(c, g_1^{\frac{1}{a+c}}\right) \in \mathbb{Z}_p \times \mathbb{G}_1$ for $c \notin \{c_1, c_2, \cdots, c_q\}$.

According to the algebraic algorithm [21] with respect to the group $\mathbb{G}_1$, h_i falls into three types:

- $h_i = g_1^{d_i}$, where d_i is chosen by the adversary. We have that

$$h_i^{\frac{1}{a+c_i}} = g_1^{\frac{d_i}{a+c_i}} .$$

  Since the exponent d_i can be removed by the adversary, the response from the oracle is equivalent to $g_1^{\frac{1}{a+c_i}}$ of the modified q-SDH assumption.

- $h_i = g_1^{ad_i}$, where d_i is chosen by the adversary. We have that

$$h_i^{\frac{1}{a+c_i}} = g_1^{\frac{ad_i}{a+c_i}} = g_1^{d_i - \frac{c_i d_i}{a+c_i}} .$$

  Since $g_1^{d_i}$ and the exponent $c_i d_i$ can be removed by the adversary, the response from the oracle is equivalent to $g_1^{\frac{1}{a+c_i}}$ of the modified q-SDH assumption.

- $h_i = g^{\frac{1}{\prod_{c_i \in \mathcal{C}}(a+c_i)}}$ or $g^{\frac{a}{\prod_{c_i \in \mathcal{C}}(a+c_i)}}$, where $\mathcal{C}$ is any subset of $\{c_1, c_2, \cdots, c_q\}$ chosen by the adversary. Without loss of generality, let $h_i = g_1^{\frac{ad_i}{(a+c_1)(a+c_2)}}$ where d_i is chosen by the adversary. We have that

$$h_i^{\frac{1}{a+c_i}} = g_1^{\frac{ad_i}{(a+c_1)(a+c_2)(a+c_i)}} = g_1^{\frac{d_i}{(a+c_1)(a+c_2)} - \frac{c_i d_i}{(a+c_1)(a+c_2)(a+c_i)}} .$$

  It is easy to check that given the pairs $(c_1, g_1^{\frac{1}{a+c_1}})$, $(c_2, g_1^{\frac{1}{a+c_2}})$ and $(c_i, g_1^{\frac{1}{a+c_i}})$, we can compute $g_1^{\frac{1}{(a+c_1)(a+c_2)}}$ and $g_1^{\frac{1}{(a+c_1)(a+c_2)(a+c_i)}}$. Therefore, the response from the oracle is equivalent to the pairs of the modified q-SDH assumption.

According to the above analysis, what the oracle responds is equivalent to q pairs of $(c_i, g_1^{\frac{1}{a+c_i}})$. In comparison with the modified q-SDH assumption, the proposed assumption is still stronger since all its random values c_i are adaptively chosen by the adversary; while they are passively given by the instance of the modified q-SDH assumption. Therefore, as long as the adversary does not query (c, h^*) for any h^* to the oracle, it seems that the oracle would be useless for computing the pair $(c, g^{1/(a+c)})$ for any $c \notin \{c_1, c_2, \cdots, c_q\}$.

Definition 3. *The Oracle q-SDH assumption is (t, ϵ)-hard if no adversary can find any pair $(c, g_1^{1/(a+c)})$ for $c \notin \{c_1, c_2, \cdots, c_q\}$ in running time t with probability ϵ at least after making q queries to the oracle.*

3   Our Signature Scheme

3.1   Construction

In our signature scheme, the message space is $\mathbb{Z}_p$, which is 160 bits for $|p| = 160$. We can extend the message space into arbitrary bit stings by utilizing a collision-resistant hash functions $H : \{0, 1\}^* \to \mathbb{Z}_p$. However, we believe that 160-bit message space is sufficient in many RFID scenarios, such as authentication in [26,22]. The message space therefore is assumed to be of $\mathbb{Z}_p$ in this paper.

Setup: Taking as input a security parameter 1^λ, the signer randomly chooses a bilinear pairing $\mathbb{BP} = (g_1, g_2, \mathbb{G}_1, \mathbb{G}_2, \mathbb{G}_T, p, e)$ and a random value $\alpha \in \mathbb{Z}_p$, and sets $h_1 = g_1^\alpha, h_2 = g_2^\alpha$. The public key and the signing key are defined as

$$pk = (\mathbb{BP}, \ h_1, h_2), \quad sk = \alpha.$$

Pre-Com: Taking as input the public key pk, the signature recipient does as follows:

- Randomly choose $r, y, \beta, x_1, x_2, \cdots, \ x_{2n} \in \mathbb{Z}_p$ and a $2n$-bit string $B = b_1 b_2 \cdots b_{2n} \in \{0, 1\}^{2n}$, where half bits are zero. Here, n is a security parameter about error probability that will be discussed later. We let B_0 be the subset of $\{1, 2, \cdots, 2n\}$ containing j if $b_j = 0$, and let B_1 be a subset with an analogous definition for $b_j = 1$.
- Compute S_i and v_i for all $i = 1, 2, \cdots, 2n$ as

$$\begin{cases} b_i = 0 : & S_i = \left(g_1^{x_i(r\alpha - y)}, \ g_1^{x_i} \right), \ v_i = g_1^{x_i r} \\[2mm] b_i = 1 : & S_i = \left(g_1^{x_i(r\beta - y)}, \ g_1^{x_i} \right), \ v_i = x_i \end{cases}.$$

- Set the one-time pre-computable token PC as

$$PC = \left(r, y, \beta, B, S_1, S_2, \cdots, S_{2n}, v_1, v_2, \cdots, v_{2n} \right).$$

Sign-Verify: Given a message $m \in \mathbb{Z}_p$ to be signed, the signer takes as input sk and the recipient takes as input PC. The interactive protocol for signature generation and verification is described as follows:

- The recipient computes $w = rm + y \pmod{p}$ and sends $S_m = (S_1, S_2, \cdots, S_{2n}, w)$ to the signer.
- Upon receiving S_m, let $S_i = (s_{1,i}, s_{2,i})$, the signer computes u_i for all $i = 1, 2, \cdots, 2n$ as

$$u_i = \left(s_{1,i} \cdot s_{2,i}^{w} \right)^{\frac{1}{\alpha + m}},$$

and forwards $U_m = (u_1, u_2, \cdots, u_{2n})$ to the recipient.
- Upon receiving U_m, the recipient checks u_i or sets σ_i for all $i = 1, 2, \cdots, 2n$ as follows

$$\begin{cases} i \in B_0 : & \text{check } u_i \overset{?}{=} v_i \\ i \in B_1 : & \text{set } \sigma_i = (u_i, v_i) \end{cases}.$$

If $u_i \neq v_i$ holds for any $i \in B_0$, return 0. Otherwise, the signature of m is

$$\sigma_m = \left(r, \beta, \sigma_i : i \in B_1 \right).$$

Re-verify: Taking as input m, σ_m and pk, the verifier checks that the pairing equation

$$e\left(u_i^{\frac{1}{v_i r (\beta + m)}}, h_2 g_2^m \right) = e(g_1, g_2)$$

holds for (r, β) and any pair (u_i, v_i) from σ_m. If it is correct, return 1; otherwise, return 0.

Remark 1. In the above signature scheme, the message m to be signed could let $\alpha + m = 0$ or $\beta + m = 0$. However, the probability is negligible, and we directly assume that both $\alpha + m$ and $\beta + m$ are nonzero during signing and verification.

Remark 2. In our **Re-verify** algorithm, if the input by both the signer and the verifier is correct, the verification is about one pairing and two exponentiations. Otherwise, it will cost n pairing computation and $n + 1$ exponentiation computations for the worst case. According to the Theorem 1, the verification will cost i pairing and $i + 1$ exponentiations with probability $1/2^i$ at most.

3.2   Correctness

In our signature scheme, the actual signing proof on a message m is the group element $g_1^{1/(\alpha + m)}$. This signature format is the same as [3], where the verification approximately requires one pairing and one exponentiation. Instead of verifying the correctness of signature, the signature recipient in our scheme verifies whether the input by the signer is valid or not.

If $S_i = (s_{1,i}, s_{2,i}) = \left(g_1^{x_i(r\alpha - y)}, \ g_1^{x_i} \right)$, we have

$$s_{1,i} \cdot s_{2,i}^{w} = g_1^{x_i(r\alpha - y)} \cdot (g_1^{x_i})^{rm+y} = g_1^{x_i r(\alpha + m)}$$

$$u_i = \left(s_{1,i} \cdot s_{2,i}^{w} \right)^{\frac{1}{\alpha + m}} = g_1^{x_i r} = v_i.$$

When the recipient provides this kind of S_i, the recipient believes that the input by the signer is $\frac{1}{\alpha+m}$ if $u_i = v_i$. However, the recipient cannot get the signing proof. We call this S_i as *verification token*.

If $S_i = (s_{1,i}, s_{2,i}) = \left(g_1^{x_i(r\beta - y)}, \ g_1^{x_i}\right)$, we have

$$\left(s_{1,i} \cdot s_{2,i}^{w}\right)^{\frac{1}{\alpha+m}} = \left(g_1^{x_i(r\beta-y)} \cdot (g_1^{x_i})^{rm+y}\right)^{\frac{1}{\alpha+m}} = g_1^{\frac{x_i r(\beta+m)}{\alpha+m}}$$

$$u_i^{\frac{1}{v_i r(\beta+m)}} = g_1^{\frac{1}{\alpha+m}}.$$

When the recipient provides this kind of S_i, the recipient will get the valid signing proof if the input is $\frac{1}{\alpha+m}$. However, the recipient cannot verify whether the input by the signer is $\frac{1}{\alpha+m}$ or not. We call this S_i as *proof token*.

In our signature scheme, verification tokens are mixed with proof tokens under on the DDH assumption. The recipient provides both tokens to the signer such that the input to the proof tokens can be checked from verification tokens. Precisely, $2n$ numbers of S_i are sent to the signer, where half of them are verification tokens and the others are proof tokens. Each S_i is generated independently, and it is actually an instance of DL problem. When the DDH assumption holds in the group $\mathbb{G}_1$, we immediately get that all S_i are indistinguishable. If U_m is passed the check, the recipient believes that there exists at least one input to the proof token is $\frac{1}{\alpha+m}$, and therefore the received signature is valid.

The only error probability of accepting an invalid signature is that the signer successfully distinguishes the function of each token. The following theorem shows that this probability is negligible when n is enough large.

Theorem 1. *Assuming that the DDH assumption holds in the group $\mathbb{G}_1$, σ_m is a valid signature with error probability*

$$\frac{1}{\binom{2n}{n}} + \binom{2n}{2} \cdot \epsilon,$$

where ϵ is the advantage of breaking the DDH assumption.

Proof. According to our scheme, the recipient was cheated only and if only $u_i = v_i$ holds for all $i \in B_0$ and $u_i^{\frac{1}{v_i r(\beta+m)}} \neq g_1^{\frac{1}{\alpha+m}}$ holds for all $i \in B_1$. To successfully cheat the recipient, the signer must do as follows:

- Guess the subset $B_0 \in \{1, 2, \cdots, 2n\}$ chosen by the recipient correctly.
- Compute u_i the same as the Sign-Verify algorithm for all $i \in B_0$.
- For all $i \in B_1$, choose $\alpha' \neq \alpha$ and compute u_i as

$$\left(s_{1,i} \cdot s_{2,i}^{w}\right)^{\frac{1}{\alpha'+m}}.$$

We let $\Pr[Success]$ be the probability that the adversary (signer) computes the subset B_0 successfully. Let $\Pr[Guess]$ be the probability that the adversary finds the subset by guessing, and let $\Pr[Dis]$ be the probability that the adversary finds the subset by distinguishing verification tokens from proof tokens. We have

$$\Pr[Success] \le \Pr[Guess] + \Pr[Dis].$$

There are $\binom{2n}{n}$ choices of B_0 set as the subset of $\{1, 2, \cdots, 2n\}$. Since B_0 is randomly chosen, we therefore have

$$\Pr[Guess] = \frac{1}{\binom{2n}{n}}.$$

The adversary is given $S_m = (S_1, S_2, \cdots, S_{2n}, w)$, where verification tokens and proof tokens are randomized. Let $\beta' = r\beta \bmod p$. Since r, y, β are randomly and independently picked from $\mathbb{Z}_p$, we have β' is also random and independent from r and y. Without loss of generality, let $r_1 = r\alpha - y$ and $r_2 = r\beta - y$. We have

$$(r_1, r_2, w) = (r, y, \beta') \cdot \begin{pmatrix} \alpha & -1 & 0 \\ 0 & -1 & 1 \\ m & 1 & 0 \end{pmatrix}^T = (r, y, \beta') \cdot \mathbf{A}^T.$$

Since the determinant of $\mathbf{A}$ is $-(\alpha + m)$ that is nonzero (Remark 1), we have r_1 and r_2 are universally random and independent of w. Therefore, $(S_1, S_2, \cdots, S_{2n})$ containing r_1, r_2 are independent of w.

According to the definition of S_i, each token $S_i = (s_{i,1}, s_{i,2}) = (g_1^{x_i r_i}, g_1^{x_i})$ is an instance of DL problem, where $r_i \in \{r_1, r_2\}$ is the solution of $s_{i,2}^{r_1} = s_{i,1}$ or $s_{i,2}^{r_2} = s_{i,1}$. Given any two tokens S_i, S_j, let $S_i = (g_1^{x_i r_i}, g_1^{x_i})$ and $S_j = (g_1^{x_j r_j}, g_1^{x_j})$, where $r_i, r_j \in \{r_1, r_2\}$. Since (x_i, r_i, x_j, r_j) are random and independent, this is an instance of DDH assumption. The adversary will distinguish whether $r_i = r_j$ with probability ϵ at most. There are $\binom{2n}{2}$ different instances from U_m in total. We yield the following union bound

$$\Pr[Dis] \le \binom{2n}{2} \cdot \epsilon.$$

Putting the above two probability bound, we obtain the theorem. $\qquad\square$

When the DDH assumption holds, ϵ is negligible such that $\binom{2n}{2}\epsilon$ is also negligible. We can choose a proper n to restrict the error probability in a small range. For example, we can set $n = 15$ for error probability bounded with 2^{-30}.

3.3   Security

Theorem 2. *Assume that the Oracle q-SDH assumption holds with (t', ϵ'), we can use it to construct (t, q_s, ϵ)-secure signature scheme.*

$$t = t' - O(nq_s \cdot T), \qquad q_s = \frac{q}{2n}, \qquad \epsilon = \epsilon',$$

where T is the average time of an exponentiation in the group $\mathbb{G}_1$.

Proof. Suppose there exists an adversary $\mathcal{A}$ who can break our signature scheme with (t, q_s, ϵ) advantage. We construct an algorithm $\mathcal{B}$ that solves the Oracle q-SDH assumption with advantage (t', ϵ') at least. The algorithm $\mathcal{B}$ is given $(g_1, g_1^a) \in \mathbb{G}_1, (g_2, g_2^a) \in \mathbb{G}_2$ and an oracle $O_a()$. The aim of $\mathcal{B}$ is to output $(c, g_1^{1/(a+c)}) \in \mathbb{Z}_p \times \mathbb{G}_1$ with a new c never queried to the oracle. $\mathcal{B}$ interacts with the adversary as follows.

Setup: The algorithm $\mathcal{B}$ sets $pk = (\mathbb{BP}, g_1^a, g_2^a)$ and forwards this public key to the adversary, where the signing key α is simulated with a in the given instance.

Query: The adversary makes a signature query by presenting (m_i, S_{m_i}), which is adaptively chosen. Let $S_{m_i} = (S_1, S_2, \cdots, S_{2n}, w_i)$ and $S_i = (s_{1,i}, s_{2,i})$ for all $i = 1, 2, \cdots, 2n$. The algorithm $\mathcal{B}$ responds by computing $u_i' = s_{1,i} \cdot s_{2,i}^{w_i}$ for all $i = 1, 2, \cdots, 2n$, and querying the following $2n$ pairs to the oracle $O_a()$

$$\Big((m_i, u_1'), \ (m_i, u_2'), \ \cdots, \ (m_i, u_{2n}') \Big).$$

Let $u_i = (u_i')^{\frac{1}{a+m_i}}$ be the response to (m_i, w_i) from the oracle. The algorithm $\mathcal{B}$ forwards $U_{m_i} = (u_1, u_2, \cdots, u_{2n})$ to the adversary.

Forgery: The adversary $\mathcal{A}$ outputs a forged signature (m^*, σ_{m^*}). Let σ_{m^*} be

$$\Big(r, \beta, (u_1, v_1), \ (u_2, v_2), \ \cdots, \ (u_n, v_n) \Big).$$

If it is a valid signature, it means that there exists one pair, e.g. (u_1, v_1), such that

$$e\Big(u_1^{\frac{1}{v_1 r(\beta + m^*)}}, \ h_2 g_2^{m^*} \Big) = e(g_1, g_2).$$

The algorithm $\mathcal{B}$ outputs $(m^*, u_1^{\frac{1}{v_1 r(\beta + m^*)}}) = (m^*, g_1^{\frac{1}{a+m^*}})$, which is the solution to the Oracle q-SDH assumption.

The main time cost for $\mathcal{B}$ is the signature simulation, where each signature query requires $O(n)$ exponentiations. The algorithm $\mathcal{B}$ makes $2n$ queries to the oracle for each signature query, and there is no aborting in the above simulation. Therefore, we obtain Theorem 2. This completes our security proof.   □

4   Application to RFID

4.1   Hardware Requirement

Applying our signature scheme to RFID, we let tag owner run the Pre-Com algorithm and RFID tags run the Sign-Verify algorithm. The tag owner computes and uploads pre-computation tokens into tags in a secure channel, such that tags enable to verify signatures generated by pre-defined readers. The remaining computation for tags is mainly dominated by a modular multiplication in the Sign-Verify algorithm.

Circuit Requirement. Our Sign-Verify algorithm is computationally efficient for tags, consisting of the modular multiplication $rm + y \pmod{p}$ and bitwise comparisons. Since the bitwise comparison is very simple in architecture, we discuss the circuit requirement of modular multiplication only.

We found that our modular multiplication falls into the type presented by Oren and Feldhofer in [20], and can be replaced with randomized multiplication [23] without modular reductions. More precisely, $rm + y \pmod{p}$ can be replaced with $rm + y + R \cdot p$ without affecting the security, as long as R is a $|p| + 80$-bit random string for 80-bit security. To avoid the modular reduction, we compute $y' = y + R \cdot p$ instead of y in the pre-computation phase in which $|y'| = 2|p| + 80$. The rest of verification is $rm + y'$. The implementation of randomized multiplication with a 1024-bit modulus in [20] fits completely into 4681 gates. Our Sign-Verify algorithm for tags merely need the randomized multiplication with a 160-bit modulus. Following the result of Table 3 in [20], our randomized multiplication only requires the components of memory for r, y', the multiplexers, multiplier, adder and accumulator, which are no more than 2000 gates available for a low-cost tag [27]. It saves a significant gates compared to the point multiplication described in [14].

Memory Requirement. Each signature verification requires a one-time token PC defined as

$$PC = \left(r, y', \beta, B, S_1, S_2, \cdots, S_{2n}, v_1, v_2, \cdots, v_{2n} \right).$$

For 2^{-30} error probability in signature verification, we have $n = 15$. For 80-bit security of signature scheme, we have $|p| = |\mathbb{G}_1| = 160$ (bits) [3]. Putting these parameter into $|PC|$, we finally have

$$|PC| = (4 + n)|p| + 2n + 5n|\mathbb{G}_1| + 80 \approx 2KB.$$

That is, each signature verification requires about 2KB memory for pre-computation token. We notice that the token size can be reduced with a pseudo random function to generate all randomness stored in PC. I.E., replacing all $v_i = x_i$ with a random seed.

The above analysis of circuit requirement and memory requirement indicates that signature verification is feasible for those tags with 2KB writable memory but very limited computational capability. For polynomial verifications, our scheme requires a large amount of memory and is impractical for tags. However, when RFID tags alternately communicate with readers and tag owners, a small rewritable memory (e.g. 4KB) is obviously sufficient. Our scheme is more suitable in those scenarios where tags are to receive few important messages signed by pre-defined readers.

4.2   Comparisons

In this section, we compare our signature scheme to the divisible online/offline signature scheme and server-aided signature verification in terms of verification structure, computational efficiency and hardware requirement.

The divisible online/offline signature scheme from the Lamport one-time signature can be described as follows. In the offline phase, the signer pre-signs on $H_{ots} = \big(H(x_{1,0}), H(x_{1,1}), H(x_{2,0}), H(x_{2,1}), \cdots, H(x_{L,0}), H(x_{L,1})\big)$ by utilizing a traditional signature scheme, and this signature is pre-verified by the verifier. In the online phase, given an L-bit message m to be signed, the signer reveals $x_{i,b}$ to the verifier if the i-bit message is b for all i. The signature verification is to check whether $x_{i,b}$ is the pre-image of $H(x_{i,b})$. In comparison with this scheme, our scheme does not require the verifier to interact with the signer in the pre-computation phase, or require the signer to store all x_i for signature generation.

The server(signer)-aided signature verification proposed in [18] is the most efficient for signature verification. In the pre-computation phase, the verifier pre-computes one exponentiation. Given a signature to be verified, with a pre-computation token, the verifier can delegate two exponentiations to the server (or signer). The rest of verification is one exponentiation with a small exponent and two modular multiplications.

Table 1. Comparison of three schemes for efficient signature verification

	Pre-computation Size	Signature Verification
DOOS	6.4KB	160 times of hashing
SAV	0.06KB	One exponentiation with a 30-bit exponent and two modular multiplications
Our scheme	2KB	One modular multiplication

We compare the efficiency and list the result in Table 1. The comparison is under the assumption of 80-bit security and 30-bit error probability. We use DOOS to denote the above divisible online/offline signature scheme, and SAV to denote the above server-aided signature verification. We observe that all verifications must perform bitwise comparisons. This computation is negligible in comparison with others, and not considered in our discussion. A hash function architecture for low-cost RFID tags has been proposed in [19], but it still requires 5527 gates. Our verification is the most efficient with one modular multiplication, and the architecture is the most cheapest compared to those schemes.

5   Signature Verification of Partially Known Messages

We have described a pre-computable signature scheme in Section 3. With the pre-computation token (r, y), given any message $m \in \mathbb{Z}_p$, the RFID tag computes $rm + y \pmod{p}$ and compares whether $u_i = v_i$ for signature verification. The main computation is the modular multiplication. In this section, we show how to remove this modular multiplication when messages to be signed are partially known by the verifier.

In our construction, messages to be signed are from $\mathbb{Z}_p$. Observe that the message can be re-written into an N-bit strings as $m = m_{[1]}m_{[2]}\cdots m_{[N]}$, where $m_{[i]}$ is the i-th bit of message. In RFID applications, messages to be signed may have been partially known. For example, the unique identification code is set as one part of messages and would never be changed in each tag. We can assume that each bit of messages to be signed is either known by the tag or decided by the reader. Under this assumption, we show how to speed up signature verification with extended pre-computations.

Let $U = \{N_1, N_2, \cdots, N_l\}$ be the subset of $\{1, 2, \cdots, N\}$, where only $m_{[i]}$ for all $i \in U$ are decided by the signer. Let $z_{N_i} = 2^{N - m_{[N_i]}}$ for all $i = 1, 2, \cdots, l$, the message m can be re-written into

$$m = m_R + z_{N_1} m_{[N_1]} + z_{N_2} m_{[N_2]} + \cdots + z_{N_l} m_{[N_l]}.$$

Let $(y_{N_1}, y_{N_2}, \cdots, y_{N_l})$ be random numbers in $\mathbb{Z}_p$ satisfying

$$y = \sum_{i=1}^{l} y_{N_i} \ (\text{mod } p),$$

where y is the randomness defined in Section 3. We enable to split $rm + y$ into

$$rm + y = r(m_R + \sum_{i=1}^{l} z_{N_i} m_{[N_i]}) + y = rm_R + \sum_{i=1}^{l}(r \cdot m_{[N_i]} \cdot z_{N_i} + y_{N_i}).$$

Table 2. Pre-computation tokens in tags instead of (r, y)

	N_1	N_2	$\cdots$	N_l
0	$rm_R + r \cdot 0 \cdot z_{N_1} + y_{N_1}$	$r \cdot 0 \cdot z_{N_2} + y_{N_2}$	$\cdots$	$r \cdot 0 \cdot z_{N_l} + y_{N_l}$
1	$rm_R + r \cdot 1 \cdot z_{N_1} + y_{N_1}$	$r \cdot 1 \cdot z_{N_2} + y_{N_2}$	$\cdots$	$r \cdot 1 \cdot z_{N_l} + y_{N_l}$

In the pre-computation phase, suppose $2l$ distinct numbers shown in Table 2 are computed and stored in the tag instead of (r, y). Signature verification without the modular multiplication is feasible in the Sign-Verify algorithm for the verifier.

Let m be the message to be signed. For $i = 1, 2, \cdots, l$, the tag does as follows:

- If $i = 1$, output $w_{N_i} = rm_R + r \cdot m_{[N_i]} \cdot z_{N_i} + y_{N_i}$.
- Otherwise $i = 2, 3, \cdots, l$, output $w_{N_i} = r \cdot m_{[N_i]} \cdot z_{N_i} + y_{N_i}$.

The tag returns $(w_{N_1}, w_{N_2}, \cdots, w_{N_l})$ instead of computing w to the signer, and the signer computes

$$w = w_{N_1} + w_{N_2} + \cdots + w_{N_l} \ (\text{mod } p)$$

before generating u_i. As a consequence, the tag does not need to perform the modular multiplication and the rest of computation is the bitwise comparisons.

We assume there are l bits of messages unknown and decided by the signer. In comparison with our first scheme, the second scheme removes the modular multiplication, at the cost of $2l$ additional elements in $\mathbb{Z}_p$ which is about $\frac{l}{25}$KB in total for the 160-bit prime p. The result of pre-computation and verification cost are listed in Table 3.

Table 3. Data storage requirement and signature verification cost

Schemes	Data Storage	Signature Verification
Our scheme 1	2 KB	Modular Multiplication+Bitwise Comparison
Our scheme 2	$(2 + \frac{l}{25})$ KB	Bitwise Comparison

6 Conclusion

We proposed a pre-computable signature scheme with efficient signature verification for RFID. Our signature verification requires a 2KB-size pre-computation token for each signature verification, but the rest of verification is mainly dominated by a modular multiplication. Our signature verification will be more computationally efficient when messages to be signed are partially known. We believe that they are good candidates for passive tags that have a weak computation capacity. The proposed signature verification is applicable to low-cost tags with a small amount of rewritable memory.

Acknowledgement. We would like to thank Sherman S.M. Chow and the anonymous reviewers of ISPEC 2012 for their helpful comments and suggestions. This work has been supported by ARC Discovery Grant DP110101951.

References

1. Bellare, M., Garay, J.A., Rabin, T.: Fast Batch Verification for Modular Exponentiation and Digital Signatures. In: Nyberg, K. (ed.) EUROCRYPT 1998. LNCS, vol. 1403, pp. 236–250. Springer, Heidelberg (1998)
2. Blass, E.O., Elkhiyaoui, K., Molva, R.: Tracker: Security and privacy for rfid-based supply chains. In: NDSS 2011. The Internet Society (2011)
3. Boneh, D., Boyen, X.: Short Signatures Without Random Oracles. In: Cachin, C., Camenisch, J.L. (eds.) EUROCRYPT 2004. LNCS, vol. 3027, pp. 56–73. Springer, Heidelberg (2004)
4. Boneh, D., Boyen, X.: Short signatures without random oracles and the sdh assumption in bilinear groups. J. Cryptology 21(2), 149–177 (2008)
5. Boneh, D., Boyen, X., Shacham, H.: Short Group Signatures. In: Franklin, M.K. (ed.) CRYPTO 2004. LNCS, vol. 3152, pp. 41–55. Springer, Heidelberg (2004)
6. Boyen, X.: The Uber-Assumption Family. In: Galbraith, S.D., Paterson, K.G. (eds.) Pairing 2008. LNCS, vol. 5209, pp. 39–56. Springer, Heidelberg (2008)
7. Chow, H.K.H., Choy, K.L., Lee, W.B., Lau, K.C.: Design of a rfid case-based resource management system for warehouse operations. Expert Syst. Appl. 30(4), 561–576 (2006)
8. Chow, S.S.M., Au, M.H., Susilo, W.: Server-aided signatures verification secure against collusion attack. In: Cheung, B.S.N., Hui, L.C.K., Sandhu, R.S., Wong, D.S. (eds.) ASIACCS 2011, pp. 401–405. ACM (2011)
9. Even, S., Goldreich, O., Micali, S.: On-Line/Off-Line Digital Signatures. In: Brassard, G. (ed.) CRYPTO 1989. LNCS, vol. 435, pp. 263–275. Springer, Heidelberg (1990)

10. Ferrara, A.L., Green, M., Hohenberger, S., Pedersen, M.Ø.: Practical Short Signature Batch Verification. In: Fischlin, M. (ed.) CT-RSA 2009. LNCS, vol. 5473, pp. 309–324. Springer, Heidelberg (2009)
11. Fiat, A.: Batch rsa. J. Cryptology 10(2), 75–88 (1997)
12. Gao, C.-z., Wei, B., Xie, D., Tang, C.: Divisible On-Line/Off-Line Signatures. In: Fischlin, M. (ed.) CT-RSA 2009. LNCS, vol. 5473, pp. 148–163. Springer, Heidelberg (2009)
13. Girault, M., Lefranc, D.: Server-Aided Verification: Theory and Practice. In: Roy, B.K. (ed.) ASIACRYPT 2005. LNCS, vol. 3788, pp. 605–623. Springer, Heidelberg (2005)
14. Hein, D.M., Wolkerstorfer, J., Felber, N.: ECC Is Ready for RFID – A Proof in Silicon. In: Avanzi, R.M., Keliher, L., Sica, F. (eds.) SAC 2008. LNCS, vol. 5381, pp. 401–413. Springer, Heidelberg (2009)
15. Juels, A.: Minimalist Cryptography for Low-Cost RFID Tags (Extended Abstract). In: Blundo, C., Cimato, S. (eds.) SCN 2004. LNCS, vol. 3352, pp. 149–164. Springer, Heidelberg (2005)
16. Lamport, L.: Constructing digital signatures from a one-way function. Tech. rep., SRI-CSL-98, SRI International Computer Science Laboratory (1979)
17. Lee, S.Y., Wang, L.H., Fang, Q.: A low-power rfid integrated circuits for intelligent healthcare systems. IEEE Transactions on Information Technology in Biomedicine 14(6), 1387–1396 (2010)
18. Lim, C.H., Lee, P.J.: Server (Prover/Signer)-Aided Verification of Identity Proofs and Signatures. In: Guillou, L.C., Quisquater, J.-J. (eds.) EUROCRYPT 1995. LNCS, vol. 921, pp. 64–78. Springer, Heidelberg (1995)
19. O'Neill, M.: Low-cost sha-1 hash function architecture for rfid tags. In: RFIDSec 2008 (2008)
20. Oren, Y., Feldhofer, M.: A low-resource public-key identification scheme for rfid tags and sensor nodes. In: Basin, D.A., Capkun, S., Lee, W. (eds.) WISEC 2009, pp. 59–68. ACM (2009)
21. Paillier, P., Vergnaud, D.: Discrete-Log-Based Signatures May Not Be Equivalent to Discrete Log. In: Roy, B.K. (ed.) ASIACRYPT 2005. LNCS, vol. 3788, pp. 1–20. Springer, Heidelberg (2005)
22. Paise, R.I., Vaudenay, S.: Mutual authentication in rfid: security and privacy. In: Abe, M., Gligor, V.D. (eds.) ASIACCS 2008, pp. 292–299. ACM (2008)
23. Shamir, A.: Memory Efficient Variants of Public-Key Schemes for Smart Card Applications. In: De Santis, A. (ed.) EUROCRYPT 1994. LNCS, vol. 950, pp. 445–449. Springer, Heidelberg (1995)
24. Shamir, A., Tauman, Y.: Improved Online/Offline Signature Schemes. In: Kilian, J. (ed.) CRYPTO 2001. LNCS, vol. 2139, pp. 355–367. Springer, Heidelberg (2001)
25. Tsang, P.P., Chow, S.S.M., Smith, S.W.: Batch Pairing Delegation. In: Miyaji, A., Kikuchi, H., Rannenberg, K. (eds.) IWSEC 2007. LNCS, vol. 4752, pp. 74–90. Springer, Heidelberg (2007)
26. Vaudenay, S.: On Privacy Models for RFID. In: Kurosawa, K. (ed.) ASIACRYPT 2007. LNCS, vol. 4833, pp. 68–87. Springer, Heidelberg (2007)
27. Weis, S.A., Sarma, S.E., Rivest, R.L., Engels, D.W.: Security and Privacy Aspects of Low-Cost Radio Frequency Identification Systems. In: Hutter, D., Müller, G., Stephan, W., Ullmann, M. (eds.) SPC 2003. LNCS, vol. 2802, pp. 201–212. Springer, Heidelberg (2004)

Redactable Signatures for Independent Removal of Structure and Content

Kai Samelin*, Henrich C. Pöhls**, Arne Bilzhause,
Joachim Posegga, and Hermann de Meer

Institute of IT-Security and Security-Law (ISL), University of Passau, Germany
{ks,hcp,ab,jp}@sec.uni-passau.de, demeer@uni-passau.de

Abstract. In this paper, we present a provably secure redactable signature scheme allowing to independently redact structure and content. We identify the problems when structure is not separated from content, resulting in an attack on the scheme proposed at VLDB '08 by *Kundu* and *Bertino*. The attack allows for changing the semantic meaning of a given tree. We introduce a rigid security model, including consecutive redaction control, to formalize the required behaviour of our scheme. Moreover, we present first performance evaluations of our implementation to demonstrate the practical use of the presented scheme.

Keywords: Structural Integrity, Redactable Signatures, Performance, XML.

1 Introduction

A redactable signature scheme (RSS) allows a third party to remove parts of a signed document m without invalidating its protecting signature σ. This action can be performed without involvement of the original signer. In more detail, a RSS allows a third party to replace parts of the original document with $\bot$, a special symbol indicating that a redaction took place. As a result, the verifier only sees a blinded version of the document, while still being able to verify that the remaining subdocuments are still valid and authentic. The RSSs we will consider allow for public redactions, i.e. no private keys are required to perform a redaction. Moreover, a RSS can allow to prohibit a consecutive third party to remove certain parts, a property named Consecutive Redaction Control [20]. The notation we use for a document is $m = m[1]||\ldots||m[\ell]$. We will call each $m[i]$ a submessage, where $\ell \in \mathbb{N}^+$ is the number of submessages and $||$ a concatenation. Current schemes just allow to redact subdocuments. In particular, no existing scheme allows redacting the ordering or other structures, which carry information as well. This may not be sufficient in some cases, which is shown show next.

Examples and Benefits of Redacting Structure Separately. Structured data comes in many forms, for example XML-Schemata describe the structure

---

* Is funded by "Regionale Wettbewerbsfähigkeit und Beschäftigung", Bayern, 2007-2013 (EFRE).
** Is funded by BMBF (FKZ:13N10966) and ANR as part of the ReSCUeIT project.

M.D. Ryan, B. Smyth, and G. Wang (Eds.): ISPEC 2012, LNCS 7232, pp. 17–33, 2012.

(and often implicitly the semantics) of tree-structured XML-Documents. Even in linear documents, e.g. a text file, the order of subdocuments is important, e.g. the ordering of chapters in a book. *Liu* et al. introduced the paradigm of separating structural integrity and content integrity in [18] without considering RSS. This implicit information stored inside the structure of a document leads to our attack on the *Kundu*-Scheme.

The "digital document sanitization problem", as introduced by *Miyazaki* et al. in [19], assumes that the signing process itself cannot be altered. This may happen, if the signer is not reachable anymore, or must not know which parts of the document are passed to third parties. Consider the following two examples clarifying why one needs to be able to redact structure: (1) In an university the exam results are published in a list. The list first gives the student's name ($m[1]$) and the grade ($m[2]$), then the next student's name ($m[3]$) and then the grade ($m[4]$) and so on. Imagine the list being ordered by grades, i.e. the student with the best grade is at the beginning. Thus, the subdocuments $m[i]$ hold information about either a grade or a student's name, while the ordering carries the information "better-than". We only want a signed list of all the students' name who took part in the exam. Hence, we need to redact all information about grades from this list. A redactable scheme allows deleting the grades, i.e. all $m[i] \leftarrow \bot$, where i is even. Using a transparent [1,4,5] RSS would also remove the trace that some parts where removed. In particular, $\bot$ would not be visible anymore. However, the original ordered relation of the remaining subdocuments is still present, invading privacy. Hence, we also need to redact the ordering among them. Current schemes are not able to redact this information; they require that the ordering cannot be redacted or work only on structureless sets [20].

(2) From a business point of view, we can derive our second example: The sales department provides a monthly overview over all sent invoices to an external auditor. However, the order in which a company sends out its invoices may leak some business critical information. Further imagine that the list must be ordered in a monthly manner, i.e. the invoices need to be grouped by month, while the internal ordering must not be made public to protect trade-secrets. This requires the RSS to explicitly sign each subdocument relation separately to allow removal of only this information at a later stage.

There are many other application scenarios, e.g. one can redact hierarchies within companies, or explicitly sign partially ordered sets, which is useful for information flow models [24]. Many more examples for the use of RSS are given in the original works, our main motivation is to maintain privacy or protect trade secrets. Hence, the RSS is required to be transparent, meaning the fact that redaction has occurred must not be known by a verifying third party. Loss of transparency would decrease the value of the redacted information, e.g. a summarized report redacted by the PR department is less valuable than a summarized report where redactions by the PR department are hidden. Hence, we require a usable scheme to be transparent and allow redactions of structure to cater for such constellations.

State of the Art and Current Limitations. The concept of removing parts from signed data without invalidating the signature was initially introduced as "content extraction signature" by *Steinfeld* et al. in [25] resp. in [12] by *Johnson* et al. Their inspiring work has lead to many RSS constructions in the last years [8,20,21]. The schemes have been extended to work on tree-structured data [4,15,16] and on arbitrary graphs [17]. However, the schemes proposed in [15] and [16] suffer from an attack vector changing the semantics of the tree. We will present this attack in this paper. A related concept are sanitizable signature schemes (SSS), introduced by *Ateniese* et al. in [1], where the choice of values for a specific submessage $m[i]$ is not per se limited to $m[i]$ or $\bot$, but to arbitrary strings $\subset \{0,1\}^*$. Limiting third parties to certain values is a well-known field [7,13,23].

Recently, *Brzuska* et al. defined and formalized a set of desired properties for redactable tree-structured documents in [4]. In this paper, we extend these definitions towards linear documents with separate structure redaction. Most of the schemes proposed up to now are not transparent, i.e. one can see that a third party redacted something [10,12,21,25,26]. Furthermore, this also impacts on privacy, as already noted in [16] and [20]. The scheme introduced in [20] also suffers from several problems: (1) It is just useable for sets, which means that the ordering, what we call structure, is not protected. (2) It does not allow multi-sets, i.e. each element, resp. subdocument must be unique. (3) This fact is not checked during their verification algorithm, hence their scheme is forgeable, i.e. by copying existing elements. The only other provably transparent schemes, i.e. [4] and [8], require $\mathcal{O}(n^2)$ operations as well, but their only gain is transparency, hence coming very costly. We have the same complexity, but allow much more freedom, i.e. removing structure and allowing consecutive redaction control.

Our Contribution and Organization. In this paper, we present the first transparent RSS for ordered linear documents which redacts content and structure separately. We introduce a precise formal model for this new paradigm. This model will also include consecutive redaction control, which has been used in several papers [11,20,21], but has not yet been formalized rigorously. We will denote the set of admissible redactable entities as ADM, following the notation of [5]. Moreover, we present an attack on the *Kundu*-Scheme in Sect. 2, allowing to exploit the implicit semantic meaning of structure. Furthermore, we propose a concrete provably secure RSS construction, which will meet all of our security requirements stated in Sect. 4. Our scheme is also secure against the probabilistic attacks on transparency described by *Brzuska* et al. in [4]. Existing schemes fell victim to this attack: The scheme by *Kundu* and *Bertino* [16] lacks provably transparency since it uses ordered random numbers [4]. Also the schemes by *Izu* et al. in [11] are suspect to this attack. This is a result of the proofs given for the *Kundu*-Scheme in [4]. Hence, we introduce a way to sign the ordering of all submessages $m[i]$ in this paper. Our solution will sign each "left-of" relation to allow transparent redactions, as already proposed by *Chang* et al. in [8] and by *Brzuska* et al. in [4]. In particular, each pair $(m[i], m[j])$ gets signed, where

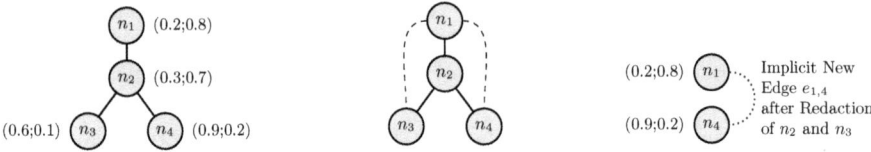

Fig. 1. Original Tree T **Fig. 2.** Transitive Closure of   **Fig. 3.** Redacted Tree T'
T, i.e. span$_\models(T)$

$0 < i < j \leq \ell$. However, their schemes do not allow to redact any structure. Our solution requires $\mathcal{O}(n^2)$ operations for signing and verification. This is similar to [4] and [8]. A more detailed theoretical cost analysis is provided as well, while a performance comparison of our implementation using real data can be found in Sect. 5. Additional preliminaries and our extended model are presented in Sect. 3. Formal proofs of the security and correctness are in the appendix.

2 Attacking the *Kundu*-Scheme

The only RSS for trees able to redact non-leafs is the *Kundu*-Scheme, introduced in [15] and revised in [16]. Their scheme builds upon the idea that a third party having the pre- and post-order traversal numbers of all nodes contained in a tree T is always able to correctly reconstruct T. Hence, signing each node $n_i \in T$ along with both numbers and the content is enough to protect T. To make the scheme transparent, these traversal numbers are randomized in an order-preserving manner, which does not have an impact on the reconstruction algorithm, which just checks for greater than relations [15,16]. Thus, verification is straight forward — with one additional step: A verifier has to check if all nodes are in the correct order using the traversal numbers. This leads to the problem that a verifier is not able to determine whether a given edge existed in the original tree T, just if it *could* have existed. However, as shown in the introduction, the structure itself does carry information as well: Assume that one removes n_2 and n_3 from T, as depicted in Fig. 3. This allows to add a new edge $e_{1,4}$, which has not explicitly been present in the original tree T. This implies, that the tree $T^{\mathcal{A}} = (\{n_1, n_4\}, \{e_{1,4}\})$ is valid in terms of the signature. For more detail we compute the traversal numbers for the example tree in Fig. 1: The pre-order traversal of T will output $(1, 2, 3, 4)$, while the post-order traversal will output $(4, 3, 2, 1)$. The randomization step may transform them into $(0.2, 0.3, 0.6, 0.9)$ and $(0.8, 0.7, 0.2, 0.1)$ resp. Hence, the node n_1 has a structural position of $\rho_1 = (0.2; 0.8)$. For n_2, n_3 and n_4 this is done accordingly. We redact n_2, an intermediate node of n_4, and n_3. For the redacted tree in Fig. 3, the traversal-numbers are still in the correct order. Hence, the signature verifies. *Kundu* and *Bertino* neither prohibit nor exclude the redaction of intermediate nodes, but claim this is a useful property [16]. This behaviour is problematic, as we will show next. The *Kundu*-Scheme signs the transitive closure of the tree

T, as depicted in Fig. 2. This is a very weak form of structural integrity protection and allows some semantic attacks: Consider a hierarchical structure of treatments inside a medical database, i.e. treatments consists of treatments, e.g. a chemotherapy consists of giving drugs against cancer and additional prophylactic drugs to avoid infections, codified into the tree's structure. If the cancer drugs and chemotherapy node is redacted, the only treatment node left is the prophylactic drug one. This does neither destroy any XML-Schemata nor can it be detected by humans. This behaviour is not acceptable, though it may have its application, e.g. to redact hierarchies within a company. However, we argue that the places where this is allowed must be explicitly denoted by the signer to avoid the mentioned attack. It remains on open question how to construct a secure scheme, which allows such constellations, along with a suitable security model, since the one introduced in [4] just allows to redact leafs.

3   Preliminaries, Notations and Security Properties

Basically, we have the same requirements as *Brzuska* et al. [4], i.e. unforgeability, privacy and transparency. However, we need to adjust the definitions as we treat structure as a redactable entity and to make statements about linear documents instead of trees. We require that the splitting of m into the subdocuments $m[i]$, along with the order, is efficiently reconstructable from any received m.

Definition 1 (RSS Algorithms for Content and Structure Redaction).
A RSS which allows separate redaction of content and structure, with consecutive redaction control, consists of five efficient algorithms. In particular, $RSS :=$ (KeyGen, Sign, Verify, Redact, Close) such that:

KeyGen. *The algorithm KeyGen outputs the public and private key of the signer, i.e. $(\mathrm{pk}, \mathrm{sk}) \leftarrow KeyGen(1^\lambda)$, where the input parameter λ is the security parameter.*

Sign. *The algorithm Sign outputs the signature σ on input of the secret key sk and the document m. It outputs $(m, \sigma) \leftarrow Sign(\mathrm{sk}, m)$.*

Verify. *The algorithm Verify outputs a bit $d \in \{0, 1\}$ indicating the correctness of the signature σ, w.r.t. pk, protecting m. In particular: $d \leftarrow Verify(\mathrm{pk}, m, \sigma)$*

Redact. *The algorithm Redact takes as input the document m, the public key pk of the signer, the signature σ and description of the redaction MOD containing either a submessage $m[i]$ or a binary relation $m[i, j]$ that shall be redacted. Calling Redact sequentially allows to redact more relations and submessages. The algorithm outputs $(m', \sigma') \leftarrow Redact(\mathrm{pk}, m, \sigma, \mathrm{MOD})$, where $m' \leftarrow \mathrm{MOD}(m)$ denotes the alteration of m w.r.t. MOD. MOD may contain more than one modification in our notation. We require that ADM, which denotes the entities of m admissible to be redacted, is always correctly recoverable from (m, σ). The algorithm doing so will be described as:*

Sanitizable. *On input of a valid message/signature pair (m, σ), Sanitizable outputs* ADM: ADM $\leftarrow$ *Sanitizable*(m, σ).
We will treat Sanitizable as part of Redact and not as a stand alone algorithm. Note, Redact allows public redactions, since just the public key pk *of the signer is required.*

Close. *The algorithm Close alters σ on input of m, the public key* pk *of the signer, the signature σ and a sanitization control description* MOD$_c$ *which contains the entities subject to redaction control. The algorithm outputs $(m, \sigma') \leftarrow$ Close*$(\text{pk}, m, \sigma, \text{MOD}_c)$. MOD$_c$ *may contain many modifications. Close does not change the message m itself, but Sanitizable(m, σ') = Sanitizable$(m, \sigma) \setminus$ MOD$_c$. This algorithm can be called by the signer and any other third party. This enables the signer to close parts of m prior to distributing.*

Signing each "left-of" relation is enough to protect the structure of an ordered document. This has already been utilized and proven in [8] and [4]. The signer is able to redact parts of the document as well, since a RSS allows public redaction. Hence, all parties can sanitize and close the document, which includes the signer and the final recipient as well.

3.1   Security Properties

We now define the required security properties of RSS. These have already been identified in [4] for trees. Therefore, we will adapt and extend their notion for our needs. We will denote the transitive closure of a message m, w.r.t. to Redact, as $\text{span}_\models(m)$, which is derived from [8]. We denote a redaction of a submessage $m[i]$ as $m \setminus m[i]$. A redaction of a relation between $m[i]$ and $m[j]$ will be denoted as $m \setminus m[i, j]$. Note, the following definitions address only the information a third party can derive from the signature; e.g., if obvious redactions took place, it may be trivial to decide whether something has been redacted. We will use the notation $\sqsubseteq$ to express a subset relation in terms of submessages and submessage relations.

Unforgeability. No one should be able to compute a valid signature on a document outside the transitive closure $\text{span}_\models(m)$, without having access to the secret key sk. That is, even if an outsider can request signatures on different documents, it remains impossible to forge a signature for a new document. This is analogous to the standard unforgeability requirement for other signature schemes. We say that a *RSS* is unforgeable, iff for any efficient (PPT) adversary $\mathcal{A}$ the probability that the game depicted in Fig. 4 returns 1, is negligible (as a function of λ).

Privacy. No one should be able to gain any knowledge about redacted parts without having access to them. This is similar to the standard indistinguishability notion for encryption schemes. We say that a *RSS* for documents is private, iff for any efficient (PPT) adversary $\mathcal{A}$ the probability that the game depicted in Fig. 5 returns 1, is negligibly close to $\frac{1}{2}$ (as a function of λ).

Experiment $\mathsf{Privacy}_{\mathcal{A}}^{\mathsf{RSS}}(\lambda)$
  $(pk, sk) \leftarrow \mathsf{KeyGen}(1^\lambda)$
  $b \xleftarrow{\$} \{0,1\}$
  $d \leftarrow \mathcal{A}^{\mathsf{Sign}(sk,\cdot),\mathsf{LoRRedact}(\dots,sk,b)}(pk)$
    where oracle $\mathsf{LoRRedact}$
    for input $m_0, m_1, \mathrm{MOD}_0, \mathrm{MOD}_1$:
    if $\mathrm{MOD}_0(m_0) \neq \mathrm{MOD}_1(m_1)$, return $\perp$
    $(m, \sigma) \leftarrow \mathsf{Sign}(sk, m_b)$
    return $(m', \sigma') \leftarrow \mathsf{Redact}(pk, m, \sigma, \mathrm{MOD}_b)$.
  return 1 iff $b = d$

Experiment $\mathsf{Unforgeability}_{\mathcal{A}}^{\mathsf{RSS}}(\lambda)$
  $(pk, sk) \leftarrow \mathsf{KeyGen}(1^\lambda)$
  $(m^*, \sigma^*) \leftarrow \mathcal{A}^{\mathsf{Sign}(sk,\cdot)}(pk)$
    let $i = 1, 2, \dots, q$ index the queries
  return 1 iff
    $\mathsf{Verify}(pk, m^*, \sigma^*) = 1$ and
    $\forall i, 1 \leq i \leq q : m^* \notin \mathrm{span}_{\models}(m_i)$

Fig. 4. Game for Unforgeability

Fig. 5. Game for Privacy

Experiment $\mathsf{DisclosureSecure}_{\mathcal{A}}^{\mathsf{RSS}}(\lambda)$
  $(pk, sk) \leftarrow \mathsf{KeyGen}(1^\lambda)$
  $(m^*, \sigma^*) \leftarrow \mathcal{A}^{\mathsf{RSign}(sk,\cdot)}(pk)$
    where oracle RSign for input m, MOD_c:
    $(\sigma, m) \leftarrow \mathsf{Sign}(sk, m)$
    return $\mathsf{Close}(pk, m, \sigma, \mathrm{MOD}_c)$
  return 1 iff
  let $i = 1, 2, \dots, q$ index the queries
  let $\mathrm{ADM}_i \leftarrow \mathsf{Sanitizable}(m_i, \sigma_i)$ and
  let $\mathrm{ADM}^* \leftarrow \mathsf{Sanitizable}(m^*, \sigma^*)$ and
  $\mathsf{Verify}(pk, m^*, \sigma^*) = 1$ and
    $\exists i : m^* \in \mathrm{span}_{\models}(m_i) \wedge m_i \setminus m^* \not\subseteq \bigcup_{0 < i \leq q} \mathrm{ADM}_i$ or
    $\exists i : \mathrm{ADM}^* \supset \mathrm{ADM}_i \wedge \forall i : \mathrm{ADM}^* \not\subseteq \bigcup_{0 < i \leq q} \mathrm{ADM}_i$

Experiment $\mathsf{Transparency}_{\mathcal{A}}^{\mathsf{RSS}}(\lambda)$
  $(pk, sk) \leftarrow \mathsf{KeyGen}(1^\lambda)$
  $b \xleftarrow{\$} \{0,1\}$
  $d \leftarrow \mathcal{A}^{\mathsf{Sign}(sk,\cdot),\mathsf{Sign/Redact}(\dots,sk,b)}(pk)$
    where oracle $\mathsf{Sign/Redact}$ for input m, MOD:
    if $\mathrm{MOD}(m) \notin \mathrm{span}_{\models}(m)$, return $\perp$
    if $b = 0$: $(\sigma, m) \leftarrow \mathsf{Sign}(sk, m)$,
          $(\sigma', m') \leftarrow \mathsf{Redact}(pk, \sigma, m, \mathrm{MOD})$
    if $b = 1$: $m' \leftarrow \mathrm{MOD}(m)$
          $(m', \sigma') \leftarrow \mathsf{Sign}(sk, m')$,
    finally return (m', σ').
  return 1 iff $b = d$

Fig. 6. Game for Transparency

Fig. 7. Game for Disclosure Secure

Transparency. The verifier should not be able to decide whether a signature has been created by the signer, or through the redaction algorithm Redact. This means, that a party cannot decide whether a freshly signed or a blinded version where some parts have already been redacted has been received. We say that a *RSS* is transparent, iff for any efficient (PPT) adversary $\mathcal{A}$, the probability that the game depicted in Fig. 6 returns 1, is negligibly close to $\frac{1}{2}$ (as a function of λ).

Disclosure Secure. No one should be able to redact parts of a document which are not part of ADM. This is analogous to the immutability requirement for SSS [5]. Note, in [20] *Miyazaki* et al. merged this with unforgeability. However, for unforgeability any message is enough to break the game; for disclosure security, an adversary has two possibilities: Either it is able to redact a part which is subject to redaction control or is able to alter ADM, such that the disclosure control is reversed. Therefore, the games are slightly different. Additionally, our game is stricter as the adversary can choose the parts of the message to be subject to disclosure control. We say that a *RSS* is disclosure secure, iff for any efficient (PPT) adversary $\mathcal{A}$ the probability that the game depicted in Fig. 7 returns 1, is negligible (as a function of λ).

Next, we will describe the needed primitives for our scheme.

3.2 Aggregate Signatures and Bilinear Pairings

Aggregate signatures ($\mathcal{AGG}$) have been introduced by *Boneh* et al. in [3]. The basic idea is as follows: Given ℓ signatures σ_i, $0 < i \leq \ell$, one constructs a compressed signature σ which contains all signatures σ_i. This allows verifying all given signatures σ_i by verifying σ. The scheme can be constructed as follows: Let $\mathbb{G}_1$ be a cyclic multiplicative group with prime order q, generated by g, i.e. $\mathbb{G}_1 = \langle g \rangle$. Further, let $\mathbb{G}_T$ denote a cyclic multiplicative group with the same prime order q. Let $\hat{e} : \mathbb{G}_1 \times \mathbb{G}_1 \to \mathbb{G}_T$ be a bilinear map such that:

1. Bilinearity: $\forall u, v \in \mathbb{G}_1 : \forall a, b \in \mathbb{Z}/q\mathbb{Z} : \hat{e}(u^a, v^b) = \hat{e}(u,v)^{ab}$
2. Non-degeneracy: $\exists u, v \in \mathbb{G}_1 : \hat{e}(u,v) \neq 1$
3. Computability: There is an efficient algorithm $\mathcal{A}_{bimap}$ that calculates the mapping $\hat{e}$ for all $u, v \in \mathbb{G}_1$

Definition 2 (The BGLS-Scheme). *The $\mathcal{AGG}$ by Boneh et al. [3] (BGLS-Scheme) with public aggregation consists of five efficient algorithms. Especially:*

$$\mathcal{AGG} = \{AKeyGen, ASign, AVerf, AAgg, AAggVerf\}$$

AKeyGen. *The algorithm KeyGen outputs the public and private key of the signer,* sk $\xleftarrow{\$} \mathbb{Z}/q\mathbb{Z}$ *denote the signer's private key and* $\mathcal{H}_k : \{0,1\}^* \to \mathbb{G}_1$ *an ordinary cryptographic hash-function from the family $\mathcal{H}_K$ and set $Q \leftarrow g^{sk}$, where g is a generator of $\mathbb{G}_1$. Set the public parameters and key* pk $\leftarrow (g, Q, \mathbb{G}_1, \mathbb{G}_T, \mathcal{H}_k, \hat{e})$. *Output* (pk, sk).

ASign. *The algorithm ASign outputs the signature σ_i on input of the secret key* sk *and a single document m_i. It outputs* $\sigma_i \leftarrow (\mathcal{H}_k(m_i))^{sk}$.

AVerf. *To verify a signature σ_i, a third party has to check, if the following equation holds:* $\hat{e}(\sigma_i, g) \stackrel{?}{=} \hat{e}(\mathcal{H}_k(m_i), Q)$.

AAgg. *To aggregate ℓ signatures σ_i, protecting m_i, into an aggregated signature σ, the aggregator computes* $\sigma \leftarrow \prod_{i=1}^{\ell} \sigma_i$, *denoted as* AAgg(pk, $\mathcal{S}$), *where $\mathcal{S}$ is a set of signatures signed using the same public parameters. Note: This can be done by untrusted parties and without knowing the private keys.*

AAggVerf. *To verify an aggregated signature σ, a verifier checks whether $\hat{e}(\sigma, g) \stackrel{?}{=} \prod_{i=1}^{\ell} \hat{e}(\mathcal{H}_k(m_i), Q)$ holds, on input of σ,* pk *and a list of signed (sub)messages. To improve efficiency, the right side can be rewritten as $\hat{e}(\prod_{i=1}^{\ell} \mathcal{H}_k(m_i), Q)$. Note, we just use one public key, Q, which allows this improvement. Using just one public key also has the advantage that we are sure that just one signing key is used. We denote the algorithm as* $d \leftarrow$ AAggVerf(pk, σ, $\{m_i\}_{0 < i \leq \ell}$).

As usual, the correctness requirements should hold. Formal proofs of those can be found in [3]. We require the expected security properties to hold, i.e. unforgeability under chosen message attacks. The proofs can also be found in [3]. We explicitly assume that splitting up an aggregate signature is not feasible, as shown for the BGLS-Scheme in [9]. However, we require that the attacker has access to a signing oracle. For the BGLS-Scheme, this has already been assumed in [20], but is not stated formally in [3]. Moreover, it is required that, if a third party knows a contained signature, it can build an inverse and actually remove the signature from the aggregate. We will denote the removal of σ_i from σ as $\sigma' \leftarrow \sigma \setminus \sigma_i$. For the BGLS-Scheme [3] this means: $\sigma' \leftarrow \sigma \cdot \sigma_i^{-1}$. We will use this behaviour to obtain secure consecutive redaction control.

4 *RSS* Construction Using Aggregate Signatures

Our construction is based upon the defined $\mathcal{AGG}$. The construction introduced will be generic, we give an instantiation afterwards. It extends the scheme introduced by *Miyazaki* et al. in [20] without inheriting its flaws and limitations. Using aggregating signatures over accumulating hashes [2] resp. distributing many signatures has three advantages: (1) We can introduce consecutive redaction control; (2) we are information theoretically secure, both in terms of transparency and privacy; (3) we speed up the verification procedure as well.

4.1 High-Level Description of Our Construction

Construction 1 (RSS). *Our construction makes use of an aggregating signature scheme $\mathcal{AGG}$ as defined earlier. We will explain every algorithm in detail next. Note, this is a high-level description; an instantiation based on the BGLS-Scheme is given in Sect. 4.2.*

Key Generation. *The key pair generation algorithm* KeyGen *outputs the key pair* $(\mathrm{sk}, \mathrm{pk})$*, i.e.:* $(\mathrm{sk}, \mathrm{pk}) \leftarrow$ AKeyGen(1^λ)*, i.e. it uses the key pair of the underlying $\mathcal{AGG}$.*

Signing. *To sign m, where all "left-of" relations $m[i,j]$ can be derived from, perform the following steps:*

1. *Choose a nonce τ, i.e. τ must be unique for each document signed. The tag is needed to avoid adding subdocuments from other documents signed with the same secret key* sk
2. *Sign τ, i.e. $\sigma_\tau \leftarrow$ ASign(sk, τ)*
3. *Draw ℓ pair-wise distinct nonces r_i from a uniform distribution. These are needed to prevent an adversary from aggregating a contained entity twice*
4. *Append each r_i to the corresponding subdocument $m[i] \sqsubseteq m$, then append τ and sign the resulting string, i.e. $\sigma_i \leftarrow$ ASign$(\mathrm{sk}, \tau || r_i || m[i])$*
5. *Sign each existing tagged "left-of" relation: $\sigma_{i,j} \leftarrow$ ASign$(\mathrm{sk}, \tau || r_i || r_j)$, for all $0 < i < j \leq \ell$, if $m[i,j] \sqsubseteq m$*
6. *Aggregate each generated signature, i.e:*

$$\sigma_c \leftarrow \mathsf{AAgg}(\mathrm{pk}, \sigma_\tau \cup \{\sigma_i \mid m[i] \sqsubseteq m\} \cup \{\sigma_{i,j} \mid m[i,j] \sqsubseteq m\})$$

7. *Output $\sigma = (\sigma_c, \tau, \{\sigma_i \mid m[i] \sqsubseteq m\}, \{\sigma_{i,j} \mid m[i,j] \sqsubseteq m\}, \{r_i \mid m[i] \sqsubseteq m \vee m[i,j] \sqsubseteq m \vee m[j,i] \sqsubseteq m\})$*

Note: This algorithm already allows to sign partially ordered sets by not requiring all relations; this is necessary to maintain privacy and transparency.

Redact. *To redact a subdocument $m[i]$, the following steps are performed:*

1. *Check σ's validity using* **Verify**. *If the signature is not valid, return $\perp$*
2. *If $m[i] \not\sqsubseteq m$, return $\perp$*
3. *Set $m' = m \setminus m[i]$. Note, this does not redact the submessage's relations*
4. *Calculate: $\sigma'_c = \sigma_c \setminus \sigma_i$*
5. *Output $\sigma' = (\sigma'_c, \tau, \{\sigma_i \mid m'[i] \sqsubseteq m'\}, \{\sigma_{i,j} \mid m'[i,j] \sqsubseteq m'\}, \{r_i \mid m'[i] \sqsubseteq m' \vee m'[i,j] \sqsubseteq m' \vee m'[j,i] \sqsubseteq m'\})$*

To redact a relation $m[i,j]$, the third party has to perform the following steps:

1. *Check σ's validity using* **Verify**. *If the signature is not valid, return $\perp$*
2. *If $m[i,j] \not\sqsubseteq m$, return $\perp$*
3. *Set $m' = m \setminus m[i,j]$. Note, this does not redact submessages m_i nor m_j*
4. *Calculate: $\sigma'_c = \sigma_c \setminus \sigma_{i,j}$*
5. *Output $\sigma' = (\sigma'_c, \tau, \{\sigma_i \mid m'[i] \sqsubseteq m'\}, \{\sigma_{i,j} \mid m'[i,j] \sqsubseteq m'\}, \{r_i \mid m'[i] \sqsubseteq m' \vee m'[i,j] \sqsubseteq m' \vee m'[j,i] \sqsubseteq m'\})$*

Verify. *The algorithm* **Verify** *performs the following steps:*

1. *Check, if all r_i are pair-wise distinct. If not, output 0*
2. *Use* **AAggVerf** *to verify τ, every $m[i]$ and the received relations which we assumed can be derived from m. In particular, all received submessages $m[i]$, appended with τ and the received r_i, τ itself, and only the submessage relations derived from m must be checked. If the validation passes, return 1, otherwise 0 resp. $\perp$ on error*

Close. *The algorithm* **Close** *prohibits the possibility of further redaction:*

1. *Check the validity of σ using* **Verify**. *If the signature is not valid, return $\perp$*
2. *If a submessage $m[k]$ is subject to redaction control, do not distribute σ_k anymore, i.e. output $\sigma' = (\sigma_c, \tau, \{\sigma_i \mid m[i] \sqsubseteq m \wedge \sigma_i \neq \sigma_k\}, \{\sigma_{i,j} \mid m[i,j] \sqsubseteq m\}, \{r_i \mid m[i] \sqsubseteq m \vee m[i,j] \sqsubseteq m \vee m[j,i] \sqsubseteq m\})$*
3. *If a submessage relation $m[k,l]$ is subject to redaction control, do not distribute $\sigma_{i,j}$ anymore, i.e. output $\sigma' = (\sigma_c, \tau, \{\sigma_i \mid m[i] \sqsubseteq m\}, \{\sigma_{i,j} \mid m[i,j] \sqsubseteq m\}, \{r_i \mid (m[i] \sqsubseteq m \vee m[i,j] \sqsubseteq m \vee m[j,i] \sqsubseteq m) \wedge \sigma_{i,j} \neq \sigma_{k,l}\})$*

The algorithms **Redact** and **Close** do not require any private keys. They only allow to remove resp. to close just a single submessage or one relation. This is done for brevity; sequentially running the given algorithms reestablishes the required and intuitive behaviour, i.e. removing a submessage along with its relations. The reason why we need to add σ_τ to the aggregate: If at least one subdocument resp. relation is closed, an adversary must be able to calculate resp. extract σ_τ, which, as will prove in the appendix, is infeasible. Thus, the verification algorithm will not accept the signature, which reestablishes our required correctness requirement. A third party having all signatures but σ_τ can calculate it by redacting all relations and all submessages. However, this does not introduce any security problems, since the third party could give away all signatures anyway.

4.2 Instantiation Using the BGLS-Scheme

To clarify the generic description given in Sect. 4.1 we will give an instantiation now. It shows how such a scheme can be implemented using the BGLS-Scheme and it allows us to give performance measurements in Sect. 5.

Construction 2 (*RSS₂*). *For brevity, we will omit the case where already partially ordered sets are subject to signing; the algorithms can be adjusted accordingly very easily, as already shown in the high-level description of our algorithms. We will use the BGLS-Scheme, since it is well known. The proof given in the appendix is done for the BGLS-Scheme as well. We will prove our generic scheme in the full version of this paper.*

Sign. *To sign a document $m = m[1]||\ldots||m[\ell]$, the signer signs each subdocument using the secret key sk and an additional tag τ. First, the signer signs τ, i.e. $\sigma_\tau \leftarrow (\mathcal{H}_k(\tau))^{\text{sk}}$. Afterwards, ℓ pair-wise distinct nonces r_i have to be drawn uniformly. Then, each submessage $m[i] \sqsubseteq m$ is signed, i.e. $\sigma_i \leftarrow (\mathcal{H}_k(\tau||r_i||m_i))^{\text{sk}}$. Note, τ must be different for each document m under sk. Afterwards, the signer calculates $\sigma_{i,j} \leftarrow (\mathcal{H}_k(\tau||r_i||r_j))^{\text{sk}}$ for all $0 < i < j \le \ell$. The tag τ is required to avoid adding subdocuments of other documents signed with the same secret key sk. Hence, τ "binds" all subdocuments to exactly one document m^τ. Afterwards, the signer aggregates all signatures σ_i and $\sigma_{i,j}$ into the final aggregated signature σ_c, i.e.:*

$$\sigma_c \leftarrow \sigma_\tau \cdot \prod_{i=1}^{\ell} \sigma_i \cdot \prod_{j=2}^{\ell} \prod_{i=1}^{i<j} \sigma_{i,j}$$

All signatures, i.e. σ_i, $\sigma_{i,j}$ and σ_τ, are sent along with the document m. Furthermore, a third party requires all random numbers r_i for verification.

Redact. *Verify σ first. To redact $m[k]$, $m[k]$ is deleted from the set of subdocuments, i.e. $m' = m \setminus m[k]$. Then the third party produces a new aggregated signature σ' over the remaining subdocuments by calculating $\sigma'_c \leftarrow \sigma_c \cdot \sigma_k^{-1}$. To redact a relation $m[i,j]$, the algorithm is similar, i.e. $m' = m \setminus m[i,j]$ and $\sigma'_c \leftarrow \sigma_c \cdot \sigma_{i,j}^{-1}$. Redacted signatures must not be further distributed. Also, all no longer required nonces must be deleted as well to maintain privacy, as shown in the generic construction.*

Verify. *To verify σ, the verifier checks whether the following equation holds:*

$$\hat{e}(\sigma_c, g) \stackrel{?}{=} \hat{e}(\mathcal{H}_k(\tau) \cdot \prod_{i=1}^{\ell} s_i \cdot \prod_{j=2}^{\ell} \prod_{i=1}^{i<j} t_{i,j}, Q)$$

where

$$s_i = \begin{cases} \mathcal{H}_k(\tau||r_i||m[i]) & \text{if } m[i] \sqsubseteq m \\ 1 & \text{otherwise} \end{cases} \quad \text{and } t_{i,j} = \begin{cases} \mathcal{H}_k(\tau||r_i||r_j) & \text{if } m[i,j] \sqsubseteq m \\ 1 & \text{otherwise} \end{cases}$$

If so, he checks if all used r_i are pair-wise distinct. If this test is passed, the ordering and the content has been verified explicitly *and the received document is valid. The case where a given submessage resp. submessage relation* *is not part of the received document, does not impact on transparency, since the document could have been signed like this; A third party always knows, if a given entity does not exist, which is crucial to have a useable verification procedure, while 1 is the neutral element in the multiplicative group. Moreover, no information from the signature is leaked, as required by our security model. Thus, the instantiation used allows a very compact representation of the verification algorithm without introducing security flaws.*

Close. *The algorithm* Close *just no longer sends the corresponding signature. This is the same behaviour as defined in the generic construction.*

Correctness and Security of the Proposed Scheme. The proofs are relegated to App. A.

Runtime and Storage Complexity. Our construction requires $n + \frac{n(n-1)}{2} + 1 + n$ steps for signing. The dominant term is $\frac{n(n-1)}{2}$, which is in $\mathcal{O}(n^2)$. Redacting a subdocument or relation just requires two steps, namely deleting the subdocument or relation $m[k]$ and adjusting the aggregated signature to σ'. Hence, the redaction algorithm is in $\mathcal{O}(1)$. Verification is in $\mathcal{O}(n^2)$. Note, this construction requires all signatures to be available. Hence, our scheme has a storage requirement of $\mathcal{O}(n^2)$, since $n + \frac{n(n-1)}{2}$ signatures are required.

4.3   Modifications

Restricting to Sanitizer and Accountability. The proposed scheme allows public redaction. To limit redaction to explicitly denoted third parties, the signature σ_c can be altered to hold an additional signature $\sigma_2 \leftarrow \text{SIGN}(sk, \mathcal{CH}(m))$, where m is the message to be signed, while $\mathcal{CH}$ is a chameleon hash [14]. The parameters of $\mathcal{CH}$ and m itself need to be delivered with σ_2. Only third parties who possess the secret key for $\mathcal{CH}$ can alter m without breaking the verification procedure. This can be enriched further to achieve third party and signer accountability [5]: $\mathcal{CH}$ could be replaced with a tag-based chameleon-hash, i.e. the one introduced by *Brzuska* et al. in [5]. Note, both types of accountability have not yet been formalized for RSS. We are confident that both formalizations are similar or even the same, though we note that this is ongoing work. The approach has already been introduced in [23] by *Pöhls* et al.

Binding Subdocuments and Relations. A third party can bind two or more subdocuments $m[i]$ resp. relations $m[i, j]$ to each other. In particular, it may be wanted that $m[1]$ and $m[3]$ can just be redacted together as one. This is also true for any relations; it may be wanted that a (maybe consecutive) third party is only able to redact all relations of, e.g., $m[6]$ at once. To do so, the corresponding signatures must be aggregated and distributed, e.g. in our first example $\sigma_{(1,3)} \leftarrow \sigma_1 \cdot \sigma_3$. For our second example this would be $\sigma_{(6)} \leftarrow \prod_{i=1}^{i=5} \sigma_{i,6} \cdot \prod_{i=7}^{i=\ell} \sigma_{6,i}$. Note, this does not affect the message m itself. This has already been proposed in [20].

Table 1. Median Runtime for the Scheme; All in ms

	Generation of σ in ms				Verification of σ in ms				Redaction in ms			
ℓ Curve	10	25	50	100	10	25	50	100	10	25	50	100
128 Bit	6,350	28,675	158,557	615,546	3,675	16,638	89,233	338,156	3	10	22	32
256 Bit	39,313	170,405	667,321	2,660,354	20,323	92,828	345,360	1,401,178	9	20	44	83
384 Bit	95,555	435,902	1,740,444	6,837,645	49,203	229,935	896,825	3,580,709	15	37	71	153

However, we can show that for our scheme, which allows much more freedom, the signer is still able to restrict the third parties in such a sophisticated way.

5 Performance Measurements

We have implemented our scheme to demonstrate the usability despite its runtime complexity of $\mathcal{O}(n^2)$ and the fact that it is based on pairings. We used the library developed by the *National University of Maynooth*[1] [22] and the tests were run on a *Lenovo Thinkpad T61* with an *Intel* T8300 Dual Core @2.40 Ghz and 4 GiB of RAM. We ran *Ubuntu* Version 10.04 LTS (64 Bit) and Java version 1.6.0_26-b03. We used a single thread to calculate the signatures; an improvement would be to parallelize signature calculations, since all but the aggregation step are independent. The source code is available upon request. We took the median of 10 runs and evaluated three sizes of curves, i.e. 128, 256 and 384 Bit. Table 1 shows the results for 10, 25, 50 and 100 subdocuments. As shown, for high security parameter sizes and high subdocument counts, we are considerably slower than a standard SHA-512 hash. For comparison, a SHA-512 on a document with 10 subdocuments takes 4ms and for 100 it takes 40ms. So, our implementation is at best 1,587 times slower than SHA-512 (10 subdocuments signed using a 128 bit curve). In comparison to other primitives based on pairings used in SSS our scheme can compete: A chameleon hash like *Zhang* et. al's [27] (128bit) takes 930ms to generate a single hash according to [23], while our scheme has a growth of $\mathcal{O}(n^2)$. However, all other *provably* secure and transparent schemes, i.e. [4] and [8], have the same complexity and therefore just differ by a constant factor. Hence, faster aggregate signatures would directly lead to a faster scheme. We note that for large security parameters, and a large submessage count, the scheme becomes very slow.

6 Conclusion and Open Questions

We presented a secure RSS for linear documents, that offers information-theoretical transparency and privacy. It treats content and structure as separate redactable parts; giving more freedom, which allows this RSS a wider applicability. Furthermore, we have introduced a formal and rigorous security model,

---

[1] http://www.nuim.ie/

which is the first to formally define the property of secure consecutive redaction control. Our scheme needs $\mathcal{O}(n^2)$ signing and verification steps. However, it allows redacting structure and content separately, which has not been possible with any scheme before, and has many applications in real world environments. Our implementation demonstrates that our construction is rather slow, but may still be useable for some real-life applications. It remains an open question, if more efficient schemes can be constructed and how we can construct an unlinkable [6] RSS with the same possibilities. Moreover, we presented an attack on the *Kundu*-Scheme [15,16], which breaks the structural integrity protection, thus allows modifying a signed document's semantic meaning.

References

1. Ateniese, G., Chou, D.H., de Medeiros, B., Tsudik, G.: Sanitizable Signatures. In: di Vimercati, S.d.C., Syverson, P.F., Gollmann, D. (eds.) ESORICS 2005. LNCS, vol. 3679, pp. 159–177. Springer, Heidelberg (2005)
2. Benaloh, J., De Mare, M.: One-way accumulators: A decentralized alternative to digital signatures, pp. 274–285. Springer, Heidelberg (1993)
3. Boneh, D., Gentry, C., Lynn, B., Shacham, H.: Aggregate and Verifiably Encrypted Signatures from Bilinear Maps. In: Biham, E. (ed.) EUROCRYPT 2003. LNCS, vol. 2656, pp. 416–432. Springer, Heidelberg (2003)
4. Brzuska, C., Busch, H., Dagdelen, O., Fischlin, M., Franz, M., Katzenbeisser, S., Manulis, M., Onete, C., Peter, A., Poettering, B., Schröder, D.: Redactable Signatures for Tree-Structured Data: Definitions and Constructions. In: Zhou, J., Yung, M. (eds.) ACNS 2010. LNCS, vol. 6123, pp. 87–104. Springer, Heidelberg (2010)
5. Brzuska, C., Fischlin, M., Freudenreich, T., Lehmann, A., Page, M., Schelbert, J., Schröder, D., Volk, F.: Security of Sanitizable Signatures Revisited. In: Jarecki, S., Tsudik, G. (eds.) PKC 2009. LNCS, vol. 5443, pp. 317–336. Springer, Heidelberg (2009)
6. Brzuska, C., Fischlin, M., Lehmann, A., Schröder, D.: Unlinkability of Sanitizable Signatures. In: Nguyen, P.Q., Pointcheval, D. (eds.) PKC 2010. LNCS, vol. 6056, pp. 444–461. Springer, Heidelberg (2010)
7. Canard, S., Jambert, A.: On Extended Sanitizable Signature Schemes. In: Pieprzyk, J. (ed.) CT-RSA 2010. LNCS, vol. 5985, pp. 179–194. Springer, Heidelberg (2010)
8. Chang, E.-C., Lim, C.L., Xu, J.: Short Redactable Signatures Using Random Trees. In: Fischlin, M. (ed.) CT-RSA 2009. LNCS, vol. 5473, pp. 133–147. Springer, Heidelberg (2009)
9. Coron, J.-S., Naccache, D.: Boneh *et al.*'s *k*-Element Aggregate Extraction Assumption Is Equivalent to the Diffie-Hellman Assumption. In: Laih, C.-S. (ed.) ASIACRYPT 2003. LNCS, vol. 2894, pp. 392–397. Springer, Heidelberg (2003)
10. Haber, S., Hatano, Y., Honda, Y., Horne, W.G., Miyazaki, K., Sander, T., Tezoku, S., Yao, D.: Efficient signature schemes supporting redaction, pseudonymization, and data deidentification. In: ASIACCS, pp. 353–362 (2008)
11. Izu, T., Kunihiro, N., Ohta, K., Sano, M., Takenaka, M.: Sanitizable and Deletable Signature. In: Chung, K.-I., Sohn, K., Yung, M. (eds.) WISA 2008. LNCS, vol. 5379, pp. 130–144. Springer, Heidelberg (2009)
12. Johnson, R., Molnar, D., Song, D., Wagner, D.: Homomorphic Signature Schemes. In: Preneel, B. (ed.) CT-RSA 2002. LNCS, vol. 2271, pp. 244–262. Springer, Heidelberg (2002)

13. Klonowski, M., Lauks, A.: Extended Sanitizable Signatures. In: Rhee, M.S., Lee, B. (eds.) ICISC 2006. LNCS, vol. 4296, pp. 343–355. Springer, Heidelberg (2006)
14. Krawczyk, H., Rabin, T.: Chameleon Hashing and Signatures. In: Symposium on Network and Distributed Systems Security, pp. 143–154 (2000)
15. Kundu, A., Bertino, E.: Structural Signatures for Tree Data Structures. In: Proc. of PVLDB 2008, New Zealand. ACM (2008)
16. Kundu, A., Bertino, E.: CERIAS Tech Report 2009-1 Leakage-Free Integrity Assurance for Tree Data Structures (2009)
17. Kundu, A., Bertino, E.: How to authenticate graphs without leaking. In: EDBT, pp. 609–620 (2010)
18. Liu, B., Lu, J., Yip, J.: XML data integrity based on concatenated hash function. International Journal of Computer Science and Information Security 1(1) (May 2009)
19. Miyazaki, K., Susaki, S., Iwamura, M., Matsumoto, T., Sasaki, R., Yoshiura, H.: Digital documents sanitizing problem. Technical Report ISEC2003-20, IEICE (2003)
20. Miyazaki, K., Hanaoka, G., Imai, H.: Digitally signed document sanitizing scheme based on bilinear maps. In: Proceedings of the 2006 ACM Symposium on Information, Computer and Communications Security, ASIACCS 2006, pp. 343–354. ACM, New York (2006)
21. Miyazaki, K., Iwamura, M., Matsumoto, T., Sasaki, R., Yoshiura, H., Tezuka, S., Imai, H.: Digitally Signed Document Sanitizing Scheme with Disclosure Condition Control. IEICE Transactions 88-A(1), 239–246 (2005)
22. Owens, L., Duffy, A., Dowling, T.: An Identity Based Encryption system. In: PPPJ, pp. 154–159 (2004)
23. Pöhls, H.C., Samelin, K., Posegga, J.: Sanitizable Signatures in XML Signature — Performance, Mixing Properties, and Revisiting the Property of Transparency. In: Lopez, J., Tsudik, G. (eds.) ACNS 2011. LNCS, vol. 6715, pp. 166–182. Springer, Heidelberg (2011)
24. Sandhu, R.S.: Lattice-Based Access Control Models. Computer 26, 9–19 (1993)
25. Steinfeld, R., Bull, L., Zheng, Y.: Content Extraction Signatures. In: Kim, K.-c. (ed.) ICISC 2001. LNCS, vol. 2288, pp. 285–304. Springer, Heidelberg (2002)
26. Wu, Z.-Y., Hsueh, C.-W., Tsai, C.-Y., Lai, F., Lee, H.-C., Chung, Y.: Redactable Signatures for Signed CDA Documents. Journal of Medical Systems, 1–14 (December 2010)
27. Zhang, F., Safavi-naini, R., Susilo, W.: ID-Based Chameleon Hashes from Bilinear Pairings. In: IACR Cryptology ePrint Archive, number 208 (2003)

A   Security and Correctness Proofs

Theorem 1 (The Construction is Correct). *Our construction is correct.*

Proof. Trivially follows from the definitions and the algorithms, i.e. every information claimed to be valueable is explicitly signed and must explicitly be verified. Signing the "left-of" relationship is enough to protect the ordering due to the transitive behaviour. See [8] and [4] for additional information. Note, the unique nonces imply that copy attacks, i.e. just aggregating a specific signature σ_i again are prohibited. The nonces also circumvent the problem of not being able to sign a document where a document is contained twice from the beginning [3].   □

Theorem 2 (The Construction is Private). *Our construction is private in the information-theoretical sense.*

Proof. Our scheme is private in the information-theoretical sense. In particular, the parts redacted are completly removed from the signature and the message. Hence, the secret bit b is perfectly hidden. The signing algorithm requires that always fresh r_i are drawn *uniformly*, while removing a random number from a uniformly distributed list leads to a uniformly distributed list again. Hence, even an unbounded adversary is not able to guess the bit better than at random. The adversary would be able to distinguish between two uniform distributions. The other way around is similar; if the redacted message would have been signed directly, while the corresponding r_i are not changed, the output is the same, prohibiting even unbounded adversaries from guessing any better than random. This implies perfect privacy.   □

Theorem 3 (The Construction is Transparent). *Our construction is transparent in the information-theoretical sense.*

Proof. Our scheme is also transparent in the information-theoretical sense. In other words, the secret bit b is perfectly hidden. Our signing algorithm requires that always fresh r_i are drawn *uniformly*, while removing a random number from a uniformly distributed list leads to a uniformly distributed list again. Hence, even an unbounded adversary is not able to guess the bit better than at random. Otherwise, the adversary would be able to distinguish between two uniform distributions, which is obviously impossible. Again, the other way around is similar: If the redacted message would have been signed directly, the distributions are still uniform and it is impossible for any adversary to guess b better than at random.   □

Theorem 4 (The Construction is Unforgeable). *Our construction is unforgeable.*

Proof. Note: We require that the tags τ_m are chosen unique for each message, while sk is fixed. The r_i are drawn uniformly as well. Hence, we will omit unlikely collisions of those and trivial mix-and-match-attacks. Knowing this, we can construct an adversary $\mathcal{B}$ with breaks the unforgeability of the BGLS-Scheme, if an adversary $\mathcal{A}$ with a non-negligible advantage ϵ exists, winning our unforgeability game. To do so, $\mathcal{B}$ uses $\mathcal{A}$ as a black box. For every signature query $\mathcal{A}$ requests, $\mathcal{B}$ forwards the queries to its signing oracle $\mathcal{O}^{Sign}$ and genuinely returns the answers to $\mathcal{A}$. Eventually, $\mathcal{A}$ will output a pair (m^*, σ^*). Given the transcript of the simulation, $\mathcal{B}$ checks, if (m^*, σ^*) is a trivial "forgery", i.e. a result of an allowed redaction. If so, $\mathcal{B}$ aborts the simulation. If, at some time, $\mathcal{B}$ does not need to restart, $\mathcal{B}$ outputs the tuple (m^*, σ^*) as its forgery attempt. Note that if $\exists i : \sigma^* \neq \sigma_i \wedge m_i = m^*$, then the pair (m^*, σ^*) does not win our unforgeability game and is therefore not a valid forgery attempt. This ends the simulation. We have to distinguish between two cases: (1) If $\exists i : \sigma^* = \sigma_i \wedge m_i \neq m^*$, $\mathcal{B}$ has found collision of the underlying random oracle or must have forged at least two messages. One can extract the colliding aggregates and output them as a valid forgery of the BGLS-Scheme itself. In both cases, m^* has never been queried. (2) If $\neg \exists i : \sigma^* = \sigma_i \vee m_i = m^*$. Then we have a valid forgery of a message m never queried. This breaks the unforgeability of the BGLS-Scheme. To avoid duplicate work, we relegate the reader to [3] and [20], where the authors show how to break the "Diffie-Hellman-Problem" using our algorithm $\mathcal{B}$, which always outputs a valid forgery, if $\mathcal{A}$ is successful, hence with probability ϵ.   □

Theorem 5 (The Construction is Disclosure Secure). *Our construction is disclosure secure.*

Proof. Note, the following proofs are given under the assumption, that the k-element-aggregate-extraction-assumption (k-EAEA) [3] yields, even if the adversary has access to a signing oracle. Let $\mathcal{A}$ be an algorithm winning our disclosure secure game. We can then use $\mathcal{A}$ to break k-EAEA and therefore also the "Diffie-Hellman Assumption" [9] resp. the unforgeability of the underlying BGLS-Scheme. To do so, we let $\mathcal{B}$ use $\mathcal{A}$ as a black-box again. For every query of $\mathcal{A}$ to the oracle $\mathcal{O}^{RSign}$, $\mathcal{B}$ forwards the queries to its oracle $\mathcal{O}^{AAggSign}$, where $\mathcal{O}^{AAggSign}$ signs and aggregates messages in one step. A full description is given in the full version of this paper. For all messages $m_c = m_i \setminus \text{MOD}_{c,i}$, $\mathcal{B}$ calls $\mathcal{O}^{Sign}$ and simulates $(m_i', \sigma_i') \leftarrow \text{Close}(pk, m_i, \sigma_i, \text{MOD}_{c,i})$. Afterwards, it forwards (m_i', σ_i') genuinely to $\mathcal{A}$. Eventually, $\mathcal{A}$ outputs its forgery attempt (m^*, σ^*). If (m^*, σ^*) is non-trivial and actually winning the disclosure secure game, $\mathcal{B}$ outputs (m^*, σ^*), otherwise $\mathcal{B}$ aborts. This ends the description of our simulation.

There are two cases:

Case 1: $\mathcal{A}$ could reconstruct parts of ADM_i
Case 2: $\mathcal{A}$ could redact parts of m_i, which were subject to disclosure control

The first case: Trivial; $\mathcal{A}$ must be able to extract signatures from the aggregate; The algorithm given in [9] can use $\mathcal{B}$ to break the DH-Assumption. The second case: Either $\mathcal{A}$ forged the signature or extracts sub-signatures as well. As before, an algorithm able to forge signatures can be used to solve the DH-Problem [3,20]. To extract the sub-signatures in the non-forgery case, one reverse calculates the signatures. In particular, one only needs to calculate $\sigma \setminus \sigma^*$ and output the result. The result was an aggregated signature, and therefore the algorithm given in [9] can use $\mathcal{B}$ to break DH.   □

Improved Efficiency of Chosen Ciphertext Secure Encryption from Factoring*

Xianhui Lu[1], Bao Li[1], Qixiang Mei[2], and Yamin Liu[1]

[1] State Key Laboratory of Information Security, Graduate University of Chinese Academy of Sciences, Beijing, 100049, China
[2] School of Information, Guangdong Ocean University, Zhanjiang, 524088, China
{xhlu,lb,ymliu}@is.ac.cn, nupf@163.com

Abstract. We propose a new variant of HK09 (proposed by Hofheinz and Kiltz in Eurocrypt 2009) which improves the decapsulation efficiency at the price of a slightly increased key size. Compared with the original HK09 scheme the decapsulation efficiency is improved by 32% (instantiated over the quadratic residuosity group) or 57.6% (instantiated over the semi-smooth subgroup) and the encapsulation efficiency remains the same.

Keywords: public key encryption, chosen ciphertext security, factoring.

1 Introduction

Indistinguishability against adaptive chosen ciphertext (IND-CCA) security [15,16] is now widely accepted as the standard security notion of public key encryption schemes. During a long period of time, IND-CCA secure schemes were designed based on decisional assumptions, such as Decisional Diffie-Hellman (DDH) assumption [5,7,12], Decisional Composite Residuosity (DCR) assumption [6,7] and Decisional Quadratic Residuosity (DQR) assumption [6,7], whereas the construction of IND-CCA secure schemes based on computational assumptions, such as factoring assumption and Computational Diffie-Hellman (CDH) assumption, remained an open problem.

The first IND-CCA secure public key encryption scheme based on a computational assumption was proposed by Canetti, Halevi and Katz [3], who obtained a IND-CCA secure scheme from the Computational Bilinear Diffie-Hellman (CBDH) assumption. Later Cash, Kiltz and Shoup proposed a IND-CCA secure scheme under the CDH assumption [4]. The efficiency was later improved in [8,9,17]. In these schemes the encapsulated key is generated by applying the hardcore predicate based on the CDH assumption. Thus, one exponentiation can only generate one bit of the key or a few bits of the key (using simultaneous hardcore bits). Hence the computational efficiency of these schemes is not suitable for practice.

---

* Supported by the National Natural Science Foundation of China (No.61070171), the National Basic Research Program of China(973 project) (No.2007CB311201) and the Postdoctoral Science Foundation of China (No.20100480514).

M.D. Ryan, B. Smyth, and G. Wang (Eds.): ISPEC 2012, LNCS 7232, pp. 34–45, 2012.

Hofheinz and Kiltz proposed the first practical IND-CCA secure public key encryption scheme based on the factoring assumption [10](HK09). Their scheme is constructed from Blum-Goldwasser encryption [2]. Thanks to the use of Blum-Blum-Shub pseudorandom generator [1], one multiplication can generate one bit of the key. The authors also proposed, in the appendix, a variant (HK09-A) of their scheme that has slightly more efficient decapsulation but suffers from a comparatively large key size (about $2l_T$ or $l_T + \log l_T$ elements, $l_T = 80$ for the security level of 80).

The construction of HK09 was latter generalized to the extractable hash proof system by Wee in [17]. In [17], Wee also proposed a conceptually simpler variant of HK09 which is more modular but less efficient (there is a linear blow-up in both ciphertext overhead and public key size over HK09).

The efficiency of HK09 was later improved in [14,13]. In [14], the authors instantiated HK09 over the semi-smooth subgroup and also proposed an ElGamal style variant of HK09. Briefly, semi-smooth subgroup consider the modulus of $N = PQ = (2p'p + 1)(2q'q + 1)$, where (p', q') are prime numbers large enough but much smaller than (P, Q), and (p, q) are product of distinct prime numbers smaller than a bound. The unique subgroup of QR_N (the quadratic residuosity group) with order $p'q'$ is called semi-smooth subgroup. Since $p'q'$ is much smaller than the order of QR_N, schemes instantiated over semi-smooth subgroup are more efficient. In [13] the authors proposed a tradeoff between the efficiency of encapsulation and decapsulation of HK09. Compared with original HK09 the efficiency of decapsulation was improved by 38.9% and the efficiency of encapsulation was dropped by 11.4% (instantiated over the semi-smooth subgroup).

1.1   Motivation

Up to now, HK09-A is the most efficient IND-CCA secure public key encryption scheme based on factoring assumption over QR_N in standard model. Unfortunately, it suffers the disadvantage of a comparatively large key size ($2l_T$ elements for private key and $2l_T + 1$ elements for public key).

In HK09, the ciphertext is $(R = g^{\mu 2^{l_K + l_T}}, S = |(g^t X)^\mu|)$ and the encapsulated key is $K = \mathrm{BBS}_N(g^{\mu 2^{l_T}})$, where $g \in \mathrm{QR}_N$, $\mu \in [(N-1)/4]$, $X = g^{x2^{l_K+l_T}}$, $x \in [(N-1)/4]$ is the private key, l_K is the length of K, l_T is the length of the hash value $t = \mathrm{T}(R)$, $N = (2p+1)(2q+1)$ is a Blum number. To recover K, the decapsulation algorithm needs to compute $g^\mu = (S/R^x)^{1/t}$. Since the exponent inversion can not be computed directly for hidden order group, the decapsulation algorithm computes $g^{\mu 2^{l_T}}$ by using the gcd (greatest common divisor) skill.

To avoid the computation of exponent inversion, in HK09-A, the authors interpret t as a bitwise selector of l_T out of $2l_T$ group elements X_{ij}, where $i \in [l_T], j \in \{0, 1\}$. Concretely, the ciphertext is $(R = g^{\mu 2^{l_K}}, S = |(\prod_{i=1}^{l_T} X_{i,t_i})^\mu|)$. Despite the improved decapsulation efficiency, the key size is comparatively large.

An interesting question is, can we construct a variant of HK09 that simultaneously enjoys the properties of high efficiency and small key size?

1.2   Our Contribution

We propose a variant of HK09 which improves the decapsulation efficiency at the price of a slightly increased key size. Compared with the original HK09 scheme the decapsulation efficiency is improved by 32% (instantiated over the quadratic residuosity group) or 57.6% (instantiated over the semi-smooth subgroup) and the encapsulation efficiency remains the same. Thus our variant simultaneously enjoys the properties of high efficiency and small key size (2 or 3 elements for private key and 3 elements for public key).

Our main idea is to avoid the computation of exponent inversion by hiding g^μ instead of $g^{\mu t}$ into S. Concretely, the ciphertext is $(R = g^{\mu 2^l K}, S = |X^{\mu t}Y^\mu|)$, the encapsulated key is $K = \text{BBS}_N(g^\mu)$, where $h \in \text{QR}_N, g = h^2, X = g^{x 2^l K}, Y = g^{y 2^l K} h, (x, y) \in [(N-1)/4]$ is the private key. Thus, the decapsulation computes $g^\mu = S^2/R^{2(xt+y)}$ directly.

The main difficulty is the security proof of this new variant. To construct the challenge ciphertext, the simulator may set $X = g^{x 2^l K} h^{-1}, Y = g^{y 2^l K} h^{t^*}$ (to construct S^* without h^{μ^*}). In this case the simulator can only compute $g^{(t^*-t)\mu} = h^{2(t^*-t)}$ in the simulation of decapsulation. A direct solution is setting $R = g^{\mu 2^l K + l_T}$ and computing $g^{\mu 2^l T}$ by using the gcd skill as in [10]. In this case we still need to use $g^{\mu 2^l T}$ as the seed for BBS. We figure out a more efficient solution by setting $g = h^{2^l T + 1}$ and computing $g^\mu = h^{\mu 2^l T + 1}$ from $h^{2(t^*-t)\mu}$ and $h^{\mu 2^l K + l_T + 1} = g^{\mu 2^l K}$ by using the gcd skill. In our new solution we can set $R = g^{\mu 2^l K}$ and use g^μ as the seed for BBS.

Note that, in [13] the authors also improved the decapsulation efficiency by avoiding the computation of exponent inversion. Their skill is to derive the encapsulated key from $g^{\mu t 2^l T}$ directly. Compared with the scheme in [13], we improve the decapsulation efficiency at the cost of one element increasing in key size, while they improved the decapsulation efficiency at the cost of 11.4% decreasing in encapsulation efficiency.

We remark that our new variant can be instantiated over the semi-smooth subgroup using the technique in [14]. The resulting scheme is more efficient than that over the QR_N group.

1.3   Outline

In section 2 we review the definition of key encapsulation mechanism and target collision resistant hash function. In section 3 we propose a new variant of HK09. Finally we give the conclusion in section 4.

2   Definitions

In describing probabilistic processes, $x \xleftarrow{R} X$ denotes that x is sampled according to the distribution X. If S is a finite set, $s \xleftarrow{R} S$ denotes that s is sampled from the uniform distribution on S. If A is a probabilistic algorithm and x an input, then

$A(x)$ denotes the output distribution of A on input x. Thus, we write $y \xleftarrow{R} A(x)$ to denote of running algorithm A on input x and assigning the output to the variable y.

2.1 Key Encapsulation Mechanism

A key encapsulation mechanism consists the following algorithms:

- KEM.KeyGen(1^k): A probabilistic polynomial-time key generation algorithm takes as input a security parameter (1^k) and outputs a public key PK and a secret key SK. We write (PK, SK) ← KEM.KeyGen(1^k)
- KEM.Enc(PK): A probabilistic polynomial-time encapsulation algorithm takes as input the public key PK, and outputs a pair (K, ψ), where $K \in K_D(K_D$ is the key space) is a key and ψ is a ciphertext. We write $(K, \psi) \leftarrow$ KEM.Enc(PK)
- KEM.Dec(SK, ψ): A decapsulation algorithm takes as input a ciphertext ψ and the secret key SK. It returns a key K. We write $K \leftarrow$ KEM.Dec(SK, ψ).

We require that for all (PK,SK) output by KEM.KeyGen(1^k), all $(K, \psi) \in$ [KEM.Enc(PK)], we have KEM.Dec(SK, ψ)=K.

Now we review the IND-CCA (Indistinguishability against adaptive chosen ciphertext attack) security of KEM. Note that we use the definition in [11] which is simpler than the original definition in [7].

Definition 1. *A KEM scheme is indistinguishability against adaptive chosen ciphertext attacks if the advantage of any adversary in the following game is negligible in the security parameter k.*

1. The adversary queries a key generation oracle. The key generation oracle computes (PK, SK) ← KEM.KeyGen(1^k) and responds with PK.
2. The adversary queries an encapsulation oracle. The encapsulation oracle computes:

$$b \xleftarrow{R} \{0,1\}, (K_1, \psi^*) \leftarrow \text{KEM.Enc(PK)}, K_0 \xleftarrow{R} K_D,$$

   and responds with (K_b, ψ^*).
3. The adversary makes a sequence of calls to the decapsulation oracle. For each query the adversary submits a ciphertext ψ, and the decapsulation oracle responds with KEM.Dec(SK, ψ). The only restriction is that the adversary can not request the decapsulation of ψ^*.
4. Finally, the adversary outputs a guess b'.

The adversary's advantage in the above game is $\text{Adv}_A^{\text{cca}}(k) = |\Pr[b' = 1|b = 1] - \Pr[b' = 1|b = 0]|$. If a KEM is secure against adaptive chosen ciphertext attacks defined in the above game we say it is IND-CCA secure.

2.2   Target Collision Resistant Hash Function

Now we review the definition of target collision resistant (TCR) hash function. We say that a function $H : X \to Y$ is a TCR hash function, if, given a random preimage $x \in X$, it is hard to find $x' \neq x$ with $H(x') = H(x)$. Concretely, the advantage of an adversary $\mathcal{A}$ is defined as:

$$\mathrm{Adv}_{\mathcal{A}}^{\mathrm{tcr}}(k) = \Pr[x \xleftarrow{R} X, x' \leftarrow A(x) : x \neq x' \wedge H(x) = H(x')].$$

We say H is a TCR hash function if $\mathrm{Adv}_{\mathcal{A}}^{\mathrm{tcr}}(k)$ is negligible.

3   New Variant of HK09

Our new variant of HK09 is described as follows.

- KeyGen: Choose uniformly at random a Blum integer $N = PQ = (2p + 1)(2q + 1)$, where P, Q, p, q are prime numbers. Then compute:

$$h \xleftarrow{R} \mathrm{QR}_N, g \leftarrow h^2, (x, y) \xleftarrow{R} [(N - 1)/4],$$

$$X \leftarrow g^{x 2^{l_K}}, Y \leftarrow g^{y 2^{l_K}} h,$$

$$pk \leftarrow (N, g, X, Y), sk \leftarrow (x, y),$$

where $T : QR_N \to \{0, 1\}^{l_T}$ is a TCR hash function, l_K is the bit length of the encapsulated key K.
- Encapsulation: Given pk, the encapsulation algorithm computes:

$$\mu \xleftarrow{R} [(N - 1)/4], R \leftarrow g^{\mu 2^{l_K}}, t \leftarrow T(R), S \leftarrow \left| (X^t Y)^{\mu} \right|,$$

$$K \leftarrow \mathrm{BBS}_N(g^{\mu}),$$

where $\mathrm{BBS}_N(\alpha) = \mathrm{LSB}(\alpha), \cdots, \mathrm{LSB}(\alpha^{2^{l_K - 1}})$, $\mathrm{LSB}(\alpha)$ denotes the least significant bit of α.
- Decapsulation: Given a ciphertext (R, S) and sk, the decapsulation algorithm verifies $R \in Z_N^*, S \in Z_N^* \cap [(N - 1)/2]$, then computes:

$$t \leftarrow T(R), \rho \leftarrow xt + y,$$

$$\text{if } \left(\frac{S^2}{R^{2\rho}} \right)^{2^{l_K + 1}} = R^2 \text{ then compute } K \leftarrow \mathrm{BBS}_N \left(\frac{S^2}{R^{2\rho}} \right),$$

else return the rejection symbol $\perp$.

The correctness of the scheme above can be verified as follows:

$$\left(\frac{S^2}{R^{2\rho}} \right) = \left(\frac{\left| (X^t Y)^{\mu} \right|^2}{g^{2\mu 2^{l_K} \rho}} \right) = \left(\frac{h^{2\mu} g^{\mu 2^{l_K + 1} \rho}}{g^{\mu 2^{l_K + 1} \rho}} \right) = (h^2)^{\mu} = g^{\mu}.$$

We remark that, if pq is added to the private key, the efficiency of decapsulation can be improved by computing $\rho = (xt + y) \mod pq$. It is clear that, our new variant above can also be instantiated over semi-smooth subgroup using the technique in [14]. In this case, (x, y) are selected from $2^{l_{p'} + l_{q'} + \lambda}$, where $l_{p'}$ is the length of p', $l_{q'}$ is the length of q', λ is a parameter for security level. If $p'q'$ is added to the private key, the efficiency of decapsulation can be further improved by selecting (x, y) from $[p'q']$ instead of $2^{l_{p'} + l_{q'} + \lambda}$.

3.1   Security Proof

Theorem 1. *If factoring N is hard and T is a TCR hash function, then the new variant is IND-CCA secure.*

Review the security proof in HK09, wherein, the reduction is divided into two phases. In the first phase the BBS distinguisher is reduced to the factoring assumption. In the second phase, the IND-CCA security of the scheme is reduced to the BBS distinguisher. The experiment for the BBS distinguish problem is defined as:

$$\text{Adv}_{\mathcal{A}}^{\text{BBS}} = |\Pr[\mathcal{A}(N, z, \text{BBS}_N(u)) = 1] - \Pr[A(N, z, U) = 1]|,$$

where N is a Blum integer ($N = PQ, P = 2p+1, Q = 2q+1$, p and q are prime numbers), $u \in QR_N$, $z = u^{2^{l_K}}$, U is a random bit string of length l_K.
    Given Theorem 2 in [10], it is clear that we only need to proof the following theorem.

Theorem 2. *If it is hard to distinguish $(N, z, \text{BBS}_N(u))$ from (N, z, U) and T is a TCR hash function, then the new variant is IND-CCA secure.*

Proof. Suppose that an adversary $\mathcal{A}$ can break the IND-CCA security of the new variant. To prove the theorem, we construct an adversary $\mathcal{B}$ to distinguish $(N, z, \text{BBS}_N(u))$ from (N, z, U). The construction of $\mathcal{B}$ is described as follows.

Setup: On receiving (N, z, V), where $V = U$ or $V = \text{BBS}_N(u)$, the adversary $\mathcal{B}$ computes:

$$h \xleftarrow{R} QR_N, g \leftarrow h^{2^{l_T + 1}}, (x, y) \xleftarrow{R} [(N-1)/4],$$

$$t^* \leftarrow T(z), X \leftarrow g^{x 2^{l_K}} h^{-1}, Y \leftarrow g^{y 2^{l_K}} h^{t^*},$$

$$pk \leftarrow (N, g, X, Y).$$

The adversary $\mathcal{B}$ sends pk to adversary $\mathcal{A}$.

Challenge: The adversary $\mathcal{B}$ constructs the challenge ciphertext as follows.

$$R^* \leftarrow z, S^* \leftarrow \left| R^{*\rho^*} \right|, K^* \leftarrow V.$$

Where $\rho^* = xt^* + y$. Let $R^* = g^{\mu^* 2^{l_K}}$, the correctness of the challenge ciphertext can be verified as follow:

$$
\begin{aligned}
S^* &= \left| R^{*\rho^*} \right| \\
&= \left| g^{\mu^* 2^{l_K} (xt^* + y)} \right| \\
&= \left| g^{\mu^* 2^{l_K} xt^*} g^{\mu^* 2^{l_K} y} \right| \\
&= \left| \left(g^{2^{l_K} xt^*} h^{-t^*} \right)^{\mu^*} \left(g^{2^{l_K} y} h^{t^*} \right)^{\mu^*} \right| \\
&= \left| \left(g^{2^{l_K} x} h^{-1} \right)^{\mu^* t^*} \left(g^{2^{l_K} y} h^{t^*} \right)^{\mu^*} \right| \\
&= \left| X^{\mu^* t^*} Y^{\mu^*} \right| \\
&= \left| (X^{t^*} Y)^{\mu^*} \right| .
\end{aligned}
\tag{1}
$$

Decapsulation: On receiving the decapsulation query (R, S), the adversary $\mathcal{B}$ verifies $R \in Z_N^*, S \in Z_N^* \cap [(N-1)/2]$, then computes:

$$
t \leftarrow T(R), \rho \leftarrow xt + y.
$$

Then the adversary $\mathcal{B}$ considers three cases:

Case 1: $t \neq t^*$. In this case, the adversary $\mathcal{B}$ acts as:

$$
\text{if } \left(\frac{S^2}{R^{2\rho}} \right)^{2^{l_K + l_T + 1}} = R^{2(t^* - t)} \text{ computes:}
$$

$$
2^c = \gcd(t^* - t, 2^{l_K + l_T}) = a(t^* - t) + b2^{l_K + l_T},
$$

$$
\text{returns } K \leftarrow BBS_N \left(\left((S^2 R^{-2\rho})^a R^b \right)^{2^{l_T - c}} \right),
$$

$$
\text{else returns the rejection symbol } \bot .
$$

Since $t \neq t^*$ we have $0 < c < l_T$. Let $R = g^{\mu 2^{l_K}}$, the correctness of the verification equation can be verified as follows:

$$
\begin{aligned}
\left(\frac{S^2}{R^{2\rho}} \right)^{2^{l_K + l_T + 1}} &= \left(\frac{|(X^t Y)^\mu|^2}{g^{2\rho 2^{l_K} \mu}} \right)^{2^{l_K + l_T + 1}} \\
&= \left(\frac{((g^{x2^{l_K}} h^{-1})^t (g^{y2^{l_K}} h^{t^*}))^{2\mu}}{g^{2\rho 2^{l_K} \mu}} \right)^{2^{l_K + l_T + 1}} \\
&= \left(\frac{(g^{(xt+y)2^{l_K}} h^{t^* - t})^{2\mu}}{g^{2\rho 2^{l_K} \mu}} \right)^{2^{l_K + l_T + 1}} \\
&= \left(\frac{(g^{\rho 2^{l_K}} h^{t^* - t})^{2\mu}}{g^{2\rho 2^{l_K} \mu}} \right)^{2^{l_K + l_T + 1}} \\
&= ((h^{t^* - t})^{2\mu})^{2^{l_K + l_T + 1}} \\
&= (h^{2^{l_T + 1}})^{2^{l_K} \mu (2(t^* - t))} \\
&= g^{2^{l_K} \mu (2(t^* - t))} \\
&= R^{2(t^* - t)}.
\end{aligned}
\tag{2}
$$

The correctness of K can be verified as follows:

$$
\begin{aligned}
K &= \mathrm{BBS}_N\left(\left(\left(S^2 R^{-2\rho}\right)^a R^b\right)^{2^l T - c}\right) \\
&= \mathrm{BBS}_N\left(\left(\left(h^{2(t^*-t)\mu}\right)^a \left(g^{\mu 2^l K}\right)^b\right)^{2^l T - c}\right) \\
&= \mathrm{BBS}_N\left(\left(\left(h^{2\mu}\right)^{a(t^*-t)} \left(\left(h^{2^l T+1}\right)^{\mu 2^l K}\right)^b\right)^{2^l T - c}\right) \\
&= \mathrm{BBS}_N\left(\left(\left(h^{2\mu}\right)^{a(t^*-t)} \left(h^{2\mu}\right)^{b 2^l K + l_T}\right)^{2^l T - c}\right) \\
&= \mathrm{BBS}_N\left(\left(\left(h^{2\mu}\right)^{a(t^*-t)+b 2^l K + l_T}\right)^{2^l T - c}\right) \\
&= \mathrm{BBS}_N\left(\left(\left(h^{2\mu}\right)^{2^c}\right)^{2^l T - c}\right) \\
&= \mathrm{BBS}_N\left(\left(h^{2\mu}\right)^{2^l T}\right) \\
&= \mathrm{BBS}_N\left(\left(h^{2^l T+1}\right)^\mu\right) \\
&= \mathrm{BBS}_N\left(g^\mu\right).
\end{aligned}
\tag{3}
$$

Case 2: $t = t^*, R \neq R^*$. Denote this case as an event $\mathrm{bad}_{\mathrm{tcr}}$. Since T is a TCR hash function, we have $\Pr[\mathrm{bad}_{\mathrm{tcr}}] \leq \mathrm{Adv}_{\mathcal{C}}^{\mathrm{tcr}}$.

Case 3: $t = t^*, R = R^*, S \neq S^*$. In this case, if $S^2 \neq R^{2\rho}$ return the rejection symbol $\perp$. If $S^2 = R^{2\rho}$, we have $|S| = S \neq S^* = |S^*|$ and $S^2 = R^{2\rho} = R^{*2\rho} = S^{*2}$. Then, $S \neq \pm S^*$ and $S^2 - S^{*2} = (S + S^*)(S - S^*) = 0$. Thus $\mathcal{B}$ can factor N directly by computing $\gcd(N, S + S^*)$ or $\gcd(N, S - S^*)$.

Guess: On receiving b' from adversary $\mathcal{A}$, the adversary $\mathcal{B}$ outputs b'.

This finishes the construction of the adversary $\mathcal{B}$. We claim that the distribution of simulated public key and the challenge ciphertext is almost identical in the simulation above and the IND-CCA game.

Lemma 1. *There exists an event* $\mathrm{bad}_{\mathrm{key}}$ *such that, conditioned on* $\neg\mathrm{bad}_{\mathrm{key}}$ *the public key and the challenge ciphertext are identically distributed in simulation and the IND-CCA game. Concretely,*

$$
\Pr[\mathrm{bad}_{\mathrm{key}}] \leq \frac{5}{2^{k-1}},
$$

where k is the parameter of security level.

Since the proof of the lemma above is very similar to that of lemma 1 in [10], we omit the detail.

It is clear that, unless bad_{tcr} or bad_{key} occurs, $\mathcal{B}$ perfectly simulates the real IND-CCA game. To be concrete:

$$\begin{aligned}
\text{Adv}_{\mathcal{B}}^{\text{BBS}} &= \text{Adv}_{\mathcal{A}}^{\text{cca}} - \Pr[\text{bad}_{\text{tcr}}] - \Pr[\text{bad}_{\text{key}}] \\
&\geq \text{Adv}_{\mathcal{A}}^{\text{cca}} - \text{Adv}_{\mathcal{C}}^{\text{tcr}} - \frac{5}{2^{k-1}}.
\end{aligned} \tag{4}$$

This completes the proof of theorem 2. □

3.2 Efficiency

In this section, we analyze the efficiency of our new variant and compare it with the previous schemes in [10,14,13]. Note that, all of these schemes can be instantiated over the QR_N group or the semi-smooth subgroup. For the sake of clarity, these two cases are discussed respectively.

The case of QR_N group. Compared with the original HK09 scheme the decapsulation efficiency of the proposed variant is improved by 32% in the case of quadratic residuosity group. The efficiency of schemes in [10,14,13] and our variant is listed in table 1, where HK09 is the scheme in [10], HK09-A is the scheme in the appendix of [10], E-HK is the ElGamal style variant of HK09 in [14], T-HK is the tradeoff variant of HK09 in [13] and NEW is the proposed variant. The parameters are the same as those in [10,14,13], $l_N = 1024, l_K = l_T = 80$.

Table 1. Schemes instantiated over the QR_N group

	Encapsulate(mul)	Decapsulate(mul)	SK (bits)	PK (bits)
HK09	$3272(3l_N + l_K + 1.5l_T)$	$2376(1.5l_N + 4l_K + 6.5l_T)$	l_N	$2l_N$
HK09-A	$3232(3l_N + l_K + 1l_T)$	$1616(1.5l_N + l_K)$	$2l_T l_N$	$(2l_T + 1)l_N$
E-HK	$4808(4.5l_N + l_K + 1.5l_T)$	$2043(1.5 \times 1.2l_N + 2.5l_T)$	$2l_N$	$3l_N$
T-HK	$3432(3l_N + 2l_K + 2.5l_T)$	$1816(1.5l_N + l_K + 2.5l_T)$	l_N	$2l_N$
NEW	$3272(3l_N + l_K + 1.5l_T)$	$1736(1.5l_N + l_K + 1.5l_T)$ $1616(1.5l_N + l_K)$	$2l_N$ $3l_N$	$3l_N$

The encapsulation of our variant can first compute $A = g^\mu$, which requires $1.5l_N$ multiplications. Then, the computation of $B = (X^t Y)^\mu$ requires $1.5l_N + 1.5l_T$ multiplications. Finally, the computations of $R = A^{2^{l_K}} = g^{2^{l_K}\mu}$ and $K = \text{BBS}_N(A)$ require l_K multiplications. Thus, the encapsulation requires $3l_N + l_K + 1.5l_T$ multiplications. The decapsulation computes $D = R^\rho$, which requires $1.5l_N + 1.5l_T$ multiplications (the length of $\rho = xt+y$ is $l_N + l_T$). Then computes $((S/D)^2)^{2^{l_K}}$ and $K = \text{BBS}_N((S/D)^2)$, which require l_K multiplications. We have that the decapsulation requires $1.5l_N + l_K + 1.5l_T$ multiplications. Note that, the decapsulation can be improved by adding pq to the private key and computing $\rho = (xt+y) \mod pq$. As a result, the decapsulation requires $1.5l_N + l_K$ multiplications.

In [10], the authors claim that the encapsulation requires $3l_N + 1l_K + 2.5l_T$ multiplications. We point out that the computation of $A^{2^{l_T}} = g^{\mu 2^{l_T}}$ and $S = A^t B = g^{\mu t} X^\mu$ can be further optimized. $A^{2^{l_T}}$ is a by-product of A^t. That is, the encapsulation of HK09 requires $3l_N + 1l_K + 1.5l_T$ multiplications.

In [14], the authors claim that the encapsulation requires $4.5l_N + l_K + 2.5l_T$ multiplications and the decapsulation requires $1.5 \times 1.2l_N + l_K + 2.5l_T$ multiplications (the authors of [14] consider the case of the semi-smooth subgroup group, we consider the QR_N group here). We point out that, g^{2^v} can be precomputed. Thus the computation of $R = g^{\mu 2^v}$ only requires l_N multiplications. As a result, the encapsulation of E-HK requires $4.5l_N + l_K + 1.5l_T$ multiplications. In decapsulation, the computation of $K = BBS_r^+(R^{\rho'})$ is a by-product of $R^{\rho' t}$. So the decapsulation only requires $1.5 \times 1.2l_N + 2.5l_T$ multiplications.

The case of semi-smooth subgroup group. Compared with the original HK09 scheme the decapsulation efficiency of our new variant is improved by 57.6% in the case of semi-smooth subgroup. The efficiency of schemes in [10,14,13] and our variant instantiated over the semi-smooth subgroup is listed in table 2, where S-HK is the instantiation of HK09, S-E-HK is the instantiation of E-HK, S-T-HK is the instantiation of T-HK, S-HK-A is the the instantiation of HK9-A and S-NEW is the instantiation of NEW. The parameters are the same as those in [10,14,13], $l_K = l_T = 80, l_{p'} = l_{q'} = 160, \lambda = 80, l_e = l_{p'} + l_{q'} + \lambda = 400, l_{e'} = l_{p'} + l_{q'} = 320$.

Table 2. Schemes instantiated over the semi-smooth subgroup

	Encapsulate(mul)	Decapsulate(mul)	SK (bits)	PK (bits)
S-HK	$1400(3l_e + l_K + 1.5l_T)$	$1440(1.5l_e + 4l_K + 6.5l_T)$ $1320(1.5l_{e'} + 4l_K + 6.5l_T)$	l_e $2l_{e'}$	$2l_N$
S-E-HK	$2000(4.5l_e + l_K + 1.5l_T)$	$920(1.5 \times 1.2l_e + 2.5l_T)$ $776(1.5 \times 1.2l_{e'} + 2.5l_T)$	$2l_e$ $3l_{e'}$	$3l_N$
S-T-HK	$1560(3l_e + 2l_K + 2.5l_T)$	$880(1.5l_e + l_K + 2.5l_T)$ $760(1.5l_{e'} + l_K + 2.5l_T)$	l_e $2l_{e'}$	$2l_N$
S-HK-A	$1360(3l_e + l_K + 1l_T)$	$680(1.5l_e + l_K)$ $560(1.5l_{e'} + l_K)$	$2l_T l_e$ $(2l_T + 1)l_{e'}$	$(2l_T + 1)l_N$
S-NEW	$1400(3l_e + l_K + 1.5l_T)$	$800(1.5l_e + l_K + 1.5l_T)$ $560(1.5l_{e'} + l_K)$	$2l_e$ $3l_{e'}$	$3l_N$

Note that, the private key of schemes instantiated over semi-smooth subgroup is selected from $[2^{l_{p'} + l_{q'} + \lambda}]$. When $p'q'$ is added to the private key, the decapsulation efficiency can be improved by selecting the private key from $[p'q']$. So we consider two cases for the decapsulation efficiency and the private key size.

4   Conclusion

We proposed a variant of HK09 which improves the decapsulation at the price of a slightly increased key size. Compared with the original HK09 scheme the decapsulation efficiency is improved by 32% (instantiated over the quadratic residuosity group) or 57.6% (instantiated over the semi-smooth subgroup) and the encapsulation efficiency remains the same. We proved that the proposed variant is IND-CCA secure under the factoring assumption.

References

1. Blum, L., Blum, M., Shub, M.: A simple unpredictable pseudo-random number generator. SIAM J. Comput. 15(2), 364–383 (1986)
2. Blum, M., Goldwasser, S.: An Efficient Probabilistic Public-Key Encryption Scheme Which Hides All Partial Information. In: Blakely, G.R., Chaum, D. (eds.) CRYPTO 1984. LNCS, vol. 196, pp. 289–302. Springer, Heidelberg (1985)
3. Canetti, R., Halevi, S., Katz, J.: Chosen-Ciphertext Security from Identity-Based Encryption. In: Cachin, C., Camenisch, J.L. (eds.) EUROCRYPT 2004. LNCS, vol. 3027, pp. 207–222. Springer, Heidelberg (2004)
4. Cash, D., Kiltz, E., Shoup, V.: The Twin Diffie-Hellman Problem and Applications. In: Smart, N.P. (ed.) EUROCRYPT 2008. LNCS, vol. 4965, pp. 127–145. Springer, Heidelberg (2008)
5. Cramer, R., Shoup, V.: A Practical Public Key Cryptosystem Provably Secure against Adaptive Chosen Ciphertext Attack. In: Krawczyk, H. (ed.) CRYPTO 1998. LNCS, vol. 1462, pp. 13–25. Springer, Heidelberg (1998)
6. Cramer, R., Shoup, V.: Universal Hash Proofs and a Paradigm for Adaptive Chosen Ciphertext Secure Public-Key Encryption. In: Knudsen, L.R. (ed.) EUROCRYPT 2002. LNCS, vol. 2332, pp. 45–64. Springer, Heidelberg (2002)
7. Cramer, R., Shoup, V.: Design and analysis of practical public-key encryption schemes secure against adaptive chosen ciphertext attack. SIAM J. Comput. 33, 167–226 (2004), http://dl.acm.org/citation.cfm?id=953065.964243
8. Hanaoka, G., Kurosawa, K.: Efficient Chosen Ciphertext Secure Public Key Encryption under the Computational Diffie-Hellman Assumption. In: Pieprzyk, J. (ed.) ASIACRYPT 2008. LNCS, vol. 5350, pp. 308–325. Springer, Heidelberg (2008)
9. Haralambiev, K., Jager, T., Kiltz, E., Shoup, V.: Simple and Efficient Public-Key Encryption from Computational Diffie-Hellman in the Standard Model. In: Nguyen, P.Q., Pointcheval, D. (eds.) PKC 2010. LNCS, vol. 6056, pp. 1–18. Springer, Heidelberg (2010)
10. Hofheinz, D., Kiltz, E.: Practical Chosen Ciphertext Secure Encryption from Factoring. In: Joux, A. (ed.) EUROCRYPT 2009. LNCS, vol. 5479, pp. 313–332. Springer, Heidelberg (2009)
11. Kiltz, E.: Chosen-Ciphertext Secure Key-Encapsulation Based on Gap Hashed Diffie-Hellman. In: Okamoto, T., Wang, X. (eds.) PKC 2007. LNCS, vol. 4450, pp. 282–297. Springer, Heidelberg (2007)
12. Kurosawa, K., Desmedt, Y.: A New Paradigm of Hybrid Encryption Scheme. In: Franklin, M. (ed.) CRYPTO 2004. LNCS, vol. 3152, pp. 426–442. Springer, Heidelberg (2004)
13. Lu, X., Li, B., Mei, Q., Liu, Y.: Improved tradeoff between encapsulation and decapsulation of hk09. In: Inscrypt 2011 (2011) (to appear)
14. Mei, Q., Li, B., Lu, X., Jia, D.: Chosen Ciphertext Secure Encryption under Factoring Assumption Revisited. In: Catalano, D., Fazio, N., Gennaro, R., Nicolosi, A. (eds.) PKC 2011. LNCS, vol. 6571, pp. 210–227. Springer, Heidelberg (2011)

15. Naor, M., Yung, M.: Public-key cryptosystems provably secure against chosen ciphertext attacks. In: Proceedings of the Twenty-Second Annual ACM Symposium on Theory of Computing, STOC 1990, pp. 427–437. ACM, New York (1990)
16. Rackoff, C., Simon, D.R.: Non-interactive Zero-Knowledge Proof of Knowledge and Chosen Ciphertext Attack. In: Feigenbaum, J. (ed.) CRYPTO 1991. LNCS, vol. 576, pp. 433–444. Springer, Heidelberg (1992)
17. Wee, H.: Efficient Chosen-Ciphertext Security via Extractable Hash Proofs. In: Rabin, T. (ed.) CRYPTO 2010. LNCS, vol. 6223, pp. 314–332. Springer, Heidelberg (2010)

Deniable Encryptions Secure against Adaptive Chosen Ciphertext Attack

Chong-zhi Gao[1,2], Dongqing Xie[1], and Baodian Wei[3]

[1] School of Computer Science, Guangzhou University,
Guangzhou 510006, China
czgao@gzhu.edu.cn, dongqing_xie@hotmail.com
[2] Key Laboratory of Network Security and Cryptology, Fujian Normal University,
Fuzhou 350007, China
[3] Department of Electronics and Communication Engineering,
Sun Yat-sen University, Guangzhou 510006, China
weibd@mail.sysu.edu.cn

Abstract. The deniable encryption is a type of encryption which can hide the true message while revealing a fake one. Even if the sender or the receiver is coerced to show the plaintext and the used random numbers in encryption, a deniable encryption scheme behaves like only an innocent message is encrypted. Because it protects privacy against malicious coercer, the deniable encryption is very useful in communication systems such as the cloud storage system when the communication channel is eavesdropped by a coercer. Previous deniable encryptions only concern the security under the adversary's chosen plaintext attack (CPA). For non-interactive deniable encryptions, this paper introduce some security notions under adaptive chosen ciphertext attack (CCA). Furthermore, the first sender-deniable construction with deniability and indistinguishability against CCA attack is constructed.

Keywords: Deniable Encryption, Chosen Plaintext Attack, Chosen Ciphertext Attack.

1 Introduction

Suppose in a communication system, a sender sends an encrypted message to a receiver. Consider a situation in which an adversary obtains the ciphertext and later asks the sender or the receiver to open the ciphertext, i.e., to show the plaintext and the randomness used in generating the ciphertext. A regular encryption scheme does not resist the coercive attack above since it also serves as a commitment and thus the plaintext will be exposed.

Canetti et al. [3] investigated this coercive attack and first introduced the notion of deniable encryption, in which the sender (or the receiver) has the ability to open a ciphertext as an encryption of another message different than the true plaintext and thus the privacy is protected. Because it protects privacy against malicious coercer, the deniable encryption is very useful in communication systems such as the cloud storage system when the communication channel is eavesdropped by a

M.D. Ryan, B. Smyth, and G. Wang (Eds.): ISPEC 2012, LNCS 7232, pp. 46–62, 2012.

coercer [8]. The deniability could be classified as sender deniability or receiver de-niability according to which parties may be coerced. For the sender-deniable case, Canetti et al.'s scheme achieves $O(\frac{1}{n})$ detection advantage and semantic security under chosen plaintext attack where n denotes the length of the ciphertext. Here "detection advantage" is the advantage that the adversary successfully detects whether the sender/receiver are cheating or not.

The deniable encryption in Canetti et al.'s definition [3] is interactive style (For self-containment, we include in Appendix a definition of interactive deniable encryptions (adapted from [3]).). In the security model for an interactive deniable scheme, a chosen plaintext attack (CPA) is considered, i.e., the adversary is given the receiver's public key pk without access to the private decryption key sk. Thus a natural question arises: can we strengthen the adversary's attacking ability by letting him have ability to access the decryption oracle? This paper considers this type of attack in non-interactive cases. The idea is similar with the regular encryption cases for which the IND-CCA2 (indistinguishability against adaptive chosen ciphertext attack [15, 1]) security is defined.

1.1   Other Related Work

To achieve negligible detection advantage, Canetti et al. [3] defined a weaker notion of deniability – flexibly deniable encryption. In this weaker framework, the sender may choose to encrypt a message in an honest mode or in a dishonest mode, and the ciphertext obtained in the dishonest mode can be opened later as being encrypted in the honest mode, but not vice versa. Most recent deniable encryption schemes are in this flexible frameworks [12, 10, 11, 8].

We call the non-flexible deniability "full deniability". In fully deniable encryptions, there is no honest or dishonest mode, i.e., all ciphertexts can be opened later as encryptions of faked messages. In 2011, Bendlin et al. showed in [2] that any non-interactive public-key deniable encryption scheme cannot achieve negligible detection advantage in the fully deniable framework. Thus, in order to obtain negligible detection advantage, resorting to interactive approaches [5] or the flexible framework seems necessary. However, Dürmuth and Freeman's interactive construction [5] which was announced achieving negligible detection advantage was broken by Peikert and Waters (this is mentioned by Dürmuth and Freeman themselves in [6]). So it is still an open problem to construct a (fully) deniable encryption scheme with negligible detection advantage.

Recently, Neill et al. [14] gave the first non-interactive public-key deniable encryption scheme which requires no third party, and is simultaneously sender and receiver deniable in the flexible framework.

1.2   Our Contribution

In the fully deniable framework, we introduce the security notions for non-interactive deniable encryptions which resist adaptive chosen ciphertext attack. Furthermore, we give the first concrete implementation which requires no third party.

1.3   Organization

The rest of this paper is organized as follows. In Section 2, we explain some security notions and some basic tools used in our construction. Section 3 gives a non-interactive deniable encryption scheme secure against adaptive chosen ciphertext attack. Section 4 concludes the paper.

2   Preliminaries

2.1   Notations

We denote by $\mathbb{N}$ the set of natural numbers, and by $\mathbb{R}$ the set of real numbers. If $k \in \mathbb{N}$, we denote by 1^k (resp. 0^k) the concatenation of k ones (resp. zeroes) and by $\{0,1\}^k$ the set of bitstrings of bitlength k. The notation $[k]$ represents the set $\{1, 2, \ldots, k\}$. "PPT" is an abbreviation for "probabilistic polynomial-time".

If S is a set, the notation $|S|$ denotes the number of elements in set S, and the notation $x \leftarrow S$ denotes that x is selected randomly from S. If $\mathcal{A}$ is an algorithm, by $y \leftarrow \mathcal{A}(x_1, x_2, \ldots)$ it means that on input $x_1, x_2, \ldots$, $\mathcal{A}$'s output is y. If $p(\cdot, \cdot, \ldots)$ is a predicate, the notation $\Pr[p(x, y, \ldots) : x \leftarrow S; y \leftarrow T; \ldots]$ denotes the probability that $p(x, y, \ldots)$ will be true after the ordered execution of the algorithms $x \leftarrow S, y \leftarrow T, \ldots$, etc.

Definition 1 (Negligible Function). *A function $\epsilon : \mathbb{N} \to \mathbb{R}$ is negligible if for all $c > 0$, $\epsilon(k) < 1/k^c$ for all sufficiently large k.*

2.2   Deniable Encryption

In the rest of this paper, all notions are under the framework of full deniability. In Section 2 and 3, encryption schemes are all non-interactive style.

A public-key deniable encryption scheme is a two-party (a sender S and a receiver R) public key encryption protocol with the additional property that later, upon coercion, the sender can convincingly lie about the encrypted value.

Deniable Encryption

A sender-deniable encryption scheme is a tuple of algorithms $\mathcal{E} = (\mathsf{Gen}, \mathsf{Enc}, \mathsf{Dec}, \phi_S)$.

– $(pk, sk) \leftarrow \mathsf{Gen}(1^k)$. The key generation algorithm, a PPT algorithm which on input a security parameter 1^k where $k \in \mathbb{N}$, outputs a public/private key pair (pk, sk).
– $c \leftarrow \mathsf{Enc}_{pk}(m, r)$. The encryption algorithm, a PPT algorithm which on input a public key pk, a plaintext m and a random local input r, outputs a ciphertext c. We write an execution of this algorithm as $c \leftarrow \mathsf{Enc}_{pk}(m)$ with the randomness omitted.
– $m \leftarrow \mathsf{Dec}_{sk}(c)$. The decryption algorithm, a deterministic polynomial time algorithm which on input a private key sk and a ciphertext c, returns a plaintext m.

– $r'' \leftarrow \phi_S(pk, m, r, m')$. The sender's opening algorithm, a PPT algorithm which on input a public key pk, a true plaintext m, a true random local input r and a fake plaintext m', outputs a fake randomness r''.

Correctness: For any message m, the probability

$$\Pr\left[\bar{m} \neq m : (pk, sk) \leftarrow \mathsf{Gen}(1^k); c \leftarrow \mathsf{Enc}_{pk}(m); \bar{m} \leftarrow \mathsf{Dec}_{sk}(c)\right]$$

should be negligible.

In the following we give two security notions defined under adaptive chosen ciphertext attack.

SDEN-CCA (Sender-deniability under adaptive chosen ciphertext attack)

For a deniable encryption scheme $\mathcal{E} = (\mathsf{Gen}, \mathsf{Enc}, \mathsf{Dec}, \phi_S)$, sender-deniability under adaptive chosen ciphertext attack (SDEN-CCA) is defined through the following experiment, in which $\mathcal{A}$ denotes the adversary.

Experiment $\mathsf{SDEN\text{-}CCA}_{\mathcal{A},\mathcal{E}}^{m,m'}(k)$:

1. $(pk, sk) \leftarrow \mathsf{Gen}(1^k)$;
2. $r, r' \leftarrow \mathcal{R}$ where $\mathcal{R}$ is the random local input space. For two messages m and m', $c \leftarrow \mathsf{Enc}_{pk}(m, r)$, $c' \leftarrow \mathsf{Enc}_{pk}(m', r')$ and $r'' \leftarrow \phi_S(pk, m, r, m')$;
3. $b \leftarrow \{0, 1\}$;

$$(m^*, r^*, c^*) = \begin{cases} (m', r', c') & \text{if } b = 0 \\ (m', r'', c) & \text{if } b = 1 \end{cases}$$

4. $b' \leftarrow \mathcal{A}^{\mathsf{Dec}_{sk}(\cdot)}(pk, m^*, r^*, c^*)$.
5. The experiment returns 1 if $b' = b$, otherwise returns 0.

The decryption oracle $\mathsf{Dec}_{sk}(\cdot)$ receives a ciphertext c and outputs c's plaintext m. If the input is the challenge ciphertext c^* or an invalid ciphertext, it just returns *null*.

We define the adversary's detection advantage in above experiment as:

$$\mathsf{Adv}_{\mathcal{A},\mathcal{E}}^{\mathsf{SDEN\text{-}CCA}}(k) = \max_{m,m' \in M} \{2 \cdot \Pr\left[\mathsf{SDEN\text{-}CCA}_{\mathcal{A},\mathcal{E}}^{m,m'}(k) = 1\right] - 1\}$$

where M is the plaintext space of $\mathcal{E}$.

Definition 2 (SDEN-CCA). *A deniable encryption scheme $\mathcal{E}$ is δ-sender-deniable under adaptive chosen ciphertext attack (δ-SDEN-CCA) if for every PPT adversary $\mathcal{A}$, $\mathsf{Adv}_{\mathcal{A},\mathcal{E}}^{\mathsf{SDEN\text{-}CCA}}(k)$ is at most δ.*

The SDEN-CCA definition captures the property that the sender can output a fake message-randomness pair (m', r'') and convincingly announce that $c = \mathsf{Enc}_{pk}(m, r)$ is generated by (m', r''), under an adversary's chosen ciphertext attack.

Remark 1 (Receiver deniability). For an interactive deniable encryption scheme, receiver deniability requires that the receiver gives his random local inputs in communication when he is coerced. In above non-interactive definition, the receiver has no random input in decrypting the ciphertext and thus defining the receiver deniability in above framework does not make sense. However, when the decryption algorithm is probabilistic or the randomness in the key generation algorithm is viewed as a random input to the decryption algorithm, defining receiver deniability is meaningful. Discussing the latter case is out of the scope of this article.

IND-CCA (Indistinguishability under adaptive chosen ciphertext attack). IND-CCA is defined in the usual way by viewing $\mathcal{E}$ as a standard encryption scheme. Previous literatures usually use the notation IND-CCA2 [15, 1] to distinguish it from the non-adaptive cases [9, 13]. Consider the following experiment for a deniable encryption scheme $\mathcal{E} = (\mathsf{Gen}, \mathsf{Enc}, \mathsf{Dec}, \phi_S)$:

Experiment $\mathsf{IND\text{-}CCA}_{\mathcal{A},\mathcal{E}}(k)$:

1. $(pk, sk) \leftarrow \mathsf{Gen}(1^k)$, and pk is sent to the adversary $\mathcal{A} = (\mathcal{A}_1, \mathcal{A}_2)$;
2. $(m_0, m_1, st) \leftarrow \mathcal{A}_1^{\mathsf{Dec}_{sk}(\cdot)}(pk)$ where st is a state information;
3. $b \leftarrow \{0, 1\}$; $c^* \leftarrow \mathsf{Enc}_{pk}(m_b)$;
4. $b' \leftarrow \mathcal{A}_2^{\mathsf{Dec}_{sk}(\cdot)}(pk, c^*, st)$;
5. The experiment returns 1 if $b' = b$, otherwise returns 0.

The decryption oracle $\mathsf{Dec}_{sk}(\cdot)$ receives a ciphertext c and outputs c's plaintext m. If the input is the challenge ciphertext c^* or an invalid ciphertext, it just returns *null*.

We define the adversary's advantage in above experiment as:

$$\mathrm{Adv}_{\mathcal{A},\mathcal{E}}^{\mathrm{IND\text{-}CCA}}(k) = 2 \cdot \Pr\left[\mathsf{IND\text{-}CCA}_{\mathcal{A},\mathcal{E}}(k) = 1\right] - 1.$$

Definition 3 (IND-CCA). *A deniable encryption scheme $\mathcal{E}$ is indistinguishable under adaptive chosen ciphertext attack (IND-CCA) if for every PPT adversary $\mathcal{A}$, $\mathrm{Adv}_{\mathcal{A},\mathcal{E}}^{IND\text{-}CCA}(k)$ is negligible in k.*

For a regular encryption scheme, in the IND-CPA (indistinguishability under chosen plaintext attack) definition [9], which is weaker than IND-CCA, the adversary is not allowed to query the decryption oracle $\mathsf{Dec}_{sk}(\cdot)$.

2.3   Building Blocks

This section reviews some cryptographic primitives that we will use in constructing deniable encryption schemes with CCA security.

Extended Hash Proof System
In the following we review the notion of subset membership problem and its related extended hash proof system.

Assume there exists a set $\mathcal{X}$ and an underlying NP-language $\mathcal{L} \subset \mathcal{X}$, and k is the system parameter. The subset membership problem (SMP) related to $\mathcal{L}$ and $\mathcal{X}$ is hard *iff* it is infeasible to distinguish a random element in $\mathcal{L}$ and a random element in $\mathcal{X} \setminus \mathcal{L}$. Formally, the SMP is hard if for every PPT distinguisher D,

$$\mathsf{Adv}_D^{smp}(k) := \Pr\left[D(X) = 1 : X \leftarrow \mathcal{X} \setminus \mathcal{L}\right] - \Pr\left[D(X) = 1 : X \leftarrow \mathcal{L}\right]$$

is negligible in the parameter k.

We denote the sampling algorithm of $\mathcal{L}$ by $\mathsf{SampL}(\mathcal{L}, W)$ with $W \in \mathcal{R}_{\mathsf{SampleL}}$ being the random input, and assume the output is uniformly distributed in $\mathcal{L}$ if W is randomly selected from $\mathcal{R}_{\mathsf{SampleL}}$. For simplicity, we may assume sampling a random element in $\mathcal{X}$ is just selecting a random element X from $\mathcal{X}$ with X itself being the random local input of the sampling algorithm.

Furthermore, A SMP has a sparse language if

$$\varsigma^{\mathcal{L}, \mathcal{X}}(k) := \Pr\left[X \in \mathcal{L} : X \leftarrow \mathcal{X}\right]$$

is negligible.

The notion of extended hash proof systems was first introduced by Cramer and Shoup [4] and later was used by Fehr et al. [7] to construct non-committing encryption schemes secure against chosen-ciphertext attacks.

Definition 4 (EHPS). *An extended hash proof system* EHPS *for a subset membership problem* SMP *consists of the following PPT algorithms:*

- $(hpk, hsk) \leftarrow \mathsf{HashGen}(1^k)$. *The key generation algorithm, a PPT algorithm which on input a security parameter 1^k where $k \in \mathbb{N}$, outputs a public key hpk and a secret key hsk.*
- $K \leftarrow \mathsf{SEval}(hsk, X, t)$. *The secret evaluation algorithm, a deterministic algorithm which on input a secret key hsk, an element from space $\mathcal{X}$ and a tag t from the tag space $\mathcal{T}$, outputs a value K in the key space $\mathcal{K}$.*
- $K \leftarrow \mathsf{PEval}(hpk, X, W, t)$. *The public evaluation algorithm, a deterministic algorithm which on input a public key hpk, an element from space $\mathcal{X}$, a witness W for language $\mathcal{L}$ and a tag t, outputs a value K in the key space $\mathcal{K}$.*

Correctness: It is required that for all $(hpk, hsk) \leftarrow \mathsf{HashGen}(1^k)$, all $t \in \mathcal{T}$ and all $X \leftarrow \mathsf{SampleL}(\mathcal{L}, W)$, $\mathsf{PEval}(hpk, X, W, t) = \mathsf{SEval}(hsk, X, t)$ holds.

The above definition guarantees that the public key hpk uniquely determines the action of the secret evaluation algorithm SEval for all $X \in \mathcal{L}$. Another key property of an extended hash proof system EHPS says that the action of SEval is undetermined for all element $X \in \mathcal{X} \setminus \mathcal{L}$. This is captured by the following definition.

Definition 5 (2-universal). *An extended hash proof system is 2-universal iff for all possible hpk, all distinct $(X_1, t_1), (X_2, t_2)$ in $(\mathcal{X} \setminus \mathcal{L}) \times \mathcal{T}$, and any $K_1, K_2 \in \mathcal{K}$, there exists a negligible function $neg(k)$ such that*

$$\Pr\left[\mathsf{SEval}(hsk, X_2, t_2) = K_2 | \mathsf{SEval}(hsk, X_1, t_1) = K_1\right] < neg(k),$$

where the probability is taken over all possible hsk with $(hpk, hsk) \leftarrow \mathsf{HashGen}(1^k)$.

Cross-Authentication Codes

This tool was first introduced by Fehr et al. [7] to construct non-committing encryption schemes secure against chosen-ciphertext attacks.

Definition 6 (L-Cross-authentication code [7]). *For $L \in \mathbb{N}$, an L-cross-authentication code (short: L-XAC) XAC consists of a key space $\mathcal{XK}$ and a tag space $\mathcal{XT}$ and of three PPT algorithms XGen, XAuth and XVer. XGen(1^k) produces a uniformly random key $K \in \mathcal{XK}$, XAuth($K_1, \ldots, K_L$) outputs a tag $T \in \mathcal{XT}$, and XVer(K, i, T) outputs a decision bit. The following properties are required:*

Correctness. *The probability*

$$\mathsf{fail}_{\mathsf{XAC}}(k) := \max_{i \in [L]} \Pr\left[\mathsf{XVer}(K_i, i, \mathsf{XAuth}(K_1, ..., K_L)) \neq 1\right],$$

is negligible, where $K_1, \ldots, K_L$ are generated by XGen(1^k) independently and the max *is taken over all $i \in [L]$.*

Security against impersonation and substitution attacks. $\mathsf{Adv}_{\mathsf{XAC}}^{imp}(k)$ *and* $\mathsf{Adv}_{\mathsf{XAC}}^{sub}(k)$ *are defined as follows and are both negligible:*

$$\mathsf{Adv}_{\mathsf{XAC}}^{imp}(k) := \max_{i, T'} \Pr\left[\mathsf{XVer}(K, i, T') = 1 : K \leftarrow \mathsf{XGen}(1^k)\right]$$

where max *is taken over all $i \in [L]$ and $T' \in \mathcal{XT}$.*

$$\mathsf{Adv}_{\mathsf{XAC}}^{sub}(k) := \max_{i, K_{\neq i}, F} \Pr\left[\begin{matrix} T' \neq T \text{ and } \mathsf{XVer}(K_i, i, T') = 1 : K_i \leftarrow \mathsf{XGen}(1^k); \\ T \leftarrow \mathsf{XAuth}(K_1, \ldots, K_L); T' \leftarrow F(T) \end{matrix}\right].$$

where max *is taken over all $i \in [L]$, all $K_{\neq i} = (K_j)_{j \neq i} \in \mathcal{XK}^{L-1}$ and all possible PPT algorithm $F : \mathcal{XT} \to \mathcal{XT}$.*

A concrete implementation of an L-cross-authentication code can be found in [7].

3   A Deniable Encryption Scheme Secure under Chosen Ciphertext Attacks

Using the building blocks introduced in Section 2.3, which are utilized to construct a CCA secure non-committing encryption scheme by Fehr et al. [7] (FHKW scheme for short), together with Canetti et al.'s parity paradigm [3], we propose a deniable encryption scheme secure under adaptive chosen ciphertext attacks. Our construction is a small variant of the FHKW scheme. On a high level, instead of encrypting multiple bits as in the original FHKW scheme, we exploit these message bits to host the bits for the parity idea in Canetti et al's deniable encryption. Therefore, there is only a conceptual difference of viewing the message bits between our construction and the FHKW scheme. Not surprisingly, the technique in FHKW scheme for obtaining the CCA security also works in our construction.

3.1   Construction

Suppose SMP is a subset membership problem instance with sparse language $\mathcal{L} \subset \mathcal{X}$, and EHPS is a 2-universal extended hash proof system for SMP with tag space $\mathcal{T}$ and key space $\mathcal{K}$. Let $L \in \mathbb{N}$ be an odd integer, suppose XAC is an L-cross-authentication code with key space $\mathcal{XK} = \mathcal{K}$ and tag space $\mathcal{XT}$. Furthermore, a collision free hash function $h : \mathcal{X}^L \to \mathcal{T}$ is needed.

The deniable encryption scheme $\mathcal{E} = (\mathsf{Gen}, \mathsf{Enc}, \mathsf{Dec}, \phi_S)$ is constructed as follows. Its plaintext space is $\{0, 1\}$.

- $\mathsf{Gen}(1^k)$. The key generation algorithm runs $(hpk, hsk) \leftarrow \mathsf{HashGen}(1^k)$, outputs $pk = (hpk, h)$ as public key and $sk = hsk$ as secret key.
- $\mathsf{Enc}_{pk}(m, r)$. $m \in \{0, 1\}$ and the random local input r has the form $(\hat{\triangle}, W_1, \hat{X}_1, \hat{K}_1, \ldots, W_L, \hat{X}_L, \hat{K}_L) \in [\frac{L+1}{2}] \times (\mathcal{R}_{\mathsf{SampleL}} \times \mathcal{X} \times \mathcal{K})^L$.
  1. To encrypt 0 (resp. 1), compute $\triangle = 2(\hat{\triangle} - 1)$ (resp. $\triangle = 2\hat{\triangle} - 1$). Thus $\triangle$ is a random even number (resp. odd number) from $\{0, 1, .., L\}$.
  2. Set a mode string $s = s_1 s_2, .., s_L \in \{0, 1\}^L$ as $s_1 = 1, s_2 = 1, \ldots, s_\triangle = 1, s_{\triangle+1} = 0, \ldots, s_L = 0$.
  3. For $j \in [L]$, set
  $$X_j = \begin{cases} \hat{X}_j & \text{if } s_j = 0 \\ \mathsf{SampleL}(\mathcal{L}; W_j) & \text{if } s_j = 1 \end{cases}$$
  and compute $t = h(X_1, ..., X_L)$.
  4. For $j \in [L]$, set
  $$K_j = \begin{cases} \hat{K}_j & \text{if } s_j = 0 \\ \mathsf{PEval}(hpk, X_j, W_j, t) & \text{if } s_j = 1 \end{cases}$$
  and compute $T = \mathsf{XAuth}(K_1, ..., K_L)$.
  5. Return the ciphertext $c = (X_1, \ldots, X_L, T)$.
- $\mathsf{Dec}_{sk}(c)$.
  1. Parse $c = (X_1, \ldots, X_L, T)$, and compute $t = h(X_1, ..., X_L)$.
  2. For $j \in [L]$, compute $\bar{K}_j = \mathsf{SEval}(hsk, X_j, t)$ and $s_j = \mathsf{XVer}(\bar{K}_j, j, T)$.
  3. Output 0 if the string $s = s_1 s_2, .., s_L$ has an even number of 1s, otherwise output 1.
- $\phi_S(pk, m, r, m')$. Return $r' = r$ if $m' = m$. Otherwise, parse $r := (\hat{\triangle}, W_1, \hat{X}_1, \hat{K}_1, \ldots, W_L, \hat{X}_L, \hat{K}_L)$, compute
$$\triangle = \begin{cases} 2\hat{\triangle} - 1 & \text{if } m = 1, \\ 2(\hat{\triangle} - 1) & \text{if } m = 0, \end{cases}$$

and set $r' := (\hat{\triangle}', W_1', \hat{X}_1', \hat{K}_1', \ldots, W_L', \hat{X}_L', \hat{K}_L')$ where
1. $\hat{\triangle}' = \begin{cases} \hat{\triangle} & \text{if } (m, m') = (1, 0) \\ \hat{\triangle} - 1 & \text{if } (m, m') = (0, 1) \end{cases}$
2. $(W_j', \hat{X}_j', \hat{K}_j') = (W_j, \hat{X}_j, \hat{K}_j)$ for all $j \neq \triangle$;

3. $W'_\triangle$ is randomly selected from $\mathcal{R}_{\mathsf{SampleL}}$;
4. $\hat{X}'_\triangle = \mathsf{SampleL}(\mathcal{L}; W_\triangle)$ and $\hat{K}'_\triangle = \mathsf{PEval}(hpk, \hat{X}'_\triangle, W_\triangle, t)$ where t is computed as in the encryption algorithm $\mathsf{Enc}_{pk}(m, r)$.

Correctness: It can be proved that the probability that an encryption is decrypted incorrectly is negligible. We suppose in encrypting a message m, the mode string is $s = s_1, \ldots, s_L$. We also suppose the corresponding mode string in decryption is $\bar{s} = \bar{s}_1, \ldots, \bar{s}_L$ and the decrypted message is $\bar{m}$. Then for any $j \in [L]$, $\Pr[\bar{s}_j = 0 | s_j = 1] = \mathsf{fail}_{\mathsf{XAC}}(k)$. And

$$
\begin{aligned}
&\Pr[\bar{s}_j = 1 | s_j = 0] \\
&= \Pr[X_j \notin \mathcal{L} \wedge \bar{s}_j = 1 | s_j = 0] + \Pr[X_j \in \mathcal{L} \wedge \bar{s}_j = 1 | s_j = 0] \\
&= \Pr[X_j \notin \mathcal{L} | s_j = 0] \cdot \Pr[\bar{s}_j = 1 | s_j = 0 \wedge X_j \notin \mathcal{L}] + \Pr[X_j \in \mathcal{L} \wedge \bar{s}_j = 1 | s_j = 0] \\
&\leq \Pr[\bar{s}_j = 1 | s_j = 0 \wedge X_j \notin \mathcal{L}] + \Pr[X_j \in \mathcal{L} | s_j = 0] \\
&\leq \mathsf{Adv}_{\mathsf{XAC}}^{imp}(k) + \varsigma^{\mathcal{L}, \mathcal{X}}(k).
\end{aligned}
$$

Let $\epsilon(k) = \max\{\mathsf{fail}_{\mathsf{XAC}}(k), \varsigma^{\mathcal{L}, \mathcal{X}}(k) + \mathsf{Adv}_{\mathsf{XAC}}^{imp}(k)\}$, which is negligible. Then $\Pr[\bar{m} \neq m] \leq \Pr[\bar{s} \neq s] \leq 1 - (1 - \epsilon(k))^L \leq L \cdot \epsilon(k)$, which is also negligible.

3.2   Security Proof

Now we prove that our construction is secure under adaptive chosen ciphertext attacks (CCA). We call an X a 0-element if X is uniformly sampled from $\mathcal{X}$, or a 1-element if X is uniformly sampled from $\mathcal{L}$. The intuition behind the proof is that a 1-element can be opened as a 0-element without being detected. As in our construction, the encryption of 1 has a mode string $s = s_1, \ldots, s_L$ where for some even number v, $s_1 = s_2 = \cdots = s_{v+1} = 1$, and $s_{v+2} = s_{v+3} = \cdots = s_L = 0$. Since the 1-element X_{v+1} of the ciphertext can be opened as a 0-element, the encryption of 1 with mode string $\overbrace{111\ldots1}^{v+1}\overbrace{0\ldots0}^{L-v-1}$ thus can be opened as encryption of 0 with a mode string $\overbrace{111\ldots1}^{v}\overbrace{00\ldots0}^{L-v}$. On the other hand, the encryption of 0 with mode string $\overbrace{111\ldots1}^{v}\overbrace{0\ldots0}^{L-v}$ where v is an even number can be opened as an encryption of 0 with a mode string $\overbrace{11\ldots1}^{v-1}\overbrace{00\ldots0}^{L-v+1}$.

Meanwhile, the extended hash proof system and L-cross-authentication code are employed to guarantee the security against the CCA attack, just as in the FHKW scheme [7]. The basic idea is that by adding the authentication part T into the ciphertext, whenever an adversary submits a valid decryption query, he must know the corresponding plaintext and randomness in advance. And thus accessing the decryption oracle is of no help to the adversary.

Remark 2. Although the technique we use is adopted from Fehr et al. [7]'s technique for proving encryption schemes' NC-CCA security (non-committing security under CCA attack), however we note that the NC-CCA and SDEN-CCA are defined in different frameworks and the NC-CCA security does not necessarily imply SDEN-CCA security (but we have no formal proof for it.).

Theorem 1 ($\frac{4}{L}$-SDEN-CCA). *The deniable encryption scheme* $\mathcal{E} = $ (Gen, Enc, Dec, ϕ_S) *constructed above is* $\frac{4}{L}$*-SDEN-CCA secure.*

Proof. We first prove there exists a negligible function $\epsilon(k)$ such that $2 \cdot \Pr[\mathsf{SDEN}\text{-}\mathsf{CCA}_{\mathcal{A},\mathcal{E}}^{1,0}(k) = 1] - 1 < \epsilon(k)$, and then we prove $2 \cdot \Pr\left[\mathsf{SDEN}\text{-}\mathsf{CCA}_{\mathcal{A},\mathcal{E}}^{0,1}(k) = 1\right] - 1 < 4/L$. Thus the theorem follows immediately.

Claim 1. There exists a negligible function $\epsilon(k)$ such that $2 \cdot \Pr[\mathsf{SDEN}\text{-}\mathsf{CCA}_{\mathcal{A},\mathcal{E}}^{1,0}(k) = 1] - 1 < \epsilon(k)$.

Proof. Our proof is generally based on Fehr et al. [7]'s technique for proving encryption schemes' SO-CCA security, which will proceed in a series of games. We define Game_0 and Game_7 as following.

Game_0

1. $(pk, sk) \leftarrow \mathsf{Gen}(1^k)$;
2. $r' \leftarrow \mathcal{R}$; $c' \leftarrow \mathsf{Enc}_{pk}(0, r')$;
3. $(m^*, r^*, c^*) \leftarrow (0, r', c')$;
4. $b' \leftarrow \mathcal{A}^{\mathsf{Dec}_{sk}(\cdot)}(pk, m^*, r^*, c^*)$;
5. The game returns b'.

Game_7

1. $(pk, sk) \leftarrow \mathsf{Gen}(1^k)$;
2. $r \leftarrow \mathcal{R}$; $c \leftarrow \mathsf{Enc}_{pk}(1, r)$; $r'' \leftarrow \phi_S(pk, 1, r, 0)$;
3. $(m^*, r^*, c^*) \leftarrow (0, r'', c)$;
4. $b' \leftarrow \mathcal{A}^{\mathsf{Dec}_{sk}(\cdot)}(pk, m^*, r^*, c^*)$;
5. The game returns b'.

Let out_ξ be the output of Game_ξ. To prove the claim, we should prove there exits a negligible $\epsilon(k)$ such that $|\Pr[out_0 = 1] - \Pr[out_7 = 1]| < \epsilon(k)$. We prove this by interpolating a series of games into Game_0 and Game_7.

Without loss of generality, we assume that $\mathcal{A}$ always makes q decryption queries. Let c^i denote $\mathcal{A}$'s i-th decryption query, and let c^* denote the challenge ciphertext. We write $c^i = (X_1^i, \ldots, X_L^i, T^i)$, $c^* = (X_1^*, \ldots, X_L^*, T^*)$ and similarly for the variables $t, (K_j)_{j \in [L]}, (s_j)_{j \in [L]}$.

Game_1

Game_1 is the same with Game_0, except that it is aborted as soon as $X_j^* = X_{j'}^*$ for some distinct $j, j' \in [L]$. by a standard counting argument, we get

$$|\Pr[out_0 = 1] - \Pr[out_1 = 1]| \leq \frac{L(L-1)}{|\mathcal{L}|}. \tag{1}$$

Game₂

Game₂ is the same with Game₁, except that it is aborted as soon as $h(X_1^i, ..., X_L^i) = h(X_1^*, ..., X_L^*)$ for some $i \in [q]$. Due to the collision resistance of $h(\cdot)$, there exists a negligible function $\epsilon_1(k)$ such that

$$|\Pr[out_1 = 1] - \Pr[out_2 = 1]| < \epsilon_1(k). \tag{2}$$

Write r^* as $(\hat{\triangle}^*, W_1^*, \hat{X}_1^*, \hat{K}_1^*, ..., W_L^*, \hat{X}_L^*, \hat{K}_L^*)$. For later analysis, we implement how $W_{\triangle+1}^*, X_{\triangle+1}^*, K_{\triangle+1}^*$ are generated in Game₂ where $\triangle = 2(\hat{\triangle}^* - 1)$. In Game₂, $\hat{\triangle}^*$ is randomly selected from $[\frac{L+1}{2}]$, $W_{\triangle+1}^*$ is randomly selected from $\mathcal{R}_{\text{SampleL}}$, and $X_{\triangle+1}^* = \hat{X}_{\triangle+1}^*$, $t^* = h(X_1^*, ..., X_L^*)$, $K_{\triangle+1}^* = \hat{K}_{\triangle+1}^*$.

Game₃

Now we transform Game₂ into Game₃, by modifying the decryption oracle. In Game₂, receiving a decryption query c, $\bar{K}_j = \mathsf{SEval}(hsk, X_j, t)$ and $s_j = \mathsf{XVer}(\bar{K}_j, j, T)$ are computed for all $j \in [L]$. Now in Game₃, for all $j \in [L]$, the decryption oracle first determines whether X_j is in $\mathcal{L}$. If $X_j \in \mathcal{L}$, the oracle finds W_j such that $X_j = \mathsf{SampleL}(\mathcal{L}; W_j)$ and computes $\bar{K}_j = \mathsf{PEval}(hpk, X_j, W_j, t)$. The value of s_j in Game₃ is now changed to $s_j = 1$ iff $X_j \in \mathcal{L}$ and $\mathsf{XVer}(\bar{K}_j, j, T) = 1$. We define bad₃ to be the event that $X_j^i \notin \mathcal{L}$ but $\mathsf{XVer}(\bar{K}_j^i, j, T^i) = 1$ for some $i \in [q], j \in [L]$. Note that the decryption oracle is now inefficient, but it doesn't need the information of hsk, i.e., the decryption oracle does not leak any information about hsk beyond hpk. By a counting argument and the fact that Game₂ and Game₃ are identical unless the event bad₃ occurs, we get

$$|\Pr[out_2 = 1] - \Pr[out_3 = 1]| \leq \Pr[\mathsf{bad}_3] \leq Lq \cdot \mathsf{Adv}_{\mathsf{XAC}}^{imp}(k). \tag{3}$$

Game₄

Now we transform Game₃ into Game₄, computing $K_{\triangle+1}^* = \mathsf{SEval}(hsk, X_{\triangle+1}^*, t^*)$, rather than as $K_{\triangle+1}^* = \hat{K}_{\triangle+1}^*$ in Game₃. Furthermore, the $\hat{K}_{\triangle+1}^*$ component of r^* is replaced by $K_{\triangle+1}^*$. Note that in Game₃, hsk is not needed in decryption oracle and thus in Game₄ the only information about hsk beyond hpk is released while computing $K_{\triangle+1}^*$. But the 2-universality of EHPS guarantees $K_{\triangle+1}^*$ looks uniform. And thus

$$\Pr[out_3 = 1] = \Pr[out_4 = 1]. \tag{4}$$

Game₅

Now we transform Game₄ into Game₅, by modifying the decryption oracle back in the sense that $s_j = \mathsf{XVer}(\bar{K}_j, j, T)$ again. The difference between Game₄ and Game₅ is almost the same with the difference between Game₂ and Game₃ except that in Game₄ and Game₅, the information about hsk beyond hpk is leaked while computing $K_{\triangle+1}^*$. We define bad₅ to be the event that $X_j^i \notin \mathcal{L}$ but $\mathsf{XVer}(\bar{K}_j^i, j, T^i) = 1$ for some $i \in [q], j \in [L]$ in Game₄ and Game₅. When $(X_i^j, t^j) \neq (X_{\triangle+1}^*, t^*)$ for all i, j, the only information about hsk beyond hpk is released while computing $K_{\triangle+1}^*$. Thus by the the 2-universality of EHPS and a counting argument, we get

$$\Pr\left[\mathsf{bad}_5 | (X_i^j, t^j) \neq (X_{\triangle+1}^*, t^*) \text{ for all } i, j\right] \leq Lq \cdot \mathsf{Adv}_{\mathsf{XAC}}^{imp}(k). \tag{5}$$

When $(X_i^j, t^j) = (X_{\triangle+1}^*, t^*)$ for some $i = i_0, j = j_0$, since we can safely assume $t^j \neq t^*$ for all j and $X_{i_1}^* \neq X_{i_2}^*$ for all $i_1 \neq i_2$ from the games after Game$_2$, we can conclude that $i_0 = \triangle +1$ and $X_i^{j_0} = X_i^*$ for all i by the collision resistance of $h(\cdot)$. Therefore, to make the decryption query $(X_1^j, \ldots, X_L^j, T^j)$ valid, $(X_1^j, \ldots, X_L^j, T^j) \neq (X_1^*, \ldots, X_L^*, T^*)$ should be hold, which implies that $T^j \neq T^*$. Thus, $\Pr[\mathsf{bad}_5]$ in this case is the probability that the adversary issues a valid decryption query, which satisfies the following inequality

$$\Pr\left[\mathsf{bad}_5 | (X_i^j, t^j) = (X_{\triangle+1}^*, t^*) \text{ for some } i, j\right] \leq Lq \cdot \mathsf{Adv}_{\mathsf{XAC}}^{sub}(k). \qquad (6)$$

Combining inequalities (5) and (6), we get

$$|\Pr[out_4 = 1] - \Pr[out_5 = 1]| \leq \Pr[\mathsf{bad}_5] \leq Lq \cdot \max\{\mathsf{Adv}_{\mathsf{XAC}}^{imp}(k), \mathsf{Adv}_{\mathsf{XAC}}^{sub}(k)\}. \qquad (7)$$

Game$_6$

Now we transform Game$_5$ into Game$_6$, computing $X_{\triangle+1}^* = \mathsf{sample}(\mathcal{L}, W_{\triangle+1}^*)$ rather than as $X_{\triangle+1}^* = \hat{X}_{\triangle+1}^*$ in Game$_5$. Furthermore, the $\hat{X}_{\triangle+1}^*$ component of r^* is replaced by $X_{\triangle+1}^*$. It is easy to see any algorithm which distinguishes Game$_6$ from Game$_5$ can break the subset membership problem. Thus there exists a negligible function $\epsilon_2(k)$ such that

$$|\Pr[out_5 = 1] - \Pr[out_6 = 1]| \leq \epsilon_2(k). \qquad (8)$$

Using the notations of Enc, ϕ_S, we may rewrite Game$_6$ into Game$_7$. Combining equations (1), (2), (3), (4), (7) and (8) together, we get that there exits a negligible $\epsilon(k)$ such that $|\Pr[out_0 = 1] - \Pr[out_7 = 1]| < \epsilon(k)$. And thus the claim is proved.

Claim 2. $2 \cdot \Pr\left[\mathsf{SDEN\text{-}CCA}_{\mathcal{A},\mathcal{E}}^{0,1}(k) = 1\right] - 1 < 4/L$.

Proof. The proof is similar to the proof of claim 1, except that the adversary can distinguish an honest opening from a dishonest opening with a probability less than $4/L$. We define Game$_{-1}$ and Game$_7$ as following.

Game$_{-1}$

1. $(pk, sk) \leftarrow \mathsf{Gen}(1^k)$;
2. $r' \leftarrow \mathcal{R}$; $c' \leftarrow \mathsf{Enc}_{pk}(1, r')$;
3. $(m^*, r^*, c^*) \leftarrow (1, r', c')$;
4. $b' \leftarrow \mathcal{A}^{\mathsf{Dec}_{sk}(\cdot)}(pk, m^*, r^*, c^*)$;
5. The game returns b'.

Game$_7$

1. $(pk, sk) \leftarrow \mathsf{Gen}(1^k)$;
2. $r \leftarrow \mathcal{R}$; $c \leftarrow \mathsf{Enc}_{pk}(0, r)$; $r'' \leftarrow \phi_S(pk, 0, r, 1)$;
3. $(m^*, r^*, c^*) \leftarrow (1, r'', c)$;
4. $b' \leftarrow \mathcal{A}^{\mathsf{Dec}_{sk}(\cdot)}(pk, m^*, r^*, c^*)$;
5. The game returns b'.

Let out_ξ be the output of Game$_\xi$. To prove the claim, we should prove $|\Pr[out_{-1} = 1] - \Pr[out_7 = 1]| < 4/L$. We prove this by interpolating a series of games into Game$_{-1}$ and Game$_7$.

Let c^* denote the challenge ciphertext and write $c^* = (X_1^*, \ldots, X_L^*, T^*)$, $r^* = (\hat{\Delta}^*, W_1^*, \hat{X}_1^*, \hat{K}_1^*, \ldots, W_L^*, \hat{X}_L^*, \hat{K}_L^*)$.

Game$_0$

Game$_0$ is the same with Game$_{-1}$, except that it is aborted as soon as $\hat{\Delta}^* = \frac{L+1}{2}$. Since in Game$_{-1}$, $\hat{\Delta}^*$ is randomly selected from $[\frac{L+1}{2}]$, we get

$$|\Pr[out_{-1} = 1] - \Pr[out_0 = 1]| \leq \frac{2}{L+1}. \tag{9}$$

The games from Game$_1$ to Game$_6$ are defined in the same way as in the proof of Claim 1, except that Δ equals $2\hat{\Delta}^* - 1$ from Game$_1$. Note that the Game$_i$ is aborted as soon as $\hat{\Delta}^* = \frac{L+1}{2}$ when $0 \leq i \leq 6$, and thus we can assume $1 \leq \hat{\Delta}^* \leq \frac{L+1}{2} - 1$ in the games from Game$_0$ to Game$_6$. By the same deduction as in the proof of Claim 1, we can prove that there exists a negligible function $\epsilon(k)$ such that

$$|\Pr[out_0 = 1] - \Pr[out_6 = 1]| \leq \epsilon(k). \tag{10}$$

Note that in Game$_7$, $\hat{\Delta}^*$ is randomly distributed in $\{0, 1, \ldots, \frac{L+1}{2} - 1\}$ by the implementation of the ϕ_S. We define bad$_7$ to be the event that $\hat{\Delta}^*$ equals 0 in Game$_7$. By the fact that Game$_6$ and Game$_7$ are identical unless the event bad$_7$ occurs, we get

$$|\Pr[out_6 = 1] - \Pr[out_7 = 1]| \leq \Pr[\mathsf{bad}_7] \leq \frac{2}{L+1}. \tag{11}$$

Combining equations (9), (10) and (11) together, we conclude that $|\Pr[out_{-1} = 1] - \Pr[out_7 = 1]| < 4/L$.

Theorem 1 follows immediately from Claim 1 and Claim 2. ∎

Theorem 2 (IND-CCA). *Our encryption scheme $\mathcal{E} = (\mathsf{Gen}, \mathsf{Enc}, \mathsf{Dec}, \phi_S)$ is IND-CCA secure.*

To prove this theorem, we will transform a game which encrypts 0 to another game which encrypts 1, and prove that any PPT adversary can distinguish successive games with only negligible probability. The proof is almost the same with that of Claim 1 and is thus omitted. We note that in the IND-CCA games, the variable r^* will not be given to adversary.

4   Conclusion

In the fully deniable framework, we introduce the security notions for non-interactive deniable encryption schemes secure against adaptive chosen ciphertext attack (CCA). Furthermore, a concrete construction is also given.

Acknowledgement. We would like to thank Sherman Chow and anonymous reviewers of ISPEC 2012 for giving valuable suggestions and corrections to this paper. This paper is supported by Natural Science Foundation of China(60903165, 60803135), Open Funds of Key Lab of Fujian Province University Network Security and Cryptology(09A008), and Fundamental Research Funds for the Central Universities(10lgpy31).

References

[1] Bellare, M., Desai, A., Pointcheval, D., Rogaway, P.: Relations among Notions of Security for Public-Key Encryption Schemes. In: Krawczyk, H. (ed.) CRYPTO 1998. LNCS, vol. 1462, pp. 26–46. Springer, Heidelberg (1998)

[2] Bendlin, R., Nielsen, J.B., Nordholt, P.S., Orlandi, C.: Receiver-deniable public-key encryption is impossible. Cryptology ePrint Archive, Report 2011/046 (2011), http://eprint.iacr.org/

[3] Canetti, R., Dwork, C., Naor, M., Ostrovsky, R.: Deniable Encryption. In: Kaliski Jr., B.S. (ed.) CRYPTO 1997. LNCS, vol. 1294, pp. 90–104. Springer, Heidelberg (1997)

[4] Cramer, R., Shoup, V.: Universal Hash Proofs and a Paradigm for Adaptive Chosen Ciphertext Secure Public-Key Encryption. In: Knudsen, L.R. (ed.) EUROCRYPT 2002. LNCS, vol. 2332, pp. 45–64. Springer, Heidelberg (2002)

[5] Dürmuth, M., Freeman, D.M.: Deniable Encryption with Negligible Detection Probability: An Interactive Construction. In: Paterson, K.G. (ed.) EUROCRYPT 2011. LNCS, vol. 6632, pp. 610–626. Springer, Heidelberg (2011)

[6] Dürmuth, M., Freeman, D.M.: Deniable encryption with negligible detection probability: An interactive construction. Cryptology ePrint Archive, Report 2011/066 (2011), http://eprint.iacr.org/

[7] Fehr, S., Hofheinz, D., Kiltz, E., Wee, H.: Encryption Schemes Secure against Chosen-Ciphertext Selective Opening Attacks. In: Gilbert, H. (ed.) EUROCRYPT 2010. LNCS, vol. 6110, pp. 381–402. Springer, Heidelberg (2010)

[8] Gasti, P., Ateniese, G., Blanton, M.: Deniable cloud storage: sharing files via public-key deniability. In: Al-Shaer, E., Frikken, K.B. (eds.) WPES, pp. 31–42. ACM (2010)

[9] Goldwasser, S., Micali, S.: Probabilistic encryption. JCSS 28(2), 270–299 (1984)

[10] Ibrahim, M.H.: A method for obtaining deniable public-key encryption. I. J. Network Security 8(1), 1–9 (2009)

[11] Ibrahim, M.H.: Receiver-deniable public-key encryption. I. J. Network Security 8(2), 159–165 (2009)

[12] Klonowski, M., Kubiak, P., Kutyłowski, M.: Practical Deniable Encryption. In: Geffert, V., Karhumäki, J., Bertoni, A., Preneel, B., Návrat, P., Bieliková, M. (eds.) SOFSEM 2008. LNCS, vol. 4910, pp. 599–609. Springer, Heidelberg (2008)

[13] Naor, M., Yung, M.: Public-key cryptosystems provably secure against chosen ciphertext attack. In: Proc. of the Twenty-Second Annual ACM Symposium on Theory of Computing, Baltimore, Maryland, pp. 427–437. ACM (1990)

[14] O'Neill, A., Peikert, C., Waters, B.: Bi-Deniable Public-Key Encryption. In: Rogaway, P. (ed.) CRYPTO 2011. LNCS, vol. 6841, pp. 525–542. Springer, Heidelberg (2011)

[15] Rackoff, C., Simon, D.R.: Non-interactive Zero-Knowledge Proof of Knowledge and Chosen Ciphertext Attack. In: Feigenbaum, J. (ed.) CRYPTO 1991. LNCS, vol. 576, pp. 433–444. Springer, Heidelberg (1992)

Appendix

Deniable Encryption in Interactive Style

We present the definition of interactive encryptions with deniability. To compare it with the non-interactive definition in Section 2.2, we rephrase Canetti et al.'s definition [3] into a game style one. In the rest of the paper, all encryption schemes are interactive.

A sender-deniable (interactive) encryption scheme is a protocol $\mathcal{E} = (\mathsf{Gen}, \mathsf{Com}, \phi_S)$ executed between a sender S and a receiver R.

- $key \leftarrow \mathsf{Gen}(1^k)$. The key generation algorithm, a PPT algorithm which on input a security parameter 1^k where $k \in \mathbb{N}$, outputs a public/private key pair $key = (pk, sk)$.
- $(\bar{m}, Trans) \leftarrow \mathsf{Com}_{key}(m, r_S, r_R)$. The communication protocol, a two party computation protocol for transmitting m with r_S being S's random local input, r_R being R's random local input, $\bar{m}$ being the output of the receiver R and $Trans$ being the (public) transcript in the communication. Here we assume S has pk as input and R has (pk, sk) as input. Let $\mathsf{Trans}_{key}(m, r_S, r_R)$ denote the second part of above output, and let $\mathsf{Trans}_{key}(m)$ denote the random variable describing $\mathsf{Trans}_{key}(m, r_S, r_R)$ with r_S and r_R being uniformly and independently selected.
- $r_S'' \leftarrow \phi_S(pk, m, r_S, m')$. The sender's opening algorithm, a PPT algorithm which on input a public key pk, a true plaintext m, a true random local input r_S of S and a fake plaintext m', outputs a fake randomness r_S'' for the sender S.

Correctness: For any message m, the probability

$$\Pr\left[\bar{m} \neq m : key \leftarrow \mathsf{Gen}(1^k); (\bar{m}, Trans) \leftarrow \mathsf{Com}_{key}(m, r_S, r_R)\right]$$

should be negligible.

In the following we give two security notions defined under chosen plaintext attack (CPA).

SDEN (Sender-deniability)

For a deniable encryption scheme $\mathcal{E} = (\mathsf{Gen}, \mathsf{Com}, \phi_S)$, sender-deniability is defined through the following experiment, in which $\mathcal{A}$ denotes the adversary.

Experiment $\mathsf{SDEN}_{\mathcal{A}, \mathcal{E}}^{m, m'}(k)$:

1. $key \leftarrow \mathsf{Gen}(1^k)$ where $key = (pk, sk)$ and pk is sent to $\mathcal{A}$;
2. $r_S, r_S' \leftarrow \mathcal{R}_S$ where $\mathcal{R}_S$ is the random local input space for S; $r_R, r_R' \leftarrow \mathcal{R}_R$ where $\mathcal{R}_R$ is the random local input space for R. For two messages m and m', the sender's opening algorithm computes $r_S'' \leftarrow \phi_S(pk, m, r_S, m')$.
3. $b \leftarrow \{0, 1\}$;

$$(m^*, r_S^*, Trans^*) = \begin{cases} (m', r_S', \mathsf{Trans}_{key}(m', r_S', r_R')) & \text{if } b = 0 \\ (m', r_S'', \mathsf{Trans}_{key}(m, r_S, r_R)) & \text{if } b = 1 \end{cases}$$

4. $b' \leftarrow \mathcal{A}(pk, m^*, r_S^*, Trans^*)$.
5. The experiment returns 1 if $b' = b$, otherwise returns 0.

We define the adversary's detection advantage in above experiment as:

$$\text{Adv}_{\mathcal{A},\mathcal{E}}^{\text{SDEN}}(k) = \max_{m,m' \in M} \left\{ 2 \cdot \text{Pr}\left[\text{SDEN}_{\mathcal{A},\mathcal{E}}^{m,m'}(k) = 1 \right] - 1 \right\}$$

where M is the plaintext space of $\mathcal{E}$.

Definition 7 (SDEN). *A deniable encryption scheme $\mathcal{E}$ is δ-sender-deniable (δ-SDEN) if for every PPT adversary $\mathcal{A}$, $\text{Adv}_{\mathcal{A},\mathcal{E}}^{\text{SDEN}}(k)$ is at most δ.*

Indistinguishable Security (IND). Consider the following experiment:

Experiment $\text{IND}_{\mathcal{A},\mathcal{E}}(k)$:

1. $key \leftarrow \text{Gen}(1^k)$ where $key = (pk, sk)$ and pk is sent to $\mathcal{A}$;
2. $(m_0, m_1, st) \leftarrow \mathcal{A}_1(pk)$ where st is a state information;
3. $b \leftarrow \{0,1\}$; $trans^* \leftarrow \text{Trans}_{key}(m_b, r_S, r_R)$ where r_S is randomly selected from $\mathcal{R}_S$, and r_R is randomly selected from $\mathcal{R}_R$.
4. $b' \leftarrow \mathcal{A}_2(pk, trans^*, st)$;
5. The experiment returns 1 if $b' = b$, otherwise returns 0.

We define the adversary's advantage in above experiment as:

$$\text{Adv}_{\mathcal{A},\mathcal{E}}^{\text{IND}}(k) = 2 \cdot \text{Pr}\left[\text{IND}_{\mathcal{A},\mathcal{E}}(k) = 1\right] - 1.$$

Definition 8 (IND). *A deniable encryption scheme $\mathcal{E}$ is indistinguishable (IND) if for every PPT adversary $\mathcal{A}$, $\text{Adv}_{\mathcal{A},\mathcal{E}}^{\text{IND}}(k)$ is negligible in k.*

Remark 3. In above definition, m_0, m_1 are selected by adversary $\mathcal{A}$. However in Canetti et al.'s security definition [3], it is required for any $m_0, m_1 \in M$, $\text{Trans}_{key}(m_0)$ and $\text{Trans}_{key}(m_1)$ are indistinguishable by $\mathcal{A}$.

Receiver deniability. The receiver deniability is defined analogously. For a receiver-deniable encryption scheme $\mathcal{E} = (\text{Gen}, \text{Com}, \phi_R)$ where ϕ_R is the receiver's opening algorithm, consider the following experiment:

Experiment $\text{RDEN}_{\mathcal{A},\mathcal{E}}^{m,m'}(k)$

1. $key \leftarrow \text{Gen}(1^k)$ where $key = (pk, sk)$ and pk is sent to $\mathcal{A}$;
2. $r_S, r_S' \leftarrow \mathcal{R}_S$ where $\mathcal{R}_S$ is the random local input space for S; $r_R, r_R' \leftarrow \mathcal{R}_R$ where $\mathcal{R}_R$ is the random local input space for R. For two messages m and m', the receiver's opening algorithm computes $r_R'' \leftarrow \phi_R(pk, m, r_R, m')$.
3. $b \leftarrow \{0,1\}$;

$$(m^*, r_R^*, Trans^*) = \begin{cases} (m', r_R', \text{Trans}_{key}(m', r_S', r_R')) & \text{if } b = 0 \\ (m', r_R'', \text{Trans}_{key}(m, r_S, r_R)) & \text{if } b = 1 \end{cases}$$

4. $b' \leftarrow \mathcal{A}(pk, m^*, r_R^*, Trans^*)$.
5. The experiment returns 1 if $b' = b$, otherwise returns 0.

We define the adversary's detection advantage in above experiment as:

$$\text{Adv}_{\mathcal{A},\mathcal{E}}^{\text{RDEN}}(k) = \max_{m,m' \in M} \{2 \cdot \Pr \left[\text{RDEN}_{\mathcal{A},\mathcal{E}}^{m,m'}(k) = 1 \right] - 1\}$$

where M is the plaintext space of $\mathcal{E}$.

Definition 9 (RDEN). *A deniable encryption scheme $\mathcal{E}$ is δ-receiver-deniable (δ-RDEN) if for every PPT adversary $\mathcal{A}$, $\text{Adv}_{\mathcal{A},\mathcal{E}}^{RDEN}(k)$ is at most δ.*

Computational Soundness of Indistinguishability Properties without Computable Parsing

Hubert Comon-Lundh[1], Masami Hagiya[2],
Yusuke Kawamoto[1], and Hideki Sakurada[3]

[1] LSV, CNRS, ENS Cachan and INRIA, France*
[2] University of Tokyo, Japan
[3] NTT Communication Science Laboratories, NTT Corporation, Japan

Abstract. We provide a symbolic model for protocols using public-key encryption and hash function, and prove that this model is computationally sound: if there is an attack in the computational world, then there is an attack in the symbolic (abstract) model. Our original contribution is that we deal with the security properties, such as anonymity, which cannot be described using a single execution trace, while considering an unbounded number of sessions of the protocols in the presence of active and adaptive adversaries. Our soundness proof is different from all existing studies in that it does not require a computable parsing function from bit strings to terms. This allows us to deal with more cryptographic primitives, such as a preimage-resistant and collision-resistant hash function whose input may have different lengths.

1 Introduction

There are two main approaches to the analysis of protocol security. The first considers an attacker modeled as a probabilistic polynomial-time (PPT) interactive Turing machine (ITM) and a protocol is an unbounded number of copies of ITMs. The attacker is assumed to control the network and can schedule the communications and send fake messages. The security property is defined as an indistinguishability game: the protocol is secure if, for any attacker A, the probability that A gets an advantage in this game is negligible. A typical example is the *anonymity* property, by which an attacker should not be able to distinguish between two networks in one of which identities have been switched. The difficulty with such computational security notions lies in the problem of obtaining detailed proofs: they are in general unmanageable, and cannot be verified by automatic tools.

The second approach relies on a formal model: bit strings are abstracted by formal expressions (terms), the attacker is any formal process, and security properties, such as anonymity, can be expressed by the observational equivalence of processes. This model is much simpler: there is no coin tossing, no complexity bounds, and the attacker is given only a fixed set of primitive operations (the function symbols in the term algebra). Therefore it is not surprising that security proofs become

---

* This work has been supporter by the ANR project ProSe.

M.D. Ryan, B. Smyth, and G. Wang (Eds.): ISPEC 2012, LNCS 7232, pp. 63–79, 2012.

much simpler and can sometimes be automatized. However, the drawback is that we might miss some attacks because the model might be too abstract.

Starting with work of Abadi and Rogaway [2] and Backes, Pfitzmann and Waidner [4], there have been several results showing the *computational soundness* of the formal models: we do not miss any attacks when considering the abstract model, provided that the security primitives satisfy certain properties; for instance IND-CPA or IND-CCA in the case of encryption. Such results avoid the weaknesses of both approaches to security.

In their original work, Abadi and Rogaway only considered symmetric encryption and a passive attacker with some other minor restrictions. This has been extended in a number of directions. For instance, Backes et al. consider active attackers and several cryptographic primitives and show simulatability theorems, which imply the computational soundness of some formal model [4,6]. There are also several other soundness results, typically for some trace properties [13,9] and, more recently, for equivalence properties [7].

In the present work, we show a soundness result for active attackers and public-key encryption and hash functions as cryptographic primitives. Our result extends the previous work in the following respects:

1. In addition to security properties that can be checked on each trace, i.e., each individual sequence of events, we consider equivalence properties. Therefore, our work does not fit into the general framework of [3], which only considers trace properties. Actually, we need rather different proof techniques, such as tree oracles and tree transformations. The only previous results concerning equivalence properties in the presence of active attackers are [7], in which only symmetric encryption and a particular class of processes is considered, and [12], in which only a fixed number of protocol instances is considered. We do not assume here any bound on the number of protocol instances.

2. Our soundness proof does not use a *computable parsing function* from bit strings to terms. This is a major difference from all existing studies on computational soundness. It allows us to deal with a *preimage-resistant and collision-resistant hash function* whose input may have different lengths, for which the soundness of process calculi cannot be obtained by [7]'s proof technique with the computable parsing function, as we detail later.

3. Unlike [7], we do not restrict ourselves to the so-called "simple processes". Simple processes are parallel compositions of replicated processes that are just finite sequences of inputs/outputs and tests, without conditional branching. We consider here a larger fragment of the applied π-calculus of [1]: we allow negative tests and non-trivial processes in both branches of conditional, as well as arbitrary replications. We keep however two important restrictions. First we assume that the processes are determinate: every copy of a process has first to generate communication channels and disclose them. In this way, the attacker can schedule to which copy of a process a message is sent. Furthermore, we do not allow private communication channels. Considering such private channels would require to consider timing attacks, or (for

   instance) to assume that an attacker cannot distinguish between terminating
   and non-terminating processes, as investigated in [15].
4. We included hash functions in our set of primitives in order to illustrate the
   usefulness of dropping the parsing assumptions. Previous (positive) results
   on the computational soundness of hash functions either assume stronger
   properties of the hash functions than the standard preimage-resistance and
   collision-resistance ([5,11,10,8]), or they assume that all plaintexts have the
   same size ([5]). In any case, all these studies do not consider both an active attacker and indistinguishability properties. On the other hand, we assume that the hash function is only applied to nonces (possibly of different
   lengths).
5. Finally, we observe that the ability of the computational attacker to observe
   the length of bit strings cannot be soundly represented using a (reasonable)
   symbolic length function. Up to our knowledge, this problem has never been
   considered in the papers on computational soundness. We propose here a new
   solution where each plaintext term is associated with a label representing its
   expected length in the symbolic model, and protocols accept only input of
   expected length in the computational model. This is a reasonable assumption
   that can be easily implemented.

Our proof relies on ideas that are similar to [7]: each process is associated with
a *computation tree*, which records all possible executions of the process. The observational equivalence between two processes implies some labeled bisimilarity
between the computation trees. Computation trees are used as *tree oracles* in
the computational model. The computational indistinguishability between two
processes is then equivalent to that between the two tree oracles. The proof
proceeds by successive transformations of the computation trees, in such a way
that the attacker wins a game (may distinguish the tree oracles) iff he wins
the game against the transformed trees. Eventually, the computation trees are
simple enough: it is straightforward that the attacker cannot win.

   There are however important differences between our work and [7], which we
summarize now. Without computable parsing, we cannot rely on the same notion
of computation trees as in [7]; in [7], when the attacker submits a bit string to the
tree oracle, the bit string is parsed into a term and the branch of the computation
tree labeled with this term is then taken. In this paper, we consider symbolic
computation trees, in which all term labels that satisfy the same conditions are
gathered together: now the computation trees are finitely branching and the
edges are labeled with formulas rather than terms. The formulas are evaluated
on the attacker's input, whether in the computational or in the symbolic model.
In addition, since the formulas are arbitrary Boolean combinations of atomic
formulas, we may allow arbitrary conditional branching (which is not the case
in [7]).

   Symbolic computation trees however introduce new difficulties, since the previous transformations are no longer valid. We need therefore additional transformations, as well as a *partial unraveling* of the computation tree.

We also differ from [7] in three other respects:

1. We consider hash functions (in the standard model), whose inputs may have different structures (we use two different constructors for nonces of different lengths): this is an example where we cannot assume a computable parsing function. On the other hand, the impossibility result of [5] shows that the BRISM/UC results cannot be extended to hash functions in the standard model, when the plaintexts may have different structures; the BRISM framework relies on the existence of a computable parsing function, allowing to translate bit strings into terms.

2. The soundness of indistinguishability requires a symbolic length function: we need to provide the symbolic attacker with a capability to distinguish terms, whose implementations are bit strings of different lengths. This is difficult because, for instance, a pair $\langle u, u \rangle$ and a ciphertext $\{u\}^r_{\mathsf{ek}(k)}$ may or not have the same length, depending on the security parameter, while a symbolic length function cannot depend on a security parameter; should $\langle u, u \rangle$ and $\{u\}^r_{\mathsf{ek}(k)}$ get the same symbolic length or not ? A symbolic length function is hardly sound with respect to the computational length.

   The solution adopted in [7] is to assume that the length of any cryptographic primitive applied to some arguments is a homogeneous function of the lengths of its arguments. Typically, in case of a linear function, the length $|[\![\langle u, v \rangle]\!]_\eta|$ of the computational interpretation of a pair, with respect to the security parameter η must be $\alpha \times |[\![u]\!]_\eta| + \beta \times |[\![v]\!]_\eta| + \gamma \times \eta$. Then, by induction, we may factor out η from the length of the interpretation of any term and get (in)equalities on lengths, independently of η.

   This is a strong restriction on the implementation since, for instance, the pairing operation does not have a constant overhead; it depends linearly on the security parameter.

   We propose another solution here, relying on labels, that is more realistic: messages received by honest agents do have expected lengths. Such an expected length is represented by a symbolic label such that two identical labels yield the same computational length of messages in an honest execution. On the computational side, we assume that the honest agents check the lengths of messages that they receive or encrypt, which is easy to implement, so that the actual length matches the expected one. It turns out that these assumptions, together with some weak length-regularity of the cryptographic primitives, are sufficient for the soundness result, as we show in this paper.

3. [7] uses a trace mapping property, whose use in the indistinguishability games is unclear. We formalize a new transformation of computation trees, in which computational traces that do not have a symbolic counterpart yield a failure node.

We do not have the space to present here the result in detail, which will appear as a research report. We sketch our symbolic model in Section 2, emphasizing the unusual components. Similarly, we sketch our computational interpretation in Section 3 and finally sketch the main steps of the proofs of our main result in Section 4.

2 The Symbolic Model

2.1 Terms

We rely on a variant of the applied π-calculus [1]. Terms are built from names (out of a set $\mathcal{N}$), variables (out of a set $\mathcal{X}$), the *constructor function symbols* $\mathsf{FuncC} = \{\mathsf{n}^1(\_), \mathsf{n}^2(\_), \langle\_, \_\rangle, \mathsf{h}(\_), \mathsf{ek}(\_), \mathsf{dk}(\_), \mathsf{cert}(\_), \{\_\}^{\_}_{\_}\}$ and the *destructor function symbols* $\mathsf{FuncD} = \{\pi_1(\_), \pi_2(\_), \mathsf{dec}(\_, \_)\}$. Let $\mathcal{F} = \mathsf{FuncC} \cup \mathsf{FuncD}$. $\mathsf{n}^1(\_)$ and $\mathsf{n}^2(\_)$ are two constructor symbols for nonces. They can get only names as arguments. They are intended to produce names of different lengths. $\mathsf{cert}(\_)$ is a constructor for public keys certificates, $\mathsf{h}(\_)$ is a hash function symbol and $\mathsf{ek}(\_), \mathsf{dk}(\_)$ are intended to represent encryption and decryption keys, respectively. These two symbols can only take names as arguments.

All the function symbols are available to the attacker, except for $\mathsf{cert}(\_)$. Term is the set of ground terms built on these function symbols, the names and a set of constants Const. $\mathsf{Term}(\mathcal{X})$ are the terms that may additionally contain variables from $\mathcal{X}$. *Constructor terms* are terms that do not contain symbols from FuncD. For any expression or set of expressions S, $\mathsf{Var}(S)$ is the set of variables occurring free in S.

The function symbols satisfy the equations of Fig. 1. In these equations, the

$$\pi_1(\langle x, y \rangle) = x$$
$$\pi_2(\langle x, y \rangle) = y$$
$$\mathsf{dec}(\{x\}^r_{\mathsf{ek}(k)}, \mathsf{dk}(k)) = x \quad \text{if } k, r \in \mathsf{Name}$$

Fig. 1. Equational specification of the algebra

variables x, y range over any ground constructor term. This corresponds to a "call-by-value" interpretation of the destructors. In other words, the implementation is strict: if an argument of a destructor is not a constructor term, we cannot apply these equations to cancel the destructor. The set of equations is infinite, as there are symbols k, r, r' that range over all possible names. Then, Term might be seen as a quotient algebra with respect to the congruence generated by the equations of Fig. 1. We ambiguously keep the same notation Term and $\mathsf{Term}(\mathcal{X})$ for the quotients. Term is then a $\mathcal{F}$-algebra: morphisms and first-order structures are defined as usual, referring to this quotient structure.

We orient all equations of Fig. 1 from left to right. This yields an infinite convergent term rewriting system on terms. The normal form of u is written as $u\!\downarrow$.

A *labeled term* is either a term or a symbolic expression obtained from a term by labeling some of its subterms with labels in Label. More formally, the set LTerm of labeled terms is defined by:

$\mathsf{LTerm} ::= \mathsf{Term} \mid \mathcal{F}(\mathsf{LTerm}, \cdots, \mathsf{LTerm}) \mid \mathsf{Term}{:}\mathsf{Label} \mid \mathcal{F}(\mathsf{LTerm}, \cdots, \mathsf{LTerm}){:}\mathsf{Label}$

For instance, $\{\langle n^1(r), n^2(r'):l_{n^2}\rangle :l_1\}^{r''}_{ek(k)}$ and $\{h(n^1(r):l_{n^1}):l_2\}^{r'}_{ek(k)}$ are labeled terms. Intuitively, $u{:}l$ represents a message whose length is expected to be l in an honest protocol execution.

The rewrite rules of Fig. 1 can only be applied to unlabeled instances of the variables; when we rewrite a labeled term, the labels of the rule instances are implicitly removed. In this way, we keep the confluence and termination of the rewrite system and rewriting a labeled term yields a labeled term (for instance, we do not get $u{:}l{:}l'$).

2.2 Predicates, Conditions, Frames and Static Equivalence

Predicates are used either in honest processes, in order to check properties of the input terms, or by the attacker, in order to distinguish sequences of terms. We consider the following predicate symbols: M, EQ, EK, $IsEK$, IsN_1, IsN_2, PL, and HL, whose (informal) meaning is as follows. $M(u)$ holds on ground terms u such that $u{\downarrow}$ is a constructor term. EQ is the strict equality predicate: $EQ(u,v)$ implies $u{\downarrow}= v{\downarrow}$ and $M(u)$ and $M(v)$. EK holds on a ciphertext $\{u\}^w_v$ and a public key $ek(k)$ when $v = ek(k)$. $IsEK$ is true on pairs of an encryption key and a certificate of that key. IsN_1 holds on terms $n^1(r)$ with $r \in$ Name and IsN_2 holds on terms $n^2(r)$ with $r \in$ Name. PL holds on two ciphertexts whose plaintexts have the same expected length, i.e. the same label. HL holds on two hash values whose plaintexts have the same label. A *condition* is a Boolean combination of atomic formulas. Examples of predicate interpretations are given in Example 1.

The *frames* usually record the messages that have been sent. Since we consider symbolic executions, we need to extend the classical definition to message templates that may contain variable. A *frame* is an an expression $\nu\overline{y}.\nu\overline{n}.\sigma$ where $\overline{y}$ is a finite set of variables, $\overline{n}$ is a finite set of names, σ is a substitution from a finite set of variables $\mathsf{dom}(\sigma)$ into $\mathsf{Term}(\mathcal{X})$ such that $\overline{y} \cap \mathsf{dom}(\sigma) = \emptyset$, and $\mathsf{Var}(\mathsf{codom}(\sigma)) \cap \mathsf{dom}(\sigma) = \emptyset$.

Given a frame ϕ, we write σ_ϕ the associated substitution, $\mathsf{bn}(\phi)$ is the associated sequence of bound names $\overline{n}$ and $\mathsf{bv}(\phi)$ is the associated sequence of bound variables $\overline{y}$. A *ground frame* ϕ is a frame such that $\mathsf{Var}(\mathsf{codom}(\sigma_\phi)) = \emptyset$. We recall here the definition of symbolic indistinguishability between ground frames (for general frames, this notion will be directly defined on computation trees).

Definition 1. Two ground frames ϕ_1 and ϕ_2 are *statically equivalent*, which is written as $\phi_1 \sim \phi_2$, if $\mathsf{dom}(\sigma_{\phi_1}) = \mathsf{dom}(\sigma_{\phi_2})$ and for any terms u and v such that cert does not occur in u, v, $\mathsf{Var}(u) \cup \mathsf{Var}(v) \subseteq \mathsf{dom}(\sigma_{\phi_1})$ and $(\mathsf{fn}(u) \cup \mathsf{fn}(v)) \cap (\mathsf{bn}(\phi_1) \cup \mathsf{bn}(\phi_2)) = \emptyset$, we have the following:

- For each $PR \in \{M, IsEK, IsN_1, IsN_2\}$, $\mathcal{M} \models PR(u\sigma_{\phi_1}{\downarrow})$ iff $\mathcal{M} \models PR(u\sigma_{\phi_2}{\downarrow})$.
- For each $PR \in \{EQ, EK, PL, HL\}$, $\mathcal{M} \models PR(u\sigma_{\phi_1}{\downarrow}, v\sigma_{\phi_1}{\downarrow})$ iff $\mathcal{M} \models PR(u\sigma_{\phi_2}{\downarrow}, v\sigma_{\phi_2}{\downarrow})$.

Example 1. In the examples, we omit the variables of the domains of σ_ϕ: they are always $x_1, \ldots, x_n$ where n is the length of the frame.

1. $\nu r.\ \mathsf{n}^1(r) \sim \nu r'.\ \mathsf{n}^1(r')$, while $\nu r.\ \mathsf{n}^1(r) \not\sim \nu r'.\ \mathsf{n}^2(r')$, since $\mathcal{M} \models IsN_1(\mathsf{n}^1(r))$ and $\mathcal{M} \not\models IsN_1(\mathsf{n}^2(r))$.

2. $\nu r.\ \{b\colon l\}^r_{\mathsf{ek}(a)} \sim \nu r.\ \{c\colon l'\}^r_{\mathsf{ek}(a)}$ iff $l = l'$, since $\mathcal{M} \models PL(\{b\colon l\}^r_{\mathsf{ek}(a)}, \{b'\colon l\}^{r'}_{\mathsf{ek}(a)})$ and $\mathcal{M} \models PL(\{c\colon l'\}^r_{\mathsf{ek}(a)}, \{b'\colon l\}^{r'}_{\mathsf{ek}(a)})$ iff $l = l'$. In this example, the recipe u is reduced to the variable x_1 and the recipe v is the ground (labeled) term $\{b'\colon l\}^{r'}_{\mathsf{ek}(a)}$.

3. $\nu a, r.\ \{b\colon l\}^r_{\mathsf{ek}(a)}, \mathsf{dk}(a) \not\sim \nu a, r.\ \{c\colon l\}^r_{\mathsf{ek}(a)}, \mathsf{dk}(a)$ if $b, c \in \mathcal{N}$ and a, b, c, r are pairwise distinct. It suffices to consider $u = \mathsf{dec}(x_1, x_2)$, $v = b\colon \mathcal{M} \models EQ(u\sigma_{\phi_1}{\downarrow}, v)$ while $\mathcal{M} \not\models EQ(u\sigma_{\phi_2}{\downarrow}, v)$.

4. $\nu a, a', r, r'.\ \{b\colon l\}^r_{\mathsf{ek}(a)}, \{b\colon l\}^{r'}_{\mathsf{ek}(a)}, \mathsf{ek}(a) \not\sim \nu a, a', r, r'.\ \{b\colon l\}^r_{\mathsf{ek}(a)}, \{b\colon l\}^{r'}_{\mathsf{ek}(a')}, \mathsf{ek}(a)$ using EK.

2.3   Processes

Processes are built as in the applied π-calculus [1], using the predicates and function symbols of the previous section. We do not recall here the syntax and the basic definitions. Let us explain the communication rule.

$$c(x\colon l).P \parallel \bar{c}(u\colon l).Q \quad \rightarrow \quad P\{x \mapsto u\} \parallel \{x \mapsto u\} \parallel Q$$

If a process $c(x\colon l).P$ is ready to receive a message on the channel c and another process is ready to emit the message u on channel c and if the two messages have the same label, then the network moves to a configuration in which x is replaced with u in P. The active substitution $\{x \mapsto u\}$ is kept (as a local memory of P).

While the attacker's processes are arbitrary processes (the attacker may re-label the terms as he wishes), protocols are specified as combinations of basic processes, using replication, name generation and parallel composition.

The basic processes are built using name generation, conditionals and sequences of input/output actions. We assume that all inputs are labeled variables. This is not a restriction, since the attacker may re-label the terms. We assume that all occurrences of plaintexts (of either ciphertexts or hashes) in the basic processes are labeled, and that before sending a message s the process always checks $M(s)$. This forbids sending ill-formed messages (or forwarding ill-formed message). Since, according to our semantics, ill-formed messages do not pass any test, the effect of message forwarding (moving the control point of some process) can be achieved with a well-formed message. We believe that this assumption is not a restriction.

The main restriction, with respect to the full applied π-calculus is that, each time a process is replicated, it must start with the generation of communication channels that are disclosed and then used as input/output channels. This ensures the determinacy of processes: when the attacker sends a message on a channel c, there is at most one basic process that is able to receive a message on c.

Example 2. This is a simple process that first generates two channel names and disclose them, hence can be later replicated.

$$B(a, b, c, d) = \nu x, y.\ \nu i_{\mathsf{in}}, i_{\mathsf{out}}, r.\ c(x\!:\!l).\overline{c}(\langle i_{\mathsf{in}}, i_{\mathsf{out}}\rangle).$$
$$i_{\mathsf{in}}(y\!:\!l).\ \text{if } EQ(\pi_1(\mathsf{dec}(y, \mathsf{dk}(a)))), b) \wedge M(\pi_2(\mathsf{dec}(y, \mathsf{dk}(a)))) \wedge \mathit{IsEK}(\mathsf{ek}(b))$$
$$\text{then } \overline{i_{\mathsf{out}}}(\{\pi_2(\mathsf{dec}(y, \mathsf{dk}(a)))\!:\!l'\}^r_{\mathsf{ek}(b)})$$
$$\text{else } \overline{i_{\mathsf{out}}}(\{d\!:\!l'\}^r_{\mathsf{ek}(b)})$$

Example 3. The following is an example of a protocol.

$$(\nu a)(\nu b)(\nu d)\ \big(\ !\,(\nu x)\ (\nu c_1, c_2)\ c(x\!:\!l)\ \overline{c}(\langle c_1,\ c_2\rangle)\ (!\ B(a, b, c_1, d))\|\ !B(b, a, c_2, d))\ \big)$$

The attacker, using the public channel c, may send a signal, which will give back fresh channel names c_1, c_2. This allows to get a copy of the (outermost) replicated process. Each of these channel names may then be used to request a copy of the corresponding instance of B.

Protocols may also include an initial setting, in which, for instance, some private keys are disclosed (static corruption).

We assume a number of (reasonable) properties of the protocols:

- Two occurrences of the same variable have the same label.
- The random seed r used in honest encryption terms $\{\_\}^r_\_$ only occur in that terms and the random seed k used for honest (i.e., certified) keys $\mathsf{ek}(k)$ and $\mathsf{dk}(k)$, are not used for any other purpose.
- Encryption keys with their certificates are sent to the attacker whenever they are generated.
- Only correct encryption keys are used for encryption (for unknown keys, *IsEK* is checked before encryption). This rules out the problem of keys that are forged by the attacker.
- Only hash values of nonces are produced by the protocols: for unknown plaintexts s, the protocol checks $\mathit{IsN}_1(s) \vee \mathit{IsN}_2(s)$ before hashing.
- There is no dynamic corruption: the protocols only disclose decryption key at the beginning of the execution.
- There is no key cycle: a key hierarchy ensures that the attacker cannot force the protocol to produce a cycle involving non-corrupted keys.

Finally, two processes P and Q are observationally equivalent, which we write $P \sim Q$ if, as usual, there is no context C such that $C[P]$ may emit on a channel a while $C[Q]$ cannot (or the converse).

3   Computational Interpretation

3.1   Computational Interpretation of Terms and Predicate Symbols

Each function symbol f is associated with a function $[\![f]\!]$ from bit strings to bit strings that can be computed in deterministic polynomial time. These interpretations are assumed to satisfy the equations of Fig. 1, hence the set of bit strings has a structure of $\mathcal{F}$-algebra. Let $\mathcal{SS}$ be a set of mappings from Name to $\{0,1\}^*$. Given $\tau \in \mathcal{SS}$, for any ground term u, $[\![u]\!]^\tau$ is the unique extension of τ into a homomorphism of $\mathcal{F}$-algebra. If u is a term with variables X and θ is a mapping from X into $\{0,1\}^*$, $[\![u]\!]^{\theta,\tau}$ is defined in a similar way. The interpretation of labeled terms is defined by ignoring the labels. Labels themselves are interpreted as natural numbers. The *security parameter* is the minimal length of $\tau(r)$ for $r \in$ Name.

In addition, we assume the following properties of the computational interpretation:

- The ranges of constructor function symbols are disjoint and disjoint from the interpretation of names. This assumption is necessary for a soundness result. However, we do not assume that the range of a function symbol is computable.
- We assume the following properties on lengths of the computational interpretation of names and nonces.
  - For each $b = 1, 2$ and any $r, r' \in$ Name, $\big|[\![n^b(r)]\!]^\tau\big| = \big|[\![n^b(r')]\!]^\tau\big|$, and that $\big|[\![n^1(r)]\!]^\tau\big| < \big|[\![n^2(r)]\!]^\tau\big| < \big|[\![r]\!]^\tau\big|$.
  - When τ is uniformly drawn (which we will assume in what follows), the distribution of $[\![n^b(r)]\!]^\tau$ is uniform and covers all bit strings of the length $\big|[\![n^b(r)]\!]^\tau\big|$.
  - $\big|[\![n^1(r)]\!]^\tau\big|$ and $\big|[\![n^2(r)]\!]^\tau\big|$ are polynomial in the security parameter η.

  Thanks to the assumptions, for instance, the lengths of keys are different from those of nonces in the computational model.
- We assume a weak notion of length regularity: Let $u{:}\,l$ be any labeled term occurring in a protocol such that $y_1{:}\,l_1, y_2{:}\,l_2, \ldots, y_n{:}\,l_n$ are all variables occurring in u. For any computational interpretation τ of names as bit strings, if terms $v_1, v_2, \ldots, v_n$ satisfy $\big|[\![v_i]\!]^\tau\big| = [\![l_i]\!]^\tau$ for $i = 1, 2, \ldots, n$, then $\big|[\![u\{y_1 \mapsto v_1, y_2 \mapsto v_2, \cdots, y_n \mapsto v_n\}]\!]^\tau\big| = [\![l]\!]^\tau$.

- For each $PR \in \{M, IsEK\}$ and any term u,
  - $\mathcal{M} \models PR(u)$ iff $[\![PR]\!]([\![u]\!]^\tau) = 1$ holds for any $\tau \in \mathcal{SS}$, and
  - $\mathcal{M} \models \neg PR(u)$ iff $[\![PR]\!]([\![u]\!]^\tau) = 0$ holds for any $\tau \in \mathcal{SS}$.

  Note that this does not imply anything on the interpretation of PR on a bit string that is not the interpretation of any term.
- For each $PR \in \{IsN_1, IsN_2\}$ and any bit string m, $[\![PR]\!](m) = 1$ iff there are $u \in$ Term and $\tau \in \mathcal{SS}$ such that $m = [\![u]\!]^\tau$ and $\mathcal{M} \models PR(u)$. For instance, we can implement $[\![IsN_b]\!](m)$ by checking whether the length of m is $[\![l_{n^b}]\!]^\tau$ or not.
- For any bit string m and any name k,
  - if $[\![M]\!]([\![\pi_i]\!](m)) = 1$ for $i = 1, 2$, then $[\![M]\!]([\![dec]\!](m, [\![dk(k)]\!]^\tau)) = 0$,
  - if $[\![M]\!]([\![dec]\!](m, [\![dk(k)]\!]^\tau)) = 1$, then $[\![M]\!]([\![dec]\!](m, [\![dk(k')]\!]^\tau)) = 0$ for any name k' such that $[\![dk(k)]\!]^\tau \neq [\![dk(k')]\!]^\tau$,
  - for any $m \in \{0,1\}^*$ and any $m' \in \{0,1\}^* \setminus \{[\![dk(k)]\!]^\tau : \tau \in \mathcal{SS}\}$, $[\![M]\!]([\![dec]\!](m, m') = 0$.

These assumptions cover the case where m is not the computational interpretation of any term. They can be ensured, for instance, by assuming that
the decryption of a ciphertext with a wrong key returns an error. The previous work on computational soundness has implemented this by appending
each ciphertext with the encryption key used to produce the ciphertext.

- The implementation is strict: For any $f \in \mathcal{F}$ and any bit string m, $[\![M]\!](m) = 0$ implies $[\![M]\!]([\![f]\!](\cdots m \cdots)) = 0$. For instance, $[\![M]\!]([\![\{u\}_{ek(k)}^r]\!]^\tau) = 0$ when $u = dec(\{s\}_{ek(k)}^{r'}, dk(k'))$.
- For any two terms u, v, $[\![EQ]\!]([\![u]\!]^\tau, [\![v]\!]^\tau) = 1$ iff $[\![M]\!]([\![u]\!]^\tau) = [\![M]\!]([\![v]\!]^\tau) = 1$ and $[\![u]\!]^\tau = [\![v]\!]^\tau$.

For a computational soundness result, we assume nothing on the computational
interpretation of the predicates EK, PL, HL, which may (not) be available to a
computational attacker.

3.2   Interactive Turing Machines

The processes are interpreted as interactive Turing machines, which we do not
recall here. Let us only highlight the specifics of our model.

The model of the network includes a store that records the IDs (interpretation of channel names) associated with each process. This allows us to consider
nested replications: the attacker may refer to a given replicated process in a
deterministic way using such channel IDs.

More importantly, each basic process, upon receiving a message on a channel
c, checks that the length of the input bit string matches the expected length. It
proceeds only there is a match: the machine in state $c(x\!:\!l).B$ may move to the
state B only if the content of its input tape has length $[\![l]\!]$.

Definition 2. Two protocols P and Q are *computationally indistinguishable*,
which we write $P \approx Q$, if, for any attacker's machine $\mathcal{A}$,

$$|\mathbf{Pr}\left[\tau : [\![P]\!]^\tau \| \mathcal{A} = 1\right] - \mathbf{Pr}\left[\tau : [\![Q]\!]^\tau \| \mathcal{A} = 1\right]|$$

is negligible in the security parameter.

3.3   Cryptographic Assumptions

We assume the public-key encryption scheme to be IND-CCA2 and the hash
function to be preimage-resistant and collision-resistant. For instance, preimage-
resistance is stated as follows.

Given a security parameter η, a *hash function* [14] is a deterministic algorithm
$\mathcal{H}$ that, given a key $k \in K_{\mathcal{H}}$ and a bit string $m \in M_{\mathcal{H}}$, outputs a hash value of m
by k, whose length only depends on η (not on m), where $K_{\mathcal{H}}$ is a key space and
$M_{\mathcal{H}}$ is a message space such that $m' \in M_{\mathcal{H}}$ implies $\{0,1\}^{|m'|} \subseteq M_{\mathcal{H}}$, and that
each bit string in $M_{\mathcal{H}}$ is so long that it cannot be guessed by the attacker (i.e.

there is a polynomial p such that $\eta \leq p(\min\{|m| \mid m \in M_{\mathcal{H}}\}))$. $\mathcal{H}$ is preimage-resistant if the following probability is negligible in η for any PPT attacker $\mathcal{A}$ and any ℓ such that $\{0,1\}^{\ell} \subseteq M_{\mathcal{H}}$:

$$\Pr[\, k \stackrel{\$}{\leftarrow} K_{\mathcal{H}} \,;\, s \stackrel{\$}{\leftarrow} \{0,1\}^{\ell} \,;\, m := \mathcal{H}(k,s) \,;\, s' \leftarrow \mathcal{A}(1^{\eta}, k, m) : \mathcal{H}(k,s') = m\,].$$

We also assume the following (which are necessary for the soundness result):

- The key certificates cannot be forged with a non-negligible probability.
- The length of a pair is longer than (or equal to) the sum of the lengths of its two components.
- The length of a ciphertext is strictly longer than the length of the corresponding plaintext.
- The length of a hash value (of a nonce) is strictly smaller than the length of the nonce. This rules out identities such as $\mathsf{h}(n) = n$ that could, otherwise, occur with a non-negligible probability.

4   The Main Result

Our main result states that we captured all distinguishing capabilities of a computational attacker in a symbolic model:

Theorem 1. *Let P and Q be two protocols. If $P \sim Q$, then $P \approx Q$.*

The rest of the paper is devoted to the sketch of the proof of this result. First we express the problem as the equivalent problem "$t_P \sim t_Q$ implies $t_P \approx t_Q$" where t_P is a *computation tree* that represents all possible execution sequences (see Section 4.1). Unlike [7], these trees have a finite outdegree, which is independent of the security parameter.

Next, we perform successive transformations T of the computation trees, transforming the problem into "$T(t_P) \sim T(t_Q)$ implies $T(t_P) \approx T(t_Q)$". The computation trees $T(t_P)$ are no longer the computation trees of processes and that is why we use the detour through computation trees. Let us consider some of these transformations in more details.

1. The first transformation aims at ensuring more properties of the computation trees and therefore enables the next step: we *partially unravel* the computation trees, unfolding some conditions (see Section 4.2). This transformation may yield computation trees whose branching degree depends on the security parameter. The difficulty lies in proving that they are still polynomially simulatable.
2. The second transformation is a classical one: thanks to the absence of key cycles, following the ordering on keys, we may replace plaintexts of encryptions by uncorrupted keys with a constant of the same length as the plaintext (see Section 4.3). This step requires the IND-CCA2 property of the public-key encryption scheme. After this step, $t \sim t'$ iff the total unravelings $U(t)$ and $U(t')$ of t and t' respectively (which are infinitely branching trees) are identical up to renaming, which we write $U(t) \simeq U(t')$.

3. The third transformation rules out coincidences (see Section 4.4): in the resulting computation tree, the conditions explicitly state that two distinct names are distinct and that two hash values of distinct terms are distinct. Though this is trivial in the symbolic model, it may happen by chance in the computational one. We also need here to rely on collision-resistance of the hash function.
4. The fourth transformation rules out guesses made in advance (see Section 4.5): in the resulting computation tree, the conditions state explicitly that a random term that has not been produced yet, cannot be computed. This is more tricky than it looks, and relies in particular on the assumption that the length of a pair is longer than the sum of the lengths of its components. It also rules out the computation of a nonce from its hash value, thanks to preimage-resistance.

After these transformations, we can conclude that $t \approx t'$, thanks to a trace mapping property (see Section 4.6).

4.1   Computation Trees

A computation tree is a finitely branching tree whose nodes are labeled with pairs consisting a process (a state) and a frame and whose each edge is labeled with a variable, a channel name and a condition. For any node of a computation tree, given a variable x and a channel name c, the disjunction of all the conditions Φ such that (x, c, Φ) labels some edge departing from the node is a tautology and any two such conditions cannot be satisfied together.

We may associate a computation tree to any protocol: Roughly speaking, if a process $P_0 \| Q$ is structurally equivalent to $(\nu \overline{n})(c(x : l).P_1 \| Q)$ and $(\nu \overline{m})(P_0 \| Q, \phi)$ is labeling a node, we add an edge $(\nu \overline{m})\,(P_0 \| Q, \phi) \xrightarrow{x, c, \Phi} (\nu \overline{m}, \overline{n})(P_2 \| Q, \phi \uplus \phi')$ if there is a (sequence of) test Φ in P_1, whose satisfaction yields the output of ϕ' and the remaining process P_2.[1] Any symbolic trace (i.e., any sequence of triples (x, c, s) where x is a variable, c is a channel name and s is a ground term) that can be produced by an attacker process corresponds to an instance θ of a path in the process computation tree, such that, at any step as above, there is a term u such that $u\sigma_\phi\theta{\downarrow} = x\theta$ (in other words, $x\theta$ is deducible from the corresponding instance of the frame).

Given a sample τ, each computation tree t is also associated with a tree oracle $\mathcal{O}_{t,\tau}$: when the oracle is queried with a bit string m, a variable x and a channel ID $[\![c]\!]^\tau$, it evaluates (in the computational model) the conditions departing from the root node and associated with (x, c). Exactly one of them is satisfied: this corresponds to an edge $t \xrightarrow{x, c, \Phi} t'$. Then the oracle replies sending the computational interpretation of the frame labeling the root of t' and then behaves as $\mathcal{O}_{t',\tau}$. Two tree oracles are indistinguishable if no polynomial time attacker can guess with a significant advantage which of the two oracles he is interacting with.

---

[1] The names that are bound in front of the state/frame cannot be renamed, unless they are renamed in the whole subtree.

Example 4. The computation tree of the protocol $P = \nu i_{\text{in}}, i_{\text{out}}, r, k.\ c_B(x).\ \bar{c}_B(\langle i_{\text{in}}, i_{\text{out}} \rangle)$. B is shown in Fig. 2 where $\bar{n} = i_{\text{in}}, i_{\text{out}}, r, k$ and B is the following basic process:

$$i_{\text{in}}(y).\text{if } EQ(\pi_1(y), \mathsf{n}^1(r))$$
$$\text{then if } M(\text{dec}(\pi_2(y), \text{dk}(k)))$$
$$\text{then } \overline{i_{\text{out}}}(\text{dec}(\pi_2(y), \text{dk}(k))).0$$
$$\text{else } 0$$
$$\text{else } 0.$$

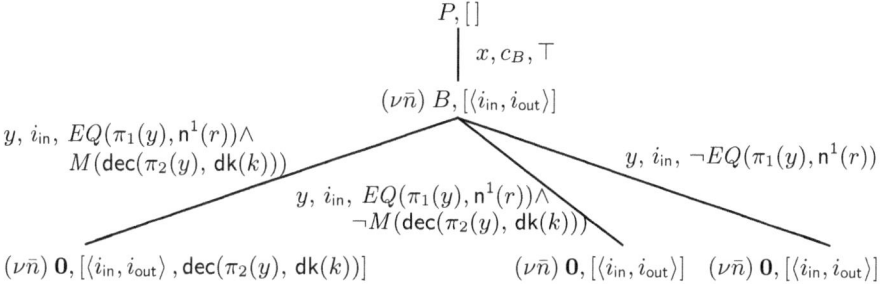

Fig. 2. Example of a computation tree

4.2 Partial Unraveling

The goal is to replace plaintexts with fixed bit strings, thanks to IND-CCA2. However, in some cases, it would not be correct, because the terms occurring in the frames or the conditions may contain variables. For instance in $\text{dec}(\{u:l\}^r_x, y)$, we may replace u with a fixed term of expected length l only if the instance of the term does not contain a redex, in other words unless $x = \text{ek}(k)$ and $y = \text{dk}(k)$ for some name k. The basic idea is to narrow these terms, which may require to split the conditions, depending on whether there is a key generated so far such that $x = \text{ek}(k)$ and $y = \text{dk}(k)$.

We prove that we can unravel a computation tree, in such a way that the resulting tree is both computationally and symbolically indistinguishable from the original tree and such that any occurrence of an encryption/decryption is *safe*: either the key is explicitly an encryption/decryption key that has been generated before, or the condition implies that this is not the case. Furthermore, we prove that the tree oracle can still be simulated in polynomial time.

For example, let us consider the computation tree t_1 shown in Fig. 3 that has only one subtree t_2. For brevity, the states and the bindings are omitted from Fig. 3.

The partial unraveling $U_{\text{ek}}(t_1)$ of t_1 is shown in Fig. 4. In $U_{\text{ek}}(t_1)$, the edge from t_2 to t_3 is split into the two edges to t_{30} and t_{31} such that $C_0 = \neg EQ(y_1, s) \land EQ(y_2, \{s:l\}^{r_1}_{\text{ek}(k)})$ and $C_1 = \neg EQ(y_1, \text{dec}(y_2, \text{dk}(k))) \land \neg EQ(y_2, \{s:l\}^{r_1}_{\text{ek}(k)})$. Similarly, the edge from t_2 to t_4 is split into the edges to t_{40} and t_{41}. Then $U_{\text{ek}}(t_1)$ is a safe computation tree.

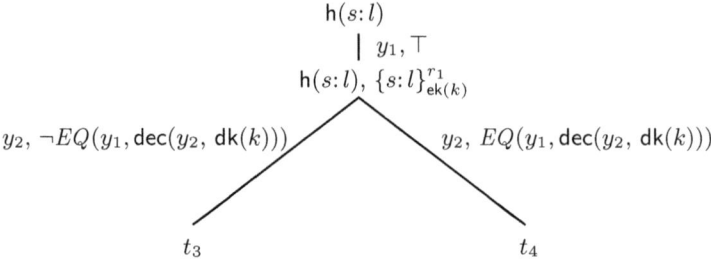

Fig. 3. Example of a computation tree t_1

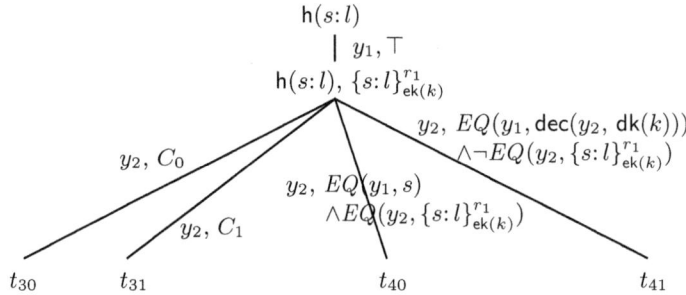

Fig. 4. The partial unraveling $U_{\mathsf{ek}}(t_1)$ of t_1

4.3 Replacing Plaintexts

To such safe computation trees, we may apply the pattern function Ω, replacing each encryption $\{u:l\}^r_{\mathsf{ek}(k)}$ with $\{\Box_l:l\}^r_{\mathsf{ek}(k)}$. This yields again a computation tree which is both symbolically and computationally indistinguishable from the original one, unless we break IND-CCA2.

For example, the tree $\Omega(U_{\mathsf{ek}}(t_1))$ is shown in Fig. 5 where $C'_0 = \neg EQ(y_1, s) \wedge EQ(y_2, \{\Box_l:l\}^{r_1}_{\mathsf{ek}(k)})$ and $C'_1 = \neg EQ(y_1, \mathsf{dec}(y_2, \mathsf{dk}(k))) \wedge \neg EQ(y_2, \{\Box_l:l\}^{r_1}_{\mathsf{ek}(k)})$. Note that the plaintext s inside the ciphertext $\{s:l\}^{r_1}_{\mathsf{ek}(k)}$ is replaced with the constant $\Box_l$, whose expected length l is the same as s.

After this step, $t \sim t'$ iff the total unravelings of t and t' respectively (which are infinitely branching trees) are identical up to renaming.

4.4 Ruling Out Coincidences

Roughly speaking, we add to any condition Φ, labeling an edge of the computation tree, the conditions $\neg EQ(r, r')$ for distinct names r, r', as well as the conditions $\neg EQ(\mathsf{h}(u), \mathsf{h}(v))$ for distinct terms $\mathsf{h}(u), \mathsf{h}(v)$ that appear either in the current frame or condition. We also add similar constraints for keys. This relies, for instance, on collision-resistance.

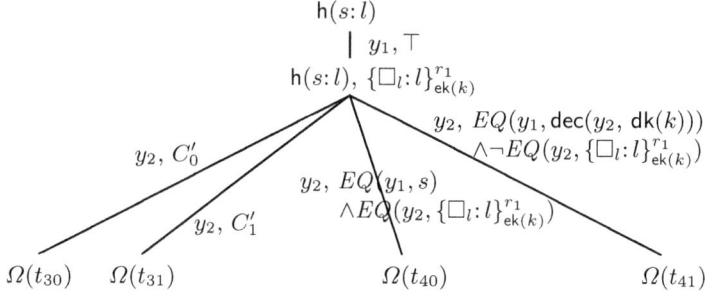

Fig. 5. $\Omega(U_{\mathsf{ek}}(t_1))$

4.5   Ruling Out Predictions

This is a bit more involved: we need to introduce new predicate symbols (for the purpose of the proof only). For instance, we consider a predicate $NP(K, u, v)$, which holds, given a substitution σ, if for any destructor context C using decryption keys in K, we have $C[u]\sigma \downarrow \neq v\sigma \downarrow$. We may express for instance that, when a name n is generated, if the currently available keys are in K, the last attacker input x cannot contain anything that depends on n. This is expressed by adding the constraint $NP(K, x, n)$. We use here preimage-resistance of the hash function, expressing that a nonce cannot be guessed from its hash.

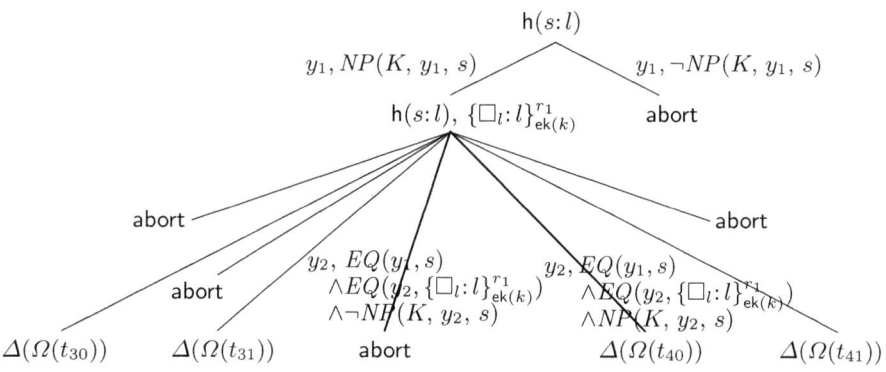

Fig. 6. $\Delta(\Omega(U_{\mathsf{ek}}(t_1)))$

For instance, if we apply the transformation Δ to $\Omega(U_{\mathsf{ek}}(t_1))$, ruling out predictions, the edge from $\Omega(U_{\mathsf{ek}}(t_1))$ to $\Omega(U_{\mathsf{ek}}(t_2))$ is split in two by adding $NP(K, y_1, s)$, which expresses the impossibility of computing the nonce s from y_1, or $\neg NP(K, y_1, s)$, and the edge from $\Omega(U_{\mathsf{ek}}(t_2))$ to $\Omega(t_{40})$ is split in two by adding $NP(K, y_2, s)$ or $\neg NP(K, y_2, s)$, as shown in Fig. 6. We omit details of the other edges that are split similarly. $\neg NP(K, y_1, s)$, for instance, implies

$EQ(C[y_1], s)$ for some destructor context C. Hence the satisfaction of this condition implies the existence of an attacker on the preimage-resistance of the hash function; the execution aborts in this case.

4.6   Trace Mapping

We show that the conditions resulting from all previous transformations are either unsatisfiable or else satisfiable both in the computational and in the symbolic model. It follows that, for every computational trace, which corresponds to a path in the computation tree and an assignment of variables that satisfies all the conditions along this path, there is also a symbolic trace that corresponds to the same path. This is what we call *trace mapping*. It is slightly different from the usual trace mapping, which states that every computational trace is an interpretation of a symbolic trace, with an overwhelming probability. First, thanks to our previous transformation steps, we get a property with the probability 1 (not with an overwhelming probability only). Next, we do not state that the computational trace is an interpretation of the symbolic one: we only state that they satisfy the same conditions. This is sufficient to conclude: thanks to trace mapping, for every sequence of attacker inputs s_i, if $\mathcal{O}_{t,\tau}$ replies the sequence $[\![u_r]\!]^\tau$, then there is a sequence of symbolic attacker inputs v_i yielding the sequence u_r of symbolic replies of $U(t)$. Now, since $U(t) \simeq U(t')$, there is also a sequence u'_r of replies of $U(t')$ such that, for some τ', $[\![u'_r]\!]^{\tau'} = [\![u_r]\!]^\tau$ is the sequence of replies of the oracle $\mathcal{O}_{t',\tau'}$ on the input sequence s_i. Hence $t \approx t'$. (And we do not need $[\![v_i]\!]^\tau = s_i$.)

5   Conclusion

We managed to get a computational soundness result for observational equivalence, without any parsing assumption. This result holds for a large subset of the applied π-calculus. We believe that the same method can be applied to other primitives, though, as this proof shows, it might be long and tedious.

However, we learned several lessons from this work. For instance, we attacked the problem of the symbolic length from another angle, using a trade-off between computational assumptions and assumptions on the protocols. We also showed how collision-resistance (resp. preimage-resistance) of hash functions can be used in soundness proofs. And maybe, more importantly, we identified several assumptions that look necessary for soundness results, showing the limitations of the method.

Acknowledgments. We thank Dominique Unruh and Véronique Cortier for valuable discussions. We also thank the anonymous reviewers for helpful comments.

References

1. Abadi, M., Fournet, C.: Mobile values, new names, and secure communication. In: Proc. of the 28th ACM Symposium on Principles of Programming Languages (POPL 2001), pp. 104–115 (2001)
2. Abadi, M., Rogaway, P.: Reconciling two views of cryptography (the computational soundness of formal encryption). Journal of Cryptology 15(2), 103–127 (2002)
3. Backes, M., Hofheinz, D., Unruh, D.: CoSP: A general framework for computational soundness proofs. Cryptology ePrint Archive, Report 2009/080 (2009), http://eprint.iacr.org/
4. Backes, M., Pfitzmann, B., Waidner, M.: A composable cryptographic library with nested operations. In: Proc. of the 10th ACM Concerence on Computer and Communications Security (CCS 2003), pp. 220–230 (2003)
5. Backes, M., Pfitzmann, B., Waidner, M.: Limits of the BRSIM/UC Soundness of Dolev-Yao Models with Hashes. In: Gollmann, D., Meier, J., Sabelfeld, A. (eds.) ESORICS 2006. LNCS, vol. 4189, pp. 404–423. Springer, Heidelberg (2006)
6. Backes, M., Pfitzmann, B., Waidner, M.: The reactive simulatability (RSIM) framework for asynchronous systems. Information and Computation 205(12), 1685–1720 (2007)
7. Comon-Lundh, H., Cortier, V.: Computational soundness of observational equivalence. In: Proc. of the 15th ACM Conference on Computer and Communications Security (CCS 2008), pp. 109–118 (2008)
8. Cortier, V., Kremer, S., Küsters, R., Warinschi, B.: Computationally Sound Symbolic Secrecy in the Presence of Hash Functions. In: Arun-Kumar, S., Garg, N. (eds.) FSTTCS 2006. LNCS, vol. 4337, pp. 176–187. Springer, Heidelberg (2006)
9. Cortier, V., Warinschi, B.: Computationally Sound, Automated Proofs for Security Protocols. In: Sagiv, M. (ed.) ESOP 2005. LNCS, vol. 3444, pp. 157–171. Springer, Heidelberg (2005)
10. Garcia, F.D., van Rossum, P.: Sound and complete computational interpretation of symbolic hashes in the standard model. Theor. Comput. Sci. 394(1-2), 112–133 (2008)
11. Janvier, R., Lakhnech, Y., Mazaré, L.: Computational soundness of symbolic analysis for protocols using hash functions. Electr. Notes Theor. Comput. Sci. 186, 121–139 (2007)
12. Kawamoto, Y., Sakurada, H., Hagiya, M.: Computationally sound symbolic anonymity of a ring signature. In: Proc. of Joint Workshop on Foundations of Computer Security, Automated Reasoning for Security Protocol Analysis and Issues in the Theory of Security (FCS-ARSPA-WITS 2008), pp. 161–175 (2008)
13. Micciancio, D., Warinschi, B.: Soundness of Formal Encryption in the Presence of Active Adversaries. In: Naor, M. (ed.) TCC 2004. LNCS, vol. 2951, pp. 133–151. Springer, Heidelberg (2004)
14. Rogaway, P., Shrimpton, T.: Cryptographic Hash-Function Basics: Definitions, Implications, and Separations for Preimage Resistance, Second-Preimage Resistance, and Collision Resistance. In: Roy, B., Meier, W. (eds.) FSE 2004. LNCS, vol. 3017, pp. 371–388. Springer, Heidelberg (2004)
15. Unruh, D.: Termination-insensitive computational indistinguishability (and applications to computational soundness). In: Proc. of the 24th IEEE Computer Security Foundations Symposium (CSF 2011). IEEE Computer Society (June 2011)

New Impossible Differential Attacks on Camellia*

Dongxia Bai[1] and Leibo Li[2,3,**]

[1] Department of Computer Science and Technology,
Tsinghua University, Beijing 100084, China
`baidx10@mails.tsinghua.edu.cn`
[2] Key Laboratory of Cryptologic Technology and Information Security,
Ministry of Education, Shandong University, Jinan 250100, China
[3] School of Mathematics, Shandong University, Jinan 250100, China
`lileibo@mail.sdu.edu.cn`

Abstract. Camellia is one of the most worldwide used block ciphers, which has been selected as a standard by ISO/IEC. In this paper, we propose several new 7-round impossible differentials of Camellia with 2 FL/FL^{-1} layers, which turn out to be the first 7-round impossible differentials with 2 FL/FL^{-1} layers. Combined with some basic techniques including the early abort approach and the key schedule consideration, we achieve the impossible differential attacks on 11-round Camellia-128, 11-round Camellia-192, 12-round Camellia-192, and 14-round Camellia-256, and the time complexity are $2^{123.8}$, $2^{121.7}$, $2^{171.4}$ and $2^{238.3}$ respectively. As far as we know, these are the best results against the reduced-round variants of Camellia. Especially, we give the first attack on 11-round Camellia-128 reduced version with FL/FL^{-1} layers.

Keywords: Camellia, Impossible Differential, Cryptanalysis, Impossible Differential Attack.

1 Introduction

Camellia is a 128-bit block cipher jointly developed by NTT and Mitsubishi in 2000, and supports 128-, 192-, and 256-bit key lengths [1]. It was adopted by cryptographic evaluation projects such as CRYPTREC [5] and NESSIE [23], as well as the standardization activities at IETF [24]. Then it was accepted by ISO/IEC [9] as an international standard.

Camellia has a Feistel structure with FL/FL^{-1} layers inserted every 6 rounds. The FL/FL^{-1} functions are keyed linear functions which are designed to provide non-regularity across rounds and destroy the differential property [1]. As one of the most widely used block cipher, Camellia has attracted a significant amount of

---

* Supported by the National Natural Science Foundation of China (Grant No. 60803125 and NO. 61133013), and the Tsinghua University Initiative Scientific Research Program(2009THZ01002).
** Corresponding author.

M.D. Ryan, B. Smyth, and G. Wang (Eds.): ISPEC 2012, LNCS 7232, pp. 80–96, 2012.
© Springer-Verlag Berlin Heidelberg 2012

attention of the cryptology researchers. The security of Camellia against various attacks are discussed in many papers, such as linear and differential cryptanalysis [25], higher order differential cryptanalysis [7,11,19], truncated differential attack [5,10,14,26], impossible differential cryptanalysis [4,16,17,18,21,22,26,27], collision attack [15,28], square attack [8,15,29], square like attack [6] et.al. Among these methods, the impossible differential attack [3,12] is the most efficient.

In recent years, there are a number of results on simple versions of Camellia which exclude the FL/FL^{-1} layers. In [4], the authors present the first 6-round impossible differentials with FL/FL^{-1} functions, and give the impossible differential attacks on Camellia-192/-256 with FL/FL^{-1} functions. Then some 7-round impossible differentials with FL/FL^{-1} functions are introduced in [16,17]. In this paper, we propose some new 7-round impossible differentials including 2 FL/FL^{-1} layers, which are the first 7-round impossible differentials including 2 FL/FL^{-1} layers. Due to our new 7-round impossible differentials including one more FL/FL^{-1} layer than all of those impossible differentials above, using our new impossible differentials could achieve better attacks. Combined with the early abort approach [20] and the key schedule considerations, we first present the attack on 11-round Camellia-128, which requires $2^{120.5}$ chosen plaintexts and $2^{123.8}$ 11-round encryptions. Then we give attacks on 11-round Camellia-192, 12-round Camellia-192, and 14-round Camellia-256, and the time complexity are $2^{121.7}$, $2^{171.4}$ and $2^{238.3}$ respectively.

The rest of this paper is organized as follows. We give some notations and briefly describe the block cipher Camellia in Section 2. Some properties of Camellia and 7-round impossible differentials with 2 FL/FL^{-1} layers are given in Section 3. Section 4 presents the impossible differential attacks on reduced-round Camellia with FL/FL^{-1} layers. Finally, we conclude the paper in Section 5.

2   Preliminaries

2.1   Notations

In this paper, we will use the following notations:
L_{r-1}, L'_{r-1} : the left 64-bit half of the r-th round input,
R_{r-1}, R'_{r-1} : the right 64-bit half of the r-th round input,
ΔS_r : the output difference of the S-box layer of the r-th round
K_r : the subkey used in the r-th round
X_l : the l-th byte of a 64-bit word X ($l = 1, \ldots, 8$)
$Y_{\{i\}}$: the i-th bit of a bit string Y ($1 \le i \le 128$)
$x \| y$: the concatenation of x and y
$x \lll_i$: the left rotation of x by i bits
$\oplus, \cap, \cup$: bitwise exclusive-OR(XOR), AND, OR

2.2   Description of Camellia

Camellia [1] is a 128-bit block cipher with Feistel structure. It has 18 rounds for 128-bit key and 24 rounds for 192-/256-bit key. We give the encryption procedure of Camellia-128 as follows, see Fig. 1.

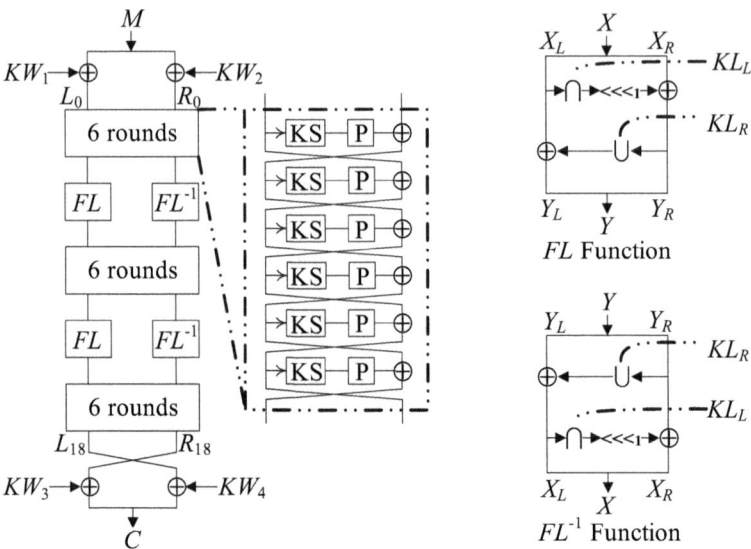

Fig. 1. Encryption procedure of Camellia-128

Encryption Procedure. First a 128-bit plaintext M is XORed with sub-keys $KW_1 \| KW_2$ and separated into two 64-bit intermediate values L_0 and R_0 : $L_0 \| R_0 = M \oplus (KW_1 \| KW_2)$. Then the following operations are performed from $r = 1$ to 18, except for $r = 6$ and 12:

$$L_r = R_{r-1} \oplus F(L_{r-1}, K_r), \ R_r = L_{r-1},$$

for $r = 6$ and 12, do the following:

$$L'_r = R_{r-1} \oplus F(L_{r-1}, K_r), \ R'_r = L_{r-1},$$
$$L_r = FL(L'_r, KL_{r/3-1}), \qquad R_r = FL^{-1}(R'_r, KL_{r/3}).$$

Finally the 128-bit ciphertext C is calculated as: $C = (R_{18} \| L_{18}) \oplus (KW_3 \| KW_4)$. F is the round function defined below:

$$F : GF(2)^{64} \times GF(2)^{64} \to GF(2)^{64}$$
$$(X, K_r) \mapsto Z = P(S(X \oplus K_r)),$$

where S and P are defined as follows:

$$S : (GF(2)^8)^8 \to (GF(2)^8)^8$$
$$(x_1, x_2, \ldots, x_8) \mapsto (y_1, y_2, \ldots, y_8),$$
$$y_1 = S_1(x_1), \ y_2 = S_2(x_2), \ y_3 = S_3(x_3), \ y_4 = S_4(x_4),$$
$$y_5 = S_2(x_5), \ y_6 = S_3(x_6), \ y_7 = S_4(x_7), \ y_8 = S_1(x_8),$$

here S_1, S_2, S_3 and S_4 are the 8×8 S-boxes.

$$P : (GF(2)^8)^8 \to (GF(2)^8)^8$$
$$(y_1, y_2, \ldots, y_8) \mapsto (z_1, z_2, \ldots, z_8),$$
$$z_1 = y_1 \oplus y_3 \oplus y_4 \oplus y_6 \oplus y_7 \oplus y_8, \quad z_5 = y_1 \oplus y_2 \oplus y_6 \oplus y_7 \oplus y_8,$$
$$z_2 = y_1 \oplus y_2 \oplus y_4 \oplus y_5 \oplus y_7 \oplus y_8, \quad z_6 = y_2 \oplus y_3 \oplus y_5 \oplus y_7 \oplus y_8,$$
$$z_3 = y_1 \oplus y_2 \oplus y_3 \oplus y_5 \oplus y_6 \oplus y_8, \quad z_7 = y_3 \oplus y_4 \oplus y_5 \oplus y_6 \oplus y_8,$$
$$z_4 = y_2 \oplus y_3 \oplus y_4 \oplus y_5 \oplus y_6 \oplus y_7, \quad z_8 = y_1 \oplus y_4 \oplus y_5 \oplus y_6 \oplus y_7.$$

The inverse of P is as follows:

$$P^{-1} : (GF(2)^8)^8 \to (GF(2)^8)^8$$
$$(z_1, z_2, \ldots, z_8) \mapsto (y_1, y_2, \ldots, y_8),$$
$$y_1 = z_2 \oplus z_3 \oplus z_4 \oplus z_6 \oplus z_7 \oplus z_8, \quad y_5 = z_1 \oplus z_2 \oplus z_5 \oplus z_7 \oplus z_8,$$
$$y_2 = z_1 \oplus z_3 \oplus z_4 \oplus z_5 \oplus z_7 \oplus z_8, \quad y_6 = z_2 \oplus z_3 \oplus z_5 \oplus z_6 \oplus z_8,$$
$$y_3 = z_1 \oplus z_2 \oplus z_4 \oplus z_5 \oplus z_6 \oplus z_8, \quad y_7 = z_3 \oplus z_4 \oplus z_5 \oplus z_6 \oplus z_7,$$
$$y_4 = z_1 \oplus z_2 \oplus z_3 \oplus z_5 \oplus z_6 \oplus z_7, \quad y_8 = z_1 \oplus z_4 \oplus z_6 \oplus z_7 \oplus z_8.$$

FL is defined below:

$$FL : GF(2)^{64} \times GF(2)^{64} \to GF(2)^{64}$$
$$(X_L \| X_R, KL_L \| KL_R) \mapsto (Y_L \| Y_R),$$
$$Y_R = ((X_L \cap KL_L) \lll_1) \oplus X_R, \quad Y_L = (Y_R \cup KL_R) \oplus X_L.$$

FL^{-1} is the inverse of FL, and all of them are linear as long as the keys are fixed [2].

Similarly to Camellia-128, Camellia-192/-256 have 24-round Feistel structure with FL/FL^{-1} layers inserted after 6, 12, 18 rounds. Before the first round and after the last round, there are pre- and post-whitening layers which use bitwise exclusive-or operations with 128-bit subkeys, respectively.

Key Schedule. Two 128-bit variables K_A and K_B are generated from the main key $K = K_L \| K_R$. For Camellia-128, K_L is the 128-bit K, and K_R is 0. For Camellia-192, K_L is the left 128-bit of K, and the concatenation of the right 64-bit of K and its complement is used as K_R. For Camellia-256, K_L is the left 128-bit of K, and K_R is the right 128-bit of K. All of the subkeys are derived from rotating K_L, K_R, K_A or K_B, and K_B is only used in Camellia-192/-256. For details of Camellia, we refer to [1].

3   New 7-Round Impossible Differentials of Camellia with 2 FL/FL^{-1} Layers

In this section, we give some useful properties of Camellia, and then present several new 7-round impossible differentials.

Property 1. *(from [13]) Let x, x', k be 32-bit values, and $\Delta x = x \oplus x'$, then the differential properties of AND and OR operations are:*

$$(x \cap k) \oplus (x' \cap k) = (x \oplus x') \cap k = \Delta x \cap k,$$
$$(x \cup k) \oplus (x' \cup k) = (x \oplus k \oplus (x \cap k)) \oplus (x' \oplus k \oplus (x' \cap k)) = \Delta x \oplus (\Delta x \cap k).$$

Property 2. *For FL^{-1} function, if the input difference is $\Delta Y = (a, 0, 0, 0, 0, 0, 0, 0)$, where a is a non-zero byte whose most significant bit is 0, then the output difference is $\Delta X = (a, 0, 0, 0, A, 0, 0, 0)$, where A is an unknown byte.*

Proof. By Property 1, apparently we can get the output difference below (note that the most significant bit of a is 0):

$$\Delta X_L = X_L \oplus X'_L = (Y_L \oplus (Y_R \cup KL_R)) \oplus (Y'_L \oplus (Y'_R \cup KL_R))$$
$$= \Delta Y_L \oplus \Delta Y_R \oplus (\Delta Y_R \cap KL_R) = \Delta Y_L = (a, 0, 0, 0),$$
$$\Delta X_R = X_R \oplus X'_R = (((X_L \cap KL_L) \lll_1) \oplus Y_R) \oplus (((X'_L \cap KL_L) \lll_1) \oplus Y'_R)$$
$$= \Delta Y_R \oplus ((\Delta X_L \cap KL_L) \lll_1) = (A, 0, 0, 0).$$

here Y and X are the 64-bit input value and output value of FL^{-1} function, and KL is the 64-bit subkey used in FL^{-1} function, and A is an unknown byte.   □

Property 3. *(from [16]) For FL^{-1} function, if the output difference is $\Delta X = (0, 0, 0, 0, b, 0, 0, 0)$, where b is a non-zero byte, then the input difference should satisfy the form $\Delta Y = (B, 0, 0, 0, b, 0, 0, 0)$, where B is an unknown byte.*

Impossible Differential. We now demonstrate that the 7-round differential

$$((0,0,0,0,0,0,0,0);(a,0,0,0,0,0,0,0)) \xrightarrow{7R} ((0,0,0,0,b,0,0,0);(0,0,0,0,0,0,0,0))$$

is impossible, where a is a non-zero byte whose most significant bit is 0, and b is an arbitrary non-zero byte, see Fig. 2.

By Property 2, the input difference of the first round is $((0, 0, 0, 0, 0, 0, 0, 0); (a, 0, 0, 0, A, 0, 0, 0))$, and then the output differences of the second and third round are

$$(P(c, 0, 0, 0, C, 0, 0, 0); (a, 0, 0, 0, A, 0, 0, 0)) \text{ and}$$

$$(P(c_1, c_2, c_3, c_4, c_5, c_6, c_7, c_8) \oplus (a, 0, 0, 0, A, 0, 0, 0); P(c, 0, 0, 0, C, 0, 0, 0)),$$

where $(c, 0, 0, 0, C, 0, 0, 0)$ is evolved from $(a, 0, 0, 0, A, 0, 0, 0)$ after key-addition layer and S-box layer, $(c_1, c_2, c_3, c_4, c_5, c_6, c_7, c_8)$ is evolved from $P(c, 0, 0, 0, C, 0, 0, 0)$ (note that $P(c, 0, 0, 0, C, 0, 0, 0) = (c, c \oplus C, c \oplus C, C, c, C, C, c \oplus C))$, c, c_1, c_5 are unknown non-zero bytes, and C, $c_i (i = 2, 3, 4, 6, 7, 8)$ are unknown bytes. So we can get that the input difference of S-box layer of the fourth round is

$$P(c_1, c_2, c_3, c_4, c_5, c_6, c_7, c_8) \oplus (a, 0, 0, 0, A, 0, 0, 0).$$

In the backward direction, the input difference of the seventh round is $((0,0,0,0,0,0,0,0);(0,0,0,0,b,0,0,0))$, and the output difference of the sixth round deduced by Property 3 is $((0,0,0,0,0,0,0,0);(B,0,0,0,b,0,0,0))$. Then the output difference of the fifth round is

$$((B,0,0,0,b,0,0,0);\ P(D,0,0,0,d,0,0,0)),$$

where $(D,0,0,0,d,0,0,0)$ is evolved from $(B,0,0,0,b,0,0,0)$ after key-addition layer and S-box layer, d is an unknown non-zero byte, and D is an unknown byte. Hence, the output difference of S-box layer of the fourth round is

$$P^{-1}(P(c,0,0,0,C,0,0,0)\oplus P(D,0,0,0,d,0,0,0))=(c\oplus D,0,0,0,C\oplus d,0,0,0).$$

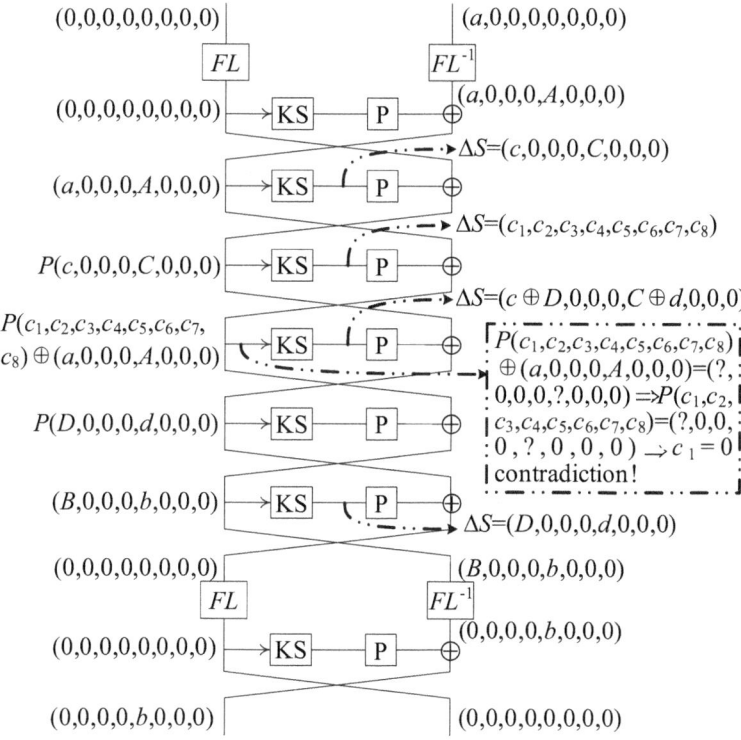

Fig. 2. 7-round impossible differential with 2 FL/FL^{-1} layers

Now the input and output differences of S-box layer of the fourth round are all determined. According to the output difference of S-box layer, the input difference of S-box layer should satisfy the form $(?,0,0,0,?,0,0,0)$ (? denotes an unknown byte). So we can get:

$$P(c_1, c_2, c_3, c_4, c_5, c_6, c_7, c_8) \oplus (a, 0, 0, 0, A, 0, 0, 0) = (?, 0, 0, 0, ?, 0, 0, 0)$$
$$\Rightarrow P(c_1, c_2, c_3, c_4, c_5, c_6, c_7, c_8) = (?, 0, 0, 0, ?, 0, 0, 0) \oplus (a, 0, 0, 0, A, 0, 0, 0)$$
$$= (?, 0, 0, 0, ?, 0, 0, 0)$$
$$\Rightarrow c_1 = 0,$$

which contradicts $c_1 \neq 0$. As a result, the differential

$$((0,0,0,0,0,0,0,0);(a,0,0,0,0,0,0,0)) \xrightarrow{7R} ((0,0,0,0,b,0,0,0);(0,0,0,0,0,0,0,0))$$

is impossible. Actually, we can get three more 7-round impossible differentials with 2 FL/FL^{-1} layers, which are:

$$((0,0,0,0,0,0,0,0);(0,a,0,0,0,0,0,0)) \xrightarrow{7R} ((0,0,0,0,0,b,0,0);(0,0,0,0,0,0,0,0)),$$
$$((0,0,0,0,0,0,0,0);(0,0,a,0,0,0,0,0)) \xrightarrow{7R} ((0,0,0,0,0,0,b,0);(0,0,0,0,0,0,0,0)),$$
$$((0,0,0,0,0,0,0,0);(0,0,0,a,0,0,0,0)) \xrightarrow{7R} ((0,0,0,0,0,0,0,b);(0,0,0,0,0,0,0,0)),$$

where a, b are non-zero bytes, and the most significant bit of a is 0.

4   Impossible Differential Attacks on Camellia with FL/FL^{-1} Layers

In this section, we present some new impossible differential attacks on 11-round Camellia-128, 11-round Camellia-192, 12-round Camellia-192, 14-round Camellia-256, using the new 7-round impossible differential proposed in Section 3. All of these attacks start from the middle round, and exclude the whitening layers to not change the structure of the algorithm.

4.1   Impossible Differential Attack on 11-Round Camellia-128

As illustrated in Fig. 3, the 7-round impossible differential is applied in rounds 7 to 13, and the attack is from round 5 to 15. The attack procedure is as follows.

1. Take 2^n structures of plaintexts $M = (L_4, R_4)$ with following form:

$$(P(x_1, \alpha_2, \alpha_3, \alpha_4, \alpha_5, \alpha_6, \alpha_7, \alpha_8); \ P(y_1, y_2, y_3, y_4, y_5, \beta_6, \beta_7, y_8)),$$

where α_i $(i = 2, \ldots, 8)$, β_j $(j = 6, 7)$ are fixed constants, x_1, y_i $(i = 1, 2, 3, 5, 8)$ take all the 8-bit values, and y_4 takes all the 7-bit values with the most significant bit fixed. As a result, each structure contains 2^{55} plaintexts which can provide about 2^{109} plaintext pairs with the difference

$$(P(e, 0, 0, 0, 0, 0, 0, 0); P(a_1, a_2, a_3, a, a_5, 0, 0, a_8)),$$

where e, a_1, a are non-zero bytes (the most significant bit of a is 0), and $a_i \neq a$ $(i = 2, 3, 5, 8)$ are unknown bytes. Aggregately, we can collect about 2^{n+109} plaintext pairs.

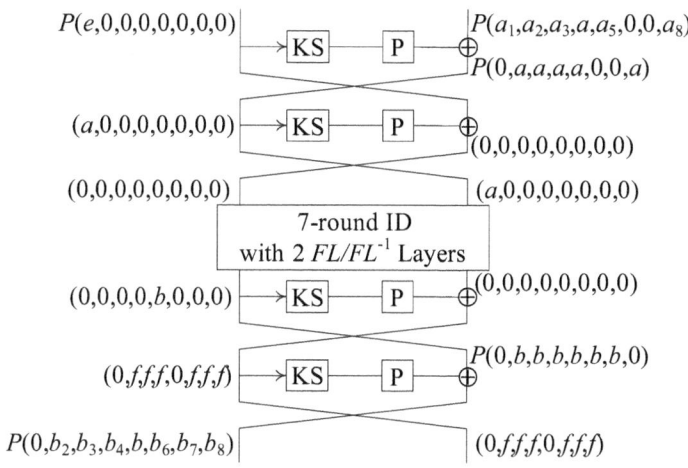

Fig. 3. Attack on 11-round Camellia-128

2. Obtain the ciphertexts of each structure and choose only the pairs that satisfy the following difference by birthday paradox

$$(P(0, b_2, b_3, b_4, b, b_6, b_7, b_8);\ (0, f, f, f, 0, f, f, f)),$$

where b, b_8, f are non-zero bytes, and $b_i \neq b$ ($i = 2, 3, 4, 6, 7$) are unknown bytes. We expect to have about $2^{n+109-64} = 2^{n+45}$ pairs remaining with this condition.

3. For each plaintext pair, we immediately get the difference $\Delta S_5 = P^{-1}(P(a_1, a_2, a_3, a, a_5, 0, 0, a_8) \oplus P(0, a, a, a, a, 0, 0, a)) = (a_1, a_2 \oplus a, a_3 \oplus a, 0, a_5 \oplus a, 0, 0, a_8 \oplus a)$. So for $l = 1, 2, 3, 5, 8$ guess $K_{5,l}$ and keep only the pairs whose $\Delta S_{5,l}$ is equal to the corresponding value above. The probability of this event is 2^{-40}, thus there remains $2^{n+45-40} = 2^{n+5}$ pairs. Note that $K_{5,l(l=1,2,3,5,8)} = K_{A\{16-39,48-55,72-79\}}$.

4. For each ciphertext pair corresponding to a remaining plaintext pair, obtain the difference $\Delta S_{15} = (0, b_2 \oplus b, b_3 \oplus b, b_4 \oplus b, 0, b_6 \oplus b, b_7 \oplus b, b_8)$. Based on the fact that the bits $K_{A\{16-30\}}$ are already known, perform the following substeps.

   4.1 The value of $K_{15,8}$ ($K_{A\{23-30\}}$) is already known, so use it to partially decrypt every remaining ciphertext pair and keep only the pairs satisfying $\Delta S_{15,8} = b_8$. The probability of this event is 2^{-8}, thus the expected number of remaining pairs is $2^{n+5-8} = 2^{n-3}$.

   4.2 Since $K_{15,7} = K_{A\{15-22\}}$, 7 bits including $K_{A\{16-22\}}$ are already known and guess the only unknown bit $K_{A\{15\}}$. Keep only the pairs satisfying $\Delta S_{15,7} = b_7 \oplus b$. The probability of this event is 2^{-8}, so we expect $2^{n-3-8} = 2^{n-11}$ pairs remain.

   4.3 The values of $K_{15,l(l=2,3,4,6)}$ ($K_{A\{7-14,103-126\}}$) are unknown, so for $l = 2, 3, 4, 6$ respectively guess $K_{15,l}$ and choose only the pairs whose $\Delta S_{15,l}$

is equal to the corresponding value above. The probability of this event is 2^{-32}, thus the expected number of such pairs is $2^{n-11-32} = 2^{n-43}$.

4.4 Guess $K_{15,1}$ and decrypt every remaining pair to get $(L_{13,5}, L'_{13,5})$, so this step does not effect the number of the remaining pairs.

5. For each remaining pair, obtain the difference $\Delta S_{14} = (0,0,0,0,f,0,0,0)$. Guess $K_{14,5}$ and choose only the pairs satisfying $\Delta S_{14,5} = f$. The probability of this condition is 2^{-8}, thus we expect $2^{n-43-8} = 2^{n-51}$ pairs remain.

6. For $l = 4, 6, 7$ guess $K_{5,l}$ and encrypt every remaining pair to get $(L_{5,1}, L'_{5,1})$.

7. For every remaining pair, guess the 8-bit value of $K_{6,1}$ and calculate the difference $\Delta S_{6,1}$. The probability that $\Delta S_{6,1}$ is equal to a fixed value e is 2^{-8}, where e is already determined by ΔL_4. Such a difference is impossible, so if there exits a pair satisfying this condition, discard the 121-bit wrong subkey guess. Unless the initial assumption on the subkeys K_5, $K_{15,l(l=1,2,3,4,6,7,8)}$ and $K_{14,5}$ is correct, it is expected that we can discard the whole 8-bit value of $K_{6,1}$ for each guessed 113-bit value above since the 121-bit wrong value remains with a very small probability by choosing a proper n. Hence if there remains a value of $K_{6,1}$ after the filtering, we can assume that the guessed value above is right.

Complexity. After analyzing the 2^{n-51} remaining pairs, the expected number of remaining 121-bit wrong keys is $N = 2^{121} \times (1 - 2^{-8})^{2^{n-51}}$. In order to let $N \ll 1$, we choose $n = 65.5$. Then the data complexity is $2^{120.5}$ chosen plaintexts. The memory complexity is dominated by storing the $2^{110.5}$ proper pairs in step 2, which requires $2^{115.5}$ bytes. Table 1 shows the time complexity of each step, so the total complexity of the attack, in encryption unit, is about $(2^{n+59} + 2^{127})/11 \approx 2^{123.8}$.

Table 1. Time Complexity of the Attack on 11-round Camellia-128

Step	Time Complexity
2	2^{n+55} E
3	$\sum_{i=0}^{4} 2 \times 2^{n+45-8i} \times 2^{8(i+1)} \times \frac{1}{8} = 2^{n+51} \times 5 \frac{1}{11} E$
4.1	$2 \times 2^{n+5} \times 2^{40} \times \frac{1}{8} = 2^{n+43} \frac{1}{11} E$
4.2	$2 \times 2^{n-3} \times 2^{40} \times 2^1 \times \frac{1}{8} = 2^{n+36} \frac{1}{11} E$
4.3	$\sum_{i=0}^{3} 2 \times 2^{n-11-8i} \times 2^{41} \times 2^{8(i+1)} \times \frac{1}{8} = 2^{n+38} \frac{1}{11} E$
4.4	$2^{n-43} \times 2^{73} \times 2^8 \times \frac{1}{8} = 2^{n+35} \frac{1}{11} E$
5	$2 \times 2^{n-43} \times 2^{81} \times 2^8 \times \frac{1}{8} = 2^{n+44} \frac{1}{11} E$
6	$\sum_{i=0}^{2} 2^{n-51} \times 2^{89} \times 2^{8(i+1)} \times \frac{1}{8} = (2^{n+43} + 2^{n+51} + 2^{n+59}) \frac{1}{11} E$
7	$2 \times 2^{113} \times 2^8 \times (1 + (1 - 2^{-8}) + \ldots + (1 - 2^{-8})^{2^{n-51}-1}) \times \frac{1}{8} \approx 2^{127} \frac{1}{11} E$

4.2 Impossible Differential Attack on 11-Round and 12-Round Camellia-192

In this section, first we give a brief description of the attack on 11-round Camellia-192, and then present the attack on 12-round Camellia-192.

Attack on 11-round Camellia-192. A similar 11-round attack as described in Section 4.1 is equally applicable to Camellia-192 from round 11 to 21, utilizing the 7-round impossible differential in rounds 13 to 19 as shown in Fig.3. According to the key schedule of Camellia-192/-256, we get

$$K_{11} = K_{A\{46-109\}}, \quad K_{12,1} = K_{A\{110-117\}},$$
$$K_{20,5} = K_{R\{63-70\}}, \quad K_{21,l(l=1,2,3,4,6,7,8)} = K_{A\{7-30,95-126\}}.$$

Considering the redundancy in $K_{11}, K_{12,1}$ and $K_{21,l(l=1,2,3,4,6,7,8)}$, in fact we only need to guess 113 bits $K_{A\{7-30,46-126\}}\|K_{R\{63-70\}}$. By choosing $n = 65.4$, then $N \ll 0$. Consequently, this attack requires $2^{120.4}$ chosen plaintexts, $2^{115.4}$ bytes of memory and an overall effort of $2^{120.4} + 2^{124.4}/11 \approx 2^{121.7}$ eleven-round Camellia-192 encryptions. The details see Table 3 in Appendix A.

Attack on 12-round Camellia-192. We add one round on the bottom of the 11-round attack, and give a 12-round attack on Camellia-192, which is from round 11 to 22, see Fig. 4. The attack procedure is as follows.

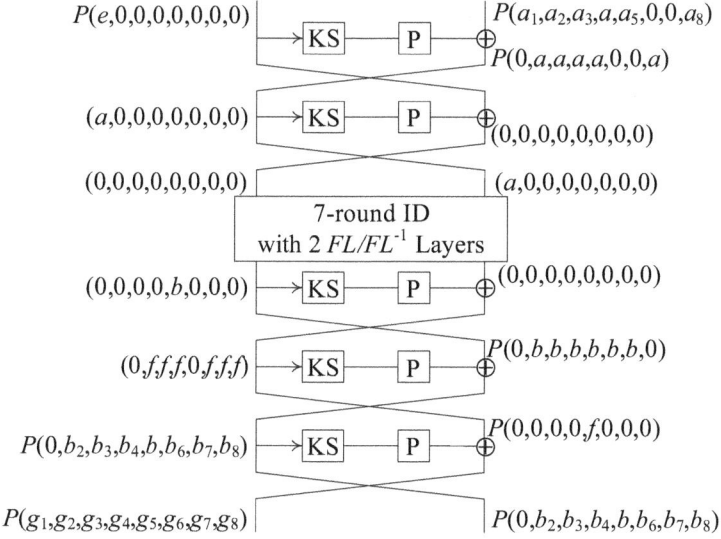

Fig. 4. Attack on 12-round Camellia-192

1. The choice of plaintexts is the same as the 11-round attack, and the ciphertext pairs are sieved by the difference

$$(P(g_1, g_2, g_3, g_4, g_5, g_6, g_7, g_8); \ P(0, b_2, b_3, b_4, b, b_6, b_7, b_8)),$$

where b, b_8 are non-zero bytes, and $g_i \ (i = 1, \ldots, 8)$, $b_j \neq b \ (j = 2, 3, 4, 6, 7)$ are unknown bytes. The probability of this condition is about 2^{-8}, so the expected number of remaining pairs is about $2^{n+109-8} = 2^{n+101}$.

2. Obtain the difference $\Delta S_{11} = (a_1, a_2 \oplus a, a_3 \oplus a, 0, a_5 \oplus a, 0, 0, a_8 \oplus a)$, then for $l = 1, 2, 3, 5, 8$ guess $K_{11,l}$ and keep the pairs whose $\Delta S_{11,l}$ is equal to the corresponding value above. So we expect $2^{n+101} \times 2^{-40} = 2^{n+61}$ pairs remain. Note that $K_{11,l(l=1,2,3,5,8)} = K_{A\{46-69,78-85,102-109\}}$.

3. We can get the difference $\Delta S_{22} = (g_1, g_2, g_3, g_4, g_5 \oplus f, g_6, g_7, g_8)$ $(\Delta S_{22,5} \neq g_5$ since $f \neq 0)$, and the bits $K_{A\{46-69,78-85\}}$ are already known. Then perform the following substeps.

   3.1 The values of $K_{22,l(l=3,4)}$ $(K_{A\{47-62\}})$ are already known, so for $l = 3, 4$ $\Delta S_{22,l}$ can be computed, then choose the pairs satisfying $\Delta S_{22,l} = g_l$. Thus there remains $2^{n+61} \times 2^{-16} = 2^{n+45}$ pairs.

   3.2 Since $K_{22,7} = K_{A\{79-86\}}$, guess the only unknown bit $K_{A\{86\}}$ and keep the pairs satisfying $\Delta S_{22,7} = g_7$. Next $K_{22,2} = K_{A\{39-46\}}$, guess the unknown 7 bits $K_{A\{39-45\}}$ and keep the pairs satisfying $\Delta S_{22,2} = g_2$. Similarly, as $K_{22,6} = K_{A\{71-78\}}$, we guess the unknown 7 bits $K_{A\{71-77\}}$ and keep the pairs satisfying $\Delta S_{22,6} = g_6$. Thus the expected number of remaining pairs is $2^{n+45} \times 2^{-24} = 2^{n+21}$.

   3.3 The values of $K_{22,l(l=1,8)}$ $(K_{A\{31-38,87-94\}})$ are unknown, so for $l = 1, 8$ guess $K_{22,l}$ and choose the pairs satisfying $\Delta S_{22,l} = g_l$. Then $2^{n+21} \times 2^{-16} = 2^{n+5}$ pairs remain. As $K_{22,5} = K_{A\{63-70\}}$, guess the only unknown bit $K_{A\{70\}}$ and keep only the pairs satisfying $\Delta S_{22,5} \neq g_5$. The probability of this event is $(2^8 - 1)/2^8 \approx 1$, thus we expect about 2^{n+5} pairs remain. And now the intermediate values $(L_{21}\|R_{21}, L'_{21}\|R'_{21})$ also can be computed.

4. We can obtain $\Delta S_{21} = (0, b_2 \oplus b, b_3 \oplus b, b_4 \oplus b, 0, b_6 \oplus b, b_7 \oplus b, b_8)$, and the bits $K_{A\{102-109\}}$ are already known. So perform the substeps below.

   4.1 As $K_{21,2} = K_{A\{103-110\}}$, guess the only unknown bit $K_{A\{110\}}$ and keep the pairs satisfying $\Delta S_{21,2} = b_2 \oplus b$. Then we expect $2^{n+5} \times 2^{-8} = 2^{n-3}$ pairs remain.

   4.2 The values of $K_{21,l(l=3,4,6,7,8)}$ $(K_{A\{7-30,111-126\}})$ are unknown, so for $l = 3, 4, 6, 7, 8$ guess $K_{21,l}$ and keep only the pairs whose $\Delta S_{21,l}$ is equal to the corresponding value above. Then the expected number of such pairs is $2^{n-3} \times 2^{-40} = 2^{n-43}$.

   4.3 Since $K_{21,1} = K_{A\{95-102\}}$, guess the unknown 7 bits $K_{A\{95-101\}}$ and get $(L_{19,5}, L'_{19,5})$.

5. Obtain the difference $\Delta S_{20} = (0, 0, 0, 0, f, 0, 0, 0)$, then guess $K_{20,5}$ and choose the pairs satisfying $\Delta S_{20,5} = f$. So there remains $2^{n-43} \times 2^{-8} = 2^{n-51}$ pairs.

6. The values of $K_{11,l(l=4,6,7)}$ $(K_{A\{70-77,86-101\}})$ are already known, so we can get $(L_{11,1}, L'_{11,1})$.

7. Since $K_{12,1}$ $(K_{A\{110-117\}})$ are already known, for every remaining pair, $\Delta S_{12,1}$ can be computed. We expect with probability of 2^{-8} that we get a pair with $\Delta S_{12,1} = e$, where e is a fixed value determined by ΔL_{10}. Such a difference is impossible, and every subkey we guessed that proposes such a difference is definitely a wrong key. If there remains a value of $K_{12,1}$ after the filtering, we can assume that the guessed value above is right.

Complexity. The number of remaining 128-bit wrong keys after analyzing all the 2^{n-51} pairs is $N = 2^{128} \times (1 - 2^{-8})^{2^{n-51}}$. In order to let $N \ll 1$, we choose $n = 65.6$. Then the data complexity is $2^{120.6}$ chosen plaintexts. The memory complexity is dominated by storing the $2^{166.6}$ pairs in step 1, which is about $2^{171.6}$ bytes. The time complexity is dominated by step 2, which is about $2^{n+107} \times 5/12 = 2^{172.6} \times 5/12 \approx 2^{171.4}$ 12-round encryptions. The details see Table 4 in Appendix A.

4.3   Impossible Differential Attack on 14-Round Camellia-256

We add one more round respectively on the top and bottom of the 12-round attack, and present a 14-round attack on Camellia-256, which is from round 10 to 23 as illustrated in Fig. 5. The attack procedure is below.

1. Take 2^n structures of plaintexts $M = (L_9, R_9)$ with following form:

$$(P(x_1, x_2, x_3, x_4, x_5, \alpha_6, \alpha_7, x_8); \ P(y_1, y_2, y_3, y_4, y_5, y_6, y_7, y_8)),$$

   where α_i ($i = 6, 7$) are fixed constants, x_i ($i = 1, 2, 3, 5, 8$), y_j ($j = 1, \ldots, 8$) take all the 8-bit values, and x_4 takes all the 7-bit values with the most significant bit fixed. It is obvious that each structure contains 2^{111} plaintexts which can provide about 2^{221} plaintext pairs with the difference

$$(P(a_1, a_2, a_3, a, a_5, 0, 0, a_8); P(h_1, h_2, h_3, h_4, h_5, h_6, h_7, h_8)),$$

   where a_1, a are non-zero byte (the most significant bit of a is 0), and $a_i \neq a$ ($i = 2, 3, 5, 8$), h_j ($j = 1, \ldots, 8$) are unknown bytes. Hence, we can collect about 2^{n+221} plaintext pairs, then obtain the ciphertexts of each structure.
2. We can get that $\Delta S_{10} = (h_1 \oplus e, h_2, h_3, h_4, h_5, h_6, h_7, h_8)$ ($\Delta S_{10,1} \neq h_1$ since $e \neq 0$), so for $l = 2, \ldots, 8, 1$ respectively guess $K_{10,l}$ and choose only the pairs with $\Delta S_{10,l}$ satisfying the condition above. Then we expect about $2^{n+221} \times 2^{-56} = 2^{n+165}$ pairs remain. Note that $K_{10} = K_{L\{1-45,110-128\}}$. In this step, we can get $(L_{10}\|R_{10}, L'_{10}\|R'_{10})$.
3. We can obtain the difference $\Delta S_{23} = (j_1, j_2 \oplus b_2, j_3 \oplus b_3, j_4 \oplus b_4, j_5 \oplus b, j_6 \oplus b_6, j_7 \oplus b_7, j_8 \oplus b_8)$ ($\Delta S_{23,5} \neq j_5$ since $b \neq 0$), and the bits $K_{L\{1-45,112-128\}}$ are already known.
   3.1 The values of $K_{23,l(l=1,\ldots,7)}$ ($K_{L\{1-39,112-128\}}$) are already known, so for $l = 1, \ldots, 7$, $\Delta S_{23,l}$ can be computed, then choose only the pairs satisfying $\Delta S_{23,1} = j_1$ and $\Delta S_{23,5} \neq j_5$. The probability of this condition is $2^{-8} \times ((2^8 - 1)/2^8) \approx 2^{-8}$, thus the expected number of remaining pairs is $2^{n+165-8} = 2^{n+157}$.
   3.2 Since $K_{23,8} = K_{L\{40-47\}}$, guess the unknown 2 bits $K_{L\{46,47\}}$ and get the intermediate values $(L_{22}\|R_{22}, L'_{22}\|R'_{22})$.

Next, we perform the steps 4 to 9, which are totally the same as steps 2 to 7 of Section 4.2. Finally we expect 2^{n+5} pairs remain.

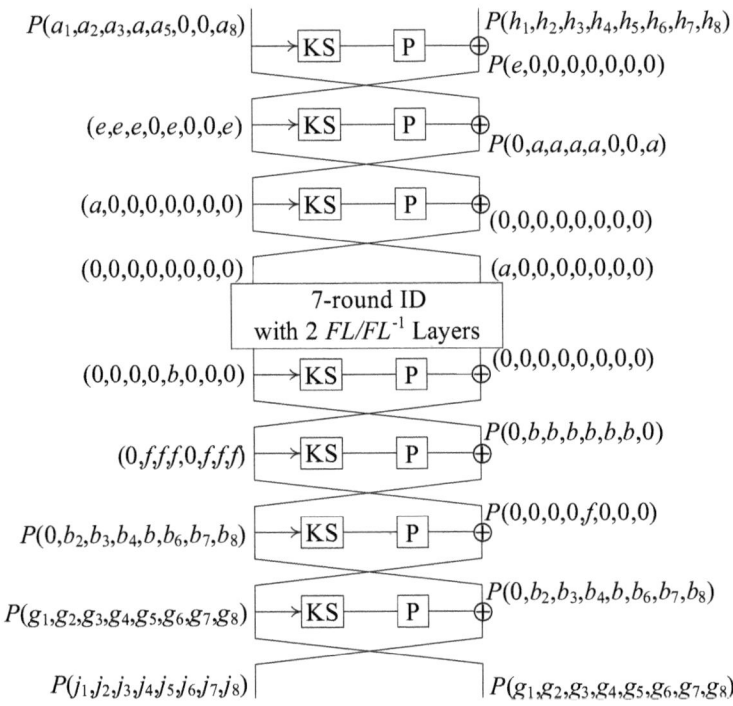

Fig. 5. Attack on 14-round Camellia-256

Table 2. Summary of Attacks on Camellia with FL/FL^{-1} Layers

Cipher	#Rounds	Attack Type	Data	Time	Source
Camellia-128	9*	Square Attack	2^{48}CP	2^{122}	[15]
	10*	Impossible DC	2^{118}CP	2^{118}	[21]
	10*	Impossible DC	$2^{118.5}$CP	$2^{123.5}$	[16]
	10 (Weak Key)	Impossible DC	$2^{110.4}$CP	$2^{110.4}$	[17]
	10	Impossible DC	$2^{112.4}$CP	2^{120}	[17]
	11*	Impossible DC	$2^{120.5}$CP	$2^{123.8}$	this paper
Camellia-192	11*	Impossible DC	2^{118}CP	$2^{163.1}$	[21]
	11 (Weak Key)	Impossible DC	$2^{119.5}$CP	$2^{138.54}$	[17]
	11	Impossible DC	$2^{113.7}$CP	2^{184}	[17]
	11*	Impossible DC	$2^{120.4}$CP	$2^{121.7}$	this paper
	12*	Impossible DC	$2^{120.1}$CP	2^{184}	[17]
	12*	Impossible DC	$2^{120.6}$CP	$2^{171.4}$	this paper
Camellia-256	12 (Weak Key)	Impossible DC	$2^{119.7}$CP	$2^{202.55}$	[17]
	12	Impossible DC	$2^{114.8}$CP/CC	2^{240}	[17]
	14*	Impossible DC	2^{120}CC	$2^{250.5}$	[17]
	14*	Impossible DC	$2^{121.2}$CP	$2^{238.3}$	this paper

*: the attack does not include the whitening layers;
Weak Key: the weak key space which contains $\frac{3}{4}$ of keys

Complexity. The expected number of remaining 194-bit wrong keys after analyzing all the 2^{n+5} pairs is $N = 2^{194} \times (1 - 2^{-8})^{2^{n+5}}$. In order to let $N \ll 1$, we choose $n = 10.2$. Then the data complexity is $2^{121.2}$ chosen plaintexts. The memory complexity is dominated by storing the $2^{n+165} = 2^{175.2}$ pairs in step 2, which is about $2^{180.2}$ bytes. The time complexity is dominated by step 2 and step 4, which is about $(2^{n+230} + 2^{n+227} + 2^{n+229} \times 5)/14 = 2^{n+228} \times 14.5/14 \approx 2^{238.3}$ encryptions. Table 5 in Appendix A shows the details of each step.

5 Conclusion

In this paper, we propose some new 7-round impossible differentials including 2 FL/FL^{-1} layers, and then present attacks on 11-round Camellia-128, 11-round Camellia-192, 12-round Camellia-192 and 14-round Camellia-256 without whitening layers. A summary of the previous works and our attacks on Camellia with FL/FL^{-1} layers is given in Table 2.

Acknowledgment. We are grateful to the anonymous reviewers for their valuable comments on this paper.

References

1. Aoki, K., Ichikawa, T., Kanda, M., Matsui, M., Moriai, S., Nakajima, J., Tokita, T.: *Camellia*: A 128-Bit Block Cipher Suitable for Multiple Platforms - Design and Analysis. In: Stinson, D.R., Tavares, S. (eds.) SAC 2000. LNCS, vol. 2012, pp. 39–56. Springer, Heidelberg (2001)
2. Aoki, K., Ichikawa, T., Kanda, M., Matsui, M., Moriai, S., Nakajima, J., Tokita, T.: Specification of Camellia–a 128-bit block cipher. version 2.0 (2001), http://info.isl.ntt.co.jp/crypt/eng/camellia/specifications.html
3. Biham, E., Biryukov, A., Shamir, A.: Cryptanalysis of Skipjack Reduced to 31 Rounds Using Impossible Differentials. In: Stern, J. (ed.) EUROCRYPT 1999. LNCS, vol. 1592, pp. 12–23. Springer, Heidelberg (1999)
4. Chen, J., Jia, K., Yu, H., Wang, X.: New Impossible Differential Attacks of Reduced-Round Camellia-192 and Camellia-256. In: Parampalli, U., Hawkes, P. (eds.) ACISP 2011. LNCS, vol. 6812, pp. 16–33. Springer, Heidelberg (2011)
5. CRYPTREC-Cryptography Research and Evaluation Committees, report, Archive (2002), http://www.cryptrec.go.jp/english/index.html
6. Duo, L., Li, C., Feng, K.: Square Like Attack on Camellia. In: Qing, S., Imai, H., Wang, G. (eds.) ICICS 2007. LNCS, vol. 4861, pp. 269–283. Springer, Heidelberg (2007)
7. Hatano, Y., Sekine, H., Kaneko, T.: Higher Order Differential Attack of Camellia (II). In: Nyberg, K., Heys, H.M. (eds.) SAC 2002. LNCS, vol. 2595, pp. 129–146. Springer, Heidelberg (2003)
8. He, Y., Qing, S.: Square Attack on Reduced Camellia Cipher. In: Qing, S., Okamoto, T., Zhou, J. (eds.) ICICS 2001. LNCS, vol. 2229, pp. 238–245. Springer, Heidelberg (2001)

9. International Standardization of Organization (ISO), International Standard-ISO/IEC 18033-3, Information technology-Security techniques-Encryption algorithms-Part 3: Block ciphers (2005)

10. Kanda, M., Matsumoto, T.: Security of Camellia against Truncated Differential Cryptanalysis. In: Matsui, M. (ed.) FSE 2001. LNCS, vol. 2355, pp. 137–286. Springer, Heidelberg (2002)

11. Kawabata, T., Kaneko, T.: A Study on Higher Order Differential Attack of Camellia. In: The 2nd Open NESSIE Workshop (2001)

12. Knudsen, L.R.: DEAL–a 128-bit Block Cipher. Technical report, Department of Informatics, University of Bergen, Norway (1998)

13. Kühn, U.: Improved Cryptanalysis of MISTY1. In: Daemen, J., Rijmen, V. (eds.) FSE 2002. LNCS, vol. 2365, pp. 61–75. Springer, Heidelberg (2002)

14. Lee, S., Hong, S.H., Lee, S.-J., Lim, J.-I., Yoon, S.H.: Truncated Differential Cryptanalysis of Camellia. In: Kim, K.-c. (ed.) ICISC 2001. LNCS, vol. 2288, pp. 32–38. Springer, Heidelberg (2002)

15. Duo, L., Li, C., Feng, K.: New Observation on Camellia. In: Preneel, B., Tavares, S. (eds.) SAC 2005. LNCS, vol. 3897, pp. 51–64. Springer, Heidelberg (2006)

16. Li, L., Chen, J., Jia, K.: New Impossible Differential Cryptanalysis of Reduced-round Camellia. In: Lin, D., Tsudik, G., Wang, X. (eds.) CANS 2011. LNCS, vol. 7092, pp. 26–39. Springer, Heidelberg (2011)

17. Li, L., Chen, J., Wang, X.: Security of Reduced-Round Camellia against Impossible Differential Attack, http://eprint.iacr.org/2011/524.pdf

18. Lu, J.: Cryptanalysis of Block Ciphers. PhD Thesis, Department of Mathematics, Royal Holloway, University of London, England (2008)

19. Lu, J.: Higher-order meet-in-the-middle attacks on 10-round Camellia-128, 11-round Camellia-192 and 12-Camellia-256. In an invited talk at ASK 2011 in August 2011, Singapore (2011)

20. Lu, J., Kim, J.-S., Keller, N., Dunkelman, O.: Improving the Efficiency of Impossible Differential Cryptanalysis of Reduced Camellia and MISTY1. In: Malkin, T.G. (ed.) CT-RSA 2008. LNCS, vol. 4964, pp. 370–386. Springer, Heidelberg (2008)

21. Lu, J., Wei, Y., Kim, J., Fouque, P.A.: Cryptanalysis of Reduced Versions of the Camellia Block Cipher. In: SAC 2011 (2011) (to appear)

22. Mala, H., Shakiba, M., Dakhilalian, M., Bagherikaram, G.: New Results on Impossible Differential Cryptanalysis of Reduced–Round Camellia–128. In: Jacobson Jr., M.J., Rijmen, V., Safavi-Naini, R. (eds.) SAC 2009. LNCS, vol. 5867, pp. 281–294. Springer, Heidelberg (2009)

23. NESSIE–New European Schemes for Signatures, Integrity, and Encryption, final report of European project IST-1999-12324. Archive (1999), https://www.cosic.esat.kuleuven.be/nessie/Bookv015.pdf

24. NTT Information Sharing Platform Laboratories: Internationally Standardized Encryption Algorithm from Japan "Camellia", http://info.isl.ntt.co.jp/crypt/index.html

25. Shirai, T.: Differential, linear, boomerang and rectangle Cryptanalysis of Reduced-Round Camellia. In: Proceedings of the Third NESSIE Workshop, Munich, Germany, November 6-7 (2002)

26. Sugita, M., Kobara, K., Imai, H.: Security of Reduced Version of the Block Cipher Camellia against Truncated and Impossible Differential Cryptanalysis. In: Boyd, C. (ed.) ASIACRYPT 2001. LNCS, vol. 2248, pp. 193–207. Springer, Heidelberg (2001)

27. Wu, W., Zhang, W., Feng, D.: Impossible differential cryptanalysis of Reduced-Round ARIA and Camellia. Journal of Computer Science and Technology 22(3), 449–456 (2007)
28. Wenling, W., Dengguo, F., Hua, C.: Collision Attack and Pseudorandomness of Reduced-Round Camellia. In: Handschuh, H., Hasan, M.A. (eds.) SAC 2004. LNCS, vol. 3357, pp. 252–266. Springer, Heidelberg (2004)
29. Yeom, Y., Park, S., Kim, I.: On the Security of Camellia against the Square Attack. In: Daemen, J., Rijmen, V. (eds.) FSE 2002. LNCS, vol. 2365, pp. 89–99. Springer, Heidelberg (2002)

A Time Complexity of Attacks in Section 4

Table 3. Time Complexity of the Attack on 11-round Camellia-192

Step	Time Complexity
2	2^{n+55} E
3	$\sum_{i=0}^{4} 2 \times 2^{n+45-8i} \times 2^{8(i+1)} \times \frac{1}{8} = 2^{n+51} \times 5 \; \frac{1}{11}E$
4.1	$2 \times 2^{n+5} \times 2^{40} \times 2^1 \times \frac{1}{8} = 2^{n+44} \; \frac{1}{11}E$
4.2	$\sum_{i=0}^{4} 2 \times 2^{n-3-8i} \times 2^{41} \times 2^{8(i+1)} \times \frac{1}{8} = 2^{n+44} \times 5 \; \frac{1}{11}E$
4.3	$2^{n-43} \times 2^{81} \times 2^7 \times \frac{1}{8} = 2^{n+42} \; \frac{1}{11}E$
5	$2 \times 2^{n-43} \times 2^{88} \times 2^8 \times \frac{1}{8} = 2^{n+51} \; \frac{1}{11}E$
6.1	$2^{n-51} \times 2^{96} \times 2^1 \times \frac{1}{8} = 2^{n+43} \; \frac{1}{11}E$
6.2	$\sum_{i=0}^{1} 2^{n-51} \times 2^{97} \times 2^{8(i+1)} \times \frac{1}{8} = (2^{n+51} + 2^{n+59}) \; \frac{1}{11}E$
7	$2 \times 2^{113} \times \left(1 + (1-2^{-8}) \ldots + (1-2^{-8})^{2^{n-51}-1}\right) \times \frac{1}{8} \approx 2^{119} \; \frac{1}{11}E$

Table 4. Time Complexity of the Attack on 12-round Camellia-192

Step	Time Complexity
1	2^{n+55} E
2	$\sum_{i=0}^{4} 2 \times 2^{n+101-8i} \times 2^{8(i+1)} \times \frac{1}{8} = 2^{n+107} \times 5 \; \frac{1}{12}E$
3.1	$\sum_{i=0}^{1} 2 \times 2^{n+61-8i} \times 2^{40} \times \frac{1}{8} = (2^{n+99} + 2^{n+91}) \; \frac{1}{12}E$
3.2	$2 \times 2^{n+45} \times 2^{40} \times 2^1 \times \frac{1}{8} = 2^{n+84} \; \frac{1}{12}E$
	$2 \times 2^{n+37} \times 2^{41} \times 2^7 \times \frac{1}{8} = 2^{n+83} \; \frac{1}{12}E$
	$2 \times 2^{n+29} \times 2^{48} \times 2^7 \times \frac{1}{8} = 2^{n+82} \; \frac{1}{12}E$
3.3	$\sum_{i=0}^{1} 2 \times 2^{n+21-8i} \times 2^{55} \times 2^{8(i+1)} \times \frac{1}{8} = 2^{n+83} \; \frac{1}{12}E$
	$2 \times 2^{n+5} \times 2^{71} \times 2^1 \times \frac{1}{8} = 2^{n+75} \; \frac{1}{12}E$
4.1	$2 \times 2^{n+5} \times 2^{72} \times 2^1 \times \frac{1}{8} = 2^{n+76} \; \frac{1}{12}E$
4.2	$\sum_{i=0}^{4} 2 \times 2^{n-3-8i} \times 2^{73} \times 2^{8(i+1)} \times \frac{1}{8} = 2^{n+76} \times 5 \; \frac{1}{12}E$
4.3	$2^{n-43} \times 2^{113} \times 2^7 \times \frac{1}{8} = 2^{n+74} \; \frac{1}{12}E$
5	$2 \times 2^{n-43} \times 2^{120} \times 2^8 \times \frac{1}{8} = 2^{n+83} \; \frac{1}{12}E$
6	$2^{n-51} \times 2^{128} \times \frac{1}{8} \times 3 = 2^{n+74} \times 3 \; \frac{1}{12}E$
7	$2 \times 2^{128} \times \left(1 + (1-2^{-8}) + \ldots + (1-2^{-8})^{2^{n-51}-1}\right) \times \frac{1}{8} \approx 2^{134} \; \frac{1}{12}E$

Table 5. Time Complexity of the Attack on 14-round Camellia-256

Step	Time Complexity
1	2^{n+111} E
2	$\sum_{i=0}^{7} 2 \times 2^{n+221-8i} \times 2^{8(i+1)} \times \frac{1}{8} = 2^{n+230} \frac{1}{14}$E
3.1	$2 \times 2^{n+165} \times 2^{64} \times \frac{1}{8} + 2 \times 2^{n+157} \times 2^{64} \times \frac{1}{8} \times 6 = (2^{n+227} + 2^{n+219} \times 6) \frac{1}{14}$E
3.2	$2 \times 2^{n+157} \times 2^{64} \times 2^{2} \times \frac{1}{8} = 2^{n+221} \frac{1}{14}$E
4	$\sum_{i=0}^{4} 2 \times 2^{n+157-8i} \times 2^{66} \times 2^{8(i+1)} \times \frac{1}{8} = 2^{n+229} \times 5 \frac{1}{14}$E
5.1	$\sum_{i=0}^{1} 2 \times 2^{n+117-8i} \times 2^{106} \times \frac{1}{8} = (2^{n+221} + 2^{n+213}) \frac{1}{14}$E
5.2	$2 \times 2^{n+101} \times 2^{106} \times 2^{1} \times \frac{1}{8} = 2^{n+206} \frac{1}{14}$E
	$2 \times 2^{n+93} \times 2^{107} \times 2^{7} \times \frac{1}{8} = 2^{n+205} \frac{1}{14}$E
	$2 \times 2^{n+85} \times 2^{114} \times 2^{7} \times \frac{1}{8} = 2^{n+204} \frac{1}{14}$E
5.3	$\sum_{i=0}^{1} 2 \times 2^{n+77-8i} \times 2^{121} \times 2^{8(i+1)} \times \frac{1}{8} = 2^{n+205} \frac{1}{14}$E
	$2 \times 2^{n+61} \times 2^{137} \times 2^{1} \times \frac{1}{8} = 2^{n+197} \frac{1}{14}$E
6.1	$2 \times 2^{n+61} \times 2^{138} \times 2^{1} \times \frac{1}{8} = 2^{n+198} \frac{1}{14}$E
6.2	$\sum_{i=0}^{4} 2 \times 2^{n+53-8i} \times 2^{139} \times 2^{8(i+1)} \times \frac{1}{8} = 2^{n+198} \times 5 \frac{1}{14}$E
6.3	$2^{n+13} \times 2^{179} \times 2^{7} \times \frac{1}{8} = 2^{n+196} \frac{1}{14}$E
7	$2 \times 2^{n+13} \times 2^{186} \times 2^{8} \times \frac{1}{8} = 2^{n+205} \frac{1}{14}$E
8	$2^{n+5} \times 2^{194} \times \frac{1}{8} \times 3 = 2^{n+196} \times 3 \frac{1}{14}$E
9	$2 \times 2^{194} \times (1 + (1 - 2^{-8}) + \ldots + (1 - 2^{-8})^{2^{n+5}-1}) \times \frac{1}{8} \approx 2^{200} \frac{1}{14}$E

Impossible Differential Attacks on Reduced-Round LBlock

Ya Liu[1], Dawu Gu[1], Zhiqiang Liu[1], and Wei Li[2,3]

[1] Department of Computer Science and Engineering,
Shanghai Jiao Tong University, Shanghai 200240, China
{liuya0611,dwgu,ilu_zq}@sjtu.edu.cn
[2] School of Computer Science and Technology,
Donghua University, Shanghai 201620, China
[3] Shanghai Key Laboratory of Integrate Administration Technologies
for Information Security, Shanghai 200240, China
liwei.edu.cn@gmail.com

Abstract. LBlock is a lightweight block cipher with 32 rounds, which can be implemented efficiently not only in hardware environment but also in software platforms. In this paper, by exploiting the structure of LBlock and the redundancy in its key schedule, we propose an impossible differential attack on 21-round LBlock based on a 14-round impossible differential. The data and time complexities are about $2^{62.5}$ chosen plaintexts and $2^{73.7}$ 21-round encryptions, respectively. As far as we know, these results are the currently best results on LBlock in the single key scenario.

Keywords: Block Cipher, LBlock, Impossible Differential Attacks.

1 Introduction

With the development of electronic and communication technologies, low-end devices such as RFID tags have been deployed in various scenarios of daily life such as access control, public transport systems, identification, eHealth, and so on. Due to some practical requirements, the primitives used in this constrained environment have to satisfy some properties, including sufficient computation speed, less gate equivalents and low power consumption. As a matter of fact, traditional block ciphers such as AES [6] are unsatisfactory for these requirements. Therefore, more and more lightweight block ciphers are proposed, e.g., PRESENT [3], KATAN/KTANTAN [4], PRINTcipher [10], LBlock [17] etc. They are dedicatedly designed with a trade-off between the security and hardware performance (i.e., good hardware performance and moderate security), and suitable for tiny computing devices which don't require the encryption of large amounts of data and strong security.

LBlock [17], proposed by Wu and Zhang in 2011, is a lightweight block cipher with 32 rounds. The block and key sizes are 64-bit and 80-bit, respectively. LBlock adopts a variant Feistel structure with left rotation operations inserted

M.D. Ryan, B. Smyth, and G. Wang (Eds.): ISPEC 2012, LNCS 7232, pp. 97–108, 2012.
© Springer-Verlag Berlin Heidelberg 2012

every round, and it can be implemented efficiently not only in hardware environment but also in software platforms. In [17], the designers carefully evaluated the security against differential cryptanalysis, linear cryptanalysis, impossible differential cryptanalysis, integral attack and related-key attack. Among them, the best results in the single key scenario were an integral attack on 20-round LBlock as well as an impossible differential attack on 20-round LBlock. Recently, Minier and Naya-Plasencia presented a new related-key impossible differential attack on 22-round LBlock [15].

Impossible differential cryptanalysis, which is a variant of differential cryptanalysis [2], was independently proposed by Knudsen [9] and Biham *et al.* [1]. Its main idea is to use impossible differentials that hold with probability zero to discard the wrong keys until only one key is left. Up to now, impossible differential cryptanalysis has received much attention and been used to attack a variety of well-known block ciphers such as AES, ARIA, CLEFIA, MISTY1 and so on [5,7,11,13,14,16,18].

In this paper, we study the security of LBlock from the aspect of impossible differential cryptanalysis. We first present some properties of the structure of LBlock. Then we observe the redundancy in the key schedule and acquire some relations between the round subkeys. Based on them, we propose a new impossible differential attack on 21-round LBlock based on a 14-round impossible differential. Among it, some techniques such as building a precomputation table, constructing a hash table and the early abort skill [12] are adopted. The data, time and memory complexities of our attack are about $2^{62.5}$ chosen plaintexts, $2^{73.7}$ 21-round encryptions and $2^{55.5}$ 4-bit words of memory, respectively. Compared to the previously best results, these results are the currently best results on LBlock in the single key scenario. In table 1, we summarize our results along with the former known ones on LBlock.

Table 1. Summary of the attacks on LBlock in the single key scenario

Rounds	Attack Type	Data (CP)	Time (Enc)	Source
18	Integral Attack	$2^{62.3}$	$2^{62.3}$	[17]
20	Integral Attack	$2^{63.7}$	$2^{63.7}$	[17]
20	Impossible DC	2^{63}	$2^{72.7}$	[17]
21	Impossible DC	$2^{62.5}$	$2^{73.7}$	Section 4.3

DC: Differential Cryptanalysis; CP: Chosen Plaintexts;
Enc: Encryptions;

The remainder of this paper is organized as follows. Section 2 gives some notations and a brief description of LBlock. Section 3 introduces some 14-round impossible differentials of LBlock. Section 4 first exploits several properties of LBlock and the redundancy in its key schedule, and then presents an impossible differential attack on 21-round LBlock. Section 5 summarizes this paper.

2   Preliminaries

In this section, we first illustrate some notations which are used in the paper. Then we briefly describe the encryption algorithm and the key schedule of LBlock.

2.1   Some Notations

Some notations are given as follows.

- P, C: the 64-bit plaintext and the 64-bit ciphertext;
- $\Delta P, \Delta C$: the differences of a plaintext pair and a ciphertext pair;
- L_{r-1}, R_{r-1}: the left half and the right half of the r-th round input;
- ΔL_{r-1}: the difference of the left half of two r-th round inputs;
- ΔR_{r-1}: the difference of the right half of two r-th round inputs;
- $X \mid Y$: the concatenation of X and Y;
- K_r: the r-th round subkey;
- S_r: the output of the S-boxes in the r-th round;
- ΔS_r: the output difference of the S-boxes in the r-th round;
- $X \lll j$: left rotation of X by j bits;
- $X_{L(32)}, X_{R(32)}$: the left half and the right half of a 64-bit word X;
- $X_{i,j}$: the j-th 4-bit word of X_i;
- $X_{l,\{i,j\}}$: the i-th and j-th 4-bit words of X_l;
- $X_{l,\{i\sim j\}}$: the i-th to the j-th 4-bit words of X_l;
- $X_{i,j}[l]$: the l-th bit of $X_{i,j}$;
- $X_{i,j}[l,t]$: the l-th and t-th bits of $X_{i,j}$;
- $X_{i,j}[l \sim t]$: the l-th to the t-th bits of $X_{i,j}$;
- $[i]_2$: binary form of an integer i

Clearly, (L_r, R_r) is the output of the r-th round.

2.2   Overview of LBlock

LBlock is a 64-bit lightweight block cipher with 32 rounds. It adopts a 80-bit key size and a variant Feistel structure with left rotations inserted every round. According to the notations above, we will describe the encryption algorithm and the key schedule of LBlock briefly.

Encryption Algorithm. Let $P = P_L \mid P_R = X_1 \mid X_0$ be a 64-bit plaintext. For $i = 2, 3, \cdots, 33$, do

$$X_i = F(X_{i-1}, K_{i-1}) \oplus (X_{i-2} \lll 8).$$

The concatenation of two binary strings X_{32} and X_{33} forms the ciphertext C, i.e.,

$$C = X_{32} \mid X_{33}.$$

Here the round function F uses the SPN structure including the key-addition layer, the nonlinear transformation S and the linear diffusion layer P. The nonlinear transformation S consists of eight 4×4 S-boxes s_i in parallel. The linear function P is defined as a permutation of eight 4-bit words, which is expressed as follows:

$$P : \{0,1\}^{32} \to \{0,1\}^{32};$$

$$Y_7 \mid Y_6 \mid Y_5 \mid Y_4 \mid Y_3 \mid Y_2 \mid Y_1 \mid Y_0 \mapsto Z_7 \mid Z_6 \mid Z_5 \mid Z_4 \mid Z_3 \mid Z_2 \mid Z_1 \mid Z_0,$$

$$Z_7 = Y_6, Z_6 = Y_4, Z_5 = Y_7, Z_4 = Y_5,$$

$$Z_3 = Y_2, Z_2 = Y_0, Z_1 = Y_3, Z_0 = Y_1.$$

The precise structure can be found in [17].

Key Schedule. The key schedule of LBlock is designed in a stream cipher way. The 80-bit master key K is stored in a key register and represented as $K = k_{79}k_{78}k_{77} \cdots k_1 k_0$. At round i, the leftmost 32 bits of current contents of register K are output as the round key K_i, i.e., $K_i = k_{79}k_{78} \cdots k_{49}k_{48}$. After extracting the round subkey K_i, the key register is updated as follows:

1. $[k_{79}k_{78}k_{77} \cdots k_1 k_0] = [k_{50}k_{49}k_{48} \cdots k_1 k_0 k_{79}k_{78} \cdots k_{52}k_{51}]$,
2. $[k_{79}k_{78}k_{77}k_{76}] = s_9[k_{79}k_{78}k_{77}k_{76}]$,
   $[k_{75}k_{74}k_{73}k_{72}] = s_8[k_{75}k_{74}k_{73}k_{72}]$,
3. $[k_{50}k_{49}k_{48}k_{47}k_{46}] = [k_{50}k_{49}k_{48}k_{47}k_{46}] \oplus [i]_2$,

where s_9 and s_8 are two 4-bit S-boxes [17].

3   14-Round Impossible Differentials of LBlock

In [17], Wu and Zhang found some 14-round impossible differential characteristics by the means of $\mathcal{U}$-method [8]. One of them is illustrated in the following: $(00000000, 00\alpha00000) \nrightarrow_{14r} (0\beta000000, 00000000)$, where $\alpha, \beta \in \{0,1\}^4 \setminus \{0\}^4$ represent non-zero 4-bit words. Similarly, Wu and Zhang obtained some other 14-round impossible differentials by changing the positions of α, β. They presented impossible differential cryptanalysis of 20-round LBlock on the basis of the above 14-round impossible differential.

We study all possible 14-round impossible differential characteristics of LBlock. By exploiting the structure of reduced-round LBlock and the redundancy in the key schedule, we select a 14-round impossible differential to attack 21-round LBlock. This 14-round impossible differential is

$$(00000000, 00\alpha00000) \nrightarrow_{14r} (0000\beta000, 00000000), \tag{1}$$

which contradicts in the middle and makes full use of the relations between the round subkeys. For other 14-round impossible differentials, the round subkeys involving in our attack on 21-round LBlock have less common or related bits. Therefore, we use the 14-round impossible differential (1) to analyze the security of LBlock. In Section 4, we will elaborate how many common or related bits exist in our attack using the 14-round impossible differential (1).

4   Impossible Differential Attacks on 21-Round LBlock

In this section, we propose an impossible differential attack on 21-round LBlock by putting three additional rounds in the plaintext side and four additional rounds in the ciphertext side of the 14-round impossible differential (1). Figure 1 shows the whole attacking procedure.

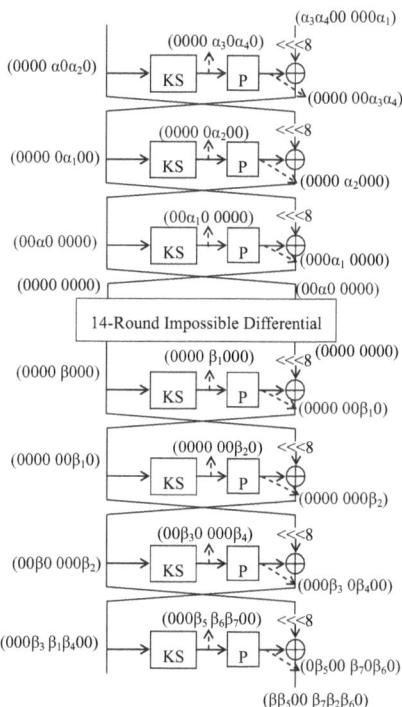

Fig. 1. Impossible Differential Attacks on 21-Round LBlock

Before introducing the whole attack, we present some properties of LBlock. In addition, we also observe the redundancy in the key schedule and gain the relations between the round subkeys. Based on them, we mount an impossible differential attack on 21-round LBlock. At last, we analyze the data and time complexities of our proposed attack.

4.1   Some Properties of LBlock

We study the structure of LBlock and present four properties, which can be used to attack 21-round LBlock. In the following, we will elaborate them.

Property 1. For 3 rounds of LBlock from rounds $i + 1$ to $i + 3$, the necessary conditions of $\Delta L_{i+3} = (0000\ 0000)$ and $\Delta R_{i+3} = (00\alpha0\ 0000)$ are:

(1) $L_i = (0000\ \alpha 0 \alpha_2 0)$, $R_i = (\alpha_3 \alpha_4 00\ 000 \alpha_1)$ and $L_{i+1} = (0000\ 0\alpha_1 00)$
(2) $\Delta S_{i+1,3} = \Delta R_{i,7}$, $\quad \Delta S_{i+1,1} = \Delta R_{i,6}$,
$\quad \Delta S_{i+2,2} = \Delta R_{i+1,1}$, $\quad \Delta S_{i+3,5} = \Delta R_{i+2,2}$,

where $\alpha_i (1 \leq i \leq 4)$ are non-zero 4-bit words.

Property 2. For 4 rounds of LBlock from rounds $i + 1$ to $i + 4$, if the input difference of the $(i + 1)$-th round is $(0000\beta 000, 00000000)$, then

(1) $\Delta L_{i+1} = (0000\ 00\beta_1 0)$, $\Delta L_{i+2} = (00\beta 0\ 000\beta_2)$ and $\Delta L_{i+3} = (000\beta_3\ \beta_1$ $\beta_4 00)$
(2) $\Delta S_{i+1,3} = \Delta L_{i+1,1}, \Delta S_{i+2,1} = \Delta L_{i+2,0}$,
$\quad \Delta S_{i+3,5} = \Delta L_{i+3,4}, \Delta S_{i+3,0} = \Delta L_{i+3,2}$,
$\quad \Delta S_{i+4,4} = \Delta L_{i+4,6}, \Delta S_{i+4,3} = \Delta L_{i+4,1}, \Delta S_{i+4,2} = \Delta L_{i+4,3}$,

where $\beta_1, \beta_2, \beta_3, \beta_4$ are non-zero 4-bit words.

The proofs of Properties 1 and 2 can be obtained from Fig 1. According to the encryption algorithm and Properties 1 and 2, we can obtain the following results.

Property 3. Let $(0000\alpha 0\alpha_2 0, \alpha_3 \alpha_4 00000\alpha_1) \rightarrow_{3r} (00000000, 00\alpha 00000)$ be a 3-round differential. $X_1 \mid X_0$ and $X_1' \mid X_0'$ are two 64-bit words, which satisfy the input difference of this 3-round differential. If we want to check whether they satisfy this 3-round differential, we have to guess at least seven 4-bit words of the round subkeys, i.e., $K_{i+1,\{6,3,1,0\}}$, $K_{i+2,\{7,2\}}$ and $K_{i+3,5}$.

Property 4. Let $(0000\beta 000, 00000000) \rightarrow_{4r} (\beta \beta_5 00\beta_7 \beta_2 \beta_6 0, 000\beta_3 \beta_1 \beta_4 00)$ be a 4-round differential. $Y_1 \mid Y_0$ and $Y_1' \mid Y_0'$ are two 64-bit words, which satisfy the output difference of this 4-round differential. If we want to check whether they satisfy this 4-round differential, we have to guess at least fourteen 4-bit words of the round subkeys, i.e., $K_{i+1,3}$, $K_{i+2,\{1,7\}}$, $K_{i+3,\{0,2,3,5\}}$ and $K_{i+4,\{0,2,3,4,5,6,7\}}$.

4.2   Some Observations on the Key Schedule of LBlock

We exploit the redundancy in the key schedule of LBlock in this section. Some relations between three or four consecutive round subkeys are presented. On the basis of them, the guessed key space of our proposed attack is reduced. In the following, we will describe them in detail.

Property 5. For rounds 1 to 3 and rounds 18 to 21, we can obtain the relations among their round subkeys, respectively.

(1) Let $K = k_{79} k_{78} k_{77} \cdots k_1 k_0$ be the current key of register. If the subkey of the first round is $K_1 = k_{79} k_{78} k_{77} \cdots k_{49} k_{48}$, then the subkeys of the second and third rounds can be expressed as follows:

$$K_2 = s_9(k_{50}, \cdots, k_{47}) \mid s_8(k_{46}, \cdots, k_{43}) \mid k_{42} \mid \cdots \mid k_{19},$$
$$K_3 = s_9(k_{21}, \cdots, k_{18}) \mid s_8(k_{17} \oplus 1, k_{16}, k_{15}, k_{14}) \mid k_{13} \mid \cdots \mid k_0 \mid k_{79} \mid \cdots \mid k_{70}.$$

(2) Let $K = k'_{79}k'_{78}k'_{77} \cdots k'_1 k'_0$ be the current key of register. If the subkey of the 18th round is $K_{18} = k'_{79}k'_{78}k'_{77} \cdots k'_{49}k'_{48}$, then the subkeys from the 19th to 21st rounds can be expressed as follows:

$$K_{19} = s_9(k'_{50}, \cdots, k'_{47}) | s_8(k'_{46}, \cdots, k'_{43}) | k'_{42} | \cdots | k'_{22} | k'_{21} \oplus 1 | k'_{20} | k'_{19},$$
$$K_{20} = s_9(k'_{21} \oplus 1, k'_{20}, k'_{19}, k'_{18} \oplus 1) | s_8(k'_{17}, \cdots, k'_{14}) |$$
$$k'_{13} | \cdots | k'_0 | k'_{79} | \cdots | k'_{73} | k'_{72} \oplus 1 | k'_{71} | k'_{70},$$
$$K_{21} = s_9(k'_{72} \oplus 1, k'_{71}, k'_{70}, k'_{69} \oplus 1) | s_8(k'_{68} \oplus 1, k'_{67}, k'_{66}, k'_{65}) | k'_{64} | \cdots | k'_{51} |$$
$$s_9(k'_{50} \cdots k'_{47}) | s_8(k'_{46} \cdots k'_{43}) \oplus 1 | k'_{42} | k'_{41} \oplus 1.$$

By Property 5, we search common or related bits of partial 4-bit words of three or four consecutive round subkeys involving in Properties 3 and 4, which is illustrated in Property 6.

Property 6. For rounds 1 to 3 and rounds 18 to 21, we can get the common or related bits of their consecutive round subkeys as follows:

(1) If four 4-bit words of K_1, $K_{1,\{6,3,1,0\}}$, are known, then we can obtain three bits information of $K_{2,7}$, i.e., $s_9^{-1}(K_{2,7})[3,2,1]$. In other words, seven 4-bit words involving in Property 3 have three related bits, i.e., $K_{1,0}[2,1,0] = s_9^{-1}(K_{2,7})[3,2,1] = k_{50}k_{49}k_{48}$.
(2) If each of the 4-bit words of K_{21} is known except for $K_{21,1}$, then we can obtain nine bits of $K_{18,3}, K_{19,\{1,7\}}$ and $K_{20,\{0,2,3,5\}}$, i.e., $K_{18,3}, K_{19}[30,31]$ and $K_{20}[0 \sim 2]$. In other words, fourteen 4-bit words involving in Property 4 have nine common or related bits, i.e., $s_9^{-1}(K_{21,7})[3 \sim 1] = K_{20,0}[2 \sim 0]$, $K_{21,2}[1,0] = K_{19,7}[3,2]$, $K_{21,5}[2 \sim 0] | K_{21,4}[3] = K_{18,3}$.

In our attack on 21-round LBlock by employing the 14-round impossible differential (1), we can reduce the guessed key space by 2^{-12} times. For other 14-round impossible differentials, we also studied the relations between the round subkeys involving in whole attacking procedure in the same way. However, we did not achieve any better result.

4.3   Attack Procedure

Based on the 14-round impossible differential (1) and properties 1 to 6, we present an impossible differential attack on 21-round LBlock. In this attack, we adopt some techniques such as constructing a hash table and building a precomputation table to reduce the complexity. Before describing our attacking algorithm, we first construct a precomputation table T from rounds 2 to 3.

Table T: For each of 2^{28} possible pairs $(L_{2,5}, \Delta L_{2,5}, K_{3,5}, K_{2,\{2,7\}}, L_{1,\{2,7\}})$, we first calculate $\Delta L_{1,2} = s_5(L_{2,5} \oplus K_{3,5}) \oplus s_5(L_{2,5} \oplus \Delta L_{2,5} \oplus K_{3,5})$. Then we continue to compute the first word of the right half of the output difference in the first round, i.e., $\Delta R_{1,1} = s_2(L_{1,2} \oplus K_{2,2}) \oplus s_2(L_{1,2} \oplus \Delta L_{1,2} \oplus$

$K_{2,2}$). Store all possible pairs $(L_{2,5}, \Delta L_{2,5}, K_{3,5}, K_{2,\{2,7\}}, L_{1,\{2,7\}})$ in a hash table T indexed by $(L_{1,\{2,7\}}, \Delta L_{1,2}, \Delta R_1, R_{1,3}, s_9^{-1}(K_{2,7})[3,2,1])$, where $\Delta R_1 = (0000\ \Delta L_{2,5} 0 \Delta R_{1,1} 0)$ and $R_{1,3} = s_7(L_{1,7} \oplus K_{2,7}) \oplus L_{2,5}$. There are 2^{27} rows in T and each row contains approximately 2 9-bit subkeys $(K_{2,2}, s_9^{-1}(K_{2,7})[0], K_{3,5})$ on average.

We can extract the proper subkeys $K_{2,2}|s_9^{-1}(K_{2,7})[0]\|K_{3,5}$ from this precomputation table T. In the following, we will elaborate the attack algorithm.

The Attack Algorithm

1. Select a set of 2^{20} plaintexts which has some fixed values in all words except for $P_{L,3}, P_{L,1}, P_{R,7}, P_{R,6}$ and $P_{R,0}$. Call this special set a structure, which contains all plaintexts with the following forms:

$$(y_1 y_2 y_3 y_4 \gamma_1 y_5 \gamma_2 y_6, \gamma_3 \gamma_4 y_7 y_8 y_9 y_{10} y_{11} \gamma_5),$$

   where $y_i(1 \leq i \leq 11)$ are fixed and $\gamma_j(1 \leq j \leq 5)$ take all possible values of $\mathbb{F}_2^4$. Clearly, each structure can form about 2^{39} plaintext pairs, of which the differences have the following forms:

$$(0000\mu_1 0 \mu_2 0, \mu_3 \mu_4 00000\mu_5),$$

   where $\mu_i(1 \leq i \leq 5)$ are non-zero 4-bit words. Take 2^n structures. Totally, we collect about 2^{n+39} plaintext pairs. Encrypt these plaintext pairs to obtain the corresponding ciphertext pairs. If the ciphertext differences have the following forms:

$$(000\nu_1 \nu_2 \nu_3 00, \nu_4 \nu_5 00 \nu_6 \nu_7 \nu_8 0),$$

   where $\nu_i(1 \leq i \leq 8)$ are non-zero 4-bit words, these pairs will be kept. The expected number of the remaining plaintext pairs is about $2^{n+39} \times 2^{-32} = 2^{n+7}$. In this step, we can simplify the selection of proper pairs by constructing a hash table.

2. Guess $K_{21,4}, K_{21,3}$ and $K_{21,2}$, respectively. By Property 2, we check whether three equations, $\Delta S_{21,4} = \Delta C_{R,6}, \Delta S_{21,3} = \Delta C_{R,1}$ and $\Delta S_{21,2} = \Delta C_{R,3}$, hold. The total probability of this event is 2^{-12}. Therefore, we expect about $2^{n+7} \times 2^{-12} = 2^{n-5}$ plaintext pairs remain. Next, guess $K_{21,\{7,6,5,0\}}$. Partially decrypt the ciphertext pairs to get partial outputs of the 20-th round, i.e., $R_{20,\{5,3,2,0\}}$ and $R'_{20,\{5,3,2,0\}}$.

3. By Property 6, we can obtain the value of $K_{20,0}[2 \sim 0]$ by the guessed 4-bit word $K_{21,7}$. Thus, guess $K_{20,0}[3]$ and $K_{20,5}$, respectively. According to Property 2, verify whether two equations, $\Delta S_{20,5} = \Delta C_{L,4}$ and $\Delta S_{20,0} = \Delta C_{L,2}$, hold. The probability for that happens is 2^{-8}. Thus, the expected number of the remaining pairs is approximately $2^{n-5} \times 2^{-8} = 2^{n-13}$. Continue to guess $K_{20,\{2,3\}}$. Partially decrypt the remaining pairs to obtain $R_{19,\{7,1\}}$ and $R'_{19,\{7,1\}}$.

4. Guess $K_{19,1}$ and verify whether $\Delta S_{19,1}$ is equal to $\Delta L_{19,0}$. The probability of this event is 2^{-4}. Thus about $2^{n-13} \times 2^{-4} = 2^{n-17}$ pairs will be kept.

According to Property 6, we can get the value of $K_{19,7}[3,2]$ by $K_{21,2}$. Next, guess $K_{19,7}[1,0]$ and partially decrypt the remaining pairs to acquire $R_{18,3}$ and $R'_{18,3}$.

5. By Property 6, we know $K_{18,3} = K_{21,5}[2 \sim 0] \mid K_{21,4}[3]$. Check whether the equation $\Delta S_{18,3} = \Delta L_{18,1}$ holds. The probability for that happens is 2^{-4}. So there remains approximately $2^{n-17} \times 2^{-4} = 2^{n-21}$ pairs.

6. Guess $K_{1,3}$ and $K_{1,1}$, respectively. Verify whether two equations, $\Delta S_{1,3} = \Delta P_{R,7}$ and $\Delta S_{1,1} = \Delta P_{R,6}$, hold. The probability of this event is 2^{-8}. So about $2^{n-21} \times 2^{-8} = 2^{n-29}$ pairs remain. Continue to guess $K_{1,\{6,0\}}$ and encrypt some 4-bit words of the remaining plaintext pairs to get $L_{1,\{7,2\}}$ and $L'_{1,\{7,2\}}$.

7. According to the precomputation table T, we get rid of some wrong subkeys. Initialize an empty table H with 2^9 rows. Each row corresponds to a different value $(K_{2,2}, s_9^{-1}(K_{2,7})[0], K_{3,5})$. For each of the remaining pairs, according to the inputs of the second round and the guessed bits $K_{1,0}[2,1,0]$ (which is equal to $s_9^{-1}(K_{2,7})[3,2,1]$ by Property 6), access the row $(L_{1,\{2,7\}}, \Delta L_{1,2}, \Delta R_1, R_{1,3}, s_9^{-1}(K_{2,7})[3,2,1])$ in the precomputation table T, which corresponds to 2 values of $(K_{2,2}, s_9^{-1}(K_{2,7})[0], K_{3,5})$. In other words, for each of 2^{n-29} proper pairs, about 2 of the subkeys $(K_{2,2}, s_9^{-1}(K_{2,7})[0], K_{3,5})$ can result in the input difference of the 14-round impossible differential (1). Remove these values from the table H. After trying all remaining pairs, if the table H is not empty, output the 9-bit value $(K_{2,2}, s_9^{-1}(K_{2,7})[0], K_{3,5})$.

8. We have obtained some 72-bit subkeys $(K_{21,\{7,6,5,4,3,2,0\}}, K_{20,0}[3], K_{20,\{5,3,2\}}, K_{19,7}[1,0], K_{19,1}, K_{1,\{6,3,1,0\}}, K_{2,2}, s_9^{-1}(K_{2,7})[0], K_{3,5})$. Let $K = k_{79} \cdots k_0$ be the secret key. According to the value of 25-bit key $(K_{1,\{6,3,1,0\}}, s_9^{-1}(K_{2,7})[0], K_{2,2}, K_{3,5})$ (which is $k_{75} \cdots k_{72} k_{63} \cdots k_{60} k_{55} \cdots k_{47} k_{30} \cdots k_{27} k_{13} \cdots k_{10}$), we guess the remaining 55-bit key of K and verify whether this key is correct by about 2^{55} trail encryptions. If this guessed key is correct, end this attack, otherwise go to step 2 and try another guess.

Up to now, we have removed all wrong keys to recover the correct one. In this attack, we consider the redundancy in the key schedule and adopt some techniques such as constructing a hash table and building a precomputation table T, which reduce the complexity.

4.4 Complexity of the Attack

For each of the remaining pairs in step 7, we remove about two subkeys $(K_{2,2}, s_9^{-1}(K_{2,7})[0], K_{3,5})$ along with the guessed subkey $(K_{21,\{7,6,5,4,3,2,0\}}, K_{20,\{5,3,2\}}, K_{20,0}[3], K_{19,7}[1,0], K_{19,1}, K_{1,\{6,3,1,0\}})$. Therefore, the probability for a wrong joint subkey surviving is about $1 - \frac{2}{2^9} = 1 - 2^{-8}$. Let ϵ be the expected number of the wrong subkeys remaining. Clearly,

$$\epsilon = 2^{72} \times (1 - 2^{-8})^{2^{n-29}}.$$

If we take $n = 42.5$, then $\epsilon \approx 2^{6.7}$. At this time, we consider that about $2^{6.7}$ wrong subkeys are left. For each of remaining subkeys, we can obtain some candidates of the main key. With about $2^{55} \times 2^{6.7} = 2^{61.7}$ trail encryptions, the correct main key will be recovered.

The data complexity is $2^{n+20} = 2^{62.5}$ chosen plaintexts. In the following, we will discuss the time complexity of each step in table 2.

Table 2. Complexity of Impossible Differential Attack on 21-Round LBlock

Step	Time Complexity
1	2^{n+20} 21-round encryptions
2	$\sum_{i=0}^{2} 2^{n+7-4\cdot i} \times 2 \times 2^{4\cdot(i+1)} + 2^{n-5} \times 2 \times 2^{28} \approx 2^{n+24}$ 1-round encryptions
3	$2^{n-5} \times 2 \times 2^{29} + 2^{n-9} \times 2 \times 2^{33} + 2^{n-13} \times 2 \times 2^{41} \approx 2^{n+29.2}$ 1-round encryptions
4	$2^{n-13} \times 2 \times 2^{45} + 2^{n-17} \times 2 \times 2^{47} \approx 2^{n+33.3}$ 1-round encryptions
5	$2^{n-17} \times 2 \times 2^{47} = 2^{n+31}$ 1-round encryptions
6	$\sum_{i=0}^{1} 2^{n-21-4\cdot i} \times 2 \times 2^{47+4\cdot(i+1)} + 2^{n-29} \times 2 \times 2^{63} \approx 2^{n+35.2}$ 1-round encryptions
7	$2^{n-29} \times 2^{63} \times 2 = 2^{n+35}$ Memory Access
8	$2^{55} \times \epsilon \approx 2^{61.7}$ 21-round encryptions

From Table 2, we know that the total time complexity is about $2^{n+31.2}$ 21-round LBlock encryptions. Furthermore, the memory complexity is about $2^{n+7} \times 4 = 2^{n+9}$ 64-bit blocks. By the value of n, we obtain the time and memory complexities are approximately $2^{73.7}$ 21-round LBlock encryptions and $2^{55.5}$ 4-bit words, respectively.

5   Conclusion

In this paper, we have presented an impossible differential attack on 21-round LBlock by setting a 14-round impossible differential (1) at rounds 4 to 17. In our attack, we study the structure of LBlock and the redundancy in its key schedule, and acquire some relations between some consecutive round subkeys. Meanwhile, some techniques such as building a hash table and constructing a precomputation table are adopted to reduce the complexity. Our proposed attack requires approximately $2^{62.5}$ chosen plaintexts, $2^{73.7}$ 21-round encryptions and $2^{55.5}$ 4-bit words of memory. To the best of our knowledge, these results, in term of the number of the attacked rounds, is better than any previously published results on LBlock in the single key scenario.

Acknowledgements. The authors are grateful to all anonymous reviewers for valuable suggestions and comments. This work has been supported by the National Natural Science Foundation of China (No. 61073150 and No. 61003278), the Opening Project of Shanghai Key Laboratory of Integrate Administration Technologies for Information Security and the Fundamental Research Funds for the Central Universities.

References

1. Biham, E., Biryukov, A., Shamir, A.: Cryptanalysis of Skipjack Reduced to 31 Rounds Using Impossible Differentials. In: Stern, J. (ed.) EUROCRYPT 1999. LNCS, vol. 1592, pp. 12–23. Springer, Heidelberg (1999)
2. Biham, E., Shamir, A.: Differential Cryptanalysis of DES-like Cryptosystems. In: Menezes, A., Vanstone, S.A. (eds.) CRYPTO 1990. LNCS, vol. 537, pp. 2–21. Springer, Heidelberg (1991)
3. Bogdanov, A.A., Knudsen, L.R., Leander, G., Paar, C., Poschmann, A., Robshaw, M., Seurin, Y., Vikkelsoe, C.: PRESENT: An Ultra-Lightweight Block Cipher. In: Paillier, P., Verbauwhede, I. (eds.) CHES 2007. LNCS, vol. 4727, pp. 450–466. Springer, Heidelberg (2007)
4. De Cannière, C., Dunkelman, O., Knežević, M.: KATAN and KTANTAN — A Family of Small and Efficient Hardware-Oriented Block Ciphers. In: Clavier, C., Gaj, K. (eds.) CHES 2009. LNCS, vol. 5747, pp. 272–288. Springer, Heidelberg (2009)
5. Chen, J., Jia, K., Yu, H., Wang, X.: New Impossible Differential Attacks of Reduced-Round Camellia-192 and Camellia-256. In: Parampalli, U., Hawkes, P. (eds.) ACISP 2011. LNCS, vol. 6812, pp. 16–33. Springer, Heidelberg (2011)
6. Daemen, J., Rijmen, V.: The Design of Rijndael: AES - The Advanced Encryption Standard. Springer, Heidelberg (2002)
7. Dunkelman, O., Keller, N.: An Improved Impossible Differential Attack on MISTY1. In: Pieprzyk, J. (ed.) ASIACRYPT 2008. LNCS, vol. 5350, pp. 441–454. Springer, Heidelberg (2008)
8. Kim, J.-S., Hong, S.H., Sung, J., Lee, S.-J., Lim, J.-I., Sung, S.H.: Impossible Differential Cryptanalysis for Block Cipher Structures. In: Johansson, T., Maitra, S. (eds.) INDOCRYPT 2003. LNCS, vol. 2904, pp. 82–96. Springer, Heidelberg (2003)
9. Knudsen, L.R.: DEAL - a 128-bit block cipher. Tech. rep., Department of Informatics, University of Bergen, Norway, technical report (1998)
10. Knudsen, L., Leander, G., Poschmann, A., Robshaw, M.J.B.: PRINTCIPHER: A Block Cipher for IC-Printing. In: Mangard, S., Standaert, F.X. (eds.) CHES 2010. LNCS, vol. 6225, pp. 16–32. Springer, Heidelberg (2010)
11. Lu, J., Dunkelman, O., Keller, N., Kim, J.-S.: New Impossible Differential Attacks on AES. In: Chowdhury, D.R., Rijmen, V., Das, A. (eds.) INDOCRYPT 2008. LNCS, vol. 5365, pp. 279–293. Springer, Heidelberg (2008)
12. Lu, J., Kim, J.-S., Keller, N., Dunkelman, O.: Improving the Efficiency of Impossible Differential Cryptanalysis of Reduced Camellia and MISTY1. In: Malkin, T. (ed.) CT-RSA 2008. LNCS, vol. 4964, pp. 370–386. Springer, Heidelberg (2008)
13. Mala, H., Dakhilalian, M., Rijmen, V., Modarres-Hashemi, M.: Improved Impossible Differential Cryptanalysis of 7-Round AES-128. In: Gong, G., Gupta, K.C. (eds.) INDOCRYPT 2010. LNCS, vol. 6498, pp. 282–291. Springer, Heidelberg (2010)
14. Mala, H., Shakiba, M., Dakhilalian, M., Bagherikaram, G.: New Results on Impossible Differential Cryptanalysis of Reduced–Round Camellia–128. In: Jacobson Jr., M.J., Rijmen, V., Safavi-Naini, R. (eds.) SAC 2009. LNCS, vol. 5867, pp. 281–294. Springer, Heidelberg (2009)
15. Minier, M., Naya-Plasencia, M.: Some preliminary studies on the differential behavior of the lightweight block cipher LBlock. In: Leander, G., Standaert, F.X. (eds.) ECRYPT Workshop on Lightweight Cryptography, pp. 35–48 (November 2011)

16. Tsunoo, Y., Tsujihara, E., Shigeri, M., Saito, T., Suzaki, T., Kubo, H.: Impossible Differential Cryptanalysis of CLEFIA. In: Nyberg, K. (ed.) FSE 2008. LNCS, vol. 5086, pp. 398–411. Springer, Heidelberg (2008)
17. Wu, W., Zhang, L.: LBlock: A Lightweight Block Cipher. In: Lopez, J., Tsudik, G. (eds.) ACNS 2011. LNCS, vol. 6715, pp. 327–344. Springer, Heidelberg (2011)
18. Wu, W., Zhang, W., Feng, D.: Impossible differential cryptanalysis of reduced-round ARIA and Camellia. J. Comput. Sci. Technol. 22(3), 449–456 (2007)

New Truncated Differential Cryptanalysis
on 3D Block Cipher

Takuma Koyama[1], Lei Wang[1], Yu Sasaki[2],
Kazuo Sakiyama[1], and Kazuo Ohta[1]

[1] The University of Electro-Communications
{t-koyama,wanglei}@ice.uec.ac.jp, {sakiyama,kazuo.ohta}@uec.ac.jp
[2] NTT Information Sharing Platform Laboratories, NTT Corporation
sasaki.yu@lab.ntt.co.jp

Abstract. This paper presents 11- and 13-round key-recovery attacks on block cipher 3D with the truncated differential cryptanalysis, while the previous best key-recovery attack broke only 10 rounds with the impossible differential attack. 3D is an AES-based block cipher proposed at CANS 2008, which operates on 512-bit blocks and a 512-bit key, and consists of 22 rounds. It was previously believed that the truncated differential cryptanalysis could not extend the attack more than 5 rounds. However, by carefully analyzing the data processing part and key schedule function simultaneously, we show the attack to 11-round 3D with 2^{251} chosen plaintext (CP), 2^{288} computations, and 2^{128} memory. Additionally, the time complexity is improved up to 2^{113} by applying the early aborting technique. By utilizing the idea of neutral bit, we attack 13-round 3D with 2^{469} CP, 2^{308} computations, and 2^{128} memory.

Keywords: 3D block cipher, key-recovery attack, truncated differential cryptanalysis, early aborting technique.

1 Introduction

At CANS 2008, Nakahara proposed a three-dimensional block cipher [10] called 3D which was based on AES (Advanced Encryption Standard) [12]. It operates on 512-bit blocks and a 512-bit key, and consists of 22 rounds. 3D was designed to have a larger block size and key size than those of AES, while the data procession can take advantage of the design of the AES round function. To enlarge the internal state size of AES (4×4-byte state), 3D puts four AES states in parallel, and regard the group as the internal state of 3D ($4 \times 4 \times 4$-byte state). See its illustration in Fig. 1. To take advantage of the three-dimensional states, 3D applies the diffusion (ShiftRows) of AES to two directions (θ_1 and θ_2 operations) in every two rounds in turn.

For block ciphers, there are two types of security evaluation standards; secret-key-type attacks and known-key-type attacks. Regarding the known-key-type attack, Le et al. [4] attacked 15 rounds with a multiple inbounds technique [9]. Although their attack works for more rounds than us, the known-key-type attack

M.D. Ryan, B. Smyth, and G. Wang (Eds.): ISPEC 2012, LNCS 7232, pp. 109–125, 2012.
© Springer-Verlag Berlin Heidelberg 2012

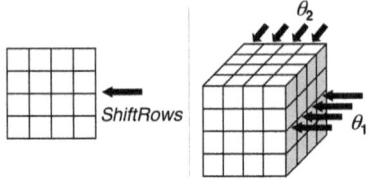

Fig. 1. Left: AES state and ShiftRows operation, Right: 3D state and θ_1 and θ_2 operations

uses the knowledge of the key, and its goal is to distinguish the permutation from a random one. The known-key-type attacks cannot be used in the secret-key-type attacks because the goal is different. Hereafter, we focus our attention on the key-recovery attack. Nakahara [11] attacked 10 rounds with an impossible-differential technique [5], which uses the fact that a certain input difference never reaches another certain output difference after a few rounds. He also considered the truncated differential cryptanalysis [6], which analyzes a set of differential transitions simultaneously. However to attack 6 rounds, the probability of the differential path he found became lower than the probability to find a pair of plaintexts with the same input and output differences for a random permutation. Moreover, even attacking 6 rounds seemed hard due to an insufficient number of valid plaintext pairs. From these observations, he predicted the hardness of applying the truncated differential cryptanalysis on 6 rounds.

In fact, however, the previous work incorrectly estimated the number of possible plaintext pairs, and thus mistakenly concluded that satisfying on 6-round path was impossible. In this paper, we show that the truncated differential cryptanalysis can still attack effectively on more than 5-round 3D. We show several improvements:

– correctly choose plaintext pairs and extend the differential path accordingly;
– carefully analyze the differential transition inside the 2-round iterated path, which raises the probability from 2^{-96} to 2^{-94};
– carefully analyze the diffusions for the data processing part and key schedule function simultaneously so that more rounds can be added to the previous differential path.

Thus, this paper presents new 11- and 13-round key-recovery attacks on 3D with the truncated differential cryptanalysis.

In our 11-round attack, we use the differential path which is satisfied with probability 2^{-376}, while the probability to find a pair of texts with the same plaintext and ciphertext differences by a random permutation is 2^{-384}. Let us denote pairs that satisfy the path by *right pairs* and that do not satisfy the path by *wrong pairs*. At the first stage of the attack, we need to collect only right pairs. Because the probability of the path is higher than the random case, we can easily detect right pairs in this attack. A simple key-recovery method recovers the key with 2^{251} CP, 2^{288} computations, and 2^{128} memory. Furthermore, we optimize its time complexity to 2^{113} by applying the early aborting technique [7,8] originally proposed by Lu, Kim, and Dunkelman [7].

In our 13-round attack, we use the differential path with probability 2^{-470}, while the probability to find a pair of texts with the same plaintext and ciphertext differences by a random permutation is 2^{-384}. Hence, right pairs cannot be detected easily in the attack. To solve this problem, we devise a technique to efficiently filter out wrong pairs. This technique comes from the general idea of neutral bit originally proposed by Biham and Chen [2].

Roughly speaking of our technique, we modify a part of plaintexts so that the modified paired values never break the differential path for the first several rounds. Hence, if the pair is a right pair, the second pair satisfying the whole path can be obtained faster than the wrong pairs. With this idea, wrong pairs can be filtered out. As a result, the key is recovered with 2^{469} CP, 2^{308} computations, and 2^{128} memory. Our attacks are currently best key-recovery attacks against reduced-round 3D. Table 1 summarizes previous key-recovery attacks and ours.

This paper is organized as follows: in Sect. 2 we describe 3D. In Sect. 3 we describe the previous results for 3D. In Sect. 4 we present our 11-round key-recovery attack and its optimization by the early aborting technique. In Sect. 5 we present our technique to detect right pairs, and extend our attack to 13-rounds. Finally, Sect. 6 concludes this paper.

Table 1. A comparison of previous results with our new attacks under key-recovery situation

Reference	Attack	Rounds	Data	Time	Memory
[10]	Multiset	4.75	2^9CP	$2^{19.5}$	2^8
[10]	ID	5.75	2^{36}CP	$2^{65.5}$	2^{32}
[10]	Multiset	5.75	2^{129}CP	2^{139}	2^{128}
[11]	ID	6	2^{256}CC	2^{256}	2^{256}
[11]	ID	10	2^{501}CP	2^{401}	2^{311}
Ours (Sect. 4:*Scenario* 1)	TD	11	2^{251}CP	2^{288}	2^{128}
Ours (Sect. 4:*Scenario* 2)	TD with EAT	11	2^{252}CP	2^{113}	2^{128}
Ours (Sect. 5:*Scenario* 3)	TD	13	2^{469}CP	2^{308}	2^{128}

ID: Impossible Differential attack; TD: Truncated Differential attack; EAT: Early Aborting Technique; CP: Chosen Plaintext; CC: Chosen Ciphertext

2   Description of 3D Block Cipher

The 3D cipher has an SPN structure. The recommended number of rounds r is 22. 512-bit message blocks and the secret key are represented as 3-dimensional cubes ($4 \times 4 \times 4$ state of bytes) or 4×16 matrices. The state of 64-byte data block $A = (a_0, a_1, ..., a_{63})$ is denoted by

$$A = \begin{pmatrix} a_0 & a_4 & a_8 & a_{12} & a_{16} & a_{20} & a_{24} & a_{28} & a_{32} & a_{36} & a_{40} & a_{44} & a_{48} & a_{52} & a_{56} & a_{60} \\ a_1 & a_5 & a_9 & a_{13} & a_{17} & a_{21} & a_{25} & a_{29} & a_{33} & a_{37} & a_{41} & a_{45} & a_{49} & a_{53} & a_{57} & a_{61} \\ a_2 & a_6 & a_{10} & a_{14} & a_{18} & a_{22} & a_{26} & a_{30} & a_{34} & a_{38} & a_{42} & a_{46} & a_{50} & a_{54} & a_{58} & a_{62} \\ a_3 & a_7 & a_{11} & a_{15} & a_{19} & a_{23} & a_{27} & a_{31} & a_{35} & a_{39} & a_{43} & a_{47} & a_{51} & a_{55} & a_{59} & a_{63} \end{pmatrix}. \tag{1}$$

The i-th round of 3D $(0 \leq i \leq r - 1)$ can be denoted by

$$\tau_i(X) = \pi \circ \theta_{i \bmod 2 + 1} \circ \gamma \circ \kappa_i(X). \tag{2}$$

The round transformations of 3D are briefly described here.

- κ_i: bitwise xor with a 512-bit round subkey, equivalent to AddRoundKey in AES;
- γ: a byte-wise S-box application. The S-box of 3D is exactly the same permutation as SubBytes in AES;
- θ_1, θ_2: equivalent to ShiftRows in AES but applied to each 4×4 square bytes of the state alternately; θ_1 in the odd-numbered rounds, θ_2 in the even-numbered rounds. We describe the transition by θ in Appendix A;
- π: matrix multiplication with columns of the state, equivalent to MixColumns in AES. The values of matrix were originally presented in [1]. The matrix has branch number 5.

For r-round 3D the round function is iterated $r - 1$ times, and in the last round the π function is replaced by the round key κ_r.

The key-schedule of 3D follows a similar framework as its encryption. For r-round 3D encryption and decryption, $(r + 1)$ 512-bit subkeys are needed. The user key $K = \kappa_0$. The i-th subkey κ_i $(1 \leq i \leq r)$ can be denoted by

$$\kappa_i = \pi \circ \theta_{i \bmod 2 + 1} \circ \gamma' \circ \kappa^*(\kappa_{i-1}). \tag{3}$$

The key-schedule works as follows:

- κ^*: bitwise xor with a 512-bit constant matrix depending on the number of rounds r;
- γ': a byte-wise S-box application to alternate columns of the state;
- θ_1, θ_2, π: these transformations are the same as encryption.

Each round transformation stands for a fraction of 0.25 (a quarter) of one round. Thus, we use the following notation: $\sharp x.yz$ denotes the number of rounds. For example, $\sharp 0$ indicates the input of 3D, and $\sharp 1.75$ indicates the intermediate state after the application of θ_2 in the second round and before the application of π in the second round.

3   Previous Works on 3D Block Cipher

In this section, in particular, we show previous results against 3D as the secret-key-type attacks. In [10], Nakahara proposed several approaches of cryptanalysis on reduced-round 3D. Among those approaches, he discussed the truncated differential cryptanalysis. He proposed a truncated differential path on 6-round 3D, which transmits the number of differences $16 \xrightarrow{1R} 16 \xrightarrow{2R} 4 \xrightarrow{3R} 16 \xrightarrow{4R} 4 \xrightarrow{5R} 16 \xrightarrow{6R} 4$. In the differential path, an attacker can use a pool of 2^{128} CP with difference at bytes in positions $(0, 5, 10, 15, 16, 21, 26, 31, 32, 37, 42, 47, 48, 53, 58, 63)$. This pool leads to about 2^{255} input pairs. The output difference contains 60 non-zero byte differences. $2^{255} \times (2^{-8})^{60} = 2^{-417} < 1$ pairs satisfy the output difference of his differential path. Thus, he concluded that there is no pair that satisfies the 6-round differential path. Since then, the truncated differential attack has not been discussed more on 3D.

Later, Nakahara improved impossible-differential attack and multiset attack to 3D [11]. His ID attack covering 10-round 3D with the time complexity of 2^{401}, the data complexity of 2^{501} CP, and the memory requirement of 2^{311} was the previous best key-recovery attack on the reduced-round 3D. We summarize these previously known results in Table 1.

4   Key-Recovery Attack on 11-Round 3D Block Cipher

In this section, firstly, we describe an 11-round truncated differential path. Secondly, we describe how to get pairs which follow the truncated differential path. In total, we will find three such pairs. Thirdly, we present how to recover the secret key. Fourth, we describe the early aborting technique and then we show how to reduce the complexity of recovering the secret key. Finally, we conclude our attack.

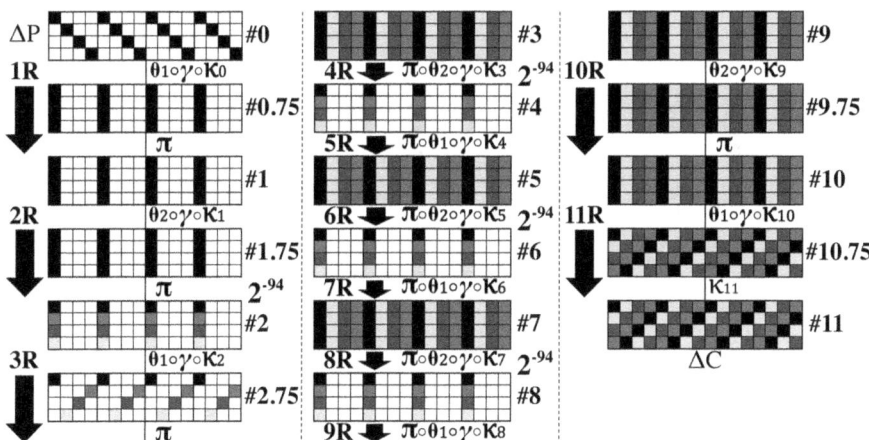

Fig. 2. Truncated differential path on 11-round 3D. Black states denote non-zero difference. White states denote zero difference. Cyan (gray), magenta (dark gray), and yellow (light gray) bytes represent four variants of our differential path (colors in brackets correspond to grayscale printing).

4.1 Truncated Differential Path

Our truncated differential path is shown in Fig. 2, where ΔP indicates the input differences, ΔC indicates the four variants of output differences. Black bytes indicate non-zero differences, and white bytes indicate zero difference. We describe the four variants of ΔC in Sect. 4.1 steps 2 and 3. The truncated differential path in Fig. 2 can be divided into three parts. In the following, we describe the three parts of the attack in detail.

1. The first part is from state $\sharp 0$ to $\sharp 1$. An adversary chooses 16-byte differences for state $\sharp 0$ diagonally. The 16-byte differences reach the 16-byte differences on the state $\sharp 1$ with the probability of almost 1.
2. The second part consists of 2 rounds, and is repeated four times; from state $\sharp 1$ to $\sharp 3$, from state $\sharp 3$ to $\sharp 5$, from state $\sharp 5$ to $\sharp 7$, and from state $\sharp 7$ to $\sharp 9$. We describe the transition by exemplifying the case that is from state $\sharp 1$ to $\sharp 3$. Focus on only the black bytes in those states. The adversary constructs such a truncated differential trail through a π function between state $\sharp 1.75$ and state $\sharp 2$ in a probabilistic way. On the each full-active column, the differences reduce four bytes to one byte with the probability of about $2^{-8\times 3} = 2^{-24}$. There are four full-active columns in state $\sharp 1.75$, thus the total probability is about $2^{-24\times 4} = 2^{-96}$. Moreover, we can use four variants of the difference transition from 16 bytes to 4 bytes on our attack scheme as in Fig. 3. In other words, we can attack the reduced-round 3D as long as the four active bytes in state $\sharp 2$ are $(a_0, a_{16}, a_{32}, a_{48})$, $(a_1, a_{17}, a_{33}, a_{49})$, $(a_2, a_{18}, a_{34}, a_{50})$, or $(a_3, a_{19}, a_{35}, a_{51})$. As a result, the probability of the path becomes four times higher; $2^{-96} \times 4 = 2^{-94}$. Repeating this part four times, so the total probability from state $\sharp 1$ to $\sharp 9$ is about $2^{-94\times 4} = 2^{-376}$.

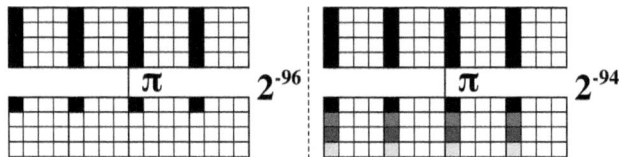

Fig. 3. Four variants of the differences transition through the π function

3. The third part is from states $\sharp 9$ to $\sharp 11$. Due to the second part, there are four variant of the differences on state $\sharp 9$. The vertical 16-byte differences on state $\sharp 9$ reach the same colored diagonal 16-byte differences on state $\sharp 11$ with the probability of about 1.

The total probability to find a *right pair* is about 2^{-376}. On the other hand, the probability to find such a pair in the random case is about $2^{-8\times 48} \times 4 = 2^{-382}$. A pair will be denoted as a *wrong pair* if it satisfies the ΔP and ΔC but does not follow the truncated differential path. For $2^{-376} > 2^{-382}$, the adversary can obtain one pair that follows the truncated differential path with a higher probability than the case that does do not follow the path. We discuss the accurate probability in Sect. 4.5.

4.2 How to Obtain Chosen Plaintext

In this section, we describe how to obtain the CP. When the adversary obtains 2^{376} pairs of $(P, P \oplus \Delta P)$, we assume he obtains one pair which fills the truncated differential path in Fig. 2. Recall he needs three pairs which satisfy the truncated differential path to recover a user key, therefore he needs to obtain $3 \times 2^{376} \approx 2^{378}$ pairs. To obtain such pairs, the adversary makes many CP structures as follows:

1. fix non-active 48-byte values of P.
2. set all the possible values (2^{128} possibilities) on the diagonal active 16-byte of P and query them to the encryption oracle.
3. make 2^{255} input and output pairs from former 2^{128} queried values.
4. repeat the above steps 2^{123} times, and obtain $2^{123+255} = 2^{378}$ pairs.

In total, the adversary queries $2^{128+123} = 2^{251}$ CP to the encryption oracle, and obtains three pairs which follow the truncated differential path from 2^{378} pairs.

4.3 How to Recover a User Key

In this section, we describe how to recover a user key from the described three pairs. In Fig. 4 and Fig. 5, the bytes noted "g" indicate guessed bytes or computed bytes for the adversary. On the other hand, stripe bytes are unknown bytes for the adversary. Figure 4 shows the first 1-round transition of the key-schedule. The adversary guesses the values of the 28 bytes of κ_0 (see Fig. 4). There are $2^{8 \times 28} = 2^{224}$ key candidates of the 28 bytes in total. Then, the attack steps are as follows:

1. guess possible values of 28 bytes of κ_0 denoted by "g" and then compute 16 bytes of κ_1.

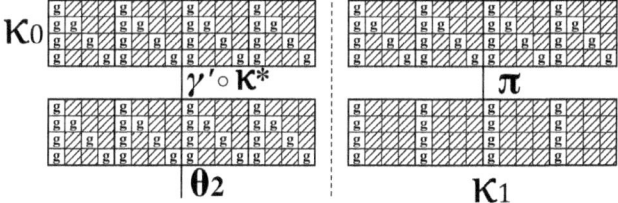

Fig. 4. The first 1-round key-schedule. "g" indicates guessed or computed value. Stripe bytes indicate unknown values.

2. compute the values P and $P \oplus \Delta P$ with the guessed key (see Fig. 5). The adversary can compute the state ♯2 named as state X from the P and the guessed key. In a similar way, he can compute the state ♯2 named as state X' from the $P \oplus \Delta P$ and the guessed key.

3. recall P and $P \oplus \Delta P$ satisfy the truncated differential path. A state of $X \oplus X'$ satisfies the truncated differential state ♯2 in Fig. 2 with the probability of 2^{-94}. Thus, the adversary checks whether the $X \oplus X'$ satisfies the differential transition under the guessed key candidate.

4. repeat the above steps with all the possible values on the "g" bytes of the κ_0. We can reduce the key space to $2^{224-94} = 2^{130}$.

5. using three pairs, we can reduce the key space $2^{224-282} < 1$. Hence, the only correct candidate remains after the above steps.

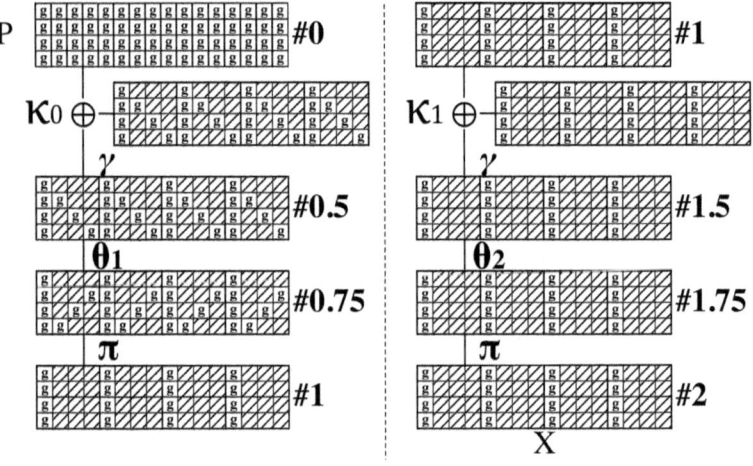

Fig. 5. Transition of guessed or computed values to recover κ_0

Thus this offline computation is $6 \times 2^{224} \times \frac{2}{11} \approx 2^{225}$ times of 1-round computation. Finally, he recovers these 28-byte of κ_0. For recovering the remaining unknown 36-byte candidates of κ_0, we present the procedure as follows:

Scenario 1

    Recover the remaining bytes exhaustively. The total amount of the data is 2^{251} CP and the offline computation is $2^{225} + 2^{8 \times 36} \approx 2^{288}$ times of 1-round computation. This attack requires 2^{128} states memory to create pairs.

4.4 Differential Attack with Early Aborting Technique

In this section, we propose how to reduce the data complexity to recover a user key by applying the early aborting technique. The early aborting technique was presented by Lu *et. al* in 2008 [7]. By using this technique, we can analyze a transition of differences even though only partial values of the transition are known.

We need a pre-computation for the technique. Fig. 6 focuses the transition of the first column (a_0, a_1, a_2, a_3) from state $\sharp 1.75$ to $\sharp 2$ in Fig. 8. The adversary computes backward all the possible differences of the first column which fill the truncated differential path in state $\sharp 2$ $((2^8 - 1) \times 4$ candidates$)$ to state $\sharp 1.75$. For four columns (the first column, the fifth column, the ninth column, and the thirteenth column), it needs about 2^{8+2+2} times of one-column π^{-1} computations in total. Since, he stores the computations in a table as the valid transitions from state $\sharp 1.75$ to $\sharp 2$.

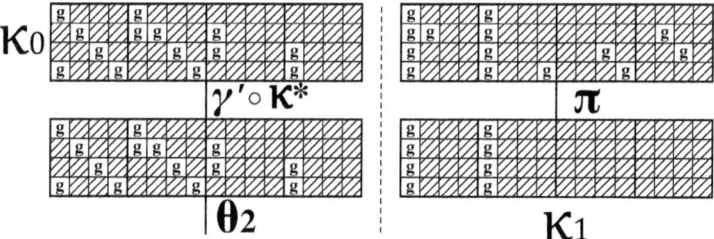

Fig. 6. Transition of differential from state $\sharp 1.75$ to $\sharp 2$ at first column with early aborting technique. Δ in a white block indicates computed non-zero difference. Δ in a black block indicates non-zero difference but cannot compute. 0 indicates zero difference. Stripe block indicates unknown bytes.

We describe how to reduce the data complexity as follows:

Scenario 2

1. guess possible values of 14 bytes of κ_0 denoted by "g" and then compute 8 bytes of κ_1 in Fig. 7.

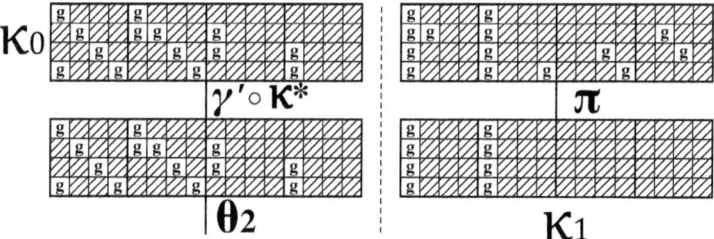

Fig. 7. The first 1-round key-schedule with early aborting technique

2. compute the state $\sharp 1.75$ from the P and the guessed key (see Fig. 8). The adversary also computes the state $\sharp 1.75$ from the $P \oplus \Delta P$ and the guessed key. Then he can compute the difference at bytes in positions $(0, 1, 16, 19, 34, 35, 49, 50)$.
3. use early aborting technique in this step. The adversary does not know the values of a_2 and a_3 in state $\sharp 1.75$. So he checks whether the computed differences satisfy the differences of a_0 and a_1 of state $\sharp 1.75$ computed

in the step 2 by using the table of the pre-computation. The probability is about $\frac{2^8-1}{(2^8-1)\times(2^8-1)} \times 4 = 2^{-6}$. Thus he can reduce the key space $2^{8\times14-6} = 2^{106}$.

4. check whether the differences of the fifth column, the ninth column, and the thirteenth column satisfy the differential transition similarly. He can reduce the key space $2^{112-6\times4} = 2^{88}$. On this *scenario*, he uses five pairs which follow the truncated differential path. Thus he repeats the above steps four times with the right pairs. In total the key space reduces to $2^{112-24\times5} < 1$.

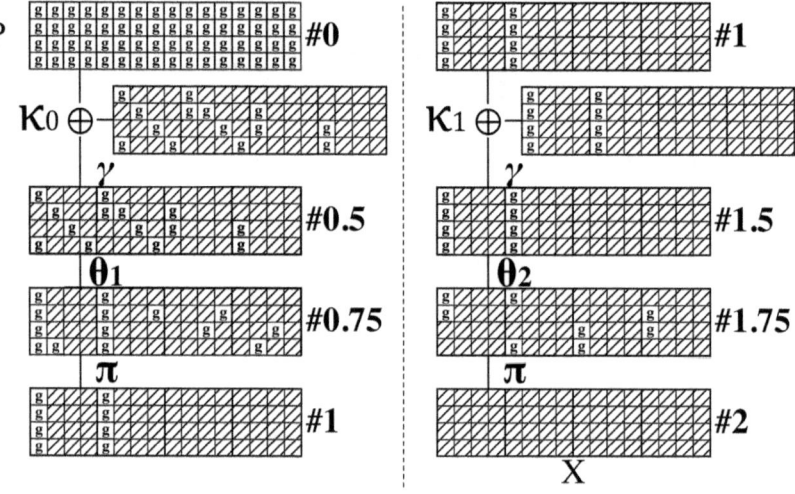

Fig. 8. Transition of guessed or computed values to recover κ_0 with early aborting technique

This procedure needs the 2-round computation from state ♯0 to ♯2. Thus this offline computation is $10\times2^{112}\times\frac{2}{11} \approx 2^{113}$ times of 1-round computation and 2^{12} times of pre-computations. Finally, he recovers these 14-byte of κ_0. For remaining unknown 50-byte candidates of κ_0, repeat the procedure with early aborting technique as follows:

1. guess 7 bytes of κ_{0_2} denoted by "g_2" in Fig. 9 and compute the above four steps similarly. The adversary has already recovered 14 bytes of κ_0 denoted as gray bytes in Fig. 9). Thus he computes the difference at bytes in positions $(0, 1, 16, 19, 34, 35, 49, 50)$ with the partial recovered key. Additionally, he computes the difference at bytes in positions $(2, 17, 32, 51)$ in state ♯1.75 with the guessed 7 bytes. By checking whether the computed differences in state ♯1.75 satisfy the transition with the table of the pre-computation, he can reduce the key space and recover the 7 bytes. On this procedures, the adversary uses the above five right pairs. The complexity to recover 7 bytes are lower clearly than 2^{113} times of 1-round encryption.

2. guess 7 bytes of κ_{0_3} denoted by "g_3" in the same way. The complexity to recover the 7 bytes are also lower than 2^{113} times of 1-round encryption.

Fig. 9. Additional guessed 7 bytes to recover κ_0. Gray bytes denotes known value.

3. guess 10 bytes of κ_{0_4} denoted by "g_4" in Fig. 10. On the step, the adversary needs to make other four plaintext/ciphertext pairs which follow the $\Delta P'$ and the $\Delta C'$ and a similar truncated differential path to above truncated differential path. The differences of the $\Delta P'$ reach the bytes in positions $(4, 5, 6, 7, 20, 21, 22, 23, 36, 37, 38, 39, 52, 53, 54, 55)$ in state $\sharp 1.75$. In other words, he reduces the key space by checking whether the computed differences of the second, sixth, tenth, and fourteenth column satisfy the transition from state $\sharp 1.75$ to $\sharp 2$. The number of guessed key candidates is $2^{8 \times 10}$. So the four pairs which satisfy the path are needed on recovering the 10 bytes, because of $2^{80-24 \times 4} < 1$. The complexity to recover the 10 bytes are lower clearly than 2^{113} times of 1-round encryption.

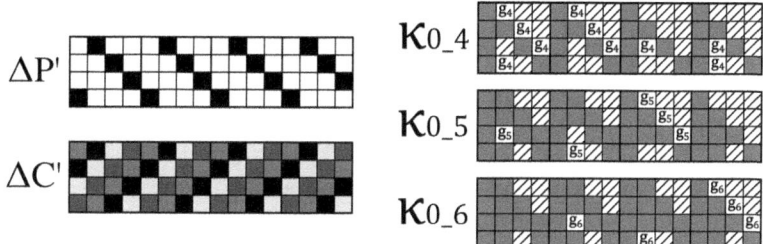

Fig. 10. Left: Another truncated differential path consisting of $\Delta P''$ and $\Delta C''$, Right: Additional guessed 10 and 5 bytes to recover κ_0

4. guess 5 bytes of κ_{0_5} denoted by "g_5" and 5 bytes of κ_{0_6} ("g_6") in Fig. 10 and recover the key like step 1 and 2 with the pairs of $\Delta P'$ and $\Delta C'$. The complexity to recover each 5 bytes are also lower clearly than 2^{113} times of 1-round encryption.

5. guess 7 bytes of κ_{0_7} ("g_7") in Fig. 11 and repeat the above procedure with the three pairs which follow the $\Delta P''$ and $\Delta C''$ like step 3. The three pairs which satisfy the path are needed on recovering the 7 bytes, because of $2^{8 \times 7 - 24 \times 3} < 1$.

The time complexity and memory requirement of the pre-computation are negligible compared with those of the main computation. In total the adversary needs $5 + 4 + 3 = 12$ pairs which follow the differential paths to recover the $14 + 7 + 7 + 10 + 5 + 5 + 7 = 55$ bytes of the κ_0. After all, recover the remaining 9 bytes exhaustively with the complexity of $2^{8 \times 9} = 2^{72}$. Thus the total offline computation is about 2^{113} times of 1-round computation and the data complexity is about 2^{252} CP.

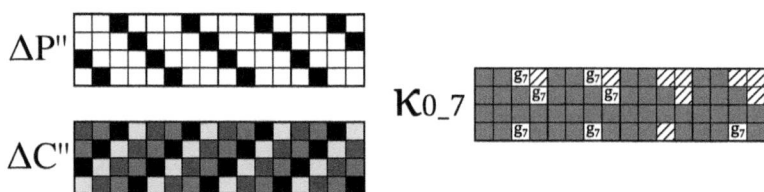

Fig. 11. Left: Another truncated differential path consisting of $\Delta P''$ and $\Delta C''$, Right: Additional guessed 7 bytes to recover κ_0

4.5   Conclusion of 11-Round Attack

In this section we conclude the 11-round attack and refer to the success probability of our attack. On Section 4.2, we have to consider the two probabilistic events on obtaining CP. The first one is whether we can obtain a pair which satisfies the input/output differential (ΔP, ΔC). Querying one pair to the encryption oracle, the probability that we cannot obtain the pair values is about $1 - 2^{-376}$. Thus, the probability that we cannot obtain any right pair from the 2^{376} is as:

$$(1 - 2^{-376})^{2^{376}} \approx \lim_{n \to \infty} (1 - 2^{-n})^{2^n} = e^{-1}. \tag{4}$$

In other words, the probability that we can obtain one right pair is described as:

$$Pr_1 = 1 - e^{-1}. \tag{5}$$

The other is whether the obtained pair follows the truncated differential path or does not follow. For $2^{-376} > 2^{-382}$, the probability that the obtained pair follows the path is as:

$$Pr_2 = 1 - 2^{-382+376} = 1 - 2^{-6}. \tag{6}$$

In total, the probability to obtain n right pairs is expressed as:

$$Pr_3(n) = (Pr_1 \times Pr_2)^n = \left\{ (1 - e^{-1})(1 - 2^{-6}) \right\}^n \approx 0.6222^n. \tag{7}$$

On 11-round attack, we need three pairs in *scenario* 1, and 12 pairs in *scenario* 2. For (7), the total probabilities that we succeed at the attack are as follows:

scenario **1** : $Pr_3(3) \approx 0.2409$.
scenario **2** : $Pr_3(12) \approx 0.0034$.

Table 2 lists the results of 11-round key-recovery attack under two *scenarios*. We note that the success probabilities of the attacks can increase about 1 by querying more CP. For (4), when we obtain a right pair from 2^{378} pairs, (4) decreases to $(1 - 2^{-376})^{2^{378}} \approx e^{-4}$. Thus (5) increases to $1 - e^{-4} \approx 0.9817$, and (7) also increases to about 1 for both *scenarios*. In this case, we need 2^{252} CP in *scenario* 1, and 2^{254} CP in *scenario* 2.

Table 2. Results of our 11-round key-recovery attacks

Reference	Attack	Rounds	Data	Time	Memory	Probability
scenario 1	TD	11	2^{251}CP	2^{288}	2^{128}	0.2409
scenario 2	TD with EAT	11	2^{252}CP	2^{113}	2^{128}	0.0034

5   Extended Attack on 13-Round 3D Block Cipher

On our attack against 13-round 3D, a user key is recovered in the same way as 11-round attack. On the other hand, we need to improve the way to obtain CP. Hence, we mainly describe how to distinguish a right pair from wrong pairs. In our technique, we modify the values of the pairs but keep them to satisfy the differential path from state ♯0 to ♯2. Hence, if the modified pair is a right pair, the pair satisfying the whole path can be obtained faster than the wrong pairs. Thus, we can generate another right pair from a right pair and wrong pairs. This technique comes from the general ideas of message modification [14,15,16,17] and especially neutral bit [2].

5.1   Truncated Differential Path

Fig. 12 indicates the truncated differential path on the 13-round 3D. The 13-round path is very similar to that of 11 rounds. The adversary needs several plaintext/ciphertext pairs which follow the truncated differential path. The total probability to obtain one pair which follows the differential path is about $2^{-94 \times 5} = 2^{-470}$. Remember that the probability to find a pair which fills the ΔP and ΔC but does not satisfy the truncated differential path is about 2^{-382}. For $2^{382-470} = 2^{-88}$, this occurrence probability of the right pair is 2^{-88} of the random case. When he obtains one pair which satisfies ΔP and ΔC and the path, he will also obtain $2^{470-382} = 2^{88}$ wrong pairs.

5.2   How to Obtain Another Right Pair

The adversary needs to distinguish a right pair from the other 2^{88} wrong pairs. We note that the vertical 16 bytes, $(a_0, ..., a_3, a_{16}, ..., a_{19}, a_{32}, ..., a_{35}, a_{48}, ..., a_{51})$, in state ♯1 only depend on the diagonal active 16 bytes, $(a_0, a_5, a_{10}, a_{15}, a_{16}, a_{21}, a_{26}, a_{31}, a_{32}, a_{37}, a_{42}, a_{47}, a_{48}, a_{53}, a_{58}, a_{63})$, in ΔP. In other words, the vertical 16 bytes are independent of the other 48 bytes in ΔP. Exploiting this characteristic, we can find a right pair as follows:

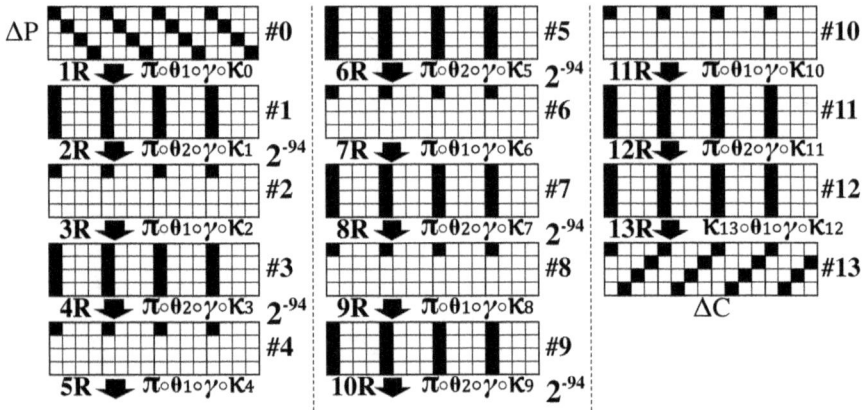

Fig. 12. Truncated differential path on 13-round 3D. Black bytes denote non-zero difference. White bytes denote zero difference.

1. choose one pair $(P, P \oplus \Delta P)$ from the $2^{88} + 1$ pairs.
2. fix their values of the above diagonal 16 bytes which hold differential and change the values of the remaining 48 non-active bytes as they satisfy ΔP. Thus we obtain a new pair $(P', P' \oplus \Delta P)$. If the pair of $(P, P \oplus \Delta P)$ is a right pair, $(P', P' \oplus \Delta P)$ also satisfy the differential state ♯2 with a probability of 1 due to the described independence.
3. check whether P' and $P' \oplus \Delta P$ satisfies the truncated differential path from state ♯2 to ♯13. The probability increases from 2^{-470} to 2^{-376}. We query P' and $P' \oplus \Delta P$ to the encryption oracle with changing the values of 48 non-active bytes. This procedure requires $2 \times 2^{376} = 2^{377}$ CP.
4. repeat the above procedure for all of the 2^{88} pairs. The wrong pairs still remain $2^{88} \times 2^{376-382} = 2^{82}$ pairs. In other words, 2^{82} pairs follow the differential path from state ♯0 to ♯2, but do not follow the differential path from ♯2 to ♯13. The procedure reduces 2^6 wrong pairs.

The adversary needs to query $2^{128} \times 2^{470-255} = 2^{343}$ CP to the encryption oracle to find $2^{88} + 1$ pairs. Furthermore he needs $2^{377} \times 2^{88} \approx 2^{465}$ CP to reduce 2^6 wrong pairs. As a result, $2^{343} + 2^{465} \approx 2^{465}$ CP are necessary to obtain one right pair and 2^{82} wrong pairs.

5.3   How to Recover a User Key

Scenario 3

Recall *scenario* 1 of the 11-round attack, he guesses the same 28-byte values of κ_0. One pair which follows the truncated differential path reduces the key space 2^{-94}. However he has 2^{82} wrong pairs, so he can reduce the key space to $2^{224-94+82} = 2^{212}$. Repeating all the above steps of 13-round attack 19 times, he reduces the key space to $2^{224-12 \times 19} = 1$. Finally, he recovers the 28-byte of κ_0 with the time complexity of $2^{224+82} \times 19 \approx 2^{310}$, the data complexity of

$2^{465} \times 19 \approx 2^{469}$ CP, and the memory requirement of 2^{128}. For the remaining 36 bytes, he recovers the key exhaustively. The total offline computation is about $2^{310} \times \frac{2}{13} + 2^{36 \times 8} \times \frac{1}{13} \approx 2^{308}$ times of 1 round computation.

5.4 Conclusion of 13-Round Attack

In this section, we conclude the 13-round attack and refer to the success probability of our attack. We need the time complexity of 2^{308}, the data complexity of 2^{469}CP, and the memory requirement of 2^{128} on the attack.

Recall (5), let Pr_4 be probability that we can obtain a right pair from 2^{470} pairs;

$$Pr_4 = 1 - (1 - 2^{-470})^{2^{470}} \approx 1 - e^{-1}. \qquad (8)$$

During reducing the wrong pairs, the probability that P' and $P' \oplus \Delta P$ created from the right pair remains after 2^{377} query is as:

$$Pr_5 = 1 - (1 - 2^{-377})^{2^{377}} \approx 1 - e^{-1}. \qquad (9)$$

So the probability that we can obtain a right pair is $Pr_4 \times Pr_5$. In total, the probability to obtain 19 right pairs is as:

$$Pr_6 = (Pr_4 \times Pr_5)^{16} = ((1 - e^{-1})(1 - e^{-1}))^{19} \approx 3.0 \times 10^{-9}. \qquad (10)$$

Recall Sect. 4.5, (10) increases about 1 by querying more CP. By querying 2^{346} CP for one right pairs, we can obtain 2^{473} pairs and (8) increases to $1 - (1 - 2^{-470})^{2^{473}} \approx 1 - e^{-8}$. Then, we also obtain about $2^{88+3} = 2^{91}$ wrong pairs. On the step of reducing wrong pairs (see Section 5.2, step 3), (9) also increases by querying more CP. By querying 2^{379} CP, (9) increases to $1 - (1 - 2^{-376})^{2^{379}} \approx 1 - e^{-8}$. Due to an increase of wrong pairs, we need to repeat all the above steps more 6 times to recover the 28-byte guessed key. And then, (10) increases to $((1 - e^{-8})(1 - e^{-8}))^{19+6} \approx 1$. In total, we need $2^{346} + 2^{379+91} \approx 2^{470}$ CP to recover the key with the probability of about 1. Thus, we can recover the user key of the 13-round 3D.

6 Conclusion

In this paper, we presented new key-recovery attacks on the 11- and 13-round 3D, by applying the truncated differential cryptanalysis technique. We showed that the truncated differential cryptanalysis can attack effectively on more than 5-round 3D. In addition we optimized the time complexity of our 11-round attack by applying the early aborting technique. Furthermore, we proposed a technique to exploit the truncated differential path with lower occurrence probability than that of a random case. This technique comes from the neutral bit concept.

Table 1 lists the complexities of previous and our new attacks described in this paper. Our attack on 13-round 3D is the currently best one on reduced-round

3D with the time complexity of 2^{308}, the data complexity of 2^{469} CP, and the memory requirement of 2^{128}.

We examined not only the encryption transition but also the key-schedule transition to construct our attack schemes. The encryption starts with θ_1. On the other hand, the key-schedule starts with θ_2. That is to say, θ_1 and θ_2 transformations are applied to the encryption and the key-schedule in reverse order. Through the examination, we deem that the inverted design makes very hard to construct efficient truncated differential paths on more than 14 rounds.

Acknowledgements. Lei Wang was supported by Grant-in-Aid for JSPS Fellows (23001043).

References

1. Barreto, P.S.L.M., Rijmen, V.: The ANUBIS Block Cipher. In: 1st NESSIE Workshop, Heverlee, Belgiunm (2000)
2. Biham, E., Chen, R.: Near-Collisions of SHA-0. In: Franklin, M.K. (ed.) CRYPTO 2004. LNCS, vol. 3152, pp. 290–305. Springer, Heidelberg (2004)
3. Cramer, R. (ed.): EUROCRYPT 2005. LNCS, vol. 3494. Springer, Heidelberg (2005)
4. Dong, L., Wu, W., Wu, S., Zou, J.: Known-Key Distinguisher on Round-Reduced 3D Block Cipher. In: Jung, S. (ed.) WISA 2011. LNCS, vol. 7115, pp. 55–69. Springer, Heidelberg (2011)
5. Knudsen, L.R.: DEAL -A 128-bit Block Cipher. Technical report no. 151, Department of Informatics, University of Bergen (1998), http://www2.mat.dtu.dk/people/Lars.R.Knudsen/newblock.html
6. Knudsen, L.R., Berson, T.A.: Truncated Differentials of SAFER. In: Gollmann, D. (ed.) FSE 1996. LNCS, vol. 1039, pp. 15–26. Springer, Heidelberg (1996)
7. Lu, J., Kim, J., Keller, N., Dunkelman, O.: Improving the Efficiency of Impossible Differential Cryptanalysis of Reduced Camellia and MISTY1. In: Malkin, T. (ed.) CT-RSA 2008. LNCS, vol. 4964, pp. 370–386. Springer, Heidelberg (2008)
8. Lu, J., Wei, Y., Kim, J., Fouque, P.A.: Cryptanalysis of Reduced Versions of the Camellia Block Cipher. In: SAC 2011 (2011) (to appear)
9. Matusiewicz, K., Naya-Plasencia, M., Nikolić, I., Sasaki, Y., Schläffer, M.: Rebound Attack on the Full LANE Compression Function. In: Matsui, M. (ed.) ASIACRYPT 2009. LNCS, vol. 5912, pp. 106–125. Springer, Heidelberg (2009)
10. Nakahara Jr., J.: 3D: A Three-Dimensional Block Cipher. In: Franklin, M.K., Hui, L.C.K., Wong, D.S. (eds.) CANS 2008. LNCS, vol. 5339, pp. 252–267. Springer, Heidelberg (2008)
11. Nakahara Jr, J.: New Impossible Differential and Known-Key Distinguishers for the 3D Cipher. In: Bao, F., Weng, J. (eds.) ISPEC 2011. LNCS, vol. 6672, pp. 208–221. Springer, Heidelberg (2011)
12. National Institute of Standards and Technology: Specification for the Advanced Encryption Standard (AES). In: Federal Information Processing Standards Publication 197 (2001), http://csrc.nist.gov/publications/fips/fips197/fips-197.pdf
13. Shoup, V. (ed.): CRYPTO 2005. LNCS, vol. 3621. Springer, Heidelberg (2005)

14. Wang, X., Lai, X., Feng, D., Chen, H., Yu, X.: Cryptanalysis of the Hash Functions MD4 and RIPEMD. In: Cramer [3], pp. 1–18
15. Wang, X., Yin, Y.L., Yu, H.: Finding Collisions in the Full SHA-1. In: Shoup [13], pp. 17–36
16. Wang, X., Yu, H.: How to Break MD5 and Other Hash Functions. In: Cramer [3], pp. 19–35
17. Wang, X., Yu, H., Yin, Y.L.: Efficient Collision Search Attacks on SHA-0. In: Shoup [13], pp. 1–16

A   Rotations of Byte Positions by θ Function

θ_1 transforms (1) into

$$
\begin{pmatrix}
a_0 & a_4 & a_8 & a_{12} & a_{16} & a_{20} & a_{24} & a_{28} & a_{32} & a_{36} & a_{40} & a_{44} & a_{48} & a_{52} & a_{56} & a_{60} \\
a_5 & a_9 & a_{13} & a_1 & a_{21} & a_{25} & a_{29} & a_{17} & a_{37} & a_{41} & a_{45} & a_{33} & a_{53} & a_{57} & a_{61} & a_{49} \\
a_{10} & a_{14} & a_2 & a_6 & a_{26} & a_{30} & a_{18} & a_{22} & a_{42} & a_{46} & a_{34} & a_{38} & a_{58} & a_{62} & a_{50} & a_{54} \\
a_{15} & a_3 & a_7 & a_{11} & a_{31} & a_{19} & a_{23} & a_{27} & a_{47} & a_{35} & a_{39} & a_{43} & a_{63} & a_{51} & a_{55} & a_{59}
\end{pmatrix},
\tag{11}
$$

and θ_2 transforms (1) into

$$
\begin{pmatrix}
a_0 & a_4 & a_8 & a_{12} & a_{16} & a_{20} & a_{24} & a_{28} & a_{32} & a_{36} & a_{40} & a_{44} & a_{48} & a_{52} & a_{56} & a_{60} \\
a_{17} & a_{21} & a_{25} & a_{29} & a_{33} & a_{37} & a_{41} & a_{45} & a_{49} & a_{53} & a_{57} & a_{61} & a_1 & a_5 & a_9 & a_{13} \\
a_{34} & a_{38} & a_{42} & a_{46} & a_{50} & a_{54} & a_{58} & a_{62} & a_2 & a_6 & a_{10} & a_{14} & a_{18} & a_{22} & a_{26} & a_{30} \\
a_{51} & a_{55} & a_{59} & a_{63} & a_3 & a_7 & a_{11} & a_{15} & a_{19} & a_{23} & a_{27} & a_{31} & a_{35} & a_{39} & a_{43} & a_{47}
\end{pmatrix}.
\tag{12}
$$

T-out-of-n Distributed Oblivious Transfer Protocols in Non-adaptive and Adaptive Settings

Christian L.F. Corniaux and Hossein Ghodosi

James Cook University, Townsville QLD 4811, Australia
chris.corniaux@my.jcu.edu.au, hossein.ghodosi@jcu.edu.au

Abstract. The unconditionally secure Distributed Oblivious Transfer (DOT) protocol introduced by Naor and Pinkas allows a receiver to contact k servers and obtain one out of two secrets held by a sender. In its generalized version presented by Blundo, D'Arco, De Santis, and Stinson, a receiver can choose one out of n secrets.

In this paper, we introduce three unconditionally secure DOT protocols which allow a receiver to obtain t out of n secrets.

The first protocol allows the receiver to obtain t secrets in one round only, provided she is able to communicate with $k + t - 1$ servers.

The settings of the second and third protocols are adaptive, i.e., the receiver sequentially sends t queries to the servers to obtain t secrets. In the second protocol, the number of receiver's queries is limited unlike in the third one, where the contacted servers need to communicate with each other.

These three protocols, like other unconditionally secure oblivious transfer protocols, guarantee the security of the sender and the privacy of the receiver. In addition, the sender's security is guaranteed against a coalition of the receiver and $k - 1$ servers and, similarly, the receiver's privacy is guaranteed against a coalition of $k - 1$ servers.

Keywords: Cryptographic Protocol, Distributed Oblivious Transfer, Unconditional Security, Adaptive Queries.

1   Introduction

Oblivious Transfer (OT) is a cryptographic protocol which allows two parties to exchange, in total privacy, one or more secret messages. The first OT protocol, introduced by Rabin [14], enables a sender to transmit a message to a receiver in such a way that the receiver gets the message with probability $\frac{1}{2}$ while the sender does not know whether the message was received. Even, Goldreich and Lempel [7] introduced a variant of the original OT for a contract signature application. This OT, identified as OT-$\binom{2}{1}$, is an exchange protocol between a receiver and a sender who has two secret messages; the receiver chooses one of the two messages and the sender transmits the chosen message to the receiver. At the end of the protocol, the sender does not know which message was selected and the receiver knows nothing of the other message.

M.D. Ryan, B. Smyth, and G. Wang (Eds.): ISPEC 2012, LNCS 7232, pp. 126–143, 2012.

A major drawback with OT-$\binom{2}{1}$ and with the more general OT-$\binom{n}{1}$ proposed by Brassard, Crépeau and Roberts [4] is the restriction in the availability of the secret messages, because if the unique sender is unavailable, the receiver cannot execute the protocol. To increase the availability of messages, the sender may distribute them to m servers, like in the first unconditionally secure Distributed Oblivious Transfer (DOT) protocol introduced by Gertner and Malkin [8] in 1997. However, the protocol does not guarantee the messages' confidentiality against curious or corrupted servers. In 2000, Naor and Pinkas [11] introduced an unconditionally secure DOT protocol which takes non-fully trusted servers into account: servers are only provided with parts – called *shares* – of the original messages. In this DOT, denoted (k, m)-DOT-$\binom{2}{1}$, the parties encompass a *sender* who has two secrets, m *servers* owning shares of the secrets, and a *receiver* whose purpose is to obtain one of the two secrets. The protocol itself is composed of two phases: (i) the *set-up phase* and (ii) the *transfer phase*. During the set-up phase, the sender generates a bivariate polynomial Q, determines shares from this polynomial and sends to each of the m servers a different set of shares. In the transfer phase, the receiver chooses the index of a secret and selects k servers she intends to contact. Then, she generates a univariate polynomial Z and sends to each of the k selected servers a value determined by the polynomial Z and the identifier of the server. Each contacted server generates a response based on its program and the value sent by the receiver. The response is sent back to the receiver. After receiving k responses, the receiver is able to determine the chosen secret. In [2,3], Blundo, D'Arco, De Santis and Stinson generalized Naor and Pinkas's protocol to n secrets. Another 1-out-of-n DOT protocol [13] was introduced by Nikov, Nikova, Preenel and Vanderwalle, highlighting the relation between the sender's security and the receiver's privacy.

However, if a receiver wishes to obtain $t > 1$ secrets, these protocols have to be executed t times, involving computation and communication overheads. Note that executing the set-up phase once and the transfer phase t times is not possible without compromising the security of the sender. Bellare and Micali [1] introduced an OT-$\binom{3}{2}$ protocol that can be generalized to an OT-$\binom{n}{n-1}$ protocol. However, this protocol as well as other OT-$\binom{n}{t}$ protocols (e.g., [12]) have been studied in computationally secure settings, not in unconditionally secure settings.

In this paper, we introduce the first unconditionally secure DOT protocol allowing a receiver to contact $k + t - 1$ servers and obtain t out of n secrets ($1 \leq t < n$) in one round only. We also introduce two unconditionally secure DOT protocols which enable a receiver to obtain t secret in an adaptive manner [10] (the choice of one secret depends on the secrets already obtained). Actually, adaptive DOT protocols are motivated by specific oblivious activities like search in databases or consultation of strongly linked documents, like website files.

Recently, Jiang, Li and Li [9] proposed an unconditionally secure DOT protocol with adaptive queries. However, their protocol consists in the repetition of the transfer phase in Nikov et al.'s protocol [13]. This technique does not guarantee the protocol's security against a dishonest – but not malicious – receiver (See Appendix).

Our two unconditionally secure DOT protocols with adaptive queries are adapted from Blundo et al.'s DOT protocol [2,3]. In the first one, the servers receive a list of t elements from the sender and use a different element of the list for each query prepared by the receiver. Thus, the receiver cannot obtain more than t secrets. This model is well adapted to a unique receiver, but for several receivers, we propose a second protocol where the number of queries accepted by the protocol is unlimited. In this second protocol, servers are allowed to communicate with each other and for each query, generate new *ad hoc* secret sharing polynomials.

Like in [11,2,3], our three protocols guarantee the security of the sender and the privacy of the receiver. Furthermore, the sender's security is guaranteed even if the receiver corrupts up to $k - 1$ servers and, symmetrically, the receiver's privacy is guaranteed even if the sender corrupts up to $k - 1$ servers. In addition, the one-round protocol is significantly more efficient than t executions of the (k, m)-DOT-$\binom{n}{1}$ protocol presented in [2,3].

This paper is organized as follows: in Sect. 2, we introduce some definitions and notations, as well as our security model. The three protocols are described, and their security is analysed, in Sects. 3, 4 and 5. Finally, the performance of the protocols is discussed in Sect. 6.

2 Preliminaries

2.1 Notations and Definitions

The settings of the different DOT protocols described in this paper encompass a sender $\mathcal{S}$ who owns n secrets $\omega_1, \ldots, \omega_n$ $(n > 1)$, a receiver $\mathcal{R}$ who wishes to learn t secrets $(1 \leq t < n)$, and m servers $S_1, \ldots, S_m$.

Each protocol is composed of a set-up phase and either one transfer phase (in a non-adaptive setting) or t transfer phases (run 1 to run t, in an adaptive setting). In a non-adaptive setting, the receiver wishes to obtain t secrets $\omega_{\sigma_1}, \ldots, \omega_{\sigma_t}$ and in an adaptive setting, the receiver wishes to learn a secret ω_{e_ℓ} $(e_\ell \in \{1, \ldots n\})$ in run ℓ.

The three protocols require the availability of private communication channels between the sender and the servers and between the receiver and the servers. We assume that these communication channels are secure, i.e., any party is unable to eavesdrop on them and they guarantee that communications cannot be tampered with.

Like in other DOT schemes where only a subset of servers are contacted by the receiver (See [11,2,3]), we assume the existence of a mechanism preventing the receiver from contacting more than the specified number of servers in each run or in the transfer phase.

All operations are executed in a finite field $\mathbb{K} = \mathbb{F}_p$ (p prime). We assume that $p > \max(n, \omega_1, \ldots, \omega_n, m)$. We denote $\mathcal{I}_n = \{1, \ldots, n\}$ the set of indices of secrets $\omega_1, \ldots, \omega_n$ held by $\mathcal{S}$ and $\mathcal{I}_m = \{1, \ldots, m\}$ the set of indices of servers $S_1, \ldots, S_m$. By an abuse of language, a polynomial and its corresponding polynomial function will not be differentiated. In addition, the Kronecker's symbol, δ_i^j, is equal to 0 if $i \neq j$ and equal to 1 if $i = j$.

We also formally define a *quasi-random* polynomial.

Definition 1. *If $(\mathbb{K}[X], +, \times)$ is the ring of polynomials over $\mathbb{K}$ and $(\mathbb{K}_d[X], +)$ the additive group of polynomials of degree at most d over $\mathbb{K}$, we say that a polynomial $F = \sum_{i=0}^{d} f_i X^i$ of $\mathbb{K}_d[X]$ is quasi-random, if the coefficients f_i $(1 \leq i \leq d)$ are randomly selected in $\mathbb{K}$ and the constant term $f_0 \in \mathbb{K}$ has a predefined value.*

2.2   Security Model

Our objective is to propose unconditionally secure DOT protocols with the same level of security as in Blundo et al.'s protocol [2,3].

Similarly to other OT protocols, our protocols must guarantee the following properties:

- Correctness - When all participants follow the protocol, $\mathcal{R}$ obtains the selected secrets.
- Sender's Security - Assuming the servers and $\mathcal{S}$ are honest, even if $\mathcal{R}$ does not follow the protocol, she cannot obtain information on the secrets she did not choose.
- Receiver's Privacy - Assuming the servers and $\mathcal{R}$ are honest, $\mathcal{S}$ who may not follow the protocol, cannot obtain any information on the receiver's selection. Because $\mathcal{S}$ is only involved in the set-up phase and other participants are not supposed to communicate with him in the transfer phase or the runs, this property is *de facto* guaranteed.

In addition, because of the distributed setting, the protocols are required to satisfy the following properties:

- The receiver's privacy against a passive coalition of $k - 1$ servers.
- The sender's security against a passive coalition of the receiver and $k - 1$ servers, before the transfer phase (or the first run) is started.

We assume that all parties wish to complete the protocols to allow $\mathcal{R}$ to obtain the chosen secrets.

Like the original protocol, our protocols do not guarantee the sender's security against a "greedy" receiver who, once the protocol is completed and she has obtained t secrets, would corrupt one server. With the additional information collected from the corrupted server, the receiver is able to determine all secrets.

3   One-Round t-out-of-n DOT Protocol

3.1   Principle of the Protocol

The (k, m)-DOT-$\binom{n}{1}$ protocol presented in [2,3] (See Fig. 1) is modified so that when the receiver collects $K = k + t - 1$ shares instead of k shares, she obtains exactly t secrets.

The key idea underlying our t-out-of-n DOT protocol is that from $K = k+t-1$ collected shares ($1 < K \le m$), a receiver is able to build t univariate polynomials of degree at most $k - 1$ agreeing with k shares. These t polynomials allow the receiver, who wishes to obtain t secrets, to build a free linear system of t equations in t unknowns. Solving this system results in the obtaining of the t chosen secrets.

During the set-up phase of the protocol, the sender generates shares of the n secrets he holds and distributes them to the m servers. The sender does not intervene in the rest of the protocol. During the transfer phase, the receiver contacts K servers to collect enough shares to construct $w_{\sigma_1}, \ldots, w_{\sigma_t}$.

Input	The sender $\mathcal{S}$ contributes with n secrets $w_0, \ldots, w_{n-1} \in \mathbb{K}$
	The receiver $\mathcal{R}$ chooses an index $e \in \{0, \ldots, n-1\}$, and
	contributes with $n-1$ private values $\delta_e^1, \ldots, \delta_e^{n-1} \in \{0,1\}$
Output	$\mathcal{R}$ receives w_e, while $\mathcal{S}$ receives nothing.

Set-up Phase

1 - *Preparation of sharing polynomials.* The sender $\mathcal{S}$ generates a quasi-random polynomial B_0 of degree at most $k - 1$, such that $B_0(0) = w_0$ and the sparse n-variate polynomial Q defined by

$$Q\left(x, y_1, \ldots, y_{n-1}\right) = B_0(x) + \sum_{j=1}^{n-1} (w_j - w_0) \times y_j \ .$$

We note that $w_0 = Q(0, \ldots, 0)$ and, for $h \in \{1, \ldots, n-1\}$, $w_h = Q(0, \ldots, 0, 1, 0, \ldots, 0)$, where the number 1 is in position $h + 1$.

2 - *Distribution of sharing polynomials.* Then, to each server S_j ($1 \le j \le m$), $\mathcal{S}$ transmits the $(n-1)$-variate polynomial $Q(j, y_1, \ldots, y_{n-1})$.

Transfer Phase

1 - *Selection of the secret index and generation of the corresponding requests.* The receiver $\mathcal{R}$ chooses the identifier e of one secret and generates $n - 1$ quasi-random polynomials D_i ($1 \le i \le n - 1$), of degree at most $k - 1$, such that $(D_1(0), \ldots, D_{n-1}(0))$ is an $(n-1)$-tuple of zeros if $\mathcal{R}$ is interested in w_0 (i.e., $e = 0$), or an $(n-1)$-tuple of zeros and a single one in position e if $\mathcal{R}$ is interested in w_e (where $e \in \{1, \ldots, n-1\}$).

2 - *Selection of servers and distribution of requests.* $\mathcal{R}$ selects a subset $\mathcal{I}_k \subset \{1, \ldots, m\}$ of k indices and sends a request $(D_1(i), \ldots, D_{n-1}(i))$ to each server S_i ($i \in \mathcal{I}_k$). When a server S_i receives such a request, it replies with the share $s_i = Q(i, D_1(i), \ldots, D_{n-1}(i))$.

3 - *Construction of the requested secret.* After having received k responses, $\mathcal{R}$ interpolates a univariate polynomial R from the k points (i, s_i) and calculates the chosen secret: $w_e = R(0)$.

Fig. 1. Simplified Blundo et al.'s DOT Protocol

3.2 Description of the Protocol

The set-up phase is similar to the one described in Fig. 1 except that, to avoid a specific processing of ω_0, we slightly modify the form of the sparse polynomial generated by the sender: first, the sender selects a random element $\alpha \in \mathbb{K}$ and then, he generates a quasi-random polynomial Q such that

$$Q(x, y_1, \ldots, y_n) = \alpha + \sum_{i=1}^{k-1} a_i x^i + \sum_{i=1}^{n} (\omega_i - \alpha) \times y_i .$$

In the transfer phase, the servers have the same behaviour as in the original protocol. On the other hand, the receiver:

- Selects $K = k + t - 1$ servers to contact instead of k servers.
- Generates t sets of n sharing polynomials instead of $n - 1$ sharing polynomials. One set of polynomials is associated with a chosen secret. Since two distinct chosen secrets produce two secret inputs with two differences (two '1' in different positions like in $(1, 0, \ldots, 0)$ and $(0, 1, \ldots, 0)$), the receiver is able to use the same polynomials to share the $(n - 2)$ '0' values in the same positions and so, minimise the number of sharing polynomials to generate. From the K collected shares, the receiver prepares t sets of k shares ($k - 1$ shares common to all sets) and interpolates t polynomials. From each of these t polynomials, the receiver is able to obtain one secret.

The resulting protocol is described in Fig. 2.

3.3 Correctness and Security of the Protocol

Correctness. To each server S_j ($1 \leq j \leq k - 1$), $\mathcal{R}$ sends a vector $\mathbf{\Theta}_j = (Z_1^{(\sigma_1)}(j), \ldots, Z_n^{(\sigma_1)}(j))$. Thus, the response returned to $\mathcal{R}$ by S_j is

$$F_j(\mathbf{\Theta}_j) = \alpha + \sum_{i=1}^{k-1} a_i j^i + \sum_{i=1}^{n} (\omega_i - \alpha) Z_i^{(\sigma_1)}(j) .$$

By construction, for $j = 1, \ldots, k - 1$ and $r = 1, \ldots, t$, we have $Z_i^{(\sigma_1)}(j) = Z_i^{(\sigma_r)}(j) = \lambda_{i,j}$. It follows that the interpolation of the k shares $F_j(\mathbf{\Theta}_j)$ ($j = 1, \ldots, k - 1, k - 1 + r$) gives a polynomial of $\mathbb{K}_{k-1}[X]$,

$$G^{(\sigma_r)}(x) = \alpha + \sum_{i=1}^{k-1} a_i x^i + \sum_{i=1}^{n} (\omega_i - \alpha) Z_i^{(\sigma_r)}(x) .$$

The evaluation of $G^{(\sigma_r)}$ for $x = 0$ is therefore:

$$G^{(\sigma_r)}(0) = \alpha + \sum_{i=1}^{k-1} a_i 0^i + \sum_{i=1}^{n} (\omega_i - \alpha) Z_i^{(\sigma_r)}(0) = \omega_{\sigma_r} .$$

We conclude that the protocol is correct.

Set-up Phase

1 - *Preparation of a sharing polynomial.* The sender $\mathcal{S}$ generates a sparse $(n+1)$-variate polynomial Q defined by

$$Q(x, y_1, \ldots, y_n) = \alpha + \sum_{i=1}^{k-1} a_i x^i + \sum_{i=1}^{n} (\omega_i - \alpha) \times y_i,$$

where the numbers α and a_i $(1 \le i \le k-1)$ are randomly selected in $\mathbb{K}$.

2 - *Distribution of sharing polynomials.* Then, to each server S_j $(1 \le j \le m)$, $\mathcal{S}$ transmits the n-variate polynomial F_j defined by

$$F_j(y_1, \ldots, y_n) = Q(j, y_1, \ldots, y_n) .$$

Transfer Phase

1 - *Selection of secret indices and servers.* The receiver $\mathcal{R}$ chooses the t secrets, $\omega_{\sigma_1}, \ldots, \omega_{\sigma_t}$, that she wishes to obtain. The set containing the indices of the t secrets is denoted $\mathcal{I}_\sigma = \{\sigma_1, \ldots, \sigma_t\} \subset \mathcal{I}_n$. The receiver also selects a subset $\mathcal{I}_K \subset \mathcal{I}_m$ of $K = k + t - 1$ indices of the servers she intends to contact. Without loss of generality, we assume that these servers are $S_1, \ldots, S_K$.

2 - *Generation of the receiver's requests.* $\mathcal{R}$ builds n lists $\Lambda_i = \{\lambda_{i,1}, \ldots, \lambda_{i,k-1}\}$ $(i \in \mathcal{I}_n)$ of $k-1$ elements randomly selected in $\mathbb{K}$. Then, for $\sigma_r \in \mathcal{I}_\sigma$, from each list Λ_i, $\mathcal{R}$ interpolates a polynomial $Z_i^{(\sigma_r)} \in \mathbb{K}_{k-1}[X]$ from the k points of $\{(0, \delta_i^{\sigma_r}), (1, \lambda_{i,1}), \ldots, (k-1, \lambda_{i,k-1})\}$.

3 - *Transmission of the requests to the servers.* $\mathcal{R}$ sends to each server S_j a vector $\Theta_j = (Z_1^{(\sigma_1)}(j), \ldots, Z_n^{(\sigma_1)}(j))$ if $1 \le j \le k-1$ and a vector $\Theta_j = (Z_1^{(\sigma_{j-k+1})}(j), \ldots, Z_n^{(\sigma_{j-k+1})}(j))$ if $k \le j \le K$.

4 - *Transmission of the requests' responses to the receiver.* When a server S_j $(j \in \mathcal{I}_K)$ receives a request Θ_j, it replies with the share $F_j(\Theta_j)$.

5 - *Construction of the requested secrets.* For each secret index $\sigma_r \in \mathcal{I}_\sigma$, $\mathcal{R}$ interpolates a univariate polynomial $G^{(\sigma_r)} \in \mathbb{K}_{k-1}[X]$ from the k values $F_j(\Theta_j)$ $(1 \le j \le k-1)$ and $F_{k-1+r}(\Theta_{k-1+r})$. Then, $\mathcal{R}$ calculates the t secrets $\omega_{\sigma_r} = G^{(\sigma_r)}(0)$ $(1 \le r \le t)$.

Fig. 2. One-Round t-out-of-n DOT Protocol

Sender's Security against a Dishonest Receiver. During the transfer phase, $\mathcal{R}$ contacts K servers to collect shares. We assume that $\mathcal{R}$ does not follow the protocol and sends a vector $\Theta_j = (y_{j,1}, \ldots, y_{j,n})$ of elements of $\mathbb{K}$ to the server S_j $(j \in \mathcal{I}_K)$. From the K collected shares, $\mathcal{R}$ is able to build a linear system of K equations in $k+n$ unknowns, namely $\alpha, a_1, \ldots, a_{k-1}, \omega_1, \ldots, \omega_n$. This system may also be written under the matrix form $\mathcal{T} \times U = \Gamma$, where:

$$\mathcal{T} = \begin{pmatrix} (1 - \sum_{i=1}^{n} y_{1,i}) & 1^1 & \cdots & 1^{k-1} & y_{1,1} & \cdots & y_{1,n} \\ \cdots\cdots\cdots\cdots\cdots\cdots\cdots\cdots\cdots\cdots\cdots\cdots\cdots\cdots\cdots \\ (1 - \sum_{i=1}^{n} y_{K,i}) & K^1 & \cdots & K^{k-1} & y_{K,1} & \cdots & y_{K,n} \end{pmatrix},$$

$$U = \begin{pmatrix} \alpha \\ a_1 \\ \cdots \\ a_{k-1} \\ \omega_1 \\ \cdots \\ \omega_n \end{pmatrix} \quad \text{and} \quad \Gamma = \begin{pmatrix} G^{(1)}(0) \\ \cdots\cdots \\ G^{(K)}(0) \end{pmatrix}.$$

To obtain s linear combinations of the secrets $\omega_1, \ldots, \omega_n$, $\mathcal{R}$ has to transform the system $\mathcal{T} \times U = \Gamma$ into an equivalent system $\mathcal{T}' \times U = \Gamma'$, where

$$\mathcal{T}' = \begin{pmatrix} A & B \\ 0 & D \end{pmatrix}$$

and $A \in \mathcal{M}_{K-s,k}(\mathbb{K})$, $B \in \mathcal{M}_{K-s,n}(\mathbb{K})$ and $D \in \mathcal{M}_{s,n}(\mathbb{K})$. In $\mathcal{T}$, we observe a Vandermonde submatrix composed of the columns 2 to k:

$$\begin{pmatrix} 1^1 & \cdots & 1^{k-1} \\ \cdots\cdots\cdots \\ k^1 & \cdots & k^{k-1} \end{pmatrix}.$$

The rank of this submatrix is $k - 1$, and so the number of rows of A is at least $k - 1$. It follows that $K - s = k + t - 1 - s \geq k - 1$ and so $s \leq t$. Therefore, $\mathcal{R}$ cannot determine more than $s = t$ linear combinations of secrets.

To force the receiver to obtain information on no more than t secrets from the t linear combinations, the technique described by Naor and Pinkas [11] may be applied; in the set-up phase, the sender randomly selects n masks $c_1, \ldots, c_n \in \mathbb{K}^*$. Two polynomials Q_1 and Q_2 are generated (See Fig. 2, first step of the set-up phase), Q_1 to share the n masked secrets $c_i \omega_i$ and Q_2 to share the n masks c_i ($i \in \mathcal{I}_n$). In the transfer phase, in response to the receiver's request $(Z_1(j), \ldots, Z_n(j))$, the contacted server S_j ($j \in \mathcal{I}_K$) returns two shares: $Q_1(j, Z_1(j), \ldots, Z_n(j))$ and $Q_2(j, Z_1(j), \ldots, Z_n(j))$. From the collected $2K$ shares the receiver is able to determine exactly t masked secrets and their corresponding masks.

It follows that the protocol is secure against a dishonest receiver.

Receiver's Privacy against a Coalition of Servers. The indices $\sigma_r \in \mathcal{I}_\sigma$ chosen by the receiver are represented under the form of vectors $(\delta_{\sigma_r}^1, \ldots, \delta_{\sigma_r}^n)$ of private values, where $\delta_{\sigma_r}^j = 0$ or $\delta_{\sigma_r}^j = 1$. The receiver's input to the protocol consists of shares of these values. That is, each server S_j ($j \in \mathcal{I}_K$) receives for each of the n elements $\delta_{\sigma_r}^i$ a share produced by a Shamir's (k, K)-threshold secret sharing scheme.

In order to breach the privacy of the receiver, a set of $k - 1$ colluding servers should be able to determine at least one of the values $\delta_{\sigma_r}^j$. The set of $k - 1$ collaborating servers, however, owns $k - 1$ shares corresponding to each values $\delta_{\sigma_r}^j$ associated with a Shamir's (k, K)-threshold scheme. Due to the perfectness of Shamir's threshold scheme, every set of $k - 1$ shares provides the coalition with absolutely no information about the relevant secret.

It follows that the receiver's privacy is guaranteed against a coalition of up to $k - 1$ servers.

Sender's Security against a Coalition of the Receiver and Servers before the Transfer Phase. Assuming the technique described above to prevent the receiver from obtaining information on more than t secrets is used, each server S_j ($j \in \mathcal{I}_m$) receives two n-variate polynomials from $\mathcal{S}$. More precisely, each server S_j receives a list of $2 \times (n + 1)$ elements: $\alpha_1 + \sum_{i=1}^{k-1} a_{1,j} j^i$, $\alpha_2 + \sum_{i=1}^{k-1} a_{2,j} j^i$, $c_1 \omega_1 - \alpha_1, \ldots, c_n \omega_n - \alpha_1$ and $c_1 - \alpha_2, \ldots, c_n - \alpha_2$. The first two elements can be considered as shares generated by (k, m)-threshold Shamir's secret sharing schemes whereas the other elements can be viewed as $2n$ secrets masked by α_1 and α_2, the masks α_1 and α_2 being unknown. To determine α_1 or α_2, a coalition of servers would need to obtain the corresponding sharing polynomial which is of degree at most $k - 1$. So, the coalition should contain at least k members. In addition, although each server is able to determine linear combinations of masks $c_1, \ldots, c_n$ they cannot obtain linear combinations of the secrets $\omega_1, \ldots, \omega_n$, as shown by Cheong, Koshiba and Nishiyama [5]. Note that in this scenario, the use of the technique preventing the receiver from obtaining information on more than t secrets makes the additional masking of secrets described in Blundo et al.'s DOT sub-protocol [2,3] unnecessary.

Furthermore, in this scenario there is no advantage for the receiver to collude with $k - 1$ servers to breach the sender's security, since the receiver has no input to contribute in an attack.

We conclude that a coalition of the receiver with $k - 1$ servers cannot obtain any information on the secrets held by the sender before the transfer phase is executed.

Sender's Security against a Coalition of Servers after the Protocol is Executed. Like in the original protocol, the security of the sender is not guaranteed if servers are corrupted by the receiver once the protocol has been executed. Actually, if the receiver corrupts only one server, she is able to obtain all secrets. Indeed, any corrupt server S_j ($j \in \mathcal{I}_m$) is able to provide the receiver with the elements $c_1 \omega_1 - \alpha_1, \ldots, c_n \omega_n - \alpha_1$, $c_1 - \alpha_2, \ldots, c_n - \alpha_2$. Moreover, the execution of the protocol gives the receiver t masks $c_{\sigma_1}, \ldots, c_{\sigma_t}$, as well as t secrets, $\omega_{\sigma_1}, \ldots, \omega_{\sigma_t}$. Consequently, simple subtractions allow the receiver to determine α_1 and α_2 and hence all masks and masked secrets. Then, simple divisions allow the receiver to calculate all the secrets $\omega_1, \ldots, \omega_n$.

4   Adaptive DOT Protocol with Limited Queries

4.1   Description of the Protocol

This protocol is a basic adaptation of Blundo et al.'s DOT protocol [2,3] (See Fig. 1) where we allow the transfer phase to be executed t times.

In addition to the secure private communication channels between the sender and the servers and between the receiver and the servers, we assume the availability of a broadcast channel.

The major characteristics of the adapted protocol are:

- In the set-up phase, the sender generates a list of polynomials $Q^{(\ell)}$ $(1 \leq \ell \leq t)$ instead of a single polynomial Q.
- In run ℓ, the contacted servers use the polynomial $Q^{(\ell)}$ to respond to the receiver's query.

To avoid a specific processing of the first secret like in the original protocol, we slightly transform the sparse polynomial generated by the sender; In the set-up phase, the sender selects a random element $\alpha \in \mathbb{K}$ and generates t quasi-random polynomials $B_0^{(\ell)}$ $(1 \leq \ell \leq t)$, of degree at most $k-1$, such that $B_0^{(\ell)}(0) = \alpha$. Then, the sender builds the t $(n+1)$-variate polynomials

$$Q^{(\ell)}(x, y_1, \ldots, y_n) = B_0^{(\ell)}(x) + \sum_{i=1}^{n} (\omega_i - \alpha) \times y_i \ .$$

Set-up Phase

1 - *Preparation of sharing polynomials.* The sender S selects a random element $\alpha \in \mathbb{K}$ and generates t quasi-random polynomials $B_0^{(\ell)} = \sum_{i=1}^{k-1} a_i^{(\ell)} X^i + \alpha$ $(1 \leq \ell \leq t)$.

2 - *Distribution of sharing polynomials.* Then, to each server S_j $(j \in \mathcal{I}_m)$, S transmits the $t + n$ values $B_0^{(1)}(j), \ldots, B_0^{(t)}(j), \omega_1 - \alpha, \ldots, \omega_n - \alpha$, as well as a local current run number initialized to 0 (we require $t \leq p - 1$).

Run ℓ $(1 \leq \ell \leq t)$

1 - *Selection of a secret index and generation of the corresponding requests.* The receiver $\mathcal{R}$ chooses the index $e^{(\ell)}$ of one secret and generates n quasi-random polynomials $D_i^{(\ell)}$ $(i \in \mathcal{I}_n)$, of degree at most $k - 1$, such that $(D_1^{(\ell)}(0), \ldots, D_n^{(\ell)}(0)) = (\delta_1^{e^{(\ell)}}, \ldots, \delta_n^{e^{(\ell)}})$.

2 - *Selection of servers and update of the current run number.* $\mathcal{R}$ selects a subset $\mathcal{I}_k^{(\ell)} \subset \mathcal{I}_m$ of k indices and broadcasts the current run number ℓ. On reception of ℓ and $\mathcal{I}_k^{(\ell)}$, a server S_j $(j \in \mathcal{I}_m)$ with a local run number ℓ' checks that $\ell \leq t$ and $\ell' < \ell$. If the two inequalities are satisfied, the local run number is updated with ℓ, otherwise, S_j shuts down.

3 - *Distribution of the requests.* $\mathcal{R}$ sends to each server S_j $(j \in \mathcal{I}_k^{(\ell)})$ a request $(D_1^{(\ell)}(j), \ldots, D_n^{(\ell)}(j))$.

4 - *Transmission of the requests' responses to the receiver.* When a server S_j receives such a request, it replies with the share $s_j^{(\ell)} = B_0^{(\ell)}(j) + \sum_{i=1}^{n} (\omega_i - \alpha) D_i^{(\ell)}(j)$.

5 - *Construction of the requested secret.* After receiving k responses $s_j^{(\ell)}$ $(j \in \mathcal{I}_k^{(\ell)})$, $\mathcal{R}$ interpolates a univariate polynomial $R^{(\ell)}$ from the k points $(j, s_j^{(\ell)})$ and calculates the chosen secret: $\omega_{e(\ell)} = R^{(\ell)}(0)$.

Fig. 3. Adaptive DOT Protocol with Limited Queries

To transmit a list of t polynomials $Q^{(1)}(j, y_1, \ldots, y_n), \ldots, Q^{(t)}(j, y_1, \ldots, y_n)$ to a server S_j, the sender just has to send to S_j the values $B_0^{(1)}(j), \ldots, B_0^{(t)}(j)$, $\omega_1 - \alpha, \ldots, \omega_n - \alpha$.

A server contacted by the receiver needs to know what polynomial $Q^{(\ell)}$ to use, i.e., what is the current run number ℓ. Therefore, we add a mechanism to synchronize the contacted servers thanks to a broadcast channel. Before sending requests, the receiver broadcasts the number of the next run. On reception of the next run number ℓ, a server with a local run number ℓ' checks if $\ell' < \ell \leq t$. If the double inequality is satisfied, then the server updates its local run number to ℓ. Otherwise it shuts down since the receiver has either reused a run number or tried to execute more than t runs.

The DOT protocol introduced by Blundo et al. [2], including the above modifications, is described in Fig. 3.

4.2 Correctness and Security of the Protocol

We show that the protocol is correct and guarantees the sender's security. In addition we consider the two scenarios involving a coalition of active parties.

Correctness. In run ℓ, a contacted server S_j ($j \in \mathcal{I}_k^{(\ell)}$) uses the $n+1$ values $B_0^{(\ell)}(j), \omega_1 - \alpha, \ldots, \omega_n - \alpha$ to prepare the response $s_j^{(\ell)}$. We have:

$$s_j^{(\ell)} = B_0^{(\ell)}(j) + \sum_{i=1}^{n} (\omega_i - \alpha) D_i^{(\ell)}(j) \ .$$

The polynomial $B_0^{(\ell)}$ is of degree at most $k-1$, as well as the polynomials $D_i^{(\ell)}$ ($i \in \mathcal{I}_n$). It follows that the degree of the polynomial $R = B_0^{(\ell)} + \sum_{i=1}^{n} (\omega_i - \alpha) \times D_i^{(\ell)}$ is at most $k-1$. With the k values $s_j^{(\ell)}$, the receiver is therefore able to interpolate this polynomial R. Thus, the receiver can calculate

$$R^{(\ell)}(0) = \left(B_0^{(\ell)} + \sum_{i=1}^{n} (\omega_i - \alpha) D_i^{(\ell)} \right)(0)$$
$$= B_0^{(\ell)}(0) + \sum_{i=1}^{n} (\omega_i - \alpha) D_i^{(\ell)}(0)$$
$$= \alpha + \sum_{i=1}^{n} (\omega_i - \alpha) \delta_i^{e^{(\ell)}}$$

It follows that $R^{(\ell)}(0) = \alpha + (\omega_{e(\ell)} - \alpha) = \omega_{e(\ell)}$. Consequently, the protocol is correct.

Sender's Security against a Dishonest Receiver. We assume that $\mathcal{R}$ does not follow the protocol and, after t runs, has collected kt shares which allow her to build a linear system of kt equations in $(k-1)t + n + 1$ unknowns.

With a demonstration similar to the demonstration detailed in the previous protocol for the sender's security against a dishonest receiver, it is not difficult to prove that from these kt equations, $\mathcal{R}$ cannot determine more than t linear combinations of secrets. Again, the technique described by Naor and Pinkas [11] may be used to force $\mathcal{R}$ to obtain information on no more than t secrets from the t linear combinations.

Thus, the sender's security is guaranteed.

Receiver's Privacy against a Coalition of Servers. In run ℓ, the index $e^{(\ell)}$ chosen by the receiver is represented under the form of a vector $(\delta_1^{e^{(\ell)}}, \ldots, \delta_n^{e^{(\ell)}})$ of private values. The receiver's input to the protocol consists of shares – generated by Shamir's k-threshold scheme – of these values. A set of $k-1$ colluding servers holds $k-1$ shares related to a value $\delta_i^{e^{(\ell)}}$, which is insufficient to determine $\delta_i^{e^{(\ell)}}$.

That is, the inputs of the receiver guarantee her privacy.

Sender's Security against a Coalition of the Receiver and Servers before the First Run. The analysis of the security property is similar to the analysis performed in the previous protocol: each server receives $2t$ shares generated by (k, m)-threshold Shamir's secret sharing schemes and $2n$ other elements which can be viewed as $2n$ secrets protected by two masks, α_1 and α_2. To determine one of these masks, a coalition of servers would need to obtain a corresponding sharing polynomial which is of degree at most $k-1$, and so would require at least k members.

We conclude that a coalition of the receiver with $k-1$ servers cannot obtain any information on the secrets held by the sender before the first run is executed.

5   Adaptive DOT Protocol with Unlimited Queries

5.1   Description of the Protocol

The major problem with the current unconditionally secure polynomial-based DOT [11,2,3,13] protocols is that the transfer phase cannot be repeated. Indeed, when the receiver sends a same request to a server in two different runs, she obtains the same response. Thus, she is able to reuse responses from previous queries, which allows her to request additional shares and obtain additional secrets. The key idea of our second adaptive protocol is to force a server contacted in different runs, with a same request, to respond with – possible – different shares. To achieve this, we propose that the servers generate a new polynomial $Q^{(\ell)}$ for the run ℓ instead of reusing the same polynomial Q in each run like in the protocol proposed by Jiang et al. [9]. We assume that to exchange information about this new polynomial, a private communication channel between any two servers are available in addition to the secure private communication channels between the sender and the servers and between the receiver and the servers.

In the original protocol, we observe that the polynomial B_0 generated by the sender can be considered as a sharing polynomial for the value ω_0. Consequently, applying the redistribution technique introduced by Desmedt and Jajodia [6], the servers contacted in run ℓ are able to calculate a new sharing polynomial, $B_0^{(\ell)}$, for ω_0. The polynomial $Q^{(\ell)}$ is then defined by:

$$Q^{(\ell)}(x, y_1, \ldots, y_{n-1}) = B_0^{(\ell)}(x) + \sum_{i=1}^{n-1} (\omega_i - \omega_0) \times y_i \ .$$

To avoid a specific processing of ω_0, we slightly transform the sparse polynomial generated by the sender and introduce the following modifications in Blundo et al.'s DOT protocol (The resulting protocol is described in Fig. 4):

- In the set-up phase, the sender randomly selects an element $\alpha \in \mathbb{K}$. The quasi-random polynomial B_0 is such that $B_0(0) = \alpha$ and the coefficient of y_i is $\omega_i - \alpha$ $(i \in \mathcal{I}_n)$.
- In run ℓ, in addition to the n values $D_1^{(\ell)}(j), \ldots, D_n^{(\ell)}(j)$ sent to the server S_j $(j \in \mathcal{I}_k^{(\ell)})$, the receiver sends the list $\mathcal{I}_k^{(\ell)}$ of contacted servers.
- Each contacted server S_j generates a quasi-random polynomial $C_j^{(\ell)}$, of degree at most $k - 1$, such that $C_j^{(\ell)}(0) = B_0(j)$. Then S_j distributes $C_j^{(\ell)}(i)$ to S_i $(i \in \mathcal{I}_k^{(\ell)})$. With k shares $C_j^{(\ell)}(i)$, each server S_i calculates

$$B_0^{(\ell)}(i) = \sum_{j \in \mathcal{I}_k^{(\ell)}} C_j^{(\ell)}(i) \times \prod_{\substack{d \in \mathcal{I}_k^{(\ell)} \\ d \neq i}} \frac{d}{d - i} \ .$$

- The response $s_i^{(\ell)}$ returned by S_i to the receiver is then built using $B_0^{(\ell)}(i)$ instead of $B_0(i)$.

5.2   Correctness and Security of the Protocol

The sender's security, the receiver's privacy against a coalition of servers and the sender's security against a coalition of the receiver and $k - 1$ servers before the first run are the same as in the previous protocol. Indeed, the redistribution protocol is secure and the receiver's contribution is exactly the same.

We now show that the protocol is correct; At the end of run ℓ, the receiver has collected k shares $s_j^{(\ell)}$ $(j \in \mathcal{I}_k^{(\ell)})$ and interpolates

$$R^{(\ell)}(0) = \sum_{i \in \mathcal{I}_k^{(\ell)}} \left(s_i^{(\ell)} \prod_{\substack{i \in \mathcal{I}_k^{(\ell)} \\ j \neq i}} \frac{j}{j - i} \right) \ .$$

Set-up Phase

1 - *Preparation of a sharing polynomial.* The sender $\mathcal{S}$ selects a random element $\alpha \in \mathbb{K}$. Then, $\mathcal{S}$ generates a quasi-random polynomial B_0, of degree at most $k-1$, such that $B_0(0) = \alpha$.

2 - *Distribution of sharing polynomials.* Then, to each server S_j ($j \in \mathcal{I}_m$), $\mathcal{S}$ transmits $B_0(j)$ and the n values $\omega_1 - \alpha, \ldots, \omega_n - \alpha$.

Run ℓ ($\ell \geq 1$)

1 - *Selection of a secret index and generation of the corresponding requests.* The receiver $\mathcal{R}$ chooses the index $e^{(\ell)}$ of a secret and generates n quasi-random polynomials $D_i^{(\ell)}$ ($i \in \mathcal{I}_n$), of degree at most $k-1$, such that $(D_1^{(\ell)}(0), \ldots, D_n^{(\ell)}(0)) = (\delta_1^{e^{(\ell)}}, \ldots, \delta_n^{e^{(\ell)}})$.

2 - *Selection of servers and distribution of the requests.* $\mathcal{R}$ selects a subset $\mathcal{I}_k^{(\ell)} \subset \{1, \ldots, m\}$ of k indices and sends to each server S_j ($j \in \mathcal{I}_k^{(\ell)}$) a request $(D_1^{(\ell)}(j), \ldots, D_n^{(\ell)}(j))$ as well as the list $\mathcal{I}_k^{(\ell)}$.

3 - *Redistribution of shares and transmission of the requests' responses to the receiver.* When a server S_j receives such a request, it generates a quasi-random polynomial $C_j^{(\ell)}$, of degree at most $k-1$, such that $C_j^{(\ell)}(0) = B_0(j)$. The server S_j distributes to each server S_i ($i \in \mathcal{I}_k^{(\ell)}$) the share $C_j^{(\ell)}(i)$. Each server S_i calculates

$$B_0^{(\ell)}(i) = \sum_{j \in \mathcal{I}_k^{(\ell)}} C_j^{(\ell)}(i) \prod_{\substack{d \in \mathcal{I}_k^{(\ell)} \\ d \neq i}} \frac{d}{d-i} \qquad (1)$$

and replies to $\mathcal{R}$ with the share $s_i^{(\ell)} = B_0^{(\ell)}(i) + \sum_{j=1}^n (\omega_j - \alpha)D_j^{(\ell)}(i)$.

4 - *Construction of the requested secret.* After receiving k responses $s_i^{(\ell)}$ ($i \in \mathcal{I}_k^{(\ell)}$), $\mathcal{R}$ interpolates a univariate polynomial $R^{(\ell)}$ from the k points $(i, s_i^{(\ell)})$ and calculates the chosen secret: $\omega_{e^{(\ell)}} = R^{(\ell)}(0)$.

Fig. 4. Adaptive DOT Protocol with Unlimited Queries

We show that $R^{(\ell)}(0) = \omega_{e^{(\ell)}}$.

$$R^{(\ell)}(0) = \sum_{i \in \mathcal{I}_k^{(\ell)}} \left(\left(B_0^{(\ell)}(i) + \sum_{j=1}^n (\omega_j - \alpha)D_j^{(\ell)}(i) \right) \prod_{\substack{i \in \mathcal{I}_k^{(\ell)} \\ j \neq i}} \frac{j}{j-i} \right)$$

$$= \underbrace{\sum_{i \in \mathcal{I}_k^{(\ell)}} \left(B_0^{(\ell)}(i) \prod_{\substack{i \in \mathcal{I}_k^{(\ell)} \\ j \neq i}} \frac{j}{j-i} \right)}_{=R_1} + \underbrace{\sum_{j=1}^n \left(\sum_{i \in \mathcal{I}_k^{(\ell)}} (\omega_j - \alpha)D_j^{(\ell)}(i) \prod_{\substack{i \in \mathcal{I}_k^{(\ell)} \\ j \neq i}} \frac{j}{j-i} \right)}_{=R_2}$$

If we replace $B_0^{(\ell)}$ with its value (1), we obtain

$$
R_1 = \sum_{i \in \mathcal{I}_k^{(\ell)}} \left(\left(\sum_{j \in \mathcal{I}_k^{(\ell)}} C_j^{(\ell)}(i) \prod_{\substack{d \in \mathcal{I}_k^{(\ell)} \\ d \neq i}} \frac{d}{d-i} \right) \prod_{\substack{i \in \mathcal{I}_k^{(\ell)} \\ j \neq i}} \frac{j}{j-i} \right)
$$

$$
= \sum_{j \in \mathcal{I}_k^{(\ell)}} \left(\left(\sum_{i \in \mathcal{I}_k^{(\ell)}} C_j^{(\ell)}(i) \prod_{\substack{d \in \mathcal{I}_k^{(\ell)} \\ d \neq i}} \frac{d}{d-i} \right) \prod_{\substack{i \in \mathcal{I}_k^{(\ell)} \\ j \neq i}} \frac{j}{j-i} \right)
$$

$$
= \sum_{j \in \mathcal{I}_k^{(\ell)}} C_j^{(\ell)}(0) \prod_{\substack{i \in \mathcal{I}_k^{(\ell)} \\ j \neq i}} \frac{j}{j-i}
$$

$$
= \sum_{j \in \mathcal{I}_k^{(\ell)}} B_0(j) \prod_{\substack{i \in \mathcal{I}_k^{(\ell)} \\ j \neq i}} \frac{j}{j-i}
$$

$$
= B_0(0) = \alpha
$$

In addition, we have

$$
R_2 = \sum_{j=1}^{n} (\omega_j - \alpha) D_j^{(\ell)}(0)
$$

$$
= \sum_{j=1}^{n} (\omega_j - \alpha) \, \delta_j^{e^{(\ell)}} = \omega_{e(\ell)} - \alpha
$$

It follows that $R^{(\ell)}(0) = R_1 + R_2 = \omega_{e(\ell)}$. Therefore, the protocol is correct.

6   Efficiency Consideration

In Table 1, we list the main computations (poly. = sharing polynomials, int. = interpolations, scp. = $(n-1)$-tuple scalar products) performed by each party, for Blundo et al.'s DOT protocol repeated t times and for our three DOT protocols. Blundo et al.'s DOT protocol is denoted [BL], our one-round DOT protocol [OR], our adaptive DOT protocol with limited queries [AL] and our adaptive DOT protocol with unlimited queries [AU].

Similarly, in Table 2, we list for each protocol the number of shares exchanged between the sender and the servers, the receiver and the servers, and among the servers.

To improve the fairness of the comparison, we do not take into account the masks of the sub-protocol described in [2,3], i.e., the $2mt(n-1)$ shares distributed by the sender to the servers and the $2kt$ shares collected by the receiver.

The computation and communication performances of all protocols are close, except for the set-up phase which is t times more efficient for [OR] and [AU] than for the other two protocols. However, [AU] requires more computation on the servers' sides than [BL] executed t times.

Table 1. Computation Efficiency of DOT protocols

	[BL]	[OR]	[AL]	[AU]
Set-up Phase(s)				
S	$2t$ poly.	2 poly.	$2t$ poly.	2 poly.
Transfer Phase(s) or Run(s)				
$\mathcal{R}$	$(n-1)t$ poly., $2t$ int.	n $(t=1)$ or $n+t$ $(t>1)$ poly., $2t$ int.	nt poly., $2t$ int.	nt poly., $2t$ int.
Contacted Server	2 scp.	2 scp.	2 scp.	2 poly., 2 int., 2 scp.

Table 2. Communication Efficiency of DOT protocols (shares)

	[BL]	[OR]	[AL]	[AU]
Set-up Phase(s)				
$S \rightarrow$ Servers	$2mtn$	$2m(n+1)$	$2m(n+t)$	$2m(n+1)$
Transfer Phase(s) or Run(s)				
$\mathcal{R} \rightarrow$ Servers	$kt(n-1)$	Kn	ktn	ktn
Servers $\rightarrow \mathcal{R}$	$2kt$	$2K$	$2kt$	$2kt$
Servers $\rightarrow$ Servers				$2k(k-1)$

The number of shares exchanged in the adaptive protocols is similar to the number of shares exchanged in [BL] executed t times, apart from the shares exchanged among the contacted servers in [AU]. On the other hand, we observe that in the set-up phase of [OR], the sender S transmits around t less shares to the servers $S_1, \ldots, S_m$ than in [BL]. Furthermore, the transfer phase of [OR] is around $e = \frac{kt}{k+t-1}$ times more efficient than the transfer phase of [BL] executed t times. Note that $e \in]1, k]$ and that $e = 1$ corresponds to the receiver's request for $t = 1$ secret only.

In conclusion, in this paper we have presented three polynomial-based unconditionally secure DOT protocols displaying the same level of security as Blundo et al.'s DOT protocol. The one-round t-out-of-n DOT protocol is more efficient than the original protocol executed t times and the other two protocols allow one or more receivers to adaptively obtain several of the sender's secrets.

Acknowledgements. We would like to thank Saša Radomirović and the anonymous reviewers of ISPEC 2012 for their helpful comments.

References

1. Bellare, M., Micali, S.: Non-interactive Oblivious Transfer and Applications. In: Brassard, G. (ed.) CRYPTO 1989. LNCS, vol. 435, pp. 547–557. Springer, Heidelberg (1990)
2. Blundo, C., D'Arco, P., De Santis, A., Stinson, D.R.: New Results on Unconditionally Secure Distributed Oblivious Transfer. In: Nyberg, K., Heys, H.M. (eds.) SAC 2002. LNCS, vol. 2595, pp. 291–309. Springer, Heidelberg (2003)
3. Blundo, C., D'Arco, P., De Santis, A., Stinson, D.R.: On unconditionally secure distributed oblivious transfer. Journal of Cryptology 20(3), 323–373 (2007)
4. Brassard, G., Crépeau, C., Robert, J.M.: All-or-Nothing Disclosure of Secrets. In: Odlyzko, A.M. (ed.) CRYPTO 1986. LNCS, vol. 263, pp. 234–238. Springer, Heidelberg (1987)
5. Cheong, K.Y., Koshiba, T., Nishiyama, S.: Strengthening the Security of Distributed Oblivious Transfer. In: Boyd, C., González Nieto, J. (eds.) ACISP 2009. LNCS, vol. 5594, pp. 377–388. Springer, Heidelberg (2009)
6. Desmedt, Y.G., Jajodia, S.: Redistributing secret shares to new access structures and its applications. Tech. rep., George Mason University (1997)
7. Even, S., Goldreich, O., Lempel, A.: A randomized protocol for signing contracts. Communications of the ACM 28, 637–647 (1985)
8. Gertner, Y., Malkin, T.: Efficient distributed (n choose 1) oblivious transfer. Tech. rep., MIT Lab of Computer Science (1997)
9. Jiang, S., Li, H., Li, B.: Distributed oblivious transfer with adaptive queries. In: 2010 International Conference on Communications and Mobile Computing, pp. 213–217. IEEE (2010)
10. Naor, M., Pinkas, B.: Oblivious Transfer with Adaptive Queries. In: Wiener, M. (ed.) CRYPTO 1999. LNCS, vol. 1666, pp. 573–590. Springer, Heidelberg (1999)
11. Naor, M., Pinkas, B.: Distributed Oblivious Transfer. In: Okamoto, T. (ed.) ASIACRYPT 2000. LNCS, vol. 1976, pp. 205–219. Springer, Heidelberg (2000)
12. Naor, M., Pinkas, B.: Computationally secure oblivious transfer. Journal of Cryptology 18(1), 1–35 (2005)
13. Nikov, V., Nikova, S., Preneel, B., Vandewalle, J.: On Unconditionally Secure Distributed Oblivious Transfer. In: Menezes, A., Sarkar, P. (eds.) INDOCRYPT 2002. LNCS, vol. 2551, pp. 395–408. Springer, Heidelberg (2002)
14. Rabin, M.O.: How to exchange secrets with oblivious transfer. Tech. rep., Aiken Computation Lab, Harvard University (1981)

Appendix: Jiang et al.'s DOT Protocol Analysis

The main difference between Blundo et al.'s DOT protocol [2,3] and Nikov et al.'s DOT protocol [13] lies in the form of the polynomial generated in the set-up phase. In Nikov et al.'s protocol, the sender S generates a quasi-random polynomial B_0 of degree at most $k-1$, such that $B_0(0) = \omega_0$ and $n-1$ quasi-random polynomials B_i $(1 \leq i \leq n-1)$, of degree at most λ_S $(\lambda_S < k)$, such that $B_i(0) = \omega_i - \omega_0$. Then, S generates a sparse n-variate polynomial Q defined by

$$Q\left(x, y_1, \ldots, y_{n-1}\right) = B_0(x) + \sum_{j=1}^{n-1} B_j(x) \times y_j \ .$$

Jiang et al. have proposed an unconditionally secure adaptive DOT protocol [9] based on Nikov et al.'s DOT protocol. The set-up phase is unchanged and the transfer phase, where the polynomials D_i ($1 \leq i \leq n-1$) are of degree at most λ_R ($\lambda_S + \lambda_R \leq k-1$), is repeated t times, allowing the receiver $\mathcal{R}$ to obtain t secrets. Jiang et al. describe a "special case" allowing $\mathcal{R}$ to determine any polynomial B_j ($1 \leq j \leq n-1$) and claim that it does not reduce the sender's security level. Actually, what is important is the number of contacted servers required to determine B_j: only $\lambda_S + 1$ instead of k, which leaves $\mathcal{R}$ with $k - (\lambda_S + 1)$ redundant shares that can be used to determine an additional secret.

Thus, assuming the set-up phase is similar to the set-up phase of Fig. 2 with the n-variate polynomial Q presented above, and that the ℓ-th adaptive transfer phase is denoted 'run $\ell - 1$', we are able to devise the following attack:

In run 0, the dishonest receiver $\mathcal{R}$ selects the secret index $e = 0$ and transmits to each server S_i ($i \in \mathcal{I}_k = \{i_1, \ldots, i_k\}$) the request $(0, \ldots, 0)$ composed of $n - 1$ zeros. The k collected shares are then $B_0(i)$ ($i \in \mathcal{I}_k$). Since B_0 is a polynomial of degree at most $k - 1$, $\mathcal{R}$ is able to fully determine it and to calculate $\omega_e = \omega_0 = B_0(0)$.

We assume that $\mathcal{R}$ wishes to obtain the secret ω_{e_ℓ} in run ℓ and in addition, the secret ω_{e_+}. Each run ℓ, from run 1, allows $\mathcal{R}$ to obtain $\lambda_S + 1$ shares to calculate the chosen secret ω_{e_ℓ}, as well as $u = k - (\lambda_S + 1)$ extra shares. It follows that the number of runs to obtain ω_{e_+} is $v = 1 + \lceil \frac{\lambda_S + 1}{u} \rceil = \lceil \frac{k}{k - (\lambda_S + 1)} \rceil$.

For each run ℓ ($1 \leq \ell \leq v - 1$), $\mathcal{R}$ prepares two lists of servers: $J^{(\ell)}$, the list of $\lambda_S + 1$ servers to contact to obtain the secret ω_{e_ℓ} and $J_+^{(\ell)}$ the list of $k - (\lambda_S + 1)$ servers to contact to obtain shares of ω_{e_+}. The list $J_+^{(\ell)}$ may be defined for example by $J_+^{(\ell)} = \{i_{(\ell-1) \times (k - \lambda_S + 1) + 1}, \ldots, i_{\ell \times (k - \lambda_S + 1)}\}$. The set $J^{(\ell)}$ is composed of the rest of the list of servers, i.e., $J^{(\ell)} = \mathcal{I}_k \setminus J_+^\ell$. Each server of $J^{(\ell)}$ receives a request $(\delta_1^{e_\ell}, \ldots, \delta_{n-1}^{e_\ell})$ whereas each server of $J_+^{(\ell)}$ receives a request $(\delta_1^{e_+}, \ldots, \delta_{n-1}^{e_+})$. A server $S_j \in J^{(\ell)}$ responds with $B_0(j) + B_{e_\ell}(j)$. Because $\mathcal{R}$ determined B_0 in run 0, she is able to calculate $B_{e_\ell}(j)$. The polynomial B_{e_ℓ} being of degree at most λ_S, $\mathcal{R}$ interpolates B_{e_ℓ} from the $\lambda_S + 1$ shares collected from the servers of $J^{(\ell)}$ and hence determines $\omega_{e_\ell} = B_{e_\ell}(0) + B_0(0)$.

At the end of run $v - 1$, $\mathcal{R}$ has collected $\lambda_S + 1$ shares $B_{e_+}(j)$ from different servers S_j of $J_+^{(1)} \cup \cdots \cup J_+^{(v-1)}$. The polynomial B_{e_+} being of degree at most λ_S, $\mathcal{R}$ interpolates B_{e_+} from the $\lambda_S + 1$ shares and calculates $\omega_{e_+} = B_{e_+}(0) + B_0(0)$.

In conclusion, if the receiver does not follow the protocol but the servers do, she is able to obtain one secret per run plus another secret at the end of run v.

This attack shows that, without modifications, Nikov et al.'s DOT protocol cannot be used as an adaptive DOT protocol.

A Code-Based 1-out-of-N Oblivious Transfer Based on McEliece Assumptions

Preetha Mathew K.[1], Sachin Vasant[2,*],
Sridhar Venkatesan[2,*], and C. Pandu Rangan[1,**]

[1] Theoretical Computer Science Lab,
Department of Computer Science and Engineering,
Indian Institute of Technology Madras, India
{kpreetha,prangan}@cse.iitm.ac.in
[2] Department of Mathematics and Computer Applications,
PSG College of Technology, Coimbatore, India
{sachin.tcs2k7,vsridhar1729}@gmail.com

Abstract. In this paper, we propose an efficient code-based 1-out-of-N oblivious transfer, OT_1^N, based on McEliece assumptions without invoking the OT_1^2 several times as in the paradigm proposed in [20,6]. We also show that the protocol is computationally secure against passive and active adversaries. To our knowledge, this is the first practical code-based OT_1^N protocol. The proposed protocol is compared with some existing number-theoretic OT_1^N protocols for efficiency.

Also, the passively secure 1-out-of-2 OT protocol proposed by Dowsley et al. [10] is reviewed. A formal argument of the computational security of the protocol against active adversaries is furnished.

Keywords: Code-based cryptography, 1-out-of-N oblivious transfer, McEliece Cryptosystem.

1 Introduction

Oblivious transfer is one of the well-established cryptographic primitives that has played a prominent role in achieving secure two-(multi-)party computation [14,17]. OT protocols are the foundation of secure distributed computation. Hence it is used for developing various applications. Some of the applications of this primitive includes Private Information Retrieval (PIR)[22], fair electronic contract signing [11], zero knowledge proofs [1,29], secure function evaluation [14] and aids in developing a one-time proxy signature [36]. A k-out-of-N oblivious transfer (OT_k^N) is a two party primitive in which the sender has N messages, and the receiver intends to read k (choices) of these N messages. This oblivious transfer protocol is said to be secure, if the receiver remains oblivious to the messages that are not within his choice set while the sender does not obtain any

---

* This material is based upon work supported by the Summer Fellowship from Indian Statistical Institute Chennai.
** Currently, Head, Indian Statistical Institute Chennai.

M.D. Ryan, B. Smyth, and G. Wang (Eds.): ISPEC 2012, LNCS 7232, pp. 144–157, 2012.
© Springer-Verlag Berlin Heidelberg 2012

information about the choices of the receiver. A specific instance of the above OT is the 1-out-of-2 OT protocol, OT_1^2, where $k = 1$ and $N = 2$, was first modeled by Rabin [26] with its security based on the assumption of hardness of quadratic residuosity problem. The definition was, later, in an equivalent manner is given in [9]. An extensive discussion of OT_1^2 is furnished in [24,22,15].

Another variant of oblivious transfer is 1-out-of-N OT, OT_1^N in which the receiver is able to retrieve only the message specified according to his choice out of N messages. Such protocols are also known as *"All-or-Nothing Disclosure Of Secrets"* (ANDOS) in which the receiver is not allowed to gain combined information of the secrets[35]. In literature, there are two flavors for constructing a OT_1^N *scheme*: (i) performing N or $logN$ invocations of a secure OT_1^2 [20,6], and (ii) constructions based on the hardness assumptions of certain fundamental problems [21,28]. The security of the former is based upon the security assumption of OT_1^2 invoked whereas, the security of latter approaches directly relies on the hard problems such as *Decisional Diffie-Hellman* problem [35], *Extended Riemann Hypothesis* [16], etc. Generic constructions of OT_1^N are also proposed using certain primitives like *Lossy Trapdoor* functions [25].

The efficiency of an OT scheme is evaluated based on communication and computational complexity incurred during the execution of the protocol. OT protocols using modular exponentiations are computationally expensive than those which use only hash functions, X-OR operations etc. [21]. The above line of thought is indicated by Naor and Pinkas in [21], discussing the *communication/computation trade-off* and render schemes which are computationally efficient under the security assumption of discrete-logarithm *(DL)* problem. The computationally intensive task of modular exponentiation is a major drawback of the number-theoretic OT protocols. Code-based protocols serve as efficient alternatives for the above, since the underlying operations are vector-matrix multiplication which are less computationally intensive than the modular exponentiation.

The notion of code-based cryptography to provide a secure cryptosystem was introduced by McEliece [27] in 1978. It did not gain popularity during that period due to its large key size. The security of the McEliece cryptosystem is based on *Bounded Decoding* problem which is NP-complete [2] and the hardness of *Goppa Code Distinguishability* [8] problem. The problem of *Bounded Decoding* is conjectured to be hard in the average case [31]. [30] discusses the security of code-based cryptosystems and presents arguments on which we can gain confidence on their security. Unlike number-theoretic schemes which are weak against Shor's algorithm[33], no quantum algorithm has been found for the solution of the code-based hard problems. Hence, code-based cryptosystems such as McEliece scheme and its secure variants are among the strong candidates for *Post-Quantum Cryptography*.

Dowsley et al. in [10] pioneered a simple and efficient code-based OT_1^2 based on McEliece security assumption which was computationally secure for both the sender and the receiver. We revisit the protocol in section 3. Almost concurrently and independently Kobara et al. in [18] proposed two code-based OT_1^2 protocols which is an extension of Rabin OT to the code-based setting. They

also discussed the methodology with which Shamir's zero-knowledge identification scheme (ZKID),[32], can be used to verify the correctness of receiver's
public keys and combining McEliece encryption with Stern's ZKID, [34], to provide verifiable encryption. With the view of providing unconditional security
for the receiver, Morozov and Savvides in [19] implement an interactive hashing subroutine [23] for generating the two public keys on the receiver's end and
base their security assumption on the hardness of the general decoding problem
on the sender's side. Although code-based OT_1^2 are computationally efficient in
comparison with number-theoretic OT_1^2 protocols, they suffer from high communication overhead. This is an inherent issue of McEliece cryptosystem attributed
to the large size of public key (100 kilobytes to several megabytes) [4].

Motivation: Various proposals on oblivious transfer including code-based OT_1^2
have been observed in the recent past, but there is no 1-out-of-N code-based OT
protocol, OT_1^N, in literature. Naïve extension of existing code-based OT_1^2 as per
[20,6], will result in high communication and computation cost. Also existence
of schemes based on different hardness assumptions is advantageous. Even if one
of the hardness assumptions is broken (as number-theoretic assumptions would
be, on the advent of quantum computers), switching over to alternatives would
be possible. Since, OT_1^N is a building block for many other cryptographic primitives, we believe that an efficient code-based OT_1^N would enable the realisation
of such primitives under code-based assumptions. Hence we propose a new approach to construct OT_1^N protocol using McEliece assumptions.

Our Contributions: Our contributions in this paper are: (i) formally argu-
ing the security of the passively secure OT_1^2 protocol proposed by Dowsley et
al. [10] against active adversaries, (ii) this is the first code-based OT_1^N protocol computationally secure against active adversaries, which is computationally
efficient, and (iii) the proposed code-based OT_1^N protocol maintains the communication overhead comparable with that of code-based OT_1^2 protocols.

Organization of the paper: Section 2 provides a brief introduction of the
security definition and the assumptions on which the proposed protocol is constructed. The security of the passive protocol in [10] against active adversaries is
formally argued in section 3. We propose a code-based OT_1^N protocol, argue its
security against active adversaries and compare its efficiency with some existing
schemes based on number-theoretic security assumptions in section 4. Finally,
conclusion and directions for future work is given in section 5.

2   Preliminaries

In this section, we state the security definition of 1-out-of-N oblivious transfer,
OT_1^N, and state the security assumptions upon which the scheme is constructed.
A brief overview of the McEliece cryptosystem [27] is provided, which acts as
the underlying trapdoor function for the proposed scheme. Henceforth, we make
use of the following notations:

- $x \in_R \mathcal{D}$ denotes a uniformly random selection of x from $\mathcal{D}$.
- $\oplus$ denotes a bit-wise X-OR operation
- $X \overset{c}{=} Y$ denotes that the random variable X is computationally indistinguishable from the random variable Y.

2.1 Security Definition of Oblivious Transfer

The security definition of OT_1^N is adapted from the definition given in [10]. Let $[\mathcal{A}, \mathcal{B}](b_1, b_2, \ldots, b_N, c)$ be an oblivious transfer protocol, where $\mathcal{A}$ is the sender entity and $\mathcal{B}$ is the receiver entity. Let $\widetilde{\mathcal{A}}$ be the dishonest sender and $\widetilde{\mathcal{B}}$ be dishonest receiver. For the protocol $[\widetilde{\mathcal{A}}, \mathcal{B}](b_1, b_2, \ldots, b_N, c)$, define $View_{\widetilde{\mathcal{A}}}(\widetilde{\mathcal{A}}(x), \mathcal{B}(b))$ to be the knowledge or view that a malicious PPT algorithm $\widetilde{\mathcal{A}}$ has of the state of the algorithm $\mathcal{B}$, corresponding to its state x. For the protocol $[\mathcal{A}, \widetilde{\mathcal{B}}](b_1, b_2, \ldots, b_N, c)$, let us define $View_{\widetilde{\mathcal{B}}}(\mathcal{A}(a), \widetilde{\mathcal{B}}(y))$ as the knowledge or view that a malicious PPT algorithm $\widetilde{\mathcal{B}}$ has of the state of the algorithm $\mathcal{A}$, corresponding to its state y. A formal definition of OT_1^N is as follows.

Definition 1. *A protocol $[\mathcal{A}, \mathcal{B}](b_1, b_2, \ldots, b_N, c)$ is said to honestly implement a secure 1-out-of-N oblivious transfer, for probabilistic polynomial time (PPT) algorithms $\mathcal{A}$ and $\mathcal{B}$, and N bit-strings ($b_1, b_2, \ldots, b_N$)of arbitrary length m and a choice $c \in \{1, \ldots, N\}$, if the following properties hold :*

- ***Completeness:*** *For honest entities $\mathcal{A}$ and $\mathcal{B}$, the entity $\mathcal{B}$ must obtain b_c correctly, and outputs it, whereas $\mathcal{A}$ does not output anything.*
- ***Security for $\mathcal{A}$:*** *For the state of honest entity $\mathcal{A}$ to remain secure against any adversary $\widetilde{\mathcal{B}}$ in $[\mathcal{A}, \widetilde{\mathcal{B}}](b_1, b_2, \ldots, b_N, c)$ the view that $\widetilde{\mathcal{B}}(x)$ obtains on the state of $\mathcal{A}$ for $b_i, \forall i \in \{1, \ldots, N\} \setminus \{c\}$, is computationally indistinguishable from the view of the state of $\mathcal{A}$ given a random string $y \in_R \{0, 1\}^m$.*
- ***Security for $\mathcal{B}$:*** *The honest entity $\mathcal{B}$ remains secure against any adversary $\widetilde{\mathcal{A}}$ in $[\widetilde{\mathcal{A}}, \mathcal{B}](b_1, b_2, \ldots, b_N, c)$, if the view that $\widetilde{\mathcal{A}}(x)$ has, when input of $\mathcal{B}$ is c, is computationally indistinguishable from the view obtained when input of $\mathcal{B}$ is any $i \in \{1, \ldots, N\} \setminus \{c\}$.*

$$View_{\widetilde{\mathcal{A}}}(\widetilde{\mathcal{A}}(x), \mathcal{B}(c)) \overset{c}{=} View_{\widetilde{\mathcal{A}}}(\widetilde{\mathcal{A}}(x), \mathcal{B}(i))$$

2.2 Security Assumptions

The following are some of the hard problems on which the security of the McEliece [27] cryptosystem and the proposed scheme is based. Incidentally, these problems are based on coding theory. Hence, before proceeding to the security assumptions, a brief overview of some of the facts of coding theory is given. A binary linear-error correcting code of length n and dimension k or a $[n, k]$-code is a *k-dimensional* subspace of $\mathbb{F}_2^n$. If the minimum hamming distance between any two codewords is d, then the code is a $[n, k, d]$ code. The hamming weight of a codeword x, $\mathsf{wt}(x)$, is the number of non-zero bits in the codeword. If $t \leq \lfloor \frac{d-1}{2} \rfloor$, the code is said to be t-error correcting, i.e, it detects and corrects errors of weight at most t. The generator matrix $G \in \mathbb{F}_2^{k \times n}$ of a $[n, k]$ linear code C is a matrix of rank k whose rows span the code C. The parity-check matrix $H \in \mathbb{F}_2^{n-k \times n}$ of a $[n, k]$ code C is defined such that $HG^T = 0$. Hence, code C can be defined as $\{mG : \forall m \in \mathbb{F}_2^k\}$ or $\{c : Hc^T = 0\}$.

The security of the proposed scheme is based on the assumption of hardness of the following problems:

Definition 2. Bounded Decoding Problem. *For a code C having parameters $[n, k, 2t + 1]$ and a generator matrix G, given a $y \in \mathbb{F}_2^n$ and an integer $t \leq \lfloor \frac{d-1}{2} \rfloor$ find $m \in \mathbb{F}_2^k$ with $e \in \mathbb{F}_2^n$ having weight $\mathsf{wt}(e) \leq t$, where $y = mG + e$.*

The advantage of a PPT algorithm $\mathcal{C}$ for solving the problem on a given code C is denoted by $\mathsf{Adv}_{\mathcal{C}}^{\mathsf{BD}}(C)$.

Assumption 1. *For any probabilistic polynomial time algorithm $\mathcal{F}$, $\mathsf{Adv}_{\mathcal{F}}^{\mathsf{BD}}(C) < \epsilon_1(n, k)$ where $\epsilon_1(n, k)$ is a negligible function, for any random linear code C.*

For Goppa codes, there is a polynomial time bounded decoding algorithm. Thus, there is a preference for most code-based cryptosystems to use the Goppa code as a trapdoor.

Definition 3. Goppa code-distinguishability. *For parameters $[n, k, 2t + 1]$ given a matrix $G \in \mathbb{F}_2^{k \times n}$, output 1 if G is a generator matrix of a Goppa code, 0 if G is a generator matrix of a random code.*

The advantage of a PPT algorithm $\mathcal{D}$ of solving the problem is denoted by $\mathsf{Adv}_{\mathcal{D}}^{\mathsf{CD}}(n)$.

Assumption 2. *For any probabilistic polynomial time distinguisher $\mathcal{D}$, $\mathsf{Adv}_{\mathcal{D}}^{\mathsf{CD}}(n) < \epsilon_2(n, k)$ where $\epsilon_2(n, k)$ is a negligible function if it is not a high rate goppa code (for a high rate code $\frac{k}{n} \to 1$), [7].*

$$|Pr[\mathcal{D}(G) = 1] - Pr[\mathcal{D}(M) = 1]| < \epsilon_2$$

where G is the generator of the goppa code and M is any random code.

2.3   Overview of McEliece PKC

In this section, an overview of the McEliece PKC [27] is presented which is based on the hardness assumptions defined in the earlier section.

- **Setup:**
  - $k \times n$ generator matrix G
  - random $n \times n$ permutation matrix T
  - random dense $k \times k$ non singular matrix S
  - $\widetilde{G} = SGT$,

  $\widetilde{G}$ and the code parameters $[n, k, 2t + 1]$ are made public and the private key is (S, G, T).

- **Encryption:** For the k bit message m, compute $y = m\widetilde{G} + e$, where e is random vector of length n and weight t. Now, y is the ciphertext sent to the receiver.
- **Decryption:** On receiving y, compute $y' = yT^{-1} = mSG + eT^{-1}$, where T^{-1} is the inverse of the permutation matrix T. On applying the list decoding algorithm [3] for G on y', an $m' = mS$ is obtained. Finally, m is retrieved as $m = m'S^{-1}$.

3 Review of the Passively Secure 1- out-of-2 Protocol for OT by Dowsley et al.

In this section, a brief description of the passively secure OT protocol by Dowsley et al., [10], is furnished and also present our argument on the security of the protocol against active adversary.

3.1 The OT Protocol

The protocol $[A, B](b_0, b_1, c)$ involves the following steps:

Protocol 1

1. $\mathcal{A}$ chooses a $Q \in_R \mathbb{F}_2^{k \times n}$ and sends it to $\mathcal{B}$
2. $\mathcal{B}$ selects a random t-error correcting Goppa Code $[n, k, 2t + 1]$ and its generator matrix G. $\mathcal{B}$ also selects an invertible matrix $S \in_R \mathbb{F}_2^{k \times n}$ and a random $n \times n$ permutation matrix T. $\mathcal{B}$ sets the decodable key $P_c = SGT$ and $P_{1-c} = P_c \oplus Q$ and sends P_0, t to $\mathcal{A}$.
3. $\mathcal{A}$ computes P_1 as $P_1 = P_0 \oplus Q$. $\mathcal{A}$ now performs McEliece encryption on two bit strings $r_0, r_1 \in_R \mathbb{F}_2^k$ using the keys P_0 and P_1 respectively, i.e., computes $y_i = r_i P_i \oplus z_i \forall i \in \{0, 1\}$ where $z_i \in \{0, 1\}^n$ with $\mathsf{wt}(z_i) \leq t$. $\mathcal{A}$ now encrypts the bits as $\widehat{b}_i = b_i \oplus \langle r_i, m_i \rangle, \forall i \in \{0, 1\}$ for some randomly selected $m_i \in \{0, 1\}^k$. $\mathcal{A}$ sends $\widehat{b}_i, y_i, m_i \ \forall i \in \{0, 1\}$.
4. $\mathcal{B}$ now decrypts r_c using the McEliece decryption algorithm, and finds $b_c = \widehat{b}_c \oplus \langle r_c, m_c \rangle$.

Completeness: The protocol is complete as $\mathcal{B}$ can decrypt r_c corresponding to the decodable trapdoor P_c and hence, retrieve b_c. r_{1-c} cannot be decrypted since it is encrypted by a random matrix where the decoding trapdoor is not available.

3.2 Security of the Protocol against Active Adversary

The authors of [10] had claimed that their scheme was not secure against a dishonest active adversary $\widetilde{\mathcal{B}}$, as $\widetilde{\mathcal{B}}$ may find some (P', P'') having reasonable decoding properties such that $P' \oplus P'' = Q$, and hence, gain partial information of b_{1-c}. We claim that, the argument is fallacious because the probability of generating such codes is negligible.

Lemma 1. *The probability that a uniformly generated matrix Q can be represented as $Q = P' \oplus P''$, where P' and P'' are matrices having good decoding properties, is negligible.*

Proof: Let us assume that the probability that a uniform matrix Q is of the form $Q = P' \oplus P''$ is a non-negligible value $\frac{1}{p}$. This would in turn imply that a non-negligible fraction $\frac{1}{p}$ of all randomly generated matrices can be expected to be of the form $P' \oplus P''$ where P' and P'' are matrices with good decoding properties.

Let $\mathcal{P}_{decode}$ be the set of all matrices that display good decoding properties, and $\mathcal{Q}_{decode}$ be the set of all uniformly generated matrices that maintain the properties. Since every element $Q \in \mathcal{Q}_{decode}$ is formed by the linear combination of some $P', P'' \in \mathcal{P}_{decode}$, therefore $|\mathcal{Q}_{decode}| = \binom{|\mathcal{P}_{decode}|}{2} \approx O(|\mathcal{P}_{decode}|^2)$. Since $|\mathcal{Q}_{decode}|$ is a non-negligible fraction $\frac{1}{p}$ of the set of all uniformly generated matrices, $|\mathcal{P}_{decode}|$ is a non-negligible fraction $\frac{1}{p^2}$ of the set of all uniformly generated matrices.

Thus, a non-negligible fraction of all uniformly generated matrices have good decoding properties. This is in contradiction with the assumption 1.   □

A more formal argument that their OT protocol is secure against active adversaries is proved by the following theorem.

Theorem 1. *The OT_1^2 protocol $[\mathcal{A}, \mathcal{B}](b_0, b_1, c)$ is secure for both entities $\mathcal{A}$ and $\mathcal{B}$ against corresponding active adversaries under Definition 1, and the assumptions 1 and 2.*

Proof: Security for $\mathcal{A}$: Let us consider the active PPT adversary $\widetilde{\mathcal{B}}$. To obtain the bit b_i, it is necessary to completely decode the given y_i to obtain r_i, and partial knowledge of r_i would not suffice.

The lemma 1 describes the infeasibility in adaptive choosing of P_c.

The proof is completed with the following argument:

With the assumption that $\mathcal{A}$ is honest, $\{y_0, y_1\}$ output by $\mathcal{A}$ is always decodable for the corresponding code generated by $\{P_0, P_1\}$, if the decoding algorithm is available. Since $\langle r_{1-c}, m_{1-c} \rangle$ is a hard-core predicate [13], to distinguish $\widehat{b_{1-c}}$ for $b_{1-c} = 0$ and $b_{1-c} = 1$, $\widetilde{\mathcal{B}}$ has to obtain r_{1-c}. Hence, for P_{1-c}, the adversary $\widetilde{\mathcal{B}}$ has to perform the following steps:

1. $r_{1-c} \leftarrow \mathsf{Decode}(y_{1-c})$.
2. Compute, $b_{1-c} = \widehat{b}_{1-c} \oplus \langle r_{1-c}, m_{1-c} \rangle,$.

Now, r_{1-c} is the solution for the *Bounded Decoding* problem with input (y_{1-c}, P_{1-c}), which is a contradiction to the assumption 1.

Security for $\mathcal{B}$: Let us assume $\widetilde{\mathcal{A}}$ is a PPT adversary in the proposed OT_1^2 protocol $[\widetilde{\mathcal{A}}, \mathcal{B}](b_0, b_1, c)$. On receiving a y_c that is not decodable, we assume that $\mathcal{B}$ accepts $b_c = 0$, instead of notifying $\widetilde{\mathcal{A}}$ of erroneous encryption. Thus, a malicious generation of y_i will lead to no knowledge of the appropriate c. Hence, the knowledge of the choice c is based on the information $\widetilde{\mathcal{A}}$ obtains from the keys.

Rewriting assumption 2 for $M = G \oplus Q, Q \in \mathbb{F}_2^{k \times n}$,

$$|Pr[\mathcal{D}(G) = 1] - Pr[\mathcal{D}(G \oplus Q) = 1]| < \epsilon_2 \tag{1}$$

where ϵ_2 is a negligible function for any PPT distinguisher $\mathcal{D}$. Assume that there exists a PPT adversary $\widetilde{\mathcal{A}}$ which finds the choice c with non-negligible probability,

$$\widetilde{\mathcal{A}}(P_0, P_1, t) \to c$$

$\widetilde{\mathcal{A}}$ can distinguish P_c from P_{1-c}. Note that,

$$P_{1-c} = P_c \oplus Q$$

Since, $\widetilde{\mathcal{A}}$ can distinguish P_c from P_{1-c}, $\widetilde{\mathcal{A}}$ can distinguish P_c from any $P_c \oplus Q$ with non-negligible probability. This is a contradiction to the equation (1)   □

With the formal argument for the security of the protocol 1, an efficient extension of the protocol to the 1-out-of-N scenario is proposed.

4   1-out-of-N Oblivious Transfer

In this section, we present the first code-based OT_1^N and provide a security argument for the same. Also, a comparison of the proposed protocol with some existing number-theoretic OT_1^N protocols is provided.

4.1   The 1-out-of-N OT Scheme

In the 1-out-of-N protocol, the sender $\mathcal{A}$ sends a random matrix Q to the receiver $\mathcal{B}$. The receiver selects a random t-error correcting Goppa code $[n, k, 2t + 1]$ and sets the generator matrix G as the key P_c. $\mathcal{B}$ derives P_1 as a function of P_c and Q_c, where Q_c is obtained by $c - 1$ circular right shifts on Q and sends (P_1, t) to $\mathcal{A}$. $\mathcal{A}$ encrypts a random r_i using McEliece encryption using the encryption key $P_i = P_{i-1} \oplus Q_{i-1}$ and masks b_i with a hard core predicate of r_i, $\forall 1 \leq i \leq N$. $\mathcal{B}$ decrypts r_c and unmasks b_c. It is to be noted that $N < n$ due to the circular shifting of matrix Q.

Following is the formal description of the protocol.

Protocol 2. *For the public parameters $[n, k, 2t + 1]$, N and a hard-core predicate $h : \{0,1\}^k \to \{0,1\}^m$, where m is the size of the secret. The protocol $[\mathcal{A}, \mathcal{B}](b_1, b_2, \ldots, b_N, c)$ is as follows:*

1. *$\mathcal{A}$ generates $Q \in_R \mathbb{F}_2^{k \times n}$, and sends it to $\mathcal{B}$.*
2. *$\mathcal{B}$ selects a random t-error correcting binary Goppa Code $[n, k, 2t + 1]$ with generator matrix G and sets $P_c = G$. If $c = 1$ then $P_1 = G$, else, $\mathcal{B}$ computes $P_1 = P_c \oplus (\oplus_{i=1}^{c-1} Q_i)$ where $Q_i = Q_{i-1}T$, $i > 1$, $Q_1 = Q$ and T is the $n \times n$ permutation matrix that represents circular right shift by 1 column. $\mathcal{B}$ sends (P_1, t) to $\mathcal{A}$.*

3. $\mathcal{A}$ generates $r_1 \in_R \mathbb{F}_2^k$ and encrypts r_1 as $y_1 = r_1 P_1 + z_1$ where $z_1 \in_R \mathbb{F}_2^n$ with $\text{wt}(z_1) \leq t$. $\mathcal{A}$ conceals b_1 as $\widehat{b}_1 = b_1 \oplus h(r_1)$ and sends $(\widehat{b}_1, y_1)$ to $\mathcal{B}$. $\mathcal{A}$ conceals the subsequent messages as follows: Compute $P_i = P_{i-1} \oplus Q_{i-1}$. Generate $r_i \in_R \mathbb{F}_2^k$. Encrypt r_i as $y_i = r_i P_i + z_i$ where $z_i \in_R \mathbb{F}_2^n$ with $\text{wt}(z_i) \leq t$ and b_i as $\widehat{b}_i = b_i \oplus h(r_i)$. Send $(\widehat{b}_i, y_i)$, $\forall i \in \{2, 3, \ldots, N\}$

4. $\mathcal{B}$ decrypts r_c from y_c and retrieves $b_c = \widehat{b}_c \oplus h(r_c)$. If y_c is not decodable, then b_c is assumed to be 0.

4.2   Security of the Scheme

In accordance with definition 1, a proof that the proposed scheme is a secure OT_1^N is presented in this section, along with its security against the active adversaries. The security of the scheme is based on the hardness assumptions 1 and 2.

The following lemma, on the security of the proposed construction of the blinding matrices $Q_i, \forall i \in \{2, \ldots, N\}$, shows that the construction does not compromise the security of $\mathcal{A}$.

Lemma 2. *For any matrix $M \in_R \mathbb{F}_2^{k \times n}$, the probability that $\oplus_{i=1}^j M_i = 0$ with $M_1 = M$ and M_i being $i - 1$ circular right shifts from M, for any $j \in \{2, \ldots, N\}$ is at most $\frac{1}{2^{k(\lfloor \frac{n}{j} \rfloor + (n \mod j) - 1)}}$.*

Proof: For $j = 2$, $M_1 \oplus M_2 = 0$. Let, c_i denote the ith column of M_1 and the indices be reduced to mod n to obtain the circular effect. M_2 is obtained by right shifting M_1 by one column. Therefore, the $i - 1^{th}$ column of M_1 becomes i^{th} column of M_2. So, $c_i \oplus c_{i-1} = 0 \implies c_i = c_{i-1}, \forall i \in \{0, 1 \ldots, n-1\}$. Therefore, all columns of M_1 must be equal. The probability of such a matrix being generated is $\frac{1}{2^{k(n-1)}} < \frac{1}{2^{k(\lfloor \frac{n}{2} \rfloor + (n \mod 2) - 1)}}$.

For $j \geq 3$, $\oplus_{i=1}^j M_i = 0$ implies $c_i \oplus c_{i-1} \ldots \oplus c_{i-(j-1)} = 0, \forall i \in \{0, 1 \ldots, n-1\}$. Substituting $i = i - 1$ in the previous equation, $c_{i-1} \oplus c_{i-2} \ldots \oplus c_{i-j} = 0$. Addition of the above two equations yields, $c_i \oplus c_{i-j} = 0 \implies c_i = c_{i-j}, \forall i \in \{0, 1 \ldots, n-1\}$. This means, every $j + 1^{th}$ column must be equal. Hence, $\forall i \in \{0, 1 \ldots, j-1\}$, it is necessary that, $c_i = c_k$, where k is of the form $i + xj \mod n$, where $x \in \mathbb{Z}^+$. There are $\lfloor \frac{n}{j} \rfloor$ such x's. When $n \mod j > 0$, for columns $c_i, \forall i \in \{0, 1, \ldots, n \mod j - 1\}$, there is one more repetition of the corresponding columns c_{i-j}. Thus, the probability of $\oplus_{i=1}^j M_i = 0$ is at most $\frac{1}{2^{k(\lfloor \frac{n}{j} \rfloor + (n \mod j) - 1)}}$.   □

From the lemma, it could be observed that the probability for $\oplus_{i=1}^j M_i = 0$ is maximum for $j = N$. The probability is at most $\frac{1}{2^{k(\lfloor \frac{n}{N} \rfloor + (n \mod N) - 1)}}$. Since $N \leq n - 1$, substituting $N = n - 1$ results in the probability $\frac{1}{2^{k(\lfloor \frac{n}{n-1} \rfloor + (n \mod n-1) - 1)}} = \frac{1}{2^{k(\lfloor \frac{n}{n-1} \rfloor)}} < \frac{1}{2^k}$. Hence, the probability of finding an M such that $\oplus_{i=1}^{n-1} M_i = 0$ is at most $\frac{1}{2^k}$

Using the above lemma for the blinding matrices, the proposed scheme is proved to be a secure OT_1^N given a multibit hardcore predicate. The protocol is argued to be conditionally secure for both the receiver and sender.

Theorem 2. *The proposed protocol* $[A, B](b_1, b_2, \ldots, b_N, c)$ *is an* OT_1^N *according to definition 1, under the assumptions 1 and 2.*

Proof: **Completeness:** Assuming the entities are honest, the entity $\mathcal{A}$ encrypts r_i using the key P_i, where $P_i = P_{i-1} \oplus Q_{i-1}$ and $P_1 = P_c \oplus (\oplus_{i=1}^{c-1} Q_i)$. Hence, r_c is encrypted with P_c', where $P_c' = P_{c-1} \oplus Q_{c-1}$. On iterating backwards, $P_c' = P_1 \oplus (\oplus_{i=1}^{c-1} Q_i) = P_c$. Hence, r_c is encrypted with P_c. Since, $\mathcal{B}$ possesses the decoding trapdoor for P_c, he is able to retrieve r_c, and compute $b_c = \widehat{b}_c \oplus h(r_c)$. For example, if we consider $c = 3, N = 4$, the key with trapdoor is P_3. P_1 is generated as $P_1 = P_3 \oplus Q_1 \oplus Q_2$. $\mathcal{B}$ sends P_1 to $\mathcal{A}$. $\mathcal{A}$ assumes the key $P_1' = P_1$. $\mathcal{A}$ constructs $P_2' = P_1' \oplus Q_1 = (P_3 \oplus Q_1 \oplus Q_2) \oplus Q_1 = P_3 \oplus Q_2$ and $P_3' = P_2' \oplus Q_2 = (P_3 \oplus Q_2) \oplus Q_2 = P_3$ and $P_4' = P_3' \oplus Q_3 = P_3 \oplus Q_3$. Hence, for the choice $c = 3$, the construction gives the key P_3 consistent to both $\mathcal{A}$ and $\mathcal{B}$. It can be seen that for $i \neq c$, $P_i = P_c \oplus R$, where R is a random matrix. Since, the decoding trapdoor for such P_i's is not known, the receiver cannot decode the corresponding r_i's. A formal proof for the same is given below.

Security for $\mathcal{A}$: Let us assume $\widetilde{\mathcal{B}}$ is a PPT adversary in the proposed OT_1^N protocol $[A, \widetilde{B}](b_1, b_2, \ldots, b_N, c)$. Lemma 2 proves that probability of obtaining $P_i = P_c$ for some $i \neq c$ is negligible. Hence, it can be assumed without loss of generality that matrices $Q_1, Q_2 \ldots Q_N$ will ensure sufficient alteration in the structure of P_c. To obtain any knowledge of b_i for some $i \neq c$ the adversary has to decode y_i completely.

Since $\mathcal{A}$ is honest, $\mathcal{A}$ computes $y_i = r_i P_i \oplus z_i, \forall i$ with $\mathsf{wt}(z_i) \leq t$. Hence, the outputs of $\mathcal{A}$, $\{y_1, y_2, \ldots, y_N\}$ are decodable for the corresponding code generated by $\{P_1, P_2, \ldots, P_N\}$ if the decoding algorithm is available. Since $h(r_i)$ is a hrad-core predicate, the distribution for $\widehat{b}_i$ can be distinguished for various b_i only by obtaining the corresponding r_i. Hence, for $P_i, i \neq c$, any PPT adversary $\widetilde{B}$ with a non-negligible success probability, has to perform the following steps:

1. $r_i \leftarrow \mathsf{Decode}(y_i)$.
2. Compute, $b_i = \widehat{b}_i \oplus h(r_i)$.

Now, r_i is the solution for the *Bounded Decoding* problem with input (y_i, P_i) found with non-negligible probability by PPT algorithm $\widetilde{B}$, which is a contradiction to the assumption 1.

Security for $\mathcal{B}$: Let us assume $\widetilde{\mathcal{A}}$ is a PPT adversary in the proposed OT_1^N protocol $[\widetilde{A}, B](b_1, b_2, \ldots, b_N, c)$. On receiving a y_c that is not decodable, $\mathcal{B}$ accepts $b_c = 0$, instead of notifying $\widetilde{\mathcal{A}}$ of erroneous encryption. Thus, a malicious generation of y_i will lead to no knowledge of the appropriate c. Hence, the knowledge of the choice c is based on the information $\widetilde{\mathcal{A}}$ obtains from the keys.

Rewriting assumption 2 for $M = G \oplus R, R \in \mathbb{F}_2^{k \times n}$.

From equation (1),

$$|Pr[\mathcal{D}(G) = 1] - Pr[\mathcal{D}(G \oplus R) = 1]| < \epsilon_2$$

where ϵ_2 is a negligible function for any PPT distinguisher $\mathcal{D}$. Assume that there exists a PPT adversary $\widetilde{A}$ which finds the choice c with non-negligible probability,

$$\widetilde{\mathcal{A}}(P_1, P_2, \ldots, P_N, t) \to c$$

$\widetilde{\mathcal{A}}$ can distinguish P_c from P_i, $\forall i \in \{1, 2, \ldots, N\} \setminus \{c\}$. Note that,

$$P_i = P_1 \oplus (\oplus_{j=1}^{i-1} Q_j) = (P_c \oplus (\oplus_{j=1}^{c-1} Q_j)) \oplus (\oplus_{j=1}^{i-1} Q_j)$$

$$\implies P_j = P_c \oplus R$$

where $R = (\oplus_{j=1}^{c-1} Q_j)) \oplus (\oplus_{j=1}^{i-1} Q_j)$. Since, $\widetilde{\mathcal{A}}$ can distinguish P_c from P_i where $i \neq c$, $\widetilde{\mathcal{A}}$ can distinguish P_c from $P_c \oplus R$ with non-negligible probability. This is a contradiction to the equation (1). □

4.3   Efficiency and Parameters of the Proposed Scheme

The asymptotic efficiency of some of the OT_1^N is given in Table 1. From the table, it is clear that the proposed protocol involves only N vector matrix multiplication. These operations are computationally less expensive than N exponentiations.

It can also be noted that the communication complexity is asymptotically comparable to any OT_1^2 protocol based on McEliece assumption.

As mentioned earlier, the security of the proposed protocol is based on the hardness of *Bounded Decoding* problem and *Goppa code distinguishability* problem. The work factor required to solve the above problems is based on the parameters of the underlying code. Table 2 gives some of the secure parameters for

Table 1. Comparison of the proposed protocol with some existing OT_1^N protocols and the original OT_1^2 protocol

Scheme	Sender computation	Receiver computation	Communication
log N-dimension protocol, Naor and Pinkas, [22]	log N encryptions due to OT_1^2 protocol	log N decryptions due to OT_1^2 protocol	log N times the communication complexity of OT_1^2 protocol
2-dimensional protocol, [22]	log N encryptions due to OT_1^2 protocol	log N decryptions due to OT_1^2 protocol	log N times the communication complexity of OT_1^2 protocol
DDH based protocol, Tzeng, [35]	$2N$ exponentiations	3 exponentiations	$2N$ elements in $\mathbb{Z}_q$, for a large prime q
1-out-of-2 protocol, Dowsley et. al., [10]	2 encryptions using McEliece cryptosystems	1 invocation of decoding algorithm	2 $k \times n$ matrices
Proposed scheme	N encryptions using McEliece cryptosystem	1 invocation of decoding algorithm	2 $k \times n$ matrices,i.e,the same complexity as the underlying OT_1^2 protocol

Table 2. Parameters of the proposed OT_1^N

Parameters $[n, k, 2t + 1]$	Key size (in bits)	Binary work factor
[2048, 1696, 65]	3473408	$2^{86.8}$
[4096, 3604, 83]	14761984	$2^{128.5}$

the proposed protocol and the corresponding work factor for solving the *Bounded Decoding* problem. The proposed parameters are as per the secure parameters mentioned in [12]. For the given parameters, the *Goppa-code distinguishability* is known to be hard [7].

5 Conclusion

In this paper, we reviewed Dowsley et al.'s passive OT_1^2 protocol and formally argued its security against active adversaries. The paper also introduces an elegant and computationally efficient 1-out-of-N code based oblivious transfer based on McEliece assumptions. To the best of our knowledge, the proposed protocol is the first practical code-based OT_1^N. The scheme is proved to be computationally secure against passive and active adversaries. On comparison with some of the existing number-theoretic OT_1^N, the proposed protocol is computationally efficient. The protocol achieves a communication complexity comparable to code-based OT_1^2 asymptotically, thus making it independent of N.

References

1. Bellare, M., Micali, S.: Non-interactive oblivious transfer and applications. In: Brassard [5], pp. 547–557
2. Berlekamp, E.R., Mceliece, R.J., Vantilborg, H.C.: On the inherent intractability of certain coding problems. IEEE Transactions on Information Theory (1978)
3. Bernstein, D.J.: List decoding for binary goppa codes (2008)
4. Bernstein, D.J., Buchmann, J., Dahmen, E.: Post Quantum Cryptography, 1st edn. Springer, Heidelberg (2008) (incorporated)
5. Brassard, G. (ed.): CRYPTO 1989. LNCS, vol. 435. Springer, Heidelberg (1990)
6. Brassard, G., Crépeau, C., Robert, J.-M.: Information theoretic reductions among disclosure problems. In: FOCS, pp. 168–173. IEEE (1986)
7. Faugère, J.C., Otmani, A., Perret, L., Tillich, J.P.: A distinguisher for high rate mceliece cryptosystems
8. Courtois, N.T., Finiasz, M., Sendrier, N.: How to Achieve a McEliece-Based Digital Signature Scheme. In: Boyd, C. (ed.) ASIACRYPT 2001. LNCS, vol. 2248, pp. 157–174. Springer, Heidelberg (2001)
9. Crépeau, C.: Equivalence between Two Flavours of Oblivious Transfers. In: Pomerance, C. (ed.) CRYPTO 1987. LNCS, vol. 293, pp. 350–354. Springer, Heidelberg (1988)
10. Dowsley, R., van de Graaf, J., Müller-Quade, J., Nascimento, A.C.A.: Oblivious Transfer Based on the McEliece Assumptions. In: Safavi-Naini, R. (ed.) ICITS 2008. LNCS, vol. 5155, pp. 107–117. Springer, Heidelberg (2008)

11. Even, S., Goldreich, O., Lempel, A.: A randomized protocol for signing contracts. Commun. ACM 28(6), 637–647 (1985)
12. Finiasz, M., Sendrier, N.: Security Bounds for the Design of Code-Based Cryptosystems. In: Matsui, M. (ed.) ASIACRYPT 2009. LNCS, vol. 5912, pp. 88–105. Springer, Heidelberg (2009)
13. Goldreich, O., Levin, L.A.: A hard-core predicate for all one-way functions. In: Johnson, D.S. (ed.) STOC, pp. 25–32. ACM (1989)
14. Goldreich, O., Micali, S., Wigderson, A.: How to play any mental game or a completeness theorem for protocols with honest majority. In: STOC, pp. 218–229. ACM (1987)
15. Haitner, I.: Semi-honest to Malicious Oblivious Transfer—The Black-Box Way. In: Canetti, R. (ed.) TCC 2008. LNCS, vol. 4948, pp. 412–426. Springer, Heidelberg (2008)
16. Kalai, Y.T.: Smooth Projective Hashing and Two-Message Oblivious Transfer. In: Cramer, R. (ed.) EUROCRYPT 2005. LNCS, vol. 3494, pp. 78–95. Springer, Heidelberg (2005)
17. Kilian, J.: Founding cryptography on oblivious transfer. In: STOC, pp. 20–31. ACM (1988)
18. Kobara, K., Morozov, K., Overbeck, R.: Coding-Based Oblivious Transfer. In: Calmet, J., Geiselmann, W., Müller-Quade, J. (eds.) MMICS 2008. LNCS, vol. 5393, pp. 142–156. Springer, Heidelberg (2008)
19. Morozov, K., Savvides, G.: Efficient computational oblivious transfer using interactive hashing. In: Proceedings of the 6th ACM Symposium on Information, Computer and Communications Security, ASIACCS 2011, pp. 448–452. ACM, New York (2011)
20. Naor, M., Pinkas, B.: Oblivious transfer and polynomial evaluation. In: STOC, pp. 245–254 (1999)
21. Naor, M., Pinkas, B.: Efficient oblivious transfer protocols. In: SODA, pp. 448–457 (2001)
22. Naor, M., Pinkas, B.: Computationally secure oblivious transfer. J. Cryptology 18(1), 1–35 (2005)
23. Ostrovsky, R., Venkatesan, R., Yung, M.: Fair games against an all-powerful adversary. In: AMS DIMACS Series in Discrete Mathematics and Theoretical Computer Science, pp. 155–169 (1991)
24. Peikert, C., Vaikuntanathan, V., Waters, B.: A Framework for Efficient and Composable Oblivious Transfer. In: Wagner, D. (ed.) CRYPTO 2008. LNCS, vol. 5157, pp. 554–571. Springer, Heidelberg (2008)
25. Peikert, C., Waters, B.: Lossy trapdoor functions and their applications. In: Dwork, C. (ed.) STOC, pp. 187–196. ACM (2008)
26. Rabin, M.O.: How to exchange secrets with oblivious transfer. Cryptology ePrint Archive, Report 2005/187 (2005), http://eprint.iacr.org/
27. McEliece, R.J.: A public-key cryptosystem based on algebraic coding theory. JPL DSN Progress Report, 114–116 (1978)
28. Salomaa, A., Santean, L.: Secret selling of secrets with several buyers. Bulletin of the EATCS 42, 178–186 (1990)
29. De Santis, A., Di Crescenzo, G., Persiano, G.: Zero-knowledge arguments and public-key cryptography. Inf. Comput. 121(1), 23–40 (1995)
30. Sendrier, N.: The tightness of security reductions in code-based cryptography. In: 2011 IEEE Information Theory Workshop (ITW), pp. 415–419 (October 2011)

31. Sendrier, N.: Decoding One Out of Many. In: Yang, B.-Y. (ed.) PQCrypto 2011. LNCS, vol. 7071, pp. 51–67. Springer, Heidelberg (2011)
32. Shamir, A.: An efficient identification scheme based on permuted kernels (extended abstract). In: Brassard [5], pp. 606–609
33. Shor, P.W.: Polynominal Time Algorithms for Discrete Logarithms and Factoring on a Quantum Computer. In: Adleman, L.M., Huang, M.-D.A. (eds.) ANTS 1994. LNCS, vol. 877, p. 289. Springer, Heidelberg (1994)
34. Stern, J.: A New Identification Scheme Based on Syndrome Decoding. In: Stinson, D.R. (ed.) CRYPTO 1993. LNCS, vol. 773, pp. 13–21. Springer, Heidelberg (1994)
35. Tzeng, W.-G.: Efficient 1-out-of-n oblivious transfer schemes with universally usable parameters. IEEE Trans. Computers 53(2), 232–240 (2004)
36. Wang, H., Pieprzyk, J.: Efficient One-Time Proxy Signatures. In: Laih, C.-S. (ed.) ASIACRYPT 2003. LNCS, vol. 2894, pp. 507–522. Springer, Heidelberg (2003)

Towards Fine-Grained Access Control on Browser Extensions*

Lei Wang, Ji Xiang, Jiwu Jing, and Lingchen Zhang

State Key Lab of Information Security, Graduate University of CAS, China
{lwang,jixiang,jing,lchzhang}@is.ac.cn

Abstract. We propose a practical and fine-grained browser extension access control framework, which regulates the misbehavior of JSEs with malicious intent at run time by means of restricting the access to resources, in order to prevent the malicious JSEs from ruining users security. The resource access of a JSE, which constrains its behavior, is the basis of the functionalities of it. Instead of the conventional static access control rules, we formulate the fine-grained access control policies dynamically in the framework while JSEs are executing within Firefox, which makes our framework more flexible and practical in real-world use. We tested 100 popular JSEs on AMO to evaluate the compatibility of our framework, and found that only two of them are not compatible due to their sensitive behavior. To evaluate the capability of restraining the misbehavior of JSEs, we tested ten malicious ones and the results show that all of them are blocked by our framework before they actually misbehave.

Keywords: framework, fine-grained access control, dynamic regulation, ordinal resource access.

1 Introduction

Fundamentally, a web browser is an environment where many kinds of codes run, such as HTML, Java, AJAX and JavaScript codes, etc. As for the JavaScript codes executing inside Mozilla Firefox, they are from the browser core, websites or JSEs (JavaScript Extensions). The browser core constitutes the browser itself and achieves its main functions. JavaScript code of websites is executed by Firefox under the constraint of SOP (Same Origin Policy) [1], which is to regulate the behavior of JavaScript code in the websites. Nevertheless, there is a lack of practical and run-time policies to restrict the behavior of JSEs while they are running inside Firefox, though Mozilla offers a strict review process to check the JSE before publishing it on AMO [2], JSEs from the wild which are absent from the review process, will be dropped onto the user's computer by some malware and run when Firefox starts the next time.

---

* This work was supported by National Natural Science Foundation of China (Grant No. 70890084/G021102, 61003274 and 61003273) and Knowledge Innovation Program of Chinese Academy of Sciences (Grant No. YYYJ-1013).

M.D. Ryan, B. Smyth, and G. Wang (Eds.): ISPEC 2012, LNCS 7232, pp. 158–169, 2012.

Up to now, there are already some run-time solutions to detect and regulate the malicious JSEs [3–7]. [3] and Sabre [4] adopt the dynamic taint technology to analyze the information flow inside Firefox, which achieves high accuracy at the cost of great overhead. [5] and [6] formulate several static access control rules to restrict the privileges of JSEs. Though it incurs low overhead, it is difficult to formulate appropriate policies for each monitored JSE while preserving the accuracy. Barth et al. [7] propose a novel security browser extension framework for ensuring users security, which may need a long time to be widely deployed. As for the policies of Mozilla [8, 9], the strict review process can be easily bypassed by dropping JSEs onto the user's computer by some malware.

In this paper, we propose a practical, flexible and fine-grained browser extension access control framework, which works at run time to ensure the security of host machines against JSEs with malicious intent while they are running within Firefox. In our framework, we dynamically formulate the fine-grained access control policies with the consideration of restricting the ordinal access to some resources, instead of prohibiting accessing some certain types of resource. For example, if one of the policies in [5, 6] is that a JSE is denied to access the cookie-related XPCOM (Cross Platform Component Object Model) components which are provided by Mozilla Firefox, it means that the JSE is unable to access cookies any longer. However, ours is quite different. In our fine-grained framework, the access control policy is formulated dynamically while the JSE is running, and we only prohibit its sending out the cookie (i.e., accessing the network communication resource) after the JSE acquired it.

JSEs achieve their versatile functionalities by accessing kinds of resources. Our framework considers the ordinal access to the sensitive resources to achieve better regulation, because some popular JSEs on AMO also access the sensitive resources, however, with different resource access sequence. Legitimate JSEs usually access their own resources, which are created by themselves, and they do not leak users privacy or compromise the host machine during their lifetime. However, most JSEs with malicious intent target at compromising users' computer to obtain the private information. Therefore, we propose two modules in our framework, the access control module, which enforces the fine-grained policies towards the resource access of JSEs, and the dynamic regulations module, which dynamically formulates the access control policies, to restrict the access to resources at run time.

We implemented the framework on Firefox, version 3.6.13Pre, and tested the top 100 popular JSEs on AMO [2] to evaluate its compatibility. Only two JSEs are not compatible with our framework because of their ordinal access to the sensitive resources, e.g., the login passwords. To evaluate the capability of restraining malicious JSEs, we tested the most famous one, FFSniFF [10] which steals users passwords, and other nine malicious ones implemented by ourselves. And the experimental results show that our framework is able to prohibit their malicious behavior at run time.

To summarize, our paper makes the following contributions:

- Our browser extension access control framework is built inside Firefox and is a run-time JSE behavior-regulating mechanism. It is a much simpler and faster deployment mechanism for wide deployment in real world, compared with the framework of [7].
- The access control policies in our framework are formulated dynamically, which makes it more flexible to restrict the resource access of JSEs, and are global ones and applicable for all the JSEs running inside Firefox.
- Our framework is fine-grained and all its policies aim at restricting the ordinal access to the sensitive resources of JSEs, instead of allowing/prohibiting the access to some single resource.

2   Background Overview

2.1   Basic Notions

Resources are those that can be accessed by invoking XPCOM components provided by Mozilla Firefox, such as files, cookies, Windows registry values, DOM tree information of websites and login information, etc. Resources are the essential components of JSEs to fulfill their functionalities. *Sensitive resources* are resources that contain private and confidential information of users and can be exploited to leak private information or to compromise the host machine, such as credit card number, login account and passwords. Otherwise, the resources are considered to be *insensitive* ones, for example the configuration file and the log file created by the JSE itself.

Resource Access is the behavior of accessing the resource by a JSE. Resource access of a JSE dominates its behavior during the lifetime. Due to the types of resources, resource access is also composed of *sensitive resource access* and *insensitive resource access.*

Ordinal Resource Access to some sensitive resources are a series of actions on the sensitive resources accessed by the JSE. For example, a JSE sends the acquired passwords back to the attacker by utilizing the network communication resource after accessing the password resource.

In this paper, we focus on restricting the resource access of JSEs while they are running inside Firefox, to ensure the users security by preventing information leakage and the compromise of host machines. Methods for detecting malicious JSEs during their distribution and installation are out of scope. Malicious JSEs launching the attack in collusion with each other are also beyond the scope of this paper.

2.2   Firefox Overview

As depicted in Figure 1, there are three kinds of JavaScript codes executed inside Firefox, and they are all processed by SpiderMonkey, which is the JavaScript engine embedded within Firefox and in charge of compiling and executing the

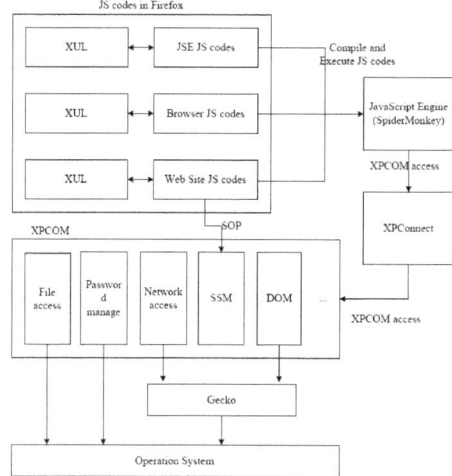

Fig. 1. JavaScript codes executing within Firefox

JavaScript codes from websites, browser core and JSEs. It also illustrates that XPCOM components of Firefox interact with OS to realize a variety of functionalities, such as communicating via network, accessing local file system, operating DOM tree of websites and so on. XPCOM components enlarge capabilities of JavaScript, and both JSEs and Firefox browser core call them to accomplish various functionalities. Therefore, XPCOM components are the essence of JSEs and almost all functionalities of JSEs are realized by invoking them, even for the simplest one, e.g., 'HelloWorld', which calls the XPCOM component of *nsIDOMJSWindow* and method of *open* to open a new window [11].

As Figure 1 shows, each calling of XPCOM components has to pass through XPConnect, which is a bridge between JavaScript and XPCOM components and is presented by Mozilla Firefox to call corresponding XPCOM components from JavaScript codes and to interact with JavaScript objects from within XPCOM components [12]. This restriction is required by Mozilla for security reasons and also becomes the main breakthrough point to realize our framework.

2.3   JavaScript Extensions of Firefox

JavaScript extensions (JSEs) are browser extensions written in JavaScript language. Up to now, there are more than seven-thousand JSEs available for download on AMO [2] and the download number of all JSEs is over 2.5 billion.

JSEs achieve versatile functionalities to extend the capabilities of Firfox. To realize its specific functionalities, a JSE accesses kinds of resources, such as files on the host machine, cookies, login information, Windows registry values and so on. Resources accessed by JSEs are the main determinant of their behavior.

3   Browser Extension Security Policy Framework

3.1   Motivation

JSEs have become the most popular extensions within Firefox, but there are no secure enough policies to prohibit them from hurting users security at run time while Firefox is running equipped with JSEs.

- Though Mozilla provides a strict review process to check JSEs, there are not sufficient policies on restricting the resource access while Firefox is running equipped with JSEs.
- Other than installing from AMO, there are some ways to install JSEs, e.g., dropping the JSE into the extension directory of Firefox. Some malware may utilize this to drop a malicious JSE into Firefox while it is running, and the malicious JSE works when Firefox starts the next time, which is absent from the review process of Mozilla.
- Ter Louw et al. [5, 6] proposed some resource access restriction rules, and they aim at restricting the resources accessed by JSEs, which is partially consistent with our idea. However, they only consider the resource access and neglect the ordinal behavior of JSEs, which makes it difficult to formulate appropriate policies for each JSE.
- Barth et al. [7] proposed a novel browser extension system that improves the browser security by adjusting the JSEs' development pattern with least privilege, privilege separation and strong isolation principles. Though it is an excellent solution, it changes the development pattern of browser extensions and needs a long time for widespread deployment.

Therefore, we propose a run-time behavior-regulating browser extension access control framework to regulate the misbehavior of JSEs with malicious intent by restricting the ordinal access to some sensitive resources for them.

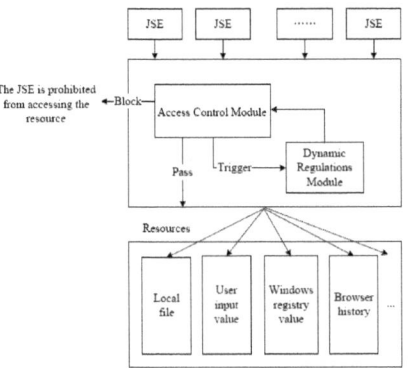

Fig. 2. The architecture of our framework

3.2   Architecture

The architecture of our framework is shown in Figure 2. It is located between JSEs and the resources to ensure that all the policies are checked before the resources are accessed by JSEs. Our framework prohibits the misbehavior of JSEs before it actually occurs. It is composed of two modules, an access control module, which enforces the fine-grained policies to restrict the resource access of JSEs, and a dynamic regulations module, which dynamically formulates the access control policies to restrict the ordinal access to some sensitive resources.

3.3   Access Control Module

The access control module is composed of resource acquiring component, resource classifying component, filtering component and triggering component, and the architecture is shown in Figure 3.

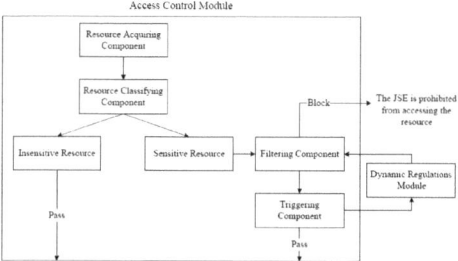

Fig. 3. The architecture of the access control module

Resource Acquiring Component.   To realize the whole functions of the framework, first of all we have to relate the JSE with its accessing resources and recognize what kinds of resources the JSE is accessing, which is the primary function of this component. Its implementation is described in detail in Section 4.2.

Resource Classifying Component.   The resource classifying component is used to determine whether the resource accessed by a JSE is sensitive. If the resource accessed by the JSE is insensitive, the resource access continues without any interference. If the resource is sensitive, the resource access enters the filtering component and the triggering component starts the dynamic regulations module subsequently.

After we analyze the behavior of top 25 popular JSEs on AMO, we found that legitimate JSEs usually access their own resources, for example files created by themselves. All the resources accessed by JSEs and their classifications are summarized in Table 1, and each type of resource in the table is given a badge to avoid verbosity in the following reference. We strive to make JSEs access the resources reasonably, because the resources are associated with the behavior of JSEs.

Table 1. Resources accessed by JSEs

Resources	Resource Instances	Label	Badge
Files	Configuration files	Insensitive	A
	Log files	Insensitive	B
	CSS (Cascading Style Sheets) files of web pages	Insensitive	C
	Temporary files	Insensitive	D
	Files created by the JSE itself	Insensitive	E
	Executable files downloaded from the Internet	Sensitive	F
	Files on the host machine apart from the above	Sensitive	G
Cookies	Cookies created by the JSE itself	Insensitive	H
	Cookies created others	Sensitive	I
Login information	Login information created by the JSE itself	Insensitive	J
	Login information created others	Sensitive	K
Windows registry values	Registry values created by the JSE itself	Insensitive	L
	Registry values created others	Sensitive	M
Browsing history	Browsing history of users	Sensitive	N
Node value of web pages	'input' node value of the web page DOM tree	Sensitive	O
	Other node values of the web page DOM tree	Insensitive	P
Network communication	HTTP/HTTPs network communication to send	Sensitive	Q
	HTTP/HTTPs network communication to receive	Sensitive	R
	Email communication to send	Sensitive	S
	Email communication to receive	Sensitive	T
Processes	processes created/launched by the JSE	Sensitive	U
	processes killed by the JSE	Sensitive	V

Filtering Component. In the beginning, there is no filtering policy in this component. Policies of this component are all formulated dynamically by the dynamic regulations module. All the sensitive resource access has to be checked by the filtering policies in this component before it actually occurs. If the access complies with the filtering policies, the access is blocked immediately and the JSE stops working. Otherwise the JSE continues working without any interference.

Triggering Component. When the resource accessed by a JSE is sensitive, the triggering component will trigger the dynamic regulations module to dynamically formulate the access control policies for the accessed resource.

3.4   Dynamic Regulations Module

The dynamic regulations module is proposed to formulate the fine-grained access control policies and to restrict the ordinal resource access of JSEs when the resources accessed by JSEs are sensitive ones.

The framework is composed of several dynamic access control policies, which target at restricting the ordinal resource access of JSEs and can be added dynamically in future. At present, there are two policies to enhance the access control policies: (1) never to send the sensitive information out after acquiring them, meaning that the JSE is prevented from accessing the sensitive resources Q and S after accessing G, I, K, M, N or O; (2) never to launch the executable files after downloading them from the Internet, meaning that if the JSE accesses the sensitive resource F, the access to U will be denied. Policies can be dynamically appended if the restriction of the resource access becomes more strict in future.

The access control policies are formulated after analyzing 25 popular JSEs on AMO. These JSEs never send any sensitive information out even if they access the information and never launch the executable file even if they download it from the Internet. In contrast, most JSEs with malicious intent aim at stealing private information of users. It inspires us to formulate the appropriate and fine-grained policies in our framework to prevent leakage of users private information and the compromise of host machines.

Malicious JSEs usually launch attacks by accessing several sensitive resources ordinally. Taking FFSniFF [10] as an example, it acquires the 'input' node value of the web page DOM tree (accessing the sensitive resource O) in the beginning, which is definitely identified by our framework. Since the accessed resource is sensitive and contains private information of users, the dynamic regulations module is triggered to append the first policy to the access control policies and its subsequent resource access is to be filtered by the filtering component. Once our framework detects that its subsequent behavior is to send the acquired information out over network (accessing the sensitive resource S), FFSniFF is terminated immediately due to the restriction policy. Though FFSniFF acquires the 'input' node values, it does not send them back to the attacker actually. Hence, users security is protected by our framework.

4   Implementation

4.1   Position to Achieve the Framework

As shown in Figure 1, while a JSE is running within Firefox, it invokes XP-COM components, which are called by XPConnect, provided by Firefox to access the resources. Therefore, we achieve the functionalities of the framework by adding codes in XPConnect. According to our analysis of XPConnect, we locate the framework in the function $XPCWrappedNative :: CallMethod$, which is used to invoke XPCOM components in XPConnect ultimately. We realize the framework just before calling XPCOM components, so that each invocation of XPCOM components is protected through the framework.

To realize our framework, the most essential procedure is to acquire all the resources accessed by the JSE, and then we enforce all the policies of the framework before the resources are accessed. Therefore, we propose the implementation of the resource acquiring component next.

4.2   Resource Acquiring Component

Because the resources accessed by a JSE are expressed in the form of XPCOM components and their arguments while it is running, the resource acquiring component of the access control module is responsible for distilling XPCOM components and their arguments and relating them with the JSE.

In this component, we intercept all the XPCOM components invoked by JSEs in XPConnect rather than SpiderMonkey and XPCOM, taking advantage of the restrictions of Mozilla. We utilize the call stack of JavaScript codes to relate the XPCOM components with a JSE in order to distinguish that invoked by Firefox browser core. For example, when FFSniFF is accessing the 'input' node value of the web page DOM tree, we identify and record the JSE name 'ffsniff' in the source filename (e.g., chrome://ffsniff/content/ffsniffOverlay.js) whose file contains the currently running JavaScript codes, in the JavaScript call stack 'JSStackFrame'. FFSniFF invokes the XPCOM component, 'nsIDOMHTMLInputElement', and its method 'getElementsByTagName' with an argument 'input' to access the 'input' node value, which is considered as the sensitive resource in our framework. Therefore, we accomplish the procedure of relating the accessed resources with the JSE.

During this distilling procedure, we found that the arguments of some XP-COM components contain all the information we want, for example *nsIXML-HttpRequest.open* (*A.B* denotes calling the method *B* of XPCOM component *A*) contains the type of request and the requested URI, when a JSE is to communicate with a remote server via network. However, in the case of reading a file in the local disk by invoking *nsIScriptableInputStream.read*, its only argument is the length of the accessed contents and there is no filename. In this scenario, we analyze the anterior XPCOM components and their arguments, e.g., we acquire the filename of the accessed file in the argument of *nsILocalFile.initWithPath*. Therefore, we are able to record XPCOM components, their arguments and the resources accessed by the JSE completely.

5   Evaluation

5.1   Compatibility with Legitimate JSEs

We have tested 100 popular JSEs on AMO [2] (including the aforementioned 25 JSEs) to evaluate the compatibility of our policy framework. For each popular JSE, we installed it from AMO and triggered its core functionalities. The experimental results show that our policy framework is efficient, accurate and compatible with most JSEs and with only 2-in-100 false positive rate.

LastPass and *StumbleUpon* are the two JSEs that violate policies of the framework and are prohibited from working, because they satisfy the characteristics of attacks, i.e., sending data over network after reading sensitive information. *LastPass* is an online password manager, and it automatically fills out forms, accesses and manages users data, thus there is security risk that *LastPass* steals users private data if the author has malicious intent. Whereas *StumbleUpon* accesses users cookies to discover great websites that match users interests during running. Therefore, the two JSEs are regulated to stop working by our framework. Actually most legitimate JSEs do not have these characteristics. Due to the popularity of *LastPass* and *StumbleUpon*, we maintain a static access control policy to whitelist them.

5.2   Effectiveness on Restricting Malicious JSEs

In this section, we evaluated the framework with obviously malicious JSEs to test the efficiency and accuracy of prohibiting malicious JSEs. Due to the difficulty of acquiring samples of malicious JSEs listed on Mozilla blocklist [13], we implemented nine JSEs that behave maliciously besides FFSniFF, which can be obtained on Internet.

- **Downloading from the Internet.** FFSniFF is acquired from the Internet and it aims at stealing the passwords input by users on web pages [10]. JSEs on Mozilla blocklist are not available for download any more, therefore, we just test this one as a popular malicious JSE towards our framework.
- **Tampering with a legitimate JSE to make it behave maliciously.** Because Firefox does not check the integrity of a JSE once it is installed, we modified the source codes of an installed JSE, NoScript, to attach malicious behavior, e.g., stealing sensitive information, downloading and executing codes.
- **Implementing malicious JSEs by ourselves.** According to our analysis on the behavior of malicious JSEs, we have implemented eight malicious JSEs that include but not limited to the malicious behavior of sensitive information theft and pernicious executive downloading.

We evaluated the policy framework with all the ten malicious JSEs listed above, and it was able to identify and prohibit all the malicious JSEs we tested. Experimental results show that our framework is an efficient mechanism to restrict the misbehavior of JSEs and is transparent to users.

5.3   Performance

To evaluate the performance of the framework, we utilized three popular browser benchmark suits, SunSpider [14], Acid3 [15] and Kraken [16] to run the comprehensive tests. Our test platform is a 2.33GHz Intel Core2 Quad machine running Microsoft Windows XP Professional SP3 with 4GB RAM and the version of Firefox we used is 3.6.13pre.

Table 2 shows the experimental results. It depicts that our policy framework brings in only 7.567% additional overhead with the SunSpider benchmark suit, and 3.236% higher overhead with Kraken, compared with original, unmodified Firefox. The framework has little influence on JavaScript compiling and executing from the score of SunSpider, and has no effect on modern technologies used on Web 2.0, as the result of Kraken shown. With Mozilla's own benchmark suit, Kraken, the framework costs only 3.236% more overhead than unmodified Firefox. The most time-consuming procedure in our framework is the dynamic formulation and enforcement procedure of the fine-grained access control policies, which has to formulate the policies and to take appropriate actions on the information cached in the computer memory that is acquired by the resource acquiring component according to the policies.

6   Related Work

Review Process [8, 9]. Mozilla provides a review process to ensure that a JSE is safe and available for download on AMO [2] only if it passes the review

Table 2. The results of performance evaluation

	Original Firefox	Modified Firefox	Overhead
SunSpider 0.91	1321.6ms	1421.6ms	7.567%
Acid3	94/100	94/100	0
Kraken 1.1	24704.0ms	25503.4ms	3.236%

process. The review process of JSEs includes two categories, full review and preliminary review. Full review requires the source codes and functionalities of JSEs to be examined cautiously by editors. Yet preliminary review process is a faster review intended for the experimental JSEs and does not check for functionality or full policy compliance. JSEs on AMO were all reviewed by the editors and installing JSEs from AMO is the most secure way. However, we can also drop JSEs into the extension directory of Firefox, e.g., *C: \Program Files \Mozilla Firefox \extensions*, to install them, which can be utilized by malwares. The existing review process of Mozilla seems helpless to this. Therefore, we need a run-time behavior-regulating mechanism against JSEs, which works while Firefox is running equipped with JSEs.

Access Control Policies. Ter Louw et al. [5, 6] are the first to address the security of JSEs and utilize XPCOM components calling to identify malicious JSEs. They monitor the XPCOM components called by JSEs to restrict the XPCOM access of JSEs by defining several static access control rules. Their mechanism just takes care of single XPCOM component called by JSEs, whereas our framework focuses on restricting the ordinal resource access of JSEs, which is reflected in both XPCOM components and their arguments, and dynamically formulating the global policies to restrict the resource access of JSEs.

Security Framework. Due to the high accuracy of the dynamic taint analysis technique, several researchers adopt this technical solution in several prior works [3, 4]. They all aim at detecting malicious JSEs and preventing them from hurting users security. Besides the dynamic taint analysis technology, some security researchers put forward overall security frameworks for securing JSEs [7, 17, 18]. Barth et al. [7] proposed a security browser extension framework within the web browser, Google Chrome. To utilize the extension framework, all extensions have to be developed by a new pattern which is not compatible with that currently used, and all the existing extensions have to be rewritten, which may need a long time for wide deployment in real world. VEX [17, 18] is another extension framework proposed to find vulnerabilities in JSEs, which adopts the static information flow technology to analyze JSEs offline. Nevertheless, our framework is working online to restrict the misbehavior of JSEs while Firefox is running. And with the advantage of the implementation, our framework is a much more fast deployment mechanism in practical real world use.

7   Conclusion

We proposed a practical, realtime, efficient and fine-grained browser extension access control framework, that is capable of regulating and restricting the misbehavior of JSEs by several global policies. Policies of our framework are dynamically formulated on the basis of the fine-grained resource access control and the ordinal resource access of JSEs, and are proposed to restrict the misbehavior of JSEs with malicious intent and to protect users' security. The framework is integrated inside Firefox, which makes it a fast deployment mechanism in real-world use. Experimental results show that the framework achieves efficiency and accuracy and is a simple and efficient restriction mechanism for restricting the resource access of JSEs at run time while Firefox is running equipped with JSEs.

References

1. SOP: The Same-Origin Policy (August 2001),
   `http://www.mozilla.org/projects/security/components/same-origin.html`
2. Amo: Addons.mozilla.org, `https://addons.mozilla.org`
3. Djeric, V., Goel, A.: Securing script-based extensibility in web browsers. In: USENIX Security (2010)
4. Dhawan, M., Ganapathy, V.: Analyzing information flow in JavaScript-based browser extensions. In: 2009 Annual Computer Security Applications Conference, pp. 382–391. IEEE (2009)
5. Ter Louw, M., Lim, J.S., Venkatakrishnan, V.N.: Extensible Web Browser Security. In: Hämmerli, B.M., Sommer, R. (eds.) DIMVA 2007. LNCS, vol. 4579, pp. 1–19. Springer, Heidelberg (2007)
6. Ter Louw, M., Lim, J.S., Venkatakrishnan, V.N.: Enhancing web browser security against malware extensions. Journal in Computer Virology 4(3), 179–195 (2008)
7. Barth, A., Felt, A., Saxena, P., Boodman, A.: Protecting browsers from extension vulnerabilities. In: Proceedings of the 17th Network and Distributed System Security Symposium (NDSS), San Diego, CA, Citeseer (2010)
8. Review process of mozilla,
   `https://addons.mozilla.org/en-US/developers/docs/policies/reviews`
9. Add-on reviews,
   `https://wiki.mozilla.org/AMO:Editors/EditorGuide/AddonReviews`
10. Ffsniff: Firefox sniffer (June 2008),
    `http://azurit.elbiahosting.sk/ffsniff`
11. Building an firefox extension,
    `https://developer.mozilla.org/en/Building_an_Extension`
12. Mozilla xpconnect, `https://developer.mozilla.org/en/XPConnect`
13. Mozilla addons blocklist, `http://www.mozilla.com/en-US/blocklist/`
14. Sunspider javascript benchmark,
    `http://www.webkit.org/perf/sunspider/sunspider.html`
15. Acid3 benchmark, `http://www.webstandards.org/action/acid3/`
16. Kraken benchmark, `http://krakenbenchmark.mozilla.org/index.html`
17. Bandhakavi, S., King, S., Madhusudan, P., Winslett, M.: VEX: vetting browser extensions for security vulnerabilities. In: USENIX Security (2010)
18. Bandhakavi, S., Tiku, N., Pittman, W., King, S.T., Madhusudan, P., Winslett, M.: Vetting browser extensions for security vulnerabilities with vex. Communications of the ACM 54(9), 91–99 (2011)

Enhanced STE3D-CAP:
A Novel 3D CAPTCHA Family

Yang-Wai Chow[1] and Willy Susilo[2,*]

[1]Centre for Multimedia and Information Processing
[2]Centre for Computer and Information Security Research
School of Computer Science and Software Engineering
University of Wollongong, Australia
{caseyc,wsusilo}@uow.edu.au

Abstract. With the growth of the Internet, its wide-ranging services are increasingly being threatened by adverse and malicious attacks. CAPTCHAs have emerged as a standard security countermeasure against Internet attacks such as distributed denial of service attacks and botnets. However, many CAPTCHA schemes themselves have been found to be susceptible to automated attacks. The task of designing a good CAPTCHA scheme is still an open and challenging question, as a good CAPTCHA must fulfil two fundamental requirements; namely, it must be secure against automated attacks whilst being human usable. This paper presents STE3D-CAP-e, a human usable text-based CAPTCHA that is robust against a variety of attacks. STE3D-CAP-e adopts a novel 3D CAPTCHA approach designed to capitalise on the inherent human ability to perceive depth from stereoscopic images. By presenting CAPTCHA challenges using stereoscopic images, humans can distinguish the main text from the background clutter in 3D. The various issues that were considered and addressed in the design of STE3D-CAP-e are described, along with a formal definition of its underlying AI problem family. This paper also presents analysis of STE3D-CAP-e in terms of its security and usability.

Keywords: CAPTCHA, stereoscopic, usability, segmentation-resistant.

1 Introduction

In recent years, CAPTCHAs (Completely Automated Public Turing test to tell Computers and Humans Apart) have become ubiquitous on the Internet as a security countermeasure against adverse attacks like distributed denial of service attacks and botnets. While the idea of 'Automated Turing Tests' has been around for some time, the term 'CAPTCHA' was introduced by von Ahn et al. [13] as automated tests that humans can pass, but current computer programs cannot pass. In their seminal work, they describe CAPTCHAs as hard Artificial Intelligence (AI) problems that can be exploited for security purposes.

---

* This work is supported by ARC Future Fellowship FT0991397.

M.D. Ryan, B. Smyth, and G. Wang (Eds.): ISPEC 2012, LNCS 7232, pp. 170–181, 2012.

This has given rise to an arms race between CAPTCHA developers, who attempt to create more secure CAPTCHAs, and attackers, who try to break them. The development of a good CAPTCHA scheme is not an easy task as it must be secure against automated attacks, and at the same time, it must be usable by humans (i.e. human-friendly). Of the different categories of CAPTCHAs (e.g. image-based CAPTCHAs, audio CAPTCHAs) that have emerged thus far, text-based CAPTCHAs are the most common and widely deployed category to date. The popularity of text-based CAPTCHAs is due, in part, to its intuitiveness to users world-wide in addition to its potential to provide strong security [15].

STE3D-CAP (pronounced 'steed-cap' /'stidkæp/)[1], or Stereoscopic 3D CAPT-CHA, was introduced as a novel CAPTCHA approach that was designed to be segmentation-resistant whilst being human usable [11]. The fundamental idea behind STE3D-CAP is to present CAPTCHA challenges to the user using stereoscopic images. This technique relies on the inherent human ability to perceive depth from stereoscopic images. If the stereoscopic CAPTCHA is designed well, this task will be easy and natural for humans but difficult for current computer programs. By incorporating stereoscopic images in the CAPTCHA challenge, segmentation-resistant methods like adding clutter and 'crowding characters together' can be implemented to a higher degree whilst still maintaining usability. This is because to humans, the text in the resulting CAPTCHA will appear to stand out from the clutter in the perceived 3D scene.

1.1   Our Contributions

This paper was inspired by the work by Susilo et al. [11], where they introduced a CAPTCHA built from stereoscopic images which they called STE3D-CAP. This paper builds on the concepts underlying STE3D-CAP, and presents a new and improved stereoscopic CAPTCHA design. We will refer to this enhanced version as STE3D-CAP-e. The work in [11] relied on the use of specialised stereoscopic display hardware to present stereoscopic images to the user [11]. However, as stereoscopic 3D devices have yet to become ubiquitous, this restricts the pervasiveness of STE3D-CAP. Therefore, the work presented here focuses on an anaglyph approach to presenting STE3D-CAP-e challenges. Nevertheless, it should be noted that this in no way precludes the use of stereoscopic display devices for STE3D-CAP-e.

Instead of adding random clutter, as used in a variety of other CAPTCHAs and in [11] in STE3D-CAP-e the clutter will consist of characters in the background. This will appear as 'text-on-text' and the resulting CAPTCHA challenge will be to distinguish the main characters from the background characters. The innovation of using text as the background clutter makes the task of segmentation all the more difficult for computers.

Two versions of STE3D-CAP-e are presented in this paper; one in which the rendered characters appear as solid objects, and the other that uses wireframe characters. Examples of these are shown in Figure 1(a) and 1(b) respectively.

---

[1] 'Steed' - a spirited horse, especially for war.

These stereoscopic CAPTCHAs can be viewed using red-cyan anaglyph glasses. To solve STE3D-CAP-e, a user must identify the foreground characters.

(a) Solid object version. Foreground characters = 'TEKX'

(b) Wireframe version. Foreground characters = 'ECFU'

Fig. 1. Examples of STE3D-CAP-e, which can be viewed in 3D using a pair of red-cyan anaglyph glasses

2   Related Work

2.1   CAPTCHA Security

CAPTCHA security has been the topic of much scrutiny. A number of researchers have demonstrated that many existing CAPTCHA schemes are vulnerable to automated attacks. Much of this vulnerability stems from certain design flaws in these CAPTCHAs.

2.2   CAPTCHA Usability

In addition to the security strength, or robustness, of a CAPTCHA scheme, the other issue that has to be considered when designing CAPTCHAs is its ease of use for humans. ScatterType is an example of a text-based CAPTCHA that was designed to resist segmentation attacks[2], however initial usability experiments showed an overall legibility rate of 53% [1]. The legibility rate was subject to the difficulty level of the CAPTCHA challenge. Baird et al. [1] stated that the CAPTCHA generation parameter range could be controlled to be within an operating regime that would result in highly human legible CAPTCHAs. However, they also reported that there was weak correlation between the generating parameters and the desired properties, thus making automatic selection of suitably legible challenges difficult.

Another usability issue is that before being able to identify individual characters in the string, humans must first be able to distinguish the text from any background clutter. In addition to its aesthetic properties, the use of colour or background textures can make the task of perceiving the text from the background easier. However, it has been shown that inappropriate use of colour and

---

[2] It is observed that for the human legible challenges in this CAPTCHA, it can probably be segmented using something similar to the vertical pixel-count attack as described in [14].

background textures can be problematic in terms of both usability and security [15]. In general, if the background colour or texture can easily be separated from the text using an automated program, then it does not contribute to the security strength of the CAPTCHA and it may be better not to use it as it can actually harm usability. This is because it may make it hard to see the actual text or be distracting for a human user.

2.3   3D CAPTCHAs

A number of attempts at designing and developing 3D CAPTCHAs have recently emerged in literature and in practice. These approaches typically generate CAPTCHA challenges by rendering 3D models of text-objects or of other objects.

Among 3D CAPTCHA ideas that have been proposed in the research community, Mitra et al. [7] proposed a technique of generating 'emerging images' by rendering extremely abstract representations of 3D models placed in 3D environments. This approach is based on 'emergence', the unique human ability to perceive objects in an image not by recognising the object parts, but as a whole [7]. Ross et al. [9] presented a pilot usability study and security analysis of a prototype implementation of their CAPTCHA called 'Sketcha'. Sketcha is based on oriented line drawings of 3D models and the user's task is to correctly orient images containing these 3D model line drawings.

3   Enhanced Stereoscopic 3D CAPTCHA: **STE3D-CAP-e**

STE3D-CAP-e is a text-based CAPTCHA that is designed to be human usable, yet at the same time robust against a variety of automated attacks. The underlying concept behind STE3D-CAP-e is to present the CAPTCHA challenge to the user via stereoscopic images. When viewed in 3D, legitimate human users should be able to distinguish the main text from the background clutter. This approach attempts to exploit the difference in ability between humans and computers in the task of 3D perception.

3.1   Design and Implementation

The security strength of a CAPTCHA is determined by the cumulative effects of its design choices [4]. A number of security flaws found in existing CAPTCHA designs was previously outlined in section 2. STE3D-CAP-e was designed to overcome these, by addressing the following issues in its design and implementation:

– Instead of using random clutter, in STE3D-CAP-e the background clutter consists of characters themselves. This 'text-on-text' approach makes it extremely difficult for a computer to correctly segment the resulting CAPTCHA. On the other hand, stereoscopy is part of the human visual system and when STE3D-CAP-e is viewed in 3D, humans should be able to identify the foreground characters from the background characters. In the Mori and Malik

[8] attack on Gimpy, they state that it is nearly impossible to determine individual characters in such severe clutter, as many parts can be occluded or highly ambiguous. Therefore, in the second part of their work they presented a holistic approach to determine entire words [8].

- STE3D-CAP-e uses random characters. As such, holistic approaches that rely on a database of dictionary words (or phonetic strings) to identify entire words will not work.
- In addition, STE3D-CAP-e is a variable length CAPTCHA. Variable length CAPT-CHAs are harder to segment as the attacker has limited prior knowledge regarding the exact length of the solution [14].
- STE3D-CAP-e uses both local and global warping. This significantly deters pixel-count attacks [16].
- Random 3D transformations are also implemented for all characters in STE3D-CAP-e. Thus, increasing the difficulty of attacks.
- All characters are rendered using the same colour. Therefore, colour cannot be used as a criteria to separate the background from the foreground.
- Furthermore, STE3D-CAP-e adopts the 'crowding characters together' approach for both the background and foreground characters, and also overlaps character rows, which makes the task of segmentation all the more difficult.

The current implementation of STE3D-CAP-e consists of 3 rows, with 7 characters per row. The character set is made up of capital letters and digits. Characters in the rows are made to overlap in the vertical direction and the characters in the columns are crowded together in the horizontal direction, at times overlapping or joining together. The foreground characters consist of 3 to 5 characters, in sequence, that can start from any location in the middle row. Initial implementations allowed foreground characters to take random locations, but this had usability implications as it confused users.

The other reason for restricting foreground characters to the middle row, is because it may be possible to identify characters in the top and bottom rows by trying to recognise the top part or bottom part of the characters in those rows. Placing the foreground characters in the middle row circumvents this. Although in doing so, attackers will have this information. Nevertheless, this does not make the task of segmentation or identifying individual characters any easier, due to the overlapping characters from both the top and bottom rows.

It should be noted that STE3D-CAP-e can easily be expanded to contain more rows and columns, and longer foreground character strings. However, this was thought to make the challenge unnecessarily confusing. In addition, a variety of factors can also be adjusted (e.g. amount of local and global warping, transformation range, etc.) Two versions of STE3D-CAP-e were implemented, one by rendering characters as solid objects and the other by rendering them in wireframe. Examples of these were previously shown in Figure 1(a) and 1(b) respectively.

3.2   Issues Unique to **STE3D-CAP-e**

In light of the fact that STE3D-CAP-e uses a novel stereoscopic approach to present CAPTCHA challenges, there are several issues unique to STE3D-CAP-e that are not relevant to other CAPTCHAs. These are discussed as follows.

Stereoscopy. Stereoscopy relates to the perception of depth in the human visual system that arises from the interocular distance (i.e. the distance between the eyes) [3]. When presented with a stereo pair, two images created for the left and right eyes respectively, the human visual system perceives the sensation of depth through a process known as stereopsis. Stereopsis relies on binocular disparity (i.e. the difference in the images that are projected onto the left and right eye retinas, then onto the visual cortex), to obtain depth cues from stereoscopic images. Stereoscopic display technologies simulate binocular disparity by presenting different images to each of the viewer's eyes independently [6]. If the stereoscopic images are generated correctly, the visual cortex will fuse the images to give rise to the sense of depth. There are a variety of different stereoscopic display technologies, a comprehensive overview can be found in McAllister [6].

There are a number of factors to consider when generating stereoscopic images. One of which is referred to as stereoscopic parallax, or simply parallax. Parallax is the distance (which can be positive or negative) between the projected positions of a point in the left and right eye views on the projection plane. A point in space that is projected onto the projection plane can be classified as having one of three relationships:

- Zero parallax occurs when the projected point coincides with the projection plane. This will result in the pixel position of the projected point being at exactly the same position in the anaglyph image.
- Positive parallax occurs when the projected point is located behind the projection plane. In this case, the pixel position of the projected point is located on the right for the right eye, and on the left for the left eye. When perceived in 3D, the point will appear at a depth 'into' the screen.
- Negative parallax occurs when the projected point is located in front of the projection plane. When this happens, the pixel position of the projected point is located on the left in the right image and on the right in the left image. Viewed in 3D, the viewer will perceive the point as coming 'out' of the screen.

Since STE3D-CAP-e challenges are generated in 3D, this allows greater flexibility in the random transformation of 3D characters. Unlike traditional 2D CAPTCHAs in which characters can only be randomly translated in the horizontal and vertical dimensions, and rotated clockwise or counter-clockwise. In STE3D-CAP-e characters can be randomly translated 'into' or 'out of' the screen. In addition to clockwise and counter-clockwise rotation, the 3D characters in STE3D-CAP-e can also have random rotations in terms of their yaw and pitch.

In normal perspective projection, objects will get smaller with distance from the viewer. However, this must be avoided in STE3D-CAP-e, otherwise separating foreground from background characters will be a simple matter of distinguishing characters based on their size. As such, the characters in STE3D-CAP-e are scaled in a way that makes them all appear to be of similar sizes when rendered in the 2D image, despite them being at different depths in 3D.

Another issue that had to be addressed was how to make it difficult for computer vision techniques to reconstruct the 3D scene. To achieve this, characters in STE3D-CAP-e are rendered in a random order with a degree of translucency. This effectively blends the colours of the foreground and background characters together and creates a 'see-through' effect (the degree of which can be adjusted), thus making it harder for attacks involving image processing and computer vision techniques. This is discussed in section 4.2.

Limitations. The unique nature of STE3D-CAP-e also results in a number of limitations:

- STE3D-CAP-e is a visual CAPTCHA, and like all other visual CAPTCHAs, it is not accessible to those with visual impairments. In addition, STE3D-CAP-e cannot be used by individuals who are stereo-blind.
- To view STE3D-CAP-e in 3D, a stereoscopic display approach has to be used. For the anaglyph approach, this requires a pair of anaglyph glasses. While these are cheap to produce, it gives rise to the limitation that individuals who are colour-blind, or have a colour defect which coincides with the anaglyph colour filters, will not be able to view STE3D-CAP-e in 3D. This can be overcome using other stereoscopic display approaches (e.g. autostereoscopic displays or active shutter glasses). However, while these devices are the way of the future, they have yet to become ubiquitous.
- To comfortably view STE3D-CAP-e challenges in 3D, its display size cannot be too small.

3.3   New AI Problem Family

This section introduces the AI problem family used to construct STE3D-CAP-e. This is based on the definitions and notations defined in von Ahn et al. [13]. To commence, the terminology that will be used throughout this section is defined as follows.

An image is defined as an $h \times w$ matrix (where h stands for height and w stands for width), whose entries are pixels. A pixel is defined as a triplet (R, G, B), where $0 \leq R, G, B \leq M$, for a constant M [13]. Let $\mathcal{I}_{2d}$ be a distribution on 2D images (i.e. anaglyph),and $\mathcal{I}_{3d}$ be a distribution on 3D images, $\mathcal{T}_{2d}$ be a distribution on 2D transformations, and $\mathcal{T}_{3d}$ be a distribution on 3D transformations, that includes rotation, scaling, translation and warping. The depth of a 3D image is denoted by d, where $d = 0$ represents a foreground image. Let $\mathcal{T}_{3d} : \mathcal{I}_{3d} \rightarrow \mathcal{I}_{3d}$ be a transformation function that accepts a 3D image and produce a distorted 3D image. Let $\mathcal{T}_{2d} : \mathcal{I}_{2d} \rightarrow \mathcal{I}_{2d}$ be a transformation function that accepts a 2D image (anaglyph) to produce a distorted 2D image. Functions $\mathcal{T}_{3d}$ and $\mathcal{T}_{2d}$ apply local warping/distortion to each 3D image and global warping/distortion to the final 2D image. Let $\mathcal{F} : \mathcal{I}_{3d} \times \mathbb{Z} \to \mathcal{I}_{3d}$ be a function that transforms a 3D image (that is originally at depth $d = 0$) to a 3D image of depth $d \in \mathbb{Z}$. Let $\mathcal{G} : \mathcal{I}_{3d} \times \mathbb{Z} \to \mathcal{I}_{3d}$ be a function that 'extracts' the 3D image at layer $d \in \mathbb{Z}$ to produce a new 3D image. Let $\mathcal{E} : \mathcal{I}_{3d} \to \mathcal{I}_{2d}$ be an anaglyph extraction function, that extracts an anaglyph image (in the $\mathcal{I}_{2d}$ set) from a 3D image (in the $\mathcal{I}_{3d}$ set). Note that for practicality, we assume that any new 3D image created will have depth $d = 0$ (i.e. in the foreground). Let $\uplus : \mathcal{I}_{3d} \times \mathcal{I}_{3d} \to \mathcal{I}_{3d}$ be a function that combine two 3D images into a single 3D image. Let $|A|$ be the cardinality of A. Let $\Delta : |\mathcal{I}_{3d}| \to \mathcal{I}_{3d}$ be a lookup function that maps an index in $|\mathcal{I}_{3d}|$ and outputs a 3D image in $\mathcal{I}_{3d}$. Let ℓ be the length of the STE3D-CAP-e challenge. Let γ be the number of layers that will be used for the clutter in STE3D-CAP-e.

For clarity, the rest of this paper will use **Roman boldface** characters to denote elements of $\mathcal{I}_{3d}$ and Sans Serif characters to denote elements of $\mathcal{I}_{2d}$.

Problem Family ($\mathcal{P}_{\mathsf{STE3D\text{-}CAP\text{-}e}}$)
Consider the following experiment.

1. Randomly select $\mathcal{I} := \{i \in |\mathcal{I}_{3d}|^{\ell}\}$.
2. For each $i \in \mathcal{I}$, compute $\widetilde{\mathcal{I}} := \{\mathbf{i} \leftarrow \Delta(i)\}$.
3. For each $\mathbf{i} \in \widetilde{\mathcal{I}}$, compute $\widetilde{\mathcal{I}} := \{\mathcal{T}_{3d}(\mathbf{i})\}$.
4. For $\beta := 1$ to γ do
   (a) Randomly select $\mathcal{C} := \{c \in |\mathcal{I}_{3d}|^{\ell}\}$.
   (b) For each $c \in \mathcal{C}$, compute $\widetilde{\mathcal{C}} := \{\mathbf{c} \leftarrow \Delta(i)\}$.
   (c) For each $\mathbf{c} \in \widetilde{\mathcal{C}}$, compute $\widetilde{\mathcal{C}} := \{\mathcal{T}_{3d}(\mathbf{c})\}$.
   (d) For each $\mathbf{c} \in \widetilde{\mathcal{C}}$, compute $\widehat{\mathcal{C}} := \{\mathcal{F}(\mathbf{c}, \beta)\}$.
   (e) For each $\mathbf{i} \in \widetilde{\mathcal{I}}, \mathbf{c} \in \widetilde{\mathcal{C}}$, compute $\widetilde{\mathcal{I}} := \{\mathbf{i} \uplus \mathbf{c}\}$.
5. Compute $\overline{\mathcal{I}} := \mathcal{E}(\widetilde{\mathcal{I}})$.
6. Compute $\widehat{\mathcal{I}} := \mathcal{T}_{2d}(\overline{\mathcal{I}})$.
7. Output $\widehat{\mathcal{I}}$ as the STE3D-CAP-e challenge.

The output of the experiment is $\widehat{\mathcal{I}}$. Note that $|\widehat{\mathcal{I}}| = \ell$, is the length of the STE3D-CAP-e challenge. The total number of objects in $\widetilde{\mathcal{I}}$ is $(\gamma + 1)\ell$, where γ is the number of layers used in the STE3D-CAP-e clutter. Assuming that $\Delta^{-1} : \mathcal{I}_{3d} \to |\mathcal{I}_{3d}|$ and $\mathcal{E}^{-1} : \mathcal{I}_{2d} \to \mathcal{I}_{3d}$ exist, then the answer to the STE3D-CAP-e challenge is

$$v = \forall_{\mathbf{c} \in \mathcal{E}^{-1}(\widehat{\mathcal{I}})} \ \left(\Delta^{-1} \left(\{\mathcal{G}(\mathbf{c}, 0)\} \right) \right).$$

$\mathcal{P}_{\mathsf{STE3D\text{-}CAP\text{-}e}}$ is to write a program that takes $\widehat{\mathcal{I}}$ as input and outputs v, assuming the program has precise knowledge of $\mathcal{I}_{3d}$ and $\mathcal{I}_{2d}$.

Hard Problem in $\mathcal{P}_{\mathsf{STE3D\text{-}CAP}}$
We believe that $\mathcal{P}_{\mathsf{STE3D\text{-}CAP\text{-}e}}$ contains a hard problem. Given $\widehat{\mathcal{I}}$, for any program $\mathcal{B}$,

$$Pr\left[\mathcal{B}_r(\widehat{\mathcal{I}}) = v\right] < \eta.$$

Based on this hard problem, we can construct a secure (α, β, η)-CAPTCHA.

4   Security Analysis

This section presents analysis on the security of STE3D-CAP-e. An adversary, $\mathcal{A}$, will have access to the STE3D-CAP-e challenge, $\widehat{\mathcal{I}}$. $\mathcal{A}$'s main goal is to output $v = \forall_{\mathbf{c} \in \mathcal{E}^{-1}(\widehat{\mathcal{I}})} \left(\Delta^{-1} \left(\{ \mathcal{G}(\mathbf{c}, 0) \} \right) \right)$. In this section, we will provide several possible attack scenarios that can be used to attack STE3D-CAP-e and the formalisation of these attacks. Please note that the sample images resulting from the proposed attacks are not included in the paper due to the page limitation.

4.1   Brute Force Attacks

To attack a STE3D-CAP-e challenge, $\widehat{\mathcal{I}}$, $\mathcal{A}$ can launch a straightforward attack by adopting the brute force strategy. In this attack, $\mathcal{A}$ will provide a random solution to the challenges until one succeeds. This means that given $\widehat{\mathcal{I}}$, $\mathcal{A}$ will try a random answer to solve the challenge. Since STE3D-CAP-e is a variable-length CAPTCHA, its length of the correct answer is ℓ. Suppose that there are 36 possible characters which comprise of case insensitive letters and digits, then the chance of a successful brute force attack is $\frac{1}{36^{\ell}}$. Having attempted n times, the overall chance will be $\left(\frac{1}{36^{\ell}} \right)^{n}$, which is negligible. Furthermore, in practice CAPTCHAs are usually combined with techniques such as token bucket algorithms to combat denial-of-service attacks [5].

4.2   Single Image Attacks

In a single image attack, $\mathcal{A}$ is provided with an anaglyph STE3D-CAP-e challenge, $\widehat{\mathcal{I}}$. Note that this image is a 2D image. $\mathcal{A}$ will be interested to extract v from $\widehat{\mathcal{I}}$. There are several strategies that $\mathcal{A}$ can employ to conduct this attack:

1. Anaglyph filtering technique.
2. Edge detection technique.
3. 3D reconstruction technique.

These techniques are discussed in detail as follows.

Edge Detection Technique. The aim of the edge detection technique is to find the edges of the objects in the given image, $\widehat{\mathcal{I}}$. Since $\widehat{\mathcal{I}}$ is a 2D image, directly conducting an edge detection method on this image will include all the clutter embedded in the image.

Anaglyph Filtering Technique. The aim of this attack is to separate the 'left' image from the 'right' image of $\widehat{\mathcal{I}}$, and then try to analyse them. This is possible because in an anaglyph image, the two images are colour encoded to produce a single image. Hence, separate left and right images can simply be obtained by filtering the anaglyph image using appropriate colour filters (usually red/cyan, red/blue, or red/green). Formally, we define two functions $\mathcal{E}_{left} : \mathcal{I}_{2d} \to \mathcal{I}_{2d}$ and $\mathcal{E}_{right} : \mathcal{I}_{2d} \to \mathcal{I}_{2d}$ as extraction functions for left and right colours, respectively.
   The attack is conducted as follows.

1. Compute $\mathcal{I}_{left} := \mathcal{E}_{left}(\widehat{\mathcal{I}})$.
2. Compute $\mathcal{I}_{right} := \mathcal{E}_{right}(\widehat{\mathcal{I}})$.

The attacker, $\mathcal{A}$, can try to run an edge detection filter on these separate images. If the foreground characters were to completely block the background characters, this would appear as completely clear regions in the resulting images. Nonetheless, one can see that this is not the case because STE3D-CAP-e challenges were rendered using a certain degree of translucency, therefore the foreground characters do not completely occlude the background characters.

With $\mathcal{I}_{left}$ and $\mathcal{I}_{right}$, $\mathcal{A}$ can also try to analyse these by obtaining the differences between them. This is because foreground characters will have a different parallax compared to background characters. Formally, let $\mathcal{I}_{diff} = \mathcal{I}_{left} - \mathcal{I}_{right}$, where $-$ denotes any preprocessing and image difference operations. This still does not yield much useful information for the task of segmentation, because of the significantly overlapping characters. In order to make a successful attack, $\mathcal{A}$ should compute

$$\mathcal{I}_{new} := \widehat{\mathcal{I}} \setminus \forall_{\mathbf{c} \in \mathcal{E}^{-1}(\widehat{\mathcal{I}}), \delta \neq 0} \{\mathcal{G}(\mathbf{c}, \delta)\}$$

and then compute $\mathcal{I}_{left} := \mathcal{E}_{left}(\mathcal{I}_{new})$ and $\mathcal{I}_{right} := \mathcal{E}_{right}(\mathcal{I}_{new})$. Upon obtaining these values, $\mathcal{A}$ can compute $\mathcal{I}_{diff} = \mathcal{I}_{left} - \mathcal{I}_{right}$ and possibly apply a thresholding or edge detection technique, either before or after $\mathcal{I}_{diff}$. Nevertheless, it is not feasible to compute $\mathcal{I}_{new}$, since the function $\mathcal{E}^{-1}$ does not exist and cannot be ascertained from $\mathcal{I}_{diff}$. Hence, this attack will not succeed.

3D Reconstruction Technique. The purpose of this attack is to estimate 3D information from the given anaglyph image. This will require the use of a stereo correspondence algorithm. Stereo correspondence, a process that tries to find the same features in the left and right images, is a heavily investigated topic in computer vision [10]. The result of this is typically to produce a disparity map, an estimate of the disparity in the left and right images, which may subsequently be used to find depth discontinuities or to construct a depth map, if the geometric arrangement of the views is known.

One of the problems in stereo matching is how to handle effects like translucency [12]. Therefore, the design of STE3D-CAP-e is such that all characters are rendered with a degree of translucency. Furthermore, many stereo matching algorithms require texture throughout the images, as untextured regions in the stereo pair gives rise to ambiguity [2]. STE3D-CAP-e is rendered without the use of textures.

5   Usability

We conducted a pilot study to determine the usability of STE3D-CAP-e. This study was also done to ascertain whether any improvements could be made to the design of STE3D-CAP-e, from a usability standpoint.

For this study, a total of 36 STE3D-CAP-e challenges were generated with an 800 x 300 resolution. Of these, 18 were generated using the solid object approach and the other 18 using the wireframe approach. Each approach contained an equal number of challenges with lengths of 3, 4 and 5, respectively (i.e. 6 challenges per category). The experiment was designed to be short to avoid participants losing concentration. Total time required to complete the experiment varied between participants, but took no longer than 7 minutes. A program was written to present the STE3D-CAP-e challenges to participants in a randomised sequence, with the same conditions maintained for all participants. The program also timed and recorded all answers.

From the results of the experiment, the overall accuracy, with accuracy being determined based on the number of correct answers, was 86.71%. The amount of time taken by participants to solve individual challenges varied rather widely, with an average response time of approximately 6.5 seconds per challenge. In general, the amount of time taken per challenge rarely exceeded 10 seconds.

Results of the solid object and wireframe approaches were compared, and it was found that the wireframe approach gave rise to a higher accuracy at 88.29%, while the accuracy of the solid object approach was 85.12%. On average, participants also took longer to solve challenges generated using the solid object approach as opposed to the wireframe approach. Nevertheless, t-tests indicated that these differences between the means were not statistically significant.

5.1   Pilot Study Conclusions

For good usability, and to avoid users getting annoyed, Chellapilla et al. [4] stated that the human success rate of a good CAPTCHA should approach 90%. The overall result from this pilot study just about satisfies this benchmark, and this suggests that both solid object and wireframe versions of STE3D-CAP-e are human usable. Furthermore, it is anticipated that the human success rate will significantly improve if digits are removed from STE3D-CAP-e challenges. This will avoid users getting confused between particular digits and letters. As this was observed to be a major source of incorrect answers in this study, the removal of digits will certainly improve the usability of STE3D-CAP-e. While it will also mean that attackers can work with a smaller set of possible characters, this is not a large concern as it is not deemed to have a major impact on the security of STE3D-CAP-e. Other usability issues that can be factored in to increase usability, is prevent confusing character combinations. For example, 'V''V', which could be mistaken to be a 'W', and vice versa.

6   Conclusion

Current CAPTCHAs generally suffer from a security-usability trade off. STE3D-CAP-e is a novel 3D CAPTCHA approach that was designed to address these limitations. The result is a CAPTCHA that is both human usable and resistant against a variety of automated attacks.

References

1. Baird, H.S., Moll, M.A., Wang, S.-Y.: A Highly Legible CAPTCHA That Resists Segmentation Attacks. In: Baird, H.S., Lopresti, D.P. (eds.) HIP 2005. LNCS, vol. 3517, pp. 27–41. Springer, Heidelberg (2005)
2. Birchfield, S., Tomasi, C.: Depth discontinuities by pixel-to-pixel stereo. International Journal of Computer Vision 35(3), 269–293 (1999)
3. Bourke, P., Morse, P.: Stereoscopy: Theory and Practice. In: Workshop at the 13th International Conference on Virtual Systems and Multimedia, VSMM 2007 (2007), http://local.wasp.uwa.edu.au/ pbourke/papers/vsmm2007/ stereoscopy_workshop.pdf
4. Chellapilla, K., Larson, K., Simard, P.Y., Czerwinski, M.: Building Segmentation Based Human-Friendly Human Interaction Proofs (HIPs). In: Baird, H.S., Lopresti, D.P. (eds.) HIP 2005. LNCS, vol. 3517, pp. 1–26. Springer, Heidelberg (2005)
5. Elson, J., Douceur, J.R., Howell, J., Saul, J.: Asirra: a CAPTCHA that Exploits Interest-Aligned Manual Image Categorization. In: Ning, P., di Vimercati, S.D.C., Syverson, P.F. (eds.) ACM Conference on Computer and Communications Security, pp. 366–374. ACM (2007)
6. McAllister, D.: 3D Displays. Wiley Encyclopedia on Imaging, Pacific Grove, CA (2002)
7. Mitra, N.J., Chu, H.-K., Lee, T.-Y., Wolf, L., Yeshurun, H., Cohen-Or, D.: Emerging Images. ACM Trans. Graph. 28(5) (2009)
8. Mori, G., Malik, J.: Recognizing Objects in Adversarial Clutter: Breaking a Visual CAPTCHA. In: CVPR (1), pp. 134–144 (2003)
9. Ross, S.A., Halderman, J.A., Finkelstein, A.: Sketcha: a CAPTCHA based on Line Drawings of 3D Models. In: Rappa, M., Jones, P., Freire, J., Chakrabarti, S. (eds.) WWW, pp. 821–830. ACM (2010)
10. Scharstein, D., Szeliski, R.: A taxonomy and evaluation of dense two-frame stereo correspondence algorithms. International Journal of Computer Vision 47(1-3), 7–42 (2002)
11. Susilo, W., Chow, Y.W., Zhou, H.: STE3D-CAP: Stereoscopic 3D CAPTCHA. In: Heng, S.-H., Wright, R.N., Goi, B.-M. (eds.) CANS 2010. LNCS, vol. 6467, pp. 221–240. Springer, Heidelberg (2010)
12. Tsin, Y., Kang, S.B., Szeliski, R.: Stereo matching with linear superposition of layers. IEEE Trans. Pattern Anal. Mach. Intell. 28(2), 290–301 (2006)
13. von Ahn, L., Blum, M., Hopper, N.J., Langford, J.: CAPTCHA: Using Hard AI Problems for Security. In: Biham, E. (ed.) EUROCRYPT 2003. LNCS, vol. 2656, pp. 294–311. Springer, Heidelberg (2003)
14. Yan, J., Ahmad, A.S.E.: A Low-Cost Attack on a Microsoft CAPTCHA. In: Ning, P., Syverson, P.F., Jha, S. (eds.) ACM Conference on Computer and Communications Security, pp. 543–554. ACM (2008)
15. Yan, J., Ahmad, A.S.E.: Usability of CAPTCHAs or Usability Issues in CAPTCHA Design. In: Cranor, L.F. (ed.) SOUPS. ACM International Conference Proceeding Series, pp. 44–52. ACM (2008)
16. Yan, J., Ahmad, A.S.E.: CAPTCHA Security: A Case Study. IEEE Security & Privacy 7(4), 22–28 (2009)

High-Entropy Visual Identification
for Touch Screen Devices

Nathaniel Wesley Filardo and Giuseppe Ateniese

Johns Hopkins University
Computer Science Department
3400 N. Charles Ave.
Baltimore, MD 21218
{nwf,ateniese}@cs.jhu.edu
http://www.cs.jhu.edu/~{nwf,ateniese}/

Abstract. We exhibit a system for improving the quality of user-derived keying material on touch-screen devices. We allow a device to recover previously generated, highly entropic data suitable for use as (part of) a strong secret key from a user's act of identifying to the device. Our system uses visual cryptography [21], using no additional electronics and no memorization on the part of the user. Instead, we require the use of a transparency overlaid on the touch-screen. Our scheme is similar to the identification scheme of [22] but tailored for constrained, touch-screen displays.

1   Introduction

Mobile devices have become pervasive features of modern life. While handy, these devices typically do not have input mechanisms that make entering secure passwords easy. (In fact, many of them use predictive text models to make entering even low entropy prose easier. This does not bode well for asking the user to enter even short, highly entropic strings such as t5Ax9zK%.) Therefore, we expect mobile devices either to not be used for storing sensitive data or to present a likely vulnerability.

Our system enhances password or pass-phrase security by pairing traditional password entry with the requirement that the user answer a randomly chosen visual challenge. The system does not require that a user memorize any static secret material beyond their extant password; instead, our challenges use visual cryptography [21] and require that the user carry a transparent slide to respond. Informally, this puts our system in the category of systems which "authenticate with something you have" (or as one factor of a multi-factor system) rather than "with something you know." Our scheme is similar to the one in [22] (a detailed comparison may be found in Appendix A).

We believe our system to be useful as a generic tool for augmenting password strength, without requiring that users memorize yet more secrets. The challenges encode many bits of entropy in their solution, and are well-suited as a drop-in augmentation to systems, both for authentication and for deriving encryption

M.D. Ryan, B. Smyth, and G. Wang (Eds.): ISPEC 2012, LNCS 7232, pp. 182–198, 2012.

keys, which have traditionally used passwords or phrases. Our system is designed so that any attacker not in possession of the user's slide gains no insight into how to answer by collecting any number of challenges (but without seeing responses).

In our demonstration prototype using OpenIntent's OI Safe [23],[1] a password store and cryptography provider for the Android environment, the entropy encoded in the challenge is **concatenated** with the user's password and fed into a traditional Password-Based Encryption (PBE) [1, 17] scheme to decrypt the (strong, random) key used to encrypt individual password entries. That is, authentication takes place by successfully decrypting a second key, rather than the more typical hash-and-compare done with password authentication schemes. The safe stores, in addition to the user's data, enough information to create challenges. A new challenge is generated and the safe is re-keyed every time it is successfully opened.

We will first give a brief review of the basic visual cryptography we use (section 2), followed by an overview of our scheme and prototype implementation (section 3) and a contrast to prior work (section 4). We then discuss our threat model more fully, and the resulting theoretical design of a parametric family of systems (section 5). Having laid out our parameter space, we exhibit our particular realization within this family and apply standard human-computer interaction tools to estimate performance of an ideal instantiation (section 6).

2   Visual Cryptography

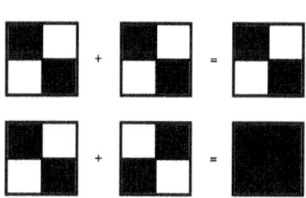

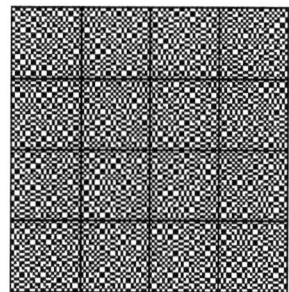

(a) The basic 2 × 2-subpixel, 2-of-2 visual secret splitting scheme. Shown here, four display pixels of each share are being combined to produce one pixel of the hidden image.

(b) An example slide, which should be scaled to match the device's display and printed on a transparent sheet of plastic. Slides are composed of random noise rendered as display pixels as per section 2. The grid lines separate independent instances of visual secret splitting (each grid cell) and are imposed only to aid in subsequent use; see Figure 1.

---

[1] All of the code used for this paper is available on the Web at http://github.com/nwf/android-vcpass and http://github.com/nwf/android-vcpass-oisafe

Visual Cryptography [21] is a method for encrypting or hiding visual information in a way where decryption may be done by a human without the use of code-books, tables, or computers. The prototypical example, and the one we use in our prototype scheme, is a two-of-two secret splitting scheme, in which a black and white secret image is split into two "black and transparent" shares, neither of which alone conveys any information about the encoded image.[2]

To hide a single pixel of the image, we follow the most basic 2-of-2 secret splitting scheme of [21]. A $b \times b$ block of pixels in the shares will have either identical (for a white pixel) or complementary (for black) diagonals set black (the other pixels will be *transparent*), as shown in 1a. The resulting shares will have b^2 as many pixels as the original image; to avoid confusion we distinguish between "display pixels" of the shares and "image pixels" of the original and reconstructed images. Information security is attained by setting one share's blocks independently, identically distributed (iid) uniformly at random, making it clearly uncorrelated with the hidden image. The other share's corresponding block is then set to the appropriate diagonal. While the image was an input to the values of this share, no information survives due to the iid uniform bit flip channel defined by the first share. Thus the secret is only recoverable from the *pair* of shares, as intended.

3   System Overview

As is typical of secure document stores, OI Safe has a "master key" which is used to encrypt individual entries. The master key is chosen at random and is itself encrypted using a salted PBE scheme fed with the user's password; this makes changing the password independent of the amount of the data being stored. OI Safe may be "opened" by entering the password, which allows it to decrypt the master key, and thereby allows the user and external applications to access stored passwords and its encryption functionality. It may be "closed" (either explicitly or after a configurable timeout) by erasing the in-memory copy of the master key plain-text.

Our prototype enhances the security of the system by combining, prior to PBE strengthening, the user's password with (roughly 36 bits of) random data, hidden using visual cryptography. To open the safe under this new scheme, the user first provides a plain-text password, as with the non-augmented OI Safe, and then decrypts the previously generated random data. The latter step involves placing a transparency (carrying a gridded image such as 1b), previously generated and printed, over the display and indicating the direction (or absence) of an arrow in each grid cell by touching and dragging in the appropriate direction. (The set of arrow and blank images we call the "vocabulary" in subsequent discussion.[3])

---

[2] Formally, the requirement is that there is zero mutual information between either of the shares in isolation and the secret.

[3] Our prototype chooses to use a vocabulary of four arrows, one for each cardinal direction, and two blanks. There are sixteen independent cells in our challenges. These choices balances the entropy of the challenge (see subsection 5.2) against the (estimated) time to answer the challenge (see subsection 6.1), but are not the only possible choice; section 5 will discuss the system, and its parameters, more fully.

We emphasize that it is possible to use the touch screen, and therefore to answer the challenge, without removing the overlay slide first.

A camera shot of the challenge prompt and slide overlay running on a Motorola Droid^{TM} phone may be found in Figure 1. This picture gives an idea of the "arrow" vocabulary used and gives an example of what a user of the system would see when answering a challenge.[4] By virtue of visual secret splitting, absent the slide, the phone appears to be displaying random noise. To answer the challenge, the user would touch each cell and drag in the direction indicated in the table. Additional details of implementation may be found in section 6.

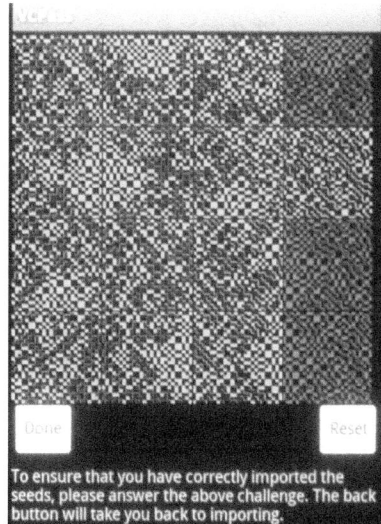

none	down	none	down
left	right	up	none
up	none	none	right
none	left	left	right

(a) Camera shot of the application's challenge prompt.

(b) Solution to challenge.

Fig. 1. Challenge and solution. To improve visibility, challenges are displayed using only one color subpixel – in this case green. As the user provides answers (correct or not), the cells are shaded blue; answers are provided by touching each triangle and dragging away from the broad side. The black lines on the slide align to yellow lines between cells on the display. Due to the difficulty of aligning the display, slide, and camera, it may be hard to make out all the triangles in the challenge; the challenge is readable only within a very narrow field of view, even when properly aligned.

The system is initialized by using a desktop computer and printer to create the user's slide. Sufficient information about the slide (i.e., the seed to a CSPRNG and other material; see section 6) are then imported into the safe at construction of the secure store, i.e., at the same time as the user first sets their traditional,

---

[4] In this case, the system is prompting for an answer to check that it knows what the user's slide looks like; in general, the user would see this after having typed in their traditional password at the prompt in OI Safe.

plain-text password, just as they would in the conventional (i.e., purely plain-text password based) OI Safe scheme. The safe then generates an initial challenge and stores these parameters under the same encryption used for its own master key. Subsequently, each time the safe is opened, the parameters are decrypted and a *new challenge* is generated, using the device's strong random number generator. This challenge is written to non-volatile store for the next authentication attempt, and the safe master key is re-crypted with the user's password and the answer to this new challenge.[5] That is, whenever the safe is opened, it updates itself to be ready for the next authentication.[6] Cycling challenges in this way helps thwart incomplete surveillance attempts: repeated observation of, say, the user solving the challenge without being able to see the challenge or slide in detail, will not lead to an in-aggregate solution to a challenge, whereas repeated incomplete obsevations of password entry might.

4   Prior Work

There are deployed systems (usually under the heading of "biometrics") which attempt to make the statement that "with high probability, the operator of the device is in fact a legitimate user" based on fingerprints [14, 18, 19], facial recognition [2, 14], typing patterns [25, 26], retinal scans [9], etc. While much of this work was based on probabilistic matching, making it untenable as a source for keying material, recent work [8] has shown how to derive good keying material from biometric data. These systems typically require cameras or specialized scanners and may involve a lengthy initial data acquisition phase; our system requires only a touch-screen display (and a printer during initialization).

There are "visual identification" schemes, such as Déjà Vu [7], which use visual recognition for (remote) authentication. The secret here is entered by the discrimination of a series of pre-selected, randomly-generated visuals from a larger set. This scheme trades entropy (it derives at most one bit per displayed image) for a more pleasant user experience (this system does not require that the user carry a slide). These systems were generally conceived of for desktop, not mobile, environments and therefore use relatively large images and can present many at a time. Further, their low entropy per challenge makes them usable for one-time passwords but less ideal for encryption keys.

The system of [11] uses visual secret splitting to authenticate bank transactions. Here, the user confirms that the bank's share decrypts to correctly identify

---

[5] This is akin to the user changing their password every time they use the safe. In fact, the same code-path is invoked when the user does change their password or chooses to change their slide; both of these actions require that the safe be already open.

[6] This act is done entirely in the background since it takes noticeable amounts of CPU time—roughly 10 seconds—on current Android phones. The safe will not close itself until it is ready to be opened again. Possibly we should require visual challenges on a different schedule than closing the safe; perhaps once per day or reboot, so that the user does not typically need their slide with them. That is, we can hold the visual challenge answer in memory on a different schedule than the user's password.

the requested transaction and then reveals the location of two markers within the image to indicate acceptance. This paper appears not to consider an adversary which accumulates information across multiple uses of the system in order to learn about the user's transparency.

There has been prior work on visual cryptography for authentication of humans to devices. [16] gives a system which requires the user to memorize a secret and (mentally) perform some unspecified "simple operation" on that secret and the message received via visual cryptography. The system of [22] proposes challenges which illuminate regions of a *multi-colored* slide, the responses to which are enumerations of the indicated colors; a detailed comparison may be found in appendix A. The system of [24] uses visual secret splitting to encode passwords in a different context: authenticating users for remote voting; that paper does not consider the amount of entropy in the secret to be split (they offer, for purposes of illustration, only a very low security example; however, as they work on larger displays than we do, and need use a slide only once, this is not really a limitation so much as an omission from the paper).

We also briefly contrast our system to a hypothetical scheme where we used a camera to scan a secret image (like a QR code). Other than the obvious need for the target device to have a camera, this system would suffer from the likely constraint that these secret images should have relatively low pixel density, for ease and reliability of picture-taking. Unfortunately, this would also ease surveillance and adversarial capture of the secret.

Our system focuses on providing a moderately sized, secure channel for entropy with a simple, touch-screen user interface. As with all visual cryptography schemes, our system comes with the added cost of needing to carry a transparency containing a visual cryptography share.

5   Design

5.1   Threat Model

Our design, as with most secret-based systems, aims to defend against semi-active attackers with incomplete surveillance capabilities. We are primarily concerned with an adversary who steals the user's mobile device or finds it after it has inadvertently been left behind and thus has **absolute control** of the hardware for the duration of their attack. Since secure erasure of long-term data (which includes challenges but *not* the user's responses thereto) may be impossible, such acts may compromise all past challenges.[7] In the case of a remote authentication system, the adversary may be able to prompt the challenger to provide a challenge at any time and then abort the protocol. Our system ensures that challenges do not leak data about their interpretation, **even in aggregate**.

---

[7] In particular, modern flash devices engage in "wear-leveling" whereby writes to a logical sector are actually spread among several physical sectors. This greatly improves the useful life of the flash, but means that many old copies of rewritten material may be extractable by an adversary.

At no time will the adversary be given both a challenge and its solution (e.g., through device compromise or surveillance). This restriction may sound severe, but recall that our system is still fundamentally password-like, and that any secret-based system fails if the secret can be observed.[8]

In the same vein, we do not consider software attacks (e.g., viruses, trojan horses, "malware") on the system, as once an adversary is able to observe our process's memory, it becomes a simple matter to read out the secret keys directly. Even in absence of such abilities, software which can capture touch screen events and screen contents can read out the user's password and answers to visual cryptography problems. In the specific case of a password safe, it may be possible to impersonate the legitimate client and simply ask for the secrets contained within the safe directly! We therefore assume that the underlying trusted computing base is indeed sufficiently worthy of the trust placed in it.[9]

The formal game we play is to give our adversary the parameters of the system and the complete set of challenges that the system may ever produce.[10] The adversary wins the game if they can gain a non-negligible advantage over merely guessing.

5.2   The Challenge Schema

Our challenge to the user is relatively simple: given N cells, each of which may each take on one of $|K|$ values (which we call the *vocabulary*), discriminate between $|D|$ ($D \subseteq K$) individual values and the remaining $|K \setminus D|$. Upon prompting, the user is required to answer with which of the cells contain a value from D and to indicate which value in particular. The remainder of the cells require no explicit user action. To generate a challenge, the cells are set unformly at random (iid) from the vocabulary (of size $|K|$). We therefore expect $N |D| |K|^{-1}$ cells to require user interaction, and each cell will contribute

$$- \sum_i p_i \log_2 p_i = - \frac{|D|}{|K|} \log_2 \frac{1}{|K|} - \frac{|K \setminus D|}{|K|} \log_2 \frac{|K \setminus D|}{|K|} \qquad (1)$$

bits of entropy. We allow systems with $|D| + 1 < |K|$, (with less than maximum potential entropic return) to let us trade between expected user actions and the resulting entropy.

---

[8] In fact, our system does marginally better than traditional password-based systems in terms of the effects of perfect observation (see the discussion in Appendix B).

[9] Perhaps if the system were being used for remote authentication, rather than decryption of local data, there would be some room for correctness even in the face of local compromise. Our focus here is, as stated, to guard against the loss of secret data if the device is stolen.

[10] Our system generates each challenge iid uniformly from this space; in a system where that is not the case, the probability of a challenge share might leak information about its contents. If such a system were to be designed, security under our game would require that the theoretical adversary be told these probabilities as well, since it may be possible for a real-world adversary to estimate them with high precision.

To generate a challenge, the generator (e.g., the safe after successful authentication) must have access to all the vocabulary entries and slide data for each cell. Naturally, this information must be kept secret, as it allows anyone in possession of it to reply correctly to challenges without being able to see the images themselves. We assume that the generator has access to sufficiently safe encrypted storage (in the case of our prototype, these secrets are stored inside the presumably secure safe). The generator also needs a (cryptographically) secure random number generator to provide the entropy that will later be read back from the challenge.

5.3   System Game

The system may be described as a game between the three parties of user (the operator of the device), generator (the device when it has the system secrets in memory), and verifier (the device when it does not have the system secrets in memory).

1. For each cell $n \in \{1, \ldots, N\}$, the user uses an initialization program to create a vocabulary of equal-length, independent bit strings, K_n, with distinguished subset D_n, subject to the criteria from subsection 5.4. The user then provides all D_n privately to the generator. We use $\boldsymbol{K}$ and $\boldsymbol{D}$ to denote the in-n-order concatenation of all K_n and D_n, respectively.
2. For each of the N cells, the user's initialization program further creates a (iid) random string of bits s_n, the slide, of the same length as strings in K_n. This string is also privately provided to the generator, and the user announces all $\{k_n \oplus s_n | k_n \in K_n\}$ (without revealing any information about D_n). We use $\boldsymbol{s}$ to denote the in-n-order concatenation of s_n.
3. For each of the N cells, the generator selects an element $k_n \in K_n$ iid uniformly at random and (privately) informs the verifier. The generator publishes the challenge, $c_n = k_n \oplus s_n$.
4. The generator stores $E_{\boldsymbol{k}}(\boldsymbol{D}, \boldsymbol{s})$ (an encrypted copy of the private parameters of the system) for later use.
5. The user now computes $\boldsymbol{k}' = \boldsymbol{s} \oplus \boldsymbol{c} = \boldsymbol{s} \oplus (\boldsymbol{k} \oplus \boldsymbol{s})$ and (privately) reveals the answer to the verifier.
6. The verifier accepts if $\boldsymbol{k}' = \boldsymbol{k}$.

An adversary wins the game if they may replace the user in the last two steps and cause the verifier to accept with odds better than $\geq 1/k + \epsilon$ for some $\epsilon > 0$. However, the adversary cannot win without successfully attacking the private exchanges (e.g., via surveillance, timing, or software attacks): an $\epsilon > 0$ implies either nonuniform selection of k_n or correlation between $s_n \oplus k_n$ and k_n, which in turn would imply nonuniform selection of s_n. (In actual usage, steps 3 through 6 are repeated many times; the publication of all the encrypted vocabulary in step 2 is intended to capture this repeated use of the system parameters.)

In our system, comparison of $\boldsymbol{k}$ against $\boldsymbol{k}'$ is checked implicitly: $\boldsymbol{k}'$ is fed through a PBE scheme and used to decrypt a block (containing the safe's random master key) encrypted with $\boldsymbol{k}$. $\boldsymbol{k}'$ and $\boldsymbol{k}$ are never compared directly: successful decryption is taken to imply that $k = k'$. Further, k and s are derived from cryptographically secure pseudo-random number generators; the seeds for these generators stand in for their outputs in step 4 and the re-keying procedure above. After every successful verification, the verifier knows k and may use it to decrypt $E_k(D, s)$, revealing the secret parameters of the system. Since, in our system, the verifier and generator are the same (i.e., the device, just at different points in time), at this point, steps 3 and 4 may be repeated to produce a new secret key and a new challenge for later authentications, which allows the system to (limitedly) frustrate even perfect surveillance (unlike a pure password scheme, where no such mitigation is possible; see appendix B).

5.4   Visual Secret Shares That Don't Leak

The constructions in [21] are all intended to produce n shares for a single message; no share is ever used for multiple messages. [22] does present a multiple-use scheme for visual identification (authentication of a human), but that scheme considers the equivalent of a cell to be entirely revealed to an adversary after a use; therefore, it requires the use of many more cells to combat an adversary. To keep the number of cells low, thereby allowing for larger cells on smaller displays, we use a standard visual secret splitting scheme to obscure the challenge. To ensure that no number of challenge visual shares will reveal any information about the user's share, we must impose some constraints on the system.

As before, we have N cells, a set of K vocabulary entries for each, $D \subseteq K$ of which are to be distinguished in some way (when combined with the user's share). The cells are each made up of some number of image pixels, P. For each image pixel, we permit only one of the D values to "claim" it. We then set, iid uniformly at random and independent of the user's share, the values of all image pixels in the $K \setminus D$ values and all unclaimed image pixels of each $d \in D$. This "vocabulary generation" happens independently for each of the N cells. Were we to permit more than one $d, d' \in D$ to claim a given pixel, then there would be correlation between challenges containing d and d', thereby leaking information to an adversary.

We assume that the parameters $|D|, |K|, N, P$, the subset of the pixels claimed by each D, and the intended decoded value (i.e., the intended image) of these claimed pixels are public. Because each pixel of the slide is only meaningfully correlated with one pixel out of all of the D, and not correlated with any element in $K \setminus D$, the information security argument continues to hold. Instantiation of this scheme requires $NP|K|$ independent uniform random bits: $NP(|K| - 1)$ of which are consumed by the $K \setminus D$ and unclaimed D image pixels, and NP of which determine the user's share.[11]

---

[11] We do run the risk of generating a confusing vocabulary: that is, one in which two elements of K may not be sufficiently distinguishable. To mitigate this risk, instantiations of the system should present the full vocabulary to the user when the system is being initialized (i.e., when the slide is being generated). We assume that this clear-text is not intercepted. We assume that any correlation between the vocabulary entries K by the user's rejection of confusing vocabularies are negligible.

5.5   Incomplete Erasure Attacks

As mentioned earlier, whenever one rewrites sensitive material, (e.g., by changing the password in a staged keying system like OI Safe's) there is always a danger that the old copy is not completely erased. In our case, however, the rewritten material is encrypted with the result of a PBE scheme, and each of those copies' keys was derived, in part, from the answer to a visual challenge. Therefore, the key is reasonably entropic. Under standard assumptions of the system used to encrypt the master key, namely IND-CPA, the multitude of messages offers no gain to the adversary.[12]

6   Implementation

We now turn our attention to the particular parameters used by our prototype implementation. Rather than being a rigid encoding of this particular choice of parameters, our prototype has been designed to encapsulate the application (e.g., OI Safe) using it from the details of visual cryptography whenever possible: the application is almost entirely oblivious to the contents of the values it passes to our visual cryptography front-end. In testing, we switched a number of these parameters and the design of the distinguished elements without having to (additionally) modify OI Safe at all.

Fig. 2. An example vocabulary for one cell, as seen when overlaid with the slide, with $|K| = 6$ and $|D| = 4$. The four distinguished values (resp. up, down, left, right) are shown at the left and would be distinguished by the user touching the cell and dragging away from the broad side of the triangle. The rightmost two cells do not call for a user's response. Each cell has an independently generated vocabulary encoding the same arrows but with different "filler" pixels.

Mobile devices by necessity do not have large displays, both in the sense that there are few pixels present and that the pixels themselves are small. The former restricts the number of cells we can reasonably fit in a challenge. Despite the small screen size limiting our cell count, we chose to present only a single challenge at a time.[13] The latter had unexpected consequences: we found that using display-native pixel size for the sub-pixels of the visual cryptography made

---

[12] Our prototype uses OI Safe's default "strong" choice storing both the encrypted master key and our the secret seeds: BouncyCastle's Java cryptography provider in mode `PBEWithSHA1And256BitAES-CBC-BC`.

[13] Presenting multiple challenges for the same slide sequentially does not yield linear increase in entropy; the marginal utility of the next challenge behaves as in Table 1.

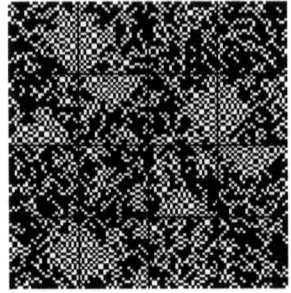

left	right	none	none
up	down	left	right
none	none	up	down
left	right	none	none

(a) An example challenge, ideally rendered, with slide overlaid.

(b) Answer to the challenge.

Fig. 3. An example of a system with $|K| = 6$, $|D| = 4$, and $N = 16$

alignment of the slide and challenge almost impossibly difficult; we therefore set the ratio of display to image pixels to $6 : 1$. With the additional impact of the inter-vocabulary-item constraints on pixels from subsection 5.4, our vocabulary tends to have images which are not immediately obvious; even an ideal rendering (see Figure 3) leaves something to be desired. It is possible that there are better vocabulary designs to be had or that the issue will be less severe on future display technologies (higher density LCDs or e-ink displays); for the moment, our design suffices.

The size of our cells are chosen so that a 4×4 grid of cells fits on a display of 312×312 (display) pixels. Given the $6 : 1$ pixel ratio, this makes our cells 13×13 image pixels and sets $P = 169$. This allows for 42 image pixels to be set by each distinguished value, which is likely large enough that confusable values are unlikely to be generated. Our prototype instantiates our scheme with $N = 16$, $|D| = 4$, and $|K| = 6$. In particular, this gives a 16 cell grid, with an expected 10.6 cells requiring user action (though some challenges will have all or no cells requiring user interaction). Each of the $|D| = 4$ cells is a direction indicator, as shown in Figure 2. The image pixels of these cells which are not fixed by the direction indicator are set randomly as described above.

This system provides roughly 2.3 bits of entropy per cell, or roughly 36 bits per challenge. If all 95 printable ASCII characters are available and used to greatest effect, then each of our challenges may be seen as having added the equivalent of 5.5 characters to the password ($36/\log_2(95) = 5.47 \ldots$). Restricting ourselves to the 26 letters of the alphabet, the requisite string length becomes 7.7 ($36/\log_2(26) = 7.65 \ldots$). See subsection 6.1 for a way to estimate how long a user would take to respond in each case.

Initial vocabulary and user share generation currently happens on a desktop computer, to make printing easier. To further the ease of use and development, we instantiate two Cryptographically Secure Pseudo-Random Number Generators (CSPRNGs) using AES in CTR mode with seeds of a few hundred random bits each (rather than store and manipulate the full string of $NP|K| = 16224$ bits). One CSPRNG is used to generate the user's slide, the other is used to generate the "noise" pixels in the vocabulary.[14] While the resulting bit stream is necessarily not an iid uniform string of bits, a CSPRNG's output should be indistinguishable from one by any probabilistic polynomial-time adversary.

Our prototype produces a new challenge after every successful opening of the safe. The secrets of the visual cryptography subsystem are themselves guarded by the same PBE-derived key as the safe's master key. To reduce space consumption, we store the CSPRNG seeds and recreate both the slide and vocabulary in memory on demand.

A few words must be said about the odd coloring of Figure 1. We use a green, rather than white, cell color as it uses only one color sub-pixel in each LCD pixel; this in turn helps the user see the reconstructed image. Yellow lines are shown between cells and corresponding thin black lines are printed on the user's slide to aid in alignment of the two. Due to the mechanics of LCD displays and perhaps also imprecise printing, there is some difficulty in aligning the slide to the screen in a way that makes the entire image clear from any single vantage point; the challenge is readable only within a very narrow field of view, even when properly aligned.

6.1   Estimating Timing

We currently have difficulties reliably both producing a slide with pixels sized correctly for the phone's display and aligning the slide and the display. More precise printing than that of a laser printer, shaping of transparencies, or some form of software-assist[15] may be sufficient to ease usage of our system. However, we do not believe that users would currently put up with the difficulty of use.[16]

In lieu of actual users, we can use Fitts's law [10, 20],

$$M_{ij} = .204 \log_2 \left[1 + \frac{D_{ij}}{W_j} \right], \qquad \overline{MT} = \sum_{i,j} P_{ij} \left[M_{ij} + RT \right]$$

to *estimate* the time it will take for a user to answer a challenge with an ideal slide and display. The left equation relates D_{ij}, the distance between objects i and j, and W_j, the width of object j, to M_{ij}, the estimated time of motion from i to j. Informally, it can be read as "short distances and large objects allow fast positioning." The right equation computes the average positioning time by weighting the positioning time of each pair M_{ij} with the probability of needing to make that move, P_{ij}; RT is the "reaction time," the time it takes the

---

[14] In our prototype, those seeds are passed to the device via a QR barcode rather than as a file, enabling us to work on devices where externally manipulating storage is annoying or impossible. This is not, however, central to the scheme.

[15] For example, we could have the user touch a series of distinguished points on the slide, giving the device a better idea of how to display the challenge. Alternatively, for devices supporting multi-touch displays, we could perhaps manufacture slides that triggered touch events merely by being placed upon the display.

[16] We acknowledge that this represents a practical weakness of our design. We do, however, believe that it can be overcome.

positioning system (i.e., the user) to find the next move. We can compare the derived estimate for our prototype with similar estimates for using touch-screen keyboards[17].

To estimate the effects of reaction time in the visual cryptography setting, where order of entry is irrelevant and there are potentially many acceptable responses at any moment (i.e., cells not yet answered), we use a weighted version of Hick's Law [12, 20]: $RT(n) = .200 \log_2 [n+1]$. Our variant is a recurrence form, which should capture that users do not re-search already searched cells:

$$RT(n) = \sum_{i=0}^{n} p_{n,i} \left[-.200 \log_2 p_{n,i} + RT(n-i) \right], \quad p_{n,i} = \begin{cases} \frac{|D|}{|K|} \left[\frac{|K \backslash D|}{|K|} \right]^i & i < n \\ \left[\frac{|K \backslash D|}{|K|} \right]^n & i = n \end{cases}$$

where $p_{n,i}$ is the probability that searching n cells for one that requires activity takes i steps. Note that in this variant there is no ambiguity about whether to respond and so no +1 inside the $\log_2$—the nonresponse case is handled as $i = n$. For our instantiation, we estimate a total of $RT(N) = 2.9$ seconds spent searching per challenge. To get expected motion time, we compute the expectation of $n\overline{MT}$:

$$\mathbb{E}\left[n\overline{MT} \right] = \sum_{n=0}^{N} p(n) n\overline{MT} = \sum_{n=0}^{N} \binom{16}{n} \left[\frac{|D|}{|K|} \right]^n \left[\frac{|K \backslash D|}{|K|} \right]^{N-n} n\overline{MT}.$$

For our instantiation, this yields an estimate of 2.2 seconds of motion. Combining these yields a grand total of 5.1 seconds to respond to a challenge, neglecting slide positioning time.

Using the Android on-screen keyboard as a prototypical example, we estimate that it would take an expert user (for whom $RT = 0$) 3.6 seconds to enter a (memorized) random 8-character mono-case string or 4.7 seconds to enter a (memorized) random 6-character mixed-case alphanumeric string.[18]

7   Future Work

Our system avails itself only of the most basic form of visual cryptography. Visual Cryptography has been actively studied by many researchers over the years. The original Naor and Shamir paper [21] discusses k-out-of-n threshold schemes more general than the 2-out-of-2 we used here. Visual cryptography has been extended to work with full-color images [6, 13, 15], with "meaningful" (i.e., non-random) cover images [5, 27, 28], and general access structures both without [3] and with [4] meaningful cover images. This prior work has tended (the identification schemes of [22] aside) to focus on the act of secret splitting itself, rather than its potential application to authentication.

---

[17] In all cases, we ignore errant entries, so these times are lower bounds. Numbers reported in this section are derived from measurements of a Motorola Droid[TM] phone running Google Android version "2.1-update1" build "ESE81."

[18] The increase in time is due to the need to transition between shifted and un-shifted modes of the on-screen keyboard.

8   Conclusion

We have developed and exhibited a system which allows users to answer high-entropy challenges without having to memorize said entropy or provide biometric information. The trade-off is carrying a visual cryptography share on a transparency and an (estimated) increase of a few seconds of entry time relative to a memorized, keyboard-based equivalent.

Acknowledgements. We are indebted to Matthew Wright for his combinatorial help in deriving the correct form of $a_M(k, i)$. The phone pictured was generously donated to JHU ISI for student use by Google, Inc. We would further like to thank our shepherd Moritz Becker and the several anonymous reviewers for their very helpful comments.

A   The Visual Identification System of Naor and Pinkas

The identification scheme with one verifier of [22] uses a transparency, known by the verifier and possessed by the human, composed of N squares, each of which is iid *colored* with one of 10 colors. The challenges in this system serve to illuminate d of these squares and keep the rest dark. The answer to the challenge is the list of colors lit, in some pre-defined order. As with our work, this system assumes incomplete surveillance; indeed, their colored slide is likely easier to observe accurately from a distance or at low resolution than our visual secret splitting share, which uses relatively small pixels.

Our goal is slightly different than the above system, as we seek to generate a large amount of entropy in addition to identifying the user. For the above system to output more than 30 bits of entropy (as ours does), it must be that $d > 10$. After M observed responses, the adversary has attack probability of $\left(\frac{1}{10} + \frac{9dM}{10N}\right)^d$. As their security threshold is 10^{-7} and goes as $1 - 5^{-d}$, to be robust to even a single answer being observed, this system requires $N > 9dM > 90$.[19] While only d of those need to be interacted with, 10 choices is enough to warrant a menu or keypad UI element, slowing response time.

If we change the system to have 5 "colors" (the four cardinal directions and blank, as in our system), then $d > 13$ (with an expected $4/5 * 13 = 10.4$ interactions required from the user) and the security threshold is $(1/5 + 4dM/5N)^{-d}$ by analogy. Making this 10^{-7} requires $N > 116$. To make layout easy, we should use an 11×11 grid of squares: the slide would contain arrows and blanks, and the display just needs to light up the requested cells. On our demo device, each

---

[19] Our system, if instantiated with $N = 16$, $|K| = 5$ and $|D| = 4$, achieves this threshold; raising $|K|$ to 6 as in our instantiation lowers our entropy moderately. Both systems quickly fall below any reasonable threshold. Our system could be augmented to generate challenges which contain voids in certain cells; this would slow the adversary's rate of information gain but would also lower the entropy were N held constant. We have not thoroughly analyzed the impact of such a change.

cell would be 5 millimeters on a side. On average, the user will have to scan $11^2/(4/5*d) \approx 11.5$ cells at a time, so Hick's search time should be on the order of $.200(121/11.5) \log_2 [11.5] \approx 7.4$ seconds. Fitts's response time should be on the order of 5.6 seconds. We expect that answering one of these challenges will therefore take between two and three times as long as one of ours (13.0 vs 5.1 seconds). It may be simpler to align and read off the challenges in this scheme, but that comes with increased risk of successful surveillance. Were we to do a user study, it would be interesting to compare the two.

B   Adversary Information Gain from Leaked Answers

The constraint that our system never yield (challenge,answer) pairs to the adversary may seem odd. However, we can demonstrate that expanding our system to work in the face of leaked answers to challenges is nontrivial by demonstrating a substantial loss of entropy for each leaked answer. Thus our system requires that the user be able to respond without the adversary's having perfect surveillance whereby they are able to see the pixel values of a challenge. For remote authentication, it should be easy to generate a novel challenge for every interaction, making surveillance-based attempts to recover (challenge,answer) pairs harder than they might otherwise be. Our prototype's situation is harder, as the challenges are necessarily created while the system secrets are available, that is, when the safe is open. An adversary may therefore collect the challenge and wait for the user to answer it; however, taking the same rudimentary precautions one takes with passwords should be sufficient.

Before we can compute the probability of an adversary's successful guess, we need to define a combinatorial relation. We need to count the number of strings of length $M > 0$ drawn from a vocabulary of $k > 0$ symbols which use exactly $0 < i \leq k$ of them. This is $a_M(k, i) \stackrel{\text{def}}{=} \binom{k}{i} \left(i^M - \sum_{j<i} \binom{i}{j} a_M(j,j) \right)$. We will not rigorously prove this, but can sketch the inductive argument. First, note that $\forall M.a_M(1, 1) = 1$, which is correct as there is only one unary string of a given length. i^M counts all possible strings for a vocabulary size i, and $\binom{k}{i}$ provides the number of such vocabularies that can be built out of our total vocabulary of size k. i^M multiply counts strings which use fewer than i symbols, and so we must subtract them off; if the undesired string uses $j < i$ symbols, it will be generated in $\binom{i}{j}$ aliases. There are, by induction, $a_M(j,j)$ such miscreant strings.

Having observed $M > 0$ answers to a given cell in a system in which $|D| = |K| - 1$, the probability of an adversary getting the right answer is

$$p(M) = |K|^{-M} \left[1 \cdot a_M(|K|, |K|) + |K|^{-1} \sum_{k=1}^{|K|-1} (k+1) \, a_M(|K|, k) \right].$$

The first term is the probability that our adversary has seen all vocabulary entries for that cell, at which point there is no guessing left. The second term is a sum over the number of entries seen, k. Having observed $k < |K|$ distinct entries, the adversary need not guess if the challenge uses one of these, which will happen with odds $k/|K|$; the adversary otherwise guesses uniformly, getting the right answer with odds $1/(|K|-k)$. All told, $1 \cdot \frac{k}{|K|} + \frac{1}{|K|-k}\frac{|K|-k}{|K|} = \frac{k+1}{|K|}$. Similarly, we can measure the expected entropy of the system:

$$H(M) = -|K|^{-M}\left[0 \cdot a_M(|K|,|K|)\right]$$

$$-|K|^{-M}\sum_{k=1}^{|K|-1} a_M(|K|,k)\left[0 + \frac{|K|-k}{|K|}\log_2\frac{1}{|K|-k}\right]$$

$$= |K|^{-M-1}\sum_{k=1}^{|K|-1} a_M(|K|,k)(|K|-k)\log_2(|K|-k).$$

The adversary's guesses are independent for each cell in the challenge, so after M challenges the odds of a successful guess is $p(M)^N$ and the entropy is $NH(M)$; see Table 1.[20] For systems instantiated with $|K| > |D| + 1$, the odds are necessarily higher and the entropies lower.

Table 1. The expectations, after M challenges' answers have been revealed, of remaining entropy (in bits) and probability of the adversary's first guess being correct. The values here are for a system instantiated with $N = 16$, $|K| = 5$, $|D| = 4$.

M	Expected entropy	Expected probability correct guess
0	37.2	6.6×10^{-12}
1	25.6	4.3×10^{-7}
2	17.3	9.4×10^{-5}
3	11.4	2.5×10^{-3}

References

[1] Abadi, M., Warinschi, B.: Password-Based Encryption Analyzed. In: Caires, L., Italiano, G.F., Monteiro, L., Palamidessi, C., Yung, M. (eds.) ICALP 2005. LNCS, vol. 3580, pp. 664–676. Springer, Heidelberg (2005)
[2] Abeni, P., Baltatu, M., D'Alessandro, R.: User authentication based on face recognition with support vector machines. In: CRV 2006: Proceedings of the The 3rd Canadian Conference on Computer and Robot Vision, p. 42. IEEE Computer Society (2006)
[3] Ateniese, G., Blundo, C., De Santis, A., Stinson, D.R.: Visual cryptography for general access structures. Inf. Comput. 129(2), 86–106 (1996)
[4] Ateniese, G., Blundo, C., Santis, A.D., Stinson, D.R.: Extended capabilities for visual cryptography. Theor. Comput. Sci. 250(1-2), 143–161 (2001)

---

[20] Note that even $M = 1$ is sufficient for the adversary to win the game, as the probability of success is dramatically increased. However, in a traditional password scheme, the probability of success after $M = 1$ revealed answers is 1. While the expected attack odds under our system will never hit 1, it rapidly falls below any reasonable security threshold, and so we would still recommend re-keying after discovered surveillance.

[5] Chang, C.C., Yu, T.X.: Sharing a secret gray image in multiple images. In: Proceedings of the First International Symposium on Cyber Worlds, pp. 230–237 (2002)

[6] Cimato, S., De Prisco, R., De Santis, A.: Colored visual cryptography without color darkening. Theor. Comput. Sci. 374(1-3), 261–276 (2007)

[7] Dhamija, R., Perrig, A.: Déjà vu: a user study using images for authentication. In: SSYM 2000: Proceedings of the 9th Conference on USENIX Security Symposium, p. 4. USENIX Association (2000)

[8] Dodis, Y., Ostrovsky, R., Reyzin, L., Smith, A.: Fuzzy extractors: How to generate strong keys from biometrics and other noisy data. SIAM J. Comput. 38, 97–139 (2008)

[9] Farzin, H., Abrishami-Moghaddam, H., Moin, M.S.: A novel retinal identification system. EURASIP Journal on Advances in Signal Processing, 10 (2008)

[10] Fitts, P.M.: The information capacity of the human motor system in controlling the amplitude of movement. Journal of Experimental Psychology 47(6), 381–391 (1954)

[11] Greveler, U.: VTANs - eine anwendung visueller kryptographie in der online-sicherheit. In: GI Jahrestagung (2) 2007, pp. 210–214 (2007)

[12] Hick, W.E.: On the rate of gain of information. Quarterly Journal of Experimental Psychology (4), 11–26 (1952)

[13] Hou, Y.C.: Visual cryptography for color images. Pattern Recognition 36(7), 1619 (2003)

[14] Jain, L., et al. (eds.): Intelligent Biometric Techniques in Fingerprint and Face Recognition. CRC Press (1999)

[15] Jin, D., Yan, W.Q., Kankanhalli, M.S.: Progressive color visual cryptography. Journal of Electronic Imaging 14(3), 33019 (2005)

[16] Kim, M.R., Park, J.H., Zheng, Y.: Human-machine identification using visual cryptography. In: Proc. the 6th IEEE Int. Workshop on Intelligent Signal Processing and Communication Systems, pp. 178–182 (1998)

[17] Laboratories, R.: Pkcs #5: Password-based cryptography standard, v2.0 (1999), ftp://ftp.rsasecurity.com/pub/pkcs/pkcs-5v2/pkcs5v2-0.pdf

[18] Lenovo: Thinkvantage® client security solution, http://www.pc.ibm.com/us/think/thinkvantagetech/security.html

[19] Ltda., A.S.: Fingerauth password manager, http://www.fingerauth.com/

[20] Mackenzie, S.I., Soukoreff, W.R.: Text entry for mobile computing: Models and methods, theory and practice. Human-Computer Interaction 17(2 & 3), 147–198 (2002)

[21] Naor, M., Shamir, A.: Visual cryptography. Tech. rep. (1994)

[22] Naor, M., Pinkas, B.: Visual Authentication and Identification. In: Kaliski Jr., B.S. (ed.) CRYPTO 1997. LNCS, vol. 1294, pp. 322–336. Springer, Heidelberg (1997)

[23] OpenIntents: OI Safe, http://www.openintents.org/en/node/205

[24] Paul, N., Evans, D., Rubin, A.D., Wallach, D.S.: Authentication for remote voting. In: Workshop on Human-Computer Interaction and Security Systems (2003)

[25] Pavaday, N., Soyjaudah, K.: A comparative study of secret code variants in terms of keystroke dynamics, pp. 133–140 (2008)

[26] Admit One Security: Keystroke dynamics, http://www.biopassword.com/keystroke_dynamics_advantages.asp

[27] Yang, C.N., Laih, C.S.: New colored visual secret sharing schemes. Des. Codes Cryptography 20(3), 325–336 (2000)

[28] Youmaran, R., Adler, A., Miri, A.: An improved visual cryptography scheme for secret hiding. In: 23rd Biennial Symposium on Communications, pp. 340–343 (2006)

A Framework for Security Analysis of Key Derivation Functions

Chuah Chai Wen, Edward Dawson,
Juan Manuel González Nieto, and Leonie Simpson

Queensland University of Technology,
{chaiwen.chuah,e.dawson,j.gonzaleznieto,lr.simpson}@qut.edu.au

Abstract. This paper presents a comprehensive formal security framework for key derivation functions (KDF). The major security goal for a KDF is to produce cryptographic keys from a private seed value where the derived cryptographic keys are indistinguishable from random binary strings. We form a framework of five security models for KDFs. This consists of four security models that we propose: Known Public Inputs Attack (KPM, KPS), Adaptive Chosen Context Information Attack (CCM) and Adaptive Chosen Public Inputs Attack(CPM); and another security model, previously defined by Krawczyk [6], which we refer to as Adaptive Chosen Context Information Attack(CCS). These security models are simulated using an indistinguisibility game. In addition we prove the relationships between these five security models and analyse KDFs using the framework (in the random oracle model).

Keywords: Key derivation function, Security framework, Indistinguishability, Cryptographic keys.

1 Introduction

Cryptographic keys are necessary for safeguarding electronic transactions, communications, and data storage. Key derivation functions (KDF) are the standard algorithm used to generate these cryptographic keys. KDFs are used to generate one or more cryptographic keys from a private seed value, such as a password, Diffie-Hellman (DH) shared secret or some non-uniformly random source material[5,7,8]. It is critical in the design of security systems that KDF proposals themselves are secure. Significant effort in designing a KDF proposal and comprehensive security analysis to evaluate the proposal is justified. The practical importance of KDFs is reflected in their adoption in industrial standard documents; for example PKCS5 [4], ISO-18033-2[9] and more recently in NIST 800-135[3]. There are KDF proposals such as [1,4,6,10] based on cryptographic hash functions.

In the current literature, formal models for the security analysis of KDFs have been introduced by Yao & Yin in [10] and Krawczyk in [6]. However, there are some limitations with each of these security models as they do not completely cover the range of realistic capabilities of the adversary. This has motivated us to extend the existing security models into a new security framework.

M.D. Ryan, B. Smyth, and G. Wang (Eds.): ISPEC 2012, LNCS 7232, pp. 199–216, 2012.

In this paper we develop a comprehensive, formal security framework to form a basis for the design and analysis of KDFs. We begin with an overview of the KDF construction and define the security of KDFs in terms of an indistinguishability game. We develop a framework in which the security can be asserted in terms of the ability of adversaries of varying capabilities to win these indistinguishability games. The adversaries considered range from passive observers of information to active adversaries of varying strength.

2   Key Derivation Functions

Generally, a key derivation function KDF is defined as

$$K \leftarrow KDF(PrivS, s, ctx, n)$$

where

- $PrivS$ is a private seed. The space of all possible private seeds is denoted by $PSPACE$ and the probability distribution of $PrivS$ is assumed to be public;
- s is a salt, a public random string chosen from the salt space $SSPACE$;
- ctx is a public context string chosen chosen from a context space $CSPACE$;
- n is a positive integer that indicates the number bits of the to be produced by the KDF;
- K is the derived cryptographic key of length n bits.

Note that all inputs are publicly known, except for the secret seed $PrivS$. The salt is uniformly random and is used to create a large set of possible keys corresponding to a given private seed value. Context information is arbitrary but application specific data; for example, a session identifier or the identities of communicating parties. The basic operation of a KDF is to transform the private seed value and public inputs into an n bit pseudorandom string which can be used as a cryptographic key. The length, n, of the cryptographic key is an application specific security parameter. From now on we will represent the key derivation function as $KDF(PrivS, s, ctx)_n$.

3   General Security Framework

The general security framework is based on an indistinguishability game played between a challenger C and an adversary A in polynomial time t, where the KDF is considered secure if no A can win the game with probability significantly greater than the probability of winning by guessing randomly. To win the game A has to determine if the challenge output given in the game is the cryptographic key generated by the KDF or a truly random binary string of the same length within a polynomial number of time steps. The game runs in two major stages: the learning stage and the challenge stage. An optional stage called the adaptive stage may be available for some powerful A, who can repeat the learning stage after receiving the challenge output. An explanation of how this game is conducted follows.

- **Learning stage**: A private seed value $PrivS$ is chosen from $PSPACE$. A can make at most q queries, either $q < |SSPACE| \times |CSPACE| < |PSPACE|$ or $q < |CSPACE| < |PSPACE|$ depending on the type of security models. For each query, a derived cryptographic key associated with a salt and context information is provided to A. A can use this information to construct a lookup table to be used in the challenge stage of the game. The capabilities of the adversary determine the level of control they have over the public inputs to KDF. A passive adversary is just an observer that obtains the cryptographic key K, but cannot query the KDF to generate a cryptographic key from their choice of public inputs. An active adversary is able to interact with the KDF to demand cryptographic keys corresponding to their choice of public inputs, with the ability to choose either salt or context information, or both.
- **Challenge stage**: A random bit $b \in_R \{0, 1\}$ is generated by C. If $b = 0$, then C computes $K' = \mathrm{KDF}(PrivS, s, ctx)$, else C outputs a random binary string K' of length of n bits. An active A may have the ability to choose either salt or context information, or both, to obtain the challenge output but this is subject to the restriction that the chosen set of public inputs were not a set of inputs from the learning stage. C sends K' to A.
- **Adaptive stage**: Give the challenge output K', a powerful active A may have the capability to learn more about K' in an adaptive stage before guessing whether K' is the cryptographic key or a binary random string. The adaptive stage consists of repeating the steps in the learning stage for up to q - q' queries, subject to the restriction that A may not ask anything directly regarding the public inputs from the challenge stage.

To complete the game, A guesses whether K' is the key or a random string. If A guesses that K' is a cryptographic key then A sends $b' = 0$, otherwise, A sends $b' = 1$. A wins the game if $b' = b$.

If the adversary is unable to distinguish between a cryptographic key derived from a private seed value using the KDF and a random string of the same length, then the KDF is secure in terms of indistinguishability. Formally, we say that the KDF is (t, q, ϵ)-secure if the probability of the adversary winning the game in time at most t with at most q queries is $\Pr[b = b'] \leq \frac{1}{2} + \epsilon$, where ϵ is negligible. If the adversary is able to distinguish the challenge output with a probability greater than $\frac{1}{2}$, then the adversary is considered to have an 'advantage' in distinguishing the cryptographic keys which are produced by the KDF and KDF is considered insecure.

4   Defining the Security Models

The major security goal for a KDF is that the cryptographic keys generated by the KDF are indistinguishable from truly random binary strings of the same length. That is, this KDF's security goal is formalized as an adversary's inability to gain any information about cryptographic keys derived from a private seed value, even though public inputs are provided to the adversary. We consider this security goal in situations where the capability of the adversary differs and use this to establish five security models: KPM, KPS, CCM, CCS and CPM. Two models, KPM and KPS, are weak security models as A is only an observer. The other models, CCM, CCS and CPM, are stronger security models as the adversary is active. The difference between these three security models lies in the capability of A in choosing the public inputs. For CCM and CCS, A can only choose ctx while A can choose both s and ctx in CPM. Table 1 briefly summarizes the capability of the adversary in the five security models. The symbol '$\sqrt{}$' indicates that the adversary is able to query the KDF to generate the cryptographic keys from their choice of public inputs. The symbol 'X' indicates that the adversary is not able to choose the public inputs although these are known by the adversaries. The symbol '-' indicates that the adversaries are not able to learn more about the challenge output at the adaptive stage. Each of these security models is discussed in greater detail in the following sections.

Table 1. Summary of the capabilities of the adversary in five security models

Security Models	KPM	KPS	CCM	CCS	CPM
Type of Adversary	Passive	Passive	Active	Active	Active
Type of Salt	Multiple	Fixed	Multiple	Fixed	Multiple
Number of Queries, $q <$	$|SSPACE| \times |CSPACE|$	$|CSPACE|$	$|SSPACE| \times |CSPACE|$	$|CSPACE|$	$|SSPACE| \times |CSPACE|$
Capability A in choosing:					
Learning Stage					
Salt	X	X	X	X	$\sqrt{}$
Context information	X	X	$\sqrt{}$	$\sqrt{}$	$\sqrt{}$
Challenge Stage					
Salt	X	X	X	X	$\sqrt{}$
Context information	X	X	$\sqrt{}$	$\sqrt{}$	$\sqrt{}$
Adaptive Stage					
Salt	-	-	X	X	$\sqrt{}$
Context information	-	-	$\sqrt{}$	$\sqrt{}$	$\sqrt{}$

4.1 Known Public Inputs Attack - KPM-Secure

For the KPM security model, the adversary can observe the salt and context information, and the resulting derived key. At the learning stage, each cryptographic key is generated from a fixed private seed value together with a different salt, and with the same or different context information. These cryptographic keys are provided to adversaries. At the challenge stage, A is presented with a binary string. If the KDF is secure, A should not be able to distinguish whether this string is a cryptographic key or a random string of the same length.

Definition 1 {KPM-secure}. *The KDF is (t, q, ϵ) KPM-secure if for all adversaries A running in polynomial time t and making at most $q < |SSPACE| \times |CSPACE|$ queries to the KDF with known multiple salt and known context information win the following indistinguishability game with probability not larger than ($\frac{1}{2} + \epsilon$).*

Learning stage	1. C chooses $PrivS \leftarrow PSPACE$. 2. For $i = 1, \ldots, q' \leq q$,	
		(2.1) C chooses $s_i \overset{R}{\leftarrow} SSPACE$ and $ctx_i \leftarrow CSPACE$. (2.2) C computes $K_i = F(PrivS, s_i, ctx_i)_n$. (2.3) A is provided with the triple (K_i, s_i, ctx_i).
Challenge stage	1. C chooses $s \overset{R}{\leftarrow} SSPACE$ and $ctx \leftarrow CSPACE$ 2. C chooses $b \overset{R}{\leftarrow} \{0, 1\}$. 3. C sends K', s and ctx to A. 4. A outputs $b' = 0$, if A believes that K' is cryptographic key, else outputs $b' = 1$.	(2.1) If $b = 0$, C outputs $K' = F(PrivS, s, ctx)_n$, (2.2) else C outputs $K' \overset{R}{\leftarrow} \{0, 1\}^n$.
	A wins the game if $b' = b$.	

4.2   Known Public Inputs Attack - KPS-Secure

For the KPS, the adversary is an observer. In this indistinguishability game, each cryptographic key is generated from a fixed private seed value together with a fixed salt, and with the different context information. The major difference between KPM-secure and KPS-secure is that for KPM-secure, multiple salts are used to generate the cryptographic keys while for KPS-secure, a fixed salt is used for generating one or more cryptographic keys.

Definition 2 {KPS-secure}. *The KDF is (t, q, ϵ) KPS-secure if for all adversaries A running in polynomial time t and making at most $q < |CSPACE|$ queries to the KDF with known fixed salt and known context information win the following indistinguishability game with probability not larger than ($\frac{1}{2} + \epsilon$).*

Learning stage	1. C chooses $PrivS \leftarrow PSPACE$. 2. C chooses $s \overset{R}{\leftarrow} SSPACE$. 3. A is provided with the value s. 4. For $i = 1, \ldots, q' \leq q$,	
		(4.1) C chooses $ctx_i \leftarrow CSPACE$. (4.2) C computes $K_i = F(PrivS, s, ctx_i)_n$. (4.3) A is provided with the pair (K_i, ctx_i).
Challenge stage	1. C chooses $ctx \leftarrow CSPACE$ (subject to restriction $ctx \notin ctx_i, \ldots, ctx'_q$). 2. C chooses $b \overset{R}{\leftarrow} \{0, 1\}$. 3. C sends K' and ctx to A. 4. A outputs $b' = 0$, if A believes that K' is cryptographic key, else outputs $b' = 1$.	(2.1) If $b = 0$, C outputs $K' = F(PrivS, s, ctx)_n$, (2.2) else C outputs $K' \overset{R}{\leftarrow} \{0, 1\}^n$.
	A wins the game if $b' = b$.	

4.3   Adaptive Chosen Context Information Attack (CCM)

For the CCM model, the adversaries are active, and are capable of choosing the context information in the indistinguishability game. For CCM, the adversaries are allowed to query multiple context information used with the same private seed value and with different randomly generated salt to form the cryptographic keys.

Definition 3 {CCM-secure}. *The KDF is (t, q, ϵ) CCM-secure if for all adversaries A running in polynomial time t and making at most $q < |SSPACE| \times |CSPACE|$ queries to the KDF with known multiple salt and chosen context information win the following indistinguishability game with probability not larger than ($\frac{1}{2} + \epsilon$).*

Learning stage	1. C chooses $PrivS \leftarrow PSPACE$.	
	2. For $i = 1, \ldots, q' \leq q$,	(2.1) C chooses $s_i \xleftarrow{R} SSPACE$.
		(2.2) A is provided s_i.
		(2.3) A chooses $ctx_i \leftarrow CSPACE$.
		(2.4) C computes $K_i = F(PrivS, s_i, ctx_i)_n$.
		(2.5) A is provided the derived cryptographic key, K_i.
Challenge stage	1. C chooses $s \xleftarrow{R} SSPACE$.	
	2. A is provided s.	
	3. A chooses $ctx \leftarrow CSPACE$.	
	4. C chooses $b \xleftarrow{R} \{0,1\}$.	(4.1) If $b = 0$, C outputs $K' = F(PrivS, s, ctx)_n$,
		(4.2) else C outputs $K' \xleftarrow{R} \{0,1\}^n$.
	5. C sends K' to A.	
Adaptive stage	1. Step 2 in **Learning stage** is repeated for up to $q - q'$ queries (subject to restriction $\{s_i, ctx_i\} \neq \{s, ctx\}$).	
	2. A outputs $b' = 0$, if A believes that K' is cryptographic key, else outputs $b' = 1$.	
	A wins the game if $b' = b$.	

4.4 Adaptive Chosen Context Information Attack (Krawczyk)

The formal security model for KDFs proposed by Krawczyk [6] is included in our framework. We refer to this model as CCS-secure. For this security model, the adversaries are capable of influencing the inputs in the indistinguishability game, and are allowed to query multiple context information under the same private seed value with the same randomly generated salt.

Definition 4 {CCS-secure}. *The KDF is (t, q, ϵ) CCS-secure if for all adversaries A running in polynomial time t and making at most $q < |CSPACE|$ queries to the KDF with known fixed salt and chosen context information win the following indistinguishability game with probability not larger than $(\frac{1}{2} + \epsilon)$.*

Learning stage	1. C chooses $PrivS \leftarrow PSPACE$.	
	2. C chooses $s \xleftarrow{R} SSPACE$.	
	3. A is provided with the value s.	
	4. For $i = 1, \ldots, q' \leq q$,	(4.1) A chooses $ctx_i \leftarrow CSPACE$.
		(4.2) C computes $K_i = F(PrivS, s, ctx_i)_n$.
		(4.3) A is provided the derived cryptographic key, K_i.
Challenge stage	1. A chooses $ctx \leftarrow CSPACE$ (subject to restriction $ctx \notin ctx_i, \ldots, ctx'_q$).	
	2. C chooses $b \xleftarrow{R} \{0,1\}$.	(2.1) If $b = 0$, C outputs $K' = F(PrivS, s, ctx)_n$,
		(2.2) else C outputs $K' \xleftarrow{R} \{0,1\}^n$.
	5. C sends K' to A.	
Adaptive stage	1. Step 4 in **Learning stage** is repeated for up to $q - q'$ queries (subject to restriction $ctx_i \neq ctx$).	
	2. A outputs $b' = 0$, if A believes that K' is cryptographic key, else outputs $b' = 1$.	
	A wins the game if $b' = b$.	

4.5 Adaptive Chosen Public Inputs Attack (CPM)

The Krawczyk security model restricts the capability of the strong active adversary. The adversary is only able to change the context information. In some situations, an active adversary may exist that can influence all the possible inputs for KDFs: the salt and the context information, as shown in [2]. This situation motivated the creation of a security model called CPM-secure. For a KDF to be CPM-secure, an adversary A who is allowed to choose both public inputs, salt and context information. For instance, the adversary may choose a null or non-random salt value. The adversary's chosen salt value and different chosen context information is used to generate the cryptographic keys. The adversaries are able to choose whether to respond to the challenger immediately or to progress to the adaptive stage. Again the adversaries are allowed to make no more than q queries.

Definition 5 {CPM-secure}. *The KDF is (t, q, ϵ) CPM-secure if for all adversaries A running in polynomial time t and making at most $q < |SSPACE| \times |CSPACE|$ queries to the KDF with chosen salt and chosen context information win the following indistinguishability game with probability not larger than $(\frac{1}{2} + \epsilon)$.*

Learning stage	1. C chooses $PrivS \leftarrow PSPACE$.	
	2. For $i = 1, \ldots, q' \leq q$,	(2.1) A chooses $s_i \leftarrow SSPACE$ and $ctx_i \leftarrow CSPACE$.
		(2.2) C computes $K_i = F(PrivS, s_i, ctx_i)_n$.
		(2.3) A is provided the derived cryptographic key, K_i.
Challenge stage	1. A chooses $s \leftarrow SSPACE$ and $ctx \leftarrow CSPACE$. (subject to restriction $\{s, ctx\} \notin \{s_i, ctx_i\}$, $\ldots, \{s'_q, ctx'_q\}$).	
	2. C chooses $b \overset{R}{\leftarrow} \{0, 1\}$.	(2.1) If $b = 0$, C outputs $K' = F(PrivS, s, ctx)_n$,
		(2.2) else C outputs $K' \overset{R}{\leftarrow} \{0,1\}^n$.
	3. C sends K' to A.	
Adaptive stage	1. Step 2 in **Learning stage** is repeated for up to $q - q'$ queries (subject to restriction $\{s_i, ctx_i\} \neq \{s, ctx\}$).	
	2. A outputs $b' = 0$, if $\mathcal{A}$ believes that K' is cryptographic key, else outputs $b' = 1$.	
	A wins the game if $b' = b$.	

5   Relating These Five Security Models

The models described above provide assurance for varying levels of security. A KDF which is considered secure under one model may not be under another. For example, a KDF may be KPM-seucre but not CPM-secure. In this section, we establish more precisely the relations between these five security models. Figure 1 gives a summary of these relations.

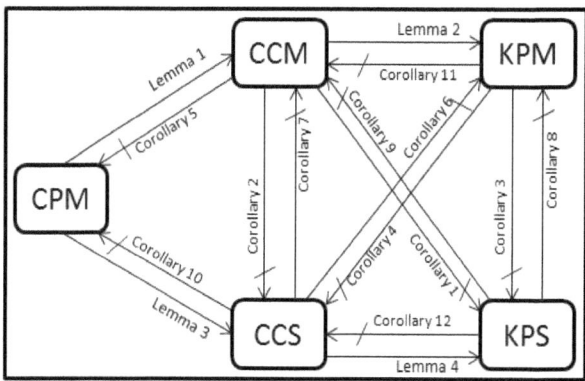

Fig. 1. The relationship between the proposed five security models

5.1 Implications between Security Models

We start by studying the implication relationships between the different security notions. These are shown as lemmas 1-4 in Figure 1.

Lemma 1. $CPM \Rightarrow CCM$.

Proof: Assume a KDF is CPM-secure but not CCM-secure. Since the KDF is not CCM-secure, then there exists an adversary A who can win the CCM game with probability greater than $\frac{1}{2} + \epsilon$. Now, we assume an adversary B who plays the CPM game with C. B will make use of the capability of A, so that A is playing the CCM game with B while B is playing the CPM game with C.

   The game is conducted as below:

- **Learning stage**
    1. C chooses $PrivS \leftarrow PSPACE$.
    2. For $i = 1, \ldots, q' \leq q$,
        (a) B chooses $s_i \leftarrow SSPACE$ and sends it over to A.
        (b) A chooses $ctx_i \leftarrow CSPACE$ and sends it over to B.
        (c) B forwards s_i and ctx_i to C. C computes $K_i = F(PrivS, s_i, ctx_i)_n$.
        (d) B is provided K_i. B forwards K_i to A.
- **Challenge stage**
    1. B chooses $s \leftarrow SSPACE$ and forwards s to A.
    2. A chooses $ctx \leftarrow CSPACE$. A sends ctx to B.
    3. B forwards s and ctx to C.
    4. C chooses $b \xleftarrow{R} \{0, 1\}$.
        (a) If $b = 0$, C outputs $K' = F(PrivS, s, ctx)_n$,
        (b) else C outputs $K' \xleftarrow{R} \{0, 1\}^n$.
    5. C sends K' to B and B forwards K' to A.
- **Adaptive stage**
    1. Step 2 in **Learning stage** is repeated for up to $q - q'$ queries (subject to restriction $\{s_i, ctx_i\} \neq \{s, ctx\}$).
    2. A outputs $b' = 0$, if A believes that K' is cryptographic key, else outputs $b' = 1$. A sends b' to B and B simply forwards b' to C.
    3. B wins the game if $b'_A = b_C$.

The probability that B wins the CPM game is equal to the probability that A wins the CCM game. Our assumption is that the KDF is not CCM-secure. That is the probability that A wins the CCM game is greater than $\frac{1}{2} + \epsilon$. Therefore, B wins the CPM game with probability greater than $\frac{1}{2} + \epsilon$. This implies that the KDF is not CPM-secure. This is a contradiction. Hence, $CPM \Rightarrow CCM$. $\square$

Lemma 2. $CCM \Rightarrow KPM$.

Lemma 3. $CPM \Rightarrow CCS$.

Lemma 4. $CCS \Rightarrow KPS$.

The proofs of these lemmas are similar to the proof of Lemma 1.

5.2 Non-implications between Security Models

To prove the non-implications between the security models (corollaries 1-12 in Figure 1), we analyse five KDFs, $KDF1$-$KDF5$, all based on an underlying hash function F (Table 2). Of these KDFs, three are proposals found in the literature. The other two are (contrived) KDF designs which are useful to demonstrate the separation between some of the security models. Perhaps the most interesting observation from our results in this section is that security when the salt value is fixed does not imply security when different salt values are used.

In what follows, all the proofs are given in the random oracle model (ROM). While proofs in the standard model would be clearly preferable, we believe that using the ROM is appropriate for our purposes. Firstly, as observed by others [6,10], many hash-based KDFs proposed in the literature and used in standards seem impossible to be proven secure based on standard properties of the underlying hash functions. Yet one would like to show that these "practical" hash-based KDFs have some level of security that justifies their use. For example, $KDF1$ in Table 2, which is standardised in PKCS#5 [4], does not seem provable without considering idealised properties of the underlying hash function. An extensive discussion on the applicability of the ROM in the analysis of KDFs is given by Krawczyk [6]. In addition, use of the ROM in this work is sufficient for our purpose of studying the relationships between the different security notions in our framework.

Table 2. Summary of the security analysis of KDF proposals based on the proposed formal security framework for KDF

Theorem	KDF proposals	KPM	KPS	CCM	CCS	CPM
1	$KDF1(PrivS, s, ctx)_n = F^{ctx}(PrivS, s)$, assuming ctx is an integer value [4]	√	X	√	X	X
2	$KDF2(PrivS, s, ctx)_n = F(PrivS\|ctx)\|F(PrivS\|s\|ctx)$	X	√	X	√	X
3	$KDF3(PrivS, s, ctx)_n = F(PrivS\|s\|ctx_1)\| F(PrivS\|s\|ctx_2)$	√	√	X	X	X
4	$KDF4(PrivS, s)_n = F(PrivS, s_1, PrivS)\| F(PrivS, s_2, PrivS)\| \ldots \| F(PrivS, s_l, PrivS)$, where $s = s_1 \| s_2 \| \ldots \| s_l$ [1]	√	√	√	√	X
5	$KDF5(PrivS, s, ctx)_n = F(F(PrivS, s), ctx)$ [6]	√	√	√	√	√

KDF1. Here we analyse the security of $KDF1$, which corresponds to $PBKDF1$, a password-based KDF standardised in PKCS#5 [4]. $KDF1$ is defined as

$$KDF1(PrivS, s, ctx)_n = F^{ctx}(PrivS, s),$$

where the context ctx is an integer value which indicates the number of iterations of the hash function F. We show that it achieves CCM security. In addition, we use the analysis of $PBKDF1$ to prove the non-implications of corollaries 1-5 in Figure 1.

Theorem 1. $KDF1$ *is secure with the respect to KPM, CCM and is not secure in KPS, CCS and CPM.*

Proof: Firstly, we show that $KDF1$ is CCM secure. The proof is in the RO model, where in order to obtain the value $F(x)$, the adversary needs to query the random oracle with input x. The random oracle queries are simulated by the challenger as follows. On input a string x, if x has not been queried before, output $F(x) \in_R \{0,1\}^n$, where n is the output length of the hash function. If x has been queried before, output the same value $F(x)$ as before. Let q_F and q_k be the number of queries made by the adversary to the random oracle and the KDF oracle, respectively.

During the learning stage, C chooses $PrivS \in_R PSPACE$, $s_i \in_R SSPACE$ and uses F to compute $K_i = F^{ctx_i}(PrivS, s_i)$, where A chooses. At the challenge stage, a challenge key is computed as $K' = F^{ctx}(PrivS, s)$, where C chooses s and A chooses ctx. A receives K' and continues to learn cryptographic keys by making up to $q - q'$ KDF queries during the adaptive stage.

Since, F is modeled as a RO, A can only distinguish whether K' is the cryptographic key generated from $KDF1$ or is a random key with probability different from $\frac{1}{2}$, if one of the following happens:

a) $s = s_i$ for some $i = 1 \ldots q_k$. This implies that s was chosen during the learning stage. When this occur, the adversary can easily win the game as follows. Without loss of generality, assume $s = s_i$ and $ctx \leq ctx_i$. Then, $F^{ctx_i - ctx}(PrivS, s) = K_i$, which can be checked by the adversary.
   The probability that this case occurs is $Pr[s = s_i] = \frac{q_k}{|SSPACE|}$.

b) The adversary queries $F(PrivS'||s')$ to the random oracle, such that $PrivS'||s' = PrivS||s$. This amounts to A guessing $PrivS$, which can happen with probability $Pr[PrivS' = PrivS] \leq \frac{q_F}{|PSPACE|}$.

The probability that A wins this indistinguishability game is:
$$Pr[A \text{ wins}] = Pr[A \text{ wins}|s = s_i]Pr[s = s_i] +$$
$$Pr[A \text{ wins}|PrivS' = PrivS]Pr[PrivS' = PrivS] +$$
$$Pr[A \text{ wins}|s \neq s_i \wedge PrivS' \neq PrivS]Pr[s \neq s_i \wedge PrivS' \neq PrivS]$$
$$\leq 1\left(\frac{q_k}{|SSPACE|}\right) + 1\left(\frac{q_F}{|PSPACE|}\right) + \frac{1}{2}\left(1 - \frac{q_k}{|SSPACE|} - \frac{q_F}{|PSPACE|}\right)$$
$$\leq \frac{1}{2} + \frac{q_k}{2|PSPACE|} + \frac{q_F}{2|PSPACE|},$$

where $\epsilon = \frac{q_k}{2|SSPACE|} + \frac{q_F}{2|PSPACE|}$ is negligible.

A only has negligible 'advantage' over random guessing the challenge output. Therefore, $KDF1$ is CCM-secure. $KDF1$ is KPM-secure by Lemma 2.

Secondly, we show $KDF1$ is not secure in CCS. Recall from Definition 4, that in CCS, the salt s is fixed for the entire indistinguishability game and A is allowed to choose ctx. An attack to the CCS security of $KDF1$ is as follows. In the learning stage, A queries ctx_1 to get K_1, such as $K_1 = F^{ctx_1}(PrivS, s)$. During the challenge stage, A asks for the challenge output corresponding to context $ctx_1 - 1$ to the KDF. A bit b is choosen randomly to output challenge output, $b = 0$, if cryptographic key, $K' = F^{ctx^* - 1}(PrivS, s)$ or $b = 1$, $K' = $ random string. Once A receives the value of K', A checks $K_1 \stackrel{?}{=} F(K')$. If so, A outputs $b' = 0$, otherwise $b' = 1$. A wins the game as $b' = b$ except with negligible probability $\frac{1}{2^n}$ (corresponding to the case where $b = 1$, but still $K_1 = F(K')$).

Next we show that $KDF1$ is not KPS-secure. The attack is similar to the strategy followed by the adversary in the CCM game above in the case where

$s = s_i$ for some $i = 1, \ldots, q_k$. In the KPS game the salt s is fixed and the context is chosen by the challenger. Without loss of generality assume that $ctx_i \leq ctx$ for some $i = 1, \ldots, q_k$. The adversary checks if $K' = F^{ctx-ctx_1}(K_i)$. If so, it outputs $b' = 0$, else outputs $b' = 1$. Again, we see that the adversary wins with all but negligible probability.

Finally, it follows from Lemma 3 that since *KDF1* is not CCS-secure, then it is not *CPM* secure.   □

The proof of Corollary 1 - 5 are an immediate result of Theorem 1:

Corollary 1. *CCM* ↛ *KPS* If a KDF is CCM-secure, it may not be KPS-secure.

Corollary 2. *CCM* ↛ *CCS* If a KDF is CCM-secure, it may not be CCS-secure.

Corollary 3. *KPM* ↛ *KPS* If a KDF is KPM-secure, it may not be KPS-secure.

Corollary 4. *KPM* ↛ *CCS* If a KDF is KPM-secure, it may not be CCS-secure.

Corollary 5. *CCM* ↛ *CPM* If a KDF is CCM-secure, it may not be CPM-secure.

KDF2. Here we analyse the security of *KDF2* which is defined as,

$$KDF2(PrivS, s, ctx)_n = F(PrivS\|ctx)\|F(PrivS\|s\|ctx)$$

We show that it achieves CCS security. Furthermore, we use the analysis of *KDF2* to prove the non-implications of corollaries 6-10 in Figure 1.

Theorem 2. *KDF2 is secure with respect to KPS, CCS and is not secure in KPM, CCM and CPM.*

Proof: Firstly, we prove that *KDF2* is CCS-secure. Again, the proof is in the RO model as in Theorem 1. In the learning stage, C chooses $PrivS \in_R PSPACE$, $s \in_R SSPACE$ and C uses F to compute $K_i = KDF2(PrivS, s, ctx_i)_n$, where A chooses ctx_i. At the challenge stage, challenge key is computed as $K' = KDF2(PrivS, s, ctx)_n$, where s is same as at the learning stage and ctx is chosen by A. C sends K' to A. Once A receives K', A continues learn the cryptographic keys which are derived from *KDF2* up to $q - q'$ queries.

Since, F is modeled as a RO, hence, A can only distinguish if K' is the key generated by *KDF2* or a random string of the same length, only if:

a) $ctx = ctx_i$ for some $i = 1 \ldots q_k$. In this case, $F(PrivS\|ctx)\|F(PrivS\|s\|ctx)$ $= F(PrivS\|ctx_i)\|F(PrivS\|s\|ctx_i)$, it means $K' = K_i$, where K_i is one of the key at the learning stage. Hence, A can distinguish K' is the key generated by *KDF2* by checking that K' is one of the key which had been generated at the learning stage. However, recall Definition 4, during the challenge stage, A is not allow to choose $ctx = ctx_i \forall i$ which had been chosen at the learning stage. It means, $ctx \neq ctx_i \forall i$. Consequently, the probability is $\Pr[ctx = ctx_i] = 0$.

b) Query $PrivS$ such as $PrivS' = PrivS$ and find $F(PrivS'\|ctx) = F(PrivS\|ctx)$ or $F(PrivS'\|s\|ctx) = F(PrivS\|s\|ctx)$. This amounts to A guessing $PrivS$, which can happen with probability $Pr[PrivS' = PrivS] \leq \frac{q_F}{|PSPACE|}$.

The probability that A winning this indistinguishability game is:

$$\Pr[A \text{ wins}] = \Pr[A \text{ wins}|PrivS' = PrivS]\Pr[PrivS' = PrivS] +$$
$$\Pr[A \text{ wins}|PrivS' \neq PrivS]\Pr[PrivS' \neq PrivS]$$
$$\leq 1\left(\frac{q_F}{|PSPACE|}\right) + \frac{1}{2}\left(1 - \frac{q_F}{|PSPACE|}\right)$$
$$\leq \frac{1}{2} + \frac{q_F}{2|PSPACE|}, \text{ where } \epsilon = \frac{q_F}{2|PSPACE|} \text{ is negligible.}$$

A only has negligible 'advantage' over random guessing the challenge output. Therefore, this KDF is CCS-secure. $KDF2$ is KPS-secure by Lemma 4.

Secondly, we show $KDF2$ is not KPM-secure. During the learning stage, C chooses $PrivS \in_R PSPACE$, $s \in_R SSPACE$, $ctx_i \in CSPACE$ and uses F to compute $K_i = KDF2(PrivS, s_i, ctx_i)_n$. A receives K_i, s_i and ctx_i. In the challenge stage, challenge key K' is computed by $K' = KDF2(PrivS, s, ctx)_n$, where $s \in_R SSPACE$ and $ctx \in CSPACE$.

F is modeled as a RO, A can distinguish if K' is the key generated by $KDF2$ or a random string of the same length, only if:

a) $ctx = ctx_i$ for some $i = 1 \ldots q_k$. Since set space of s is greater than set space of ctx, therefore, ctx will be reused with a high probability. The probability of choosing $ctx = ctx_i, \forall i$ in the challenge stage is $\frac{q_k}{|CSPACE|}$. This implies that ctx has been chosen at the learning stage, where the first half of K' is similar with the first half of K_i for some $i = 1 \ldots q_k$ at the learning stage. A can distinguish the challenge output is cryptographic key by observing the first component part of K'. The probability is, $\Pr[ctx = ctx_i] \leq \frac{q_k}{|CSPACE|}$.

b) Query $PrivS$ such as $PrivS' = PrivS$ and find $F(PrivS'\|ctx) = F(PrivS\|ctx)$ or $F(PrivS'\|s\|ctx) = F(PrivS\|s\|ctx)$. This implies that A guessing $PrivS$ which can happen with probability $Pr[PrivS' = PrivS] \leq \frac{q_F}{|PSPACE|}$.

Hence, the probability that A can win this indistinguishability game is:

$$\Pr[A \text{ wins}] = \Pr[A \text{ wins}|ctx = ctx_i]\Pr[ctx = ctx_i] +$$
$$\Pr[A \text{ wins}|PrivS' = PrivS]\Pr[PrivS' = PrivS] +$$
$$\Pr[A \text{ wins}|ctx \neq ctx_i \wedge PrivS' \neq PrivS]\Pr[ic \neq ctx_i \wedge PrivS' \neq PrivS]$$
$$\leq 1\left(\frac{q_k}{|CSPACE|}\right) + 1\left(\frac{q_F}{|PSPACE|}\right) + \frac{1}{2}\left(1 - \frac{q_k}{|CSPACE|} - \frac{q_F}{|PSPACE|}\right)$$
$$\leq \frac{1}{2} + \frac{q_k}{2|CSPACE|} + \frac{q_F}{2|PSPACE|},$$

where $\epsilon = \frac{q_k}{2|CSPACE|} + \frac{q_F}{2|PSPACE|}$,

$$\frac{q_k}{2|CSPACE|} > \frac{|SSPACE\|CSPACE|}{2|CSPACE|} \text{ is not negligible.}$$

Therefore, $KDF2$ is not KPM-secure. Hence, $KDF2$ is not CCM-secure by Lemma 2 and is not CPM-secure by Lemma 1.   □

The proof of Corollary 6 - 10 are an immediate result of Theorem 2:

Corollary 6. $CCS \nrightarrow KPM$ If a KDF is CCS-secure, it may not be KPM-secure.

Corollary 7. $CCS \nrightarrow CCM$ If a KDF is CCS-secure, it may not be CCM-secure.

Corollary 8. $KPS \nrightarrow KPM$ If a KDF is KPS-secure, it may not be KPM-secure.

Corollary 9. $KPS \nrightarrow CCM$ If a KDF is KPS-secure, it may not be CCM-secure.

Corollary 10. $CCS \nrightarrow CPM$ If a KDF is CCS-secure, it may not be CPM-secure.

KDF3. Now we analyse the security of *KDF3*, which we defined it as,

$$KDF3(PrivS, s, ctx)_n = F(PrivS\|s\|ctx_1)\| F(PrivS\|s\|ctx_2), \text{ where } ctx = ctx_1\|ctx_2.$$

We show that it only achieves KPS and KPM security. In addition, we use this analysis to prove the non-implications of corollaries 11 and 12 in Figure 1.

Theorem 3. *KDF3 is secure with respect to KPM, KPS and is not CCM, CCS and CPM.*

Proof: Firstly, we show that *KDF3* is KPM-secure. During the learning stage, C chooses $PrivS \in_R PSPACE$, $s_i \in_R SSPACE$, $ctx_i \in CSPACE$ and C uses F to compute $K_i = KDF3(PrivS, s_i, ctx_i)_n$. A is provided K_i, s_i and ctx_i. In the challenge stage, challenge key is computed as $K' = KDF3(PrivS, s, ctx)_n$, where $s \in_R SSPACE$ and ctx is chosen by C.

Since F is modeled as a RO, A can only distinguish if K' is the key generated by *KDF3* or a random string of the same length, only if:

a) C chooses $ctx \in CSPACE$, $ctx = ctx_1\|ctx_2$ and $ctx_1 = ctx_2$. In this case, A can check the challenge key K', the first half is equal with the second half of K', such as $F(PrivS\|s\|ctx_1) = F(PrivS\|s\|ctx_2)$. However, with a high probability the chosen ctx by C is most likely different such that $ctx_1 \neq ctx_2$. Hence, the probability is, $\Pr[ctx_1 = ctx_2] \leq \frac{1}{|CSPACE|}$.

b) $s = s_i$ and $ctx = ctx_i$ for some $i = 1 \ldots q_k$. In this case, A will distinguish K' is one of the cryptographic key at the learning stage, such as $K' = K_i$ for some $i = 1 \ldots q_k$, where $F(PrivS\|s\|ctx_1)\|F(PrivS\|s\|ctx_2) = F(PrivS\|s_i\|ctx_1^i)\|F(PrivS\|s_i\|ctx_2^i)$. The probability is, $\Pr[s = s_i \wedge ctx = ctx_i] \leq \frac{q_k}{|SSPACE|\times|CSPACE|}$.

c) Query $PrivS$, $PrivS' = PrivS$ and find $F(PrivS'\|s\|ctx_1) = F(PrivS\|s\|ctx_1)$ or $F(PrivS'\|s\|ctx_2) = F(PrivS\|s\|ctx_2)$. This implies that A guessing $PrivS$ which can happen with probability $Pr[PrivS' = PrivS] \leq \frac{q_F}{|PSPACE|}$.

The probability that A winning the game is:

$$\Pr[A \text{ wins}] = \Pr[A \text{ wins}|ctx_1 = ctx_2]\Pr[ctx_1 = ctx_2] + \\ \Pr[A \text{ wins}|s = s_i \wedge ctx = ctx_i]\Pr[s = s_i \wedge ctx = ctx_i] +$$

$$\Pr[A \text{ wins}|PrivS' = PrivS]\Pr[PrivS' = PrivS] +$$
$$\Pr[A \text{ wins}|ctx_1 \neq ctx_2 \wedge s \neq s_i \& ctx \neq ctx_i \wedge PrivS' \neq PrivS] \times$$
$$\Pr[ctx_1 \neq ctx_2 \wedge s \neq s_i \& ctx \neq ctx_i \wedge PrivS' \neq PrivS]$$
$$\leq 1 \left(\frac{1}{|CSPACE|}\right) + 1 \left(\frac{q_k}{|SSPACE\|CSPACE|}\right) + 1 \left(\frac{q_F}{|PSPACE|}\right) +$$
$$\frac{1}{2}\left(1 - \frac{1}{|CSPACE|} - \frac{q_k}{|SSPACE\|CSPACE|} - \frac{q_F}{|PSPACE|}\right)$$
$$\leq \frac{1}{2} + \frac{1}{2|CSPACE|} + \frac{q_k}{2|SSPACE\|CSPACE|} + \frac{q_F}{2|PSPACE|},$$

where $\epsilon = \frac{1}{2|CSPACE|} + \frac{q_k}{2|SSPACE\|CSPACE|} + \frac{q_F}{2|PSPACE|}$ is negligible.

A only has negligible 'advantage' over random guessing the challenge output. Therefore, $KDF3$ is KPM-secure.

Secondly, we show that $KDF3$ is KPS-secure. During the learning stage, C chooses $PrivS \in_R PSPACE$. C choose a fixed $s \in_R SSPACE$ which is used for entire game and chooses different $ctx_i \in CSPACE$. Then, C uses F to compute $K_i = KDF3(PrivS, s, ctx_i)_n$. A is provided K_i, s and ctx_i. In the challenge stage, challenge key is computed as $K' = KDF3(PrivS, s, ctx)_n$, where ctx is chosen by C.

Since F is modeled as a RO, A can only distinguish if K' is the key generated by $KDF3$ or a random string of the same length, only if:

a) C chooses $ctx \in CSPACE$, $ctx = ctx_1\|ctx_2$ and $ctx_1 = ctx_2$. Hence, A can distinguish the challenge key K' such as the first half of the K' is equal with the second half of the K', where $F(PrivS\|s\|ctx_1) = F(PrivS\|s\|ctx_2)$. However, the chosen ctx by C is most likely different such that $ctx_1 \neq ctx_2$. Therefore, the probability if $\Pr[ctx_1 = ctx_2] \leq \frac{1}{|CSPACE|}$.

b) Query $PrivS$, $PrivS' = PrivS$ and find $F(PrivS'\|s\|ctx_1) = F(PrivS\|s\|ctx_1)$ or $F(PrivS'\|s\|ctx_2) = F(PrivS\|s\|ctx_2)$. This implies that A guessing $PrivS$ which can happen with probability $Pr[PrivS' = PrivS] \leq \frac{q_F}{|PSPACE|}$.

The probability that A winning the game is:

$$\Pr[A \text{ wins}] = \Pr[A \text{ wins}|ctx_1 = ctx_2]\Pr[ctx_1 = ctx_2] +$$
$$\Pr[A \text{ wins}|PrivS' = PrivS]\Pr[PrivS' = PrivS] +$$
$$\Pr[A \text{ wins}|ctx_1 \neq ctx_2 \wedge PrivS' \neq PrivS]\Pr[ctx_1 \neq ctx_2 \wedge PrivS' \neq$$
$$PrivS]$$
$$\leq 1\left(\frac{1}{|CSPACE|}\right) + 1\left(\frac{q_F}{|PSPACE|}\right) + \frac{1}{2}\left(1 - \frac{1}{|CSPACE|} - \frac{q_F}{|PSPACE|}\right)$$
$$\leq \frac{1}{2} + \frac{1}{2|CSPACE|} + \frac{q_F}{2|PSPACE|},$$

where $\epsilon = \frac{1}{2|CSPACE|} + \frac{q_F}{2|PSPACE|}$ is negligible.

A only has negligible 'advantage' over random guessing the challenge output. Hence, $KDF3$ is KPS-secure.

Thirdly, we show $KDF3$ is not CCM-secure. In the learning stage, C chooses $PrivS \in_R PSPACE$ and $s_i \in_R SSPACE$, then C uses F to compute $K_i = KDF3(PrivS, s_i, ctx_i)_n$, where ctx_i is chosen by A. A receives K_i and s_i.

In the challenge stage, the challenge key K' is computed by C such as $K' = KDF3(PrivS, s, ctx)_n$, where $s \in_R SSPACE$ by C and ctx is chosen by A.

Once C sends K' to A, A continues learn the cryptographic keys $KDF3$ up to $q - q'$ queries at the adaptive stage.

F is modeled as a RO, A can only distinguish if K' is the key generated by $KDF3$ or a random string of the same length, only if, A chooses $ctx \in CSPACE$, $ctx = ctx_1\|ctx_2$ and $ctx_1 = ctx_2$. In this case, $F(PrivS\|s\|ctx_1) = F(PrivS\|s\|ctx_2)$, A can distinguish the challenge key K' where the first half of K' is equal with the second half of K'. Since A chooses ctx, hence, the probability is, $\Pr[ctx_1 = ctx_2] = 1$. Thus, $KDF3$ is not CCM-secure and $KDF3$ is not CPM-secure by Lemma 1.

Next, we show $KDF3$ is not CCS-secure. During the learning stage, C chooses $PrivS \in_R PSPACE$ and $s \in_R SSPACE$, which are fixed for entire game, then C uses F to compute $K_i = KDF3(PrivS, s, ctx_i)_n$, where ctx_i is chosen by A. A receives K_i and s. In the challenge stage, challenge key is computed as $K' = KDF3(PrivS, s, ctx)_n$, where ctx is chosen by A. C sends K' to A, A continues learn the cryptographic keys $KDF3$ up to $q - q'$ queries at the adaptive stage.

Since, F is modeled as a RO, A can only distinguish if K' is the key generated by $KDF3$ or a random string of the same length, only if, A chooses $ctx \in CSPACE$, $ctx = ctx_1\|ctx_2$ and $ctx_1 = ctx_2$, A can distinguish the challenge key K' where the first half of K' is equal with the second half of K', such as $F(PrivS\|s\|ctx_1)\|F(PrivS\|s\|ctx_2)$. ctx is chosen by A, hence, the probability is, $\Pr[ctx_1 = ctx_2] = 1$. Therefore, $KDF3$ is not CCS-secure and $KDF3$ is not CPM-secure by Lemma 3.   □

The proof of Corollary 11 - 12 are an immediate result of Theorem 3.

Corollary 11. $KPM \nrightarrow CCM$ If a KDF is KPM-secure, it may not be CCM-secure.

Corollary 12. $KPS \nrightarrow CCS$ If a KDF is KPS-secure, it may not be CCS-secure.

KDF4. Here we analyse the security of $KDF4$, which proposed by Adam *et. al* in 2004 [1]. $KDF4$ is defined as,

$$KDF4(PrivS, s)_n = F(PrivS, s_1, PrivS)\| F(PrivS, s_2, PrivS)\| \ldots \| F(PrivS, s_l, PrivS), \text{ where } s = s_1 \| s_2 \| \ldots \| s_l.$$

We show that it achieves CCM and CCS security.

Theorem 4. *If $q = 0$ and $l > 1$, then $KDF4$ is secure in CCM, CCS, KPM and KPS but is not secure in CPM.*

Proof: Firstly, we prove that $KDF4$ is secure in KPM, KPS, CCM and CCS when $q = 0$ and $l > 1$ as follows. If $q = 0$, it means, A can play neither at the learning stage nor at the adaptive stage. During the challenge stage, the challenge key is computed as $K' = KDF4(PrivS, s)_n$, where $PrivS$ and s are chosen by C, such as $PrivS \in_R PSPACE$ and $s \in_R SSPACE$. K' is provided to A.

Since F is modeled as a RO, A can only distinguish if K' is the key generated by $KDF4$ or a random string of the same length, only if:

a) If the chosen s where $s = s_1\|s_2\| \ldots \|s_l$ and $s_1 = s_2 = \ldots = s_l$. Then, A can distinguish K' it the cryptographic key which is derived from $KDF4$ by checking is there has l repetition component parts, such as $F(PrivS, s_1, PrivS)$ $= F(PrivS, s_2, PrivS) = \ldots = F(PrivS, s_l, PrivS)$. However, s is chosen randomly by C. Hence, the probability is $\Pr[s = s_1\|s_2\| \ldots \|s_l] \leq \frac{1}{|SSPACE|}$.

b) Query $PrivS$, $PrivS' = PrivS$ and find $KDF4(PrivS', s)_n = KDF4(PrivS, s)_n$. This amounts to A guessing $PrivS$, with probability $Pr[PrivS' = PrivS] \leq \frac{q_F}{|PSPACE|}$.

The probability that A winning this indistinguishability game is:

$$\begin{aligned}
\Pr[A \text{ wins}] = &\Pr[A \text{ wins}|s = s_1\|s_2\| \ldots \|s_l]\Pr[s = s_1\|s_2\| \ldots \|s_l] + \\
&\Pr[A \text{ wins}|PrivS' = PrivS]\Pr[PrivS' = PrivS] + \\
&\Pr[A \text{ wins}|s = s_1 \neq s_2 \neq \ldots \neq s_l \wedge PrivS' \neq PrivS] \times \\
&\Pr[s = s_1 \neq s_2 \neq \ldots \neq s_l \wedge PrivS' \neq PrivS] \\
\leq &1 \left(\frac{1}{|SSPACE|} \right) + 1 \left(\frac{q_F}{|PSPACE|} \right) + \frac{1}{2} \left(1 - \frac{1}{|SSPACE|} - \frac{q_F}{|PSPACE|} \right) \\
\leq &\frac{1}{2} + \frac{1}{2|SSPACE|} + \frac{q_F}{2|PSPACE|},
\end{aligned}$$

where $\epsilon = \frac{1}{2|SSPACE|} + \frac{q_F}{2|PSPACE|}$ is negligible.

A has negligible 'advantage' in making random guessing the challenge output. $KDF4$ is secure in KPM, KPS, CCM and CCS.

Secondly, we show that KDF4 is not CPM-secure ($q = 0$, $l > 1$). When $q = 0$, A is not allowed to play at the learning stage and at the adaptive stage. In the challenge stage, the challenge key is computed as $K' = KDF4(PrivS, s, PrivS)_n$, where s is chosen by A. F is modeled as a RO, A can only distinguish if K' is the key generated by $KDF4$ or a random string of the same length, only if, A chooses $s = s_1\|s_2\| \ldots \|s_l$, $s_1 = s_2 = \ldots = s_l$, such as $K' = F(PrivS\|s_1\|PrivS)$ $\| \ldots \|F(PrivS\|s_l\|PrivS)$ and $F(PrivS\|s_1\|PrivS) = \ldots = F(PrivS\|s_l\|PrivS)$. A can distinguish K' is the cryptographic key when A observes there is a l repetition component parts. Since s is chosen by A, hence the probability is $\Pr[s_1 = s_2 = \ldots = s_l] = 1$. Therefore, A can distinguish between a derived cryptographic key and a truly random string based on the observation of the l repetition component parts. Thus, $KDF4$ is not CPM-secure. $\square$

KDF5. Here we analyse the security of $KDF5$, which corresponds to the KDF proposal presented by Krawczyk in [6]. $KDF5$ is defined as,

$$KDF5(PrivS, s, ctx)_n = G(F(PrivS, s), ctx)$$

In the following analysis, both G and H are modelled as random oracles, and we show that $KDF5$ is CPM-secure.

Remark: We must note that Krawczyk [6] proved that $KDF5$ is CCS-secure in the standard model. Specifically, Krawczyk proves that if F is a good (randomised) computational extractor and G is a pseudorandom function, then the composition shown above is CCS-secure. He then goes on to show that the standard MAC algorithm HMAC satisfies both requirements under standard assumptions in the underlying hash function. Extending Krawczyk's result to CPM security in the standard model would necessitate the modification of the given definition of computational extractor, to relax the requirement on the salt being chosen uniformly at random. This notion of extractor would be trivially satisfied by deterministic extractors, such as those mentioned by Krawczyk himself [6]. We leave the formalisation of these changes as future work and now focus in showing that CPM-security is achievable in the ROM.

Theorem 5. *KDF5 is secure with respect to all five security models.*

Proof: Firstly, we show that $KDF5$ [6] is CPM-secure. During the learning stage, C chooses $PrivS \in_R PSPACE$. C uses F to compute $K_i = KDF5(PrivS, s_i, ctx_i)$, where s_i and ctx_i are chosen by A from $SSPACE$ and $CSPACE$ respectively. A is provided K_i. In the challenge stage, challenge key is computed as $K' = KDF5(PrivS, s, ctx)$, where s and ctx are chosen by A. C sends K' to A, A continues learn the cryptographic keys up to $q - q'$ queries.

Since F is modeled as a RO, A can only distinguish if K' is the key generated by $KDF5$ or a random string of the same length, only if:

a) $(s, ctx) = (s_i, ctx_i)$ for some $i = 1 \ldots q_k$, it means, $G(F(PrivS, s), ctx) = G(F(PrivS, s_i), ctx_i)$. A will distinguish K' is one of the key at the learning stage. However, based on Definition 5, the chosen pair (s, ctx) is restricted not the similar pair $(s_i, ctx_i) \, \forall \, i$ in the learning stage. Hence, the probability is $\Pr[(s, ctx) = (s_i, ctx_i)] = 0$.
b) Query $PrivS$ such as $PrivS' = PrivS$ and find $F(PrivS'\|s) = F(PrivS\|s)$ or $F(PrivS'\|s\|ctx) = F(PrivS\|s\|ctx)$. This implies that A guessing $PrivS$ with with probability $Pr[PrivS' = PrivS] \leq \frac{q_F}{|PSPACE|}$.

The probability that A winning this indistinguishability game is:
$$\Pr[A \text{ wins}] = \Pr[A \text{ wins}|PrivS' = PrivS]\Pr[PrivS' = PrivS] +$$
$$\Pr[A \text{ wins}|PrivS' \neq PrivS]\Pr[PrivS' \neq PrivS]$$
$$\leq 1\left(\frac{q_F}{|PSPACE|}\right) + \frac{1}{2}\left(1 - \frac{q_F}{|PSPACE|}\right)$$
$$\leq \frac{1}{2} + \frac{q_F}{2|PSPACE|}, \text{ where } \epsilon = \frac{q_F}{2|PSPACE|} \text{ is negligible.}$$

A is only has negligible 'advantage' to distinguish the challenge output. Therefore, $KDF5$ is CPM-secure. Hence $KDF5$ is secure in CCM, KPM, CCS and KPS by Lemma 1, Lemma 2, Lemma 3 and Lemma 4 respectively.   □

6   Conclusion

We propose four new security models known as KPM, KPS, CCM and CPM. Together with the CCS security model (proposed by Krawczyk), we believe these security models form a comprehensive security framework for KDFs. This allows for consideration of the security of a KDF against adversaries of varying capabilities. We establish the relations between these five security models. These relations are established using existing and modified KDF proposals.

As future work, we plan to use our proposed security framework to analyse the security level of other existing KDF proposals and, where possible, extend our analyses to the standard model (i.e without random oracles).

References

1. Adams, C., Kramer, G., Mister, S., Zuccherato, R.: On The Security of Key Derivation Functions. In: Zhang, K., Zheng, Y. (eds.) ISC 2004. LNCS, vol. 3225, pp. 134–145. Springer, Heidelberg (2004)
2. Barak, B., Shaltiel, R., Tromer, E.: True Random Number Generators Secure in a Changing Environment. In: Walter, C.D., Koç, Ç.K., Paar, C. (eds.) CHES 2003. LNCS, vol. 2779, pp. 166–180. Springer, Heidelberg (2003)
3. Dang, Q.: Recommendation for Existing Application-Specific Key Derivation Functions. NIST Special Publication 800, 135 (2010)
4. Kaliski, B.: PKCS# 5: Password-based cryptography specification version 2.0. Technical report, RFC 2898 (September 2000)
5. Krawczyk, H.: On Extract-then-Expand Key Derivation Functions and an HMAC-based KDF (2008), http://citeseerx.ist.psu.edu/viewdoc/download?doi=10.1.1.131.8254&rep=rep1&type=pdf
6. Krawczyk, H.: Cryptographic Extraction and Key Derivation: The HKDF Scheme. In: Rabin, T. (ed.) CRYPTO 2010. LNCS, vol. 6223, pp. 631–648. Springer, Heidelberg (2010)
7. Krawczyk, H., Eronen, P.: HMAC-based Extract-and-Expand Key Derivation Function (HKDF). Technical report, RFC 5869 (May 2010)
8. McGrew, D., Weis, B.: Key Derivation Functions and Their Uses (2010), http://www.ietf.org/id/draft-irtf-cfrg-kdf-uses-00.txt
9. Shoup, V.: ISO 18033-2: An emerging standard for public-key encryption. Final Committee Draft (December 2004)
10. Yao, F.F., Yin, Y.L.: Design and Analysis of Password-Based Key Derivation Functions. In: Menezes, A. (ed.) CT-RSA 2005. LNCS, vol. 3376, pp. 245–261. Springer, Heidelberg (2005)

On the Equivalence of Two Definitions of Visual Cryptography Scheme[*]

Teng Guo[1,2], Feng Liu[1], and ChuanKun Wu[1]

[1] State Key Laboratory of Information Security,
Institute of Information Engineering,
Chinese Academy of Sciences, Beijing 100029, China
[2] Graduate University of Chinese Academy of Sciences, Beijing 100190, China
{guoteng,liufeng,ckwu}@is.iscas.ac.cn

Abstract. A visual cryptography scheme (VCS) is a secret sharing method, for which the secret can be decoded by human eyes without needing any cryptography knowledge nor any computation. To the best of our knowledge, there are two different definitions of basis matrix (k, n)-VCS. The definition of unconditional secure basis matrix (k, n)-VCS is the generally accepted one, and has been widely used since the pioneer work of Naor and Shamir in 1994, while the definition of stacking secure basis matrix (k, n)-VCS is relatively new, and has been used in many studies in recent years. Our study shows that the above two definitions are actually equivalent. Furthermore, we generalize the equivalence relation to general access structure basis matrix VCS and general access structure size invariant VCS. But the equivalence relation does not hold for non-basis matrix (k, n)-VCS.

Keywords: Visual cryptography, Secret sharing, Unconditional secure, Stacking secure.

1 Introduction

Naor and Shamir first formally gave the definition of k out of n threshold visual cryptography scheme in [19], which is also denoted as (k, n)-VCS. In a (k, n)-VCS, an original secret image is split into n shares, where the stacking of any k shares can reveal the content of the secret image but any less than k shares should provide no information (in an information-theoretic sense) of the secret image, except the size of it. In [1], Ateniese et al. extended the model of Naor and Shamir to general access structure and formally brought up the concept of basis matrices, which are widely used to construct VCSs and to prove bounds of VCS (see [19, 1, 9, 4, 10, 30, 11, 20, 26, 2, 22, 7, 14, 24, 6, 17, 18]). A VCS based on basis matrices is also referred to as a basis matrix VCS for short. Ito et al. and Yang separately introduced size invariant visual cryptography scheme (SIVCS) in [21] and [25] respectively, which has no pixel expansion.

---

[*] This work was supported by NSFC No.60903210.

M.D. Ryan, B. Smyth, and G. Wang (Eds.): ISPEC 2012, LNCS 7232, pp. 217–227, 2012.
© Springer-Verlag Berlin Heidelberg 2012

Ateniese et al. first formally give the definition of unconditional secure basis matrix (k, n)-VCS, which is the most widely used definition of VCS (see [19, 1, 10, 15, 23, 16, 3, 30, 14, 24, 6, 17, 18]). Unconditional secure means that we cannot get any information from less than k shares (also called perfect security). On the other hand, in recent years, many studies use the definition of stacking secure basis matrix (k, n)-VCS (see [6, 5, 8, 28, 27, 13, 29, 12, 25]). Stacking secure means that the stacking of less than k shares will not disclose the secret. When the adversary cannot analyze the shares from the pixel level with the assistances of computers and scanners, stacking secure is enough. It is easy to see that unconditional security surely implies stacking security, on the other hand, stacking security may not guarantee unconditional security. To the best of our knowledge, no rigorous treatment has been paid to the relationship between the above two definitions of basis matrix (k, n)-VCS, except an illustration which took a $(2, 3)$ threshold structure as an example in [6]. Intuitively, the unconditional secure condition is stronger than the stacking secure condition. For non-basis matrix (k, n)-VCSs, which are based on two collections of share matrices, we have proved that this is in fact true by giving a (k, n)-VCS that is stacking secure but not unconditional secure. However, for basis matrix (k, n)-VCSs, surprisingly, we have proved that the two security conditions are actually equivalent, which leads to the equivalence of the above two definitions of basis matrix (k, n)-VCS. Our result provides a firm foundation for the using of the definition of stacking secure basis matrix (k, n)-VCS. Finally, we point out the following:

1. Many researches have obtained stacking secure basis matrix (k, n)-VCSs (see [6, 5, 8, 28, 27, 13, 29, 12, 25]), our results show that they also guarantee unconditional security.
2. The study of optimal (k, n)-VCS in [6] is based on the definition of stacking secure basis matrix (k, n)-VCS, on the other hand, their conclusion is for unconditional secure basis matrix (k, n)-VCSs. However, it only took a $(2, 3)$ threshold structure as an example to illustrate the equivalence of the above two definitions of basis matrix (k, n)-VCS. From this perspective, its derivation process is not rigorous, and our study can be seen as a rigorous complement and generalization to the study of [6].
3. To the best of our knowledge, most optimization algorithms and linear programmings that are used to study optimal (k, n)-VCS (see [6, 5, 13]) describe their constraints by the stacking secure condition of basis matrix VCS. On the other hand, the schemes obtained by those researches in [6, 5, 13] are expected to guarantee unconditional security. Hence there is a gap between what is obtained and what is expected. Our results fill up this gap, and provide a firm foundation to this type of researches.

This paper is organized as follows. In Section 2, we give some preliminaries of VCS. In Section 3, we prove the equivalence of the two definitions of basis matrix (k, n)-VCS. Then the equivalence relation is generalized to general access structure basis matrix VCS. Finally, it is proved that the equivalence relation cannot be extended to non-basis matrix VCS. The paper is concluded in Section 4.

2   Preliminaries

In this section, we first formally give the definition of unconditional secure basis matrix (k, n)-VCS. Then we formally give the definition of stacking secure basis matrix (k, n)-VCS.

Before moving any further, we first set up our notations. Let X be a subset of $\{1, 2, \cdots, n\}$ and let $|X|$ be the cardinality of X. For any $n \times m$ Boolean matrix M, let $M[X]$ denote the matrix M constrained to rows in X, then $M[X]$ is a $|X| \times m$ matrix. We denote by $H(M[X])$ the Hamming weight of the OR result of rows of $M[X]$. Let C_0 and C_1 be two collections of $n \times m$ Boolean matrices, we define $C_0[X] = \{M[X] : M \in C_0\}$, and define $C_1[X] = \{M[X] : M \in C_1\}$. We define $H(C_0[X]) = \{H(M[X]) : M \in C_0\}$, and define $H(C_1[X]) = \{H(M[X]) : M \in C_1\}$.

Remark: $H(C_0[X])$ and $H(C_1[X])$ are two collections (multi-sets) of numbers between 0 and m.

In a visual cryptography scheme with n participants, we share one pixel at a time. The pixel is either white or black. If the pixel to be shared is white (resp. black), we randomly permutate the columns of S_0 (resp. S_1) and distribute the j-th $(0 \le j \le n)$ row to share j, in which 0 denotes a white pixel and 1 denotes a black pixel. Formally, unconditional secure basis matrix (k, n)-VCS is defined as follows:

Definition 1 (Unconditional secure basis matrix (k, n)-VCS [1]). *The two $n \times m$ Boolean matrices (S_0, S_1) constitute an unconditional secure basis matrix (k, n)-VCS if the following conditions hold:*

1. *(Contrast) For any participant set X with $|X| \ge k$, we denote $l = H(S_0[X])$, and denote $h = H(S_1[X])$. It holds that $0 \le l < h \le m$.*
2. *(Security) For any participant set Y with $|Y| \le k - 1$, $S_0[Y]$ and $S_1[Y]$ are equal up to a column permutation.*

Remark: From another viewpoint, if we take $S_0[Y]$ and $S_1[Y]$ as two multi-sets with their column vectors as elements, then the above security condition can be stated as follows: the two multi-sets $S_0[Y]$ and $S_1[Y]$ are the same for any Y with $|Y| \le k - 1$. To verify the security condition, we need to verify the equality of the two multi-sets $S_0[Y]$ and $S_1[Y]$. Finally, we point out that S_0 and S_1 are also referred to as the basis matrices.

Now, we formally give the definition of stacking secure basis matrix (k, n)-VCS as follows:

Definition 2 (Stacking secure basis matrix (k, n)-VCS [27, 8, 6]). *The two $n \times m$ Boolean matrices (S_0, S_1) constitute a stacking secure basis matrix (k, n)-VCS if the following conditions hold:*

1. *(Contrast) For any participant set X with $|X| \ge k$, we denote $l = H(S_0[X])$, and denote $h = H(S_1[X])$. It holds that $0 \le l < h \le m$.*
2. *(Security) For any participant set Y with $|Y| \le k-1$, it holds that $H(S_0[Y]) = H(S_1[Y])$.*

Remark: The contrast conditions of the above two definitions of basis matrix (k, n)-VCS are the same. The differences lie in the security condition. The unconditional secure condition of basis matrix (k, n)-VCS requires that $S_0[Y]$ and $S_1[Y]$ are equal up to a column permutation for any Y with $|Y| \leq k - 1$, while the stacking secure condition of basis matrix (k, n)-VCS requires that $H(S_0[Y]) = H(S_1[Y])$ holds for any Y with $|Y| \leq k - 1$. Intuitively, the stacking secure condition is easier to characterize and verify than the unconditional secure condition. That is the very reason that a lot of papers use the definition of stacking secure basis matrix (k, n)-VCS (see [6, 5, 8, 28, 27, 13, 29, 12, 25]).

3   The Equivalence of Two Definitions of Basis Matrix VCS

In this section, we first prove that the two definitions of basis matrix (k, n)-VCS are actually equivalent. Then we extend the equivalence relation to general access structure basis matrix VCS and general access structure SIVCS. At last, it is proved that the equivalence relation cannot be extended to non-basis matrix (k, n)-VCS.

3.1   The Equivalence of Two Definitions of Threshold Basis Matrix VCS

To begin with our proof, we first illustrate the terminologies we will use. Numbers $0, 1, 2, \ldots, 2^m - 1$ can be represented as m-tuple Boolean row vectors $(\underbrace{00 \ldots 0})$,

$(\underbrace{00 \ldots 0}_{m-1} 1), (\underbrace{00 \ldots 0}_{m-2} 10), \ldots, (\underbrace{11 \ldots 1}_{m})$. To get m-tuple Boolean column vectors,

we transpose the above m-tuple Boolean row vectors. Now we have a $1 - 1$ mapping between the set of all m-tuple Boolean column vectors and the set of numbers $\{0, 1, 2, \ldots, 2^m - 1\}$. The above $1 - 1$ mapping is also referred to as the coding rule.

Given two numbers $a, b \in \{0, 1, 2, \ldots, 2^m - 1\}$, if the m-tuple Boolean column vector of b can be obtained by turning some (possibly 0) '1' bits of the m-tuple Boolean column vector of a into '0' bits, then we say that a covers b or that b is covered by a, which is denoted as $a \trianglerighteq b$.

Remark: Obviously, a trivially covers a. If $a \trianglerighteq b$ and $a \neq b$, we say that a non-trivially covers b or that b is non-trivially covered by a, which is denoted as $a \triangleright b$. It is convenient to know that, if $a \triangleright b$, then $a > b$. However, the converse is not true.

According to the coding rule, the column vectors of the $n \times m$ Boolean matrix can be mapped to numbers in $\{0, 1, 2, \ldots, 2^n - 1\}$. Thus the $n \times m$ Boolean matrix can also be viewed as a multi-set of cardinality m, with its column vectors as elements. Given two $n \times m$ Boolean matrices S_0 and S_1, which can also be viewed as two multi-sets, the following two propositions about them are equivalent: (1) S_0 and S_1 are equal up to a column permutation; (2) the two multi-sets S_0 and

S_1 are equal. Since the OR result of a column vector is 0 if and only if it is a zero vector, the Hamming weight of the OR result of the rows of S_0 (resp. S_1) is equal to the number of non-zero column vectors in the multi-set S_0 (resp. S_1). From another viewpoint, it is equal to m minus the number of zero vector in the multi-set S_0 (resp. S_1).

Lemma 1. *Given two $n \times m$ Boolean matrices (S_0, S_1) and a participant set X with $|X| \geq 1$, if it holds that $H(S_0[Y]) = H(S_1[Y])$ for any participant set Y with $Y \subseteq X$, then $S_0[Y]$ and $S_1[Y]$ are equal up to a column permutation for any participant set Y with $Y \subseteq X$.*

Proof: For any participant set Y with $Y \subseteq X$, according to the coding rule, the values of the column vectors in $(S_0[Y], S_1[Y])$ may be $0, 1, 2, \ldots, 2^{|Y|} - 1$. The number of column vectors of value i ($0 \leq i \leq 2^{|Y|} - 1$) in $S_0[Y]$ (resp. $S_1[Y]$) is denoted as l_i^Y (resp. h_i^Y). Obviously, for all i with $0 \leq i \leq 2^{|Y|} - 1$, we have $l_i^Y \geq 0$ and $h_i^Y \geq 0$. We also have $\displaystyle\sum_{i=0}^{2^{|Y|}-1} l_i^Y = \sum_{i=0}^{2^{|Y|}-1} h_i^Y = m$. The conclusion trivially holds for empty participant set Y. So we only need to prove that the conclusion holds for any non-empty participant set Y with $Y \subseteq X$.

From another viewpoint, we only need to prove that $l_i^Y = h_i^Y$ holds for any non-empty participant set Y with $Y \subseteq X$ and any i with $0 \leq i \leq 2^{|Y|} - 1$. We use proof by contradiction to reach our conclusion.

Assume that the conclusion does not hold, more specifically speaking, there exists a non-empty participant set $Y \subseteq X$ ($1 \leq t = |Y| \leq |X|$) such that, for some j ($0 \leq j \leq 2^t - 1$), we have $h_j^Y \neq l_j^Y$. The minimum j with $h_j^Y \neq l_j^Y$ is denoted as j^*. As we have $H(S_0[Y]) = H(S_1[Y])$, for the above Y, we get $h_0^Y = l_0^Y$ (for $H(S_0[Y]) = m - l_0^Y$ and $H(S_1[Y]) = m - h_0^Y$). Thus we have $j^* > 0$. It cannot be true that $j^* = 2^t - 1$, otherwise, as j^* is the minimum j with $h_j^Y \neq l_j^Y$, we get $\displaystyle\sum_{i=1}^{2^t-2}(l_i^Y) + l_{2^t-1}^Y = H(S_0[Y]) \neq H(S_1[Y]) = \sum_{i=1}^{2^t-2}(h_i^Y) + h_{2^t-1}^Y$, contradicting with the given condition that $H(S_0[Y]) = H(S_1[Y])$ holds for any Y with $Y \subseteq X$. Thus we have $0 < j^* < 2^t - 1$. Besides we have $h_e^Y = l_e^Y$ for any e with $0 \leq e < j^*$, for j^* is the minimum j with $h_j^Y \neq l_j^Y$.

Suppose that the '1' bits of the column vector of value j^* are on rows $Z = \{a_1, a_2, \ldots, a_w\}$, then we must have $1 \leq w < t$ (for $0 < j^* < 2^t - 1$). We define participant set $V = Y \setminus Z$ ($|Y| = t, |V| = t - w$). The number of column vectors of value i ($0 \leq i \leq 2^{|V|} - 1$) in $S_0[V]$ (resp. $S_1[V]$) is denoted as l_i^V (resp. h_i^V). Take any column vector from $S_0[Y]$ (resp. $S_1[Y]$), its value is denoted as d, if d is covered by j^*, then its corresponding $|V|$-tuple Boolean column vector in $S_0[V]$ (resp. $S_1[V]$) must be of value 0 (for all the '1' bits of that t-tuple Boolean column vector have been removed). Thus we have $h_0^V = \displaystyle\sum_{j^* \trianglerighteq d} h_d^Y = \sum_{j^* \vartriangleright d}(h_d^Y) + h_{j^*}^Y$ and $l_0^V = \displaystyle\sum_{j^* \trianglerighteq d} l_d^Y = \sum_{j^* \vartriangleright d}(l_d^Y) + l_{j^*}^Y$. Because j^* is the minimum j with $h_j^Y \neq l_j^Y$, we have $h_j^Y = l_j^Y$ for all j with $0 \leq j < j^*$. From the coding rule, we know if $j^* \rhd d$, then $d < j^*$. Hence we get $\sum\limits_{j^* \rhd d} h_d^Y = \sum\limits_{j^* \rhd d} l_d^Y$. As $h_{j^*}^Y \neq l_{j^*}^Y$, we get $h_0^V \neq l_0^V$. Furthermore, since $H(S_0[V]) = m - l_0^V$ and $H(S_1[V]) = m - h_0^V$, we get $H(S_0[V]) \neq H(S_1[V])$, which contradicts with the given condition that $H(S_0[Y]) = H(S_1[Y])$ holds for any Y with $Y \subseteq X$. Hence the assumption cannot be true, and we get the conclusion.   □

Theorem 1. *The definition of stacking secure basis matrix (k, n)-VCS and the definition of unconditional secure basis matrix (k, n)-VCS are equivalent.*

Proof: The contrast conditions of the above two definitions are the same. So we only need to prove the equivalence of the security conditions of the above two definitions. For basis matrix (k, n)-VCS, the unconditional secure condition trivially implies the stacking secure condition. Now we turn to prove the converse. Take any participant set X with $|X| = k - 1$, the condition that $H(S_0[Y]) = H(S_1[Y])$ holds for any participant set Y with $|Y| \leq k - 1$ implies the given condition of Lemma 1. Hence we know that $S_0[Y]$ and $S_1[Y]$ are equal up to a column permutation for any participant set Y with $Y \subseteq X$. Because the selection of X is arbitrary, the conclusion of Theorem 1 holds.   □

Remark: The above equivalence relationship means that a basis matrix (k, n)-VCS is stacking secure if and only if it is unconditional secure. From another viewpoint, a stacking secure basis matrix (k, n)-VCS also guarantees unconditional security.

3.2   The Equivalence of Two Definitions of General Access Structure Basis Matrix VCS

First we give some preliminaries of general access structure. Suppose the participant set is denoted as $P = \{1, 2, 3, \ldots, n\}$. A general access structure is a specification of qualified participant sets $\Gamma_{Qual} \in 2^P$ and forbidden participant sets $\Gamma_{Forb} \in 2^P$. Any participant set $X \in \Gamma_{Qual}$ can reveal the secret by stacking their share images, but any participant set $Y \in \Gamma_{Forb}$ cannot obtain any information of the secret image, except the size of it. All the minimal qualified sets are defined as $\Gamma_0 = \{A \in \Gamma_{Qual} : \forall A' \subsetneq A, A' \notin \Gamma_{Qual}\}$. If for any $A \in \Gamma_{Qual}$, any superset of A is also in Γ_{Qual}, then Γ_{Qual} is said to be monotone increasing. If for any $B \in \Gamma_{Forb}$, any subset of B is also in Γ_{Forb}, then Γ_{Forb} is said to be monotone decreasing. If Γ_{Qual} is monotone increasing and Γ_{Forb} is monotone deceasing and $\Gamma_{Qual} \cup \Gamma_{Forb} = 2^P$, then the access structure is said to be strong. In a strong access structure, $\Gamma_{Qual} = \{A \subseteq P : \exists B \in \Gamma_0, A \supseteq B\}$, and we say that Γ_{Qual} is the *closure* of Γ_0. If $\Gamma_{Qual} = \Gamma_0$, then the access structure is said to be weak. In (k, n) threshold access structure, $\Gamma_0 = \{B \subseteq P : |B| = k\}$ and $\Gamma_{Forb} = \{B \subseteq P : |B| \leq k - 1\}$. If the (k, n) threshold access structure is strong, $\Gamma_{Qual} = \{B \subseteq P : |B| \geq k\}$. On the other hand, if the (k, n) threshold access structure is weak, $\Gamma_{Qual} = \Gamma_0 = \{B \subseteq P : |B| = k\}$. Hence, in a strong (k, n)-VCS, it is required that the stacking of more than or equal to k shares can reveal the secret, while in a weak (k, n)-VCS, it is only required that the stacking of k shares can reveal the secret. All the maximal forbidden sets are defined as $\Gamma_M = \{A \in \Gamma_{Forb} : \forall a \in P \setminus A, A' = A \cup \{a\}, A' \in \Gamma_{Qual}\}$. In (k, n) threshold access structure, $\Gamma_M = \{B \subseteq P : |B| = k - 1\}$.

Formally, unconditional secure basis matrix $\{\Gamma_{Qual}, \Gamma_{Forb}\}$-VCS is defined as follows:

Definition 3 (Unconditional secure basis matrix $\{\Gamma_{Qual}, \Gamma_{Forb}\}$-VCS [1]). *The two $n \times m$ Boolean matrices (S_0, S_1) constitute an unconditional secure basis matrix $\{\Gamma_{Qual}, \Gamma_{Forb}\}$-VCS if the following conditions hold:*

1. *(Contrast) For any participant set $X \in \Gamma_{Qual}$, we denote $l = H(S_0[X])$, and denote $h = H(S_1[X])$. It holds that $0 \leq l < h \leq m$.*
2. *(Security) For any participant set $Y \in \Gamma_{Forb}$, $S_0[Y]$ and $S_1[Y]$ are equal up to a column permutation.*

Now, we formally give the definition of stacking secure basis matrix $\{\Gamma_{Qual}, \Gamma_{Forb}\}$-VCS as follows:

Definition 4 (Stacking secure basis matrix $\{\Gamma_{Qual}, \Gamma_{Forb}\}$-VCS). *The two $n \times m$ Boolean matrices (S_0, S_1) constitute a stacking secure basis matrix $\{\Gamma_{Qual}, \Gamma_{Forb}\}$-VCS if the following conditions hold:*

1. *(Contrast) For any participant set $X \in \Gamma_{Qual}$, we denote $l = H(S_0[X])$, and denote $h = H(S_1[X])$. It holds that $0 \leq l < h \leq m$.*
2. *(Security) For any participant set $Y \in \Gamma_{Forb}$, it holds that $H(S_0[Y]) = H(S_1[Y])$.*

Theorem 2. *The definition of stacking secure basis matrix $\{\Gamma_{Qual}, \Gamma_{Forb}\}$-VCS and the definition of unconditional secure basis matrix $\{\Gamma_{Qual}, \Gamma_{Forb}\}$-VCS are equivalent.*

Proof: The contrast conditions of the two definitions are the same. So we only need to prove the equivalence of the security conditions of the two definitions. For basis matrix $\{\Gamma_{Qual}, \Gamma_{Forb}\}$-VCS, the unconditional secure condition trivially implies the stacking secure condition. Now we turn to prove the converse. Take any participants set X with $X \in \Gamma_{Forb}$, since Γ_{Forb} is monotone deceasing, we have $H(S_0[Y]) = H(S_1[Y])$ for any participant set Y with $Y \subseteq X$. From Lemma 1, we know that $S_0[Y]$ and $S_1[Y]$ are equal up to a column permutation for any participant set Y with $Y \subseteq X$. Because the selection of X is arbitrary, we get the conclusion. ☐

3.3 The Equivalence of Two Definitions of General Access Structure SIVCS

The two definitions of general access structure SIVCS are the same as the two definitions of general access structure basis matrix VCS. However, their encoding processes are different. In SIVCS (see [21], [25]), to share a black (resp. white) pixel, we randomly choose a column from the black (resp. white) basis matrix, and then distribute the i-th row of the column to participant i, while in VCS, to share a black (resp. white) pixel, we randomly permutate the columns of the black (resp. white) basis matrix, and then distribute the i-th row of the permuted matrix to participant i. From Theorem 2, we know that the following Theorem also holds.

Theorem 3. *The definition of stacking secure* $\{\Gamma_{Qual}, \Gamma_{Forb}\}$-*SIVCS and the definition of unconditional secure* $\{\Gamma_{Qual}, \Gamma_{Forb}\}$-*SIVCS are equivalent.*

3.4   The Inequivalence of Two Definitions of Non-basis Matrix VCS

A more general definition of (k, n)-VCS is given by two collections of $n \times m$ Boolean matrices C_0 and C_1. To share a white pixel, we randomly choose a share matrix from C_0 and distribute the j-th $(0 \leq j \leq n)$ row to share j. (k, n)-VCS can also be classified as unconditional secure and stacking secure. Similarly, the contrast conditions are the same, both require that, for any participant set X with $|X| \geq k$, if we denote $l_X = \max\limits_{M \in C_0[X]} H(M)$ and denote $h_X = \min\limits_{M \in C_1[X]} H(M)$, then it must hold that $0 \leq l_X < h_X \leq m$. On the other hand, the security conditions are different. The unconditional secure condition requires that $C_0[Y]$ and $C_1[Y]$ contain the same matrices with the same frequencies for any participant set Y with $|Y| \leq k-1$, while the stacking secure condition requires that the two multi-sets of numbers $H(C_0[X])$ and $H(C_1[X])$ are the same for any participant set Y with $|Y| \leq k - 1$.

Formally, unconditional secure (k, n)-VCS is defined as follows:

Definition 5 (Unconditional secure (k, n)-VCS [1]). *The two collections of $n \times m$ Boolean matrices (C_0, C_1) constitute an unconditional secure (k, n)-VCS if the following conditions hold:*

1. *(Contrast) For any participant set X with $|X| \geq k$, we denote $l_X = \max\limits_{M \in C_0[X]}$ $H(M)$, and denote $h_X = \min\limits_{M \in C_1[X]} H(M)$. It holds that $0 \leq l_X < h_X \leq m$.*
2. *(Security) For any participant set Y with $|Y| \leq k - 1$, $C_0[Y]$ and $C_1[Y]$ contain the same matrices with the same frequencies.*

Now, we formally give the definition of stacking secure (k, n)-VCS as follows:

Definition 6 (Stacking secure (k, n)-VCS). *The two collections of $n \times m$ Boolean matrices (C_0, C_1) constitute a stacking secure (k, n)-VCS if the following conditions hold:*

1. *(Contrast) For any participant set X with $|X| \geq k$, we denote $l_X = \max\limits_{M \in C_0[X]}$ $H(M)$, and denote $h_X = \min\limits_{M \in C_1[X]} H(M)$. It holds that $0 \leq l_X < h_X \leq m$.*
2. *(Security) For any participant set Y with $|Y| \leq k-1$, it holds that $H(C_0[Y]) = H(C_1[Y])$.*

Remark: $H(C_0[Y])$ and $H(C_1[Y])$ are two collections (multi-sets) of numbers between 0 and m. Readers can refer to Section 2 for full definitions of $H(C_0[Y])$ and $H(C_1[Y])$.

For (k, n)-VCS, the unconditional secure condition trivially implies the stacking secure condition. However, the following Lemma shows that the converse does not hold.

Lemma 2. *For (k, n)-VCS, the stacking secure condition does not imply the unconditional secure condition.*

Proof: In order to reach our conclusion, we only need to construct a (k, n)-VCS, which is stacking secure but not unconditional secure. Suppose $\{C_0, C_1\}$ are two collections of share matrices of an unconditional secure (k, n)-VCS, C_0 for sharing a white pixel and C_1 for sharing a black pixel. Suppose the pixel expansion is m. We pad each share matrix in C_0 with a $n \times m$ all-zero matrix on the left of it, and pad each share matrix in C_1 with a $n \times m$ all-zero matrix on the right of it. The two padded collections of share matrices are denoted as $\{C_0', C_1'\}$. Since padding all-zero matrix will not affect the contrast condition and the stacking secure property, $\{C_0', C_1'\}$ constitutes a stacking secure (k, n)-VCS. However we can distinguish black pixels from white pixels by observing the relative padding positions (e.g. By observing a block on a single share, if the left half pixels are all white, we know the shared pixel is white, on the other hand, if the right half pixels are all white, we know the shared pixel is black). Hence $\{C_0', C_1'\}$ does not constitute an unconditional secure (k, n)-VCS. □

Although the above two definitions of (k, n)-VCS have the same contrast condition, however, from Lemma 2, we know that their security conditions are inequivalent. Hence we have the following Theorem.

Theorem 4. *The definition of stacking secure (k, n)-VCS and the definition of unconditional secure (k, n)-VCS are inequivalent.*

Remark: Since (k, n) threshold structure is a special case of general access structure, from Theorem 4, we know that stacking secure VCS and unconditional secure VCS are inequivalent. The above inequivalence relationship means that a stacking secure VCS may not guarantee unconditional security.

To illustrate our ideas more specifically, we give the following example.

Example 1. The following two share matrix collections define a $(2, 2)$-VCS.

$$C_0 = \left\{ \begin{bmatrix} 0010 \\ 0010 \end{bmatrix}, \begin{bmatrix} 0001 \\ 0001 \end{bmatrix} \right\} \text{ and } C_1 = \left\{ \begin{bmatrix} 1000 \\ 0100 \end{bmatrix}, \begin{bmatrix} 0100 \\ 1000 \end{bmatrix} \right\}$$

The above two collections satisfy the stacking secure condition, yet violate the unconditional secure condition.

4   Conclusions

In this paper, we have examined the intuitive differences between the stacking secure condition and the unconditional secure condition. Surprisingly, we have proved their equivalence with respect to basis matrix (k, n)-VCS. The generalizations to general access structure basis matrix VCS and general access structure SIVCS are given sequently. At last, it is proved that the equivalence relationship does not hold for non-basis matrix (k, n)-VCS.

Acknowledgements. This work was supported by NSFC No.60903210. Many thanks to the anonymous reviewers for their valuable comments.

References

1. Ateniese, G., Blundo, C., De Santis, A., Stinson, D.R.: Visual cryptography for general access structures. Information and Computation 129, 86–106 (1996)
2. Blundo, C., Cimato, S., De Santis, A.: Visual cryptography schemes with optimal pixel expansion. Theoretical Computer Science 369, 169–182 (2006)
3. Blundo, C., D'Arco, P., De Santis, A., Stinson, D.R.: Contrast optimal threshold visual cryptography schemes. SIAM Journal on Discrete Mathematics 16(2), 224–261 (2003)
4. Blundo, C., De Santis, A., Stinson, D.R.: On the contrast in visual cryptography schemes. Journal of Cryptology 12(4), 261–289 (1999)
5. Bose, M., Mukerjee, R.: Optimal (2, n) visual cryptographic schemes. Designs, Codes and Cryptography 40, 255–267 (2006)
6. Bose, M., Mukerjee, R.: Optimal (k, n) visual cryptographic schemes for general k. Designs, Codes and Cryptography 55, 19–35 (2010)
7. Cimato, S., De Prisco, R., De Santis, A.: Colored visual cryptography without color darkening. Theoretical Computer Science 374, 261–276 (2007)
8. Ciou, C.B., Yang, C.N.: Image secret sharing method with two-decoding-options: Lossless recovery and previewing capability. Image and Vision Computing 28(12), 1600–1610 (2010)
9. Droste, S.: New Results on Visual Cryptography. In: Koblitz, N. (ed.) CRYPTO 1996. LNCS, vol. 1109, pp. 401–415. Springer, Heidelberg (1996)
10. Hofmeister, T., Krause, M., Simon, H.U.: Contrast-optimal k out of n secret sharing schemes in visual cryptography. Theoretical Computer Science 240(2), 471–485 (2000)
11. Horng, G.B., Chen, T.H., Tsai, D.S.: Cheating in visual cryptography. Designs, Codes and Cryptography 38, 219–236 (2006)
12. Hou, Y.C., Xu, C.S.: A probability-based optimization model for sharing multiple secret images without pixel expansion (in chinese). Journal of Information, Technology and Society 2, 19–38 (2003)
13. Hsu, C.S., Tu, S.F., Hou, Y.C.: An Optimization Model for Visual Cryptography Schemes with Unexpanded Shares. In: Esposito, F., Raś, Z.W., Malerba, D., Semeraro, G. (eds.) ISMIS 2006. LNCS (LNAI), vol. 4203, pp. 58–67. Springer, Heidelberg (2006)
14. Hu, C.M., Tzeng, W.G.: Cheating prevention in visual cryptography. IEEE Transactions on Image Processing 16(1), 36–45 (2007)
15. Koga, H.: A General Formula of the (t,n)-Threshold Visual Secret Sharing Scheme. In: Zheng, Y. (ed.) ASIACRYPT 2002. LNCS, vol. 2501, pp. 328–345. Springer, Heidelberg (2002)

16. Krause, M., Simon, H.U.: Determining the optimal contrast for secret sharing schemes in visual cryptography. Combinatorics, Probability & Computing 12(3), 285–299 (2003)
17. Liu, F., Wu, C.K., Lin, X.J.: The alignment problem of visual cryptography schemes. Designs, Codes and Cryptography 50, 215–227 (2009)
18. Liu, F., Wu, C.K., Lin, X.J.: Step construction of visual cryptography schemes. IEEE Transactions on Information Forensics & Security 5(1), 27–38 (2010)
19. Naor, M., Shamir, A.: Visual Cryptography. In: De Santis, A. (ed.) EUROCRYPT 1994. LNCS, vol. 950, pp. 1–12. Springer, Heidelberg (1995)
20. De Prisco, R., De Santis, A.: Cheating Immune $(2,n)$-Threshold Visual Secret Sharing. In: De Prisco, R., Yung, M. (eds.) SCN 2006. LNCS, vol. 4116, pp. 216–228. Springer, Heidelberg (2006)
21. Ito, R., Kuwakado, H., Tanaka, H.: Image size invariant visual cryptography. IEICE Transactions on Fundamentals of Electronics, Communications and Computer Science E82-A(10), 2172–2177 (1999)
22. Tsai, D.S., Chen, T.H., Horng, G.B.: A cheating prevention scheme for binary visual cryptography with homogeneous secret images. Pattern Recognition 40, 2356–2366 (2007)
23. Tzeng, W.G., Hu, C.M.: A new approach for visual cryptography. Designs, Codes and Cryptography 27, 207–227 (2002)
24. Wang, Z.M., Arce, G.R., Di Crescenzo, G.: Halftone visual cryptography via error diffusion. IEEE Transactions on Information Forensics and Security 4(3), 383–396 (2009)
25. Yang, C.N.: New visual secret sharing schemes using probabilistic method. Pattern Recognition Letters 25, 481–494 (2004)
26. Yang, C.N., Chen, T.S.: Reduce shadowsize in aspect ratio invariant visual secret sharing schemes using a square block-wise operation. Pattern Recognition 39, 1300–1314 (2006)
27. Yang, C.N., Chen, T.S.: Visual secret sharing scheme: prioritizing the secret pixels with different pixel expansions to enhance the image contrast. Optical Engineering 46(9), 097005 (2007)
28. Yang, C.N., Chen, T.S.: Colored visual cryptography scheme based on additive color mixing. Pattern Recognition 41, 3114–3129 (2008)
29. Yang, C.N., Chung, T.H.: A general multi-secret visual cryptography scheme. Optics Communications 283(24), 4949–4962 (2010)
30. Zhou, Z., Arce, G.R., Di Crescenzo, G.: Halftone visual cryptography. IEEE Transactions on Image Processing 15(8), 2441–2453 (2006)

Key Length Estimation of Pairing-Based Cryptosystems Using η_T Pairing

Naoyuki Shinohara[1], Takeshi Shimoyama[2],
Takuya Hayashi[3], and Tsuyoshi Takagi[3]

[1] National Institute of Information and Communications Technology
[2] FUJITSU LABORATORIES Ltd.
[3] Kyushu University

Abstract. The security of pairing-based cryptosystems depends on the difficulty of the discrete logarithm problem (DLP) over certain types of finite fields. One of the most efficient algorithms for computing a pairing is the η_T pairing over supersingular curves on finite fields whose characteristic is 3. Indeed many high-speed implementations of this pairing have been reported, and it is an attractive candidate for practical deployment of pairing-based cryptosystems. The embedding degree of the η_T pairing is 6, so we deal with the difficulty of a DLP over the finite field $GF(3^{6n})$, where the function field sieve (FFS) is known as the asymptotically fastest algorithm of solving it. Moreover, several efficient algorithms are employed for implementation of the FFS, such as the large prime variation. In this paper, we estimate the time complexity of solving the DLP for the extension degrees $n = 97, 163, 193, 239, 313, 353, 509$, when we use the improved FFS. To accomplish our aim, we present several new computable estimation formulas to compute the explicit number of special polynomials used in the improved FFS. Our estimation contributes to the evaluation for the key length of pairing-based cryptosystems using the η_T pairing.

Keywords: pairing-based cryptosystems, discrete logarithm problem, finite field, key length, suitable values.

1 Introduction

Pairing-based cryptosystems such as identity-based encryption [9] have recently become one of the main research topics in cryptography. Their security is based on the intractability of the discrete logarithm problem (DLP) over certain types of finite fields. Once the underlying DLP is broken, the pairing-based cryptosystems are no longer secure. Therefore, evaluating the intractability of a DLP is an important task.

One of the most efficient algorithms for computing a pairing is the η_T pairing defined over supersingular curves on finite fields whose characteristic is 3 [7]. Many high-speed implementations of the η_T pairing have been reported in previous literature [4,8,15,16,22], and there are many efficient algorithms for Tate

M.D. Ryan, B. Smyth, and G. Wang (Eds.): ISPEC 2012, LNCS 7232, pp. 228–244, 2012.
© Springer-Verlag Berlin Heidelberg 2012

pairing over finite fields whose characteristic is 3 [6,11,12,17,24,28]. The timings reported in the literature are appealing for using the η_T pairing in practices; therefore in this paper we deal with the DLP over finite fields whose characteristic is 3. Moreover, since the embedding degree of the η_T pairing is 6, we are interested in finite fields $GF(3^{6n})$ for some integers n.

In this paper, we try to estimate the time complexity of solving the DLP over $GF(3^{6n})$ for extension degrees $n = 97, 163, 193, 239, 313, 353, 509$, using the following background facts. In 2010, Hayashi et al. solved a 676-bit DLP (over $GF(3^{6 \cdot 71})$) [18]. Joux and Lercier estimated that the time complexity of solving the DLP over $GF(3^{6 \cdot 97})$ is around 2^{71} [21]. And Smart et al. showed that the difficulty of solving the DLP over $GF(3^{6 \cdot 193})$ is roughly equivalent to that of factoring a 1024-bit RSA key (80-bit security) [31]. NIST recommended using a key size of more than 80 bits after 2011 [5]. Ahmadi et al. assumed that the DLP with $n = 509$ has the security level of 128 bits [4].

To estimate the time complexity, we consider an efficient algorithm to solve a DLP over $GF(3^{6n})$. Adleman proposed the function field sieve (FFS) to practically solve a DLP over finite fields whose characteristic is small [1,3]. The time complexity of the FFS for a DLP over $GF(3^{6n})$ is asymptotically

$$L_{3^{6n}}[1/3, (32/9)^{1/3}] = \exp(((32/9)^{1/3} + o(1))(\log 3^{6n})^{1/3}(\log\log 3^{6n})^{2/3}),$$

for $n \to \infty$. In 2002, Joux and Lercier proposed a practical improvement of the FFS called JL02-FFS [20], and in 2006 another new variant of the FFS (JL06-FFS) for $GF(q)$, where the characteristic is small and q is a medium-sized prime power [21]. Hayashi et al. reported that JL06-FFS has an advantage over JL02-FFS when we try to solve a DLP over $GF(3^{6n})$ [18]. Additionally, there are well-known efficient algorithms for implementation of JL06-FFS: the large prime variation [26], the lattice sieve [27], the filtering [10], the Galois action [18] and the free relation [18]. Thus, we estimate the time complexity of solving a DLP over $GF(3^{6n})$ by JL06-FFS with these efficient algorithms. We call this FFS "the improved FFS" in this paper.

There is an elemental parameter $(\kappa, d_H, d_m, B, R, S)$ commonly-utilize in JL06-FFS (FFS) and the improved FFS. There is also an advanced parameter (λ, θ, β) for the improved FFS, where λ is for the large prime variation, θ for the lattice sieve, and β for the filtering. For our estimation of the time complexity, we require the value of the parameter $(\kappa, d_H, d_m, B, R, S, \lambda, \theta, \beta)$, such that the computational cost of the improved FFS is almost minimum, when the extension degrees n are fixed. In this paper, such values are called the "suitable values" of $(\kappa, d_H, d_m, B, R, S, \lambda, \theta, \beta)$. To find suitable values for the fixed extension degrees n, we performed an experiment via a personal computer with an Intel Quad-Core (2.8 GHz) CPU and 8 GB RAM, and it took roughly 57 hours. Specifically, we checked certain computable criteria to solve a DLP with the improved FFS, changing the values of $(\kappa, d_H, d_m, B, R, S, \lambda, \theta, \beta)$. The criteria are checkable by using our new formulas (22), etc., which are extended from Granger's formula [13]. (Section 5 provides details on our experiment.)

Table 1. Estimation of the time complexity of solving DLP over $GF(3^{6n})$

n	97	163	193	239	313	353	509
$\log_2 C_{sieve}$	52.79	68.17	71.90	78.08	90.04	94.42	111.35

n: extension degree of the field $GF(3^{6n})$ over its base field $GF(3^6)$.

C_{sieve}: computational cost of the sieving step of the improved FFS
(In this paper, we ultimately regard C_{sieve} as the time complexity
of solving the DLP over $GF(3^{6n})$.)

Through the experiment we obtained Table 3 of the suitable values, and were able to eventually regard the computational cost C_{sieve} of the sieving step of the improved FFS as the time complexity of solving the DLP over $GF(3^{6n})$. On the strength of the costs C_{sieve}, we present Table 1 of the time complexity estimation of solving the DLP over $GF(3^{6n})$.

The hardness of the DLP over $GF(3^{6 \cdot 509})$ was estimated to be equivalent to 128-bit security [4], however, the DLP over $GF(3^{6 \cdot 509})$ actually accomplishes only about 111-bit security. To safely utilize a cryptographic schemes with η_T pairing over $GF(3^n)$, we must be aware of this fact.

2   Outline of Function Field Sieve

This section briefly explains the importance of the discrete logarithm problem (DLP) of $GF(3^{6n})$ where n is prime. It is well known that a function field sieve (FFS) is the most efficient method for solving a DLP of a finite field, so we provide an overview of it.

2.1   DLP and η_T Pairing

We first refer to a discrete logarithm (DLP) over the multiplicative group $GF(3^{6n})^*$. Let g be a generator of the multiplicative group $GF(3^{6n})^*$ and $A \in \langle g \rangle$. We then try to solve the DLP over $\langle g \rangle$; namely, we compute the smallest positive integer $\log_g A$ such that $g^{\log_g A} = A$.

It is expected that the η_T paring over the supersingular curve on $GF(3^n)$ realizes practical pairing-based cryptosystems. The safety of these cryptosystems is based on the difficulty of the DLP over $GF(3^{6n})$, since the map η_T is a bilinear map from $G_1 \times G_2$ to $GF(3^{6n})$, where G_1 and G_2 are cyclic groups. For example, let α be a secret integer such that $v_1 = [\alpha]v_2$ for given $v_1, v_2 \in G_1$. We then prepare arbitrary $w \in G_2$ and compute $\eta_T(v_1, w), \eta_T(v_2, w)$. Since $\eta_T(v_1, w) = \eta_T([\alpha]v_2, w) = \eta_T(v_2, w)^\alpha \in GF(3^{6n})^*$, we can obtain α by solving the DLP over $GF(3^{6n})^*$.

2.2   FFS

There are several variants of FFS. Adleman proposed the first FFS in 1994 [1], and Adleman and Huang later proposed a practical FFS [3]. Joux and Lercier proposed two more practical FFS's; JL02-FFS [20] and JL06-FFS [21]. Hayashi et al. reported that JL06-FFS has an advantage over JL02-FFS in solving a DLP over $GF(3^{6n})$ [18], so we introduce JL06-FFS. From this section, FFS means JL06-FFS.

We begin with an overview of the FFS, and suppose that we try to obtain $\log_g A$ in this section. This consists of four steps: polynomial selection, sieving, linear algebra, and individual logarithm. The parameter $(\kappa, d_H, d_m, B, R, S)$ of FFS is called the elemental parameter of the FFS.

Polynomial Selection: Let κ be the extension degree of the coefficient field of $GF(3^\kappa)[x]$, where $\kappa = 1, 2, 3, 6$. We select a monic irreducible polynomial $f \in GF(3^\kappa)[x]$, a polynomial $m \in GF(3^\kappa)[x]$, and a bivariate polynomial $H(x, y) = x + y^{d_H} \in GF(3^\kappa)[x, y]$ such that

$$H(x, m) \equiv 0 \pmod f, \quad \deg f = 6n/\kappa. \tag{1}$$

Note that, by letting d_m be $\deg m$, the following property holds:

$$d_m \cdot d_H \geq \deg f. \tag{2}$$

Then the finite field $GF(3^{6n})$ is described as $GF(3^\kappa)[x]/(f)$. And $H(x, y)$ satisfies the eight conditions proposed by Adleman [1]. There is a surjective homomorphism

$$\Phi : \begin{cases} GF(3^\kappa)[x, y]/(H) \rightarrow GF(3^{6n}) \cong GF(3^\kappa)[x]/(f) \\ \quad\quad y \quad\quad\quad \mapsto \quad\quad\quad m. \end{cases}$$

Here we select the smoothness bound B and define a rational factor base $\bar{F}(B)$ and an algebraic factor base $\hat{F}(B)$ as follows:

$\bar{F}(B) = \{\mathfrak{p} \in GF(3^\kappa)[x] \mid \deg(\mathfrak{p}) \leq B, \mathfrak{p} \text{ is monic irreducible}\},$
$\hat{F}(B) = \{\langle\mathfrak{p}, y - t\rangle \in \mathrm{Div}(GF(3^\kappa)[x, y]/(H)) \mid \mathfrak{p} \in \bar{F}(B), H(x, t) \equiv 0 \pmod{\mathfrak{p}}\},$

where $\mathrm{Div}(GF(3^\kappa)[x, y]/(H))$ is the divisor group of $GF(3^\kappa)[x, y]/(H)$ and $\langle\mathfrak{p}, y - t\rangle$ is a divisor generated by $\mathfrak{p}$ and $y - t$.

Sieving: For given positive integers R, S, we find pairs $(r, s) \in (GF(3^\kappa)[x])^2$ such that

$$\deg r \leq R, \deg s \leq S, \gcd(r, s) = 1, r \text{ is monic}, \tag{3}$$

$$rm + s = \prod_{\mathfrak{p}_i \in \bar{F}(B)} \mathfrak{p}_i^{a_i} \tag{4}$$

$$\langle ry + s\rangle = \sum_{\langle\mathfrak{p}_j, y - t_j\rangle \in \hat{F}(B)} b_j \langle\mathfrak{p}_j, y - t_j\rangle \tag{5}$$

by a sieving algorithm. The property (5) can be translated into the following equation:

$$(-r)^{d_H} H(x, -s/r) = (-r)^{d_H} x + s^{d_H} = \prod_{\langle\mathfrak{p}_j, y - t_j\rangle \in \hat{F}(B)} \mathfrak{p}_j^{b_j}. \tag{6}$$

Thus, in particular, we collect (r, s) satisfying (3), (4) and (6). And such (r, s) is called a B-smooth pair. Here, we assume $(3^{6n} - 1)/(3^\kappa - 1)$ is coprime to h which is the class number of the quotient field of $GF(3^\kappa)(x)[y]/(H)$. Then, we obtain the following congruent:

$$\sum_{\mathfrak{p}_i \in \bar{F}(B)} a_i \log_g \mathfrak{p}_i \equiv \sum_{\langle \mathfrak{p}_j, y - t_j \rangle \in \hat{F}(B)} b_j \log_g \kappa_j \quad (\mathrm{mod}\ (3^{6n} - 1)/(3^\kappa - 1)), \quad (7)$$

where $\kappa_j = \Phi(\lambda_j)^{1/h}$, $\langle \lambda_j \rangle = h\langle \mathfrak{p}_j, y - t_j \rangle$. The congruent (7) is called a *relation*. Let $\mathcal{R}_{sieve}$ be the number of relations obtained in the sieving step, and then we require the following criteria that

$$\mathcal{R}_{sieve} \geq (\#\bar{F}(B) + \#\hat{F}(B)). \quad (8)$$

Linear Algebra: After generating a linear equation from relations, we translate it into a smaller linear equation by an algorithm such as the filtering. The smaller one is solved via an algorithm such as the Lanczos method [2,25], and then we obtain

$$\log_g \mathfrak{p}_1, ..., \log_g \mathfrak{p}_{\#\bar{F}(B)}, \log_g \kappa_1, ..., \log_g \kappa_{\#\hat{F}(B)}.$$

Individual Logarithm: Using the special-Q descent method [21], we compute integers e_i, f_j such that

$$\log_g A \equiv \sum_{\mathfrak{p}_i \in \bar{F}(B)} e_i \log_g \mathfrak{p}_i + \sum_{\langle \mathfrak{p}_j, y - t_j \rangle \in \hat{F}(B)} f_j \log_g \kappa_j \quad (\mathrm{mod}\ (3^{6n} - 1)/(3^\kappa - 1)).$$

Then we obtain the discrete logarithm $\log_g A$.

3   Known Evaluation Methods

The computational cost of FFS is greatly influenced by the parameter selection of the FFS. For example, if we add only 1 to the value of the parameter R of the FFS given in equation (3), the computational cost of sieving increases 3^κ-fold. Therefore, the value of the parameter of the FFS must be meticulously selected.

The elemental parameter $(\kappa, d_H, d_m, B, R, S)$ of the FFS is given in section 2.2. For a fixed pair (n, κ), there is a well known method for evaluating the value of the parameter, such that the computational cost of solving our DLP by FFS is estimated as approximately minimum. Such parameter values are called "suitable values" in this paper. (Note that it is difficult to identify the most suitable values, namely the value of parameters of FFS for which the cost is truly the minimum.) In general, an approximate suitable value is actually adopted to solve a DLP by FFS. However, we expect there might be more suitable values around the approximate one. For our aim, we introduce a sharp probability evaluation method in section 4.3 by extending Granger's method. Therefore, in this section, we explain how to compute the approximate suitable values, and Granger's method.

Table 2. Approximate suitable values of elemental parameter of FFS

n	97				163				193				239				313				353				509			
κ	1	2	3	6	1	2	3	6	1	2	3	6	1	2	3	6	1	2	3	6	1	2	3	6	1	2	3	6
d_H	6	6	6	6	7	7	7	7	7	7	7	7	8	8	8	8	8	8	8	8	9	9	9	9	10	10	10	10
d_m	97	49	33	17	140	70	47	24	166	83	56	28	180	90	60	30	235	118	79	40	236	118	79	40	306	153	102	51
B	18	9	6	3	23	11	7	4	24	12	8	4	27	13	9	4	30	15	10	5	31	16	10	5	37	18	12	6
R	18	9	6	3	23	11	7	4	24	12	8	4	27	13	9	4	30	15	10	5	31	16	10	5	37	18	12	6
S	18	9	6	3	23	11	7	4	24	12	8	4	27	13	9	4	30	15	10	5	31	16	10	5	37	18	12	6

n: extension degree of the field $GF(3^{6n})$ over its base field $GF(3^6)$
κ: extension degree of the coefficient field of $GF(3^\kappa)[x]$ such that $GF(3^{6n}) \simeq GF(3^\kappa)[x]/(f)$,
    where $f \in GF(3^\kappa)[x]$ is a monic irreducible polynomial of degree $6n/\kappa$.
d_H: degree in y of the bivariate polynomial $H(x,y) = x + y^{d_H} \in GF(3^\kappa)[x,y]$ used for FFS
d_m: degree of the polynomial m in $GF(3^\kappa)[x]$ such that $H(x,m) \equiv 0 \pmod{f}$
B: smoothness bound for FFS
R: maximum degree of polynomial $r \in GF(3^\kappa)[x]$ used in the sieving step of FFS
S: maximum degree of polynomial $s \in GF(3^\kappa)[x]$ used in the sieving step of FFS

3.1 Asymptotic Evaluation Formulas

From asymptotic analysis in [21], when we solve a DLP over a finite field $GF(3^\kappa)[x]/(f)$ for given integers $\kappa, \deg f$ by FFS, the smallest positive integer satisfying (9) is generally selected as the value of B:

$$(B+1)\log 3^\kappa \geq \sqrt{\frac{\deg f}{B}} \log \frac{\deg f}{B}. \tag{9}$$

We then assume that $R = S = B$ and

$$d_H = \left\lceil \sqrt{\deg f / B} \right\rceil. \tag{10}$$

We also calculate the smallest integer d_m satisfying (2) for the given d_H and $\deg f$. We then have Table 2 of approximate suitable values of the elemental parameter of FFS.

3.2 Granger's Evaluation Formula

Granger proposed a sharp evaluation formula in (15) to estimate the running time of FFS. By extending ρ_1 in (15) we obtain our new functions ρ_2 and ρ_3 in section 4.3. Here we briefly explain Granger's method, and more detail is given in [13].

There is a problem about deciding on the smoothness bound B of factor bases $\bar{F}(B)$ and $\hat{F}(B)$. The numbers of factor bases increase exponentially, and take discrete values since B is an integer. To correct this problem, Granger naturally extends B-smooth to (B, β)-smooth with a new parameter $\beta \in (0,1]$. The new parameter β means the ratio of the number of polynomials in $\bar{F}(B)$ of degree B to that of all monic irreducible polynomials in $GF(3^\kappa)[x]$ of degree B.

In fact, factor bases $\bar{F}(B)$ and $\hat{F}(B)$ are extended to $\bar{F}(B,\beta)$ and $\hat{F}(B,\beta)$ such that

$$\bar{F}(B,\beta) = \bar{\Lambda} \sqcup \bar{F}(B-1), \ \hat{F}(B,\beta) = \hat{\Lambda} \sqcup \hat{F}(B-1),$$

where $\bar{A} \subset \bar{F}(B)$, $\hat{A} \subset \hat{F}(B)$ and the degree of an element in $\bar{A}$ or $\hat{A}$ is B. Elements of $\bar{A}$ and $\hat{A}$ are called large primes. We call a monic polynomial g in the rational side (B, β)-smooth if every prime factor of g is in the factor base $\bar{F}(B, \beta)$. In the same manner as the rational side, (B, β)-smooth is also introduced in the algebraic side. Therefore, B-smooth pair in section 2.2 can be naturally extended to (B, β)-smooth pair. In fact, a pair (r, s) is said to be a (B, β)-smooth pair if the (r, s) satisfies (3) and the following properties that

$$rm + s = \prod_{\mathfrak{p}_i \in \bar{F}(B-1)} \mathfrak{p}_i^{a_i} \prod_{\mathfrak{P}_j \in \bar{A}} \mathfrak{B}_j^{a_j}, \tag{11}$$

$$(-r)^{d_H} x + s^{d_H} = \prod_{\langle \mathfrak{p}_i, y-t_i \rangle \in \hat{F}(B-1)} \mathfrak{p}_i^{b_i} \prod_{\langle \mathfrak{P}_j, y-t_j \rangle \in \hat{A}} \mathfrak{B}_j^{b_j}, \tag{12}$$

which correspond to (4) and (6) respectively.

The criteria (8) is described as

$$\mathcal{R}_{sieve} \geq 2\#\bar{F}(B, \beta), \tag{13}$$

since $\bar{F}(B, \beta)$ and $\hat{F}(B, \beta)$ have almost the same cardinality in practice. For checking this criteria, Granger proposed two formulas to compute $\mathcal{R}_{sieve}$ and $\#\bar{F}(B, \beta)$. First, we discuss how to compute $\#\bar{F}(B, \beta)$. Let $I_q(k)$ be the number of monic irreducible polynomials in $GF(q)$ of degree k. $I_q(k)$ is computable by the equation $I_q(k) = \frac{1}{k} \sum_{d \mid k} \mu(d) q^{k/d}$, where μ is the *mobius function*. We then have the following formula:

$$\#\bar{F}(B, \beta) = \sum_{k=1}^{B-1} I_q(k) + \lfloor \beta I_q(B) \rfloor. \tag{14}$$

Next we consider $\mathcal{R}_{sieve}$, namely the number of (B, β)-smooth pairs (r, s) collected in the sieving step. Let $\rho_1(q, B, \beta, k)$ be the probability that a monic polynomial in $GF(q)[x]$ of degree k is (B, β)-smooth. For given non-negative integers i, j, let $\bar{a}_{i,j}$ be the number of pairs (r, s) satisfying (3). We denote $D_{NR}(i,j)$, $D_{NA}(i,j)$ by the degrees of $rm + s$ and $(-r)^{d_H} x + s^{d_H}$ respectively, where $i = \deg r$ and $j = \deg s$. Then $\mathcal{R}_{sieve}$ is described as

$$\sum_{i=0}^{R} \sum_{j=0}^{S} \rho_1(q, B, \beta, D_{NR}(i,j)) \rho_1(q, B, \beta, D_{NA}(i,j)) \bar{a}_{i,j}, \tag{15}$$

and the detail of the function $\bar{a}_{i,j}$ is given in the full version [30] of this paper.

4   New Evaluation Formulas for Efficient Implementation of FFS

To solve the DLP over $GF(3^{6n})$ for $n \geq 97$, we employ several efficient algorithms for implementation of the FFS; the large prime variation [26], the lattice sieve [27], the filtering [10], the Galois action [18], and the free relation [18]. These algorithms are not considered in Granger's method. Especially, for the lattice sieve and the large prime variation, new parameters θ and λ are respectively introduced. We extend Granger's formula for the FFS with those efficient algorithms. (We call this FFS the "improved FFS.") Then the number $\mathcal{R}_{sieve}$ of the relations given by the sieving step of the improved FFS is computable by exchanging ρ_1 in (15) with our new formulas ρ_2 and ρ_3 in section 4.3. As mentioned in section 3.2, we also suppose that $\bar{F}(B, \beta)$ and $\hat{F}(B, \beta)$ have almost the same cardinality in this section.

4.1   Well-Used Efficient Algorithms for FFS

This section provides brief explanations of efficient algorithms.

Large Prime Variation: The large prime variation is employed to reduce the computational cost of a sieving algorithm. To provide a simple explanation, we discuss only in rational side. On the algebraic side, the same discussion can be made.

In fact, we sieve with all factors $\mathfrak{p} \in \bar{F}(B, \beta)$ where $\deg \mathfrak{p} \leq B - 1$ not B; namely, we aim to effectively collect pairs (r, s) such that $rm + s$ is (B, β)-smooth with high probability. For a pair (r, s), $rm + s$ is separated into the two products $\mathcal{P}$ and $\mathcal{Q}$ such that $\mathcal{P} = \prod_{\deg \mathfrak{p}_i \leq B-1} \mathfrak{p}_i^{a_i}$, $\mathcal{Q} = \prod_{\deg \mathfrak{q}_j \geq B} \mathfrak{q}_j^{a_j}$, where $\mathfrak{p}_i$, $\mathfrak{q}_j \in GF(3^\kappa)[x]$ are irreducible. We can compute $\deg \mathcal{Q} = \deg(rm + s) - \deg \mathcal{P}$ effectively since $\deg \mathcal{P}$ is easily computable by sieving. If $\deg \mathcal{Q}$ is small enough, the $rm + s$ is (B, β)-smooth with high probability. Therefore, we prepare a threshold value $\lambda B \in \mathbf{Z}$, and eliminate (r, s) for which $\deg \mathcal{Q}$ is larger than λB. Hence the most suitable value of λ is required.

Lattice Sieve: Sieving in the lattice sieve is performed for only every (r, s) such that $rm + s$ (resp. $\langle ry + s \rangle$) is divisible by a fixed $Q \in \bar{\Lambda}$ (resp. $Q \in \hat{\Lambda}$). Such Q is called *special-Q*. It is usually chosen from $\hat{\Lambda}$ if $D_{NR}(R, S) < D_{NA}(R, S)$, where functions D_{NR} and D_{NA} are defined in section 3.2, and otherwise from $\bar{\Lambda}$. Let $\bar{\Theta}$ (resp. $\hat{\Theta}$) be the set of special-Q's on the rational side (resp. algebraic side). We then have that $\bar{\Theta} \subset \bar{\Lambda}$ and $\hat{\Theta} \subset \hat{\Lambda}$. Therefore, by letting θ be the ratio of the number of special-Q's to $\#(\bar{F}(B)\backslash\bar{F}(B-1))$ (resp. $\#(\hat{F}(B)\backslash\hat{F}(B-1))$), it holds that $0 < \theta \leq \beta \leq 1$. Moreover, the number of special-Q's is $\lfloor \theta I_{3^\kappa}(B) \rfloor$.

When we use the lattice sieve, (r, s) is represented as $c(r_1, s_1) + d(r_2, s_2)$, where $c, d, r_1, s_1, r_2, s_2 \in GF(3^\kappa)[x]$. Sieving is then performed on the c-d plane. The size of the c-d plane is roughly estimated at about $3^{\kappa(R+S+1-B)}$, since the degrees of r_1, s_1, r_2, and s_2 are about $B/2$ in most cases. The time complexity of the lattice sieve depends on the frequency of memory access, and the frequency is proportional to the size of the c-d plane. Therefore, we can assume that the complexity of sieving for one special-Q is almost the same as the size of c-d plane. Sieving is performed on both the rational side and algebraic side, so the complexity C_{sieve} of sieving in the lattice sieve is described as

$$2 \cdot 3^{\kappa(R+S+1-B)} \lfloor \theta I_{3^\kappa}(B) \rfloor. \tag{16}$$

In practice, to collect relations efficiently, sieving is performed with $\mathfrak{p} \in \bar{F}(B)$ and $\mathfrak{p} \in \hat{F}(B)$, not $\bar{F}(B, \beta)$ and $\hat{F}(B, \beta)$. After sieving, $\bar{F}(B)$ and $\hat{F}(B)$ are reduced to $\bar{F}(B, \beta)$ and $\hat{F}(B, \beta)$ via singleton and clique in the filtering described below.

Filtering: In the linear algebra step, the filtering [10] removes inessential variables and equations to solve the linear equation efficiently. It consists of three phases. The singleton phase removes an equation containing a variable whose frequency is one in the linear equation (such an equation is called *singleton.*) The clique phase deletes excess equations to produce more singletons. And the merge phase combines equations to produce singletons. The singleton phase and clique phase need little computation, and the merge phase needs a great deal. In order to produce many singletons in the clique phase, it is better to gather more relations. If we find many singletons, the number of variables in the linear equation can be reduced. Then the linear equation can be solved faster.

    The explanation of the lattice sieve mentions that sieving is performed with $\bar{F}(B)$ and $\hat{F}(B)$. After that, we reduce variables in these factor bases by filtering. In most cases, a reduced variable corresponds to some large prime, so we estimate that the size of the matrix is $2\#\bar{F}(B, \beta)$.

Free Relation: By using the free relation, we can obtain a relation virtually for free, without the sieving. Details of the method are discussed in [18,30], and the advantage is as follows. Let $\mathcal{R}_{free}$ be the number free relations. Then the following property holds:

$$\mathcal{R}_{free} \approx \begin{cases} \#\hat{F}(B)/d_H & \text{if } \gcd(d_H, 3) = 1 \\ \#\hat{F}(B)/2 & \text{if } d_H = 2, 6 \\ \#\hat{F}(B) & \text{if } d_H = 3, 9 \end{cases} \tag{17}$$

where $d_H \leq 10$. It seems that the suitable value of d_H is divisible by 3, so we check both cases where d_H is an approximate value and an integer divisible by 3. We therefore must pay attention to the selection of d_H.

Galois Action: Via the Galois action, we can reduce the size of the matrix from $2\#\bar{F}(B, \beta)$ to $2\#\bar{F}(B, \beta)/\kappa$. Therefore, the computational cost C_{linear} of the linear algebra step is described as

$$C_{linear} = \left(\frac{2\#\bar{F}(B, \beta)}{\kappa} \right)^2. \tag{18}$$

In order to use the Galois action, a primitive polynomial $f \in GF(3^\kappa)[x]$ is selected so that all coefficients of f are in $GF(3)$. Then x is fixed by a function $\phi : x \mapsto x^{3^{6n/\kappa}}$ but $c \in GF(3^\kappa) \setminus GF(3)$ is not. This means that the logarithm of the element of the factor base $\mathfrak{p}$ that has at least one coefficient in $GF(3^\kappa) \setminus GF(3)$ corresponds to the logarithm of the other element of the factor base $\phi(\mathfrak{p})$ as $3^{6n/\kappa} \log_g \mathfrak{p} \equiv \log_g \phi(\mathfrak{p})$. Since the order of ϕ is κ, the number of variables in the linear algebra step can be reduced about $1/\kappa$ times itself.

4.2   Criteria for Sufficient Number of Relations

In the same manner in section 3.2, we change criteria (8). In fact, (13) is changed for FFS with five efficient algorithms in section 4.1. First, since we use the free relation, (13) is translated into $\mathcal{R}_{sieve} + \mathcal{R}_{free} \geq 2\#\bar{F}(B,\beta)$. With consideration for the filtering, it is better to collect more relations[1], so we assume that the constraint property is that $\mathcal{R}_{sieve} + \mathcal{R}_{free} \geq 4\#\bar{F}(B,\beta)$. Finally, applying the Galois action, it is translated into

$$\mathcal{R}_{sieve} + \mathcal{R}_{free} \geq \frac{4\#\bar{F}(B,\beta)}{\kappa}. \tag{19}$$

To solve the DLP in our case, the values of parameters of the improved FFS must satisfy (19).

4.3   New Evaluation Formulas

New evaluation formulas enable us to estimate the complexity of the improved FFS by considering the parameters, κ, d_H, d_m in the polynomial selection step, B, R, S in the sieving step, λ for the large prime variation, θ for the lattice sieve, and β for the filtering. As discussed in section 3.2, Granger gave the evaluation formula ρ_1 to compute the number $\mathcal{R}_{sieve}$ of the relations. On the other hand, with consideration for the large prime variation and the lattice sieve, we introduce new evaluation formulas ρ_2 and ρ_3 for (B,β,λ)-smooth and (B,β,λ,Θ)-smooth, which are variants of (B,β)-smooth, respectively.

Granger considers a case employing the FFS with (B,β)-smooth, so he requires the number of (r,s) satisfying (3), (11), and (12). However, we consider the improved FFS. Therefore, if $D_{NR}(R,S) < D_{NA}(R,S)$, we require the number of (r,s) satisfying (3) and the following properties

$$rm + s = (\prod_{\mathfrak{p}_i \in \bar{F}(B-1)} \mathfrak{p}_i^{e_i})(\prod_{\mathfrak{P}_j \in \bar{A}} \mathfrak{P}_j^{e_j}), \text{ (where } e_i, e_j \geq 0, \sum e_j \leq \lambda) \tag{20}$$

and

$$(-r)^{d_H} x + (-s)^{d_H}$$
$$= (\prod_{\langle \mathfrak{p}_i, y-t_i \rangle \in \hat{F}(B-1)} \mathfrak{p}_i^{e_i})(\prod_{\langle \mathfrak{P}_j, y-t_j \rangle \in \hat{A} \backslash \hat{\Theta}} \mathfrak{P}_j^{e_j})(\prod_{\langle \mathfrak{P}_\ell, y-t_\ell \rangle \in \hat{\Theta}} \mathfrak{P}_\ell^{e_\ell}) \tag{21}$$

where at least one e_ℓ is larger than 0 and $e_i, e_j \geq 0, \sum e_j + \sum e_\ell \leq \lambda$. Such $rm + s$ and $(-r)^{d_H} x + (-s)^{d_H}$ are called (B,β,λ)-smooth and $(B,\beta,\lambda,\hat{\Theta})$-smooth respectively. Conversely, if $D_{NR}(R,S) \geq D_{NA}(R,S)$, we search (r,s) such that $rm + s$ and are $(B,\beta,\lambda,\bar{\Theta})$-smooth and (B,β,λ)-smooth. In this paper, (B,β,λ,Θ)-smooth means $(B,\beta,\lambda,\hat{\Theta})$-smooth if $D_{NR}(R,S) < D_{NA}(R,S)$, otherwise $(B,\beta,\lambda,\bar{\Theta})$-smooth.

---

[1] In [23] for the factorization of RSA768, the authors collected about two time more relations than the number of factor base.

In the same manner as Granger's method, we introduce two new formulas ρ_2 and ρ_3 of the probabilities for (B, β, λ)-smooth and $(B, \beta, \lambda, \Theta)$-smooth. The details are given in the full version [30] of this paper. Let $\rho_2(q, B, \beta, \lambda, k)$ be the probability that a monic polynomial in $GF(q)[x]$ of degree k is (B, β, λ)-smooth. Then ρ_2 is described as follows:

$$\rho_2(q, B, \beta, \lambda, k) =$$

$$\frac{1}{q^k} \left\{ N_q(k, B-1) + \sum_{\ell \geq 1}^{\lfloor k/B \rfloor} N_q(k - \ell B, B-1) \left\{ \sum_{i=1}^{\min\{\ell, \lambda\}} \binom{\lfloor \beta I_q(B) \rfloor}{i} \binom{\ell - 1}{\ell - i} \right\} \right\}.$$

Let $\rho_3(q, B, \beta, \Theta, \lambda, k)$ be the probability that a monic polynomial $g \in GF(q)[x]$ of degree k is $(B, \beta, \Theta, \lambda)$-smooth. Then ρ_3 is described as follows:

$$\rho_3(q, B, \beta, \lambda, \Theta, k) =$$

$$\frac{1}{q^k} \sum_{\ell=1}^{\lfloor k/B \rfloor} N_q(k - \ell B, B-1) \left\{ \sum_{\ell_Q=1}^{\ell} \sum_{\lambda_Q=1}^{Min_1} \binom{\#\Theta}{\lambda_Q} \binom{\ell_Q - 1}{\ell_Q - \lambda_Q} \tau_{B,\beta,\lambda,\Theta}(\ell, \ell_Q, \lambda_Q) \right\}$$

where

$$Min_1 = \min\{\ell_Q, \lambda, \#\Theta\},$$

$$\tau_{B,\beta,\lambda,\Theta}(\ell, \ell_Q, \lambda_Q) = \begin{cases} \sum_{\lambda_t=1}^{Min_2} \binom{\lfloor \beta I_q(B) \rfloor - \#\Theta}{\lambda_t} \binom{\ell - \ell_Q - 1}{\ell - \ell_Q - \lambda_t} & (Min_2 \geq 1), \\ 1 & (\ell = \ell_Q), \\ 0 & (\text{others}), \end{cases}$$

$$Min_2 = \min\{\ell - \ell_Q, \lambda - \lambda_Q, \lfloor \beta I_q(B) \rfloor - \#\Theta\}.$$

Consequently, we obtain the following theorem:

Theorem 1. *By replacing ρ_1 in the formula (15) with ρ_2, ρ_3, we have that*

$$\mathcal{R}_{sieve} = \sum_{i=0}^{R} \sum_{j=0}^{S} \rho_v(q, B, \beta, D_{NR}(i,j)) \rho_w(q, B, \beta, D_{NA}(i,j)) \bar{a}_{i,j}. \quad (22)$$

where (ρ_v, ρ_w) is (ρ_2, ρ_3) if $D_{AR}(R, S) > D_{NR}(R, S)$, and (ρ_3, ρ_2) otherwise.

To find suitable values of parameters of the improved FFS, we check the criteria (19) for a given value of the parameter $(\kappa, d_H, d_m, B, R, S, \lambda, \theta, \beta)$. Namely, with changing the value of the parameter, we compute $\mathcal{R}_{sieve}$, $\mathcal{R}_{free}$ and $\#\bar{F}(B, \beta)$ many times, by using (22), (17), and (14). (Note that, since we supposed that $\#\bar{F}(B, \beta) = \#\hat{F}(B, \beta)$, the value of (17) is given by (14).) When κ is small and n is large, it takes a long time to compute (22). However, if $\kappa \neq 1$ and $n \leq 509$, we can actually compute it. For example, in our experiments, it takes roughly about 57 hours to make Table 3, using a PC with an Intel Quad-Core (2.8 GHz) $\times$ 1 CPU and 8 GB RAM.

5   Estimation of Key Length

In order to estimate the key length of pairing-based cryptosystems for the fixed extension degrees $n = 97, 163, 193, 239, 313, 353, 509$, we estimate the time complexity of solving the DLP over $GF(3^{6n})$ by the FFS (introduced in section 2.2) with the five efficient algorithms in section 4.1. (This FFS with efficient algorithms is called the "improved FFS" in this paper.) The improved FFS has two kinds of parameters: the elemental parameter $(\kappa, d_H, d_m, B, R, S)$ commonly utilized in the FFS without efficient algorithms, and the advanced parameter (λ, θ, β) for the efficient algorithms, where λ, θ, and β are used for the large prime variation, the lattice sieve, and, the filtering, respectively. For our estimation of the time complexity, we search the values of parameter $(\kappa, d_H, d_m, B, R, S, \lambda, \theta, \beta)$, such that the computational cost C_{sieve} of solving the DLP by the improved FFS is almost minimum. Such parameter values are called "suitable values" in this paper. (Note that it is not realistic to identify the most suitable value of the parameter for fixed extension degrees n, since there are infinitely many values of $(\kappa, d_H, d_m, B, R, S, \lambda, \theta, \beta)$.) To find suitable values of $(\kappa, d_H, d_m, B, R, S, \lambda, \theta, \beta)$ for the fixed extension degrees n, we performed an experiment to check the criteria (19) to solve the DLP, for many values of $(\kappa, d_H, d_m, B, R, S, \lambda, \theta, \beta)$. Criteria (19) is computable by using our new estimation formula (22) corresponding to the explicit number of the relations (defined in section 4.3), and so on. In this section, for the fixed extension degrees n, we present Table 5 of the suitable values of $(\kappa, d_H, d_m, B, R, S, \lambda, \theta, \beta)$ and the computational costs C_{sieve} when those suitable values are given. From Table 5, we obtain Table 1 meaning our estimation of the time complexity of solving the DLP over $GF(3^{6n})$, in section 1.

We performed an experiment to develop Table 5, using a PC with an Intel Quad-Core (2.8 GHz) $\times$ 1 CPU and 8 GB RAM. As mentioned in section 1, for fixed extension degrees n, we suppose that if there are more suitable values than the approximate ones in Table 2, they are close to those in Table 2. Therefore, we select several values of (d_H, d_m, B, R, S) around each value in Table 2. For example, if $(n, \kappa) = (193, 6)$, then the approximate suitable value of (d_H, d_m, B, R, S) is $(7, 28, 4, 4, 4)$. We select values of (d_H, d_m, B, R, S) such as $(7, 28, 4, 4, 4)$, $(7, 28, 4, 3, 4)$, $(7, 28, 4, 4, 5)$ and so on. For such a single value, we change the values of λ, β, θ many times in that order. (We have empirically confirmed that this order has no impact on the estimation of suitable values.) Then, to check the property (19) we compute (22), (17), and (14) for given values of $(d_H, d_m, B, R, S, \lambda, \theta, \beta)$.

From now, the value of $(n, \kappa, d_H, d_m, B, R, S)$ is fixed. Through experiments, we obtain the fact that the cost C_{sieve} of sieving decreases if λ increases, and there exists an integer λ_0 such that C_{sieve} does not decrease for any $\lambda \geq \lambda_0$. Therefore, λ_0 is the most suitable value of λ. To find the integer λ_0, the value of λ is started from 1 and in steps of 1 in our computation.

For a fixed λ, we move β in $[0, 1]$, and next θ is also moved in $[0, \beta]$ for the given β, by binary search, since $0 < \theta \leq \beta \leq 1$. As mentioned in section 4.1, our sieving is performed with $\beta = 1$, so the cost C_{sieve} of sieving is given by the

Table 3. Suitable values of parameter of improved FFS to solve DLP over $GF(3^{6n})$

n	κ	d_H	d_m	B	R	S	λ	θ_{min}	β_{min}	$\log_2 C_{linear}$	$\log_2 C_{sieve}$
97	2	6	49	9	9	9	6	0.08436	0.420	49.06	54.49
	3	6	33	6	6	6	6	0.01292	0.280	47.49	53.95
	6	6	17	3	3	3	6	0.00010	0.225	46.44	52.79
163	2	7	70	11	12	12	7	0.03786	0.297	60.42	72.06
	3	7	47	7	8	8	8	0.01358	0.424	57.60	72.82
	6	6	28	4	4	4	6	0.00001	0.002	53.49	68.17
193	2	7	83	12	12	12	7	0.26513	0.727	68.49	74.74
	3	7	56	8	8	8	7	0.03672	0.471	67.00	74.06
	6	7	28	4	4	4	7	0.00015	0.230	64.69	71.90
239	2	8	90	13	14	14	7	0.06879	0.421	73.33	85.36
	3	8	60	9	9	9	7	0.01221	0.227	74.31	81.81
	6	8	30	4	4	4	8	0.01105	0.668	67.75	78.08
313	2	8	118	15	15	15	7	0.21124	0.653	86.59	93.11
	3	8	79	10	10	10	8	0.02540	0.373	84.75	92.23
	6	9	35	5	5	5	7	0.00010	0.173	82.25	90.04
353	2	9	118	16	16	16	7	0.09357	0.414	91.70	98.18
	3	9	79	10	11	11	8	0.01749	0.416	85.03	101.20
	6	9	40	5	5	5	8	0.00214	0.484	85.20	94.42
509	2	9	170	18	19	19	8	0.12474	0.547	104.67	117.45
	3	9	114	12	12	12	9	0.25254	0.847	105.43	114.30
	6	9	57	6	6	6	8	0.00060	0.342	102.69	111.35

n: extension degree of the field $GF(3^{6n})$ over its base field $GF(3^6)$
κ: extension degree of the coefficient field of $GF(3^\kappa)[x]$ such that $GF(3^{6n}) \simeq GF(3^\kappa)[x]/(f)$,
    where $f \in GF(3^\kappa)[x]$ is a monic irreducible polynomial of degree $6n/\kappa$
d_H: degree in y of the bivariate polynomial $H(x,y) = x + y^{d_H} \in GF(3^\kappa)[x,y]$ used for FFS
d_m: degree of the polynomial m in $GF(3^\kappa)[x]$ such that $H(x,m) \equiv 0 \pmod{f}$
B: smoothness bound for FFS
R: maximum degree of polynomial $r \in GF(3^\kappa)[x]$ used in the sieving step of FFS
S: maximum degree of polynomial $s \in GF(3^\kappa)[x]$ used in the sieving step of FFS
λ: threshold value for the large prime variation θ_{min}:] minimal ratio of the required special-Q's to
    all monic irreducible polynomials in $GF(3^\kappa)[x]$ of degree B
β_{min}: minimal ratio of the required large primes to all monic irreducible polynomials in $GF(3^\kappa)[x]$
    of degree B
C_{linear}: computational cost of the linear algebra step of FFS
C_{sieve}: computational cost of the sieving step of FFS

formula (16), where θ is minimum number such that (19) holds for $\theta \leq \beta = 1$.
Such θ is described as θ_{min} in Table 5.

Next, we consider the cost C_{linear} of the linear algebra step. This is evaluated
by the formula (18), and $2\#\bar{F}(B,\beta)/\kappa$ means the size of the matrix appearing
in the linear algebra step. As mentioned in section 4.1, by the filtering, the size
is reduced from $2\#\bar{F}(B)$ to $2\#\bar{F}(B,\beta)$. Therefore, we compute C_{linear} given
by (18) for β_{min}, where β_{min} is explained as follows. For the explanation of
β_{min}, we consider the case in which filtering is not employed. In other words,

in the sieving step, we set β as small as possible under the condition that (19) holds. If we reduce the β, then the relations given by sieving decrease since the numbers of the factor bases decrease. We therefore must collect more relations by performing the lattice sieve more times. This implies that larger θ is required, so there exists the minimum β satisfying (19) since $0 < \theta \leq \beta \leq 1$. The β_{min} is denoted by the minimum β. If we set β smaller than β_{min}, then (19) does not hold, and so we suppose that the filtering reduces the size of the matrix from $2\#\bar{F}(B)$ to $2\#\bar{F}(B, \beta_{min})$.

In Table 5, we omit the case of $\kappa = 1$ for the following reason. For each pair (n, κ) where $n = 71, 79, 89, 97$ and $\kappa = 1, 2, 3, 6$, we check (19) for many values of parameter $(d_H, d_m, B, R, S, \theta, \lambda, \beta)$. Then, for every fixed n, there are no suitable values when $\kappa = 1$. In other words, for each candidate of the suitable values when $\kappa = 1$, there exist more suitable values when $\kappa = 2, 3$, or 6. Therefore, we suppose that the same property holds for $n > 97$. Since the computational costs of (22) are very heavy when $\kappa = 1$ and $n \geq 163$, we omit the test for the condition.

Finally, for each fixed value of $(n, \kappa, d_H, d_m, B, R, S, \lambda)$ mentioned above, we have computed $\beta_{min}, \theta_{min}$, and obtained the costs C_{sieve}, C_{linear}. Comparing these costs where (n, κ) is fixed and $(d_H, d_m, B, R, S, \lambda)$ is changed, we obtain Table 5 of suitable values of $(d_H, d_m, B, R, S, \lambda, \theta, \beta)$ for each fixed (n, κ).

Notice that in Table 5, C_{sieve} for a fixed (n, κ) is larger than C_{linear} for the same (n, κ). Moreover, for each n, the C_{sieve} with $\kappa = 6$ is less than the C_{sieve} with $\kappa = 2, 3$. Therefore, we estimate that the time complexity of solving our

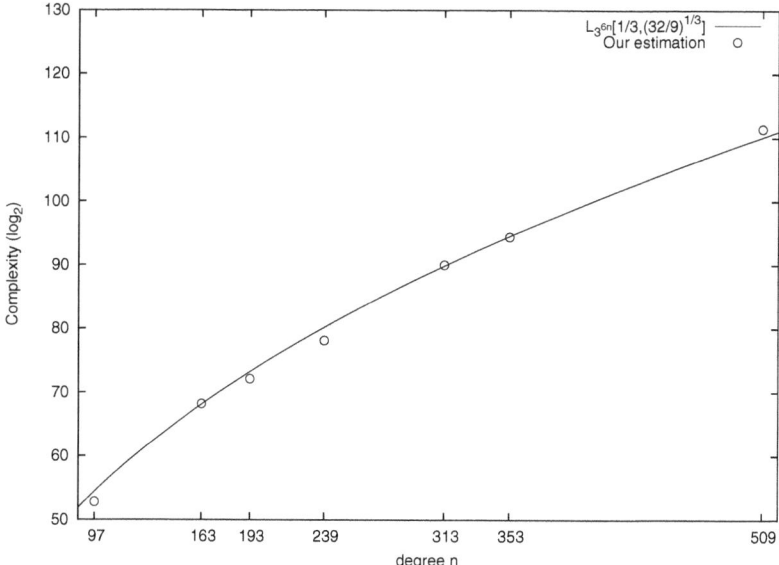

Fig. 1. Time complexity estimation of solving DLP over $GF(3^{6n})$ and $L_{3^{6n}}[1/3, (32/9)^{1/3}]$ with $o(1) = -0.18$

DLP by the improved FFS is C_{sieve} with $\kappa = 6$, so we obtain Table 1 and Figure 1. For each pair (n, κ, d_H, d_m) in Table 5, we have confirmed the existence of polynomials f, m, H satisfying (1), and these are given in the full version [30] of this paper.

6   Conclusions

In this paper, we evaluated the security of pairing-based cryptosystems using the η_T pairing defined over finite fields whose characteristic is 3. For the evaluation, we consider the time complexity of solving the discrete logarithm problem (DLP) over the extension field $GF(3^{6n})$ of the embedding degree 6 by the asymptotically fastest function field sieve (FFS). The extension degree 6 allows us to improve the speed of FFS by efficient algorithms such as the large prime variation, the lattice sieve, the filtering, the Galois action, and the free relation. We therefore estimated the precise time complexity of solving our DLP by FFS with the efficient algorithms, called the "improved FFS" in this paper. By using our new formulas to count the explicit number of smooth polynomials used in the improved FFS, our experiment obtain the precise time complexity. Finally, we adapted the formulas to the degree n appeared in several studies in the literature, and then estimated that the time complexity of solving the DLP over $GF(3^{6n})$ for $n = 193, 239, 509$ is $2^{72}, 2^{78}, 2^{111}$, respectively. Therefore, n must be larger than 239 to keep 80 bit security.

Many high-speed implementations of the η_T pairing have been reported, which have attracted us to achieve practical use of the η_T pairing. Our estimation in this paper contributes to evaluating the key length of the pairing-based cryptosystems using the η_T pairing.

References

1. Adleman, L.M.: The Function Field Sieve. In: Huang, M.-D.A., Adleman, L.M. (eds.) ANTS 1994. LNCS, vol. 877, pp. 108–121. Springer, Heidelberg (1994)
2. Aoki, K., Shimoyama, T., Ueda, H.: Experiments on the Linear Algebra Step in the Number Field Sieve. In: Miyaji, A., Kikuchi, H., Rannenberg, K. (eds.) IWSEC 2007. LNCS, vol. 4752, pp. 58–73. Springer, Heidelberg (2007)
3. Adleman, L.M., Huang, M.-D.A.: Function field sieve method for discrete logarithms over finite fields. Inform. and Comput. 151, 5–16 (1999)
4. Ahmadi, O., Hankerson, D., Menezes, A.: Software Implementation of Arithmetic in F_{3^m}. In: Carlet, C., Sunar, B. (eds.) WAIFI 2007. LNCS, vol. 4547, pp. 85–102. Springer, Heidelberg (2007)
5. Barker, E., Barker, W., Burr, W., Polk, W., Smid, M.: Recommendation for key management - Part 1: General (Revised). NIST Special Publication 800-57 (2007)
6. Barreto, P.S.L.M., Kim, H.Y., Lynn, B., Scott, M.: Efficient Algorithms for Pairing-Based Cryptosystems. In: Yung, M. (ed.) CRYPTO 2002. LNCS, vol. 2442, pp. 354–368. Springer, Heidelberg (2002)
7. Barreto, P.S.L.M., Galbraith, S., ÓhÉigeartaigh, C., Scott, M.: Efficient pairing computation on supersingular abelian varieties. Des., Codes Cryptogr. 42(3), 239–271 (2007)

8. Beuchat, J.-L., Brisebarre, N., Detrey, J., Okamoto, E., Shirase, M., Takagi, T.: Algorithms and arithmetic operators for computing the η_T pairing in characteristic three. IEEE Trans. Comput. 57(11), 1454–1468 (2008)

9. Boneh, D., Franklin, M.: Identity based encryption from the Weil pairing. SIAM J. Comput. 32(3), 586–615 (2003)

10. Cavallar, S.: Strategies in Filtering in the Number Field Sieve. In: Bosma, W. (ed.) ANTS 2000. LNCS, vol. 1838, pp. 209–231. Springer, Heidelberg (2000)

11. Galbraith, S., Harrison, K., Soldera, D.: Implementing the Tate Pairing. In: Fieker, C., Kohel, D.R. (eds.) ANTS 2002. LNCS, vol. 2369, pp. 324–337. Springer, Heidelberg (2002)

12. Gorla, E., Puttmann, C., Shokrollahi, J.: Explicit Formulas for Efficient Multiplication in $F_{3^{6m}}$. In: Adams, C., Miri, A., Wiener, M. (eds.) SAC 2007. LNCS, vol. 4876, pp. 173–183. Springer, Heidelberg (2007)

13. Granger, R.: Estimates for Discrete Logarithm Computations in Finite Fields of Small Characteristic. In: Paterson, K.G. (ed.) Cryptography and Coding 2003. LNCS, vol. 2898, pp. 190–206. Springer, Heidelberg (2003)

14. Granger, R., Holt, A.J., Page, D., Smart, N.P., Vercauteren, F.: Function Field Sieve in Characteristic Three. In: Buell, D.A. (ed.) ANTS 2004. LNCS, vol. 3076, pp. 223–234. Springer, Heidelberg (2004)

15. Granger, R., Page, D., Stam, M.: Hardware and software normal basis arithmetic for pairing-based cryptography in characteristic three. IEEE Trans. Comput. 54(7), 852–860 (2005)

16. Hankerson, D., Menezes, A., Scott, M.: Software implementation of pairings. In: Identity-Based Cryptography, pp. 188–206 (2009)

17. Harrison, K., Page, D., Smart, N.P.: Software implementation of finite fields of characteristic three, for use in pairing-based cryptosystems. LMS Journal of Computation and Mathematics 5, 181–193 (2002)

18. Hayashi, T., Shinohara, N., Wang, L., Matsuo, S., Shirase, M., Takagi, T.: Solving a 676-Bit Discrete Logarithm Problem in GF(3^{6n}). In: Nguyen, P.Q., Pointcheval, D. (eds.) PKC 2010. LNCS, vol. 6056, pp. 351–367. Springer, Heidelberg (2010)

19. Joux, A., et al.: Discrete logarithms in GF(2^{607}) and GF(2^{613}). Posting to the Number Theory List (2005), http://listserv.nodak.edu/cgi-bin/wa.exe?A2=ind0509&L=nmbrthry&T=0&P=3690

20. Joux, A., Lercier, R.: The Function Field Sieve Is Quite Special. In: Fieker, C., Kohel, D.R. (eds.) ANTS 2002. LNCS, vol. 2369, pp. 431–445. Springer, Heidelberg (2002)

21. Joux, A., Lercier, R.: The Function Field Sieve in the Medium Prime Case. In: Vaudenay, S. (ed.) EUROCRYPT 2006. LNCS, vol. 4004, pp. 254–270. Springer, Heidelberg (2006)

22. Kawahara, Y., Aoki, K., Takagi, T.: Faster Implementation of η_T Pairing Over $GF(3^m)$ Using Minimum Number of Logical Instructions for $GF(3)$-Addition. In: Galbraith, S.D., Paterson, K.G. (eds.) Pairing 2008. LNCS, vol. 5209, pp. 282–296. Springer, Heidelberg (2008)

23. Kleinjung, T., Aoki, K., Franke, J., Lenstra, A.K., Thomé, E., Bos, J.W., Gaudry, P., Kruppa, A., Montgomery, P.L., Osvik, D.A., te Riele, H., Timofeev, A., Zimmermann, P.: Factorization of a 768-Bit RSA Modulus. In: Rabin, T. (ed.) CRYPTO 2010. LNCS, vol. 6223, pp. 333–350. Springer, Heidelberg (2010)

24. Kerins, T., Marnane, W., Popovici, E., Barreto, P.S.L.M.: Efficient Hardware for the Tate Pairing Calculation in Characteristic Three. In: Rao, J.R., Sunar, B. (eds.) CHES 2005. LNCS, vol. 3659, pp. 412–426. Springer, Heidelberg (2005)

25. Lanczos, C.: Solution of systems of linear equations by minimized iterations. J. Res. Nat. Bureau of Standards 49(1), 33–53 (1952)
26. Lenstra, A.K., Lenstra Jr., H.W., Manasse, M.S., Pollard, J.M.: The number field sieve. LNIM, vol. 1554, pp. 43–49 (1993)
27. Pollard, J.M.: The lattice sieve. LNIM, vol. 1554, pp. 43–49 (1993)
28. Page, D., Smart, N.P.: Hardware Implementation of Finite Fields of Characteristic Three. In: Kaliski Jr., B.S., Koç, Ç.K., Paar, C. (eds.) CHES 2002. LNCS, vol. 2523, pp. 529–539. Springer, Heidelberg (2003)
29. Pomerance, C., Wagstaff Jr., S.S.: Implementation of the continued fraction integer factoring algorithm. Congress Numer. 37, 99–118 (1983)
30. Shinohara, N., Shimoyama, T., Hayashi, T., Takagi, T.: Key Length Estimation of Pairing-based Cryptosystems using η_T Pairing, Cryptology ePrint Archive: Report 2012/042 (2012), http://eprint.iacr.org/2012/042
31. Smart, N., Page, D., Vercauteren, F.: A comparison of MNT curves and supersingular curves. Applicable Algebra in Engineering, Communication and Computing 17, 379–392 (2006)

Lightweight Integrity for XOR Network Coding in Wireless Sensor Networks

Kazuya Izawa, Atsuko Miyaji, and Kazumasa Omote

Japan Advanced Institute of Science and Technology (JAIST)
{s0910201,miyaji,omote}@jaist.ac.jp

Abstract. In INFOCOM 2009, Yu, Wei, Ramkumar and Guan have proposed the novel mechanism (called Yu's scheme), in which a forwarder can filter polluted messages before spreading the pollution in the XOR network coding systems. In order to perform such filtering, two or more message authentication codes (MACs) are used for this scheme. However, Yu's scheme has a problem that the number of MACs increases at every coding point, since it cannot operate MACs with the XOR network coding. This means that the MAC of Yu's scheme does not have homomorphic property.

In this paper, we propose the first symmetric-key-based scheme not only to filter polluted messages but also to operate MACs with the XOR network coding on a forwarder. The XOR network coding of MACs produces improvement which does not increase the number of MACs at a coding point. Our scheme uses the UHFs-based MAC with a homomorphic property to hold homomorphic MAC, and hence it can aggregate MACs in our XOR network coding systems. We emphasize that a forwarder cannot straightforward filter polluted messages even if our scheme uses the UHFs-based MACs.

1 Introduction

Wireless Sensor Networks (WSNs) consist of small, battery-operated, limited memory and limited computational power sensor nodes. Most of existing secure schemes in WSNs are not based on public key cryptography. More importantly, reducing communication traffic is desirable to save the energy of the relay nodes (forwarders). It is especially necessary to reduce the amount of useless communication. For instance, it is important to remove polluted messages quickly or to conduct data aggregation.

Unlike the traditional message forwarding approaches, network coding [1] allows forwarders to combine multiple input messages into one or more encoded ones. This technique has novel advantages to maximize network throughput and to reduce the number of retransmissions. While a network coding is normally operated over large finite fields (called normal network coding), we focus on a special network coding based only on XOR operations, named *XOR network coding* [3,6,10,11,13,16,17,18]. It is easy to apply XOR network coding to wireless networks such as WSNs, owing to its simplicity.

M.D. Ryan, B. Smyth, and G. Wang (Eds.): ISPEC 2012, LNCS 7232, pp. 245–258, 2012.

Network coding systems are vulnerable to *pollution attacks*, in which adversaries inject polluted messages into the systems on the compromised forwarders. In a worst case scenario, a single corrupted message can end up corrupting all the information reaching a destination. These attacks not only prevent the sinks from recovering the source messages but also drain out the energy of the forwarders. Hence, it is crucial to filter polluted messages in network coding systems as early as possible. In order to achieve such filtering in the XOR network coding systems, Yu, Wei, Ramkumar and Guan [16] have proposed the novel mechanism (called Yu's scheme), in which a forwarder can filter polluted messages before spreading the pollution. In this scheme, two or more message authentication codes (MACs) are used to filter polluted messages.

However, Yu's scheme has a problem that the number of MACs increases at every coding point, since it cannot operate MACs with the XOR network coding. This means that the MAC of Yu's scheme does not have homomorphic property. If two or more MACs are operated with XOR network coding, their MACs are aggregated (encoded) to one MAC. Otherwise, as Yu's scheme, their MACs are just forwarded to downstream nodes without XOR network coding. It is meaningless that in spite of coding a message, their MACs is not aggregated (encoded). On the other hand, Apavatjrut et al. [3] have simply applied the homomorphic MAC based on universal hash functions (UHFs) to the XOR network coding systems, in which two or more MACs are operated with XOR network coding. However, a forwarder cannot filter polluted messages in this scheme. More particularly, a forwarder cannot verify the MACs for filtering since the UHFs-based MAC has one-time pad. Only a sink can verify the encoded (aggregated) MACs since it knows all the seeds which generate one-time pad.

In this paper, we propose the first symmetric-key-based scheme not only to filter polluted messages but also to operate MACs with the XOR network coding on a forwarder. The XOR network coding of MACs produces improvement which does not increase the number of MACs at a coding point. Our scheme uses the UHFs-based MAC with a homomorphic property to hold homomorphic MAC, and hence it can aggregate MACs in our XOR network coding systems. As a result, it can reduce the amount of extra space associated with communication complexity for integrity protection. We emphasize that a forwarder cannot straightforward filter polluted messages even if our scheme uses the UHFs-based MAC. Our scheme improves how to generate a pseudo-random function (PRF) in the UHFs-base MAC so that a forwarder can filter polluted messages.

2   Related Work

Working on network coding started with the pioneering paper by Ahlswede et al. [1], which established the value of coding in the routers and provided theoretical bounds on the capacity of such networks. Network coding systems can be divided into two classes of normal and XOR network coding [16]. There are several lightweight authentication schemes for both of network coding, based on symmetric-key-cryptography such as message authentication codes (MACs).

For a lightweight authentication scheme in a normal network coding against pollution attacks, the homomorphic MAC [2] and RIPPLE [12] have been proposed so far. Agrawal and Boneh [2] design a homomorphic MAC which allows checking the integrity of normal network encoded data. It converts a homomorphic MAC into a broadcast homomorphic MAC, in which a forwarder can verify the integrity of MACs. Li et al. [12] have proposed a symmetric-key-based scheme for network coding authentication (named RIPPLE). Despite using symmetric-key-based homomorphic MAC algorithms, RIPPLE achieves asymmetry by delayed disclosure of the MAC keys, inspired by TESLA [14]. While these schemes focus on normal network coding systems, the following two recent schemes [16,3] focus on a lightweight authentication in a XOR network coding against pollution attacks, which is more suitable for WSNs.

Yu's scheme [16] exploits probabilistic key pre-distribution and MACs. In this scheme, the source node generates multiple MACs for each message using its secret keys, where each MAC can authenticate only a part of the message and the parts authenticated by different MACs are overlapped. Every encoded message is attached with the MACs of the source messages. Therefore, multiple downstream forwarders can collaboratively verify different parts of the encoded message using the MACs and their own shared keys. However, Yu's scheme has a problem that the number of MACs increases at every coding point, since it cannot operate MACs with the XOR network coding. The details of Yu's scheme will be described in Section 4.

Apavatjrut et al. [3] have naively applied the homomorphic MAC based on UHFs to the XOR network coding systems. Such a XOR homomorphic MAC is given by $MAC_k(M) = h_k(M) \oplus r$, where h_k is a homomorphic UHF with the secret key k, M is a message, and r is one-time pad. However, a forwarder cannot filter the polluted messages in this scheme. We explain this reason as follows. We assume that a forwarder F_3 is connected with two upstream nodes F_1 and F_2, for example. Let M_1 and M_2 denote the source messages of s_1 and s_2, respectively. F_3 receives M_1, M_2, $MAC_k(M_1) = h_k(M_1) \oplus r_1$ and $MAC_k(M_2) = h_k(M_2) \oplus r_2$ from F_1 and F_2. Then, F_3 can compute the encoded message $M_1 \oplus M_2$ and its MAC ($MAC_k(M_1 \oplus M_2) = h_k(M_1 \oplus M_2) \oplus (r_1 \oplus r_2)$). However, F_3 cannot compute $r_1 \oplus r_2$, since $r_1 \oplus r_2$ is random number generated by s_1 and s_2. Therefore, in this scheme, a forwarder cannot filter the polluted messages because it cannot verify the MACs.

3   Preliminaries

3.1   Requirements

The following requirements need to be considered when designing a lightweight integrity of XOR network coding systems in WSNs.

Early Filtering of Polluted Messages. Network coding systems (including XOR and normal network coding) suffer from pollution propagation, i.e., a small number of polluted messages can quickly propagate in the systems and infect a large proportion messages. When a forwarder receives a polluted message, all of its encoded messages will be polluted. Then, these polluted messages are further used by downstream forwarders for encoding, thus, more messages will be polluted. It is therefore necessary to filter polluted messages as early as possible.

Encoding of MACs. The MAC is computed from the source message. The forwarder, who is not directly connected with source nodes, cannot obtain the source message but can obtain only the encoded messages. So, it is necessary for a forwarder to verify the MAC of encoded messages in order to filter the polluted messages. Hence, the encoding of MACs is essential for a forwarder to check the integrity of encoded messages. This MAC encoding also has an advantage of traffic reduction.

Restricted Resources. It is required that the WSNs consist of small, battery-operated devices with limited memory and limited computational power. XOR network coding and the symmetric-key-based MAC are more suitable for such resource-constrained WSNs.

3.2 Notation

We explain the following common notations in the paper:

Symbol	Explanation
n	the number of source messages transmitted $(n \geq 2)$
m	the number of codewords of each message
$M_i, m_{i,j}$	i-th source message and its j-th codeword; $M_i = (m_{i,1} \cdots m_{i,m})$
t	the number of random keys each node has
u	the number of codeword hashed in each MAC
q	security parameter (e.g., $q = 128$)
$\mathcal{K}_{\mathsf{UHF}}, \mathcal{K}'_{\mathsf{PRF}}$	global key pools for UHF and PRF
$k_{s,i}, k'_{s,i}$	i-th (q-bit) keys of the source node; $k_{s,i} \in \mathcal{K}_{\mathsf{UHF}}, k'_{s,i} \in \mathcal{K}_{\mathsf{PRF}}$
sid	the session ID $(sid \in \{0,1\}^q)$
mid	the set of message indeces
h_k	universal hash function using key k: $\{0,1\}^* \mapsto \{0,1\}^q$
$f_{k'}$	pseudo-random function family indexed by the key k': $\{0,1\}^* \mapsto \{0,1\}^q$
g	pseudo-random permutation function: $[1,m] \to [1,m]$
H	Non-cryptographic hash function: $\{0,1\}^q \to [1,m]$

3.3 System and Network Assumptions

We consider a general multicast network in which there are one source node, multiple sinks (receivers) and a number of forwarders. The source node sends n messages $M_1, \ldots, M_n$ in every unit of time, that is, session (the source can actually generate messages continuously). A forwarder can use XOR network coding technique to generate and forward the encoded messages.

In XOR network coding for n source messages $M_1, \ldots, M_n$, an encoded message can be represented as $E = \alpha_1 M_1 \oplus \cdots \oplus \alpha_n M_n$, where $\alpha_i \in \{0, 1\}$ for $i = 1, \ldots, n$. The bit string $(\alpha_1 \cdots \alpha_n)$ is called the encoding vector of E. Of course, M_i can be the encoded message. We adopt the model used in [8] and divide each message into m codewords of the same length. Our scheme partitions codewords only for constructing MACs.

We also assume that all of the nodes have been assigned some random secret keys using the probabilistic key pre-distribution schemes such as [7]. In particular, we assume that each node picks a fixed number of keys randomly from a large global key pool. By carefully controlling the key pool size and the number of keys that each node picks, we assure that any two nodes have certain probability to find some shared keys. The source node uses its keys to generate MACs for its messages, while each forwarder or sink verifies the MACs of received messages using their shared keys with the source node.

3.4   Threat Model [16]

We assume that the source and multiple sinks are always trusted, but the forwarders can be compromised. The adversaries can fully control the compromised forwarders and launch pollution attacks. In such attacks, they may either pollute the output messages of the compromised nodes, or inject the forged messages into systems. Formally speaking, we identify that an encoded message E has been polluted or forged, if and only if its content is not consistent with its encoding vector, for example, $E \neq \alpha_1 M_1 \oplus \alpha_2 M_2 \oplus \cdots \alpha_n M_n$ for n source messages $M_1, \ldots, M_n$.

3.5   Universal Hash Functions (UHFs)

Following Carter and Wegman [5], a universal hash function (UHF) is a family of functions indexed by a parameter called the key with the following property: for all distinct inputs, the probability over all keys that they collide is small.

Definition 1. *Let h_k be a function of an (ℓ, q)-family H from an ℓ-bit set A to an q-bit set B with the parameter k taken in a set of $\mathcal{K}_{\mathsf{UHF}}$. Let ϵ be any positive real number. Then, h_k is an ϵ-almost universal class (or ϵ-AU class) of hash function if $\forall x, x' \neq x \in A : \Pr_k\{h_k(x) = h_k(x')\} \leq \epsilon$.*

Definition 2. *h_k is $\oplus$-linear if $\forall x, x' \neq x \in A : h_k(x \oplus x') = h_k(x) \oplus h_k(x')$.*

Definition 3. *h_k is an ϵ-almost XOR universal class (or ϵ-AXU class) of hash function if $\forall x, x' \neq x \in A$ and $\forall \Delta \in B : \Pr_k\{h_k(x) = h_k(x') \oplus \Delta\} \leq \epsilon$.*

3.6   MAC Based on UHFs

UHF is not a cryptographically secure primitive. That is, it is not generally collision-resistant against an adversary who can choose messages after selection of k. Thus UHF is not in general a MAC. The UHFs can be used for message authentication if the output is processed with another function.

A MAC algorithm based on UHFs consists of two building blocks: an efficient keyed compression function that reduces long inputs to a fixed length and a method to process the short hash result and an output transformation. In practical constructions, the encryption with the one-time pad is typically replaced by applying a pseudo-random function with secret key $k' \in \mathcal{K}_{\mathsf{PRF}}$. In this case, one obtains computational rather than unconditional security. Informally, a pseudo-random function family is a function that a computationally limited adversary cannot distinguish with probability substantially better than $1/2$ from a function chosen uniformly at random from all functions with the same range and domain.

Let $f_{k'}$ denote a pseudo-random function family indexed by the key k', which is computationally indistinguishable from a random family of functions from D to R. We define the prf-advantage of an adversary $\mathcal{A}$ for family f as $\mathsf{Adv}_f^{\mathsf{prf}}(\mathcal{A}) = \left| \Pr[k' \leftarrow \mathcal{K}_{\mathsf{PRF}} : \mathcal{A}^{f_{k'}(\cdot)} = 1] - \Pr[\zeta \leftarrow \mathcal{F}^{D \to R} : \mathcal{A}^{\zeta(\cdot)} = 1] \right|$, where $\mathcal{F}^{D \to R}$ is the set of all functions from D to R. We denote by $\mathsf{Adv}_f^{\mathsf{prf}}(q_1, t_1)$ the maximum prf-advantage of an adversary making q_1 queries to its oracle and running in time t_1.

We assume that the sender keeps the state with the counter (nonce) $c \in \mathcal{C}$. Note that we need to guarantee that c is not reused during the MAC generation. The design of MAC obtained from an ϵ-AXU and $\oplus$-linear hash function h_k is given by the following equation [9]:

$$MAC_{k||k'}(x) = h_k(x) \oplus f_{k'}(c). \tag{1}$$

Given a UHF family $h : \mathcal{K}_{\mathsf{UHF}} \times A \to B$ and a PRF family $f : \mathcal{K}_{\mathsf{PRF}} \times \mathcal{C} \to B$, we construct the MAC $\mathsf{UMAC} = (\mathsf{UGen}, \mathsf{UTag}, \mathsf{UVer})$ such as : $\mathsf{UGen}(1^q)$ generates the key (k, k') uniformly at random from $\mathcal{K}_{\mathsf{UHF}} \times \mathcal{K}_{\mathsf{PRF}}$; $\mathsf{UTag} : \mathcal{K}_{\mathsf{UHF}} \times \mathcal{K}_{\mathsf{PRF}} \times A \to \mathcal{C} \times B$ is defined as $\mathsf{UTag}_{k,k'}(M) = (c, h_k(M) \oplus f_{k'}(c))$; $\mathsf{UVer} : \mathcal{K}_{\mathsf{UHF}} \times \mathcal{K}_{\mathsf{PRF}} \times A \times C \times B$ is defined as $\mathsf{UVer}_{k,k'}(M, (c, tag)) = 1$ if and only if $h_k(M) + f_{k'}(c) = tag$.

We denote by $\mathsf{Adv}_{\mathsf{UMAC}}^{\mathsf{uf\text{-}mac}}(q_1, q_2, t_1)$ the maximum advantage of all adversaries against existentially unforgeability under an adaptive chosen message attack, making q_1 queries to UTag, q_2 queries to UVer and running in time at most t_1. The tagging algorithm of UMAC outputs, in addition to the composition of UHF and PRF, a unique counter c incremented at each invocation. Thus, the UMAC is stateful and its properties are as follows [15,4].

Fact 1. *Assume that h is an ϵ^{UHF}-AXU family of hash functions and f is a PRF family. Then* UMAC *is a stateful MAC with advantage:* $\mathsf{Adv}_{\mathsf{UMAC}}^{\mathsf{uf\text{-}mac}}(q_1, q_2, t_1) \leq \mathsf{Adv}_f^{\mathsf{prf}}(q_1 + q_2, t_1) + \epsilon^{\mathsf{UHF}} q_2$.

4   The Yu's Scheme

Yu et al. [16] have proposed the novel mechanism, in which a forwarder can filter polluted messages before spreading the pollution in the XOR network coding systems. This scheme exploits probabilistic key pre-distribution and MACs. We describe the brief procedure of each phase of Yu's scheme.

Parameter Setup Phase: The source node chooses t, u and $\{r_1, \ldots, r_t\}$. Any node can compute a hash chain from a given seed r_j using a pseudo-random permutation function g. The source node has t random keys $k_{s,1}$, ..., $k_{s,t}$ from a global key pool $\mathcal{K}$, where s is the index of the source node. The index of each key $k_{s,j}$ in the key pool for $j = 1, \ldots, t$ is denoted as $id(k_{s,j})$. A forwarder picks t random keys from $\mathcal{K}$. Note that sinks have the same t keys as the source node for complete verification of messages.

MAC Calculation Phase: The source node attaches t MACs to each message M_i for $i = 1, \ldots, n$. More concretely, M_i is attached with $MAC_{i,1}, \ldots, MAC_{i,t}$ as well as the corresponding indeces of the random keys that are used to generate MACs. Thus, the source node actually generates and transmits:

$$M_i, (id(k_{s,1}), MAC_{i,1}), \ldots, (id(k_{s,t}), MAC_{i,t}). \tag{2}$$

For $j = 1, \ldots, t$, MAC is defined as $MAC_{i,j} = \mathsf{Enc}_{k_{s,j}}(id(k_{s,j}), r_j, \sigma_{i,j})$, where Enc denotes symmetric-key encryption function using key $k_{s,j}$ and $\sigma_{i,j}$ is the hash of u randomly selected codewords of M_i. Note that the MAC is decryptable in this scheme. The positions of codewords in M_i are randomly selected by the outputs of hash chain with a random seed r_j. The hash is computed by $\sigma_{i,j} = \bigoplus_{\ell=1}^{u} m_{i,r_{j,\ell}}$, where $r_{j,1}, \ldots, r_{j,u}$ are the indeces of selected codewords and also the output values of hash chain. Each source message is attached with t MACs, and each MAC is computed from u codewords. In other words, each MAC authenticates u codewords of M_i.

Message Verification Phase: Each forwarder or sink verifies its input messages based on the MACs for which it has the shared key(s) with the source node. When receiving a message along with the MACs of source messages, it first checks the indeces prefixed to each MAC to find a shared key. Then, it decrypts the corresponding MACs of source messages and generates the indeces of u codewords from r_j. After identifying the indeces of codewords, it takes the corresponding codewords out of the received message and calculates the hash of these codewords. It further takes out the hashes embedded into the decrypted MACs of source messages and encodes them using the encoding vector transmitted along with the received message. Finally, it checks if the hash of the received message equals the combination of the hashes embedded in the corresponding MACs. If equals, the verification succeeds. Otherwise, the received message is assumed to be polluted and will be discarded.

When each forwarder generates its output message, it always attaches the MACs of all source messages from which this output message is produced. For example, when a forwarder generates $E = M_1 \oplus M_2$, it will attach $MAC_{1,1}$, ..., $MAC_{1,t}$ and $MAC_{2,1}$, ..., $MAC_{2,t}$ to its output message E.

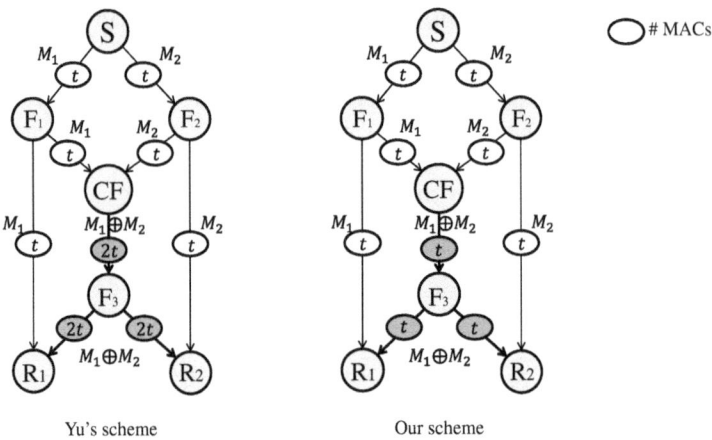

Fig. 1. The problem of Yu's scheme

4.1   Problem Statement

In Yu's scheme, all the forwarders just forward their MACs to downstream nodes without XOR network coding of MACs. Actually, the MAC is decrypted to verify the corresponding codewords of a message. Due to such a special (decryptable) mechanism, the contents embedded into the decrypted MACs are operated with XOR network coding and hence MACs are verified, although MACs are not directly operated. Therefore, the number of MACs increases at a coding point, that is, the MACs cannot be suppressed to a certain number. In a worst case scenario, a forwarder transmits nt MACs to downstream nodes.

Figure 1 shows the difference between Yu's scheme and our scheme to explain the problem of Yu's scheme in an example. The source node S wants to send two messages M_1 and M_2 to two sinks R_1 and R_2. Let CF and F denote a coding forwarder and a mere forwarder, respectively. Where a forwarder performs coding is dependent on a network topology (CF receives two or more messages). At first, S sends M_1 and M_2 to F_1 and F_2 with their MACs, respectively. Then, a forwarder broadcasts the message and its MACs to downstream nodes. The source node attaches t MACs to each message M_1 and M_2. While CF has to forward $2t$ MACs to downstream nodes in Yu's scheme, CF has only to forward t MACs in our scheme. Hence, the communication amount of MACs from CF to sinks in Yu's scheme is twice our scheme in this example.

5   Our Scheme

In this section, we propose the first symmetric-key-based scheme not only to filter polluted messages but also to operate MACs with the XOR network coding on a forwarder. The primary aim of our scheme is to reduce the amount of extra space

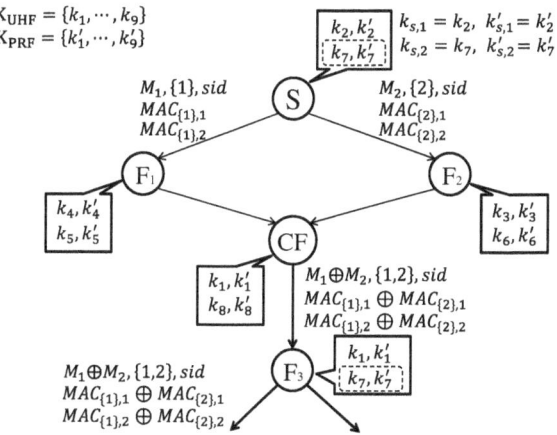

Fig. 2. Example of XOR network coding in our scheme ($t = 2$, $n = 2$)

for integrity protection, i.e., the number of MACs on communication traffic. The XOR network coding of MACs produces improvement which does not increase the number of MACs at a coding point. We describe the detailed procedure of each phase of our scheme in the rest of this section.

Parameter Setup Phase: System parameters m and q are given in advance, since they are related to pre-determined parameters of some functions. The source node chooses t, u *mid* and sid. Any node can compute a hash chain from the seed r_j using a pseudo-random permutation function g. Any node can also compute an universal hash function h and a pseudo-random function[1] f. The source node has random keys $k_{s,1}$, ..., $k_{s,t}$ from a global key pool $\mathcal{K}_{\mathsf{UHF}}$ and $k'_{s,1}$, ..., $k'_{s,t}$ from another global key pool $\mathcal{K}_{\mathsf{PRF}}$. The index of each key $k_{s,j}$ is $id(k_{s,j})$. A forwarder picks t random keys from each of $\mathcal{K}_{\mathsf{UHF}}$ and $\mathcal{K}_{\mathsf{PRF}}$, i.e., $2t$ random keys in total. Note that sinks have the same $2t$ keys as the source node for complete verification of messages.

MAC Calculation Phase: The source node attaches t MACs to each message M_i for $i = 1, \ldots, n$. The source node generates and transmits:

$$M_i, \{i\}, sid, (id(k_{s,1}), MAC_{\{i\},1}), \ldots, (id(k_{s,t}), MAC_{\{i\},t}), \tag{3}$$

where $id(k_{s,j}) = id(k'_{s,j})$. For $j = 1, \ldots, t$, MAC is defined as follows:

$$MAC_{\{i\},j} = h_{k_{s,j}}(\sigma_{i,j}) \oplus f_{k'_{s,j}}(sid||i), \tag{4}$$

where $||$ denotes concatenation and the $\sigma_{i,j}$ is the hash of u randomly selected codewords of M_i, same as Yu's scheme. The random seed r_j, which is used to generate hash chain for $\sigma_{i,j}$, is computed as $r_j = H(f_{k'_{s,j}}(sid||i))$ in our scheme.

---

[1] In practice, AES acts as a pseudo-random function (PRF). Other even more practical constructions of PRFs deployed in standards use MAC functions, such as HMAC.

MAC Coding Phase: Two or more MACs can be operated with XOR network coding in this UHFs-based MAC. The forwarder generates and transmits:

$$E_\tau, mid, sid, (id(k_{s,1}), MAC_{mid,1}), \ldots, (id(k_{s,t}), MAC_{mid,t}), \tag{5}$$

where E_τ is encoded message of τ source messages $M_1, \ldots, M_\tau$ and mid is a set of message indeces which constitutes E_τ, that is, $mid = \{1, \ldots, \tau\}$ ($\tau \geq 2$). For $j = 1, \ldots, t$, the coded MAC is defined as follows:

$$MAC_{mid,j} = h_{k_{s,j}}(\sigma_{mid,j}) \oplus F_{k'_{s,j}}(sid\|mid), \tag{6}$$

where we define $F_{k'_{s,j}}(sid\|mid) = f_{k'_{s,j}}(sid\|1) \oplus \cdots \oplus f_{k'_{s,j}}(sid\|\tau)$ and $\sigma_{mid,j} = \sigma_{1,j} \oplus \cdots \oplus \sigma_{\tau,j}$. We assume that $F_{k'_{s,j}}()$ is a pseudo random function. The $\sigma_{i,j}$ is the hash of u randomly selected codewords of E_τ. The r_j is computed as $H(F_{k'_{s,j}}(sid\|mid))$.

Figure 2 shows an example of XOR network coding in our scheme. The source node S sends M_1 and M_2 ($n = 2$) to F_1 and F_2 with their MACs, respectively. Each source message attaches two MACs ($t = 2$). Hence, the number of their keys in each forwarder is four ($= 2t$) in total. A forwarder broadcasts the message and its MACs to downstream nodes. Since this MAC has homomorphic property, two MACs are operated with XOR network coding by the node CF as follows:

$$
\begin{aligned}
MAC_{\{1\},j} \oplus MAC_{\{2\},j} &= h_{k_{s,j}}(\sigma_{1,j}) \oplus f_{k'_{s,j}}(sid\|1) \oplus h_{k_{s,j}}(\sigma_{2,j}) \oplus f_{k'_{s,j}}(sid\|2) \\
&= h_{k_{s,j}}(\sigma_{\{1,2\},j}) \oplus F_{k'_{s,j}}(sid\|\{1,2\}), \quad (j = 1, 2). \tag{7}
\end{aligned}
$$

Note that $id(k_{s,j})$ is omitted in this figure.

Message Verification Phase: We consider the verification of MACs by a forwarder. This verification phase has three status; *impossible, valid* and *failed*. In the case of *impossible* and *valid*, the forwarder transmits data to the downstream nodes. Otherwise, it discards them. The coding forwarder conducts the XOR network coding of the message and their MACs before forwarding them.

1. A forwarder first checks $id(k_{s,j})$ prefixed to each MAC to see if it has any shared key with the source node. If it does not find any shared key (i.e., *impossible*), it forwards the messages and their MACs.
2. Once finding a shared key, it computes the seed r_j of the corresponding MACs and generates the indeces of u codewords from r_j using hash chain.
3. After identifying the indeces of codewords, it takes the corresponding codewords out of the received message and calculates the hash $\sigma_{i,j}$ of these codewords.
4. It computes $MAC_{\{i\},j}$ using the $\sigma_{i,j}$ in Equation (4) or (6). The values sid and mid are public information.
5. Finally, it checks if the MACs of the received messages equals the computed MACs. If equals (i.e., *valid*), the verification succeeds. Otherwise (i.e., *failed*), the received message is assumed to be polluted and will be discarded.

In Figure 2, we show an example of verification by the forwarder F_3 which shares the keys $k_{s,2}$ and $k'_{s,2}$ with S. This means that F_3 can verify the coded MAC: $MAC_{\{1\},2} \oplus MAC_{\{2\},2}$ by using $k_{s,2}$ and $k'_{s,2}$. More concretely, after F_3 computes $\sigma_{\{1,2\},2} = \sigma_{1,2} \oplus \sigma_{2,2}$ directly from $M_1 \oplus M_2$, it then computes $MAC_{\{1,2\},2} = MAC_{\{1\},2} \oplus MAC_{\{2\},2}$ as Equation (7). Note that F_3 knows neither M_1 nor M_2. It finally checks if this value equals the received MAC. But other forwarders F_1, F_2 and CF cannot verify MACs since they do not share any key with S.

6   Discussion

6.1   Security

In this section, we discuss both the security of MAC used in our scheme (in the case that a MAC key is not revealed) and the security against pollution attacks (in the case that some MAC-keys are revealed).

For the composition of UHF and PRF to be a MAC, it is important that the counters used as input into the PRF be unique. In our scheme, we use as input (counter) to the PRF, the session ID and the index i of source message when computing the MAC for the message M_i. As Fact 1 shows, assuming a pseudo random function, as long as no nonce is re-used during the generation of tags, forging a new valid $(M_i, sid||mid, tag)$ tuple is infeasible, even after the attacker has seen many such tuples before, either by eavesdropping or by active manipulation of tag generation. We can prove security of our MAC by the same framework as the security proof of the MAC based on universal hash. More specifically, we can prove security of our homomorphpic MAC, assuming h is an ϵ^{UHF}-AXU family of hash functions, f is a PRF family and F is also a PRF family.

Since a UHFs-based MAC has homomorphic property, different MAC value can be generated by operating two or more MACs with network coding. Such MAC value may be considered to be forgery. However, such operation is not forgery in network coding system since it is the coding operation itself in the redundant message processing. This is implicitly included in the security definition of [2].

It is important to filter polluted messages, as described in Section 3.1. On the other hand, it is also important to reduce the amount of extra space associated with communication complexity for integrity protection in WSNs. Our scheme probabilistically prevents the pollution attack and operates MACs with the XOR network coding for communication efficiency. This means that our scheme aims to satisfy both security and efficiency for XOR network coding in WSNs. Note that our scheme uses the same probabilistic technique to prevent pollution attacks as Yu's scheme and hence we can obtain the same results, in which the number of hops from polluted node until a pollution is detected is evaluated (i.e., a forwarder can filter polluted messages in a few hops with high probability.).

The tag pollution attack and its countermeasure are described in [12]. This scheme prevents the tag pollution attack under the assumptions of time synchronous and delayed authentication, since it is based on TESLA [14]. We do not consider that our scheme prevents perfectly the tag pollution attack. Both Yu's scheme and our scheme probabilistically prevents this attack without their assumptions.

6.2   Efficiency

Sensors are usually resource-limited and power-constrained. The energy savings of performing network coding are crucial for energy-constrained WSNs. Since the nodes with the heaviest traffic are typically the nodes which are most essential to the connectivity of the network (e.g., area near sink), their failure may cause the network to partition. It is thus important to achieve constant congestion in large-scale WSNs. Actually, all of the MACs for all messages need to be gathered to each sink. The communication complexity should not depend on the number of source nodes n because of its power-constrained.

In this section, we compare our scheme with Yu's scheme in respect to the maximum communication complexity of MACs, storage amount of MAC keys and verification cost of one MAC for integrity protection of a forwarder at each session. Let UMAC, Dec, H and G be the computation costs of UHFs-based MAC, symmetric decryption over $|2^q|$, non-cryptographic hash function and pseudo-random permutation function, respectively. While the maximum number of MACs sent by a forwarder in Yu's scheme becomes nt, that in our scheme is constant t, described in Table 1. Hence, the maximum number of MACs in our scheme becomes $1/n$ compared with Yu's scheme, although the number of keys (i.e., storage amount) doubles. In verification cost of one MAC, Dec operation is required in Yu's scheme[2]. Note that H and G are very lightweight since the size of their outputs is quite small. The XOR operation is assumed to be negligible here because of very lightweight computation. Consequently, the maximum communication complexity of MACs of our scheme is superior to those of Yu's scheme, although the storage amount of MAC keys in our scheme is somewhat worse. The verification cost of our scheme is almost the same as that of Yu's scheme.

For example, we use well-chosen parameters in WSNs described in [16], e.g., $m = 16$, $n = u = 8$, $t = 5$, $q = 128$ (bits) and $|\mathcal{K}_{\mathsf{UHF}}| = |\mathcal{K}_{\mathsf{PRF}}| = 100$, in order to evaluate the congestion of MACs on a forwarder in each session. For such parameters, it is assumed that the size of M_i is 256 bytes. While the maximum communication complexity of MACs for M_i in Yu's scheme is 720 bytes $((128 + 8 + 8) \cdot 5 \cdot 8/8)$, that in our scheme is 80 bytes $(128 \cdot 5/8)$. Hence, the maximum ratio of the size of MACs for each M_i is 280% in Yu's scheme and 32% in our scheme. Especially, in Yu's scheme, the size of attached MACs is much larger than that of M_i. The primary aim of our scheme is to reduce the amount of extra space associated with communication complexity for integrity protection. This result shows that the XOR network coding (aggregation) of MACs is pretty effective to reduce the number of MACs on communication traffic.

---

[2] If a block cipher is used as Dec then two Dec operations are required since the size of the input or output is beyond $|2^q|$.

Table 1. The maximum communication complexity of MACs, storage amount and verification cost for integrity protection of a forwarder at each session

	Max comm. of MACs	Storage amount of keys	Verification cost per MAC
Yu's scheme	$n|2^q|t$	$|2^q|t$	Dec $+ (u-1)$G
Ours	$|2^q|t$	$2|2^q|t$	UMAC+H+$(u-1)$G

7 Conclusion

We have proposed the first symmetric-key-based scheme not only to filter polluted messages but also to operate MACs with the XOR network coding on a forwarder. Our scheme uses the UHFs-based MAC with a homomorphic property to hold homomorphic MAC, and hence it can aggregate MACs in our XOR network coding systems. The evaluation results show that our scheme is very effective to reduce the amount of extra space associated with communication complexity for integrity protection. While the maximum ratio of the size of MACs for each M_i is 280% in Yu's scheme, that is 32% in our scheme.

References

1. Ahlswede, R., Cai, N., Li, S.-Y.R., Yeung, R.W.: Network information flow. IEEE Transactions on Information Theory 46(4), 1204–1216 (2000)
2. Agrawal, S., Boneh, D.: Homomorphic MACs: MAC-Based Integrity for Network Coding. In: Abdalla, M., Pointcheval, D., Fouque, P.-A., Vergnaud, D. (eds.) ACNS 2009. LNCS, vol. 5536, pp. 292–305. Springer, Heidelberg (2009)
3. Apavatjrut, A., Znaidi, W., Fraboulet, A., Goursaud, C., Lauradoux, C., Minier, M.: Energy Friendly Integrity for Network Coding in Wireless Sensor Networks. In: NSS 2010, pp. 223–230 (2010)
4. Bowers, K.D., Juels, A., Oprea, A.: HAIL: a high-availability and integrity layer for cloud storage. In: ACM Conference on Computer and Communications Security 2009, pp. 187–198 (2009)
5. Carter, L., Wegman, M.N.: Universal Classes of Hash Functions. J. Comput. Syst. Sci. 18(2), 143–154 (1979)
6. Dong, Q., Wu, J., Hu, W., Crowcroft, J.: Practical network coding in wireless networks. In: MOBICOM 2007, pp. 306–309 (2007)
7. Eschenauer, L., Gligor, V.D.: A key-management scheme for distributed sensor networks. In: ACM Conference on Computer and Communications Security 2002, pp. 41–47 (2002)
8. Gkantsidis, C., Rodriguez, P.: Cooperative Security for Network Coding File Distribution. In: INFOCOM 2006 (2006)
9. Handschuh, H., Preneel, B.: Key-Recovery Attacks on Universal Hash Function Based MAC Algorithms. In: Wagner, D. (ed.) CRYPTO 2008. LNCS, vol. 5157, pp. 144–161. Springer, Heidelberg (2008)
10. Katti, S., Rahul, H., Hu, W., Katabi, D., Medard, M., Crowcroft, J.: XORs in the air: practical wireless network coding. In: SIGCOMM 2006, pp. 243–254 (2006)
11. Kuo, F.-C., Tan, K., Li, X., Zhang, J., Fu, X.: XOR Rescue: Exploiting Network Coding in Lossy Wireless Networks. In: SECON 2009, pp. 1–9 (2009)

12. Li, Y., Yao, H., Chen, M., Jaggi, S., Rosen, A.: RIPPLE Authentication for Network Coding. In: INFOCOM 2010, pp. 2258–2266 (2010)
13. Nage, T., Yu, F.R., St-Hilaire, M.: Adaptive Control of Packet Overhead in XOR Network Coding. In: ICC 2010, pp. 1–5 (2010)
14. Perrig, A., Canetti, R., Tygar, J.D., Song, D.X.: Efficient Authentication and Signing of Multicast Streams over Lossy Channels. In: IEEE Symposium on Security and Privacy, pp. 56–73 (2000)
15. Shoup, V.: On Fast and Provably Secure Message Authentication Based on Universal Hashing. In: Koblitz, N. (ed.) CRYPTO 1996. LNCS, vol. 1109, pp. 313–328. Springer, Heidelberg (1996)
16. Yu, Z., Wei, Y., Ramkumar, B., Guan, Y.: An Efficient Scheme for Securing XOR Network Coding against Pollution Attacks. In: INFOCOM 2009, pp. 406–414 (2009)
17. Zhang, S., Liew, S.C., Lam, P.P.: Hot topic: physical-layer network coding. In: MOBICOM, pp. 358–365 (2006)
18. Zhang, Z., Lv, T., Su, X., Gao, H.: Dual XOR in the Air: A Network Coding Based Retransmission Scheme for Wireless Broadcasting. In: ICC 2011, pp. 1–6 (2011)

iPIN and mTAN for Secure eID Applications

Johannes Braun[1], Moritz Horsch[1], and Alexander Wiesmaier[2]

[1] Technische Universität Darmstadt
Hochschulstraße 10, 64283 Darmstadt, Germany
{jbraun,horsch}@cdc.informatik.tu-darmstadt.de
[2] AGT Group (R&D) GmbH
Hilpertstraße 20a, 64295 Darmstadt, Germany
awiesmaier@agtgermany.com

Abstract. Recent attacks on the German identity card show that a compromised client computer allows for PIN compromise and man-in-the-middle attacks on eID cards. We present a selection of new solutions to that problem which do not require changes in the card specification. All presented solutions protect against PIN compromise attacks, some of them additionally against man-in-the-middle attacks.

Keywords: eID, iPIN, onetime PIN, nPA, mTAN, man-in-the-middle, PIN compromise, identity theft, smartcard.

1 Introduction

1.1 Motivation

Electronic identity (eID) cards play an important role in trustworthy authentication and many countries already employ elaborated national eID cards. The German eID card [1], for example, provides machine readable travel document functionality as specified by the International Civil Aviation Organization [2,3,4] and is equipped with an eID functionality allowing the owner to electronically prove his identity. Furthermore, it supports an eSign functionality to generate (qualified) electronic signatures to be used in eBusiness and eGovernment applications. The eID and eSign functions are protected by separated personal identification numbers (PIN).

The German eID card is a representative of the newest generation of eID cards and may serve as blueprint for others cards to come. The card provides a contactless interface according to ISO14443 [5] and to supports version 2 of the Extended Access Control (EAC) protocol according to BSI-TR-03110 [6]. The EAC protocol provides a mutual authentication and may in particular be used together with the Password Authenticated Connection Establishment (PACE) [6, Section 4.2] protocol, which protects the communication over the wireless channel and ensures user consent. EAC and PACE have been proven secure against active adversaries having access to the communication channels between the involved components [7,8,9]. To use the card, a terminal is required where the user enters his PIN.

M.D. Ryan, B. Smyth, and G. Wang (Eds.): ISPEC 2012, LNCS 7232, pp. 259–276, 2012.

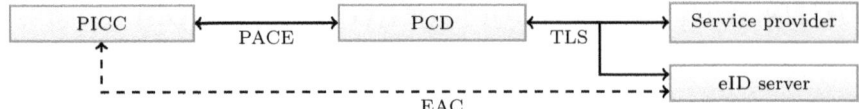

Fig. 1. eID infrastructure

However, terminals are not necessarily trustworthy, especially if the terminal consists of a simple card reader (without key pad) connected to a computer. Entering the PIN on a compromised terminal can leak it to an adversary and allow for identity theft attacks. Several attacks bypassing the security of the protocols based on compromised computers and eavesdropping on the PIN have been presented (cf. Section 1.3). The work at hand focuses on that threat concerning the eID functionality as implemented by the German eID card. We propose a new solution to protect the PIN without requiring changes to the card specification.

1.2   The eID Functionality of the German Identity Card

The German eID card allows its cardholder to electronically prove his identity to service providers on the Internet. To use the eID functionality a terminal is needed, which in general consists of a computer connected to a card reader. A client application which implements the required communication and cryptographic protocols as well as the user interaction needs to be installed on the computer. In the following, we simply refer to the German eID card as the *card* or synonymously as Proximity Integrated Circuit Card (PICC) and to the terminal (including computer, card reader and client application) as Proximity Coupling Device (PCD). The terms PICC and PCD originate from BSI-TR-03110 [6]. As the legitimate user is always the cardholder we use the term *user* and denote his PIN with π to distinguish it from other constructs, such as temporary passwords.

In contrast to a common one-factor authentication by username and password, the eID functionality enables a two-factor authentication based on the ownership of the card and the knowledge of π. This enables a high level of trust between the service provider and the user which in fact is backed by a sovereign document. But it also implies big trouble if such a card is used illegitimately.

Any service provider (e.g. web mail service or online shop) that uses authentication via this card needs to present a certificate to the card to proof its identity and its permission for data access. These certificates are emitted by the German administration. However, the authentication process is not performed by the service providers themselves. Dedicated eID servers perform it in the name of the service providers. An eID server manages certificates issued for service providers, performs the security protocols, and reads the personal data stored on the card. The service providers only receive the data and perform a local authentication process based on their environment. The corresponding infrastructure is shown in Figure 1. The authentication process is as follows:

1. The user (using the PCD) opens the website of a service provider and clicks on a link to perform the login process and the client application starts.

2. The client application establishes a TLS connection to the eID server and receives the service provider's certificate.
3. The certificate description (e.g. issuer, URL, terms of usage) is displayed to the user, who agrees to the data transmission by entering the PIN π.
4. A secure channel is established between both parties by performing PACE.
5. The eID server and the card perform a mutual authentication using the EAC protocol. Hereby, the PCD serves as bridge between the secure messaging channel and the TLS channel. The certificate received in step 2 is used during the protocol to prove the access rights of the eID server.
6. The personal data is read by the eID server and passed to the service provider which grants access to the user upon receipt.

1.3   Identity Theft Attacks Concerning the eID Functionality

Given a non compromised PCD, the usage of the German identity card is secure. The necessity to enter a PIN to enable the communication with the card provides protection against the unauthorized usage of the card. Furthermore, the communication is secured against eavesdropping by the establishment of strong ephemeral session keys and encrypted communication. As detailed in this section, in case of a compromised PCD, the secure usage of the card cannot be guaranteed. As current attacks show, the major threat is PIN compromise.

PIN Compromise Attacks. As shown by the Chaos Computer Club [10] an adversary can obtain the PIN by using key loggers or Trojan horses. Once holding the PIN, the attacker still needs to access the card. Aside from stealing the card, the attacker can establish a remote connection to the card via the compromised PCD, if the card holder leaves the card on the PCD or is tricked into doing so. The adversary is then able to impersonate the victim.

Man-in-the-Middle (MitM) Attack. A MitM attack also requires the manipulation of the client application on the PCD. An adversary controlling the PCD presents the user the correct service certificate but sends another one to the card. Therewith, the user is tricked into entering his PIN and authenticating at a service different from the one he intended to. Taking over the session by the adversary after authentication and showing an error message to the user might leave the attack undetected.

1.4   Approach and Outline

At present, the only way to prevent the attacks presented above is using card readers with a secure key pad and display. Such readers are expensive and might not always be available, for example in Internet cafés or other public places.

By adding an additional trustworthy identity provider, we propose a new solution working with a common basic card reader and leaving existing infrastructure components and protocols untouched.

In Section 2, we present the PACE protocol and address some background on multiparty computation. In Section 3, we present our solution involving different levels of trust. In Section 4, we give a security analysis and discuss the feasibility of our approach. The paper closes with future work and the conclusion.

PICC		PCD
(a) $K_\pi = \text{KDF}(\pi)$		$K_\pi = \text{KDF}(\pi)$
(b) $z = \text{E}(K_\pi, s)$	$\xrightarrow{z}$	$s = \text{D}(K_\pi, z)$
(c) $Y = y \cdot G$	$\xleftarrow{X}$	$X = x \cdot G$
	$\xrightarrow{Y}$	
(d) $H = y \cdot X$		$H = x \cdot Y$
(e) $G' = s \cdot G + H$		$G' = s \cdot G + H$
(f) $\widehat{PK}_{\text{PICC}} = \widetilde{SK}_{\text{PICC}} \cdot G'$	$\xleftarrow{\widehat{PK}_{\text{PCD}}}$ $\xrightarrow{\widehat{PK}_{\text{PICC}}}$	$\widehat{PK}_{\text{PCD}} = \widetilde{SK}_{\text{PCD}} \cdot G'$
(g) $K = \widetilde{SK}_{\text{PICC}} \cdot \widehat{PK}_{\text{PCD}}$		$K = \widetilde{SK}_{\text{PCD}} \cdot \widehat{PK}_{\text{PICC}}$
(h) $K_{\text{ENC}} = \text{KDF}_{\text{ENC}}(K)$		$K_{\text{ENC}} = \text{KDF}_{\text{ENC}}(K)$
(i) $K_{\text{MAC}} = \text{KDF}_{\text{MAC}}(K)$		$K_{\text{MAC}} = \text{KDF}_{\text{MAC}}(K)$
(j) $T_{\text{PICC}} = \text{MAC}(K_{\text{MAC}}, \widehat{PK}_{\text{PCD}})$	$\xleftarrow{T_{\text{PCD}}}$ $\xrightarrow{T_{\text{PICC}}}$	$T_{\text{PCD}} = \text{MAC}(K_{\text{MAC}}, \widehat{PK}_{\text{PICC}})$

Fig. 2. PACE [6, Chapter 4.2]

2   Background

2.1   PACE

The Password Authenticated Connection Establishment (PACE) protocol [6] was developed by the German Federal Office for Information Security, is designed to be free of patents, and can be classified as a password-based key agreement protocol [11, Section 7]. PACE uses a password with low entropy to perform a user authentication and to establish a secure connection with strong ephemeral session keys. Usually, the password is a PIN π, which is permanently stored in PICC and is to be entered by the user into PCD for a successful protocol execution. Entering a wrong password leads to invalid session keys and the connection establishment fails. Generally speaking, PACE makes sure that only the owner has access to the card and unauthorized access is prohibited. PACE can be instantiated in different variants. Here, we focus on the elliptic curve variant with *Generic Mapping* [6, A.3.4.1] as used by the German eID card.

Figure 2 provides an overview of the protocol steps. Before it starts both parties agree on common domain parameters $\mathcal{D}$, containing elliptic curve parameters and a base point G. The numbers x, y, $\widetilde{SK}_{\text{PCD}}$ and $\widetilde{SK}_{\text{PICC}}$ are smaller than the order r of the elliptic curve and are chosen uniformly at random.

1. As depicted in step (a), both parties derive a key K_π from the shared password π using the key derivation function (KDF). The KDF enables to derive one or more secret keys from a common secret value and is basically a SHA-1 hash computation. In step (b) the PICC chooses a nonce s, encrypts it using the encryption function $\text{E}(key, \cdot)$ with the key K_π, and sends the resulting ciphertext z to the PCD. The PCD decrypts z to obtain the nonce s.
2. In steps (c) – (e), both parties use s to generate a new common base point $G' = s \cdot G + H$, where H is agreed upon by the two communication partners in an anonymous Diffie-Hellman (DH) key agreement.

3. As shown in steps (f) – (g) a second DH key agreement based on G' is performed. Both, the PICC and the PCD choose an ephemeral private key $(\widetilde{SK}_{\text{PICC}}, \widetilde{SK}_{\text{PCD}})$ and calculate a common secret point K.
4. Steps (h) and (i) depict the key derivation of the keys K_{ENC} for encryption and K_{MAC} for message authentication from the common secret K.
5. In step (j) both parties calculate an authentication token $(T_{\text{PICC}}, T_{\text{PCD}})$ using a MAC function and the shared key K_{MAC}.

The authentication tokens $(T_{\text{PICC}}, T_{\text{PCD}})$ represent a mutual key confirmation and include a checksum of the ephemeral public keys $(\widetilde{PK}_{\text{PICC}}, \widetilde{PK}_{\text{PCD}})$. By checking the token, both parties can verify that the opponent calculated the same new base point G' and therefore knows the shared password π.

2.2 Multiparty Computation

Perfect Secret Sharing means dividing a secret s into n so called shares, such that it is possible to reconstruct the secret if given at least $k \leq n$ shares. Less than k shares, however, provide absolute no information about the secret. I.e. the secret is information theoretically secure as long as an adversary only obtains less than k shares. An example is Shamir's secret sharing scheme [12].

Secure Multiparty Computation (SMPC) denotes the distributed computation of a function f by n participants. Thereby, a so called non qualified subset of $t < n$ participants cannot learn anything about the function output besides their own inputs and outputs. SMPC can be realized based on Shamir's secret sharing scheme, where $t < n/2$ is required [13,14,15] to guarantee perfect security against passive adaptive adversaries. Thus, $n = 3$ and $t = 1$ are the smallest possible parameters. Note that this means, that two participants can reconstruct the inputs and outputs without involving the third participant. An SMPC scheme providing computational security can be realized for $n = 2$ and $t = 1$ [16,14] based on the Paillier cryptosystem [17].

Secure Multiparty AES (MPC AES) is based on an SMPC scheme and implements the AES encryption and decryption interactively in a distributed manner as shown in [14]. For the MPC AES execution, each participant initially has to hold a share of the AES key as well as a share of the clear- or ciphertext. These have to be shared bytewise. At the end of the protocol execution each participant holds a share of the ciphertext (encryption) or of the cleartext (decryption). These shares can then be combined to a valid cipher- or cleartext.

3 iPIN and mTAN for eID Cards

We provide solutions to prevent from the aforementioned identity theft attacks, even though the user only has access to an insecure PCD (e.g. without secure key pad and display). We use onetime passwords in different flavors, leading to the different solutions we present here.

To facilitate the use of onetime passwords and to ensure the desired security properties without changing the existing infrastructure and its protocols, we introduce an additional trustworthy infrastructure component, called Universal Identity Provider (uIdP). Keeping existing components untouched is a crucial requirement, as several million German eID cards have already been issued and have to work with our solution. The uIdP is involved in the PACE protocol execution and interacts with an adapted client software installed on the PCD such that the involvement of the uIdP is transparent to the other components such as cards, eID servers, or service providers.

Concerning the onetime passwords, we differentiate between so-called iPIN and mTAN variants. iPIN denotes indexed onetime passwords, from which the PIN π can be reconstructed given the user's iPIN and the uIdP's iPIN with the same index. It is also possible to construct iPINs directly from K_π, which then can be reconstructed directly. From a security point of view, the knowledge of the derived key K_π is equivalent to the knowledge of π.

The mTAN variants are closely related to the mobile TransAction Number (mTAN) procedure known from online banking services. In online banking, a randomized TAN and some transaction details are send by the bank to the customer's mobile phone via SMS. The user confirms his consent by entering the TAN into the online banking application, thereby sending the TAN back to the banking server. The mobile phone is a so-called Out Of Band Device (OOBD). That means it realizes an additional communication channel (out of band channel) which is independent from the previously established communication channel between the two parties. In our mTAN variants, the uIdP takes the role of the banking server and sends the TAN to the user.

The several variants are justified by the different security goals they achieve, yet have their advantages and disadvantages. iPINs allow a stronger protection of the user PIN but require the precomputation and distribution of lists containing the iPINs, while the mTAN technique is more usable and allows to prevent from the MitM attack. We describe the variants along with their security assumptions, required setup steps, and detailed protocol steps in the following sections. Variants 1 and 2 apply iPINs while Variants 3 and 4 make use of the mTAN technique. Variant 5 combines both. Note that Variants 1 and 5 in addition to the uIdP technically require a second remote server we denote with uIdP-2. We refer the reader to Section 4.2 for a discussion on practical realizations.

Depending on the respective variant, a potential adversary requires different specific capabilities for a successful identity theft concerning different possible attacks. These capabilities are summarized in Table 1, which lists the attacks in its columns, the PACE variants (i.e. our solutions) in its rows, and the necessary attacker capabilities at the respective intersections. Basically, 'PIN comp. attack' and 'MitM attack' denote the attacks described in Section 1.3. Thereby, 'PIN comp. attack' only includes remote connections to the card, while 'physical card usage' denotes the physical theft of the card and its application to impersonate the owner. 'PIN compromise' means that the PIN is revealed to an adversary.

Regarding the attacker capabilities, 'r' denotes read access, while 'rwx' denotes read-write-execute access. Thus, e.g. 'uIdP:rwx' means, that an adversary must be capable to read the uIdP's memory, as well as change and run malicious

Table 1. Required adversarial strength for identity theft

		Threat			
		PIN compromise	PIN comp. attack	MitM attack	physical card usage
PACE variant	PACE	client:r	client:rwx	client:rwx	PIN + card theft
	V1	two out of {client, uIdP, uIdP-2}:r	PIN + client:rwx	client:rwx	iPIN + card theft, OR PIN + card theft
	V2	uIdP:r (during protocol run)	PIN + client:rwx	client:rwx	iPIN + card theft, OR PIN + card theft
	V3	uIdP:r (anytime)	PIN + client:rwx, OR OOBD:r + client:rwx	client:rwx	OOBD + card theft, OR PIN + card theft
	V4	uIdP:r (anytime)	PIN + client:rwx, OR OOBD:r + client:rwx	uIdP:rwx + client:rwx	OOBD + card theft, OR PIN + card theft
	V5	two out of {client, uIdP, uIdP-2}:r	PIN + client:rwx	uIdP:rwx + client:rwx	OOBD + card theft, OR PIN + card theft

r = read access, rwx = read-write-execute access, theft = physical theft

code, whereas 'uIdP:r' means only reading is required, which also includes key logging and so forth. With 'theft' we denote the physical theft of things. 'PIN' as an adversarial strength means, that the adversary must be able to compromise the PIN, implying the required strengths for that purpose.

3.1 Preliminaries

The preliminaries and principles are common to all five variants.

In general, we assume an adversary with the goal to compromise the PIN and/or perform the mentioned identity theft attacks but not to break up the flow of the protocols. Denial of service attacks are out of scope. Thus, even a compromised participant acts according to the protocol, as deviant behavior will be detected and responded with protocol abortion by honest participants, which is not in the interest of the attacker. The channels between PCD, uIdP, eID server, and service provider are always secured applying TLS, thus an adversary cannot eavesdrop on the communication between non compromised participants.

For each variant, a non recurring setup involving registration of the user at the uIdP(s) and establishing a unique user ID (e.g. a unique pseudonym) is necessary. The actual realization of the registration depends on the uIdP, but is essentially the same for all variants. In case of the involvement of two uIdPs, however, we assume for simplicity reasons that the user ID is the same for both. Depending on the actual variant, the setup phase involves the generation and transmission of pre-shared data such as iPINs to support later protocol executions. As this data is security sensitive, a non compromised system is necessary. Thus, we assume that this is temporarily available to the user during setup. We discuss how such a system can be practically provided in Section 4.2.

Protocol runs are initiated by the user. To do so, he starts the client application on the PCD, provides his ID, and applies his identity card upon request. As the uIdP needs the public domain parameters $\mathcal{D}$ (including the base point G) to enable dedicated computations of the PACE protocol, the PCD reads $\mathcal{D}$ from the card and initially sends it along with the user's ID to the uIdP.

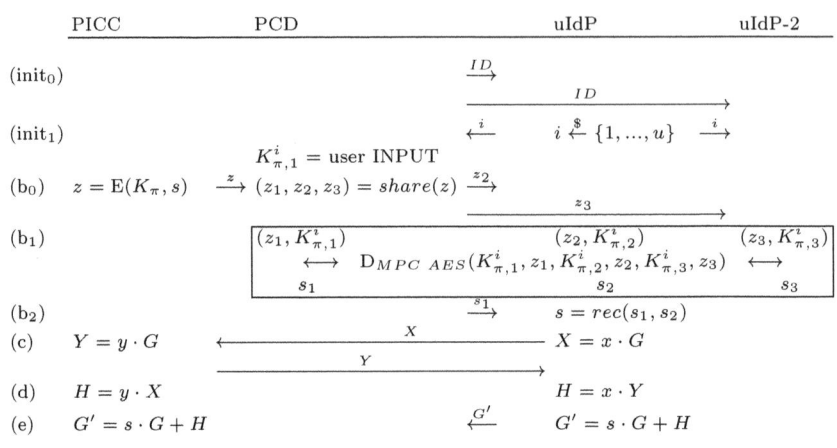

Fig. 3. PACE with multiparty decryption

3.2 Variant 1: Multiparty Decryption of Nonce

Variant 1 is designed to provide the highest possible security concerning the user PIN π respectively the derived key K_π. That is, they are never available in cleartext on any of the systems participating in the protocol execution. This goal is achieved by applying MPC AES to decrypt the nonce s. As MPC AES based on Shamir's secret sharing is necessarily a three party protocol [14], two trusted remote servers are required to implement this variant. We denote the trusted remote systems with uIdP and uIdP-2. The first uIdP server takes the main role, while the second one only provides support to facilitate MPC AES.

Assumptions. The adversary is able to compromise any participant, but at most one at the same time. uIdPs are trustworthy, meaning that they do not collude to obtain the PIN and act reasonably to protect themselves and the user.

Setup. To enable MPC AES, the key K_π must be shared in advance among the participants. The generation of iPIN lists works as follows: K_π is derived from π. Then, the sharing of K_π for three participants is repeated u times always storing each share in one of three indexed lists. Finally, each list has length u. Hence, they can be used u times before new iPIN lists must be generated. The lists are securely transmitted to the uIdPs and the user. E.g., the corresponding lists are sent to the uIdPs via TLS and the user receives a print-out.

Protocol Execution. Figure 3 shows the steps of one protocol execution of Variant 1. To initialize the protocol run (step (init$_0$)), the PCD sends the user ID to the remote servers uIdP and uIdP-2. With the ID, the remote servers identify the user account and load the user specific information, e.g. iPIN lists.

To start the multiparty decryption, the shared key K_π must also be available to the participants. This was achieved by the distribution of the iPIN lists during the setup phase. To apply a specific iPIN, the uIdP chooses (uniformly at

PICC	PCD	uIdP

(init_0) $\xrightarrow{\;ID\;}$

(init_1) $\xleftarrow{\;i\;}$ $i \xleftarrow{\$} \{1, ..., u\}$

(init_2) $\text{iPIN}_1^i = \text{user INPUT} \xrightarrow{\;iPIN_1^i\;} \pi = rec(\text{iPIN}_1^i, \text{iPIN}_2^i)$

(a) $K_\pi = \text{KDF}_\pi(\pi)$ $K_\pi = \text{KDF}_\pi(\pi)$

(b) $z = \text{E}(K_\pi, s)$ $\xrightarrow{\hspace{2cm} z \hspace{2cm}}$ $s = \text{D}(K_\pi, z)$

(c)-(j) *equal to Variant 1, cf. Figure 3*

Fig. 4. PACE with PIN sharing

random) a fresh index i and announces it in step (init_1). Now, the user must enter the correct iPIN $K_{\pi,1}^i$ taken from his list into the PCD to show his consent, while uIdP and uIdP-2 load the iPINs with the announced index from their lists.

Now the PICC gets involved. In step (b_0) the PCD receives the encrypted nonce z from the PICC. Remember, z is an AES ciphertext under the key K_π and does not reveal information about π. However, in combination with its decryption s, it is easily possible to brute force π. Thus, z must not be sent to the uIdP, to not expose both values to one system. The PCD shares z and sends one share to the uIdP, another one to the uIdP-2 and the third one is kept by the PCD.

In step (b_1) the PCD, uIdP and uIdP-2 jointly execute the decryption using MPC AES and each participant obtains a different share of the nonce s. The used iPINs are now securely deleted by uIdP and uIdP-2, thus a reuse of the user's iPIN (now known to the PCD) is impossible. From now on, the uIdP-2 is not needed anymore and it deletes all values computed during that session.

In step (b_2) the PCD transmits its share to the uIdP where s is reconstructed. The subsequent Diffie-Hellman key exchange (steps (c)-(d)) is executed between PICC and the uIdP. The PCD only forwards the data not being able to learn s.

In step (e) G' is transmitted from the uIdP to the PCD. Afterwards, the standard PACE steps are executed between PICC and PCD (see Figure 2).

3.3   Variant 2: Secret Shared PIN

In Variant 2, the protocol is less complicated and much easier to implement than in Variant 1 as it requires only one trusted remote server and no MPC AES. However, the user PIN is temporarily revealed (by reconstruction from the iPINs) to the uIdP. But it can be deleted afterwards, thus limiting the time span the user PIN can be compromised by a potential intrusion into the uIdP.

Assumptions. Compared to Variant 1, we increase the security assumptions by requiring the uIdP not to be compromised during protocol execution. Also, the uIdP is trusted not to misuse the PIN, and to erase it securely after usage.

Setup. The generation and distribution of iPIN lists is as in Variant 1 with the differences that: first, π is shared instead of the derived key K_π and second,

PICC	PCD		uIdP	OOBD

(init_0) $\xrightarrow{ID}$

(init_1) $\qquad\qquad\qquad\qquad\qquad\qquad$ TAN $\overset{\$}{\leftarrow} \{1, ..., u\}$ $\xrightarrow{TAN}$

(init_2) $\qquad$ TAN* = user INPUT $\xrightarrow{TAN^*}$ TAN $\overset{?}{=}$ TAN*

(a)-(j) *equal to Variant 2, cf. Figure 4*

Fig. 5. PACE with mTAN

any perfect secret sharing scheme for two participants can be used, in particular XOR secret sharing which is very efficient and easy to implement.

Protocol Execution. Figure 4 shows the protocol execution. Initially (step (init_0)), the PCD sends the user ID to the uIdP. With the ID, the uIdP again identifies the user and loads the specific information, in particular the iPIN list.

In step (init_1), the uIdP chooses (uniformly at random) a fresh index i and requests the ith iPIN from the PCD, thus from the user. In step (init_2), the user enters the correct iPIN into the PCD to show his consent. The iPIN is then sent to the uIdP, which reconstructs π and derives K_π (step (a)).

From now on, the PICC is involved into the protocol. z is sent by the PICC (see PACE specification [6]) and the PCD forwards it to the uIdP for decryption.

Afterwards, the protocol follows exactly Variant 1. After finishing its tasks, the uIdP deletes all session data including π, K_π and the used iPINs.

3.4 Variant 3: PACE with mTAN

This variant introduces the mTAN mechanism to circumvent the need for iPIN lists. The uIdP sends a onetime password (here called TAN) to the user's mobile phone, which serves as an OOBD. To show consent the user enters the TAN instead of an iPIN into the PCD upon request.

Compared to Variants 1 and 2, Variant 3 allows a much easier setup phase as no iPIN lists have to be generated and transferred in advance. Also, the usability is improved as the user is not required to keep a iPIN list (e.g. a piece of paper with iPINs printed on it). Yet the uIdP stores the user PIN π permanently leading to the disadvantage, that a compromise of the uIdP might reveal π at any time. Note that a large amount of PINs from different users might be revealed at once. Thus, advanced security mechanisms for the uIdP are indispensable.

Assumptions. In Variant 3, the security assumptions are further increased compared to Variants 1 and 2. The uIdP is assumed not to be compromised and is considered completely trustworthy.

Setup. Apart from the registration, only the user PIN π has to be transferred to the uIdP and the out of band channel must be defined. To define the out of band channel, the user might in particular deposit his mobile phone number at the uIdP, e.g. during registration or in a subsequent step, e.g. by yellow mail.

PICC	PCD	uIdP	OOBD

(init_0) $\xrightarrow{ID,SI}$

(init_1) $\text{TAN} \xleftarrow{\$} \{1,...,u\} \xrightarrow{SI.TAN}$

(init_2) $\text{TAN}^* = \text{user INPUT} \xrightarrow{TAN^*} \text{TAN} \overset{?}{=} \text{TAN}^*$

(a)-(j) *equal to standard PACE, though between PICC and uIdP, cf. Figure 2*

Fig. 6. Remote PACE

Protocol Execution. As seen in Figure 5, the protocol execution of Variant 3 is very similar to that of Variant 2. The differences concern the initialization part of the protocol before the PICC is involved.

To initialize the protocol run (step (init_0)), the PCD sends the ID to the uIdP. With the ID, the uIdP identifies the account and loads π. Afterwards, the uIdP chooses a TAN uniformly at random, i.e. a six digit number and sends it to the user's mobile phone (step (init_1)). The uIdP appends additional information, e.g. to identify itself and the purpose and context of the message.

In step (init_2), upon receipt, the user enters the TAN into the PCD, to show his consent. The PCD forwards it to the uIdP, which compares it to the one it sent. If the TAN is positively verified, the uIdP proceeds, otherwise the protocol is aborted by the uIdP. Following a positive TAN verification, the PICC is involved and the following protocol steps are executed as in Variant 2.

3.5 Variant 4: Remote PACE and EAC

In Variant 4, the entire PACE protocol is executed remotely by the uIdP, while the PCD only forwards messages between card and uIdP. This means the uIdP is necessarily involved into the EAC protocol. Thus, the uIdP can check the service provider's certificate and reconfirm its identity by sending it together with a TAN to the user by applying the mTAN mechanism. Thus, this variant

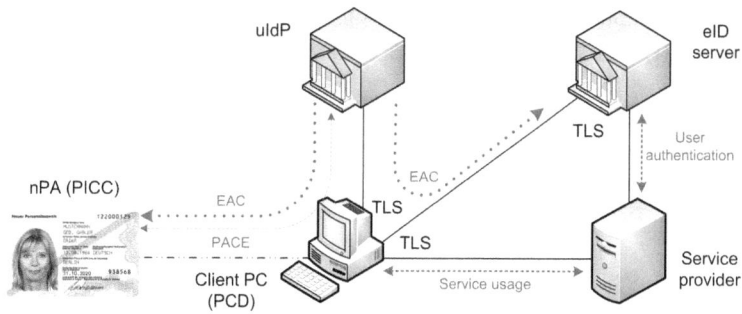

Fig. 7. Remote PACE and EAC Architecture

additionally provides protection from active adversaries and the MitM attack described above. On the negative side the user PIN π is permanently stored at the uIdP and the entire traffic of the eID functionality is routed over the uIdP.

Assumptions. The uIdP is assumed not to be compromised at all and is considered completely trustworthy. The PCD might try to manipulate the service's certificate as described for the MitM attack in Section 1.3. Thus, we assume a stronger adversary, that can manipulate the client application during execution. ***Setup.*** The setup is identical to Variant 3 (cf. Section 3.4).

Protocol Execution. Figure 6 shows the steps of Variant 4. Remember, that the service's certificate is obtained from the eID server before PACE is actually started and sent during EAC to the PICC after PACE was executed.

To initialize the protocol run (step (init_0)), the PCD sends the user ID and the service's certificate (SI) to the uIdP. With the ID, the uIdP identifies the user and loads the user's data. The uIdP chooses a TAN uniformly at random, i.e. a six digit number, and sends it to the user's OOBD (step (init_1)). Additionally, the uIdP appends the certificate's main information to the mTAN message.

That additional information allows the user to verify, that the certificate shown to him by the PCD and the one sent to the PICC are identical. In case this is true, the user enters the received TAN, which then is sent back to and verified by the uIdP (step (init_2)). A positive verification of the TAN, shows the user's consent. Then, the uIdP performs the standard PACE steps (a)-(j) jointly with the PICC. The PCD only forwards the data between uIdP and PICC.

As the complete PACE protocol is executed between PICC and uIdP, the PACE channel is established between them, and the PCD does not hold the keys for the PACE channel. Hence, all following messages for EAC must be routed over the uIdP for encryption when sent to and decryption when received from the PICC. The uIdP checks if the service's certificate is the same as the one the user confirmed during PACE. Only if this is true, the uIdP encrypts the certificate with the PACE keys and sends it via the PCD to the PICC. The PCD cannot tamper with that message as it lacks the keys.

Figure 7 shows the remote PACE and EAC architecture resulting from Variant 4. The PCD is the central element connecting the participants but mainly forwarding messages. The PACE channel is established between uIdP and PICC. During EAC, the eID server communicates via a TLS secured channel with the PCD that hands all messages to the uIdP to put these into the PACE channel and vice versa. Thus, from the point of view of the eID server the involvement of the uIdP is not visible. The same holds for the PICC.

3.6   Variant 5: Combination

Variant 5 is a combination of Variants 1 and 4. It makes use of iPINs and combines this with the mTAN mechanism and the remote PACE execution. Therewith, the reconfirmation of a specific service's certificate is possible. Hence, the user PIN π is never revealed and protection from MitM attacks can be guaranteed. However, this comes at the cost of the setup phase of Variant 1 and

$$
\begin{array}{lllll}
\text{PICC} & \text{PCD} & \text{uIdP} & \text{uIdP-2} & \text{OOBD}
\end{array}
$$

(init$_0$) $\xrightarrow{ID,SI}$

(init$_1$) $i \xleftarrow{\$} \{1,...,u\}$ $\xrightarrow{\quad SI,i \quad}$

$\xrightarrow{i}$

(init$_2$) $K^i_{\pi,1} =$ user INPUT

(b$_0$) $z = E(K_\pi, s) \xrightarrow{z} (z_1, z_2, z_3) = share(z) \xrightarrow{z_2}$

$\xrightarrow{z_3}$

(b$_1$) $\longleftrightarrow D_{MPC\ AES}(K^i_{\pi,1}, z_1, K^i_{\pi,2}, z_2, K^i_{\pi,3}, z_3) \longleftrightarrow$

(b$_2$) $\xrightarrow{s_1}\ s = rec(s_1, s_2)$

(c)-(j) *equal to standard PACE, though between PICC and uIdP, cf. Figure 2*

Fig. 8. Remote PACE with multiparty decryption

the uIdP being able to monitor the traffic of the eID functionality. As in Variant 1, a second uIdP-2 is required to support MPC AES decryption.

Note that other combinations of the different techniques used in the above presented variants are also possible, but not explained here.

Assumptions. We assume an adversary, that is able to compromise any participant, but at most one at the same time. Furthermore, the uIdPs are trustworthy in the sense that they do not collude to obtain the PIN and act reasonably to protect themselves and the user. This includes, for example, that the main uIdP is assumed not to store communication transcripts of the user.

Setup. The setup of Version 5 is the combination of the setups of Variants 1 and 4. It includes the generation of iPIN lists from the key K_π within a secure environment and their distribution (cf. Section 3.2). In addition, the user deposits his mobile phone number at the main uIdP to enable out of band communication (cf. Section 3.5). Note that the PIN π is not transferred to any of the uIdPs.

Protocol execution. The protocol steps are depicted in Figure 8. To initialize the protocol run (step (init$_0$)), the PCD sends the user ID and the service's certificate (SI) to the uIdP. With the ID, the uIdP identifies the user and loads the user's data. In step (init$_1$), the uIdP randomly chooses an iPIN index i and sends i along with the service's certificate to the user's OOBD. At the same time the uIdP sends i to uIdP-2. In step (init$_2$), the user enters the correct iPIN $K^i_{\pi,1}$ taken from his list into the PCD to show his consent, while uIdP and uIdP-2 load the iPINs with the announced index from their lists.

In step (b$_0$), the PCD receives the encrypted nonce z from the PICC. The PCD shares z and sends one share to the uIdP and another one to the uIdP-2, while the third one is kept by the PCD. In step (b$_1$) the PCD, uIdP and uIdP-2 jointly execute the decryption function using MPC AES (see Section 2.2) and each participant obtains a different share of the nonce s. The used iPINs are now securely deleted by uIdP and uIdP-2. In step (b$_2$), the PCD transmits its share to the uIdP where s is reconstructed.

Then, the standard PACE steps (c)-(j) (see Figure 2) are executed between PICC and uIdP, while the PCD only forwards the messages between them.

4   Analysis

4.1   Security Analysis

PIN Compromise. The user PIN π or the derived key K_π can be compromised only if available on a compromised device or when it is computable from any of the exchanged messages or values computed during protocol execution. This is especially relevant, as the knowledge of a single cleartext-ciphertext pair of the nonce, i.e. s and z, allows for an offline brute force attack on the 6 digit PIN π.

The secret π cannot be compromised via the PCD in any of the variants, as: first it is never entered by the user. The entered iPINs in Variants 1,2 and 5 do not enable reconstruction due to perfect secret sharing as the other shares are never available on the PCD (uIdP and uIdP-2 do not reveal this values). The TANs entered in Variants 3 and 4 are random numbers by definition and cannot reveal the PIN. Second, the PCD learns z, so the question is does it learn s? We show in the following, that it does not.

In Variants 1 and 5, z is decrypted to s by MPC AES. The multiparty computation based on Shamir's secret sharing scheme is unconditionally secure thus does not leak any information. The PCD does not get any of the other output shares besides its own one and s is reconstructed on the uIdP. In Variants 2 – 4, s is decrypted by the uIdP.

In Variants 1 – 3, the new base point G' is sent back to the PCD, ending the involvement of the uIdP(s). However, from G' one cannot recover s due to the difficulty of computing discrete logarithms. The steps after this mapping do not involve π, K_π, z or s besides their incorporation into G', hence need no further analysis. Note that in case of the remote Variants 4 and 5, the PCD actually has no informational advantage over a wiretapper eavesdropping on the contactless channel, and PACE has been proven secure against such an adversary [7].

In Variants 1 and 5, the PIN additionally cannot be compromised by intrusion into one of the uIdP's systems. The uIdPs learn their iPINs, one (unconditionally secure) share of z and the output of the secure multiparty computation respectively. The main uIdP additionally learns s from the reconstruction, but due to the lack of z cannot recover the user PIN.

In Variants 2 – 4, the PIN is revealed when the uIdP is compromised. The advantage of Version 2 is, that the PIN is only temporarily available, thus the compromise must occur at that certain time frame when the PIN is reconstructed.

To conclude, we note that a compromised participant, either PCD or uIdP, might reveal more than intended by the protocol, e.g. the PCD might reveal z to the uIdP. However, the other participant, not being compromised, would ignore such additional input or even detect the compromise and report it to the user.

MitM Attack. This concerns only Variants 4 and 5, as the others do not provide protection from that attack.

An exchange of the service's certificate with another one by a compromised PCD is always revealed as explained in the following. If the uIdP receives the exchanged certificate during initialization, it sends it via the OOBD to the user who detects the exchange by comparison with the service's certificate. If the certificate is exchanged during EAC, the exchange is detected by the uIdP by comparison with the formerly received one. As the uIdP encrypts all messages sent to the PICC with the PACE key, which the PCD in both variants does not know, the PCD cannot exchange the certificate at any other protocol stage.

If the uIdP is compromised, the PCD is not compromised by assumption. The uIdP can now send an exchanged certificate to the PICC without being recognized by the user or PCD. However, the eID server applies the correct certificate as the PCD and eID server agree on the service without involving the uIdP. Thus, PICC and eID server apply different certificates and the mutual authentication fails.

We conclude that the MitM attack is prevented as long as either PCD or uIdP are not compromised.

Discussion. All variants hand over some control to the uIdP, which makes it an attractive target for attackers. But remember, any adversary additionally needs control over the eID card to maliciously use the eID functionality. This requires either additionally compromising the PCD or stealing the card. Furthermore, in case the user does not trust the uIdP anymore, he can change the PIN on his own at any time, thereby withdrawing all rights of the uIdP.

Besides that, the preliminaries for security are changed compared to the standard scenario. That is, the security in the standard scenario relies on two factors: the knowledge of the PIN and the possession of the card. This is changed to the possession of the card and the possession of either the iPIN list or the OOBD (e.g. mobile phone), which is an issue concerning physical theft. However, the factor 'knowledge' can be kept by requiring an additional user password when contacting the uIdP or accessing the OOBD. To provide the same level of security against physical theft, the password has to be handled in the same way as the PIN in the standard scenario. This means in particular that after three wrong entries the account is locked and a separate pre-defined substantially longer password is requested to unlock the account again.

4.2   Feasibility

For practical application several feasibility issues have to be discussed. One is the need for a trustworthy system accessible by the user for iPIN generation. This can be resolved by offering a secure system at the office of the authority that distributes the card. Another possibility is bundling the card with a bootable live CD containing a secure environment for iPIN generation. In this case, the user boots once in a while his own system from the live CD to create a new set of iPINs. It might even be reasonable to trust the user's home system with generating the iPINs. In this case, the security increase kicks in when using the card on other systems e.g. in Internet cafés. For the mTAN variants, which in fact do not require precomputations, the secure system could be omitted at all, e.g. by transferring his PIN, ID and phone number by yellow mail to the uIdP.

Concerning the required infrastructure, the need for two uIdP servers for Variants 1 and 5 is in question. Aiming at the highest possible security level, this comes with the registration at two independent service providers. Having one provider operating two independent servers requiring only one registration is more usable, but we have to trust the operator of the uIdP servers not to reconstruct the PIN. In both cases an adversary has to compromise two systems for a successful attack. Remember that 2-party SMPC is possible using Paillier's cryptosystem, but the application to our solution is left to future work.

The encryption with MPC AES takes two seconds [14] for one AES block based on a reference implementation [18]. As s has a length of 128 bit, only one AES block has to be decrypted. Hence, this is not a serious performance issue. Yet, the implementation of the multiparty computation is clearly non standard. The other variants only involve standard methods, as mTAN used for online banking and elliptic curve cryptography provided by several major crypto providers such as Bouncy Castle [19].

In practice, the uIdP service(s) could be provided by governmental authorities as part of the eID card infrastructure which is necessary anyway. It is also possible to have the private economy provide the uIdP services, as done with PKI services. Besides certificate authorities, banks seem to be reasonable candidates. The trusted infrastructure is already available as well as methods such as mTAN. The bank could also provide the system for iPIN generation at its offices.

Except the client application, all components of the standard infrastructure remain unchanged. The client application hides the involvement of the uIdP from the eID server, the service provider, and the PICC. Thus, they adhere to the standard protocols. Long delays might indeed lead to an abortion. Yet, with current high speed Internet connections we do not consider this to be a problem.

5   Conclusion and Future Work

We have shown five PACE variants that increase the security against identity theft. Our approaches allow the secure usage of identity cards, even though no trusted system is available to the user. All variants prevent from PIN compromise in case of a compromised client. Variants 4 and 5 even provide protection against the described MitM attack. The only security requirement is a trustworthy identity provider. It is a valid assumption that, as a part of its core business, the uIdP's security mechanisms are far more sophisticated than the ones on a usual client PC. The necessity of iPIN lists might lead to a decrease of usability. But for a scenario, where the user applies the card for authentication mainly from his home, this seems to be an acceptable effort compared to the increase in security. For the mobile scenario, where the user applies his card en route, the mTAN based approaches allow a secure and convenient usage even from Internet cafés. Thus, we provided possibilities to securely apply smartcard based authentication using insecure devices only, by adding a special infrastructure component to allow one time passwords without requiring any changes in existing protocol implementations on the smartcard or the existing infrastructure.

As mentioned in Section 2.2, using the Paillier cryptosystem Variants 1 and 5 can also be implemented as two party protocols with the advantage, that only one remote server is needed which can still not learn the PIN. But there are several drawbacks: first, the setup is much more complicated, in particular the iPIN generation. Second, MPC is only computationally secure, not being prohibitive but clearly needs further consideration concerning the security parameters to not weaken the overall protocol. Third, there exist no timings and performance estimations. Hence, the Paillier-based solutions are left for future work.

One of the next tasks will be the implementation of the introduced PACE variants based on an existing client implementation such as MONA [20]. The remote execution of the PACE protocol (Variant 4) has additional applications in scenarios where the card is used with resource restricted PCDs, such as a mobile phone as considered in [21,22,23,24]. Variant 4 hands all expensive computations to the remote server and the PCD only forwards messages. Thus, the client software on the PCD is much less involved and easy to implement.

References

1. Federal Office for Information Security. Architektur elektronischer Personalausweis und elektronischer Aufenthaltstitel. Technical Guideline BSI-TR-03127, Version 1.14 (2011),
   https://www.bsi.bund.de/SharedDocs/Downloads/DE/BSI/
   Publikationen/TechnischeRichtlinien/TR03127/BSI-TR-03127_pdf.pdf
2. International Civil Aviation Organization (ICAO). Machine Readable Travel Documents - Part 1: Machine Readable Passport, Specifications for electronically enabled passports with biometric identification capabilities. ICAO Doc 9303 (2006)
3. International Civil Aviation Organization (ICAO). Machine Readable Travel Documents - Part 3: Machine Readable Official Travel Documents, Specifications for electronically enabled official travel documents with biometric identification capabilities. ICAO Doc 9303 (2008)
4. International Civil Aviation Organization (ICAO). Supplemental Access Control for Machine Readable Travel Documents. ISO/IEC JTC1 SC17 WG3/TF5 for ICAO, Version 0.8, Draft of 12.10.2009 (2009)
5. ISO/IEC. ISO/IEC 14443-1: Identification cards - Contactless integrated circuit(s) cards - Proximity cards - Part 1-4. International Standard (2001)
6. Federal Office for Information Security (Bundesamt für Sicherheit in der Informationstechnik). Advanced Security Mechanism for Machine Readable Travel Documents - Extended Access Control (EAC), Password Authenticated Connection Establishment (PACE), and Restricted Identification (RI). Technical Directive (BSI-TR-03110), Version 2.05 (2010),
   https://www.bsi.bund.de/SharedDocs/Downloads/EN/BSI/Publications/
   TechGuidelines/TR03110/TR-03110_v205_pdf.pdf
7. Bender, J., Fischlin, M., Kügler, D.: Security Analysis of the PACE Key-Agreement Protocol. In: Samarati, P., Yung, M., Martinelli, F., Ardagna, C.A. (eds.) ISC 2009. LNCS, vol. 5735, pp. 33–48. Springer, Heidelberg (2009)
8. Ullmann, M., Kügler, D., Neumann, H., Stappert, S., Vögeler, M.: Password Authenticated Key Agreement for Contactless Smart Cards. Communications of the ACM (2008)

9. Dagdelen, Ö., Fischlin, M.: Security Analysis of the Extended Access Control Protocol for Machine Readable Travel Documents. In: Burmester, M., Tsudik, G., Magliveras, S., Ilić, I. (eds.) ISC 2010. LNCS, vol. 6531, pp. 54–68. Springer, Heidelberg (2011)

10. Chaos Computer Club. Practical demonstration of serious security issues concerning swissid and the german electronic identity card, November 01 (2010), http://www.ccc.de/de/updates/2010/sicherheitsprobleme-bei-suisseid-und-epa

11. Boyd, C., Mathuria, A.: Protocols for Authentication and Key Establishment. Springer, Heidelberg (2003)

12. Shamir, A.: How to share a secret. Communications of the ACM 22, 612–613 (1979)

13. Ben-Or, M., Goldwasser, S., Wigderson, A.: Completeness theorems for non-cryptographic fault-tolerant distributed computation. In: Proceedings of the Twentieth Annual ACM Symposium on Theory of Computing, STOC 1988, pp. 1–10. ACM, New York (1988)

14. Damgård, I., Keller, M.: Secure Multiparty AES. In: Sion, R. (ed.) FC 2010. LNCS, vol. 6052, pp. 367–374. Springer, Heidelberg (2010)

15. Cramer, R., Damgård, I., Maurer, U.M.: General Secure Multi-party Computation from any Linear Secret-Sharing Scheme. In: Preneel, B. (ed.) EUROCRYPT 2000. LNCS, vol. 1807, pp. 316–334. Springer, Heidelberg (2000)

16. Cramer, R., Damgård, I.B., Nielsen, J.B.: Multiparty Computation from Threshold Homomorphic Encryption. In: Pfitzmann, B. (ed.) EUROCRYPT 2001. LNCS, vol. 2045, pp. 280–299. Springer, Heidelberg (2001)

17. Paillier, P.: Public-Key Cryptosystems Based on Composite Degree Residuosity Classes. In: Stern, J. (ed.) EUROCRYPT 1999. LNCS, vol. 1592, pp. 223–238. Springer, Heidelberg (1999)

18. VIFF. VIFF, the Virtual Ideal Functionality Framework, January 19 (2012), http://viff.dk/

19. Bouncy Castle. Bouncy Castle Crypto APIs, January 19 (2012), http://www.bouncycastle.org

20. Horsch, M.: Mobile Authentisierung mit dem neuen Personalausweis (MONA). Master thesis, Technische Universität Darmstadt (July 2011)

21. Buchmann, J., Wiesmaier, A., Hühnlein, D., Braun, J., Horsch, M., Kiefer, F., Strenzke, F.: Towards a mobile eCard Client. Tagungsband zum 13. KryptoTag, p. 4 (December 2010)

22. Wiesmaier, A., Horsch, M., Braun, J., Kiefer, F., Hühnlein, D., Strenzke, F., Buchmann, J.: An efficient mobile PACE implementation. In: Proceedings of the 6th ACM Symposium on Information, Computer and Communications Security, ASIACCS 2011, pp. 176–185. ACM, New York (2011)

23. Braun, J., Horsch, M., Wiesmaier, A., Hühnlein, D.: Mobile Authentisierung und Signatur. In: Schartner, P., Taeger, J. (eds.) D-A-CH Security 2011: Bestandsaufnahme, Konzepte, Anwendungen, Perspektiven, pp. 32–43. Syssec Verlag (September 2011)

24. Hühnlein, D., Petrautzki, D., Schmölz, J., Wich, T., Horsch, M., Wieland, T., Eichholz, J., Wiesmaier, A., Braun, J., Feldmann, F., Potzernheim, S., Schwenk, J., Kahlo, C., Kühne, A., Veit, H.: On the design and implementation of the Open eCard App. In: GI SICHERHEIT 2012 Sicherheit - Schutz und Zuverlässigkeit (2012)

Secure Distributed Computation
of the Square Root and Applications

Manuel Liedel

Fakultät für Wirtschaftswissenschaften,
University of Regensburg
`Manuel.Liedel@wiwi.uni-regensburg.de`

Abstract. The square root is an important mathematical primitive whose secure, efficient, distributed computation has so far not been possible. We present a solution to this problem based on Goldschmidt's algorithm. The starting point is computed by linear approximation of the normalized input using carefully chosen coefficients. The whole algorithm is presented in the fixed-point arithmetic framework of Catrina/Saxena for secure computation. Experimental results demonstrate the feasibility of our algorithm and we show applicability by using our protocol as a building block for a secure QR-Decomposition of a rational-valued matrix.

Keywords: Square Root, Fixed-Point Arithmetic, Secure Computation, QR-Decomposition.

1 Introduction

Secure Multi-Party-Computation (SMPC) is an important branch of cryptography which enables a number of distinct entities (or parties) to securely evaluate any function without any of them having to reveal their particular input. The problem was first presented in [16] and (mostly) theoretically solved in ([1], [2], [6], [9]). However due to their high complexity these protocols are unsuitable for all but the most elementary computations.

In 2010 in [3], [4] and [5], Catrina et al. presented a framework for secure computation with fixed-point numbers. It can be used in conjunction with any linear Secret Sharing Scheme with a multiplication protocol such as Shamir's ([14]) and is the most versatile and practical scheme for secure computations with non-integer numbers developed so far. We describe how it can be extended by a protocol that securely computes the square root. It is based on Goldschmidt's algorithm for square root rather than Newton-Raphson iterations mainly because each iteration contains fewer dependent multiplications for virtually identical computation complexity. However, since Goldschmidt's algorithm is not self-correcting, the last iteration is Newton-Raphson to correct for accumulated rounding errors ([13]). The starting point - correct up to 5.4 bits - is computed by linear approximation.

M.D. Ryan, B. Smyth, and G. Wang (Eds.): ISPEC 2012, LNCS 7232, pp. 277–288, 2012.

We view our protocol not so much as a stand-alone application, but rather as a building block for more intricate algorithms. One such application is the secure computation of the QR-Decomposition of matrices, which can be used to securely solve linear systems of equations[1] and is an important building block in many other numerical algorithms such as optimization algorithms and finding zeroes of functions.

In section 2 we will define cryptographic primitives and terminology. In sections 3 and 4 we will describe our algorithm and its implementation. In section 5 we will apply our algorithm to the QR-Decomposition of matrices and in section 6 we will present our experimental results. Lastly in section 7 we will draw a conclusion.

2   Cryptographic Primitives and Definitions

The cryptographic primitive underlying our algorithms is a linear Secret Sharing Scheme (LSSS), such as Shamir's, with a multiplication protocol. Any secret shared number x will be written with braces $[x]$, while any public constant c will be written without braces. To signify a secret-shared vector v we will add an arrow: $[\vec{v}]$. A secret-shared matrix A will be written $[[A]]$. All matrices - unless stated differently - will be assumed to be quadratic with n rows and columns.

On top of the LSSS we employ the fixed-point arithmetic presented in [3],[4] and [5] to facilitate computations with non-integer numbers. We assume that all numbers have total bit-length k of which f are fractional, i.e. are elements of $\mathbb{Q}_{<k,f>}$ (cf. [5]). In order to be able to represent these in a Secret Sharing Scheme all fixed-point numbers are scaled by 2^f before being secret-shared yielding the set $\mathbb{Z}_{<k,f>}$. Any number in $\mathbb{Z}_{<k,f>}$ representing $\frac{x}{2^f}$ will be denoted by $\bar{x}$. Since secret-sharing requires a finite field we will treat $\mathbb{Z}_{<k,f>}$ as if it were part of $\mathbb{Z}/q\mathbb{Z}$ for a very large q (e.g. $\log_2 q \approx l = 1024$, $k = 110$). Note that because of this no wrap-around will occur and thus computations will *not* be affected by the fact that numbers are actually part of the much bigger $\mathbb{Z}/q\mathbb{Z}$. At some points in our protocols (pseudo-)random sharings of zero (PRSZ) need to be computed. We refer the reader to [8] for details.

We aim to develop algorithms secure in the so-called honest-but curious scenario in which parties may not deviate from the protocol. In addition we only require statistical and not information-theoretic security, i.e. the protocols can be simulated such that the distributions of the real and the simulated view are statistically indistinguishable ([5]).

In the analysis of our algorithm we measure computation complexity using the unit of one secure multiplication.

---

[1] This has been done already (cf. [7] and others), but only for fields with characteristic > 0.

3 Mathematical Foundations

Both algorithms - Goldschmidt's as well as Newton-Raphson's - work by iterative approximation, i.e. iteratively improving an initial estimate. They converge quadratically: If a good initial estimate is given, the number of correct digits doubles in every iteration.

3.1 Newton-Raphson Method

The aim of the Newton-Raphson method is to approximate the zero of a continuous, once differentiable function f. Starting with iterate x_0 a new iterate is given by (cf. [15]).

$$x_{k+1} = x_k - \frac{f(x_k)}{f'(x_k)} \tag{1}$$

We assume that the input is always greater than 0 and apply (1) to the function $f(R) = \frac{1}{R^2} - x$, whose zero is given by $\frac{1}{\sqrt{x}}$. The iterating function is thus $R_{j+1} = \frac{1}{2} \cdot R_j \cdot \left(3 - x \cdot R_j^2\right)$. At the end we multiply by x and gain $\sqrt{x}$.

3.2 Goldschmidt's Algorithm

If $x > 0$ is the number whose radicand is desired, Goldschmidt's algorithm ([10]) iteratively computes approximations of $\sqrt{x}$ and $\frac{1}{\sqrt{x}}^2$. The description of the software-friendly version can be seen in Fig. 1. An initial estimate y_0 of $\frac{1}{\sqrt{x}} = \frac{1}{\sqrt{x_0}}$, such that

$$\frac{1}{2} < x_0 \cdot y_0^2 < \frac{3}{2} \tag{2}$$

is assumed to be given. We set $g_0 = x_0 \cdot y_0$ and $h_0 = \frac{y_0}{2}$. The iterates for $\sqrt{x}$ and $\frac{1}{2\sqrt{x}}$ are given by g_i and h_i respectively. Note that the multiplications in lines 3 and 4 are independent.

Algorithm 1: Goldschmidt's algorithm for square root

1 While $|g_i - g_{i-1}| > \varepsilon$
2 $r_{i-1} = \frac{1}{2} - g_{i-1} \cdot h_{i-1}$
3 $g_i = g_{i-1} \cdot (1 + r_{i-1})$
4 $h_i = h_{i-1} \cdot (1 + r_{i-1})$

Fig. 1. Goldschmidt's algorithm for square root with starting point y_0

---

[2] It is actually a variation of the Newton-Raphson method described above; this can be shown using the original definition of the algorithm shown in [13]. Thus the convergence properties of Newton-Raphson iterations also apply here

3.3   Computation of the Starting Value

We compute the starting value by linear approximation:

$$L(x) = \alpha \cdot x + \beta. \tag{3}$$

Since the domain of our linear approximating function is the interval $[\frac{1}{2}, 1[$, we first have to normalize the input x_0 to this range giving x_{normal}. This is done in such a way that the resulting value is actually a very close approximation of $\frac{1}{\sqrt{x_0}}$ (see section 4)! To compute the coefficients α and β the idea (cf. [12][3]) is to minimize the relative error function

$$E(x) = \frac{\alpha \cdot x + \beta - \frac{1}{\sqrt{x}}}{\frac{1}{\sqrt{x}}} \tag{4}$$

Differentiating E gives its maximum at $x_{max} = -\frac{\beta}{3\alpha}$. Evaluating at x_{max} we get

$$M := E(x_{max}) = \frac{\sqrt{3}}{3} \cdot \sqrt{\frac{-\beta}{\alpha}} \cdot \left(\frac{2}{3} \cdot \beta - \frac{\sqrt{3}}{\sqrt{\frac{-\beta}{\alpha}}} \right) \tag{5}$$

Plugging this back into E and solving the system

$$E\left(\frac{1}{2}\right) = -M \tag{6}$$

$$E(1) = -M \tag{7}$$

for α and β gives us the values $\alpha = -0.8099868542$ and $\beta = 1.787727479$ which allow us to compute a linear approximation to $\frac{1}{\sqrt{x}}$ for $\frac{1}{2} \leq x < 1$ with relative error no more than 0.0222593752. This means the result is exact to almost 5.5 bits.

4   Description and Analysis of the Algorithms

We approximate $\frac{1}{\sqrt{x}}$ by first normalizing the input value to the interval $[\frac{1}{2}, 1[$ and then applying function (3) using the constants computed in section 3.3. The final result is computed by Goldschmidt and Newton-Raphson iterations.

4.1   Norm

Protocol Norm from [5] returns values $2^{k-1} \leq [c] < 2^k$ and $[v]$ such that $[x] \cdot [v] = [c]$. If $2^{m-1} \leq [x] < 2^m$ then $[v] = [2^{k-m}]$. We modify Norm so that in addition it also returns $[m]$ as well as $[w] = [2^{\frac{m}{2}}]$, if m is even and $[w] = [2^{\frac{m-1}{2}}]$, if m is odd. $[w]$ is computed by sub-protocol HalfIndex, which works by rearranging

---
[3] The coefficients used in [5] can be computed in a similar way.

Protocol 2: $([c], [v], [m], [w]) \leftarrow$ **NormSQ**$([x], k, f)$

---

1 $\left([x_{k-1}]^{\mathbb{F}_2^8}, \ldots, [x_0]^{\mathbb{F}_2^8}\right) \leftarrow$ BitDec$([x], k, k)$

2 $\left([y_{k-1}]^{\mathbb{F}_2^8}, \ldots, [y_0]^{\mathbb{F}_2^8}\right) \leftarrow$ PreOR $\left([x_{k-1}]^{\mathbb{F}_2^8}, \ldots, [x_0]^{\mathbb{F}_2^8}\right)$

3 foreach $i \in [0, \ldots, k-1]$**do parallel**

4 $[y_i] \leftarrow$ BitF2MtoZQ $\left([y_i]^{\mathbb{F}_2^8}\right)$

5 foreach $i \in [0, \ldots, k-2]$**do**

6 $[z_i] \leftarrow [y_i] - [y_{i+1}]$

7 $[z_{k-1}] \leftarrow [y_{k-1}]$

8 $\overrightarrow{[W]} \leftarrow$ HalfIndex $\left(\overrightarrow{[z]}, k\right)$

9 $[w] \leftarrow \sum_{i=0}^{\frac{k}{2}} 2^i \cdot [W_i]$

10 $[m] \leftarrow \sum_{i=0}^{k-1} 2^i \cdot [z_i]$

11 $[v] \leftarrow \sum_{i=0}^{k-1} 2^{k-i-1} [z_i]$

12 $[c] \leftarrow [x][v]$

13 return$([c], [v], [m], [w])$

Fig. 2. Modified protocol NormSQ

the entries of $\overrightarrow{[z]}$ and can thus be implemented without additional expense. The modified protocol NormSQ is depicted in Fig. 2. Note that - in contrast to Norm - we leave out computation of the sign, since we assume the radicand to be greater than zero.

4.2 Approximation

Correctness: Let us assume that m is even. After evaluating the linear approximating function (3) we get $\alpha \cdot 2^{2k} + \beta \cdot 2^k \cdot [c]$. Multiplication by $[v] = [2^{k-m}]$ then yields $\alpha \cdot 2^{3k-m} + \beta \cdot 2^{2k-m} \cdot [c]$. But since $[c]$ is nothing but the Secret-Sharing of $\frac{x}{2^m} \cdot 2^k = \frac{x \cdot 2^f}{2^m} \cdot 2^k$ this equals[4] $\alpha \cdot 2^{3k-m} + \beta \cdot 2^{3k-m} \cdot \frac{x \cdot 2^f}{2^m}$. After truncating[5] this by $3k - 2f$ Bits, we get

$$2^{2f-m} \cdot \left(\alpha + \beta \cdot \frac{x \cdot 2^f}{2^m}\right), \tag{8}$$

which is a linear approximation to the inverse square root of the normalized value $\frac{x \cdot 2^f}{2^m}$ of $[x]$, scaled by the factor 2^{2f-m}. This means equation (8) equals

$$K \cdot 2^{2f-m} \cdot \frac{1}{\sqrt{\frac{x \cdot 2^f}{2^m}}} = \frac{2^{\frac{3f}{2}}}{2^{\frac{m}{2}}} \cdot K \cdot \frac{1}{\sqrt{x}}, \tag{9}$$

---

[4] For ease of presentation we will drop braces from here.

[5] We neglect rounding errors at this point; for computational reasons the order in Protocol 3 is slightly different.

Protocol 3: $[w] \leftarrow \mathsf{LinAppSQ}([b], k, f)$

---
1 $\alpha \leftarrow \mathsf{fld}_k(-0.8099868542)$
2 $\beta \leftarrow \mathsf{fld}_{2k}(1.787727479)$
3 $([c], [v], [m], [W]) \leftarrow \mathsf{NormSQ}([b], k, f)$
4 $[w] \leftarrow \alpha[c] + \beta$
5 $[m] \leftarrow \mathsf{Mod2}([m], \lceil \log_2 k \rceil)$
6 $[w] \leftarrow [w] \cdot [W] \cdot [v]$
7 $[w] \leftarrow \mathsf{DivConst}\left([w], 2^{\frac{f}{2}}\right)$
8 $[w] \leftarrow \mathsf{TruncPr}\left([w], 3k, 3k - 2f\right)$
9 $[w] \leftarrow (1 - [m]) \cdot [w] \cdot 2^f + \left(\sqrt{2} \cdot 2^f\right) \cdot [m] \cdot [w]$
10 $[w] \leftarrow \mathsf{TruncPr}([w], k, f)$
11 **return** $[w]$

Fig. 3. Linear approximation of $\frac{1}{\sqrt{x}}$

where K is factor very close to 1, determined by the approximation. Multiplication by $[W] = 2^{\frac{m}{2}}$ and division by $2^{\frac{f}{2}}$ thus yields an approximation to $\frac{1}{\sqrt{x}}$ scaled by 2^f which is just what is needed. If m is odd (to distinguish between even and odd we employ the protocol Mod2 from [3]), function NormSQ returns $[W] = 2^{\frac{m-1}{2}}$. Thus multiplication by $[W] \cdot 2^{-\frac{f}{2}}$ only gives $K \cdot \frac{1}{\sqrt{2}} \cdot \frac{1}{\sqrt{x}}$. In this case we thus subsequently multiply the equation by $\sqrt{2}$ and get the desired result.

Complexity: The cost is dominated by the protocol NormSQ and - to a lesser degree - by the protocol $\mathsf{TruncPr}([w], 3k, 3k - 2f)$. All other steps only add a small constant number of multiplications. The complexity of LinAppSQ can be seen in Table 1.

4.3 Goldschmidt's Algorithm

Given an approximation $[y_0]$ that fulfills the requirement (2) all we we have left to do is turn Algorithm 1 into a Secure Multi-Party Algorithm (Fig. 4).

In contrast to Algorithm 1 the number of iterations is fixed at $\theta = \lceil \log_2 \left(\frac{k}{5.4}\right) \rceil$ which ensures accuracy to k bits. We have replaced the last iteration (lines 19-23) by a Newton-Raphson iteration, because - in contrast to a Goldschmidt iteration - it is self-correcting and accumulated errors can be eliminated[6] ([13], except perhaps for the last bit which may be wrong due to the inexactness of probabilistic rounding). Since $[g]$ and $[gh]$ are no longer needed at this point,

---

[6] Due to accumulated rounding errors it is theoretically possible that the result after the last Goldschmidt iteration has less than $\frac{k}{2}$ correct bits, and thus one Newton-Raphson iteration might not suffice to eliminate them. However this did not occur once in our experiments. See section 6.2 for more details.

Protocol 4: $[g] \leftarrow$ **SQR**$([x], k, f)$

1 $\theta \leftarrow \left\lceil \log_2 \left(\frac{k}{5.4} \right) \right\rceil$	16 $[r] \leftarrow \frac{3}{2} \cdot 2^f - [gh]$
2 $[y_0] \leftarrow$ LinAppSQ$([x], k, f)$	17 $[h] \leftarrow [h] \cdot [r]$
3 $[g_0] \leftarrow [y_0] \cdot [x]$	18 $[h] \leftarrow$ TruncPr$([h], k, f)$
4 $[g_0] \leftarrow$ TruncPr$([g_0], k, f)$	19 $[H] \leftarrow (2 \cdot [h])^2$
5 $[h_0] \leftarrow$ DivConst$([g_0], 2)$	20 $[H] \leftarrow [H] \cdot [x]$
6 $[gh] \leftarrow [g_0] \cdot [h_0]$	21 $[H] \leftarrow \left(3 \cdot 2^{2f}\right) - [H]$
7 $[gh] \leftarrow$ TruncPr$([gh], k, f)$	22 $[H] \leftarrow [h] \cdot [H]$
8 **For** $i = 1, \ldots, \theta - 2$	23 $[g] \leftarrow [H] \cdot [x]$
9 $\quad [r] \leftarrow \frac{3}{2} \cdot 2^f - [gh]$	24 $[g] \leftarrow$ DivConst$([g], 2)$
10 $\quad [g] \leftarrow [g] \cdot [r]$	25 $[g] \leftarrow$ TruncPr$([g], 4k, 4f)$
11 $\quad [h] \leftarrow [h] \cdot [r]$	26 **return**$([g])$
12 $\quad [g] \leftarrow$ TruncPr$([g], k, f)$	
13 $\quad [h] \leftarrow$ TruncPr$([h], k, f)$	
14 $\quad [gh] \leftarrow [g] \cdot [h]$	
15 $\quad [gh] \leftarrow$ TruncPr$([gh], k, f)$	

Fig. 4. Goldschmidt's square root algorithm for SMPC

their computation is omitted in the last Goldschmidt iteration (lines 16-18). Note that computation (and truncation) of $[g]$ and $[h]$ in the loop can be parallelized. Complexity again can be read off from Table 1.

4.4 Security

All our protocols consist of building blocks that have been proven secure either perfect or statistical ([3],[4],[5]). No information is revealed in our additional protocols. All counters are public parameters and thus do not leak any information. We conclude our protocols are secure in the honest-but-curious scenario.

5 Application to QR-Decomposition

The QR-Decomposition of a matrix is an important numerical primitive, that can be used to solve linear systems of equations and is part of many numerical algorithms. For any matrix A, the goal is to compute an orthogonal matrix Q and an upper-triangular matrix R such that $Q \cdot R = A$. For details see [11].

5.1 Secure Computation of the QR-Decomposition

We compute the QR-Decomposition by the sequential application of *Householder-Matrices*. Each such Householder-Matrix is responsible for computing one column of R. Their product forms Q. To compute a Householder-Matrix one first needs to compute the *Householder-Vector* $\overrightarrow{v}$ from the respective column $\overrightarrow{v}$. The Householder-Matrix P is then defined by $P = \left(Id - 2 \cdot \frac{\tilde{v}\tilde{v}^t}{\tilde{v}^t\tilde{v}}\right)$. The secure version

Table 1. Complexity of the protocols. The bit-length of k is assumed to be a power of 2, e.g. $k = 2^l$. All vectors are assumed to be of length n and all matrices are assumed to be quadratic with n rows and n columns.

	Secure Multiplications	Rounds	Field
LinAppSqr	10	$\frac{k}{2} + l + 9$	$\mathbb{Z}_q$
	$7k + 1$	7	$\mathbb{Z}_{q_1}$
	$2k^2 - 2k + kl$	$l + 1$	$\mathbb{F}_{2^8}$
SQR	$6\theta + 11$	$\frac{k}{2} + l + 4\theta + 14$	$\mathbb{Z}_q$
	$3f \cdot (\theta + 1) + 7k + 1$	$2\theta + 9$	$\mathbb{Z}_{q_1}$
	$2k^2 - 2k + kl$	$l + 1$	$\mathbb{F}_{2^8}$
House	$6\theta + 15$	$\frac{k}{2} + l + 4\theta + 17$	$\mathbb{Z}_q$
	$8k + 4f + 3\theta f$	$2\theta + 10$	$\mathbb{Z}_{q_1}$
	$2k^2 + kl - 4$	$l + 1$	$\mathbb{F}_{2^8}$
Pre-Mult-House	$2n^2 + 3n + 3\theta + 9$	$l + 3\theta + 13$	$\mathbb{Z}_q$
	$k \cdot (2\theta + 6) + nf \cdot (n + 2) - 1$	12	$\mathbb{Z}_{q_1}$
	$2k^2 + kl$	$2l + 2$	$\mathbb{F}_{2^8}$
QRDecomp	$\mathcal{O}(n^3 + \theta n)$	$(n - 1) \cdot (\frac{k}{2} + 2l + 7\theta + 30)$	$\mathbb{Z}_q$
	$\mathcal{O}(n^3 f + \theta kn)$	$(n - 1) \cdot (2\theta + 22)$	$\mathbb{Z}_{q_1}$
	$\mathcal{O}(+kln + k^2 n)$	$3(n - 1) \cdot (l + 1)$	$\mathbb{F}_{2^8}$

of the algorithm used to compute the Householder-Vector $\overrightarrow{v}$ from a vector $\overrightarrow{v}$ is based on the one described in [11], but differs in that the first component is not normalized to one which saves one division. It can be seen in Fig. 5.

We assume the vector to be non-zero.[7] In steps 1-3 the norm of the input-vector is computed using the routine described in [3] that reduces the cost of the inner-product to one secure multiplication. Protocol SQR is utilized in step 3. In step 5 the sign of $[x_1]$ is computed. Steps 1-3 and 4-5 can be parallelized.

5.2 Multiplication with a Householder-Matrix

If a secret-shared Householder-Vector $\overrightarrow{[v]}$ and a matrix $[[A]]$ are given, the algorithm for Pre-Multiplication of $[[A]]$ by the respective Householder-Matrix is described in Fig. 6. Correctness can be easily verified using the equation in section 5.1. Post-Multiplication is only slightly different.

5.3 Computation of the QR-Decomposition

With these tools it is easy to describe the QR-Decomposition based on Householder-Multiplications (Fig. 7). The matrix R is saved in the upper-triangular part, while the Householder-Vectors - except for the first component,

---

[7] This condition could be checked prior to the computation, but this should rarely be necessary. For $\overrightarrow{[x]} = 0$ the respective Householder-Vector is not defined.

Protocol 5: $\overrightarrow{[v]} \leftarrow \mathsf{House}\left(\overrightarrow{[x]}, n\right)$

---

1 $[\mu] \leftarrow \mathsf{Inner}\left(\overrightarrow{[x]}, \overrightarrow{[x]}\right)$
2 $[\mu] \leftarrow \mathsf{TruncPr}([\mu], k, f)$
3 $[\mu] \leftarrow \mathsf{SQR}([\mu], k, f)$
4 $\overrightarrow{[v]} \leftarrow \overrightarrow{[x]}$
5 $[\sigma] \leftarrow 1 - 2 \cdot \mathsf{LTZ}([x_1], k)$ $\backslash\backslash \sigma = [sign([x_1])]$
6 $[\beta] \leftarrow [x_1] + [\sigma] \cdot [\mu]$
7 $[v_0] \leftarrow [\beta]$
8 return $\overrightarrow{[v]}$

Fig. 5. Computation of a Householder-Vector

Protocol 6: $[[A]] \leftarrow \mathbf{Pre\text{-}Mult\text{-}House}\left([[A]], \overrightarrow{[v]}, m, n\right)$

---

1 $[\tilde{v}] \leftarrow \mathsf{Inner}\left(\overrightarrow{[v]}, \overrightarrow{[v]}\right)$
2 $[\tilde{v}] \leftarrow \mathsf{TruncPr}([\tilde{v}], k, f)$
3 $[\beta] \leftarrow -2 \cdot \mathsf{DivNR}(1, [\tilde{v}], k, f)$
4 $\overrightarrow{[v]} \leftarrow \mathsf{Matrix\text{-}Mult\text{-}Vector}([[A]]^t, \overrightarrow{[v]})$
5 $\overrightarrow{[w]} \leftarrow [\beta] \cdot \overrightarrow{[v]}$
6 $\overrightarrow{[w]} \leftarrow \mathsf{TruncPr}(\overrightarrow{[w]}, 2k, 2f)$
7 $[[V]] \leftarrow \mathsf{Matrix\text{-}Matrix\text{-}Multiply}\left(\overrightarrow{[v]}, \overrightarrow{[w]}^t\right)$
8 $[[V]] \leftarrow \mathsf{TruncPr}([[V]], 3k, 3f)$
9 $[[A]] \leftarrow [[A]] + [[V]]$
10 return $[[A]]$

Fig. 6. Pre-Multiplication of A by the Householder-Matrix determined by the House-holder vector $\overrightarrow{[v]}$

which is stored in an additional vector $[\delta]$ - are stored below the diagonal. If necessary the matrix Q can then be computed by repeated application of protocol 6.

6 Experimental Results

6.1 The Setup

All protocols were tested with an underlying (5,2) Shamir Secret Sharing Scheme. In contrast to "real" Multi-Party-Computations all computations were performed on one machine so network-latency is not included in the computation times. We tested our protocols using our own C++-implementation of the fixed-point arithmetic from [3], [4] and [5]. For computations with very large numbers we employed the GNU MP 5.0.2. The machine was running Linux Mint 10 with an Athlon II Quad-Core CPU @2.6GHz and 4GB RAM.

Protocol 7: $\left([[A]], \overrightarrow{[\delta]}\right) \leftarrow \mathbf{QR}\left([[A]], n\right)$

---

1 For $(j = 1, \ldots, n-1)$

2     $\overrightarrow{[v(j:n)]} \leftarrow \mathsf{House}\left(\overrightarrow{[A(j:n,j)]}, n-j+1\right)$

3     $[[A(j:n,j:n)]] \leftarrow \mathsf{Pre\text{-}Mult\text{-}House}\left([[A(j:n,j:n)]], \overrightarrow{[v(j:n)]}, n-j, n-j\right)$

4   **If** $(j < n)$

5         $[[A(j+1:n,j)]] \leftarrow \overrightarrow{[v(j+1:m)]}$

6         $[\delta_j] \leftarrow [v_1]$

7 return $\left([[A]], \overrightarrow{[\delta]}\right)$

Fig. 7. Secure Computation of the QR-Decomposition of a square matrix using Householder-Matrices

6.2   Computation of the Square Root

In our experiments we computed 8 square roots from numbers $a = 0.008585937$, $b = 0.146234375$, $c = 0.6326875$, $d = 11.19$, $e = 197.04$, $f = 3110.4$, $g = 489,291.776$, $h = 3,701,997.568$. Since in our protocol numbers are normalized first, the size of the number should matter less than how close or how far a number $2^{k-1} \le s < 2^k$, $s \in \{a, b, c, d, e, f, g, h\}$ is to the respective 2^k and 2^{k-1}. Care was taken that the numbers are evenly distributed, i.e. irrespective of size there is one number for each eighth of the interval $[2^{k-1}, 2^k[$. We used fixed-point numbers with 110 bits of which 80 were fractional. The absolute value of the absolute error (the difference between the exact result and the computed result) was always less than 2^{-80}, i.e. exact in our fixed-point setting. Computation times were $\approx 4.89s$ ($\approx 0.98s$ per player) for all numbers. One full Goldschmidt iteration took about 0.57s ($\approx 0.114s$ p.p.) to compute (the abbreviated one took 0.19s ($\approx 0.038s$ p.p.)). What stands out is that the Newton-Raphson iteration at the end at about 0.19s p.p. was more than 60% more expensive! Even though communication did not actually take place, this is remarkable and vindicates our decision to use Goldschmidt iterations for all but one iteration. Figures for average precision gained from testing our algorithm on 1400 random numbers can be seen in Table 2.

Table 2. Exactness for computation of the square root

x	a	b	c	d	e	f	g	h
abs. error	$< 2^{-81}$	$< 2^{-82}$	$< 2^{-81}$	$< 2^{-82}$	$< 2^{-81}$	$< 2^{-80}$	$< 2^{-81}$	$< 2^{-82}$
rel. error	$< 2^{-78}$	$< 2^{-81}$	$< 2^{-81}$	$< 2^{-84}$	$< 2^{-85}$	$< 2^{-86}$	$< 2^{-90}$	$< 2^{-93}$

6.3   Computation of the QR-Decomposition

We tested our secure implementation of the QR-Decomposition on a symmetric positive definite 3×3-matrix A and a random 5×5-matrix B. To quantify the exactness of our results $(\tilde{Q}, \tilde{R})$ we compared them to the exact ones using the Frobenius-Norm:

$$\|A\|_F := \sqrt{\sum_{i=1}^{n}\sum_{j=1}^{n} a_{ij}^2} \tag{10}$$

The results can be found in Table 3. Note that the Frobenius-Norm is just one of a number of (equivalent) matrix-norms. Using another norm could yield slightly smaller or bigger numbers.

Table 3. Experimental results of the QR-Decomposition

Matrix	A	B
$\|\tilde{Q}\|_F - \|Q\|_F$	$4.7 \cdot 10^{-20}$	$\approx 1.6 \cdot 10^{-24}$
$\|\tilde{R}\|_F - \|R\|_F$	$3.2 \cdot 10^{-14}$	$\approx 7 \cdot 10^{-12}$
$\|\tilde{Q} \cdot \tilde{R}\|_F - \|A, B\|_F$	$3.1 \cdot 10^{-14}$	$\approx 7 \cdot 10^{-12}$

7   Conclusion and Further Work

We have for the first time described a practical way to securely compute the square root of a shared value. We have demonstrated the feasibility of our approach experimentally and applied it to the QR-Decomposition of a square-matrix which can be used to securely solve linear systems of equations and can serve as a building block for many other numerical algorithms.

Acknowledgment. The author is funded by "Ausbau der Kompetenzpartnerschaft zum Themenschwerpunkt 'IT-Sicherheit' an den Standorten Passau und Regensburg" which is co-funded by the European Regional Development Fund (EFRE).

References

1. Beaver, D., Micali, S., Rogaway, P.: The round complexity of secure protocols. In: Proceedings of the Twenty-second Annual ACM Symposium on Theory of Computing, STOC 1990, pp. 503–513. ACM, New York (1990)
2. Ben-Or, M., Goldwasser, S., Wigderson, A.: Completeness theorems for non-cryptographic fault-tolerant distributed computation. In: Proceedings of the Twentieth Annual ACM Symposium on Theory of Computing, STOC 1988, pp. 1–10. ACM, New York (1988)

3. Catrina, O., de Hoogh, S.: Improved Primitives for Secure Multiparty Integer Computation. In: Garay, J.A., De Prisco, R. (eds.) SCN 2010. LNCS, vol. 6280, pp. 182–199. Springer, Heidelberg (2010)
4. Catrina, O., de Hoogh, S.: Secure Multiparty Linear Programming Using Fixed-Point Arithmetic. In: Gritzalis, D., Preneel, B., Theoharidou, M. (eds.) ESORICS 2010. LNCS, vol. 6345, pp. 134–150. Springer, Heidelberg (2010)
5. Catrina, O., Saxena, A.: Secure Computation with Fixed-Point Numbers. In: Sion, R. (ed.) FC 2010. LNCS, vol. 6052, pp. 35–50. Springer, Heidelberg (2010)
6. Chaum, D., Crépeau, C., Damgård, I.: Multiparty unconditionally secure protocols. In: Proceedings of the Twentieth Annual ACM Symposium on Theory of Computing, STOC 1988, pp. 11–19. ACM, New York (1988)
7. Cramer, R., Damgård, I.: Secure Distributed Linear Algebra in a Constant Number of Rounds. In: Kilian, J. (ed.) CRYPTO 2001. LNCS, vol. 2139, pp. 119–136. Springer, Heidelberg (2001)
8. Cramer, R., Damgård, I., Ishai, Y.: Share Conversion, Pseudorandom Secret-Sharing and Applications to Secure Computation. In: Kilian, J. (ed.) TCC 2005. LNCS, vol. 3378, pp. 342–362. Springer, Heidelberg (2005)
9. Goldreich, O., Micali, S., Wigderson, A.: How to play any mental game. In: Proceedings of the Nineteenth Annual ACM Symposium on Theory of Computing, STOC 1987, pp. 218–229. ACM, New York (1987)
10. Goldschmidt, R.E.: Applications of division by convergence. Master's thesis, M.I.T. (1964)
11. Golub, G.H., van Loan, C.F.: Matrix Computations, 3rd edn. The Johns Hopkins University Press (1996)
12. Ito, M., Takagi, N., Yajima, S.: Efficient initial approximation for multiplicative division and square root by a multiplication with operand modification. IEEE Transactions on Computers 46, 495–498 (1997)
13. Markstein, P.: Software division and square root using goldschmidt's algorithms. In: 6th Conference on Real Numbers and Computers, pp. 146–157 (2004)
14. Shamir, A.: How to share a secret. Commun. ACM 22, 612–613 (1979)
15. Stoer, J., Bulirsch, R.: Introduction to numerical analysis. Texts in applied mathematics. Springer, Heidelberg (2002)
16. Yao, A.C.: Protocols for secure computations. In: Proceedings of the 23rd Annual Symposium on Foundations of Computer Science, SFCS 1982, pp. 160–164. IEEE Computer Society, Washington, DC, USA (1982)

Prevent Kernel Return-Oriented Programming Attacks Using Hardware Virtualization

Tian Shuo[1,2], He Yeping[1], and Ding Baozeng[1,2]

[1] Institution of Software, Chinese Academy of Sciences
[2] Graduate University of Chinese Academy of Sciences
{tianshuo,baozeng}@nfs.iscas.ac.cn, yeping@iscas.ac.cn

Abstract. ROP attack introduced briefly in this paper is a serious threat to compute systems. Kernel ROP attack is great challenge to existing defenses because attackers have system privilege, little prerequisite to mount attacks, and the disability of existing countermeasures against runtime attacks. A method preventing kernel return-oriented programming attack is proposed, which creates a separated secret address space for control data taking advantage of VMM architecture. The secret address space is implemented as a shadow stack on the same host with the target OS facilitated by hardware virtualization techniques. The experience result shows the performance overhead in our implementation is about 10% and acceptable in practical.

Keywords: Return-Oriented Programming, kernel attacks, virtualization, shadow stack.

1 Introduction

ROP(Return Oriented Programming) was introduced by Shacham in[1] for x86 architecture, and allowed attackers to induce arbitrary behaviors in the target program without injecting new code. It was subsequently extended to various architectures, such as Atmel AVR, SPARC, ARM, Z80, and PowerPC[2-5]. ROP attacks are increasingly used in practical, in particular, ROP-based attacks happened on applications such as Adobe Reader, Adobe Flashplayer, and Quicktime Player. Moreover, ROP has been adapted to kernel exploits, such as ROP-based rootkit for Windows operating system which bypasses kernel integrity protection mechanisms. Finally, tools have been developed enabling the automatic constructing of ROP instruction sequences[6] . ROP attack is a severe threaten to computer system security.

ROP attack is one of code-reuse run-time attacks, which can execute unintended operations using valid code existing in memory. A pioneering runtime attack is stack smashing, which hijacks control flow to injected shell code in stack data region taking advantage of memory vulnerabilities. Instead of injecting code, code-reuse attacks, such as return-to-libc attacks, make use of valid functions in program memory for malicious intention. In further, ROP-based attacks is Turing-complete without injecting shell code or calling function in kernel space. Return-oriented programming

M.D. Ryan, B. Smyth, and G. Wang (Eds.): ISPEC 2012, LNCS 7232, pp. 289–300, 2012.

constructing program operation units by contacting together pieces of binary code terminated with return in memory, which are called gadgets. The basic operation units can be created with ROP include memory operation, algorithm/logic operation, (un)conditional jump, and system call.

There are many challenges for preventing ROP-based kernel attacks in practical. First, there are many runtime attacks countermeasures[7, 8] based on preventing code injection, however, ROP attack is immunity to these defenses because of its code-reuse. Second, probability countermeasures[9-11] for runtime attacks can be bypassed by attackers in case of memory leak[12]. Third, while randomizing the address space layout[13] increased the difficulty of issuing attack, attackers can still have enough code pieces for their malicious program[14, 15]. In the end, There are also ad-hoc ROP attacks defenses on the assumption of ROP gadgets terminated with return instruction[16, 17]. These ad-hoc defenses cannot adapted to kernel ROP attacks because target OS cannot run on the prevention framework[18] or the countermeasures might be bypassed by attackers with high privilege.

In this paper, we introduce ROP attack briefly, and induce the challenges for defeating kernel level ROP attack. The essential element of ROP attack is hijacking control flow by changing control data to arbitrary value during program running. And the challenges for kernel ROP attack countermeasures are shown as following: First, attacks on kernel level with system privilege are able to cheat the host to bypass the defense mechanism; Second, various of implementations of ROP attack are able to bypass the ad-hoc ROP attack countermeasures and nowadays existing runtime attacks prevention methods; Third, the performance overhead introduced by the defense must not be heavy, otherwise, it will be unpractical during system running. Under this circumstance, we propose a mechanism based on shadow stacking, and a secret address space with one-way view for control data is proposed, which is implemented taking advantage of VMM architecture. The secret address space is on the same physical host but different logical address space with the target kernel based on memory paging table maintained by hypervisor. Therefore, the isolation between target kernel and shadow stack enable the mechanism defeating system privilege ROP attacks. On the other hand, the switching between the two address spaces requires hypervisor involvement, and incurs heavy overhead by context switch. We make use of the hardware virtualization features to mitigate the overhead, and evaluation of our experiment result shows that the overhead is about 10%, which makes our kernel ROP attacks defenses practical. Therefore, there are ROP attacks without return and jump-oriented programming attacks proposed recently, our work is mainly for defeating ROP attacks in which gadgets are terminated with return instruction.

This paper is constructed as follow: In section 2, the ROP attack is briefly introduced, and the challenges for kernel ROP attacks defense is proposed; In section 3, we introduce our solution based on VMM, including the briefly overview, implementation and evaluation; Section 4 is the related works and section 5 concludes the paper.

2   Return-Oriented Programming Attack

2.1   ROP Introduction

ROP(Return-Oriented Programming) allows an adversary to introduce arbitrary (Turing-complete) behavior into target program without injecting any malicious code in the program address space, it is based generalization of the original return-into-libc. Instead invokes functions residing in libc for malicious aims, ROP enables attackers constructing desired semantics by contacting gadgets, which are short instruction sequences terminated with return instruction. The address pointer of gadgets is inserted in stack data region as instruction register content. Generally, a program consists of code and data, and there are several kinds of data: some are related to control flow, such as stored registers in stack frame, and regular data like the local variables of a function, as depicted in Fig 1.

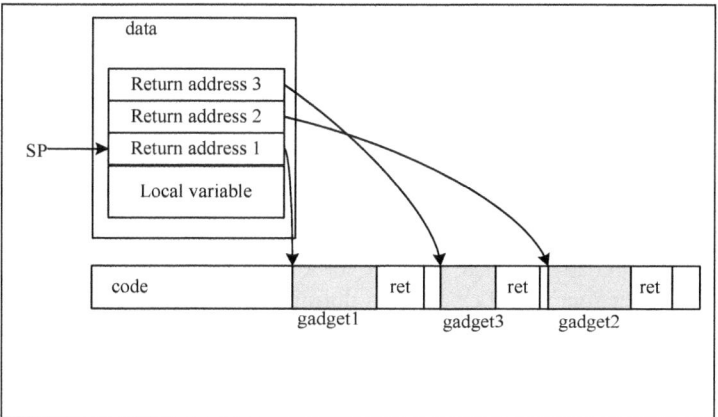

Fig. 1. The abstraction of program and the ROP elements

Mounting ROP attack includes three steps as shown in Fig.1. First, attackers identify gadgets in binary code for basic operations, and a gadget can be instruction sequence start from intermediate part of valid instruction and terminate with byte c3 which is the instruction of ret. As shown in Fig. 1, gadgets are identified by start address in code segments of the program. As described in Fig 2, valid code is wrong interpreted starting at two byte offseting the real start location, forming a garget. The finding of usable gadgets is collateral to our work, and details refer to [32].

Second, the control data is overwritten pointing to and scheduling gadgets for specific operations, as in Fig. 1 the return addresses in stack is modified to be the address of gadgets, it can be realized by buffer overflow or indirect pointer exploitation. Third, attackers must make sure register SP pointing to the first return address in stack to mount the attack, on Intel x86, while function returns, SP will transfer to stack frame of return address automatically, on the other hand, this can be performed by stack-pivot sequence   allowing to change SP to arbitrary value.

bytes   assembler

valid code

| b8 13 00 00 00 | mov $0x13, %eax |
| e9 c3 f8 ff ff | jmp 3aae9 |

gadget

00 00	add %al, (%eax)
00 e9	add %cd, %cl
c3	ret

Fig. 2. Example of gadget in valid code

2.2   Challenges for Defense Kernel ROP Attacks

There are many state-of-the-art approaches against runtime attacks, however, they don't work well for kernel ROP attack because of its new features.

First, ROP attack requires neither malicious code injection nor libc function calling, and bytes in the program's code segments are sufficient for arbitrary execution. The general defense against runtime attacks managing to prevent adversary from injecting shell code, such as W ⊕ X[7] and instruction set randomization[8], makes no sense to ROP attacks defense. On the other hand, existing control flow monitoring measures are too coarse-grained, such as stack shepherding[19] which checking the matching between source and destination during function call, are not able to detect the disorder of control flow on instruction level.

Second, there are various methods for adversary modifies control data to contact gadgets executed sequentially. It's necessary for adversary to change the return address pointing to the start of gadget in code segment, which is typical result of buffer overflow exploiting, and can also be performed using stack-pivot sequence [18]. Therefore, countermeasures against buffer overflow are not enough for ROP attack defense.

Third, for kernel ROP attack, an adversary executes malicious operations with system privilege. It's hard to ensure the integrity of defending mechanism running in kernel, which is likely be cheated by adversary such as rootkit. On the assumption that kernel and applications are not trusted, any measures on the host system may be controlled by attackers. Therefore, traditional in-host defenses on target operating system might be bypassed by kernel attack.

Existing runtime attack countermeasures can't defeat kernel ROP attack because of its powerful new features. Overwriting control data in function stack is an essential step for adversary mounting ROP attacks. And the uniform treatment of all data in program memory makes it hard to guarantee the integrity of control flow transferring caused by function return. Based on the observation, keeping control data integrity during function running can effectively defense ROP attack. On the other hand, kernel ROP attack defense requires the countermeasure have high privilege, and the architecture of VMM provides the opportunity of enforce defense with hypervisor privilege, facilitating keeping control data secret to avoid contaminated by adversary.

3   Our Solution

3.1   ROP Attack Defense Overview

Our solution prevents kernel ROP-based attack transparently to users by keeping control structure secret from adversary. A secret address space is in parallel to the system address space of target kernel, and can't be observed from running operating system and applications. The data stack in the secret address space is used for containing control data, and is called secret stack. Taking advantage of compiler interface, operations of keeping control data integrity can be inserted into function prologue and epilogue like stack smashing countermeasures [7]. As shown in Figure 3, when CALL instruction executed, function prologue will store the return address of callee function, which is the address next to CALL instruction, into the secret stack instead of program stack. On the other hand, when RET instruction executed, function epilogue pops out the top value of secret stack, which will change the program counter value and program execution control will transfer to the address.

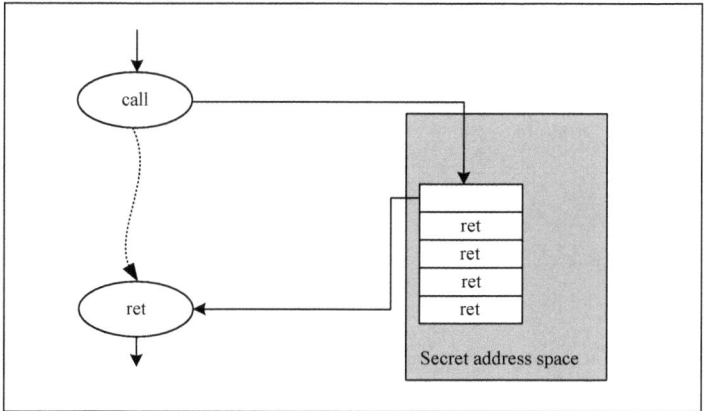

Fig. 3. Overview of ROP attack defense framework

The overall design of kernel ROP attacks defense framework is shown as Figure 4. The target kernel is a guest OS running on VMM(Virtual Machine Monitor). Two address spaces in parallel is provided in the same VM domain by creating two page tables, one for system kernel virtual memory, and another for secret address space. A page table is required for mapping virtual address space to physical address; therefore, when an instruction is executed the current page table is used by the hardware to perform address translation. Page based virtual memory is generated by creating page table that map virtual address to physical address. OS creates separated page table for each process so that its own virtual memory address space and the necessary isolation can be achieved. A new page table for secret virtual address space is created after kernel booting, and a continual physical address is allocated In the system virtual memory, there is no mapping between page table entries and the physical memory for secret address space. Therefore, there is one-way view between the two virtual address spaces.

Generally, kernel is mapped into fixed address range, which is called system address space. We denote the code and data in this range as kernel code and kernel data.

We assume that the pages containing kernel data can be write protected, while the data regions will have all access rights. In generally, the dynamically LKM code should be maintained in the kernel data region. In secret address space, all kernel code and data are set to non-executable and it avoids malicious modification of the secret page table by target kernel.

The entry and exit gates are the only regions that mapped into both address spaces, and are used to store and load control data while OS running. As mentioned early, the entry and exit gates are used for switching between system and secret virtual address sapce. They are written-protected by the hypervisor so that their contents could not be modified by any code in the system address space. The main function of entry and exit gates are switching address spaces by modify the CR3 value.

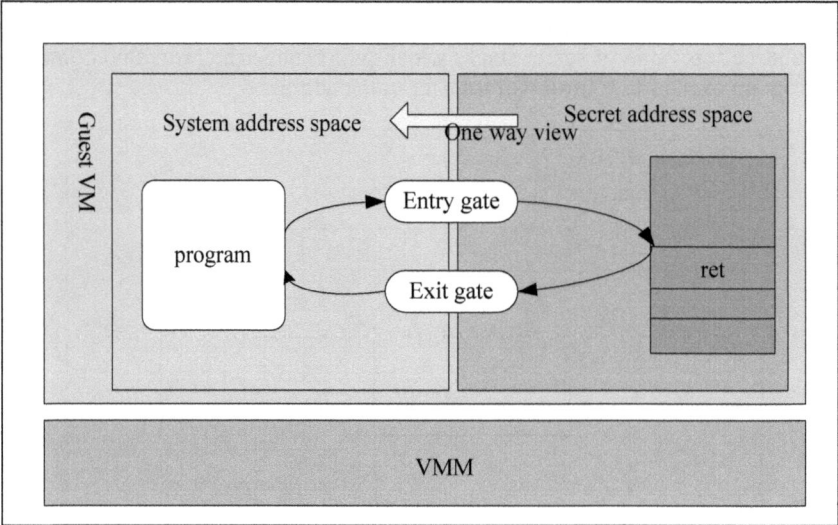

Fig. 4. Overall design of kernel ROP attacks defense framework

3.2   Hardware Virtualization

The switching between kernel system and secret address spaces needs to modify the CR3 register directly. However, changing the value of CR3 is a privileged operation which will cause trapping into the hypervisor. All accesses to guest CR3 register in the guest OS cause VMExit, which switching guest to hypervisor. The context switching brings heavy performance overhead and makes the defense mechanism unpractical. For this reason, hardware virtualization feature available in Intel VT[20] is utilized for the practical of our method.

The current virtual address space is identified by CR3 register, which contains the physical address of the root of current page table data structure, and in two-level paging mechanism the root of page table structure is called the page directory. While switching between processes, the CR3 register is updated by the kernel to appropriated page table structures. Any process running on privilege of kernel-level can update CR3 register to switch process context. In VMM architecture, the page table in guest OS is used for translating virtual address to virtual physical addresses, which share real physical address with various VMs on the same VMM. Shadow page tables are used to map guest virtual to real physical memory and there are different VMM implementations to maintain consistency among the guest page tables and shadow page tables.

With Intel VT, VMExit will not be triggered if the CR3 is updated to a page table root addresses in a list (CR3_TARGET_LIST) maintained by hypervisor. In order to avoid hypervisor intervention while directly modifying CR3 register to switch address spaces between guest OS and secret virtual space, the page table directories of both the address spaces are added into CR3_TARGET_LIST, as shown in Figure 5. The secret address space has only shadow page table without virtual page table in guest OS, and whose root is pointed by page table directory SEC_SHADOW. The hypervisor also maintain the page table directory of shadow page tables of process running on guest OS, denoted by SHADOW. Therefore, the switching between guest OS and secret address spaces just need to directly modify CR3 register with SHADOW or SEC_SHADOW, which is transparent to the normal process in guest OS .

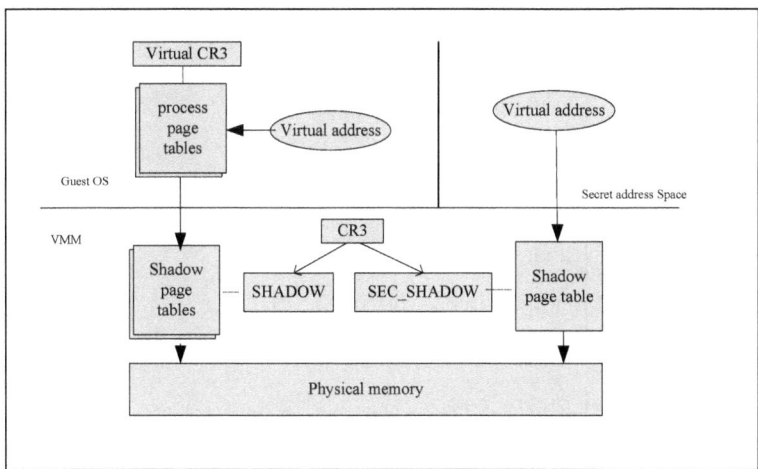

Fig. 5. Virtual memory manged by page table utilizing hardware virtualization

3.3 Implementation and Evaluation

In our prototype, we use Xen as the hypervisor and HVM domU of Ubuntu as our target. A secret address space is created in the same domU, and a modification for libc changes all function call and return operations, keeping return addresses are stored into and loaded from stack in the secret space.

First, we generate a separate hypervisor-protected secret address space by creating a separate page table sec_pg_dir. A separate section allocation description file is added in the guest kernel, and the kernel linker script files are modified to control the memory layout of output object file. A function sec_space_nomapping_init(start, end) is defined to set the kernel page table entries of the virtual address from start to end of secret space to be invalid. If the guest OS tries to access secrete address space in kernel mode, it will be trapped into hypervisor.

Then, we create entry gates and exit gates in guest source tree and the control data is migrated to secret address using compiler interface. As shown in Table1, the execution of call instruction will store the address of next instruction in program code into the stack frame, and then the program counter is pointing to the callee and callee stack is initialized beginning with push %ebp. After modified, the operation of function call is shown as the second column of Table1, entry gate swithing address space by assigning CR3 with sec_pg_dir, and the return address is stored in the data stack of in secret virtual memory. Then, exit_gate switches back into the guest OS and continue the callee execution. The modified operation for return instruction execution is similar to call as shown in Table1.

Table 1. The modified code with *entry_gate* and *exit_gate* for function call and return

original code	modified code

```call```
 	
```push %ebp```
	```;entry_gate:```
	
	```current_pg_dir = read_cr3```
	
	```push %eax```
	
	```mov %eax, sec_pg_dir```
	
	```mov %cr3, %eax```
	
	```call```
	
	```;exit_gate:```
	
	```mov %eax, current_pg_dir```
	
	```mov %cr3, %eax```
	
	```push %ebp```

```leave```
 	
```ret```
	```Leave```
	
	```;entry_gate:```
	
	```current_pg_dir = read_cr3```
	
	```push %eax```
	
	```mov %eax, sec_pg_dir```
	
	```mov %cr3, %eax```
	
	```ret```
	
	```;exit_gate:```
	
	```mov %eax, current_pg_dir```
	
	```mov %cr3, %eax```

Since the CR3 register cannot be directly loaded with data, the value of sec_pg_dir first needs to be moved to a general purpose register, eax. In order to prvent the execution from diverting to somewhere else due to interrupt, we use CLI instruction to disable interrupt. Moreover, we also put the variable current_pg_dir and sec_pg_dir into the CR3_TAGET_LIST maintained by hypervisor just like SIM[21], therefore, it could avoid the hypervisor intervention when switching the address spaces. This would greatly improve the performance.

In experiment, we worked on libc linked to the target operating system instead of the whole kernel. Code of libc is most likely used for adversary constructing gadget according to Chen et al[17]. Although there might be ROP attacks without gadgets in libc, the experiment shows the overhead bring by in-host secret address space and the practical of our defense to certain degree. We make use of UnixBench[22] measure the performance reduction brought by the countermeasure. The result shown in Fig 6 is performance ration of with countermeasure and original guest system. The overhead is around 10%, and is acceptable.

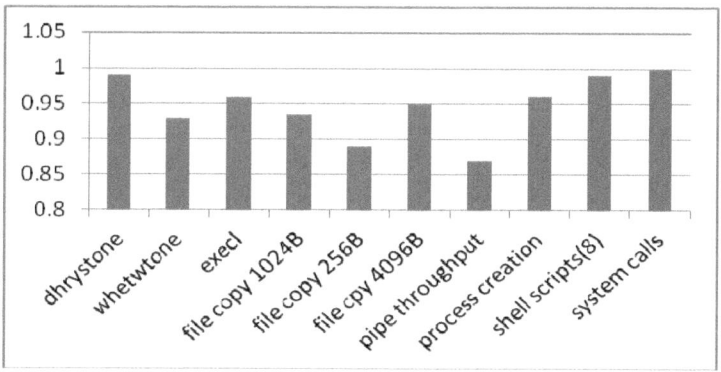

Fig. 6. Result of performance measured by UnixBench

4   Related Work

There are many approaches trying to prevent runtime attacks from malicious behavior. Operating system and processor manufactures enable memory pages to set attribute W ⊕ X(Writable XOR Executable)[7], current Windows versions enabled it by default[23]. However, W ⊕ X unable to against attacks without code injection, such as return-to-libc, and ROP attacks. Probability countermeasures are proposed against runtime attacks, and mainly contain three classes. The first ones, such as StackGuard[9, 10]and its enforcement ProPolice[24], based on canary protect return address from stack smashing. The second ones utilize obfuscation technique, randomizing the address space layout[13] or program instructions[8] increasing the difficulty of issue attacks. The third class attempts to protect against attacks by reorganizing the layout of stack memory[24, 25]. However, all the countermeasures depend on the assumption of keep memory secret[12], which is broken in case of memory over-read vulnerability coexist with buffer overflow in program.

Approaches defeating ROP attacks are proposed recent years, however, none of them aims to prevent kernel-level ROP attacks. ROP attack defenses based on new hardware features are applied to embedded microprocessor system[26], and Stack-Ghost[27] is used on SPARC architecture, both of witch can hardly apply to general system. Shepherding[19] and ROPdefender[18] monitor program control transfer while running taking advantage of dynamic binary instrumentation, however, they can't be extend to kernel running monitoring. Return instruction and gadget are essential elements for ROP, G-free [28] eliminates the condition of constructing gadgets by unaligned branch instructions deletion, and Jinku Li et al[16] rewrite the binary code of Linux kernel for a system without both intended and unintended return instructions. There are also ROP defense methods based on measure of return frequency [17, 29], which can be bypassed by executing longer gadgets sequence.

CFI(Control Flow Integrity)[30] principle is the basic for verifying that a program running according to the intention of programmer. CFI is enforced on VMM architecture in order to prevent kernel rootkits which hijack control flow of guest operating system [31], it monitor the kernel state and checking the target of control transferring based on the memory and registers values, so it can't defense against kernel ROP attacks but detecting the attacks happened yet on the guest os. VMM architecture facilitate the implementation of guest OS code integrity using shadow memory [32], and a secret address space secret for adversary on kernel[21]. Our solution make use of the idea of shadow stack, such as RAD[33], Stack Shield[34], and further, in order to avoid contaminated by adversary on kernel level, we constructed secret address space for control data provided by feature of VMM.

5   Conclusion

ROP attack is considered a major threaten in practical computing environment. ROP attack can be divided into three parts, first, attackers identify gadgets in binary code representing basic operations, second, the control data is overwritten pointing to and scheduling gadgets for specific operations, third, attackers must make sure register SP pointing to the first return address in stack to mount the attack. The challenges for preventing kernel ROP attacks are the system privilege of attacks, little prerequisite to mount attacks, and the disability of exiting runtime attack countermeasures. We propose a method preventing kernel ROP attack taking advantage of hardware virtualization, disable the attack by enforce control data integrity which is in a secret address space. We implemented our solution on libc measuring overhead caused by separated secret address space and virtual space switching. The result of experience shows that the performance loss is about 10%, which is acceptable in practical.

Acknowledgement. We thank the anonymous reviewers for comments that helped to improve the paper. This work was supported by the National Science Foundation of China under Grant No.90818012, the National Science and Technology Major Projcet No.2010ZX01036-001-002 and the Knowledge Innovation Key Directional Program of Chinese Academy of Sciences under Grant No.KGCX2-YW-125.

References

1. Shacham, H.: The geometry of innocent flesh on the bone: return-into-libc without function calls (on the x86). In: Proceedings of the 14th ACM Conference on Computer and Communications Security, pp. 552–561 (2007)
2. Buchanan, E., Roemer, R., Shacham, H., Savage, S.: When good instructions go bad: generalizing return-oriented programming to RISC. In: Proceedings of the 15th ACM Conference on Computer and Communications Security, pp. 27–38 (2008)
3. Checkoway, S., A. J. F., Kantor, B., Halderman, J.A., Felten, E.W., Schacham, H.: Can DREs provide long-lasing security? The case of return-oriented programming and the AVC Advantage. USENIX/ACCURATE/IVAoSS (2009)
4. Kornau, T.: Return oriented programming for the ARM achitecture (2010)
5. Lidner, F.: Developments in Cisco IOS forensics (2009)
6. Dullien, T., Kornau, T., Weinmann, R.-P.: A framework for automated architecture-independent gadget search. In: Proceedings of the 4th USENIX Conference on Offensive Technologies, p. 1 (2010)
7. PaXTeam. Documentation for the PaX project
8. Barrantes, E.G., Ackley, D.H., Palmer, T.S., Stefanovic, D., Zovi, D.D.: Randomized instruction set emulation to disrupt binary code injection attacks. In: Proceedings of the 10th ACM Conference on Computer and Communications Security, pp. 281–289 (2003)
9. Cowan, C., Pu, C., Maier, D., Hintony, H., Walpole, J., Bakke, P., Beattie, S., Grier, A., Wagle, P., Zhang, Q.: StackGuard: automatic adaptive detection and prevention of buffer-overflow attacks. In: Proceedings of the 7th Conference on USENIX Security Symposium, vol. 7, pp. 63–78 (1998)
10. Madan, B., Phoha, S., Trivedi, K.: StackOFFence: a technique for defending against buffer overflow attacks. In: Information Technology: Coding and Computing, ITCC 2005, pp. 656–661 (2005)
11. Tian Shuo, H.Y.: Ding Liping: SSGuard: a Nonlinear-enhanced Countermeasure against Stack-smashing Attacks. In: Proceedings of ICIMT 2010, vol. 1, pp. 427–433 (2010)
12. Strackx, R., Younan, Y., Philippaerts, P., Piessens, F., Lachmund, S., Walter, T.: Breaking the memory secrecy assumption. In: Proceedings of the Second European Workshop on System Security, pp. 1–8 (2009)
13. Shacham, H., Page, M., Pfaff, B., Goh, E.-J., Modadugu, N., Boneh, D.: On the effectiveness of address-space randomization. In: Proceedings of the 11th ACM Conference on Computer and communications Security, pp. 298–307 (2004)
14. Roglia, G.F., Martignoni, L., Paleari, R., Bruschi, D.: Surgically returning to randomized lib (c). In: Computer Security Applications Conference, pp. 60–69 (2009)
15. Le, L.: Payload already inside: data re-use for ROP exploits. Black Hat (2010)
16. Li, J., Wang, Z., Jiang, X., Grace, M., Bahram, S.: Defeating return-oriented rootkits with "Return-Less" kernels. In: Proceedings of the 5th European Conference on Computer systems, pp. 195–208 (2010)
17. Chen, P., Xiao, H., Shen, X., Yin, X., Mao, B., Xie, L.: DROP: Detecting Return-Oriented Programming Malicious Code. In: Prakash, A., Sen Gupta, I. (eds.) ICISS 2009. LNCS, vol. 5905, pp. 163–177. Springer, Heidelberg (2009)
18. Davi, L., Sadeghi, A.-R., Winandy, M.: ROPdefender: a detection tool to defend against return-oriented programming attacks. In: Proceedings of the 6th ACM Symposium on Information, Computer and Communications Security, pp. 40–51 (2011)
19. Vladimir Kiriansky, D.B.: Saman Amarasinghe Secure Execution via Program Shepherding. In: 11th USENIX Security Symposium, pp. 191–206 (2002)

20. Intel. IA-32 Intel Architecture Software Developer's Mannual Volume 3B: System Programming Guide, Part 1 (January 2006)
21. Sharif, M.I., Lee, W., Cui, W., Lanzi, A.: Secure in-VM monitoring using hardware virtualization. In: Proceedings of the 16th ACM Conference on Computer and Communications Security, pp. 477–487 (2009)
22. http://www.Tux.org
23. Microsoft. Data Execution Prevention (2006)
24. Eto, H., Yoda, K.: Propolice: Improved stack-smashing attack detection. Transactions of Information Processing Society of Japan 43(12), 4034–4041 (2002)
25. Younan, Y., Pozza, D., Piessens, F., Joosen, W.: Extended protection against stack smashing attacks without performance loss. In: 22nd Annual Computer Security Applications Conference, ACSAC 2006, pp. 429–438 (2006)
26. Francillon, A., Perito, D., Castelluccia, C.: Defending embedded systems against control flow attacks. In: Proceedings of the First ACM Workshop on Secure Execution of Untrusted Code, pp. 19–26 (2009)
27. Frantzen, M., Shuey, M.: StackGhost: Hardware facilitated stack protection. In: SSYM 2001: Proceedings of the 10th Conference on USENIX Security Symposium, pp. 55–66 (2001)
28. Onarlioglu, K., Bilge, L., Lanzi, A., Balzarotti, D., Kirda, E.: G-Free: defeating return-oriented programming through gadget-less binaries. In: Proceedings of the 26th Annual Computer Security Applications Conference, pp. 49–58 (2010)
29. Davi, L., Sadeghi, A.-R., Winandy, M.: Dynamic integrity measurement and attestation: towards defense against return-oriented programming attacks. In: Proceedings of the 2009 ACM Workshop on Scalable Trusted Computing, pp. 49–54 (2009)
30. Abadi, M., Erlingsson, M.B., Ligatti, J.: Control-flow integrity principles, implementations, and applications. ACM Trans. Inf. Syst. Secur. 13(1), 1–40 (2009)
31. Nick, L., Petroni, J., Hicks, M.: Automated detection of persistent kernel control-flow attacks. In: Proceedings of the 14th ACM Conference on Computer and Communications Security, pp. 103–115 (2007)
32. Riley, R., Jiang, X., Xu, D.: Guest-transparent prevention of kernel rootkits with vmm-based memory shadowing (2008)
33. Tzi-Cker Chiueh, F.-H.H.: RAD: a compile-time solution to buffer overflow attacks. icdcs. In: 21st IEEE International Conference on Distributed Computing Systems (ICDCS 2001), pp. 409–417 (2001)
34. Vendicator. Stack Shield: A "stack smashing" technique protection tool for Linux

Structure-Based RSA Fault Attacks

Benjamin Michéle, Juliane Krämer, and Jean-Pierre Seifert

Security in Telecommunications
Technische Universität Berlin and Telekom Innovation Laboratories
{ben,juliane,jpseifert}@sec.t-labs.tu-berlin.de

Abstract. Fault attacks against cryptographic schemes as used in tamper-resistant devices have led to a vibrant research activity in the past. This area was recently augmented by the discovery of attacks even on the public key parts of asymmetric cryptographic schemes like RSA, DSA, and ECC. While being very powerful in principle, all existing attacks until now required very sophisticated hardware attacks to mount them practically – thus excluding them from being a critical break-once-run-everywhere attack.

In contrast, this paper develops a purely software-based fault attack against the RSA verification process. This novel attack consists in completely replacing the modulus by attacking the structures managing the public key material. This approach contrasts strongly with known attacks which merely change some bits of the original modulus by introducing hardware faults. It is important to emphasize that the attack described in this paper poses a real threat: we demonstrate the practicality of our new public key attack against the RSA-based verification process of a highly protected and widely deployed conditional access device – a set-top box from Microsoft used by many IPTV providers. Furthermore, we successfully applied our attack method against a 3G access point, leading to root access.

Keywords: Fault attacks, RSA, signature verification, public key cryptography.

1 Introduction

Throughout the last years there has been a great amount of research on hardware-based fault attacks against cryptographic schemes [2,21,27]. The threat that these attacks pose to cryptographic protocols has been adequately demonstrated. In our work we develop a completely new fault attack against the verification process of asymmetric signature schemes, which we call a *structure-based* fault attack. The objective of our attack is the forgery of signatures for arbitrary files. Contrary to other atacks, e.g., [2,21], we do not want to reveal the secret key. Although our novel attack augments the possibilities of hardware-based fault attacks, it is particularly useful for enabling purely software-based fault attacks. Our attack can also be seen as an extension of non-control-data attacks [6] to cryptographic protocols.

M.D. Ryan, B. Smyth, and G. Wang (Eds.): ISPEC 2012, LNCS 7232, pp. 301–318, 2012.
© Springer-Verlag Berlin Heidelberg 2012

The general goal of our approach is to attack the verification process of asymmetric signature schemes such as RSA so that signatures for arbitrary files can be forged. Instead of introducing faults to the verification key itself, we introduce faults to the structures managing the key. We use this approach to launch a purely software-based break-once-run-everywhere attack against a highly secure, widely deployed consumer electronics device: the set-top box (STB) used for Microsoft's IPTV system Mediaroom [17]. Additionally, we present a second successful structure-based attack we conducted against a highly security-sensitive device, a 3G residential femtocell from Ubiquisys [28]. Both of the attacked systems[1] use the RSA signature scheme.

Since it is not possible to factorize RSA moduli with currently used bit lengths [13], many attacks rely on modifying some bits of the modulus by inducing hardware faults [1,20,27]. These attacks are probabilistic and involve the danger of destroying the attacked device as well. The attack presented in this paper avoids directly factorizing the modulus or a hardware-based modified version of it, i.e., the memory area containing the original key remains unmodified. Instead, the entire RSA modulus is replaced by attacking the structures managing it. This results in a different memory region being used as the modulus. Thus, our novel attack is another proof that the public key parts have to be protected, a demand that has been heard for several years [3,7].

The main contributions of this paper are:

- **Development of a New Fault Attack:** We introduce a novel attack against signature verification processes, which we call a structure-based fault attack. The main advantage of our attack is that we only modify the (dynamic) structures managing the public key material, but not the key material itself. For RSA, this means that the memory region containing the original modulus remains unmodified.
- **A Compromise of Two Highly Security-Sensitive Devices:** We prove the practical applicability of our attack by compromising the security of two highly tamper-resistant, security-sensitive devices: an STB by Microsoft and a 3G access point.

The paper is organized as follows: In Section 2 we provide necessary background information. The theory behind our structure-based fault attack is explained in Section 3. Then we describe a proof-of-concept practical attack in Section 4, i.e., the application of our attack against a real system and key. In Section 5 we explain related attacks like our successful attack against a 3G access point. Finally, we close with our conclusions in Section 6.

2   Background

This section provides some background information necessary for understanding the novel attack. First, we explain the de facto standard method for establishing file integrity and authenticity by using digital signature schemes as defined in PKCS#1. Then we evaluate existing attacks against these schemes.

---

[1] Both vendors were notified of the vulnerabilities in their products.

2.1 Protection of Integrity and Authenticity

Cryptographic Hash Function – SHA-1. A cryptographic hash function is an algorithm that turns a possibly variable-sized amount of data into a fixed-size output, the *hash value*. The SHA-1 [22] hash function produces 160-bit values. Though there is distinct data being mapped to the same hash value due to the domain being considerably larger than the image set, the design of good hash functions ensures three characteristics: It must not be possible to calculate data having a certain hash value (*preimage resistance*), to calculate data distinct to given data, having the same hash value as these (*second preimage resistance*), and to find two inputs that hash to the same output (*collision resistance*).

Asymmetric Cryptography with RSA. RSA is an asymmetric cryptographic algorithm publicly described for the first time in 1978 [26]. Given sufficiently large keys and the use of up-to-date implementations, RSA is believed to be secure.

An RSA signature scheme consists of a modulus $N = pq$, where p and q are two distinct large primes of the same bit size, and two integers $e, d < N$ such that $ed \equiv 1 \mod \varphi(N)$, where $\varphi(N)$ is Euler's totient function. The public key consists of the pair (N, e), whereas $(p, q, d, \varphi(N))$ form the secret key. If an attacker learns any part of the secret key, he can determine the other parts, too.

Messages m satisfying $0 < m < N$ are signed with $s = m^d \mod N$. The message-signature pair (m, s) is verified if $m = s^e \mod N$. Recovering the secret key is equivalent to factorizing N, which is computationally infeasible for the size of primes used: Nowadays, p and q consist of at least 1024 bits each, thus N is a 2048-bit semiprime.

Digital Signature Scheme Standard PKCS#1. The de facto standard digital signature scheme used to protect the integrity and authenticity of files is defined in PKCS#1 [11]. From the two presented signature schemes with appendix, we will focus on RSASSA-PKCS1-v1_5.

The first step in creating a digital signature for a file is to calculate the file's cryptographic hash value. This hash value is then embedded in an ASN.1 [10] structure indicating the used hash function, e.g., SHA-1. This string is padded to the bit length used by the RSA algorithm, e.g., 2048 bits, to form the encoded message. The standard requires a minimum length of 8 octets for the padding string, resulting in a minimum length of 368 bits for the encoded message. Table 1 illustrates an exemplary PKCS#1 encoded message. Finally, the RSA signature primitive is applied to the encoded message to generate the signature.

The recipient can check the authenticity of the file by verifying its signature. First, the verification primitive is applied to the signature and the RSA public key. The resulting string has to be carefully checked, i.e., it must conform to the previously explained format of an encoded message including padding, etc. Failure to do so can create attack vectors that may lead to forged signatures and compromised systems [5,19]. Then, the ASN.1 structure has to be analyzed to identify the hash function that was used to create the hash value in the signature. Finally, this hash value has to be compared against a freshly calculated hash of the file. If the encoding is valid and the hash values are identical, the recipient will treat the file as authentic.

Table 1. 2048-bit PKCS#1 encoded message using the SHA-1 hash function

221 bytes			15 bytes	20 bytes
prefix	padding	postfix	ASN.1 object identifier for SHA-1	SHA-1 hash
00 01	FF .. FF	00	30 21 30 09 06 05 2B 0E 03 02 1A 05 00 04 14	22 59 .. 11

2.2 Related Work

This section summarizes why pure mathematical attack strategies do not work against SHA-1 and RSA, and explains attacks based on various fault injections.

Breaking SHA-1 and RSA. Attacking a hash function in the PKCS#1 setting means conducting a *second preimage attack*. Having a 160-bit output, SHA-1 is resistant to brute force second preimage attacks [24]. Thus, SHA-1 is *weak collision resistant*, which is crucial for any system relying on digital signatures. In 2005, it was shown that SHA-1 is not *strong collision resistant* [31]. Due to these results, Federal US agencies had to stop relying on digital signatures using SHA-1 by the end of 2010 [23]. Yet, the lack of strong collision resistance cannot be used to forge signatures in our case.

Attacking RSA effectively means factorizing the public modulus. Except for quantum computers, there is no publicly known algorithm to date that can factorize an n-bit RSA modulus in polynomial time, i.e., in time $\mathcal{O}\left(n^k\right)$ for some natural constant k. The most efficient algorithm known is the *general number field sieve* whose expected running time is subexponential in the modulus' bit length [15]. This was used for the factorization of the largest RSA modulus that has been factorized publicly so far [13], a 768-bit integer. However, this does not pose any threat to 2048-bit moduli to date.

Xbox TEA Vulnerability. In 2003, a vulnerability [8] was reported on Microsoft's Xbox that allows the execution of unauthorized code. Microsoft uses a two-stage boot loader: Stage one, the secret boot ROM, is hardwired in silicon whereas stage two, the Flash Boot Loader (FBL), is stored in FLASH ROM along with a public key used to verify the authenticity of the kernel. The stage one boot loader checks the integrity of the FBL and, if successful, executes its code. The integrity is verified by calculating a hash value of the FBL and public key using the Tiny Encryption Algorithm (TEA) and comparing it to a hash stored in the secret boot ROM.

TEA, however, has a related-key weakness [12] that allows an attacker to generate hash collisions by complementing the most significant bit of adjacent double words in the FBL. Whereas in [8] this was exploited to change jump instructions, the same weakness was exploited in [9] to modify the modulus stored in the FBL in a way that the resulting modulus was prime *and* the hash would not change. This faulty modulus allowed the creation of a new private key, which could be used to sign modified kernel images accepted by the FBL.

Hardware-Based Fault Attacks. A hardware-based fault attack against the RSA verification process was presented in 2005 [27] and generalized one year later [20]. The attack consists of forcing the attacked cryptographic device to use a slightly modified modulus instead of the original one by inducing hardware faults. Since the factorization of the altered modulus is known, the attacker can calculate a new private key so that the device accepts the signature of any arbitrary message signed with this new key. Besides the fact that this attack involves the danger of destroying the attacked device, it is probabilistic, i.e., the modulus cannot be modified deterministically. It also requires complex hardware to be conducted. In contrast, our attack is completely software-based and thus does not suffer from these limitations.

Non-Control-Data Attacks. The authors of [6] state that most memory corruption attacks are control-data attacks. This means that these attacks alter the program flow by corrupting data that is loaded to the processor's program counter, such as return addresses and function pointers. This allows an attacker to execute previously injected code or existing library code in a malicious way.

On the other hand, there are non-control-data attacks [6] that use memory corruption attacks to manipulate the data the program is working with. The authors identified the following types of data to be critical for software security: configuration data, user input, user identity data, and decision-making data. They demonstrate that by manipulating this data, security compromises equivalent to control-data attacks are possible in many real-world software applications.

Regarding non-control-data attacks, we extend the list of security critical data types to cryptographic key data used for signature verification. However, we do not introduce faults to the data itself, but rather to the structures managing this data such as pointers.

3   Structure-Based Fault Attack

In this section we describe our novel attack against signature verification processes that we call a *structure-based* fault attack. It forces the verification process to use a faulty public key instead of the original key. Knowledge of this faulty public key is exploited to calculate a corresponding private key. This key can then be used to sign arbitrary files that will be accepted by the verification process. The impact on vulnerable systems can therefore be seen as comparable to a universal forgery of digital signatures.

The novel idea of our attack is to introduce faults into the structures managing the data needed for the public key operations. This attack scheme can be used in different scenarios to attack a variety of systems. Depending on the system being attacked, different privileges are required to carry out the attack. For example, the ability to write to certain memory addresses is required for some scenarios. Section 3.1 lists possible ways to corrupt a program's memory, which can be seen as memory fault injections [6]. Section 3.2 explains how the attack can be applied to RSA-based signatures. Section 3.3 lists scenarios where our novel attack succeeds whereas obvious known attacks like disabling the signature check would be unsuccessful.

3.1 Enabling the Attack

In general, a system performing cryptographic operations needs a structure managing the relevant key material. For example, if the system is to verify an RSA-based signature, the responsible process will need at least the public exponent, a reference to the modulus, and its length. If it was possible to introduce faults into any part of this structure, this would enable an attacker to forge signatures. Faults to the program's memory can be introduced in a number of different ways:

Stack-Based Buffer Overflows. Using a stack-based buffer overflow, an attacker may be able to replace the exponent, modulus size information, or the pointer to the modulus stored in memory. Depending on the system, this may also be possible with heap-based buffer overflows as well as format string vulnerabilities.

Missing Boundary Checks. A process copying data from one memory location to another might fail to correctly check boundaries, possibly due to signed integer overflows. This could enable an adversary to overwrite key material structures or parts of the modulus by providing malicious boundaries to the process. We give an example of a similar type of vulnerability in Section 4.5.

Certificate Chains. The public key used for verification can be supplied on unprotected media like hard disks. In this case it has to be protected by a certificate chain, whose root certificate is securely stored inside the verifying device. This adds more flexibility to the system, as certificates can be issued to third parties. However, parsing the ASN.1 in certificate chains is complex and error prone, and may lead to vulnerabilities [29,30]. Therefore system designers may be tempted to amend certificates with an easily parsable header containing the public key information needed for signature verification. This information includes at least the exponent, the modulus size, and an offset indicating the start address of the modulus bits. This optimization, however, introduces a new vulnerability: An adversary can alter the header information which will ultimately enable the forgery of signatures. Microsoft uses this optimization for their otherwise highly secured IPTV system. In Section 4 we describe our proof-of-concept attack against Microsoft's IPTV system leading to forged signatures.

Hardware-Based. Classical hardware-based fault attacks modify bits of the modulus while it is being loaded, e.g., from memory to processor registers. There are various methods that can be used to induce faults in semiconductors [1]. Our structure-based attack can be applied to this hardware-based scenario as well. Instead of modifying the modulus bits directly, an adversary could introduce faults while the key material structures are being calculated or loaded. For example, if an adversary knows the exact time when the pointer to the modulus is calculated, a glitch attack can be used to introduce faults to this pointer. This would result in a completely new modulus as seen by the verifying process.

3.2 Conducting the Attack

This section explains how to perform our structure-based attack against an RSA modulus and shows that the resulting moduli are indeed well suited for this attack. For completeness, we also describe how to apply our attack against the public exponent of an RSA key.

Attacking the Modulus

Our attack is very powerful as it does not require altering the modulus itself [20,27], but rather the structures managing it: The attack starts with searching the exploitable memory space for a number that can be used as a new modulus. The exploitable memory space depends on the attacker's ability to modify the structures managing the modulus: An adversary may attack the size of the modulus, the address information, or both.

By deterministically introducing faults into these structures, the attacker provides a new memory region to be used as modulus data, as illustrated in Figure 1. Thus, the new modulus depends on the fault introduced to the pointer as well as the current content of the memory at this address. The verification process loads the data from the faulty address, which results in a new modulus $\widehat{N}$ being used during verification.

The introduced fault is chosen so that the factorization and with that the totient of this new modulus are known and its totient is coprime to e. Thus, the attacker can calculate $\widehat{d}$, so that $e\widehat{d} \equiv 1 \mod \varphi(\widehat{N})$. As the verification process now uses $(\widehat{N}, e)$ for verifying signatures, it accepts the signature of any given message signed with $(\widehat{d}, \widehat{N})$.

Size. The first parameter that can be altered is the modulus' size information, which will be limited by a minimum bit length (cf. Section 2.1).

Pointer to Memory Address. The other parameter that can be modified is the pointer to the memory area in which the modulus bits are stored. Detection of a modified pointer might be difficult in a running system as the memory address in which the modulus is stored may be dynamically calculated.

Combination of Size and Address. Both parameters can be modified in combination, too. Yet, some constraints may be imposed on the size and memory address parameters. For example, in the case of certificate chains with additional headers as described in Section 3.1, the resulting modulus may be checked to be within the original key material memory address range. Nevertheless, a combination of

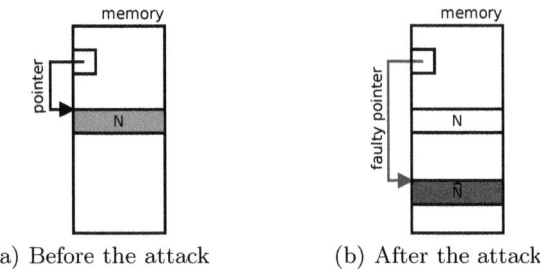

(a) Before the attack   (b) After the attack

Fig. 1. Structure-based fault attack: After inducing a fault in the pointer to the modulus N, the verification process will use the faulty modulus $\hat{N}$.

size and address modification can be used to generate a wide variety of possible moduli in this case.

Our proof-of-concept uses exactly this combined attack with the described constraint to forge signatures on a real system, which we describe in Section 4.

Combination with TOCTTOU Attacks. Another advantage of our attack is the ability to combine it with time-of-check-to-time-of-use (TOCTTOU) attacks. For example, if certificate chains are involved, a typical application flow will be similar to the one shown in Figure 3(a). First, the verification process will call a function to verify the validity of the public key by verifying the certificate chain. The function will need the memory address of the modulus as an argument passed to it. Typically, the pointer to this address will be copied when the function is called. If the certificate chain is valid, the verification process will call a second function to verify the signature. This function will also need a pointer to the modulus data, which will be copied when the function is called. This can enable an adversary to provide two distinct moduli to these signature validation functions, without modifying the original modulus data.

Methods for applying faults to the arguments passed to the verification functions are listed in Section 3.1.

Suitable Moduli

In practice, factorizing an integer becomes infeasible if at least two of its prime factors are above a critical size. With commodity hardware, this critical size is somewhere between 30 and 50 digits. The probability $G(\beta)$ for a random integer $\leq x$ to have its second largest prime factor $\leq x^\beta$ is given in [14, p. 383]. Note that this probability depends only on β, not on x.

To show that this formula can be applied in practice, we used freely available software [32] to factorize random integers of varying bit length. For each bit length, we tried to factorize 100 integers by finding prime factors of up to 30 digits using the *Elliptic Curve Method* (ECM) with the optimal settings from [33]. The results given in Figure 2 demonstrate that it is indeed feasible to expect a high percentage of random integers to be easily factorizable, depending on

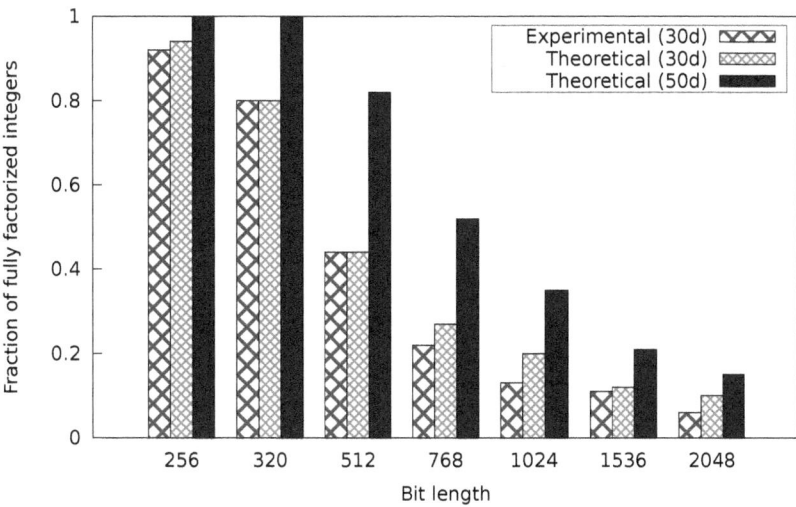

Fig. 2. Factorization of 100 random integers of varying bit length: Experimental results (ECM, B1=250k, 430 curves) vs. theoretical probability that the second largest prime factor of an integer has no more than 30 and 50 digits, resp.

the integers' bit length. Note that the candidate moduli are not independently distributed random numbers, as their respective bitstrings overlap. They are, however, sufficiently random to yield good factorization results.

Figure 2 illustrates the fraction of random integers whose second largest prime factor has no more than 30 and 50 digits, respectively. In other words, this fraction of integers can be fully factorized using these prime factors.

With these settings and considering primes of up to 30 digits, the factorization of 100 integers for each bit length given in Figure 2 required less than a day on a computer with two Intel six-core Xeon X5650 CPUs running at 2.67GHz. In contrast, trying to find prime factors of up to 50 digits for a single 2048-bit integer took more than a week on the same machine. An adversary will therefore always try to modify the modulus in a way that it becomes either small or that it results in many modulus candidates of which one can be easily factorized.

Attacking the Exponent

The part of the public key that can be attacked easily is the public exponent e. The attack consists of replacing the original exponent with $e = 1$. This can be done either directly or by modifying the pointer to the memory containing the exponent. The adversary can then provide a simple encoded message (cf. Section 2.1) as a signature, i.e., without having to apply the signing primitive. The verification process will raise such a signature to the power of 1, yielding the same valid encoded message. Hence, the signature will be treated as valid.

3.3   Infeasibility of Trivial Attacks

If we are able to manipulate data structures, naturally the question arises as to why we do not disable the signature check directly in the program code in memory. Another option would be to overwrite the original modulus with our modulus. The answer is that there are at least six scenarios that prevent an adversary from taking this route:

Read-Only Program Memory. If the memory region of the executable code is write-protected, we cannot disable the signature check by overwriting the corresponding memory region. However, references to cryptographic keys or the keys themselves are normally kept on the stack or heap. In general, these memory regions are not write-protected. Data kept in these structures might be prone to buffer overflow attacks and may allow the insertion of faults into key structures.

Key Stored in Read-Only Memory (ROM). The above mentioned limitation for executable code holds true for the key material, too. The key cannot be replaced if it is stored in ROM. However, by changing the references to the key material an adversary effectively introduces faults to the key being used for verification.

Length Restriction for Fault Insertion. If an adversary is able to overwrite the entire modulus, he can overwrite it with his own modulus and therefore create valid signatures. However, the amount of modulus bits that can be altered by an adversary using buffer overflows or hardware fault attacks might be limited and thus not sufficient to create an easily factorizable modulus. With our attack, the change of a single bit results in a completely different modulus.

Locality of Fault Insertion. The memory area that can be altered depends on the attack used to introduce faults to the verifying process' memory. For example, if an adversary can provoke a stack buffer overflow, he may only be able to overwrite memory used by the stack. If the modulus is stored on the heap, the adversary cannot overwrite the modulus directly.

Certificate Chains. If the system uses certificate chains to verify the authenticity of a file, the modulus of the signed certificate cannot be modified. Any direct modification would lead to an invalid certificate and an untrusted signature.

Run-Time Monitoring. The system being attacked could use run-time monitoring to ensure the integrity of critical data structures such as public key material. This would make it very difficult for an adversary to change the public key data itself. However, introducing faults to management structures, such as function arguments or local variables pointing to key material, are likely to go undetected.

4   Proof-of-Concept Practical Attack

As a proof-of-concept we applied our structure-based fault attack against the set-top box (STB) used by Microsoft's IPTV system *Mediaroom* [17]. We must emphasize that the companies involved in designing the STB and its software spent a great amount of effort in securing it. Many leading TV service providers around the world are offering this IPTV service to their customers. According to Microsoft, more than 7 million consumers have a subscription [17].

We start with a short overview of the STB used for Mediaroom and its file verification mechanism. Then we explain how we applied our attack to forge file signatures. We used the simple attack against the exponent described in Section 3.2 to successfully forge signatures verified by the boot loader. Due to additional checks on the exponent, this attack did not succeed against the file verification process used by the kernel. Therefore we applied the attack against the modulus structure of the certificates as described in Section 3.2 to forge signatures for the configuration files.

4.1 System Overview

Microsoft offers its IPTV system to big telecommunication companies to provide IPTV to their customers. An example is British Telecom, which offers this product under the brand name BT-Vision. Every customer needs a special STB that will connect to the IPTV backend system to receive IPTV streams. Due to the strong security required by the copyright holders of the streamed content, all HD content is encrypted by the streaming servers. The encrypted stream is then passed through the main CPU of the STB to the secure coprocessor, which decrypts and outputs the content over HDMI. Even the main CPU of the STB never has access to decrypted video content. This setup results in a complete end-to-end encryption from the IPTV backend to the customer's TV.

Accordingly, the STB uses a trusted boot mechanism to ensure that only software signed by Microsoft can be executed. In addition, every configuration and customization file is signed by the IPTV provider. These files and the software are provided on the built-in hard disk, along with signed files containing the corresponding hash values and the certificates required to verify these signatures. The STB periodically checks for software and configuration updates, which are automatically downloaded from the IPTV provider and placed on the disk. This enables the provider to remotely fix vulnerabilities, add features, etc. The only part of the software that cannot be updated remotely on older STB generations is the encrypted boot loader stored in flash memory.

4.2 File Verification

During startup, the boot loader makes use of the secure coprocessor to verify the authenticity of operating system files using a securely stored public key from Microsoft. Some operators display custom splash screen images during startup, which are verified in the same way, but with a certificate from the operator. After handing over control to the kernel, every file containing executable code is verified with the public key of MS before being loaded. Additionally, every customization and configuration file used for the IPTV client application is verified with the

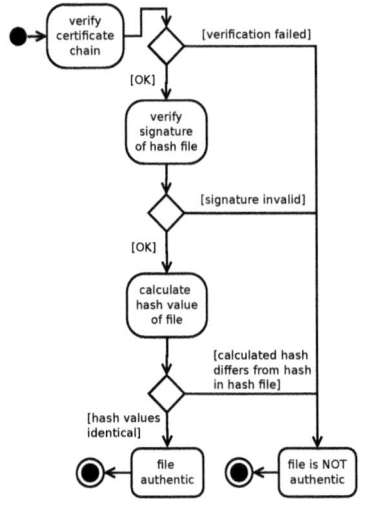

(a) Verification process for signed files

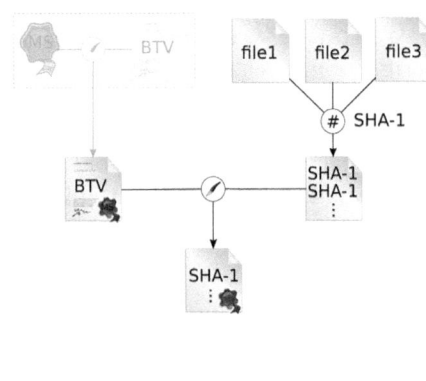

(b) Microsoft issues a certificate to BT-Vision, which is used to sign files

Fig. 3. Microsoft STB: signature verification and generation

operator's certificate. The signature verification process for operator-signed files is illustrated in Figure 3(a) and consists of the following steps:

Certificate Chain Validation. The operator's certificate is loaded from the hard disk and must contain a valid PKCS#1 signature from Microsoft. This signature is verified on the secure coprocessor, using a separate public key from Microsoft that cannot be replaced.

Signature Validation. A file containing hash values as shown in Figure 3(b) is loaded from the hard disk. Each line of this file contains a triple of name, size, and SHA-1 hash value of a corresponding file on the disk, e.g., a splash screen image. The signature of this hash value file is verified with the operator's public key. If the signature is valid, the signed hash values are treated as authentic.

Comparison of Hash Values. The file is loaded from the hard disk and the corresponding SHA-1 hash value is calculated. The verification process compares this value with the signed value from the list. If they are equal, the file is treated as authentic and will be processed. For the boot loader this means that the splash screen image can be displayed on the screen. Regarding the IPTV client, options from a configuration file can be applied, for example.

The binary format of the certificate used to verify the signatures is proprietary. It basically contains a public RSA key consisting of the modulus and the public exponent, as well as a PKCS#1 signature over the modulus. This prevents an adversary from replacing the modulus, because he cannot forge the PKCS#1 signature that has to be issued by Microsoft. However, the exponent and the structural information about the modulus, i.e., its size and starting address within the file, are not protected by the signature. This enables us to launch our structure-based fault-attack against the signature verification.

4.3   Attacking the Exponent

One easily exploitable weakness of the binary format described in Section 4.2 is the public exponent not being protected by the signature. This allows an attacker to modify the public key file and set the exponent to 1. He may then replace the signature in the signature file with a plain PKCS#1 encoded message. The verification process will verify the signature by raising it to the power of e, which in this case is 1. The result will be the same value, that is, the plain PKCS#1 encoded message. Hence, the forged signature will be accepted.

4.4   Attacking the Modulus

The goal of this section is to practically demonstrate that a structure-based fault attack against a public key modulus can be used to sign arbitrary files used by the IPTV client process running on Microsoft's STB.

We use the 2048-bit modulus of the public RSA key from BT-Vision, which is stored on the hard disk of BT-Vision's STB. Alternatively, the entire software package containing the key can be downloaded from [4] using [25]. The Windows CE kernel uses this public RSA key to verify signatures of various files when they are loaded, including all the configuration files for the IPTV client software. The modulus is embedded in the previously explained binary format and has the following hexadecimal representation. The characters printed in italics denote the faulty modulus $\widehat{N}$ that was chosen for the proof-of-concept.

```
CDCDBFC0FE0E908A43AB41070DAB8F33F1914186C3F66BCCED9769571A681BFA
D4560C4A15315E3C2BAA00CD353C779FB49DAA5517484C5E78593F92C221DD1C    ←
48D3C31404DE9507171E5B1FCE3A6B3BBDE04CE161C983B6F1F0B942F4ED9AC0    ←
756FAD62CD09E96E83FA42DE6323B8CD740665C57BF064D034427BEB114136C8    ←
ECC7F4134988385A51F39C1BFA8D0D5FF0E737EEE42DCBC3F8AE350ED24992DE    ←
4EEA8B2BF5B46273CBDBEBDAB936E97A03C589504A31CC71DA2DD1079AABE468    ←
298E89E1FA52D62FACB13FC9F159CE6C7C9660A7719C5C0C79CAC5FFDF2D3AAC    ←
DAE36E57853C44839D9665AE347A73750AA7DAA142FE37A095793B6E8ED180E7₁₆  ←
```

In this real-world example, neither the starting address nor the bit length of the original 2048-bit modulus is protected. The new modulus $\widehat{N}$, however, has to be within the memory range of the original one, i.e., it has to be a continuous part of the original modulus. Another restriction stems from the signature complying to PKCS#1, which requires the modulus' bit length to be at least 368 (cf. Section 2.1). The standard, however, is not implemented correctly on the STB and allows padding strings of only two octets in length. This results in a minimum bit length of only 320. Due to the file format of the certificate file, size and starting address of the new modulus can be chosen only bytewise. Thus, we get n-bit strings as key candidates with $n \in \{320 + i \cdot 8 \mid i \in \{0, \ldots, 215\}\}$ and $\lfloor (2048 - n)/8 \rfloor + 1$ strings of bit length n for a fixed n. Altogether, the set of available numbers consists of $\sum_{i=0}^{215} \lfloor (2048 - (320 + i \cdot 8))/8 \rfloor + 1 = 23652$ integers.

For our attack to succeed, only one of these integers has to be fully factorized. Due to the large number of available candidates with short bit length, chances are high that at least one of them can be factorized very easily (cf. Section 3.2). Using even the small set of primes $\{2, 3\}$, trial division indicates the 36th out of 217 analyzed 320-bit numbers to be a suitable $\widehat{N}$:

$$4A15315E3C2BAA00CD353C779FB49DAA5517484C$$
$$5E78593F92C221DD1C48D3C31404DE9507171E5B_{16}$$

$\widehat{N}$ has the small prime factor 3 with multiplicity 1. As its quotient is also prime after dividing $\widehat{N}$ by 3, we know the factorization of $\widehat{N}$. Its totient is, as expected, coprime to $e = 65537$. The STB will accept any configuration and customization file signed with the corresponding private exponent d:

$$18D4F063FFE8903C0DE226F9DF44715CCE2CD705$$
$$1232BB9252FA537E2EA43D51B45220319FDB75F1_{16}$$

4.5   Impact on the STB

The goal of our proof-of-concept is to demonstrate the efficiency and practical applicability of our structure-based fault attack against a highly secured and widely deployed device designed by very experienced large companies. It was not our goal, however, to completely destroy the security of Microsoft's STB. Using our attack, we were thus able to replace various signature-protected files:

Configuration Files. These files control every aspect of the IPTV client software running on the STB. Using our attack, anyone can freely change these parameters on his own STB. This includes enabling various locked down features, e.g., DVB-T receivers with time-shift functionality, USB connectivity, stand-alone mode, etc. In addition, the menus can be changed and extended to include new services from unauthorized providers.

Customization Files. The bitmap files used for the boot loader splash screens as well as those used for the IPTV client can be exchanged. This does not seem to be a threat at first sight, but it is. Obviously, to some degree Microsoft trusts the companies deploying their IPTV service. Therefore it allows them to provide custom images for splash screens as long as they are signed and therefore cannot be replaced by a malicious end user.

Using our attack we can replace these images, which in itself does not pose a threat. But due to additional flaws in the boot loader, a specially crafted bitmap file causes the boot loader to overwrite significant parts of the memory. These parts include mapped memory from the hardware, interrupt vectors, encrypted flash memory, and other unidentified parts.

In this particular case it seems difficult to exploit the vulnerability for control-data attacks [6]. The reason for this is that the function copying the image data replaces the most significant byte of every 4-byte integer with hexadecimal FF_{16}. In MIPS machine code [18], there is no valid machine instruction starting with FF_{16}. Additionally, with regard to overwriting return addresses, those addresses starting with FF_{16} do not offer a promising attack vector. Finally, the overwritten memory parts do not seem to be used as stack memory.

However, if key material was stored in this memory area, we could launch an attack against the modulus again. The advantage is obvious: We do not depend on specific data to overwrite the modulus. Even with the restriction of the MSB being FF_{16} there is a high probability to easily factorize the resulting modulus. Interesting targets would be the keys used to ensure that only signed code is executed. These keys, however, are not stored in the main memory and therefore not vulnerable to this attack.

5   Further Attacks

The STB is not the only device being susceptible to structure-based attacks. We were able to root a 3G access point by manipulating public key structures as shown in the next section. Furthermore, we recall a similar vulnerability described by Paul Leyland in PGP 2.x.

5.1   3G Access Point

During our research we analyzed a commercially deployed 3G residential femto-cell, produced by Ubiquisys [28]. This device was found to be vulnerable to our structure-based attack, too. It enabled us to flash a modified firmware to the device resulting in full root access.

Essentially, a structure consisting of four elements is stored in memory and passed to a function. We attack this structure by introducing a fault to one of its parts while it is being loaded from the network. This effectively forces the function to use a modulus supplied by us rather than the one securely stored on flash memory. The result is a compromise of this security-sensitive function and subsequently the entire device.

Normally only firmware images signed by the provider can be flashed to the device, because an open 3G access point could be abused for all sorts of malicious activity. As the RSA modulus used for verifying authentic firmware images has a length of 2048 bit, it is unfeasible to attack it directly (cf. Section 2.2). Therefore, we attacked the process supplying the verification process with the modulus. Listing 1.1 shows the vulnerable code section:

Listing 1.1. Vulnerable Code on 3G Femtocell

```
echo "Checking␣downloaded␣file␣signature..."
FILESIZE = 'stat −c %s rootfs.tgz'
FILESIG  = 'cat rootfs.sig'
if [ 'sigcheck rootfs.tgz $SIZE $SIG $MODULUS' != OK ]; then
  echo "Signature␣check␣failed"
  DOWNLOADFAIL=1;
fi
```

The `sigcheck` function processes the first four arguments as firmware file, size, signature, and modulus. It uses the fixed value of $e = 65537$ as the public exponent. If the signature *rootfs.sig* can be verified using the supplied modulus, the firmware file *rootfs.tgz* belonging to the signature will be treated as authentic.

Now our structure-based fault attack is launched: We provide `sigcheck` with a faulty argument, in this case a faulty signature in *rootfs.sig*. This signature consists of two strings instead of the expected single string. The first string resembles a signature whereas the second string is a modulus; both are provided by us. Now effectively five arguments are being passed to `sigcheck`: our firmware file, its size, our new signature, our new modulus, and the original modulus. `sigcheck` accepts a second modulus as an optional fifth parameter, which is only used if the signature cannot be verified using the first modulus; otherwise it is ignored.

Obviously, the implemented file verification method does not sufficiently protect the data structures involved in signature verification. Using our attack we were able to forge signatures for manipulated firmware images which were accepted by the verification process running on the device. The impact is devastating as our attack allows us to flash custom firmware images to the device and also gives us a root shell on this powerful device.

5.2 PGP Key Vulnerability

In 1997, a vulnerability in PGP 2.x public keys was described [16]. The public key file contains the public exponent and the modulus as well as the respective bit length. A fingerprint can be generated using the command "pgp -kvc" to verify the key's authenticity. This fingerprint is the MD5 hash of the key bits, but not of their lengths. This design misfeature of PGP 2.x allows an adversary to generate a PGP key that will have the same fingerprint as the original.

The attack is conducted by changing the bit length information of the exponent and modulus, leaving the sum of the bit lengths as well as the fingerprint unaltered. The modified exponent and modulus can then be exploited to generate a new private key either by using an exponent $\widehat{e} = 1$ or by finding an easily factorizable modulus.

6   Conclusion

In this paper we introduced a novel attack against signature verification processes. Instead of attacking the public key used for verification directly, we attack the structures managing the public key material. Our approach opens the door to a whole new class of attacks.

We demonstrated that the effort to launch our attack is minimal, once a vulnerable system is found. We showed that even the most secure software from one of the world's largest software companies is vulnerable to our attack. This leads us to conclude that system designers are not aware of these kinds of attacks. Even large companies have to be reminded that they should reuse existing proven cryptographic libraries and not try to enhance them. It is important to note that we were able to apply our attack so easily due to software designers not expecting this kind of attack. However, we have described how our structure-based attack can be applied in other less obvious ways. Thus, we emphasize the necessity to protect public key material against fault attacks.

We have also proved that our structure-based fault attacks are powerful yet feasible for attackers with limited resources. Except for the hardware-based application of our attack, all attacks are software-based. Required computing resources are negligible, which we demonstrated in practice.

Interestingly, our attack on the STB would not have been possible if the implementors of the relevant certificate format had been familiar with the PGP key vulnerability. A detailed knowledge of the Xbox vulnerabilities might have prevented our attack as well. It is therefore strongly advisable for implementors of security critical components to familiarize themselves with all previously performed attacks.

References

1. Bar-El, H., Choukri, H., Naccache, D., Tunstall, M., Whelan, C.: The sorcerer's apprentice guide to fault attacks. In: Proceedings of the IEEE 1994, pp. 370–382 (2006)
2. Biehl, I., Meyer, B., Müller, V.: Differential Fault Attacks on Elliptic Curve Cryptosystems. In: Bellare, M. (ed.) CRYPTO 2000. LNCS, vol. 1880, pp. 131–146. Springer, Heidelberg (2000)
3. Brier, E., Chevallier-Mames, B., Ciet, M., Clavier, C.: Why One Should Also Secure RSA Public Key Elements. In: Goubin, L., Matsui, M. (eds.) CHES 2006. LNCS, vol. 4249, pp. 324–338. Springer, Heidelberg (2006)
4. BT-Vision. STB Software Package (2010),
   `http://ref-bootstrap.nevis.btopenworld.com/upgrade/upgrade-files/005/`
   `Philips_DiT9719_05_L3/1.6.25077.835/PKG.DIR`
5. Bushing, Marcan: Console Hacking 2008: Wii Fail (2008),
   `http://events.ccc.de/congress/2008/Fahrplan/events/2799.en.html`
6. Chen, S., Xu, J., Sezer, E.C., Gauriar, P., Iyer, R.K.: Non-Control-Data Attacks Are Realistic Threats. In: USENIX Security Symposium, pp. 177–192 (2005)
7. Gueron, S., Seifert, J.-P.: Is It Wise to Publish Your Public RSA Keys? In: Breveglieri, L., Koren, I., Naccache, D., Seifert, J.-P. (eds.) FDTC 2006. LNCS, vol. 4236, pp. 1–12. Springer, Heidelberg (2006)
8. Huang, A.: Hacking the Xbox. No Starch Press (2003)

9. Huang, A.: Xbox Hardware Hacking (2003),
   http://events.ccc.de/congress/2003/fahrplan/event/604.en.html
10. ITU. Abstract Syntax Notation One (ASN.1): Specification of basic notation (ITU-T Recommendation X.680). International Telecommunications Union, Nov. 2208
11. Jonsson, J., Kaliski, B.: Public-Key Cryptography Standards (PKCS) #1: RSA Cryptography Specifications Version 2.1. RFC 3447 (Informational) (February 2003)
12. Kelsey, J., Schneier, B., Wagner, D.: Key-Schedule Cryptanalysis of IDEA, G-DES, GOST, SAFER, and Triple-DES. In: Koblitz, N. (ed.) CRYPTO 1996. LNCS, vol. 1109, pp. 237–251. Springer, Heidelberg (1996)
13. Kleinjung, T., et al.: Factorization of a 768-bit RSA modulus. Cryptology ePrint Archive, 2010/006
14. Knuth, D.E.: The Art of Computer Programming, 3rd edn., vol. 2. Addison-Wesley (1997)
15. Lenstra, A.K., Hendrik, J., Lenstra, W. (eds.): The development of the number field sieve. Lecture Notes in Mathematics, vol. 1554. Springer, Berlin (1993)
16. Leyland, P.: The comp.security.pgp FAQ (1997),
   http://www.pgp.net/pgpnet/pgp-faq/#KEY-PUBLIC-KEY-FORGERY
17. Microsoft. Mediaroom, http://www.microsoft.com/mediaroom/you/
18. MIPS Technologies. MIPS32 Architecture (2008),
   http://www.mips.com/products/architectures/mips32/#specifications
19. Mitre. Common Vulnerabilities and Exposures: CVE-2006-4339, RSA Signature Forgery (2006),
   http://cve.mitre.org/cgi-bin/cvename.cgi?name=CVE-2006-4339
20. Muir, J.A.: Seiferts RSA fault attack: Simplified analysis and generalizations. IACR Eprint archive (2005)
21. Naccache, D., Nguyên, P.Q., Tunstall, M., Whelan, C.: Experimenting with Faults, Lattices and the DSA. In: Vaudenay, S. (ed.) PKC 2005. LNCS, vol. 3386, pp. 16–28. Springer, Heidelberg (2005)
22. National Institute of Standards and Technology. Secure Hash Standard. Federal Information Processing Standard (FIPS) 180-1 (April 1993)
23. National Institute of Standards and Technology. NIST's Policy on Hash Functions (2008), http://csrc.nist.gov/groups/ST/hash/policy.html
24. Paar, C., Pelzl, J.: Understanding Cryptography. A Textbook for Students and Practitioners. Springer, Heidelberg (2010)
25. Plenkk. Pkgtool (2010),
   http://www.t-hack.com/wiki/index.php/Download_Update_Files
26. Rivest, R., Shamir, A., Adleman, L.: A method for obtaining digital signatures and public-key cryptosystems. Communications of the ACM 21, 120–126 (1978)
27. Seifert, J.-P.: On authenticated computing and RSA-based authentication. In: Proceedings of the 12th ACM Conference on Computer and Communications Security, CCS 2005, pp. 122–127. ACM, New York (2005)
28. Ubiquisys. Residential femtocells,
   http://www.ubiquisys.com/residential-3g-femtocells
29. US-CERT. Vulnerability note vu#748355 (2002),
   http://www.kb.cert.org/vuls/id/748355
30. US-CERT. Technical cyber security alert ta04-041a (2004),
   http://www.us-cert.gov/cas/techalerts/TA04-041A.html
31. Wang, X., Yin, Y.L., Yu, H.: Finding Collisions in the Full SHA-1. In: Shoup, V. (ed.) CRYPTO 2005. LNCS, vol. 3621, pp. 17–36. Springer, Heidelberg (2005)
32. Zimmermann, P.: GMP-ECM, http://ecm.gforge.inria.fr/
33. Zimmermann, P.: Optimal parameters for ECM,
   http://www.loria.fr/~zimmerma/records/ecm/params.html

Fault Analysis of the KATAN Family of Block Ciphers

Shekh Faisal Abdul-Latip[1,2], Mohammad Reza Reyhanitabar[1], Willy Susilo[1], and Jennifer Seberry[1]

[1] Centre for Computer and Information Security Research,
School of Computer Science and Software Engineering,
University of Wollongong, Australia
{sfal620,rezar,wsusilo,jennie}@uow.edu.au
[2] Information Security and Digital Forensics Lab (INSFORLAB),
Faculty of Information and Communication Technology,
Universiti Teknikal Malaysia Melaka, Malaysia
shekhfaisal@utem.edu.my

Abstract. In this paper, we investigate the security of the KATAN family of block ciphers against differential fault attacks. KATAN consists of three variants with 32, 48 and 64-bit block sizes, called KATAN32, KATAN48 and KATAN64, respectively. All three variants have the same key length of 80 bits. We assume a single-bit fault injection model where the adversary is supposed to be able to corrupt a single random bit of the internal state of the cipher and this fault injection process can be repeated (by resetting the cipher); i.e., the faults are transient rather than permanent. First, we determine suitable rounds for effective fault injections by analyzing distributions of low-degree (mainly, linear and quadratic) polynomial equations obtainable using the cube and extended cube attack techniques. Then, we show how to identify the exact position of faulty bits within the internal state by precomputing difference characteristics for each bit position at a given round and comparing these characteristics with ciphertext differences (XOR of faulty and non-faulty ciphertexts) during the online phase of the attack. The complexity of our attack on KATAN32 is 2^{59} computations and about 115 fault injections. For KATAN48 and KATAN64, the attack requires 2^{55} computations (for both variants), while the required number of fault injections is 211 and 278, respectively.

Keywords: Block ciphers, cube attack, differential fault analysis, KATAN.

1 Introduction

Fault analysis as a type of side channel attack (or implementation attack) was originally introduced by Boneh et al. [6] by an attack against implementations of public key algorithms. The method was then adapted and extended by Biham and Shamir [5] to differential fault analysis, making it applicable to implementations of symmetric key algorithms as well [9, 10]. Several models for fault

M.D. Ryan, B. Smyth, and G. Wang (Eds.): ISPEC 2012, LNCS 7232, pp. 319–336, 2012.
© Springer-Verlag Berlin Heidelberg 2012

attacks have been introduced in the literature, among which we adopt a popular model, called transient single-bit fault model, as used for example in [10, 9]. In this model it is assumed that the adversary can inject one bit of error into the internal state of a cipher during its execution (e.g. using a laser beam) without damaging the bit position permanently; that is, the cipher can be reset to resume its normal (unfaulty) operation and this fault injection can be repeated as many times as required. For some interesting practical settings for carrying out these attacks we refer to [15].

In this paper we present fault attacks on the KATAN family of block ciphers [7]. KATAN consists of three variants with 32, 48 and 64-bit block sizes, named KATAN32, KATAN48 and KATAN64, respectively. All three variants have the same key length of 80 bits. KATAN aims at meeting the needs of an extremely resource-limited environment such as RFID tags. Assuming the transient single-bit fault attack model as used for example in [10, 9], we present a differential fault attack empowered by the algebraic techniques of the cube attack [8] and its extended variants [1].

The cube attack, put forth by Dinur and Shamir at EUROCRYPT 2009 [8], is a generic type of algebraic attack that may be applied against any cryptosystem, provided that the attacker has access to a bit of information that can be represented by a low-degree multivariate polynomial over $GF(2)$ of the secret and public variables of the target cryptosytem. Dinur and Shamir in [8] compared the cube attack to some of the previously known similar techniques [14, 16]. Recently, we have presented an extended variant of the cube attack in [1] to extract low-degree (mainly quadratic) sparse system of equations in addition to the linear equations obtainable from the original cube attack. In this paper, we employ these techniques together with fault analysis to build a hybrid attack against KATAN.

PREVIOUS WORK. Cryptanalytical results on the KATAN family have been presented in [13, 3]. Recall that all three members of the KATAN family (i.e. KATAN32, KATAN48, and KATAN64) have 254 rounds. Knellwolf et al. [13] presented partial key recovery attacks (called "conditional differential cryptanalysis") against 78 rounds of KATAN32, 70 rounds of KATAN48, and 68 rounds of KATAN64 and concluded that the full versions of these ciphers seem to have sufficiently large number of rounds (254 rounds) to provide a confident security margin against their proposed attack. Bard et al. [3] presented cube attacks against 60, 40, and 30 rounds, and algebraic attacks against 79, 64, 60 rounds of KATAN32, KATAN48 and KATAN64, respectively. They also showed a side channel attack against the full 254 rounds of KATAN32, which has been the only attack against a full-round member of the KATAN family, so far. Bard et al.'s attack against the full-round KATAN32 combines the cube attack technique with a side channel attack model; namely, it assumes that adversary can obtain one bit of information from the internal state of the cipher and this one-bit information leakage must be *error free*. Bard et al. stated that such information is supposed to be captured by some side channels; for example, power or timing analysis or electromagnetic emanation, but we note that such measurements are not error (noise) free in practice and it is not clear whether Bard et al's attack can be adapted to handle such errors. Another way to capture such information leakage (albeit again hardly error free) is to use intrusive probing techniques which are expensive and usually are destructive to the underlying device. We also note that the Bard et al.'s attack is not a fault attack. The idea behind a fault attack, as introduced by Boneh et al. [6], is that if a wrong (faulty) result is released from a cryptosystem (as well as the normal unfaulty results) then adversary can use that information to break the cryptosystem. (Bard et al. do not assume and do not use any faulty computations in their side channel model).

OUR CONTRIBUTION. We combine the cube attack [8] and its extended variant (as presented in our previous work) [1] with *fault analysis* to form successful hybrid attacks against the full-round versions of all three members of the KATAN family. To the best of our knowledge, this is the first time that the cube attack and its extended variants are combined with *"fault analysis"* to form a successful hybrid attack against a block cipher. We assume a single-bit transient fault injection model as our side channel model, where the adversary is supposed to be able to corrupt a single random bit of the internal state of the cipher and this fault induction process can be repeated (by resetting the cipher); i.e., the faults are transient rather than permanent.

First, we determine effective rounds for fault inductions by analyzing distributions of low-degree polynomial equations obtainable using the cube and extended cube attack methods. Then, we show how to identify the exact position of faulty bits within the internal state by precomputing difference characteristics for each bit position at a given round and comparing these characteristics with ciphertext differences during the online phase of the attack. Finally, we show how to recover a low-degree (linear and quadratic) system of multivariate polynomial equations in the internal state and subkey bits that are easily solvable. The complexity of our attack on KATAN32 is 2^{59} and it requires about 115 fault injections. For KATAN48 and KATAN64, the attack requires 2^{55} computations (for both variants), while the required number of fault injections is 211 and 278, respectively.

Our fault attack on KATAN32 turns out to need about 2^8 times more (offline) operations compared to the previous side channel attack by Bard et al. [3] which requires 2^{51} computations; nevertheless, our attack model (namely, the transient fault injection at random bit positions in the internal state) is essentially *different* from the (noise free) information leakage assumption by Bard et al. in [3], and is arguably more practical as supported by previously known results such as [15]. Furthermore, our attack is directly adapted to the cases of KATAN48 and KATAN64 (both requiring 2^{55} computations) and, so far, is the only attack against the latter variants of KATAN in the side channel attack model.

2   A Brief Description of KATAN

KATAN is a family of block ciphers [7] consisting of three variants, namely: KATAN32, KATAN48 and KATAN64. Each variant accepts an 80-bit secret key and performs 254 rounds to produce a ciphertext. All variants also share the same key schedule as well as the same nonlinear functions. KATAN ciphers aim at constrained environments such as hardware implementations with limited resources (power consumption, clock frequency and gate counts). KATAN32 with

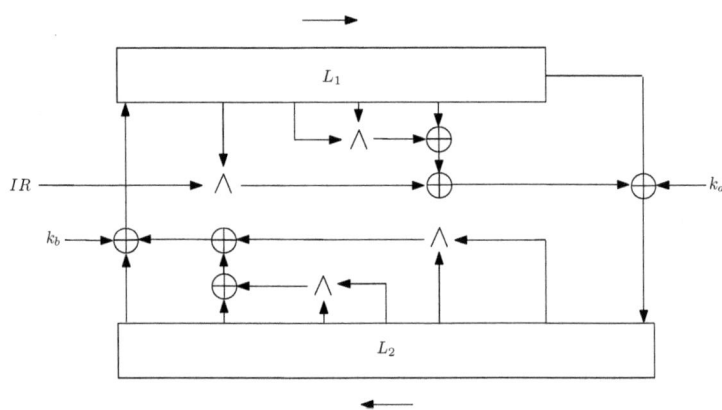

Fig. 1. The Outline of the KATAN Family of Block Ciphers

block size of 32 bits is the lightest variant in the family. A 32-bit plaintext block is loaded into two registers L_1 and L_2, respectively, of length 13 and 19 bits. The bits are indexed in the right-to-left order, from 0 to 12 for L_1 (i.e. $L_1 = (L_1[12], \cdots, L_1[0])$) and from 0 to 18 for L_2 (i.e. $L_2 = (L_2[18], \cdots L_2[0])$). The least significant bit (LSB) of the plaintext block is loaded to bit 0 of register L_2 followed by the other bits until the 18-th bit, and then remaining bits are loaded into register L_1 until the most significant bit (MSB) of the plaintext is loaded into bit 12 of register L_1. One round of KATAN32 consists of shifting the register L_1 and L_2 one bit to the left, and computing two new bit values using nonlinear functions f_a and f_b, respectively. These new bits are then loaded into the LSB bits of registers L_2 and L_1, respectively. The nonlinear functions f_a and f_b are defined as follows:

$$f_a(L_1) = L_1[x_1] \oplus L_1[x_2] \oplus (L_1[x_3] \cdot L_1[x_4]) \oplus (L_1[x_5] \cdot IR) \oplus k_a \qquad (1)$$
$$f_b(L_2) = L_2[y_1] \oplus L_2[y_2] \oplus (L_2[y_3] \cdot L_2[y_4]) \oplus (L_2[y_5] \cdot L_2[y_6]) \oplus k_b \qquad (2)$$

where IR specifies an irregular update rule (i.e. $L_1[x_5]$ is used only when $IR = 1$), and k_a and k_b are two subkey bits. We refer to [7] for the details on the irregular update rules (IRs) for each round.

The key schedule for all variants of KATAN expands an 80-bit secret key K to 508 subkey bits using the following linear mapping

$$k_i = \begin{cases} K_i, & \text{for } 0 \leq i \leq 79, \hfill (3) \\ k_{i-80} \oplus k_{i-61} \oplus k_{i-50} \oplus k_{i-13}, & \text{otherwise} \hfill (3') \end{cases}$$

Given the precomputed subkey values, the values of k_a and k_b for a particular round t are defined as k_{2t} and k_{2t+1}, respectively. Thus the subkey for round t is defined as $k_a||k_b = k_{2t}||k_{2t+1}$. The selection for tap positions, x_is ($1 \leq i \leq 5$) and y_js ($1 \leq j \leq 6$), and the length of registers L_1 and L_2 are defined independently for each variant as shown in Table 1. Besides the tap positions and the length

Table 1. Parameters for the KATAN Family of Block Ciphers

Cipher	$|L_1|$	$|L_2|$	x_1	x_2	x_3	x_4	x_5	y_1	y_2	y_3	y_4	y_5	y_6
KATAN32	13	19	12	7	8	5	3	18	7	12	10	8	3
KATAN48	19	29	18	12	15	7	6	28	19	21	13	15	6
KATAN64	25	39	24	15	20	11	9	38	25	33	21	14	9

of the registers, the difference between all the three variants is the number of times the nonlinear functions f_a and f_b are applied in each round using the same subkey. One round of KATAN48 is shifting the registers L_1 and L_2 two bits to the left (i.e. requires two clock cycles). In each shift within the same round, the function f_a and f_b are applied using the same subkey $k_a||k_b$. Hence, full round of KATAN48 requires 508 clock cycles (i.e. 254 rounds $\times$ 2 clocks per round) to produce the ciphertext.

In contrast, one round of KATAN64 requires the registers L_1 and L_2 to be shifted three bits to the left (i.e. requires three clock cycles). Similarly, in each shift within the same round, the function f_a and f_b are applied using the same subkey $k_a||k_b$. As a result, the full round KATAN64 requires 762 clock cycles to produce the ciphertext. Fig. 1 shows the generic structure of the KATAN family of block ciphers. The initial state of KATAN-v (for v=32, 48, 64) is denoted by $IS = (s_{v-1}, \cdots, s_1, s_0) = L_1||L_2$ for the associated L_1 and L_2 registers.

3   An Overview of the Cube and Extended Cube Attacks

The main idea underlying the cube attack [8] is that the multivariate "master" polynomial $p(v_1, \cdots, v_m, k_1, \cdots, k_n)$, representing an output bit of a cryptosystem over $GF(2)$ of secret variables k_i (key bits) and public variables v_i (i.e. plaintext or initial values), may inject algebraic equations of low degrees, in particular *linear* equations. The cube attack provides a method to derive such lower degree (especially linear) equations, given the master polynomial only as a black-box which can be evaluated on the secret and public variables.

Let's ignore the distinction between the secret and public variables' notations and denote all of them by $x_i, \cdots, x_\ell$, where $\ell = m + n$. Let $I \subseteq \{1, ..., \ell\}$ be a subset of the variable indexes, and t_I denote a monomial term containing multiplication of all the x_is with $i \in I$. By factoring the master polynomial p by the monomial t_I, we have:

$$p(x_1, \cdots, x_\ell) = t_I \cdot p_{S(I)} + q(x_1, \cdots, x_\ell) \tag{4}$$

where $p_{S(I)}$, which is called the *superpoly* of t_I in p, does not have any common variable with t_I, and each monomial term t_J in the residue polynomial q misses at least one variable from t_I. A term t_I is called a *"maxterm"* if its superpoly in p is linear polynomial which is not a constant, *i.e.* $deg(p_{S(I)}) = 1$.

The main observation of the cube attack is that, the summation of p over t_I, i.e. by assigning all the possible combinations of 0/1 values to the x_is with $i \in I$ and fixing the value of all the remaining x_is with $i \notin I$, the resultant polynomial equals $p_{S(I)} \pmod 2$. Given access to a cryptographic function with public and secret variables, this observation enables an adversary to recover the value of the secret variables (k_is) in two steps, namely the preprocessing and online phases.

During the preprocessing phase, the adversary first finds sufficiently many maxterms, i.e. t_Is, such that each t_I consists of a subset of public variables $v_1, \cdots, v_m$. To find the maxterms, the adversary performs a probabilistic linearity test (such as the BLR test of [4]) on $p_{S(I)}$ over the secret variables $k_i \in \{k_1, \cdots, k_n\}$ while the value of the public variables not in t_I are fixed (to 0 or 1) (cf. [8] for more details).

Then the next step is to derive linearly independent equations in the secret variables k_is from $p_{S(I)}$ that are closely related to the master polynomial p, such that, solving them enables the adversary to determine the values of the secret variables. Once sufficiently many linearly independent equations in the secret variables are found, the preprocessing phase is completed. In the online phase, the adversary's aim is to find the value of the right-hand side of each linear equation by summing the black box polynomial p over the same set of maxterms t_Is which are obtained during the preprocessing phase. Now, the adversary can easily solve the resultant system of the linear equations, e.g. by using the Gaussian elimination method, to determine the values of the secret (key) variables.

A generalized variant of the cube attack, called extended cube, has been shown in [1] for extracting "low-degree nonlinear" equations efficiently. It revises the notion of tweakable polynomials from the original cube attack as

$$p(x_1, ..., x_\ell) = t_I \cdot X_K \cdot p_{S(I \cup K)} + q(x_1, ..., x_\ell) \tag{5}$$

where t_I is a subterm of size s over x_is with $i \in I$; X_K is a subterm of size r over x_is with $i \in K$, and $p_{S(I \cup K)}$ is the superpoly of $t_I \cdot X_K$ in p. Note that since both subterms t_I and X_K are factored out from p, the superpoly $p_{S(I \cup K)}$ does not contain any common variable with t_I and X_K, and each term t_J in the residue polynomial q misses at least one variable from $t_I \cdot X_K$. Now using the main observation of the cube attack, the summation of p over '$t_I \cdot X_K$', by assigning all the possible combinations of 0/1 values to the x_is with $i \in I \cup K$ and fixing the value of all the remaining x_is with $i \notin I \cup K$, the resultant polynomial equals to $p_{S(I \cup K)} \pmod 2$.

The only difference between the original cube attack and the extended cube attack is in the preprocessing phase; the online phase for both of the methods are the same. During the preprocessing phase of the extended cube attack, the adversary finds many monomials t_Is, such that each t_I consists of a subset of public variables $v_1, \cdots, v_m$, and the corresponding superpoly $p_{S(I)}$ is a polynomial of degree D. To find those t_Is, the adversary performs the generalized version of the BLR test as proposed by Dinur and Shamir in [8] on $p_{S(I)}$ over the secret variables $k_1, \cdots, k_n$.

To derive efficiently a nonlinear equation $p_{S(I)}$ of degree D over secret variables k_is, the adversary should identify the subset $S \subseteq \{1, \cdots, n\}$ that consists of the secret variable indexes within $p_{S(I)}$, in which each k_i with $i \in S$ is either a term or a subterm of $p_{S(I)}$. To do this, the subterm X_K (cf. equation (5)) is assigned with each secret variable $k_i \in \{k_1, \cdots, k_n\}$ one at a time while the subterm t_I is fixed to the monomial in which its superpoly $p_{S(I)}$ is of degree D, and all public variables v_is with $i \notin I$ are fixed to 0 or 1. For each assignment of X_K, the adversary chooses κ sets of vector $\mathbf{x} \in \{0,1\}^{n-1}$ representing samples of $n-1$ secret variables k_is with $i \notin K$ independently and uniformly at random, and verify that X_K (or similarly the secret variable k_i that is assigned to X_K) exists as a variable in the superpoly $p_{S(I)}$ if $p_{S(I \cup K)} = 1$ for at least an instance vector $\mathbf{x}$.

Having the set of secret variables k_is with $i \in S$ of the nonlinear superpoly $p_{S(I)}$ of degree D enables the adversary to derive the nonlinear equation over the secret variables by finding all terms of degrees $0, 1, \cdots, D$ within the superpoly equation. Suppose $N = |S|$ is the number of secret variables k_is with $i \in S$ of the superpoly $p_{S(I)}$ of degree D. To derive $p_{S(I)}$, firstly the adversary assigns the subterm X_K one at a time with a monomial indexed by a subset $K \in T$ where T is a set of cube indexes of monomials constructed from all combinations of k_is from degree 1 until degree D with $i \in S$. In each assignment, all $v_i, k_i \notin t_I \cdot X_K$ are set to zero. Then to verify the existence of the monomial $X_K \in T$ as a term in $p_{S(I)}$, the adversary sums p over the monomial $t_I \cdot X_K$. If the result is equal to 1, then with probability 1, X_K is a term in the superpoly $p_{S(I)}$. Finally, the existence of a constant term (i.e. a term of degree 0) in the superpoly $p_{S(I)}$ is also determined by setting all public variables, v_is, for $i \notin I$ and all secret variables $k_1, \cdots, k_n$ to zero, and sum the polynomial p over t_I. Similarly, if the result is equal to 1, then with probability 1, a constant term exists within the superpoly $p_{S(I)}$.

4   Fault Analysis of KATAN

We simulate a fault attack assuming that the adversary can cause one transient single-bit error at a time in the internal state during the encryption/decryption process. It is assumed that the adversary can choose the target round(s) in which faults should be injected, for example, based on the side channel information inferred from power consumption traces and/or the clocking sequence (e.g., this can be done by triggering a laser beam with the target number of clocks of the cryptographic module). However, it is assumed that adversary cannot influence the exact position of the faulty bit within the internal state; he can only inject the fault randomly with the hope that it will hit the target bit positions by chance.

Using this fault model, our aim is to recover the 80-bit secret key used in KATAN. Our attack consists of two phases, namely offline and online phases. During the offline phase, firstly we identify the rounds (of the enciphering process) that can provide linear and quadratic equations due to single-bit faults. We call such rounds as *effective rounds* for our fault attacks.

Next, we determine the position of the faulty bits within the internal state using *difference characteristics* which we construct using the cube methods. Given a faulty ciphertext resulting from a random fault injection into an "unknown" internal state bit s_{j+t} after t-th round, to determine the position j, first we compute the ciphertext differential, Δc, by XORing (summing modulo 2) the non-faulty ciphertext c with the faulty ciphertext c' such that $\Delta c_j = c_j \oplus c'_j$, for $0 \leq j < |L_1| + |L_2|$. Then, guided by the lookup table, we refer to positions with values '0' and '1' (and ignore those with a '-' sign) within each characteristic and compare them with bits in the same positions in Δc. If all the corresponding bits in Δc match the bits in the characteristic of the faulty bit s_{j+t} then we can ensure that a fault has been injected into the bit at position j.

Finally, we extract a *low-degree* system of multivariate polynomial equations which are obtainable within the effective rounds using the difference between faulty and non-faulty ciphertexts facilitate by the cube and extended cube methods. More precisely, we only concentrate on extracting simple independent linear and quadratic equations that are easily solvable. After having a sufficient number of independent equations, we determine the target internal state bit positions for fault injections.

Knowing both the rounds and bit positions to be aimed, next the adversary moves to the online phase. In the online phase, the adversary repeatedly clocks the ciphers from the beginning until achieving one of the target rounds. Upon achieving this round, the adversary randomly injects a fault to the internal state with the hope to effect one of the target bits by chance. As the fault injection might not hit any one of the target bits, and the effect of one injection should be mutually exclusive from the effect of other injections, the error caused by the injections need to be transient rather than permanent. This is to enable the adversary to inject faults into the internal state repeatedly until all the target bits of each target round have been injected successfully. The aim of the online phase is to determine the value of right hand side of each equation obtained during the offline phase. Having the value of right-hand side of the equations, enables the adversary to recover the subkey bits provided by the key schedule algorithm. The knowledge about the value of the subkey bits enables the adversary to exploit the key schedule algorithm to recover the 80-bit secret key.

Our attack on the KATAN ciphers exploits the observation that after recovering n neighboring "subkey bits", the adversary can recover the 80-bit "secret key" with time complexity of 2^{80-n} computations. This is because the 80-bit secret key is directly loaded into an 80-bit LFSR (the key register) and the sub-key bits for round $t > 79$ are computed using a linear update function and shift operations (cf. Equation 3 and Equation 3'). Therefore, at any round $t > 79$, if we can recover the value of some of the LFSR bits (or similarly the value of the subkey bits), we can guess the remaining $80 - n$ values of the LFSR internal state bits and iteratively clock the LFSR backward until round $t = 0$ to recover the secret key. Suppose the highest and the lowest index values of the subkey bits to be recovered are H and L respectively. Hence, our aim is to recover the subkey bits such that $H - L \leq 79$, as all subkey bits between these index range will be the content of the 80-bit LFSR at a particular round t.

4.1 Attack on KATAN32

To apply differential fault attack on KATAN, first we determine the effective rounds for fault injection. To do this, we find the number of linear and quadratic equations within each round during the offline phase using cube methods. For each faulty round t, we consider each internal state bit as the monomial t_I (cf. equation 4) one at a time, and each bit of the ciphertext as a polynomial p over the internal state bits at round t. Next we detect the linear and quadratic equations by applying linearity and quadraticity tests using the BLR and generalized BLR tests as described in Section 3. Each time an equation (linear and quadratic) being detected, we accumulate the number of equations accordingly until all the internal state bits of round t have been considered. We repeat this procedure for each round of all KATAN's variants. As a result, Fig. 2 is derived indicating the range of rounds that should be considered for fault injections. In the figure, "Faulty Round" denotes the number of rounds that the cipher has run before injecting a fault into the internal state.

In order to examine the actual internal state position of faulty round t which has been affected by a random fault injection, the difference characteristic for each of the internal state bit of round t needs to be constructed. To construct the difference characteristics, we select each of the internal state bit of round t as the monomial, t_I, one at a time and apply the BLR linearity test on the corresponding superpoly, $p_{S(I)}$, to determine whether the test will result constant 0, constant 1, linear or higher degree superpoly. Constant 0 and constant 1 superpolys indicate values '0' and '1' in the difference characteristic bits, respectively. However linear and higher degree superpolys indicate unknown values in the characteristic bits, i.e. the '-' sign. Table 6 in Appendix shows an example of difference characteristics for KATAN32 for faulty round $t = 237$.

The fault attack can be efficiently applied if the rounds that have high number of quadratic equations are considered. As for KATAN32, this refers to the fault injections after $t = 237$ rounds as shown in Fig. 2. Considering this faulty round, we provide a sample set of linear and quadratic equations that can help in recovering the target subkey bits as shown in Table 3 in Appendix.

In the table, $L_2 = (s_{18+t}, \cdots, s_{0+t})$ and $L_1 = (s_{31+t}, \cdots, s_{19+t})$. Δc_j denotes a ciphertext bit difference where the difference is obtained by XORing the non-faulty ciphertext bit c_j with the faulty ciphertext bit c'_j, i.e. $\Delta c_j = c_j \oplus c'_j$, for

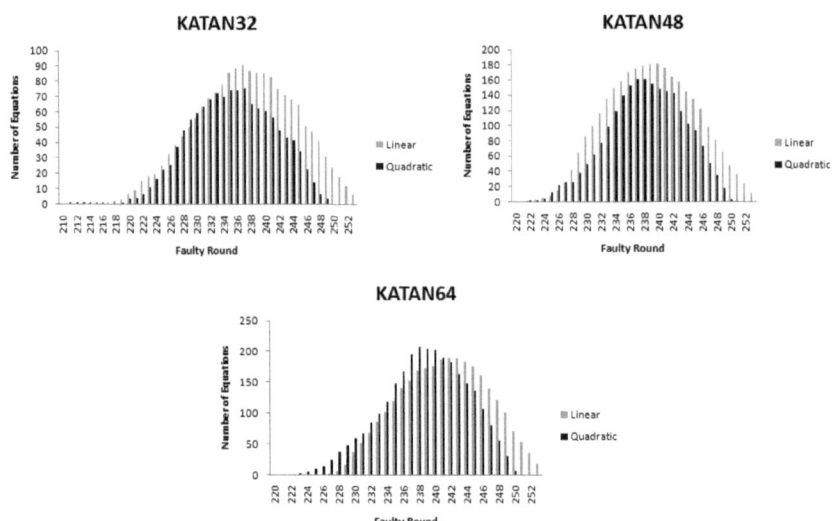

Fig. 2. Distribution of Linear and Quadratic Equations in KATAN

$0 \leq j \leq 31$. For subkey bits we use a slightly different notation to facilitate our analysis, in which we denote the k_is as subkey bits whose indexes range from $0 \leq i \leq 507$ (in which bits indexed 0 until 79 are from the original secret key bits). We do not consider each subkey bit indexed $i > 79$ as a boolean function over the 80 secret key bits. Instead, to facilitate our analysis we only consider each one of them as an independent new variable.

Considering fault injection after $t = 237$ rounds, 10 subkey bits can be found within the quadratic equations, i.e. $k_{474}, \ldots, k_{482}$ and k_{484} (cf. Table 3 for the polynomial equations and Table 6 for the difference characteristics in Appendix). Recovering these subkey bits, requires solving the corresponding quadratic equations in which some of the linear equations listed in the table should also be involved, as they can provide the solution for the internal state bits of registers L_1 and L_2 within the quadratic equations. For example, to find the solution for k_{474}, we consider s_{1+t} as the faulty bit after $t = 237$ rounds. Considering the difference between non-faulty and faulty ciphertext bit c_{24}, i.e. Δc_{24}, the symbolic representation of the differential is

$$s_{22+t} + s_{26+t} + s_{31+t} + k_{474} + s_{24+t}s_{27+t} = \Delta c_{24}. \qquad (6)$$

The value of the right hand side (RHS) of this equation (either 0 or 1) can be determined by numerically computing Δc_{24}, such that $\Delta c_{24} = c_{24} \oplus c'_{24}$. To recover the value of k_{474} for example, requires the values of all other bits within the equation to be known. If there exist a case in which the value of certain bits cannot be recovered considering the equations derived from the faulty round t

only, the adversary needs to consider earlier rounds to find equivalent bits since the value of the internal state bits are only shifted from the LSB to MSB except the LSB bits. Tables 2–5 in Appendix show the set of equations that are solvable and resulting from faulty rounds $t = 231, 237, 243$ and 249, respectively. Note that, comparing more earlier rounds results in having difficulty to determine the faulty bit positions within register L_1 and L_2. This is because the uniqueness of the difference characteristics will slowly disappear as we consider earlier rounds.

4.2   Attack on KATAN48

Following the method used on KATAN32, we consider the KATAN48 block cipher as our next target. Since KATAN48 requires two clocks for each round, if a certain internal state bit s_{j+t} cannot be solved directly in certain faulty round t, then its solution may be found by referring to bit s_{j-2n+t} in an earlier faulty round $t - n$, for $j - 2n \geq 29$ and $31 \leq j \leq 47$, or $j - 2n \geq 0$ and $2 \leq j \leq 28$.

Our attack on KATAN48 considers faulty rounds $t = 234, 238, 242, 246$ and 250 as the target rounds. Similar to the analysis of KATAN32, the selection of these rounds is based on the number of quadratic equations that can be found within the effective rounds. Fig. 2 shows that the highest number of quadratic equations for KATAN48 can be found at faulty rounds $t = 237$ and $t = 238$. Since the difference characteristics are more clearly defined when we consider later rounds, we choose $t = 238$ rather than $t = 237$ as our first target round. Table 8 in Appendix shows the polynomial equations obtained using the difference between non-faulty and faulty ciphertexts for fault induction after $t = 238$ rounds of KATAN48. Table 7 in Appendix shows the equations obtained using fault induction after $t = 234$ rounds of KATAN48. For equations obtainable using fault induction after $t = 242, 246, 250$ rounds of KATAN48 we refer to the full version of this paper in [2].

4.3   Attack on KATAN64

Now we consider a fault attack on the third variant of the KATAN block cipher, namely, KATAN64. In KATAN64 we have $L_2 = (s_{38+t}, \cdots, s_{0+t})$ and $L_1 = (s_{63+t}, \cdots, s_{39+t})$. Since each round in KATAN64 requires 3 clocks, if certain internal state bits s_{j+t} cannot be recovered at faulty round t, we can try to recover their values from bit s_{j-3n+t} of faulty round $t - n$, for $j - 3n \geq 39$ and $42 \leq j \leq 63$, or $j - 3n \geq 0$ and $3 \leq j \leq 38$. Our attack on KATAN64 considers faulty rounds $t = 236, 238, 242, 246$ and 250 as the target rounds. Equations obtainable using fault induction after these rounds are provided in the the full version of this paper in [2].

4.4   Attack Complexity

Result on KATAN32. Our experimental simulation of the attack on KATAN32 shows that 21 subkey bits from faulty rounds $t = 231, 237, 243, 249$ can be recovered, requiring collectively 20 specific internal state bit positions (regardless of the round number) to be considered as target faulty bits, as shown in Tables 2–5 in Appendix. The average number of fault injections needed to successfully hit these 20 target faulty bits is 115 (where the average is taken over 10,000 trials).

Since the highest index of the subkey bits is $H = 498$ and the lowest index is $L = 474$ (hence $H - L = 24 < 80$) the target subkey bits can be found in the 80-bit key register within rounds $209 \leq t \leq 236$. Therefore, to recover the secret key, we need to guess the remaining 59 bits of the key register and then to clock the key register backward until round $t = 0$. This reduces the complexity of the attack to 2^{59} computations compared to 2^{80} by exhaustive key search.

Result on KATAN48. The attack on KATAN48 results in recovering 25 sub-key bits considering faulty rounds $t = 234, 238, 242, 246, 250$ which requires collectively 27 specific internal state bits positions to be considered as target faulty bits (refer to Tables 7 and 8 in Appendix and the full version of this paper in [2]). The average number of required fault injections to successfully hit these 27 target faulty bits is 211 (where the average is taken over 10,000 trials). The highest and the lowest subkey bit indexes are $H = 500$ and $L = 476$, respectively (hence $H - L = 24 < 80$), so all the subkey bits can be found within the content of the 80-bit key register at rounds $210 \leq t \leq 237$. Therefore, to recover the secret key we need to guess the remaining 55 bits of the key register and then to clock backward until round $t = 0$ to recover the secret key. Thus, finding the correct key requires 2^{55} computations in this attack.

Result on KATAN64. In attacking KATAN64 we consider faulty rounds $t = 236, 238, 242, 246, 250$ to recover (at least) the same 25 subkey bits as in the attack on KATAN48 which requires collectively 44 specific internal state bit positions to be faulty (refer to the full version of this paper in [2]). The average number of required fault injections to successfully hit these 44 target faulty bits is 278 (where the average is taken over 10,000 trials). This results in an attack with complexity 2^{55} (Noticing that the highest index of the subkey bits is $H = 491$ and the lowest index is $L = 476$ (i.e. $H - L = 15 < 80$); hence, these 25 target subkey bits can be found in the 80-bit secret key register and we only need to guess the remaining 55 bits of the key register).

5 Conclusion

In this paper, we showed fault attacks using a transient single-bit fault model against all three members of the KATAN family; namely, KATAN32, KATAN48 and KATAN64. Our attacks employ the cube attack and its extensions to determine the effective fault injection rounds, to generate the difference characteristics and to generate linear and quadratic equations. The complexity of our attack on KATAN32 is 2^{59} computations and about 115 fault injections. For KATAN48 and KATAN64, the attack requires 2^{55} computations (for both variants), while the required number of fault injections is 211 and 278, respectively. Our fault attacks on KATAN48 and KATAN64, so far, are the only attacks against the full-round versions of these ciphers.

Acknowledgments. We thank Flavio D. Garcia and the anonymous reviewers of ISPEC 2012 for their constructive comments and suggestions.

References

[1] Abdul-Latip, S.F., Reyhanitabar, M.R., Susilo, W., Seberry, J.: Extended Cubes: Enhancing the Cube Attack by Extracting Low-Degree Non-Linear Equations. In: Cheung, B., et al. (eds.) ASIACCS 2011, pp. 296–305. ACM (2011)

[2] Abdul-Latip, S.F., Reyhanitabar, M.R., Susilo, W., Seberry, J.: Fault Analysis of the KATAN Family of Block Ciphers. Cryptology ePrint Archive: Report 2012/030 (full version of this paper)

[3] Bard, G.V., Courtois, N.T., Nakahara Jr., J., Sepehrdad, P., Zhang, B.: Algebraic, AIDA/Cube and Side Channel Analysis of KATAN Family of Block Ciphers. In: Gong, G., Gupta, K.C. (eds.) INDOCRYPT 2010. LNCS, vol. 6498, pp. 176–196. Springer, Heidelberg (2010)

[4] Blum, M., Luby, M., Rubinfield, R.: Self-Testing/Correcting with Application to Numerical Problems. In: STOC, pp. 73–83. ACM, New York (1990)

[5] Biham, E., Shamir, A.: Differential Fault Analysis of Secret Key Cryptosystems. In: Kaliski Jr., B.S. (ed.) CRYPTO 1997. LNCS, vol. 1294, pp. 513–525. Springer, Heidelberg (1997)

[6] Boneh, D., DeMillo, R., Lipton, R.: On the Importance of Checking Cryptographic Protocols for Faults. In: Fumy, W. (ed.) EUROCRYPT 1997. LNCS, vol. 1233, pp. 37–51. Springer, Heidelberg (1997)

[7] De Cannière, C., Dunkelman, O., Knežević, M.: KATAN and KTANTAN — A Family of Small and Efficient Hardware-Oriented Block Ciphers. In: Clavier, C., Gaj, K. (eds.) CHES 2009. LNCS, vol. 5747, pp. 272–288. Springer, Heidelberg (2009)

[8] Dinur, I., Shamir, A.: Cube Attacks on Tweakable Black Box Polynomials. In: Joux, A. (ed.) EUROCRYPT 2009. LNCS, vol. 5479, pp. 278–299. Springer, Heidelberg (2009)

[9] Hoch, J.J., Shamir, A.: Fault Analysis of Stream Ciphers. In: Joye, M., Quisquater, J.-J. (eds.) CHES 2004. LNCS, vol. 3156, pp. 240–253. Springer, Heidelberg (2004)

[10] Hojsík, M., Rudolf, B.: Differential Fault Analysis of Trivium. In: Nyberg, K. (ed.) FSE 2008. LNCS, vol. 5086, pp. 158–172. Springer, Heidelberg (2008)

[11] Hojsík, M., Rudolf, B.: Floating Fault Analysis of Trivium. In: Chowdhury, D.R., Rijmen, V., Das, A. (eds.) INDOCRYPT 2008. LNCS, vol. 5365, pp. 239–250. Springer, Heidelberg (2008)

[12] Hu, Y., Zhang, F., Zhang, Y.: Hard Fault Analysis of Trivium. Cryptology ePrint Archive, Report 2009/333 (2009)

[13] Knellwolf, S., Meier, W., Naya-Plasencia, M.: Conditional Differential Cryptanalysis of NLFSR-Based Cryptosystems. In: Abe, M. (ed.) ASIACRYPT 2010. LNCS, vol. 6477, pp. 130–145. Springer, Heidelberg (2010)

[14] Lai, X.: Higher Order Derivatives and Differential Cryptanalysis. In: Communication and Cryptology, pp. 227–233. Kluwer Academic Publisher (1994)

[15] Skorobogatov, S.P., Anderson, R.J.: Optical Fault Injection Attacks. In: Kaliski Jr., B.S., Koç, Ç.K., Paar, C. (eds.) CHES 2002. LNCS, vol. 2523, pp. 31–48. Springer, Heidelberg (2003)

[16] Vielhaber, M.: Breaking ONE.FIVIUM by AIDA an Algebraic IV Differential Attack. IACR ePrint Archive, Report 2007/413 (2007),
http://eprint.iacr.org/2007/413

[17] Vielhaber, M.: AIDA Breaks BIVIUM (A&B) in 1 Minute Dual Core CPU Time. Cryptology ePrint Archive, Report 2009/402, IACR (2009)

A   Appendix

Table 2. Polynomial equations obtained using the difference between non-faulty and faulty ciphertexts for fault induction after $t = 231$ rounds of KATAN32

Faulty Bit	Ciphertext Bit Differential	Polynomial Equations
s_{8+t}	Δc_7	s_{10+t}
s_{9+t}	Δc_8	s_{11+t}
s_{10+t}	Δc_9	s_{12+t}
s_{11+t}	Δc_{17}	s_{9+t}
s_{19+t}	Δc_{28}	s_{22+t}
s_{20+t}	Δc_{29}	s_{23+t}
s_{21+t}	Δc_{30}	s_{24+t}
s_{22+t}	Δc_{31}	s_{25+t}

Table 3. Polynomial equations obtained using the difference between non-faulty and faulty ciphertexts for fault induction after $t = 237$ rounds of KATAN32

Faulty Bit	Ciphertext Bit Differential	Polynomial Equations
s_{1+t}	Δc_{28}	$s_{19+t} + s_{23+t} + s_{28+t} + k_{480} + s_{21+t}s_{24+t}$
	Δc_{24}	$s_{22+t} + s_{26+t} + s_{31+t} + k_{474} + s_{24+t}s_{27+t}$
	Δc_6	s_{6+t}
	Δc_4	$s_{4+t} + s_{15+t} + k_{481} + s_{0+t}s_{5+t} + s_{7+t}s_{9+t}$
s_{2+t}	Δc_{29}	$s_{20+t} + s_{24+t} + s_{29+t} + k_{478} + s_{22+t}s_{25+t}$
	Δc_{27}	s_{4+t}
	Δc_{25}	s_{0+t}
	Δc_5	$s_{5+t} + s_{16+t} + k_{479} + s_{1+t}s_{6+t} + s_{8+t}s_{10+t}$
s_{3+t}	Δc_{30}	$s_{25+t} + s_{30+t} + k_{476} + s_{23+t}s_{26+t}$
	Δc_{28}	s_{5+t}
	Δc_{26}	s_{1+t}
	Δc_{12}	s_{8+t}
	Δc_6	$s_{6+t} + s_{17+t} + k_{477} + s_{2+t}s_{7+t} + s_{9+t}s_{11+t}$
s_{4+t}	Δc_{27}	s_{2+t}
	Δc_7	$s_{7+t} + s_{18+t} + k_{475} + s_{3+t}s_{8+t} + s_{10+t}s_{12+t}$
s_{5+t}	Δc_{30}	s_{7+t}
	Δc_{28}	s_{3+t}
	Δc_{21}	$s_{21+t} + s_{26+t} + k_{484} + s_{19+t}s_{22+t}$
	Δc_8	s_{19+t}
s_{9+t}	Δc_2	s_{11+t}
s_{10+t}	Δc_{12}	s_{12+t}
s_{11+t}	Δc_7	s_{9+t}
s_{12+t}	Δc_{12}	s_{10+t}
s_{19+t}	Δc_{22}	s_{22+t}
s_{20+t}	Δc_{23}	s_{23+t}
s_{21+t}	Δc_{24}	s_{24+t}
s_{22+t}	Δc_{25}	s_{25+t}
s_{23+t}	Δc_{26}	s_{26+t}
	Δc_{12}	s_{20+t}
s_{24+t}	Δc_{27}	s_{27+t}
	Δc_{20}	$s_{7+t} + s_{18+t} + s_{22+t} + s_{27+t} + k_{475} + k_{482} + s_{3+t}s_{8+t} + s_{10+t}s_{12+t} + s_{20+t}s_{23+t} + 1$
	Δc_{13}	s_{21+t}

Table 4. Polynomial equations obtained using the difference between non-faulty and faulty ciphertexts for fault induction after $t = 243$ rounds of KATAN32

Faulty Bit	Ciphertext Bit Differential	Polynomial Equations
s_{0+t}	Δc_{21}	$s_{22+t} + s_{27+t} + k_{494} + s_{20+t}s_{23+t}$
s_{1+t}	Δc_{27}	s_{6+t}
	Δc_{22}	$s_{23+t} + s_{28+t} + k_{492} + s_{21+t}s_{24+t}$
	Δc_{20}	s_{3+t}
s_{2+t}	Δc_{28}	s_{7+t}
	Δc_{23}	$s_{24+t} + s_{29+t} + k_{490} + s_{22+t}s_{25+t}$
	Δc_{21}	s_{4+t}
	Δc_{19}	s_{0+t}
s_{3+t}	Δc_{24}	$s_{25+t} + s_{30+t} + k_{488} + s_{23+t}s_{26+t}$
	Δc_{22}	s_{5+t}
	Δc_{20}	s_{1+t}
	Δc_{0}	$s_{6+t} + s_{17+t} + k_{489} + s_{2+t}s_{7+t} + s_{9+t}s_{11+t}$
s_{4+t}	Δc_{25}	$s_{26+t} + s_{31+t} + k_{486} + s_{24+t}s_{27+t}$
	Δc_{21}	s_{2+t}
	Δc_{1}	$s_{7+t} + s_{18+t} + k_{487} + s_{3+t}s_{8+t} + s_{10+t}s_{12+t}$
s_{18+t}	Δc_{4}	s_{21+t}
	Δc_{1}	$s_{4+t} + s_{15+t} + k_{493} + s_{0+t}s_{5+t} + s_{7+t}s_{9+t}$
s_{19+t}	Δc_{5}	s_{22+t}
	Δc_{2}	$s_{5+t} + s_{16+t} + k_{491} + s_{1+t}s_{6+t} + s_{8+t}s_{10+t}$
s_{21+t}	Δc_{7}	s_{24+t}
s_{22+t}	Δc_{8}	s_{25+t}
	Δc_{5}	s_{19+t}
s_{23+t}	Δc_{9}	s_{26+t}
	Δc_{6}	s_{20+t}
s_{24+t}	Δc_{10}	s_{27+t}
	Δc_{7}	s_{21+t}
s_{26+t}	Δc_{20}	$s_{21+t} + s_{23+t} + s_{31+t} + k_{486} + k_{496} + s_{19+t}s_{22+t} + s_{24+t}s_{27+t} + 1$
	Δc_{9}	s_{23+t}

Table 5. Polynomial equations obtained using the difference between non-faulty and faulty ciphertexts for fault induction after $t = 249$ rounds of KATAN32

Faulty Bit	Ciphertext Bit Differential	Polynomial Equations
s_{4+t}	Δc_{19}	$s_{22+t} + s_{26+t} + s_{31+t} + k_{498} + s_{24+t}s_{27+t}$
s_{5+t}	Δc_{20}	s_{0+t}
s_{21+t}	Δc_1	s_{24+t}
s_{23+t}	Δc_3	s_{26+t}
	Δc_0	s_{20+t}
s_{25+t}	Δc_2	s_{22+t}

Table 6. Difference characteristics for KATAN32 (faulty round t=237). '0' and '1' denote differential values 0 and 1 of the corresponding ciphertext bit differential Δc_j, and '-' denotes an unknown differential value.

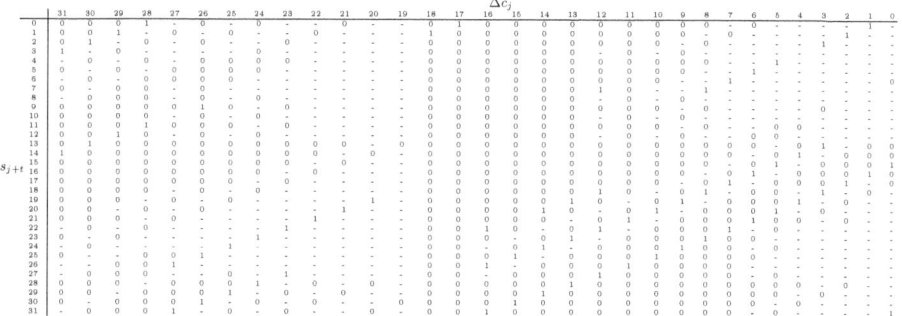

Table 7. Polynomial equations obtained using the difference between non-faulty and faulty ciphertexts for fault induction after t=234 rounds of KATAN48

Faulty Bit	Ciphertext Bit Differential	Polynomial Equations
s_{6+t}	Δc_{26}	s_{15+t}
	Δc_{25}	s_{14+t}
s_{9+t}	Δc_{28}	s_{17+t}
s_{11+t}	Δc_{18}	$s_{19+t} + 1$
s_{29+t}	Δc_{41}	s_{37+t}
s_{30+t}	Δc_{42}	s_{38+t}

Table 8. Polynomial equations obtained using the difference between non-faulty and faulty ciphertexts for fault induction after t=238 rounds of KATAN48

Faulty Bit	Ciphertext Bit Differential	Polynomial Equations
s_{4+t}	Δc_9	$s_{12+t} + 1$
	Δc_{16}	s_{13+t}
s_{5+t}	Δc_{17}	s_{14+t}
s_{6+t}	Δc_{24}	s_{15+t}
s_{8+t}	Δc_{47}	s_{0+t}
	Δc_{13}	s_{16+t}
s_{9+t}	Δc_{14}	s_{17+t}
s_{10+t}	Δc_{15}	s_{18+t}
s_{11+t}	Δc_{16}	s_{19+t}
s_{12+t}	Δc_{17}	s_{20+t}
	Δc_{16}	s_{29+t}
	Δc_{15}	s_{3+t}
s_{13+t}	Δc_{17}	s_{30+t}
s_{14+t}	Δc_{18}	s_{31+t}
	Δc_{17}	s_{5+t}
s_{15+t}	Δc_{19}	s_{32+t}
	Δc_6	s_{7+t}
s_{16+t}	Δc_{20}	s_{33+t}
	Δc_{13}	s_{8+t}
s_{17+t}	Δc_{38}	$s_{29+t} + s_{35+t} + s_{41+t} + k_{482} + s_{30+t}s_{38+t}$
	Δc_{21}	s_{34+t}
	Δc_{14}	s_{9+t}
	Δc_{12}	$s_{16+t} + s_{25+t} + k_{479} + s_{3+t}s_{12+t} + s_{10+t}s_{18+t}$
s_{18+t}	Δc_{22}	s_{35+t}
	Δc_{15}	s_{10+t}
s_{19+t}	Δc_{46}	s_{1+t}
	Δc_{40}	$s_{31+t} + s_{37+t} + s_{43+t} + k_{480} + s_{32+t}s_{40+t}$
	Δc_{14}	$s_{18+t} + s_{27+t} + k_{477} + s_{5+t}s_{14+t} + s_{12+t}s_{20+t}$
s_{29+t}	Δc_{33}	s_{37+t}
s_{30+t}	Δc_{25}	s_{38+t}
	Δc_{17}	$s_{13+t} + s_{22+t} + k_{483} + s_{0+t}s_{9+t} + s_{7+t}s_{15+t}$
s_{31+t}	Δc_{36}	$s_{33+t} + s_{39+t} + s_{45+t} + k_{478} + s_{34+t}s_{42+t} + 1$
	Δc_{35}	s_{39+t}
	Δc_{18}	$s_{14+t} + s_{23+t} + k_{481} + s_{1+t}s_{10+t} + s_{8+t}s_{16+t}$
	Δc_7	s_{4+t}
	Δc_1	$s_{4+t} + s_{40+t} + s_{46+t} + k_{476} + s_{35+t}s_{43+t}$
s_{32+t}	Δc_{36}	s_{40+t}
s_{33+t}	Δc_{37}	s_{41+t}
s_{34+t}	Δc_{38}	s_{42+t}
s_{35+t}	Δc_{39}	s_{43+t}

Biclique Cryptanalysis of Reduced-Round Piccolo Block Cipher

Yanfeng Wang[1,2], Wenling Wu[1], and Xiaoli Yu[1]

[1] State Key Laboratory of Information Security,
Institute of Software, Chinese Academy of Sciences, Beijing 100190, P.R. China
[2] Graduate University of Chinese Academy of Sciences, Beijing 100049, P.R. China
wangyanfengok1@gmail.com, {wwl,yuxiaoli}@is.iscas.ac.cn

Abstract. Piccolo is a lightweight block cipher, with a fixed 64-bit block size and variable key length 80- or 128-bit, which was proposed at CHES 2011. The iterative structure of Piccolo is a variant of Generalized Feistel Network. The transformation utilizing different-size-word based permutation improves diffusion property of Piccolo and the simple key schedule algorithm reduces hardware costs. By analyzing the distribution of the subkeys, we present a biclique cryptanalysis of full round Piccolo-80 without postwhitening keys and 28-round Piccolo-128 without prewhitening keys. The attacks are respectively with data complexity of 2^{48} and 2^{24} chosen ciphertexts, and with time complexity of $2^{78.95}$ and $2^{126.79}$ encryptions.

Keywords: Lightweight block cipher, Piccolo, Meet-in-the-middle, Biclique cryptanalysis, Complexity.

1 Introduction

The large development of low resource devices such as RFID tags and sensor nodes increases the need to provide security among such devices. The implementation costs should be taken into account when choosing security algorithms for resource-limited devices. Symmetric-key algorithms, especially block ciphers, still play an important role in the security of embedded systems. Recently, a lot of block ciphers suitable for these environments have been designed, such as PRESENT[1], MIBS[8], KATAN & KTANTAN[4], TWIS[10], PRINT[9], LBlock[13], KLEIN[6], LED[7] etc.

Piccolo[12] is a 64-bit block cipher and is designed to be particularly suitable for low-cost devices. According to the different key length, we denote the ciphers by Piccolo-80/128 respectively. The designers evaluated the security of Piccolo by various attacks and attacked Piccolo-80 to 17 rounds and Piccolo-128 to 21 rounds under the related-key model. The best result of actual single-key attack is 3-Subset Meet-in-the-Middle(MITM) attacks on 14-round Piccolo-80 and 21-round Piccolo-128 without whitening keys whose complexity is not presented. Designers also took the worst setting into consideration.

M.D. Ryan, B. Smyth, and G. Wang (Eds.): ISPEC 2012, LNCS 7232, pp. 337–352, 2012.

MITM attack[5], introduced by Diffe and Hellman, is a typical method in the cryptanalysis of block cipher, whose outstanding property is the extremely low data complexity. Over the past few years, variants have also been developed, for example 3-Subset MITM[3]. The method has been improved with many techniques to carry out the preimage attack on the hash function[11]. These techniques include spice-and-cut framework, initial structure, partial matching etc. Using the characteristic of key expansion in cipher algorithm, adversary can construct an initial structure and filter out wrong keys based on the result of partial matching, which is the main idea of the method. Recently, [2] gave the first attack on the full AES-128/-192/-256 with the biclique technique.

In this paper, 6-round bicliques of dimension 8 are constructed for both Piccolo-80 and Piccolo-128. Taking advantage of the 8-dimension bicliques, we give an attack on full round Piccolo-80 without postwhitening keys and another attack on 28-round Piccolo-128 without prewhitening keys. The attacks are respectively with data complexity of 2^{48} and 2^{24} chosen ciphertexts, and with time complexity of $2^{78.95}$ and $2^{126.79}$ encryptions. As far as we know, these are currently the best results on Piccolo.

This paper is organized as follows. Section 2 provides a brief description of Piccolo and the notations used throughout this paper. Section 3 presents the structure of the biclique cryptanalysis of reduced-round Piccolo. Section 4 presents the key recovery attacks on full round Piccolo-80 and 28-round Piccolo-128. Finally, we present conclusions in Section 5.

2   A Brief Description of Piccolo

We first introduce some notations used throughout this paper and then give a simple description of the block cipher Piccolo.

2.1   Notations

r: iterative rounds.
k_i: i-th[1] 16-bit group of the key k.
$a|b$:concatenation.
$a_{(b)}$: b denotes the bit length of a.
$\{a\}_b$: representation in base b.
$a_{[c-d]}$: c-th bit to d-th bit of a.
X_t: t-th byte of X.
$X_{t,s}$: t-th and s-th bytes of X, 16 bits in total.
$P^r_{(64)}$: 64-bit input of r-th round.
$T^r_{(64)}$: state after F-function in r-th round.
$C^r_{(64)}$: 64-bit output of r-th round.

---

[1] All counts involved in the text always start from 0.

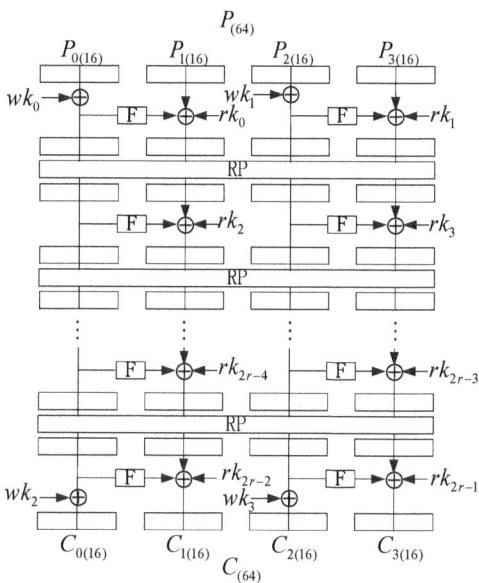

Fig. 1. The structure of the block cipher Piccolo

2.2   Description of Piccolo

Encryption Algorithm. The general structure of Piccolo is a variant of Generalized Feistel Network, which is depicted in Figure 1. The number of iterative rounds is 25 for Piccolo-80 and is 31 for Piccolo-128. Each round is made up of two functions $F : \{0,1\}^{16} \rightarrow \{0,1\}^{16}$ and one round permutation $RP : \{0,1\}^{64} \rightarrow \{0,1\}^{64}$. F consists of two S-box layers separated by a diffusion matrix M. RP divides a 64-bit input into eight bytes and then permutes them(Figure 2).

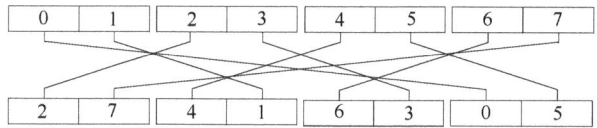

Fig. 2. Round permutation of the block cipher Piccolo

Key Schedule. To reduce the cost of hardware and to decrease key set-up time, the key schedule of Piccolo, referred to as KS_r^{80} and KS_r^{128}, is rather simple. A series of 16-bit constants, con_i^{80} and con_i^{128}, are used in the key schedule.

Key Schedule for 80-Bit Key Mode: The key scheduling function for the 80-bit key mode divides an 80-bit key $K_{(80)}$ into five 16-bit words $k_{i(16)}$ $(0 \le i < 5)$ and provides the subkeys as follows:

Algorithm $KS_r^{80}(K_{(80)})$:

$wk_0 \leftarrow k_0^L|k_1^R, \ wk_1 \leftarrow k_1^L|k_0^R, \ wk_2 \leftarrow k_4^L|k_3^R, \ wk_3 \leftarrow k_3^L|k_4^R$

for $i \leftarrow 0$ to $(r-1)$ do

$$(rk_{2i}, rk_{2i+1}) \leftarrow (con_{2i}^{80}, con_{2i+1}^{80}) \oplus \begin{cases} (k_2, k_3) \text{ if } i \bmod 5 = 0 \text{ or } 2 \\ (k_0, k_1) \text{ if } i \bmod 5 = 1 \text{ or } 4 \\ (k_4, k_4) \text{ if } i \bmod 5 = 3 \end{cases}$$

Key Schedule for 128-Bit Key Mode: The key scheduling function for the 128-bit key mode divides a 128-bit key $K_{(128)}$ into eight 16-bit words $k_{i(16)}(0 \le i < 8)$ and provides subkeys as follows:

Algorithm $KS_r^{128}(K_{(128)})$:

$wk_0 \leftarrow k_0^L|k_1^R, \ wk_1 \leftarrow k_1^L|k_0^R, \ wk_2 \leftarrow k_4^L|k_7^R, \ wk_3 \leftarrow k_7^L|k_4^R$

for $i \leftarrow 0$ to $(2r-1)$ do

if $(i+2) \bmod 8 = 0$ then

$(k_0, k_1, k_2, k_3, k_4, k_5, k_6, k_7) \leftarrow (k_2, k_1, k_6, k_7, k_0, k_3, k_4, k_5)$

$rk_i \leftarrow k_{(i+2) \bmod 8} \oplus con_i^{128}$

3   Biclique Cryptanalysis of Piccolo

3.1   Definition of Biclique

Now we introduce the notion of biclique[2]. Let f be a subcipher that connects 2^d states $\{S_j\}$ to 2^d ciphertexts $\{C_i\}$ with 2^{2d} keys $\{K[i,j]\}$:

$$\{K[i,j]\} = \begin{bmatrix} K[0,0] & K[0,1] & \dots & K[0, 2^d - 1] \\ \dots & \dots & & \\ K[2^d - 1, 0] & K[2^d - 1, 1] & \dots & K[2^d - 1, 2^d - 1] \end{bmatrix}.$$

The 3-tuple $[\{C_i\}, \{S_j\}, \{K[i,j]\}]$ is called a d-dimensional biclique, if $C_i = f_{K[i,j]}(S_j)$ for all $i, j \in \{0, \dots, 2^d - 1\}$. Figure 3 stands for the relations between 3-tuple. What's more, the vertexes of the graph stand for states while the edges stand for keys. Besides dimension, the length, which is defined as the number of rounds that f covered, is also a significant characteristic of a biclique. According to the definition of biclique, a d-dimensional biclique needs to establish 2^{2d} relationships simultaneously. [2] proposed an approach to find a d-dimensional biclique from related-key differentials. And it is difficult to construct a long biclique of high dimension for many cipher algorithms, especially for the algorithm with well diffusion. As a result, the availability of the Biclique Cryptanalysis depends on the cipher's diffusion property and key schedule. In detail, MITM with biclique attack works well for block ciphers having simple key schedule and slow diffusion.

After analyzing the key schedule algorithm of Piccolo, we can come up with the conclusion that the subkeys are linearly derived from the master key. Furthermore, six rounds (19-24 rounds) in Piccolo-80 and six rounds (22-27 rounds)

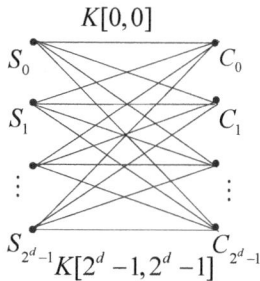

$K[0,0]$

S_0 C_0

S_1 C_1

$\vdots$ $\vdots$

S_{2^d-1} $K[2^d-1,2^d-1]$ C_{2^d-1}

Fig. 3. d-dimensional biclique

in Piccolo-128 use k_4 and k_0 only once, respectively. Taking advantage of these properties and in consideration of the data complexity, we construct 6-round biclique for both Piccolo-80 and Piccolo-128, with the same dimension of 8.

3.2 Pattern of Biclique Cryptanalysis of Piccolo

In fact, the biclique cryptanalysis of Piccolo is a meet-in-the-middle attack with biclique, which follows the strategy of initial structure and partial matching. At first, we construct a series of bicliques with high dimension by tools like related-key differentials. Then, we filter out wrong keys in every biclique by matching the internal variable in two directions. The attacks described in our paper are always in the single-key model and the procedures are described as follows:

Step 1. *Part Key Space.* Part the key space into groups, in other words, the key groups cover the full key space and do not intersect.

Step 2. *Build Biclique.* Construct a biclique of appropriate dimension for each key group.

Step 3. *Filter Out Keys.* Delete wrong keys that don't match for every biclique.
1. Choose the position of the matching internal variable v.
2. Ask the decryption oracle to decrypt the ciphertext C_i obtained during the building of biclique, then get the corresponding plaintexts P_i. In our attack, the dimension of the biclique is 8, so the number of P_i is 2^8.
3. Let $P_i \rightarrow v$ be forward direction computation and $v \leftarrow S_j$ be backward direction computation. If one of the tested keys $K[i,j]$ is the correct key, it will map state S_j to the plaintext P_i. Therefore, the adversary can delete the wrong key that does not match.

Step 4. *Search Candidates.* Exhaustively test the remaining key candidates until the correct key is found.

The structure of the Biclique Cryptanalysis aimed at Piccolo can be described as Figure 4.

By using the technique of partial matching, the computational complexity of matching will be reduced significantly. Therefore, the complexity of the whole attack will be reduced and moreover we probably find a better attack.

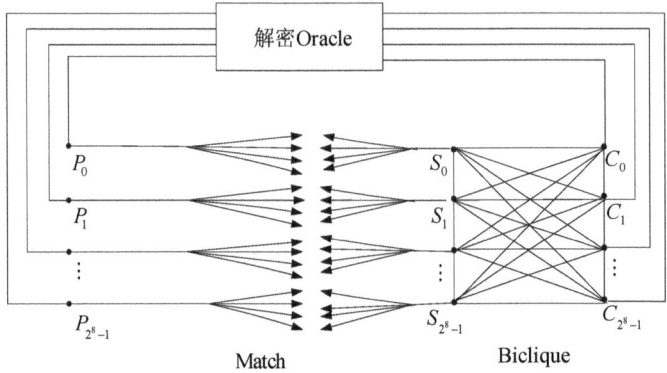

Fig. 4. Structure of Biclique Cryptanalysis

4   Key Recovery for Reduced-Round Piccolo

In this section, the key recoveries for full round Piccolo-80 without postwhitening and 28-round Piccolo-128 without prewhitening are given. The parameters of the key recovery are summarized in Table 1.

Table 1. Parameters of the key recovery in Piccolo

Piccolo-n	Rounds	BDimension	Matching v	Forward Rounds	Backward Rounds	BLength
Piccolo-80	25(0-24)	8	$T_{1,4}^{11}$	0-11	18-12	6(19-24)
Piccolo-128	28(0-27)	8	$T_{1,4}^{15}$	0-15	21-16	6(22-27)

† v :matching variable.
† BLength: Length of Biclique; † BDimension: Dimension of Biclique.

4.1   Key Recovery for Full Round Piccolo-80

According to the key schedule, we know that the subkeys are linearly derived from the master key (Table 2). Moreover, six rounds (19-24 rounds) in Piccolo-80 use k_4 only once. Using this property, we can build 6-round biclique of dimension 8 and then explore a MITM attack with biclique on full round Piccolo-80 without postwhitening keys.

Key Partitioning. For more clarity we define the key groups with respect to the master key and enumerate the groups of keys by 2^{64} base keys. The base keys $K[0,0]$ are all possible 2^{64} 80-bit values, with the last 16 bits fixed to $0_{(16)}$ and the remaining 64 bits running over all values. The keys $K[i,j]$ ($i,j \in \{0,1\}^8$) of one group are defined as follows:

$$K_4[0,0] = 00 \quad K_4[i,0] = i0$$
$$K_4[0,j] = 0j \quad K_4[i,j] = ij$$

Table 2. Key schedule of Piccolo-80

Piccolo-80					
whitening keys	$wk_0 = k_0^L|k_1^R, \;\; wk_1 = k_1^L|k_0^R, \;\; wk_2 = k_4^L|k_3^R, \;\; wk_3 = k_3^L|k_4^R$				
round i	$rk_{2i} \oplus con_{2i}^{80}$	$rk_{2i+1} \oplus con_{2i+1}^{80}$	round i	$rk_{2i} \oplus con_{2i}^{80}$	$rk_{2i+1} \oplus con_{2i+1}^{80}$
0	k_2	k_3	13	k_4	k_4
1	k_0	k_1	14	k_0	k_1
2	k_2	k_3	15	k_2	k_3
3	k_4	k_4	16	k_0	k_1
4	k_0	k_1	17	k_2	k_3
5	k_2	k_3	18	k_4	k_4
6	k_0	k_1	19	k_0	k_1
7	k_2	k_3	20	k_2	k_3
8	k_4	k_4	21	k_0	k_1
9	k_0	k_1	22	k_2	k_3
10	k_2	k_3	23	k_4	k_4
11	k_0	k_1	24	k_0	k_1
12	k_2	k_3			

† light grey color: position of key difference;
† italic: rounds covered by bicliques.

This yields the partition of the Piccolo-80 key space into 2^{64} groups of 2^{16} keys each. *The following two procedures are exhaustively applied to every key group.*

6-Round Biclique of Dimension 8. We will construct a 6-round (f: 19-th round to 24-th round) biclique of dimension 8 for every key group. Having known the keys covered by the biclique, we need to determine 2^8 states and 2^8 ciphertexts that satisfy the definition of the biclique.

The state S is defined as $P_{(64)}^{19}$, which is the input of the 19-th round encryption, and C is the output of the 24-th round i.e. the ciphertext of Piccolo-80 without postwhitening keys. Procedure of computing the states and ciphertexts is depicted in Figure 5:

Step 1. The adversary fixes $C_0 = 0_{(64)}$ and derives $S_0 = f_{K[0,0]}^{-1}(C_0)$ (Figure 5, Left). The process is called basic computation.

Step 2. Encrypt S_0 under different keys $K[i,0]$ ($0 < i < 2^8$) and the corresponding ciphertexts are denoted by C_i (Figure 5, Middle). The key differences between keys $K[i,0]$ and $K[0,0]$ will cause states' differences which are noted with black color and the computational complexity is determined by the influence of the key difference.

Step 3. Decrypt C_0 under different keys $K[0,j]$ ($0 < j < 2^8$) and the corresponding results are denoted by S_j (Figure 5, Right). Similarly, the influence of the key difference is noted with black color.

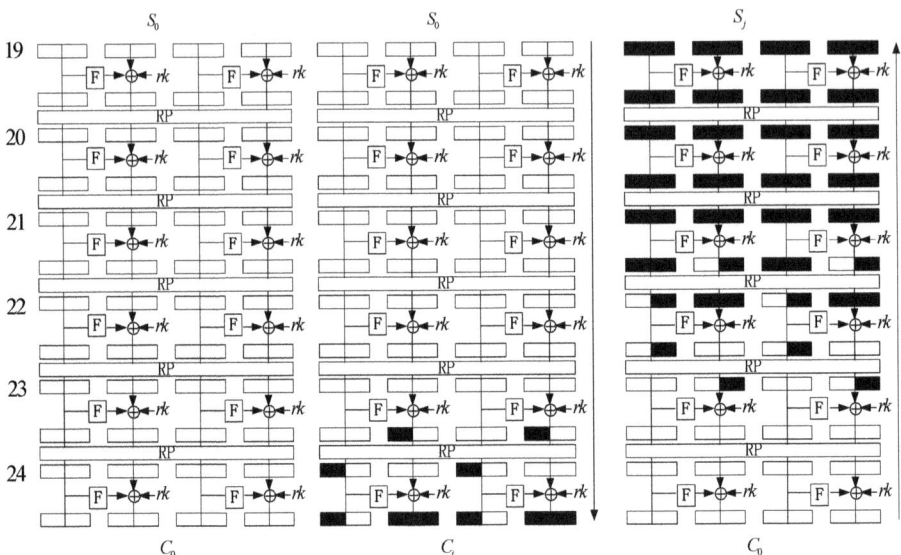

Fig. 5. Biclique construction in Piccolo-80

The black color in the figure represents that the computation process is different with the basic computation. Thanks to the simple key schedule of Piccolo, two differential trails caused by key difference share no active area. Luckily, it is easy to prove that the tuples also conform to combined differentials, that is to say: $S_j \xrightarrow{K[i,j]} C_i$ $(i, j \in \{0, 1\}^8)$ are always true.

Until now, for every key group, we obtain a corresponding 8-dimensional biclique as discussed above.

Matching over 19 Rounds. Taking the computational complexity into account we choose $v = T_{1,4}^{11}$, which is a 16-bit length of the state after F-function in round 11, as the internal matching variable. Other positions also can be chosen as internal matching variable, such as $T_{0,5}^{11}$, $T_{1,4}^{10}$, $T_{0,5}^{10}$ and so on. The choosing is according to the principle that the attack complexity is better than the brute force attack. Next, we compute the values of the matching variables in both directions and delete the wrong key that doesn't match.

Backward direction: Now we evaluate the amount of computation in backward direction. Let S_j be fixed and use keys $K[i, j]$ $(0 \le i < 2^8)$ to partly decrypt S_j. We can get the corresponding values of $T_{1,4}^{11}$, denoted by $V_{i,j}$. Because of the same starting point, the computational complexity is determined by the influence caused by key differences between $K[i, j]$ $(i \ne 0)$ and $K[0, j]$. As shown in the right part of Figure 6, there is no difference between the states noted by grid line and we can skip the computation of the states with white color obtaining the matching variables.

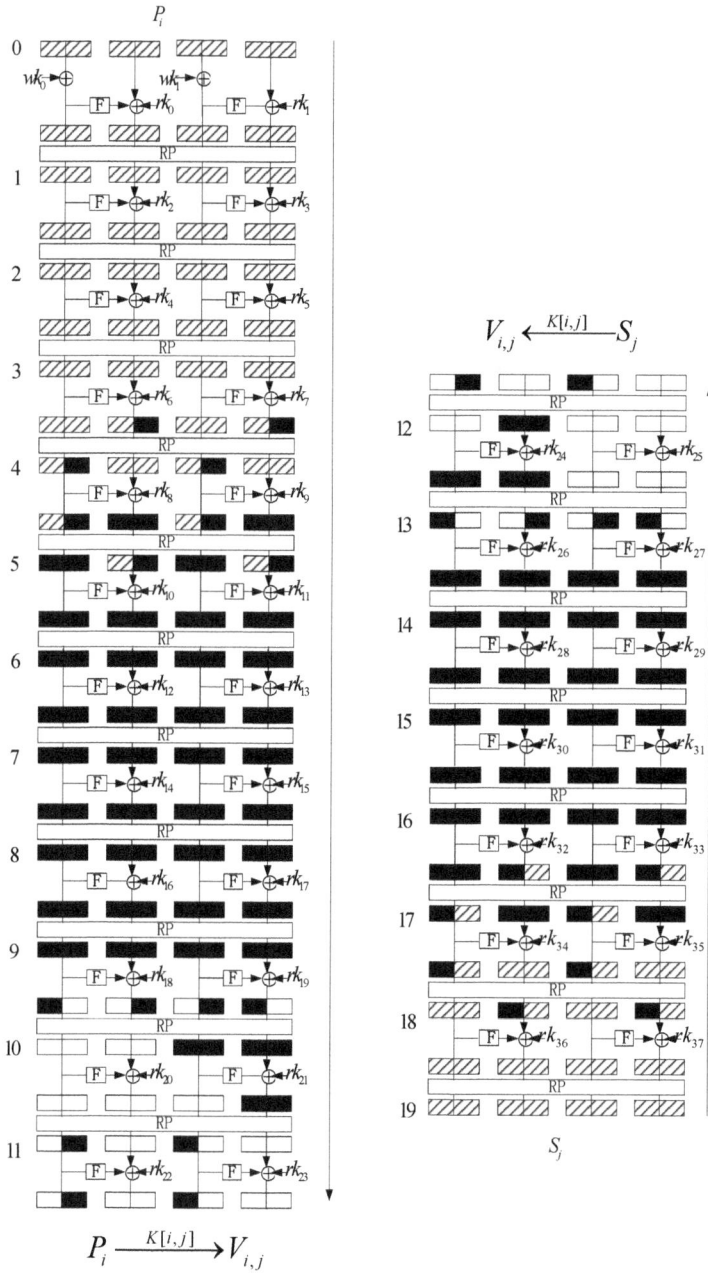

Fig. 6. Process of MITM : Biclique analysis of full round Piccolo-80

F functions are the major contributor to the computational complexity of the attack. Therefore, in order to simply evaluate the complexity, we firstly count the number of F functions that we need to compute and compare it with that in the round-reduced cipher.

Moreover, for a single S_j, the matching values can be obtained after computing 2 F functions(noted with grid line) once and 11 F functions (noted with black color) 2^8 times.

Forward direction: The process of forward computation is a little more complex than that of backward direction. Firstly, we ask for the decryptions of the ciphertexts C_i ($0 \leq i < 2^8$) and get 2^8 plaintexts P_i. Then we encrypt the plaintexts P_i with the keys $K[i,j]$ ($0 \leq j < 2^8$) to $T_{1,4}^{11}$.

As demonstrated in the left part of Figure 6, it makes no difference between the encryptions of the first 4 rounds (0-3 rounds), which is not true for the following rounds. As a result, for a single P_i, the area to be computed 2^8 times includes 13 F-functions and the area to be computed only once includes 8 F-functions.

Search Candidates. In the last stage of the attack, the attacker exhaustively tests the remaining key candidates in each key group, until the correct key is found.

Complexities. When evaluating the performance of the attack described above, we need to consider both the data complexity and the computational complexity.

Data Complexity. The data complexity is directly determined by the number of ciphertexts that we need to decrypt (Figure 5). We fix $C_0 = 0_{(64)}$ for every biclique and all the ciphertexts share the same values in bytes $C_{1,5}$, so the data complexity does not exceed 2^{48}.

Computational Complexity. First, let us see the complexity of constructing a single biclique with $C_0 = 0_{(64)}$. As before, we aim at counting the F functions that we need to compute. Firstly, the basic computation costs 12 F functions. In order to get C_i ($0 \leq i < 2^8$), we need to compute 2 F functions 2^8 times. Similarly, computing S_j ($0 \leq j < 2^8$) involves 8 F functions 2^8 times. Thus, a biclique is constructed with complexity of $2^{5.7}$ full round Piccolo-80 encryptions.

In the matching part we compute the internal variable with 16 bits in two directions for each biclique, which spends $2^8(11 \times 2^8 + 2)$ F functions in backward direction and $2^8(13 \times 2^8 + 8)$ F functions in forward direction. In total, it costs $2^8(24 \times 2^8 + 10)$ F functions, which is about $2^{14.94}$ Piccolo-80 encryptions. Because we test 2^{16} keys to see whether the 16-bit positions match or not, the number of remaining key candidates in each key group is $2^{16-16} = 1$ on the average. Altogether, we need 2^{64} bicliques. The whole computational complexity is estimated as:

$$C = 2^{64}(2^{5.7} + 2^{14.94} + 1) \approx 2^{78.95}.$$

The probability to recovery the right key of full round Piccolo-80 without post-whitening keys is 1, since we have generated biclique for every key group.

4.2   Key Recovery for 28-Round Piccolo-128

The relationship between the master key and the subkeys used in the first 28 rounds is described in Table 3. Obviously, six rounds (22-27 rounds) in Piccolo-128 only use k_0 once. This property is used to build a biclique of dimension 8 and we explore biclique cryptanalysis of 28-round Piccolo-128 without prewhitening keys.

Table 3. Key schedule of the first 28 rounds in Piccolo-128

Piccolo-128				
whitening keys	$wk_0 = k_0^L\|k_1^R,\ wk_1 = k_1^L\|k_0^R,\ wk_2 = k_4^L\|k_7^R,\ wk_3 = k_7^L\|k_4^R$			
round i	$rk_{2i} \oplus con_{2i}^{128}$	$rk_{2i+1} \oplus con_{2i+1}^{128}$	round i	$rk_{2i} \oplus con_{2i}^{128}$	$rk_{2i+1} \oplus con_{2i+1}^{128}$
0	k_2	k_3	14	k_2	k_7
1	k_4	k_5	15	k_0	k_1
2	k_6	k_7	16	k_2	k_7
3	k_2	k_1	17	k_4	k_3
4	k_6	k_7	18	k_6	k_5
5	k_0	k_3	19	k_2	k_1
6	k_4	k_5	20	k_6	k_5
7	k_6	k_1	21	k_0	k_7
8	k_4	k_5	22	k_4	k_3
9	k_2	k_7	23	k_6	k_1
10	k_0	k_3	24	k_4	k_3
11	k_4	k_1	25	k_2	k_5
12	k_0	k_3	26	k_0	k_7
13	k_6	k_5	27	k_4	k_1

† light grey color: position of key difference;
† italic: rounds covered by bicliques.

Key Partitioning. The base keys $K[0,0]$ are all possible 2^{112} 128-bit values where the first 16 bits are fixed to $0_{(16)}$ and the remaining 112 bits run over all values. The keys $\{K[i,j]\ (i,j \in \{0,1\}^8)\}$ in one group are defined as:

$$K_0[0,0] = 00 \quad K_0[i,0] = i0$$

$$K_0[0,j] = 0j \quad K_0[i,j] = ij$$

This divides the Piccolo-128 key space into the 2^{112} groups of 2^{16} keys each. *And the following two phases are exhaustively applied to every key group.*

6-Round Biclique of Dimension 8. The process of building a 6-round (f: 22-th round to 27-th round) biclique for every key group is similar to that in Piccolo-80. The state is defined as $P_{(64)}^{22}$ and the procedure of obtaining the 2^8 states and 2^8 ciphertexts is shown in Figure 7:

Step 1. Basic computation. The adversary fixes $C_0 = 0_{(64)}$ and computes the value of $S_0 = f_{K[0,0]}^{-1}(C_0)$ (Figure 7, Left).

Step 2. Encrypt S_0 under different keys $K[i,0]$ $(0 < i < 2^8)$ and get C_i (Figure 7, Middle). Similarly, the influence of the key difference is noted with black color.

Step 3. Decrypt C_0 under different keys $K[0,j]$ $(0 < j < 2^8)$ to derive S_j and the differences are noted with black color (Figure 7, Right).

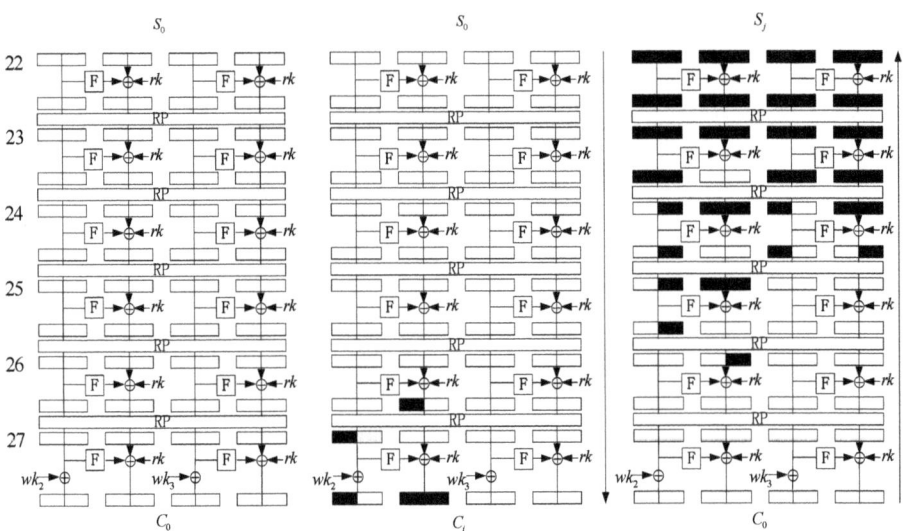

Fig. 7. Biclique construction in Piccolo-128

As before, the three tuples $[\{C_i\}, \{S_j\}, \{K[i,j]\}]$ satisfy the definition of biclique:

$$S_j \xrightarrow{K[i,j]} C_i \ (i,j \in \{0,1\}^8).$$

Matching over 22 Rounds. Though the general pattern is similar, the procedure of partial matching in this attack has a little difference with that in Piccolo-80 because of the different key schedule algorithm. In the partial matching process, we choose $T_{1,4}^{15}$ as the internal matching variable.

Backward direction. Now we evaluate the amount of computation in backward direction. Similarly, as shown in the right part of Figure 8, there is no difference between the states noted by grid line and we can skip the computation of the states with white color obtaining the matching variables. And the matching values can be obtained by decrypting 8 F functions 2^8 times and 3 F functions once for every S_j.

Forward direction. Firstly, we ask for the decryption of the ciphertexts C_i $(0 \leq i < 2^8)$ and get 2^8 plaintexts P_i. Then encrypt the plaintexts P_i with the keys $K[i,j]$ $(0 \leq j < 2^8)$ to $v = T_{1,4}^{15}$. As demonstrated in the left of Figure 8, there

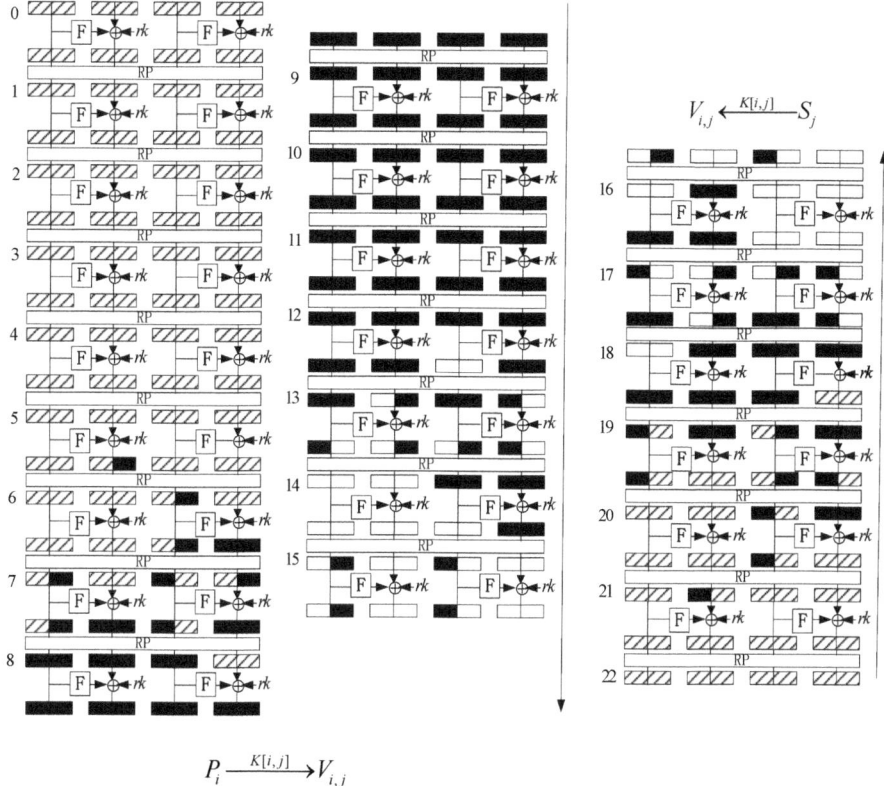

Fig. 8. Process of MITM : Biclique analysis of 28-round Piccolo-128

is no difference in the process during the encryption of the first 6 rounds (0-5 rounds) and the left-half-round of the sixth round, which is not true for the other parts. Besides, we can skip the 3 F functions of 14-th round and 15-th round because of the variant of GFN. As a result, for a single P_i, the area to be computed 2^8 times includes 16 F functions and the area to be computed only once includes 13 F functions.

Search Candidates. Test the remaining key candidates until finding the correct key.

Complexities. Next we will evaluate the complexity of the key recovery on 28-round Piccolo-128.

Data Complexity. We fix $C_0 = 0_{(64)}$ for every biclique and all the ciphertexts share the same values in bytes $C_{1,4,5,6,7}$. So the data complexity does not exceed 2^{24} (Figure 7).

Computational Complexity. First, let us see the complexity of constructing a single biclique with $C_0 = 0_{(64)}$. Basic computation spends 12 F-functions. Deriving C_i $(0 \le i < 2^8)$ needs to compute 1 F-functions 2^8 times. Similarly, it needs to compute 7 F-functions 2^8 times to obtain S_j $(0 \le j < 2^8)$. So a biclique can be constructed with complexity of about $2^{5.2}$.

In the matching part we compute 16 bits in two directions per biclique spending 8 F functions 2^8 times and 3 F functions once for every S_j, that is $2^8(8 \times 2^8 + 3)$, in backward direction and $2^8(16 \times 2^8 + 13)$ F functions in forward direction. In total, it costs $2^8(24 \times 2^8 + 16)$ F functions, which is about $2^{14.78}$ 28-round Piccolo-128 encryptions. Because we test 2^{16} keys to find whether the 16-bit match or not, the number of remaining key candidates in each key group is $2^{16-16} = 1$ on the average. Altogether, we totally need 2^{112} bicliques.

The whole computational complexity C is estimated as:

$$C = 2^{112}(2^{5.2} + 2^{14.78} + 1) \approx 2^{126.79}.$$

Since the groups around base keys has fully covered the key space, the success probability is 1.

5   Conclusion

Designers had provided various attacks including differential cryptanalysis, linear cryptanalysis, boomerang-type cryptanalysis, impossible differential cryptanalysis and MITM attack on security analysis for Piccolo[12]. The best result of actual single-key attack was 3-subset meet-in-the-middle(MITM) attacks on 14-round Piccolo-80 and 21-round Piccolo-128 without whitening keys. By analyzing the key schedule and the structure of encryption, we gave biclique cryptanalysis of full round Piccolo-80 without postwhitening keys and 28-round Piccolo-128

Table 4. Summary of previous results on Piccolo

Single-Key Model			
Piccolo-80	Piccolo-128	Method	Reference
7	7	Differential	[12]
8	8	Linear	[12]
9	9	Boomerang	[12]
9	9	Impossible Differential	[12]
14	21	3-Subset MITM	[12]
19	23	MITM Expectation	[12]
25	28	Biclique Cryptanalysis	**This paper**

without prewhitening keys. The attacks are respectively with data complexity of 2^{48} and 2^{24} chosen ciphertexts, and with time complexity of $2^{78.95}$ and $2^{126.79}$ encryptions. Furthermore, the result of the attack presented in our context has an advantage over the MITM attack which was evaluated in the worst setting by designers. Table 4 summarized the previous results on Piccolo.

We noticed that the data complexity of key recovery can be significantly reduced by sacrificing only a small factor of computational advantage. The high computational complexity has something to do with the biclique cryptanalysis itself. By deeply analyzing the biclique cryptanalysis, we know that all bicliques should cover the full key space if we want the success rate to be 1. Then, two main reasons for reducing computational complexity would be as follows. Firstly, it costs little complexity to construct long biclique of high dimension. Secondly, the key difference affects the internal matching value slightly in the process of partial matching. As discussed above, we can draw the conclusion that biclique cryptanalysis is available to the cipher having simple key schedule and slow diffusion.

Acknowledgments. We would like to thank anonymous referees for their helpful comments and suggestions. The research presented in this paper is supported by the National Natural Science Foundation of China (No.60873259) and The Knowledge Innovation Project of The Chinese Academy of Sciences.

References

1. Bogdanov, A., Knudsen, L., Leander, G., Paar, C., Poschmann, A., Robshaw, M., Seurin, Y., Vikkelsoe, C.: PRESENT: An Ultra-Lightweight Block Cipher. In: Paillier, P., Verbauwhede, I. (eds.) CHES 2007. LNCS, vol. 4727, pp. 450–466. Springer, Heidelberg (2007)
2. Bogdanov, A., Khovratovich, D., Rechberger, C.: Biclique Cryptanalysis of the Full AES. In: Lee, D.H., Wang, X. (eds.) ASIACRYPT 2011. LNCS, vol. 7073, pp. 344–371. Springer, Heidelberg (2011)
3. Bogdanov, A., Rechberger, C.: A 3-Subset Meet-in-the-Middle Attack: Cryptanalysis of the Lightweight Block Cipher KTANTAN. In: Biryukov, A., Gong, G., Stinson, D.R. (eds.) SAC 2010. LNCS, vol. 6544, pp. 229–240. Springer, Heidelberg (2011)
4. De Cannière, C., Dunkelman, O., Knežević, M.: KATAN and KTANTAN — A Family of Small and Efficient Hardware-Oriented Block Ciphers. In: Clavier, C., Gaj, K. (eds.) CHES 2009. LNCS, vol. 5747, pp. 272–288. Springer, Heidelberg (2009)
5. Diffie, W., Hellman, M.E.: Special feature exhaustive cryptanalysis of the NBS data encryption standard. Computer 10(6), 74–84 (1977)
6. Gong, Z., Nikova, S., Law, Y.W.: KLEIN: A New Family of Lightweight Block Ciphers. In: Juels, A., Paar, C. (eds.) RFIDSec 2011. LNCS, vol. 7055, pp. 1–18. Springer, Heidelberg (2012)
7. Guo, J., Peyrin, T., Poschmann, A., Robshaw, M.: The LED Block Cipher. In: Preneel, B., Takagi, T. (eds.) CHES 2011. LNCS, vol. 6917, pp. 326–341. Springer, Heidelberg (2011)

8. Izadi, M., Sadeghiyan, B., Sadeghian, S., Khanooki, H.: MIBS: A New Lightweight Block Cipher. In: Garay, J.A., Miyaji, A., Otsuka, A. (eds.) CANS 2009. LNCS, vol. 5888, pp. 334–348. Springer, Heidelberg (2009)
9. Knudsen, L., Leander, G., Poschmann, A., Robshaw, M.J.B.: PRINTCIPHER: A Block Cipher for IC-Printing. In: Mangard, S., Standaert, F.-X. (eds.) CHES 2010. LNCS, vol. 6225, pp. 16–32. Springer, Heidelberg (2010)
10. Ojha, S.K., Kumar, N., Jain, K., Sangeeta: TWIS – A Lightweight Block Cipher. In: Prakash, A., Sen Gupta, I. (eds.) ICISS 2009. LNCS, vol. 5905, pp. 280–291. Springer, Heidelberg (2009)
11. Sasaki, Y.: Meet-in-the-Middle Preimage Attacks on AES Hashing Modes and an Application to Whirlpool. In: Joux, A. (ed.) FSE 2011. LNCS, vol. 6733, pp. 378–396. Springer, Heidelberg (2011)
12. Shibutani, K., Isobe, T., Hiwatari, H., Mitsuda, A., Akishita, T., Shirai, T.: *Piccolo*: An Ultra-Lightweight Blockcipher. In: Preneel, B., Takagi, T. (eds.) CHES 2011. LNCS, vol. 6917, pp. 342–357. Springer, Heidelberg (2011)
13. Wu, W., Zhang, L.: LBlock: A Lightweight Block Cipher. In: Lopez, J., Tsudik, G. (eds.) ACNS 2011. LNCS, vol. 6715, pp. 327–344. Springer, Heidelberg (2011)

On the CCA-1 Security of Somewhat Homomorphic Encryption over the Integers*

Zhenfei Zhang, Thomas Plantard, and Willy Susilo

Centre for Computer and Information Security Research
School of Computer Science & Software Engineering (SCSSE)
University Of Wollongong, Australia
{zz920,thomaspl,wsusilo}@uow.edu.au

Abstract. The notion of fully homomorphic encryption is very important since it enables many important applications, such as the cloud computing scenario. In EUROCRYPT 2010, van Dijk, Gentry, Halevi and Vaikuntanathan proposed an interesting fully homomorphic encryption scheme based on a somewhat homomorphic encryption scheme using integers. In this paper, we demonstrate a very practical CCA-1 attack against this somewhat homomorphic encryption scheme. Given a decryption oracle, we show that within $O(\lambda^2)$ queries, we can recover the secret key successfully, where λ is the security parameter for the system.

Keywords: Fully Homomorphic Encryption, Somewhat Homomorphic Encryption, CCA-1 attack, Approximate GCD.

1 Introduction

Fully homomorphic encryption is a very important notion for cloud computing. It allows the cloud to process users' encrypted data without the need to decrypt them.

Essentially, fully homomorphic encryption schemes enable one to apply homomorphic operations over arbitrary number (n) of given ciphertexts c_1, c_2, ..., c_n without the need to know the corresponding plaintexts m_1, m_2, ..., m_n.

This notion, which was initially named "data homomorphisms", was proposed by Rivest, Shamir and Dertouzos [1] shortly after the introduction of RSA [2]. For many years, schemes that support partial homomorphism have been proposed. Nevertheless, the construction of fully homomorphic encryption had been a long standing open research problem, until the recent Gentry's breakthrough work [3,4], where a fully homomorphic scheme was proposed.

The initial construction of Gentry's FHE scheme (referred to as GENTRY scheme throughout this paper) uses ideal lattices. His work was then refined and optimized by Smart and Vercauteren [5] (referred to as SMART-VERCAUTEREN variant), Stehlé and Steinfeld [6], and Gentry and Halevi [7] (referred to as GENTRY-HALEVI variant). Meanwhile, van Dijk et al. proposed a FHE scheme

---

* This work is supported by ARC Future Fellowship FT0991397.

M.D. Ryan, B. Smyth, and G. Wang (Eds.): ISPEC 2012, LNCS 7232, pp. 353–368, 2012.

using integers (referred to as VDGHV variant) [8], which is later extended by
Coron et al. [9] (referred to as CMNT variant), Coron et al. [10], whose security
was re-evaluated by Chen and Nguyen [11]. There is also a third type of FHE
variants that are based on coding theory proposed recently [12], whose structure
is very close to the construction from ideal lattices.

The essential idea of such a scheme is to construct a somewhat homomorphic encryption (SHE) scheme and then convert it to a fully one using Gentry's
bootstrapping technique (see section 2.2) [3,13]. Therefore, usually a fully homomorphic encryption scheme contains two parts, a somewhat homomorphic
encryption scheme whose ability of homomorphic operations is limited, and a
bootstrapping technique that breaks such a limitation.

It is known that any FHE scheme that adopts Gentry's bootstrapping technique cannot be CCA-1 secure (see Subsection 2.4 for definitions). Since the
bootstrapping technique requires one to publish the encryption of their secret
keys, therefore, if there exists a decryption oracle, then the attacker can recover
the secret key by incorporating this oracle within k queries, where k is the number of bits of the security key (in the case of VDGHV scheme, the secret key
of the squashed decryption algorithm has $O(\lambda^5)$ bits, hence, a CCA-1 attack is
successful in $O(\lambda^5)$ queries). As a result, the CCA-1 security cannot be achieved
by FHE schemes that use bootstrapping technique.

We should highlight that it is important to investigate a somewhat homomorphic encryption (SHE) scheme by itself, since it has many applications, such as
medical, financial and the advertising domains as mentioned in [14]. It is noted
that in these applications, only SHE schemes are required.

As far as a SHE is concerned, the CCA-2 security is also not achievable. As
a SHE allows certain level of homomorphic operations on ciphertexts, one can
modify the CCA-2 challenge ciphertext and submit it to the decryption oracle.
Therefore, the attacker can recover the plaintext.

However, whether a SHE can be CCA-1 secure remains an open problem.
Indeed, in [15], Loftus et al. showed a CCA-1 attack against GENTRY-HALEVI
SHE scheme and SMART-VERCAUTEREN SHE scheme (we refer to this work
as LMSV attack), and proposed a CCA-1 secure SHE scheme (referred to as
LMSV variant).

Our Contributions

In this paper, we propose a CCA-1 attack against VDGHV SHE scheme, which
is *different* from the LMSV attack. We should highlight that the technique used
in the LMSV scheme to stop the LMSV attack *is not* applicable to our case.
With a decryption oracle of VDGHV SHE scheme, we can recover the secret key
successfully. Also, since the ciphertexts of VDGHV SHE scheme and CMNT
SHE scheme share the same structure, our attack can be applied to CMNT SHE
scheme as well. Moreover, our CCA-1 attack against VDGHV FHE scheme uses
$O(\lambda^2)$ queries, where λ is the security parameter of the system, while a trivial
CCA-1 attack uses $O(\lambda^5)$ queries.

2 Preliminaries

2.1 Notations

Let λ be the security parameter of the system, i.e., it takes at least 2^λ operations to break the system. For integers z and d, denote $[z]_d$ for the reduction of z mod d within $(-d/2, d/2]$. For a rational number q, let $\lfloor q \rceil$ be the closest integer to q, $[q]$ the fractional part of q.

2.2 Gentry's Framework

As stated earlier, a fully homomorphic encryption scheme essentially consists of two parts: a somewhat homomorphic encryption scheme and a bootstrapping technique.

The somewhat homomorphic encryptions scheme enables basic additions and multiplications over $\mathbb{F}_2$. Hence, it is arithmetically "complete", because essentially any circuit is derived from additions and multiplications over $\mathbb{F}_2$ [3]. However, in such a scheme, in order to bring some security strength, the ciphertexts contain a random "noise". The size of the noise is limited, to ensure a valid decryption. Nevertheless, it grows in size as the ciphertext is processed to homomorphically evaluate the function on its plaintext. Once the size of the noise in the ciphertext exceeds a certain threshold, then the ciphertext can no longer be decrypted correctly.

The "bootstrapping technique" is to solve such a limitation. If there is a guarantee that the maximum evaluation circuit depth of this somewhat homomorphic scheme is greater than its decryption circuit depth, then one can reduce the noise by evaluating its own decryption circuit, and consequently, convert the somewhat homomorphic scheme to a fully homomorphic scheme.

The general idea of bootstrapping is to "refresh" a ciphertext, namely given a ciphertext c for some plaintext m, compute a ciphertext c' such that the size of the noise in c' is smaller than the size of the noise in c. The algorithm to conduct this ciphertext refreshing operation is called "RECRYPT", which enables one to evaluate arbitrarily large circuits.

To enable RECRYPT, one publishes an encryption of the (SHE) secret key. The new ciphertext c' encrypts the same message, but it maintains a smaller noise,

$$c' = \text{RECRYPT}(\text{ENCRYPT}(sk), \text{ENCRYPT}(c)),$$

$$\text{DECRYPT}(sk, c') = \text{DECRYPT}(sk, c).$$

2.3 Overview of vDGHV SHE Scheme

In this subsection, we briefly review the vDGHV SHE scheme. We omit the description of CMNT scheme. However, it is important to note that the ciphertexts of those two schemes resemble the same structure (i.e., $c_i = g_i p + 2r_i$), and their decryption algorithms are identical.

Parameters. The following are the parameters used in the vDGHV somewhat homomorphic encryption scheme.

- α: the maximum length of the noise r_i, i.e.: $r_i \in [-2^\alpha, 2^\alpha)$;
- β: the length of the secret key p, i.e.: $p \in (2^\beta, 2^{\beta+1})$
- γ: the maximum length of an integer in the public key;
- σ: the number of public keys used in one encryption;
- n: the number of integers in the public key;

Table 1. Parameter Configurations

	α	β	γ		n
Minimum	λ	λ^2	$\lambda^4 \log \lambda$	$\lambda^4 \log \lambda + \lambda$
Recommended	λ	λ^2	λ^5		$\lambda^5 + \lambda$

In their paper, the author also gave two sets of parameters, one for the minimum requirement of the system, and another for the recommended configuration. We briefly list their configurations in table 1.

The Scheme. Now we describe vDGHV SHE scheme. The somewhat homomorphic encryption scheme consists of four algorithms:

KeyGen(λ)

- Generate parameters $\alpha, \beta, \gamma, \sigma, n$ in function of λ;
- Generate a random odd integer $p \in [2^\beta, 2^{\beta+1})$;
- Generate n random integers $\{r_i \in [-2^\alpha, 2^\alpha)\}$;
- Generate n random integers $\{g_i \in [0, 2^{\gamma-\beta})\}$;
- $sk \leftarrow p$;
- $x_0 \leftarrow g_0 p + 2r_0$;
- $x_i \leftarrow g_i p + 2r_i \bmod x_0$, $0 < i \leq n$;
- Reorder $\{x_i\}$ such that x_0 is the smallest;
- $pk \leftarrow \{x_i, \alpha, \sigma\}$.

Encrypt(m, pk)

- Generate a bit sequence $\{s_i\}$, such that $\sum s_i = \sigma$;
- $c \leftarrow m + 2 \times r + \sum_{i=1}^{n-1}(s_i \times x_i) \pmod{x_0}$, where $r \in [-2^\alpha, 2^\alpha)$;

Decrypt(c, sk)

- $m \leftarrow (c \bmod 2) \oplus (\lfloor c/p \rceil \bmod 2)$.

Remark 1. *Essentially, the* Decrypt *algorithm is simplified from* $[c - \lfloor c/p \rceil]_2$, *where* $\lfloor z \rceil$ *is to find the closest integer to* z, *while* $[z]_p$ *is to find the residue of* $z \bmod p$ *in* $(-p/2, p/2]$. *This is slightly different from* $c \bmod p \bmod 2$. $c \bmod p$ *returns an integer in* $[0, p)$, *while* $c - p \times \lfloor c/p \rceil$ *finds an integer in* $(-p/2, p/2]$.

EVALUATE(c_1, c_2, ..., c_k, $\mathcal{P}$, pk)

- Return $\mathcal{P}(c_1, c_2, ..., c_k)$.

$\mathcal{P}$ is a k-inputs evaluation polynomial while the depth of its circuit $\mathcal{C}_D$ is lower than the maximum circuit depth allowed by this SHE.

This SHE supports homomorphic additions and multiplications, when $\alpha \ll \beta$. For instance, suppose $c_1 = m_1 + g_1 p + 2r_1$ and $c_2 = m_2 + g_2 p + 2r_2$ for certain g_1, r_1, g_2, r_2, the product of two ciphertexts $c_1 c_2 = m_1 m_2 + 2(r_1 m_2 + r_2 m_1 + 2r_1 r_2) + p(g_1 m_2 + 2g_1 r_2 + g_2 m_1 + 2g_2 r_1 + g_1 g_2 p)$. One can observe that the decryption of $c_1 c_2$ is $m_1 m_2$, as long as $2(r_1 m_2 + r_2 m_1 + 2r_1 r_2) \in (-p/2, p/2]$. Therefore, the above scheme is somewhat homomorphic.

However, the homomorphic circuit depth is limited, i.e., the noise grows after each operation, and eventually the absolute value of the noise will be greater than $p/2$ and a decryption error is then possibly generated.

Suppose we want to evaluate a circuit whose depth is greater than this SHE permits, we break the circuit into several sub-circuits. For each sub-circuit, the resulting noise is less than the threshold $(p/2)$. Then we refresh the resulting ciphtertext using the bootstrapping technique. We refer the readers to the original scheme for more details. In the following, we describe the bootstrapping technique in general.

To bootstrap, firstly, decryption circuit in Remark 1 need to be modified. The original decryption requires at least one division, while the modified one consists of only additions. As we have shown earlier, the noise grows significantly faster in a multiplication than in an addition.

Remark 2. *The squash technique transfers an original secret key of $O(\lambda^2)$ bits into a new secret key of $O(\lambda^5)$ bits. As a requirement of bootstrapping, one is obliged to publish the encryption of the secret key, which in this case is the new one. Therefore, a trivial CCA-1 attack to the vDGHV FHE uses $O(\lambda^5)$ queries.*

Then, because the modified decryption circuit depth is relatively low, now it is possible to carry out the decryption circuit homomorphically, through the proposed SHE. In practice, we encrypt ciphertexts, denoted by $Enc(c)$ and the public keys, denoted by $Enc(pk)$. Let $\mathcal{C}_D$ be the decryption circuit, then EVAL($\mathcal{C}_D$, $Enc(c)$, $Enc(pk)$) $= Enc(m)$. This is because firstly $\mathcal{C}_D(c, pk) = m$ and secondly, $\mathcal{C}_D$ can be carried out homomorphically. Therefore, we obtain a new ciphertext $Enc(m)$.

The new ciphertext, $Enc(m)$ has a refreshed noise level (less than 2^α), which means $Enc(m)$ can be evaluated again. By doing this repeatedly, we can evaluate circuit with any depth homomorphically. Therefore, a fully homomorphic encryption scheme is achieved.

2.4   Security Models

In the following, we describe briefly both CCA-1 and CCA-2 attacks for completeness [16]. The IND-CCA-1/2 security game is defined as follows:

1. The challenger runs KEYGEN algorithm and output a secret key sk and a public key pk;
2. The attacker is given two oracles, an encryption oracle and a decryption oracle;
3. The challenger generates $c = $ ENCRYPT(m_b, sk), where $b \in \{0, 1\}$;
4. (Only for CCA-2) The attacker is given two oracles again, but it can not query on c;
5. The attacker output b'.

We say that an encryption scheme is CCA-1/2 secure if the advantage of the attacker to win the game $(Pr[b = b'] - 1/2)$ is negligible.

2.5 LMSV CCA-1 Attack

In this subsection we briefly revisit the LMSV attack against GENTRY-HALEVI SHE and SMART-VERCAUTEREN SHE schemes. For completeness, we show the above SHE schemes first, as well as LMSV SHE scheme, which is resistant against their own CCA-1 attack.

Recall that all three SHE schemes consist of four algorithms, KEYGEN, EN-CRYPT, DECRYPT and EVALUATE. The LMSV attack requires the first three algorithms.

KEYGEN(λ)

- Generate parameters n, t, ρ in function of λ;
- Set $f(x) \leftarrow x^n + 1$, n is a power of 2;
- Pick a random $n - 1$ degree polynomial $v(x)$, with coefficients $v_i \in (0, 2^t)$, denote $\boldsymbol{v}$ the vector form of coefficients of $v(x)$;
- Generate a matrix V from $\boldsymbol{v}$ and check if the Hermite Normal Form (HNF) of V has the correct form (as shown below) and if d is an odd number;

$$
V = \begin{vmatrix}
v_0 & v_1 & v_2 & \cdots & v_n \\
-v_n & v_0 & v_1 & \cdots & v_{n-1} \\
-v_{n-1} & -v_n & v_0 & \cdots & v_{n-2} \\
\vdots & \vdots & \vdots & \ddots & \vdots \\
-v_1 & -v_2 & -v_3 & \cdots & v_0
\end{vmatrix}, \quad
HNF(V) = \begin{vmatrix}
d & 0\,0\ldots0 \\
[-a]_d & 1\,0\ldots0 \\
[-a^2]_d & 0\,1\ldots0 \\
\vdots & \vdots\,\vdots\ddots\vdots \\
[-a^{n-1}]_d & 0\,0\ldots1
\end{vmatrix}.
$$

- Find the polynomial $w(x)$, such that $w(x) \times v(x) = d \bmod f(x)$;
- $sk \leftarrow w$, where w is one of odd coefficients of $w(x)$;
- $pk \leftarrow \{a, d, \rho\}$.

ENCRYPT(m, pk)

- Generate a degree $n - 1$ polynomial $r(x)$, with coefficients $r_i \in (0, \rho)$;
- $c(x) \leftarrow m + 2 \times r(x)$, where $m \in \{0, 1\}$;
- $c \leftarrow [m + c(a)]_d$.

The three SHE schemes have different decryption algorithms. We firstly introduce DecryptGH and DecryptSV that are used in Gentry-Halevi SHE
and Smart-Vercauteren SHE, respectively.

DecryptGH/DecryptSV(c, sk)

 – $m \leftarrow [c \times w]_d \bmod 2$.

The decryption algorithm for LMSV SHE uses a ciphertext check procedure to
stop the LMSV attack. Here, T is the threshold used for the ciphertext check.
T need to be greater than a function of ρ.

DecryptLMSV(c, sk)

 – $c(x) \leftarrow c - \lfloor c \times w(x)/d \rceil \times g(x) \bmod f(x)$;
 – $c' \leftarrow [c(a)]_d$;
 – If $c' \neq c$ or $\|c(x)\|_\infty \geq T$ return $\perp$;
 – Else, return $c(x) \bmod 2$

Now we describe the LMSV attack. Decrypt algorithms for Gentry-Halevi
SHE and Smart-Vercauteren SHE schemes are $m \leftarrow [c \times w]_d \bmod 2$. This
decryption will be valid as long as $[c \times w/d] \leq 1/2$. Therefore, for a certain
key set (w, d), the maximum value c' allowed is a fixed integer. The adversary
picks several different "ciphertexts", and pass them to the decryption oracle to
check if they can be decrypted correctly. Eventually, the attacker will recover
the threshold c' which is the maximum integer that can be decrypted correctly.
This c' in return gives the attacker w, the secret key.

    To stop this attack, Loftus et al. proposed a ciphertext check procedure. The
ciphertext that is to be decrypted, will be "disassembled" into the generating
polynomial $c(x)$. Recall that $c(x) = 2 \times r(x) + m$, hence, for valid ciphertexts,
$\|c(x)\|_\infty$ is bounded by a certain threshold smaller than T, while for invalid
"ciphertexts" (i.e., integers picked by attacker), the corresponding $c(x)$ can have
arbitrary coefficients. Therefore, in the latter case, an error $\perp$ is generated, and
the decryption stops.

3   Our CCA-1 Attack

In this section we present our CCA-1 attack. We use vDGHV SHE scheme to
demonstrate our attack. However, the following attack can be applied to CNMT
with a trivial modification.

    The security strength of vDGHV SHE comes from the noise that is added to
ciphertexts. If we can somehow reduce the noise in ciphertext, then the scheme
will no longer be secure. With the help of a decryption oracle, we can eliminate
the noise. Hence, we achieve a CCA-1 attack.

    We propose two variants that follow the same idea. The first variant requires
several ciphertexts. The main idea is to eliminate the noise and then, to find the
GCD of the remaining parts. The second variant requires only *one* ciphertext,
and we are able to recover the secret key directly.

We note that our attack recovers the secret key that allows us to decrypt any valid ciphertexts, and does *not* require any access to $\mathcal{O}_D$ at Stage 5 in the CCA attack model. Thus, our attack falls in the category of CCA-1. However, we also note that essentially, our attack is stronger than CCA-1, because instead of solving one challenge, we recover the secret key.

3.1   The Attack

Essentially, in vDGHV SHE scheme, the public keys (x_i-s) can be treated as ciphertexts encrypting 0-s with smaller noise. Therefore, the following algorithms can be applied on public keys with less cost. However, in order to strictly follow the definition of CCA-1 attack, we apply our algorithms on real ciphertexts.

We note that for any correct ciphertext c_i, the following holds that

$$c_i = m_i + 2r'_i + g'_i p$$

for certain $r'_i \in (-p/4, p/4]$ and integer g'_i, since if $|2r'| > p/2$ decryption error will be induced. For convenience, denote $\alpha' = \beta - 1$.Using the recommended parameter configuration, we have $\alpha' = \lambda^2 - 1$.

Now we show our attack against vDGHV SHE scheme. Suppose we have k ciphertexts $c_1, c_2, ..., c_k$ of encrypted 0-s, i.e.: $c_i = g'_i p + 2r'_i$. It holds that $\text{DECRYPT}(c_i, sk) = 0$. The length of r'_i-s is no greater than α'.

Let $\mathcal{O}_D(c)$ be the decryption oracle that returns $\text{DECRYPT}(c, sk)$. The following pieces of pseudo-code describe two variants of our attack.

Algorithm 1. NOISEELI(c)

$l_p \leftarrow 2^\beta - 2^{\alpha'+1}$
$r_p \leftarrow 2^{\beta+1} + 2^{\alpha'+1}$
while $r_p - l_p > 2$ **do**
    $s \leftarrow \lfloor (l_p + r_p)/4 \rfloor \times 2$
    if $\mathcal{O}_D(c+s) = 0$ **then**
        $l_p \leftarrow s$
    end if
    if $\mathcal{O}_D(c+s) = 1$ **then**
        $r_p \leftarrow s$
    end if
end while
if $\mathcal{O}_D(c+s+1) = 1$ **then**
    $s \leftarrow s+1$
end if
return $c' \leftarrow c + s$

Algorithm 1: NOISEELI is to help to eliminate the noise in ciphertext. Instead of generating a ciphertext with no noise, this algorithm generates a ciphertext with a fixed noise.

Algorithm 2: CCA-GCD describes the first variant of our attack, while Algorithm 3 CCA-P describes the second variant of our attack.

Algorithm 2. CCA-GCD$(c_0, c_1, ..., c_k)$

$c'_0 \leftarrow \text{NOISEELI}(c_0)$
$c'_1 \leftarrow \text{NOISEELI}(c_1)$
$c'_2 \leftarrow \text{NOISEELI}(c_2)$
$p' \leftarrow \gcd(c'_2 - c'_1, c'_1 - c'_0)$
$t \leftarrow 3$
while $p' \geq 2^{\beta+1}$ **and** $t \leq k$ **do**
    $c'_t \leftarrow \text{NOISEELI}(c_t)$
    $p' \leftarrow \gcd(c'_t - c'_{t-1}, p')$
    $t \leftarrow t + 1$
end while
return p'

The first algorithm inputs a ciphertext $c = 2r' + g'p$ with any noise r', it outputs a new ciphertexts $c' = g'p + \lfloor p/2 \rfloor$. The new ciphertext contains a constant noise of $\lfloor p/2 \rfloor$.

For any ciphertext $c = 2r + gp$, the DECRYPT algorithm will always output 0, as long as $|2r| \leq \lfloor p/2 \rfloor$, and output 1 if $2r > \lfloor p/2 \rfloor$. Denote $l = \lfloor p/2 \rfloor - 2r$. l represents the threshold, such that $\mathcal{O}_D(c + l) = 0$ and $\mathcal{O}_D(c + l + 2) = 1$. Also, we know that $l \in (2^\beta - 2^{\alpha'+1}, 2^{\beta+1} + 2^{\alpha'+1})$. Therefore, we set l_p and r_p to be the lower and upper bound of l. Then we start a while loop to narrow the bound as in Algorithm 1.

Algorithm 3. CCA-P(c)

$a \leftarrow \text{NOISEELI}(c)$
$b \leftarrow \text{NOISEELI}(-c)$
return $a + b + 1$

3.2   Correctness

In this subsection we prove the correctness of our attack.

For any *even* integer $s \in (2^\beta - 2^{\alpha'+1}, 2^{\beta+1} + 2^{\alpha'+1})$, decrypting $c + s$ has two possible consequences:

- If $\mathcal{O}_D(c + s) = 1$, we know that the threshold l for this ciphertext is smaller than s, then we move the upper bound r_p to s;
- One the other hand, if $\mathcal{O}_D(c + s) = 0$, we know that the threshold l for this ciphertext is greater than s, then we move the lower bound l_p to s;

By the end of the loop, we have $s = l_p = r_p - 2$. Also, it holds that $\mathcal{O}_D(c + s) = 0$ and $\mathcal{O}_D(c + s + 2) = 1$. If $\lfloor p/2 \rfloor$ is an even integer, then $s = \lfloor p/2 \rfloor$, and $\mathcal{O}_D(c + s + 1) = 1$. By contrast, if $\lfloor p/2 \rfloor$ is odd, then $s = \lfloor p/2 \rfloor - 1$, and $\mathcal{O}_D(c + s + 1) = 0$. In this case, we increase s by 1.

Hence, s is the threshold l we were looking for, and $c + s = gp + \lfloor p/2 \rfloor$. Therefore, we successfully generate a fixed noise ciphertext in $\log(2^\beta + 2^{\alpha'+2}) + 1$ queries.

The second algorithm is more straightforward. Given $k + 1$ outputs of Algorithm 1, we obtain k linear independent noise free ciphertexts. By running a classic GCD algorithm we obtain p'. It holds that either $p = p'$ or $p|p'$.

To have $p = p'$ it requires $\gcd(g_2 - g_1, g_3 - g_2, ..., g_k - g_{k-1}) = 1$. The probability of k random integers from $\mathbb{Z}$ to be coprime is $1/\zeta(k)$, where $\zeta(x)$ is the Riemann Zeta function $\sum_{i=1}^{\infty} \frac{1}{i^x}$ (see [17] for more details), while the probability of having k numbers randomly chosen form $(0, 2^{\lambda^5})$ to be coprime is greater than $1/\zeta(k)$.

In practice, 4 random integers has $1/\zeta(4) > 92\%$ probability of being coprime, while 7 random integers has $1/\zeta(7) > 99\%$ probability of being coprime. Our test (see subsection 3.5) confirmed this result, where on average cases, 3 random integers are coprime.

For the last algorithm, we generate $a = \text{NOISEELI}(c)$ and $b = \text{NOISEELI}(-c)$. It holds that:

$$a = gp + \lfloor p/2 \rfloor, \qquad b = -gp + \lfloor p/2 \rfloor.$$

Therefore, we obtain $2 \times \lfloor p/2 \rfloor$ from $a + b$. Because p is an odd integer, we recover the secret key by $p = a + b + 1$.

3.3   Efficiency

We examine the efficiency of our last two algorithms. For original ciphertexts (no homomorphic operations have been evaluated on them), it requires $\log(2^\beta + 2^{\alpha'+2}) + 1 < \beta + 3$ queries to find the fixed noise ciphertext. CCA-GCD algorithm requires a minimum 3 fixed noise ciphertexts. Therefore, in best cases we recover the secret key in $3(\beta + 3)$ queries. As $\beta = \lambda^2$, Algorithm 2 recovers the secret key in $O(\lambda^2)$ operations.

Algorithm 3 also works on $O(\lambda^2)$ but with better performance. To be more precise, it uses one ciphertext only, therefore to eliminate the noise requires at most $2(\beta + 3)$ queries.

It is true that Algorithm 3 is more efficient that Algorithm 2. The reason that we propose Algorithm 2 is that we observe Algorithm 3 will fail if we modify the decryption circuit. For instance, if $c \bmod p$ returns an integer within $[0, p)$ instead of $(-p/2, p/2]$, then Algorithm 3 will be unsuccessful. However, in this case Algorithm 2 is still valid.

3.4   An Example

In this subsection, we give an example of our CCA-1 attack. In our example, the security parameter λ is 2. Therefore, the noise r'_i and the multiplier g'_i are bounded by 2^2 and 2^{28}, respectively. The secret key p is an odd integer between 2^4 and 2^5. The ciphertext is in form of $c'_i = 2r'_i + g'_i p$. Table 2 lists three ciphertexts.

The results below indicate that we retrieve the secret key successfully. Table 3 shows that the noise is successfully eliminated within maximum 5 queries for each ciphertext. We recover s_i for each ciphertext such that $c_i + s_i = g_i p + (p - 1)/2$.

Table 2. Three sample ciphertexts

	r_i'	p	g_i'	c_i'
c_1	-3	19	343759059	6531422115
c_2	1	19	230194545	4373696357
c_3	2	19	276209466	5247979858

3.5 Implementation

In this subsection, we show the result of our implementation of our attack with different λ. This implementation is based on the NTL library [18].

The implementation was conducted in a 2.66 GHz CPU. The memory was always sufficient, as it merely required more than 600 Mbs. We started from $\lambda = 2$, and increased λ continuously until it reached 32. For each λ, we fed the program with 100 different seeds, and recorded the average time to find the secret key p, as well as average number of ciphertexts required for Algorithm 2.

The average number of ciphertexts required for Algorithm 2 for different choice of λ is quite stable. Approximately 3.8 ciphertexts are required to recover the secret key p. This implies that on average case the number of integers required to have them being coprime is 2.8.

Fig. 1 shows the timing results of our implementation. The x axis shows the choice of λ, while the y axis indicates the average time (in seconds) for each attack. Statistically, attack CCA-P uses approximately 1.9 times less time in comparison to attack CCA-GCD (this is due to the number of ciphertexts required to be noise-eliminated), and this is consistent with our result.

4 Discussions

4.1 On the Difference between Our Attack and LMSV Attack

We note that the LMSV attack is different from the attack described in this paper. The LMSV attack uses the decryption oracle to find the integer s such that $[w \times s/d] = 1/2$, and eventually recover the secret key, while our attack aims to manipulate the noise in the ciphertexts. By recovering the noise, our attack will recover the secret key of vDGHV variant.

A proof of such a difference is that our attack can be adapted to recover the noise for LMSV SHE scheme as well. However, this does not help us to recover the secret key or break the CCA-1 security (see subsection 4.2). Another evidence is that using LMSV SHE's solution (i.e., generating $\perp$ for invalid ciphertext) *will not* stop our attack either (see subsection 4.3).

4.2 On Adapting Our Attack to SHE Schemes with Ideal Lattice

We note that our method cannot be adapted to attack SHE schemes that use ideal lattices. In a typical SHE scheme with ideal lattice, a message is encrypted in a similar way:

NoiseEli(c_1)				
l_p	r_p	s_1	$\mathcal{O}_D(c_1 + s_1)$	action
0	24	12	0	$l_p \leftarrow 12$
12	24	18	1	$r_p \leftarrow 18$
12	18	14	0	$l_p \leftarrow 14$
14	18	16	1	$r_p \leftarrow 16$
14	16	14		end of loop
$\mathcal{O}_D(c_1 + s_1 + 1) = 1 \Longrightarrow s_1 = 15$				

NoiseEli(c_2)				
l_p	r_p	s_2	$\mathcal{O}_D(c_2 + s_2)$	action
0	24	12	1	$r_p \leftarrow 12$
0	12	6	0	$l_p \leftarrow 6$
6	12	8	1	$r_p \leftarrow 8$
6	8	6		end of loop
$\mathcal{O}_D(c_2 + s_2 + 1) = 1 \Longrightarrow s_2 = 7$				

Table 4 and 5 show how to extract p from c'_i in two ways. Both of the two examples uses NoiseEli to find constant noise ciphertext. As displayed in the tables, in GCD-CCA we recover $3p$ instead of p, and we did not further proceed the algorithm, since it is merely an example. This example requires access to the oracle for 14 times for the GCD-CCA variant and 10 times for CCA-P.

Table 3. Eliminate the noise of three ciphertexts

NoiseEli(c_3)				
l_p	r_p	s_3	$\mathcal{O}_D(c_3 + s_3)$	action
0	24	12	1	$r_p \leftarrow 12$
0	12	6	1	$r_p \leftarrow 6$
0	6	2	0	$l_p \leftarrow 2$
2	6	4	0	$l_p \leftarrow 4$
4	6	4		end of loop
$\mathcal{O}_D(c_3 + s_3 + 1) = 1 \Longrightarrow s_3 = 5$				

Table 4. Find p with CCA-GCD

CCA-GCD(c_1,c_2)	
$c'_1 = c_1 + 15 - c_2 - 7$	$c'_2 = c_2 + 7 - c_3 - 5$
$p' = \gcd(c'_1, c'_2) = 57$	

Table 5. Find p with CCA-P

NOISEELI(c_1)				
l_p	r_p	s_1	$\mathcal{O}_D(c_1 + s_1)$	action
0	24	12	0	$l_p \leftarrow 12$
12	24	18	1	$r_p \leftarrow 18$
12	18	14	0	$l_p \leftarrow 14$
14	18	16	1	$r_p \leftarrow 16$
14	16	14		end of loop
$\mathcal{O}_D(c_1 + s_1 + 1) = 1 \Longrightarrow s_1 = 15$				

NOISEELI($-c_1$)				
l_p	r_p	s_{-1}	$\mathcal{O}_D(c_1 + s_{-1})$	action
0	24	12	1	$r_p \leftarrow 12$
0	12	6	1	$r_p \leftarrow 6$
0	6	2	0	$l_p \leftarrow 2$
2	6	4	1	$r_p \leftarrow 4$
2	4	2		end of loop
$\mathcal{O}_D(-c_1 + s_{-1} + 1) = 1 \Longrightarrow s_{-1} = 3$				

CCA-P(c_1)	
$a \leftarrow c_1 + 15$	$b \leftarrow -c_1 + 3$
$p \leftarrow (a + b) + 1 = 19$	

$$c = m + rB_I + gB_J^{pk},$$

where I and J are two ideal lattices that are co-prime. r and g are some random elements generated during encryption. Lattice I is usually $< 2 >$, which are all even numbers, and B_I is a basis of I. As for lattice J, it generates a good basis B_J^{sk} and a bad basis B_J^{pk}. Then B_J^{pk} is used for encryption, while B_J^{sk} becomes the secret key.

Therefore, even we can somehow eliminate r through our attack, we still need to solve such a problem: given as many $g_i B_J^{pk}$, find B_J^{sk}. This is a GGH type cryptosystem [19]. As a result, we cannot recover B_J^{sk} directly using our technique.

Take LMSV SHE scheme for instance, for a ciphertext $c = 2r(a) + m \pmod{d}$, our attack recovers $r(x)$. To recover the i-th coefficient of $r(x)$, one passes $c + 2 \times r' \times a^i$ to the decryption oracle, where r' is a random integer picked by the attacker. By observing if the oracle returns m or $\bot$, one increases or decrease r' accordingly. Eventually, the attacker obtains $r' + r_i = T$. As a result, the attacker recovers one coefficient of $r(x)$. By doing this repetitively, one recovers the entire $r(x)$.

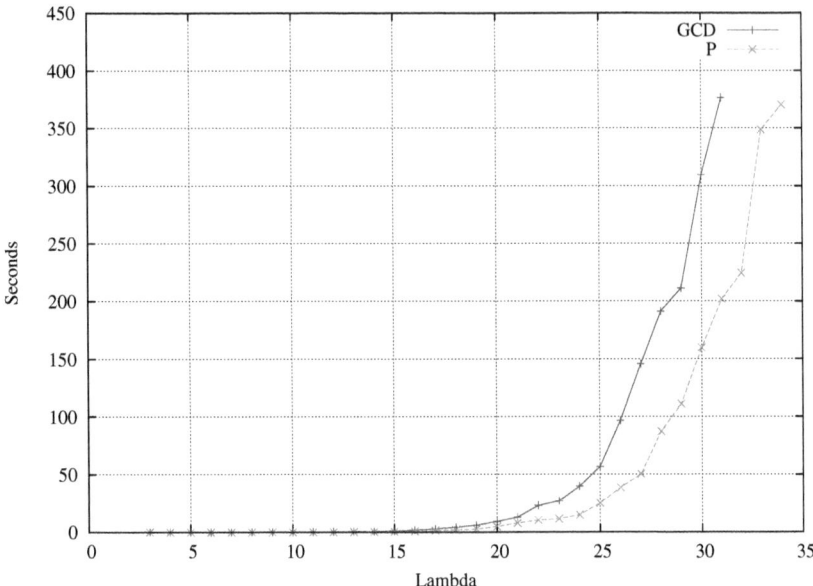

Fig. 1. Average time for recovering p

However, we note that this does not lead to a CCA-1 attack or a secret key attack. To recover the secret key one still need to solve the following problem: given an ideal lattice in the form of a, d, find a good basis of this lattice.

4.3 On LMSV SHE CCA-1 Approach

In this subsection we consider the existing proposed solution to make vDGHV SHE scheme CCA-1 secure. We note that our attack is successful, since we are able to eliminate the noise. Therefore, if there exist some techniques to disturb the noise elimination, our attack will fail.

Loftus et al. [15] showed a solution to combat their own CCA-1 attack against GENTRY-HALEVI SHE scheme/SMART-VERCAUTEREN SHE scheme (which we refer to as the LMSV SHE scheme). However, the solution in LMSV SHE scheme is *not applicable* in our case. Their possible solution is to generate some error $\perp$ (or even some random 0-s or 1-s), when the decryption oracle detects that the noise r is very close to $\pm(p-1)/2$. The decryption algorithm sets a bound T, such that when $(p-1)/2 - |r| < T$, it will not proceed decryption. However, essentially it will still leak some information. We can modify our attack to find T and consequently find a fixed noise ciphertext.

We modify our attack as follows: for each round, we query to the oracle multiply times. If the feedbacks are consistent (meaning that the attacker is not confused by random 0-s and 1-s) and not $\perp$, we proceed to the next round. Otherwise, we recover a fixed noise ciphertext with a noise level of T. Hence, our attack will still be successful even after the "patch" suggested by Loftus et al. [15].

5 Conclusion

Fully homomorphic encryption schemes play an important role in the security of many practical applications, such as cloud computing. Although the CCA-1 security for a FHE scheme is not achievable, whether its SHE scheme is CCA-1 secure remains an interesting research question, since a SHE scheme has potential to enable promising applications.

In this paper, we proposed a CCA-1 attack against vDGHV SHE scheme with integers. Unlike other schemes where the ciphertexts are protected by some noise and lattices, the strength of ciphertexts in SHE scheme with integers comes *only* from the noise. We demonstrated that we successfully eliminated the noise and recovered the secret key. Hence, we achieve a CCA-1 attack against vDGHV SHE scheme.

References

1. Rivest, R., Adleman, L., Dertouzos, M.: On data banks and privacy homomorphisms. In: Foundations of Secure Computation, pp. 169–177. Academic Press (1978)
2. Rivest, R.L., Shamir, A., Adleman, L.M.: A method for obtaining digital signatures and public-key cryptosystems. Commun. ACM 21(2), 120–126 (1978)
3. Gentry, C.: Fully homomorphic encryption using ideal lattices. In: [13], pp. 169–178
4. Gentry, C.: A Fully Homomorphic Encyrption Scheme. PhD thesis, Stanford University (2009)
5. Smart, N.P., Vercauteren, F.: Fully Homomorphic Encryption with Relatively Small Key and Ciphertext Sizes. In: Nguyen, P.Q., Pointcheval, D. (eds.) PKC 2010. LNCS, vol. 6056, pp. 420–443. Springer, Heidelberg (2010)
6. Stehlé, D., Steinfeld, R.: Faster Fully Homomorphic Encryption. In: Abe, M. (ed.) ASIACRYPT 2010. LNCS, vol. 6477, pp. 377–394. Springer, Heidelberg (2010)
7. Gentry, C., Halevi, S.: Implementing Gentry's Fully-Homomorphic Encryption Scheme. In: Paterson, K.G. (ed.) EUROCRYPT 2011. LNCS, vol. 6632, pp. 129–148. Springer, Heidelberg (2011)
8. van Dijk, M., Gentry, C., Halevi, S., Vaikuntanathan, V.: Fully Homomorphic Encryption over the Integers. In: Gilbert, H. (ed.) EUROCRYPT 2010. LNCS, vol. 6110, pp. 24–43. Springer, Heidelberg (2010)
9. Coron, J.-S., Mandal, A., Naccache, D., Tibouchi, M.: Fully Homomorphic Encryption over the Integers with Shorter Public Keys. In: Rogaway, P. (ed.) CRYPTO 2011. LNCS, vol. 6841, pp. 487–504. Springer, Heidelberg (2011)
10. Coron, J.S., Naccache, D., Tibouchi, M.: Optimization of fully homomorphic encryption. Cryptology ePrint Archive, Report 2011/440 (2011), http://eprint.iacr.org/
11. Chen, Y., Nguyen, P.Q.: Faster algorithms for approximate common divisors: Breaking fully-homomorphic-encryption challenges over the integers. Cryptology ePrint Archive, Report 2011/436 (2011), http://eprint.iacr.org/

12. Brakerski, Z., Vaikuntanathan, V.: Fully homomorphic encryption from ring-lwe and security for key dependent messages. In: [20], pp. 505–524
13. Mitzenmacher, M. (ed.): Proceedings of the 41st Annual ACM Symposium on Theory of Computing, STOC 2009, Bethesda, MD, USA, May 31-June 2. ACM (2009)
14. Lauter, K., Naehrig, M., Vaikuntanathan, V.: Can homomorphic encryption be practical? IACR Cryptology ePrint Archive 2011, 405 (2011)
15. Loftus, J., May, A., Smart, N., Vercauteren, F.: On cca-secure fully homomorphic encryption. Cryptology ePrint Archive, Report 2010/560 (2010), http://eprint.iacr.org/
16. Bellare, M., Desai, A., Pointcheval, D., Rogaway, P.: Relations among Notions of Security for Public-Key Encryption Schemes. In: Krawczyk, H. (ed.) CRYPTO 1998. LNCS, vol. 1462, pp. 26–45. Springer, Heidelberg (1998)
17. Nymann, J.E.: On the probability that k positive integers are relatively prime ii. Journal of Number Theory 7(4), 406–412 (1975)
18. Shoup, V.: NTL - A Library for Doing Number Theory, http://www.shoup.net/ntl/index.html
19. Goldreich, O., Goldwasser, S., Halevi, S.: Public-Key Cryptosystems from Lattice Reduction Problems. In: Kaliski Jr., B.S. (ed.) CRYPTO 1997. LNCS, vol. 1294, pp. 112–131. Springer, Heidelberg (1997)
20. Rogaway, P. (ed.): CRYPTO 2011. LNCS, vol. 6841. Springer, Heidelberg (2011)

Partial Key Exposure on RSA with Private Exponents Larger Than N

Marc Joye[1] and Tancrède Lepoint[2,3,⋆]

[1] Technicolor, Security & Content Protection Labs
1 avenue de Belle Fontaine, 35576 Cesson-Sévigné Cedex, France
marc.joye@technicolor.com
[2] CryptoExperts
41 boulevard des Capucines, 75002, Paris, France
[3] Laboratoire d'Informatique de l'École Normale Supérieure
45 rue d'Ulm, 75230 Paris Cedex 05, France
tancrede.lepoint@cryptoexperts.com

Abstract. In 1998, Boneh, Durfee and Frankel described several attacks against RSA enabling an attacker given a fraction of the bits of the private exponent d to recover all of d. These attacks were later improved and extended in various ways. They however always consider that the private exponent d is smaller than the RSA modulus N. When it comes to implementation, d can be enlarged to a value larger than N so as to improve the performance (by lowering its Hamming weight) or to increase the security (by preventing certain side-channel attacks). This paper studies this extended setting and quantifies the number of bits of d required to mount practical partial key exposure attacks. Both the cases of known most significant bits (MSBs) and least significant bits (LSBs) are analyzed. Our results are based on Coppersmith's heuristic methods and validated by practical experiments run through the SAGE computer-algebra system.

Keywords: RSA cryptosystem, cryptanalysis, key exposure, Coppersmith's methods, lattice reduction.

1 Introduction

For efficiency reasons, it might be tempting to select a small RSA private exponent d. In 1990, Wiener [30] showed that this results in an insecure system when $d < N^{0.25}$, where N denotes the RSA modulus. His attack made use of the continued fractions method. The bound was subsequently improved to $d < N^{0.292}$ by Boneh and Durfee [3] (see also [14, Section 3]) from powerful LLL-based techniques due to Coppersmith [8].

A related problem is that of partial key exposure: What is the fraction of the private exponent d that has to be made available to an attacker in order to break the system. This question was posed by Boneh, Durfee and Frankel [4]

⋆ This work was done while the author was with Technicolor.

M.D. Ryan, B. Smyth, and G. Wang (Eds.): ISPEC 2012, LNCS 7232, pp. 369–380, 2012.
© Springer-Verlag Berlin Heidelberg 2012

in 1998. They present several attacks where the attacker gains knowledge of most significant bits of d or of least significant bits of d. (Observe that Wiener's attack corresponds to a partial key exposure where the most significant bits are known to be zero.) Further partial key exposure attacks are presented by Blömer and May in [2] for larger values of public exponent e. The attacks in [4] require $e < N^{1/2}$. For attacks that work up to full-size exponents e, we refer to the paper of Ernst, Jochemsz, May and de Weger [12].

One may argue that partial key exposure attacks are unimportant. If an attacker is able to recover some bits of d then it should likewise be able to recover the entire private key d. While this may hold true in theory, in practice things are not so easy. Revealing some bits of d can be a lengthy and costly process. Partial key exposure attacks then facilitate the recovery of the entire private key. This especially applies to RSA implementations since it is likely that precautions were taken to prevent an adversary to obtain the private key d. Examples of implementation attacks include side-channel attacks [18, 19, 20]. Such attacks exploit differences in running times, power consumption traces, or other side channels resulting from the execution of the cryptographic algorithm. Yet another use case of partial key exposure is in covert communication channels (a.k.a. subliminal channels) [27, 28, 31]. A covert channel enables users to exchange secret information (e.g., an RSA private key) through messages that appear to be innocuous. Partial key exposure then reduces the number of exchanged messages.

All partial key exposure results on RSA presented so far have in common that the private exponent d is defined as an element in $\mathbb{Z}_{\phi(N)}^*$, where $\phi(N)$ denotes Euler's totient function of N —namely, the order of the multiplicative group of integers modulo N. In a number of implementations, a multiple of $\phi(N)$ is added to d prior to the exponentiation. In more detail, the RSA exponentiation $x^d \bmod N$ is carried out as $x^{d+k\phi(N)} \bmod N$ for some $k > 0$, that is, with an exponent whose size is at least that of N. There are mainly two reasons to do so. One of them is to offer better resistance against implementation attacks like side-channel attacks (e.g., [9, §5.1]). The other reason is efficiency. An appropriate choice of k can lower the Hamming weight of the exponent and reduce the total number of multiplications, leading to an expected performance improvement of up to 9.3% [5].

This paper deals with private exponents d that are larger than N (or more exactly than $\phi(N)$). We follow the heuristic strategy put forward by Jochemsz and May [16, 17] for solving multivariate polynomials with small integer or modular roots. The main advantage resides in its generality. The method is nevertheless heuristic in the sense that it is not guaranteed to succeed. We therefore ran many experiments with different parameter sets and none of them failed. Two practical cases are considered. The first case assumes that the attacker knows the most significant bits (MSBs) of d. Informally, we then show that if the public/private exponents verify $(e, d) \sim (N^\alpha, N^\beta)$ with $\beta \geqslant 1$ the fraction of d that is sufficient to recover it entirely is given by

$$\begin{cases} \dfrac{1-\alpha}{\beta} & \text{when } 1 < \alpha + \beta \leqslant \frac{3}{2} \\[2ex] \dfrac{2\beta - \alpha + 2\sqrt{(\alpha+\beta)(\alpha+\beta-\frac{3}{2})}}{3\beta} & \text{when } \frac{3}{2} \leqslant \alpha + \beta < 2 \end{cases} .$$

In some scenarios, the least significant bits (LSBs) can be easier to obtain; for example, when the underlying exponentiation algorithm processes the bits of d from the right to the left. Informally, with the above notation, we then show that the fraction of d that is sufficient to recover it entirely is given by

$$\frac{(6\beta - 5) + 2\sqrt{6\alpha + (6\beta - 5)}}{6\beta} .$$

The rest of this paper is organized as follows. In the next section, we introduce some useful background on lattice basis reduction. We also sketch the strategy of Jochemsz and May. We apply it to the cases of known MSBs in Section 3 and known LSBs in Section 4. Section 5 provides various data obtained through numerical experiments. Finally, we conclude in Section 6 and discuss some open issues for further research.

2   LLL and Multivariate Polynomials

2.1   Lattices

A *lattice* is a discrete additive subgroup of $\mathbb{R}^n$. For any integer lattice $L \neq \{0\}$, there exist $w \leqslant n$ linearly independent vectors $b_1, \ldots, b_w$ over $\mathbb{R}$ such that $L = b_1\mathbb{Z} \oplus \cdots \oplus b_w\mathbb{Z}$. This set of vectors is called a *basis* of the lattice. A lattice can be so represented by its basis matrix B; i.e., the matrix of the b_i's in the canonical basis of $\mathbb{R}^n$. The *determinant* of a lattice is defined as $\det(L) = (\det(BB^t))^{\frac{1}{2}}$. When the lattice is full-rank ($w = n$), the formula simplifies to $\det(L) = |\det B|$. The determinant of a lattice is well-defined since it is independent of the choice of the basis: lattice bases are obtained one from the others through a unimodular transformation (i.e., a multiplication by a matrix with determinant ± 1).

Among all the bases of a lattice L, some are 'better' than others. The goal of lattice reduction is to shorten the basis vectors and thus, since the determinant is invariant, to make them more orthogonal. The LLL algorithm, named after Lenstra, Lenstra and Lovász [21], produces in polynomial time a set of reduced basis vectors. The following lemma, as presented in [22], gives bounds on LLL-reduced basis vectors.

Lemma 1 (LLL). *Let L be a lattice of dimension w. In polynomial time, the LLL algorithm outputs reduced basis vectors v_i, $1 \leqslant i \leqslant w$, satisfying*

$$\|v_1\| \leqslant \|v_2\| \leqslant \cdots \leqslant \|v_i\| \leqslant 2^{\frac{w(w-1)}{4(w+1-i)}} \det(L)^{\frac{1}{w+1-i}} .$$

2.2   Strategy for Finding Small Roots of Multivariate Polynomials

In [6, 7, 8], Coppersmith presents rigorous methods based on LLL to find small roots of univariate modular polynomials or of bivariate integer polynomials. The methods can be extended to polynomials in more variables, but only heuristically.

The methods for finding small roots of a polynomial f mainly depend on the shape of its Newton polytope (in others words, of the monomials that appear in f). In [16], Jochemsz and May presents a heuristic strategy that applies to any multivariate polynomial with either modular or integer roots, based on Howgrave-Graham [15] lemma for the univariate case, and the improvements of Coron [10, 11]. We briefly review hereafter their root-finding strategy.

For the sake of illustration, consider without loss of generality a trivariate polynomial $f(x, y, z)$ over the integers. Let (x_0, y_0, z_0) be a (small) root of f, and let (X, Y, Z) be a upper bound of this root; i.e., $|x_0| < X$, $|y_0| < Y$ and $|z_0| < Z$. Define $W = \|f(xX, yY, zZ)\|_\infty$ the maximal coefficient (in absolute value) of $f(xX, yY, zZ)$. A basis B of a lattice L is defined via the so-called *shift polynomials* $x^i y^j z^k f(x, y, z)$ (resp. $x^i y^j z^k$) for $\{i, j, k\}$ determined by a set S (resp. $M \setminus S$) which depends on the monomials of f. The set M then consists of all the monomials that appear in the shift polynomials $x^i y^j z^k f(x, y, z)$. LLL reduction algorithm is then performed on B in order to reduce the lattice L. From a result of [16], provided that

$$X^{s_x} Y^{s_y} Z^{s_z} < W^s \, , \quad \text{where} \quad \begin{cases} s_x = \sum_{x^i y^j z^k \in M \setminus S} i + (m-1) \\ s_y = \sum_{x^i y^j z^k \in M \setminus S} j + (m-1) \\ s_z = \sum_{x^i y^j z^k \in M \setminus S} k + (m-1) \end{cases} \quad \text{and} \quad s = |S| - 1 \, ,$$

the first vectors, say f_0 and f_1, of the reduced basis produced by LLL provide two polynomials with root (x_0, y_0, z_0) over the integers. The common roots of $\{f, f_0, f_1\}$ are revealed under the assumption that two variables can be eliminated from the system $\{f = 0, f_0 = 0, f_1 = 0\}$. This can be done through the evaluation of resultants or of Gröbner bases.

Again, it is worth remembering that the strategy is heuristic. It is assumed that the aforementioned use of resultants produces a non-zero univariate polynomial, for which finding integer roots is easy. So, in our example, f_0 and f_1 need to be algebraically independent. More generally, the following assumption is supposed to hold true for n-variate polynomials, $n \geqslant 3$.

Assumption 1. *The resultant computations for the polynomials f_i yield non-zero polynomials.*

This heuristic assumption has proven to be useful in many attacks (e.g., [2, 4, 10, 11, 12, 16, 17, 24, 25]).

3   Key Recovery from Known MSBs

Most key recovery attacks on RSA cryptosystem use a similar technique. The goal is to derive, from an RSA equation, a multivariate polynomial in some of the unknowns of RSA, like p, q, d or $\phi(N)$.

Let $N = pq$ be an RSA modulus where p and q are two equal-size (balanced) primes. The public exponent is denoted e and the corresponding private exponent is $d = e^{-1} \bmod \phi(N)$. In this section, we assume that the attacker succeeded in getting the most significant bits of $d^* = d + \ell\phi(N)$ for some unknown integer $\ell > 0$. We write

$$d^* = \tilde{d} + d_0$$

where $\tilde{d}$ is a known approximation for d^* and d_0 is the value to be found. The upper bound on d_0 is defined as $d_0 \leqslant N^\delta$. The next theorem states how large δ can be in order to recover d_0 (and thus the entire private key d^*). Note that the knowledge of d^* yields a non-zero multiple of $\phi(N)$ as $ed^* - 1$ and consequently the two secret factors of N [23].

Theorem 1. *With the previous notations, suppose that $e \sim N^\alpha$ and $d^* \sim N^\beta$. Then under Assumption 1 and up to a small error factor ϵ, there exists, for sufficiently large N, a polynomial-time algorithm that computes all of d^*, provided that*

$$\delta \leqslant \begin{cases} \alpha + \beta - 1 - \epsilon & \text{for } 1 < \alpha + \beta < \frac{3}{2} \\ \frac{\alpha+\beta-\sqrt{4(\alpha+\beta)^2-6(\alpha+\beta)}}{3} - \epsilon & \text{for } \frac{3}{2} \leqslant \alpha + \beta < 2 \end{cases}.$$

The rest of this section will be devoted to the proof of Theorem 1. Notice also that it leads to the following result:

Corollary 1. *Using the notation of Theorem 1, recovering a fraction of d^* larger than*

$$\begin{cases} \frac{1-\alpha}{\beta} & \text{when } 1 < \alpha + \beta \leqslant \frac{3}{2} \\ \frac{2\beta-\alpha+2\sqrt{(\alpha+\beta)\left(\alpha+\beta-\frac{3}{2}\right)}}{3\beta} & \text{when } \frac{3}{2} \leqslant \alpha + \beta < 2 \end{cases}.$$

is sufficient to recover the entire private exponent d^* in polynomial time.

A graphical interpretation of this corollary, representing the fraction of d^* required to recover the entire exponent d^* in polynomial time, is depicted in Fig. 1.

Proof (of Corollary 1). This is a immediate consequence of Theorem 1 since the fraction of d^* corresponding to the unknown d_0 is given by $1 - \frac{\delta}{\beta}$.   □

3.1   Preliminaries

Since $ed \equiv 1 \pmod{\phi(N)}$ and $d^* = d + \ell\phi(N)$, we can write $ed^* = 1 + k^*\phi(N)$ for some integer k^*, or equivalently,

$$e\tilde{d} + ed_0 = 1 + (\tilde{k} + k_0)(N - (p + q - 1)) \tag{1}$$

with $\tilde{k} = \left\lfloor \frac{e\tilde{d}-1}{N+1} \right\rfloor$ and $\tilde{k} = k^* - k_0$. Moreover, since p and q are assumed to be balanced, we have $p + q \leqslant 3\sqrt{N}$. Hence, as shown in [2], it follows that

$$|k_0| = |k^* - \tilde{k}| \leqslant \left| \frac{ed^* - 1}{\phi(N)} - \frac{e\tilde{d} - 1}{N + 1} \right| \leqslant \frac{e}{\phi(N)} \left(|d_0| + 3N^{-\frac{1}{2}}\tilde{d} \right).$$

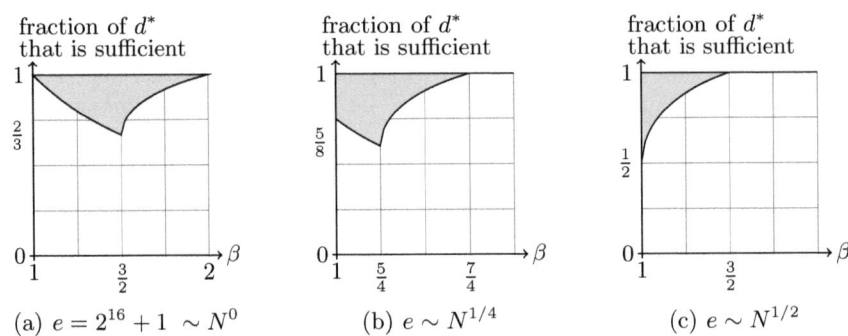

Fig. 1. Graphical representations of the results of Corollary 1

We define δ such that $|d_0| \leqslant N^\delta$. Assuming that $\delta \leqslant \beta - \frac{1}{2}$, the conditions $e \sim N^\alpha$, $\phi(N) \sim N$, $|d_0| \leqslant N^\delta$, $\tilde{d} \sim N^\beta$ immediately yield, up to some small error factor ϵ, the bound

$$|k_0| \leqslant N^{\alpha-1+\max(\delta,-\frac{1}{2}+\beta)} = N^{\alpha+\beta-\frac{3}{2}} \ . \qquad (2)$$

3.2 Trivariate Approach: $\beta \geqslant 3/2 - \alpha$

Equation (1) yields the trivariate polynomial

$$f(x,y,z) = (e\tilde{d} - 1 - \tilde{k}N) + ex - yN + \tilde{k}z + yz \, ,$$

of which $(x_0, y_0, z_0) = (d_0, k_0, p+q-1)$ is a root. Furthermore, up to a small error factor ϵ, we have the upper bounds

$$|d_0| \leqslant X = N^\delta, \quad |k_0| \leqslant Y = N^{\alpha+\beta-\frac{3}{2}}, \quad \text{and} \quad |p+q-1| \leqslant Z = N^{\frac{1}{2}} \ .$$

We now apply the strategy of Jochemsz and May [16]. The goal is to maximize δ with respect to β, when α is a fixed value. Define two integers m and t. As sketched in §2.2, the set S describing the monomials used for the shift polynomials contains the monomials of f^{m-1}, and the set M is defined as the set of monomials of $x^i y^j z^k f(x,y,z)$ with $x^i y^j z^k \in S$. Since Y is much smaller than X and Z for $\alpha + \beta < 3/2 + \delta$ (a posteriori we shall see that it was the good choice to make), we use extra-shifts on y. Therefore, we get

$$x^i y^j z^k \in S \iff \begin{cases} i = 0, \ldots, m-1 \\ j = 0, \ldots, m-1-i+t \\ k = 0, \ldots, m-1-i \end{cases}$$

and

$$x^i y^j z^k \in M \iff \begin{cases} i = 0, \ldots, m \\ j = 0, \ldots, m-i+t \\ k = 0, \ldots, m-i \end{cases} \ .$$

The parameter t has to be optimized with respect to m in order to maximize δ.

From the discussion in §2.2, we know that two polynomials sharing the root (x_0, y_0, z_0) can be computed thanks to LLL algorithm as long as $X^{s_x} Y^{s_y} Z^{s_z} < W^s$ with the notation of §2.2. First notice that, up to a small error factor ϵ, we have $W = N^{\alpha+\beta-\frac{1}{2}}$. Now defining τ such that $t = \tau m$, we obtain

$$
\begin{cases}
s = \left(\frac{1}{3} + \frac{1}{2}\tau\right) m^3 & + o(m^3) \\
s_x = \left(\frac{1}{3} + \frac{1}{2}\tau\right) m^3 & + o(m^3) \\
s_y = \left(\frac{1}{2} + \tau + \frac{1}{2}\tau^2\right) m^3 & + o(m^3) \\
s_z = \left(\frac{1}{2} + \frac{1}{2}\tau\right) m^3 & + o(m^3)
\end{cases}
.
$$

In order to get the asymptotic bound, we let m grow to infinity and all the lower-order terms contribute to some error factor ϵ. The latter equation then becomes $X^{2+3\tau} Y^{3+6\tau+3\tau^2} Z^{3+3\tau} < W^{2+3\tau}$. If we substitute the values for the upper bounds, we get:

$$
\delta(2 + 3\tau) + \left(\alpha + \beta - \tfrac{3}{2}\right)(3 + 6\tau + 3\tau^2) + \tfrac{1}{2}(3 + 3\tau) < \left(\alpha + \beta - \tfrac{1}{2}\right)(2 + 3\tau) .
$$

The optimal value for τ is given by $\frac{1 - \frac{\alpha}{2} - \frac{\beta}{2} - \frac{\delta}{2}}{\alpha + \beta - \frac{3}{2}}$ (valid until $\alpha + \beta + \delta \leqslant 2$) and leads to

$$
\delta < \frac{\alpha + \beta - \sqrt{4(\alpha + \beta)^2 - 6(\alpha + \beta)}}{3} - \epsilon .
$$

3.3   Bivariate Approach: $\beta < 3/2 - \alpha$

Analogously to what was done in the previous section, a lattice reduction leads directly to the bound $\delta < \alpha + \beta - 1 - \epsilon$.[1] However, this latter bound can simply be obtained with a straightforward argument. As $k^* \sim N^{\alpha+\beta-1}$, we can consider the bivariate polynomial

$$
f(x, y) = (e\tilde{d} - 1 - k^*N) + ex + k^*y
$$

modulo k^*. Indeed, when $\delta < \alpha + \beta - 1$ holds, we immediately obtain the value of d_0 over the integers as $d_0 = x_0 \bmod k^* = \frac{1 - e\tilde{d}}{e} \bmod k^*$.

4   Key Recovery from Known LSBs

We now assume that the attacker succeeded to recover the least significant bits (LSBs) of $d^* = d + \ell\phi(N)$. More generally, we write $d^* = d_l + d_0 M$, where d_l is known to the attacker, together with its higher bound $M = N^\mu$, but d_0 is unknown. (In the particular case of known LSBs, M is a power of two.) We prove the following theorem:

---

[1] Due to the shape of the bivariate polynomial (linear in each variable), no extra-shift is necessary.

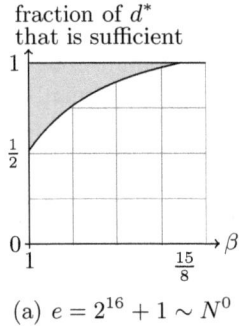
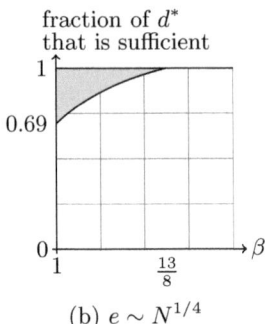

(a) $e = 2^{16} + 1 \sim N^0$ (b) $e \sim N^{1/4}$

Fig. 2. Graphical representation of the results of Corollary 2

Theorem 2. *With the previous notations, suppose that $e \sim N^\alpha$ and $d^* \sim N^\beta$. Then under Assumption 1 and up to a small error factor ϵ, there exists, for sufficiently large N, a polynomial-time algorithm that computes all of d^*, provided that*

$$\mu \geqslant \left(\frac{(6\beta - 5) + 2\sqrt{6\alpha + (6\beta - 5)}}{6} - \epsilon \right) .$$

The proof of this theorem can be seen as an application of the strategy offered in [12]. We omit it due to space limitations.

We then obtain:

Corollary 2. *Using the notation of Theorem 2, recovering a fraction of d^* larger than*

$$\frac{(6\beta - 5) + 2\sqrt{6\alpha + (6\beta - 5)}}{6\beta} .$$

is sufficient to recover the entire private exponent d^* in polynomial time.

Proof (of Corollary 2). This immediately follows from Theorem 2 by noting that the fraction of d^* corresponding to the unknown d_0 is given by $\frac{\mu}{\beta}$.   □

A graphical interpretation of Corollary 2, representing the fraction of d^* required to recover the entire exponent d^* in polynomial time, is depicted in Fig. 2.

5   Practical Experiments

The attacks described in Section 3 and 4 were implemented with the SAGE computer-algebra system [29] using Shoup's NTL [26], and run on a 2.8 GHz Intel Core i5 running Mac OS X 10.7.2. In all the listed experiments, we were able to recover the factorization of N, i.e., in each case, Assumption 1 held. One can notice that our attacks are much better than predicted (when computing the theoretical value with the used values of m and t). This difference between theoretical results and practical ones is studied in [14, 25].

Table 1. Experimental results for the attack on MSBs with a 1000-bit N

(a) $e = 65537 \sim N^0$					(b) $e \sim N^{1/2}$				
β	δ	Γ	Parameters	LLL	β	δ	Γ	Parameters	LLL
1.501	0.39	0.475	$m = 4, t = 3$ dim $= 40$	42 sec	1.001	0.41	0.475	$m = 4, t = 3$ dim $= 40$	57 sec
1.55	0.34	0.331	$m = 3, t = 2$ dim $= 24$	4 sec	1.05	0.29	0.331	$m = 4, t = 3$ dim $= 40$	1 min 45 sec
1.60	0.25	0.267	$m = 2, t = 2$ dim $= 15$	1 sec	1.10	0.23	0.267	$m = 3, t = 3$ dim $= 28$	13 sec
1.65	0.20	0.218	$m = 3, t = 3$ dim $= 28$	20 sec	1.15	0.20	0.218	$m = 4, t = 2$ dim $= 35$	1 min 19 sec
1.70	0.10	0.178	$m = 6, t = 1$ dim $= 56$	27 min	1.20	0.17	0.178	$m = 4, t = 2$ dim $= 35$	1 min 43 sec

5.1 Results for Attack on MSBs

As an illustration, consider an RSA application making use of a 2048-bit modulus N and public exponent e. Further, in order to prevent DPA-type attacks, assume that a 128-bit random multiple ℓ of $\phi(N)$ is added to d, defining the private exponent $d^* = d + \ell\phi(N)$. Thus, $\beta = \frac{2048+128}{2048} = 1.06$.

Consider the following practical settings:

Case 1: $e = 65537$, i.e. $\alpha \sim 0$. From Corollary 1, it follows that it suffices to recover the $1/\beta = 94\%$ of d^* rather than all of it, allowing 128 bits of d^* to remain unknown. However, a practical implementation does not require lattice reduction (see § 3.3) and verifying the latter result is easy.

Case 2: $e \sim N^{1/2}$, i.e. $\alpha \sim 1/2$. Corollary 1 then tells us that it suffices to recover the 71% of d^* rather than all of it, theoretically allowing 640 bits of d^* to remain unknown.

A practical implementation with $\delta = 0.19$ (i.e. $0.19 \times 2048 = 389$ bits of d^* unknown), and parameters $m = 7, t = 1$ (dim $= 72$), allowed us to recover the 389 unknown bits of d^* in 5 hours and 48 minutes.[2]

Since the bounds of the algorithms do not depend of the length of the modulus N, all the following experiments for this attack were performed with a 1000-bit N, and three different values for the public exponent, $e = 2^{16} + 1 = 65537$ and $e \sim N^{1/2}$.

For every β value between 1 and $2 - \alpha$, we looked for the bigger δ that gave us enough small vectors to recover the root (x_0, y_0, z_0). We tried for each δ different values of $m \geqslant 2$ and $t \geqslant 1$. The results are presented in Table 1. In our tests, the bound δ given in the table is reached by d_0, and the Γ-column gives the asymptotic bound which is reached when the lattice dimension goes to infinity.

---

[2] Notice that one can get closer to the theoretical bound by increasing the size of the lattice (at the expense of an increased running time: for $\delta = 0.18$, with parameters $m = 4$, $t = 1$, dim $= 30$, the 368 unknown bits were recovered in 2 minutes).

Table 2. Experimental results for the attack on LSBs with a 1000-bit N

(a) $e = 2^{16} + 1 \sim N^0$

β	μ	Γ	Parameters	LLL
1.01	0.58	0.535	$m = 2, t = 1$ dim $= 16$	1 sec
1.10	0.76	0.700	$m = 2, t = 1$ dim $= 16$	1 sec
1.20	0.96	0.871	$m = 2, t = 1$ dim $= 16$	1 sec
1.30	1.16	1.033	$m = 2, t = 1$ dim $= 16$	1 sec

(b) $e \sim N^{1/4}$

β	μ	Γ	Parameters	LLL
1.01	0.77	0.710	$m = 2, t = 1$ dim $= 16$	1 sec
1.10	0.92	0.854	$m = 4, t = 1$ dim $= 50$	20 sec
1.20	1.08	1.008	$m = 5, t = 1$ dim $= 77$	2 min 1 sec
1.30	1.26	1.158	$m = 4, t = 1$ dim $= 50$	22 sec

5.2 Results for Attack on LSBs

All experiments for this attack were conducted with a 1000-bit N, and two different values for the public exponent, $e = 2^{16} + 1 = 65537$ and $e \sim N^{1/4}$.

For every β value between 1 and $15/8 - \alpha$, we looked for the smaller μ that gave us enough small vectors to recover the root (x_0, y_0, z_0). We tried for each μ different values of $m \geqslant 2$ and $t \geqslant 1$. The results are presented in Table 2.

In our tests, the bound μ given in the table is reached by d_l and the Γ-column gives the asymptotic bound which is reached when the lattice dimension goes to infinity.

6   Conclusion

In this paper we established sufficient conditions to successfully mount partial key exposure attacks on RSA. Unlike previous works, we focused on the practical setting of a private exponent d larger than the modulus N. We derived theoretical bounds that were validated through numerical experiments for various parameter sets. Our results illustrated once more the importance of careful implementation.

Our work raises several open issues. For the interested reader, here some possible venues for further research. Is it possible to derive bounds when $\beta \geqslant 2$? Is it possible to mount a key recovery attack when random key bits of d^* are exposed? This problem naturally finds applications in so-called cold-boot attacks; see [13, 24]. Is it possible to extend the results to CRT implementations for arbitrary values for ℓ and/or e?[3] How does the use of unbalanced primes modify the attack [1]?

References

1. Bleichenbacher, D., May, A.: New Attacks on RSA with Small Secret CRT-Exponents. In: Yung, M., Dodis, Y., Kiayias, A., Malkin, T. (eds.) PKC 2006. LNCS, vol. 3958, pp. 1–13. Springer, Heidelberg (2006)

---

[3] One can apply the same strategy as above to mount a partial key recovery attack on LSBs for a low public-exponent e.

2. Blömer, J., May, A.: New Partial Key Exposure Attacks on RSA. In: Boneh, D. (ed.) CRYPTO 2003. LNCS, vol. 2729, pp. 27–43. Springer, Heidelberg (2003)
3. Boneh, D., Durfee, G.: Cryptanalysis of RSA with private key d less than $N^{0.292}$. IEEE Transactions on Information Theory 46(4), 1339–1349 (2000), extended abstract in Proc. of EUROCRYPT 1998
4. Boneh, D., Durfee, G., Frankel, Y.: An Attack on RSA Given a Small Fraction of the Private Key Bits. In: Ohta, K., Pei, D. (eds.) ASIACRYPT 1998. LNCS, vol. 1514, pp. 25–34. Springer, Heidelberg (1998)
5. Cohen, G.D., Lobstein, A., Naccache, D., Zémor, G.: How to Improve an Exponentiation Black-Box. In: Nyberg, K. (ed.) EUROCRYPT 1998. LNCS, vol. 1403, pp. 211–220. Springer, Heidelberg (1998)
6. Coppersmith, D.: Finding a Small Root of a Bivariate Integer Equation; Factoring with High Bits Known. In: Maurer, U.M. (ed.) EUROCRYPT 1996. LNCS, vol. 1070, pp. 178–189. Springer, Heidelberg (1996)
7. Coppersmith, D.: Finding a Small Root of a Univariate Modular Equation. In: Maurer, U.M. (ed.) EUROCRYPT 1996. LNCS, vol. 1070, pp. 155–165. Springer, Heidelberg (1996)
8. Coppersmith, D.: Small solutions to polynomial equations, and low exponent RSA vulnerabilities. Journal of Cryptology 10(4), 233–260 (1997)
9. Coron, J.S.: Resistance against Differential Power Analysis for Elliptic Curve Cryptosystems. In: Koç, Ç.K., Paar, C. (eds.) CHES 1999. LNCS, vol. 1717, pp. 292–302. Springer, Heidelberg (1999)
10. Coron, J.S.: Finding Small Roots of Bivariate Integer Polynomial Equations Revisited. In: Cachin, C., Camenisch, J.L. (eds.) EUROCRYPT 2004. LNCS, vol. 3027, pp. 492–505. Springer, Heidelberg (2004)
11. Coron, J.S.: Finding Small Roots of Bivariate Integer Polynomial Equations: A Direct Approach. In: Menezes, A. (ed.) CRYPTO 2007. LNCS, vol. 4622, pp. 379–394. Springer, Heidelberg (2007)
12. Ernst, M., Jochemsz, E., May, A., de Weger, B.: Partial Key Exposure Attacks on RSA up to Full Size Exponents. In: Cramer, R. (ed.) EUROCRYPT 2005. LNCS, vol. 3494, pp. 371–386. Springer, Heidelberg (2005)
13. Heninger, N., Shacham, H.: Reconstructing RSA Private Keys from Random Key Bits. In: Halevi, S. (ed.) CRYPTO 2009. LNCS, vol. 5677, pp. 1–17. Springer, Heidelberg (2009)
14. Herrmann, M., May, A.: Maximizing Small Root Bounds by Linearization and Applications to Small Secret Exponent RSA. In: Nguyen, P.Q., Pointcheval, D. (eds.) PKC 2010. LNCS, vol. 6056, pp. 53–69. Springer, Heidelberg (2010)
15. Howgrave-Graham, N.: Finding Small Roots of Univariate Modular Equations Revisited. In: Darnell, M.J. (ed.) Cryptography and Coding 1997. LNCS, vol. 1355, pp. 131–142. Springer, Heidelberg (1997)
16. Jochemsz, E., May, A.: A Strategy for Finding Roots of Multivariate Polynomials with New Applications in Attacking RSA Variants. In: Lai, X., Chen, K. (eds.) ASIACRYPT 2006. LNCS, vol. 4284, pp. 267–282. Springer, Heidelberg (2006)
17. Jochemsz, E., May, A.: A polynomial time attack on RSA with private CRT-exponents smaller than $N^{0.073}$. In: Menezes, A. (ed.) CRYPTO 2007. LNCS, vol. 4622, pp. 395–411. Springer, Heidelberg (2007)
18. Kocher, P., Jaffe, J., Jun, B.: Differential Power Analysis. In: Wiener, M. (ed.) CRYPTO 1999. LNCS, vol. 1666, pp. 388–397. Springer, Heidelberg (1999)
19. Kocher, P., Jaffe, J., Jun, B., Rohatgi, P.: Introduction to differential power analysis. Journal of Cryptographic Engineeering 1(1), 5–27 (2011)

20. Kocher, P.C.: Timing Attacks on Implementations of Diffie-Hellman, RSA, DSS, and Other Systems. In: Koblitz, N. (ed.) CRYPTO 1996. LNCS, vol. 1109, pp. 104–113. Springer, Heidelberg (1996)
21. Lenstra, A.K., Lenstra Jr., H.W., Lovász, L.: Factoring polynomials with rational coefficients. Mathematische Annalen 261(4), 515–534 (1982)
22. May, A.: New RSA Vulnerabilities Using Lattice Reduction Methods. Ph.D. thesis, University of Paderborn (2003)
23. Miller, G.L.: Riemann's hypothesis and tests for primality. Journal of Computer and System Sciences 13(3), 300–317 (1976)
24. Sarkar, S.: Partial Key Exposure: Generalized Framework to Attack RSA. In: Bernstein, D.J., Chatterjee, S. (eds.) INDOCRYPT 2011. LNCS, vol. 7107, pp. 76–92. Springer, Heidelberg (2011)
25. Sarkar, S., Sen Gupta, S., Maitra, S.: Partial Key Exposure Attack on RSA – Improvements for Limited Lattice Dimensions. In: Gong, G., Gupta, K.C. (eds.) INDOCRYPT 2010. LNCS, vol. 6498, pp. 2–16. Springer, Heidelberg (2010)
26. Shoup, V.: Number Theory Library (Version 5.5.2). A library for doing Number Theory (2011), http://www.shoup.net/ntl
27. Simmons, G.J.: The prisoners' problem and the subliminal channel. In: Chaum, D. (ed.) Advances in Cryptology, Proceedings of CRYPTO 1983, pp. 51–67. Plenum Press (1984)
28. Simmons, G.J.: The Subliminal Channel and Digital Signatures. In: Beth, T., Cot, N., Ingemarsson, I. (eds.) EUROCRYPT 1984. LNCS, vol. 209, pp. 364–378. Springer, Heidelberg (1985)
29. Stein, W.A., et al.: Sage Mathematics Software (Version 4.7). The Sage Development Team (2011), http://www.sagemath.org
30. Wiener, M.J.: Cryptanalysis of short RSA secret exponents. IEEE Transactions on Information Theory 36(3), 553–558 (1990)
31. Young, A., Yung, M.: Malicious Cryptography: Exposing Cryptovirology. John Wiley & Sons (2004)

Linear Cryptanalysis of Reduced-Round ICEBERG

Yue Sun and Meiqin Wang

School of Mathematics, Shandong University, Jinan 250100, China
yuesun@mail.sdu.edu.cn, mqwang@sdu.edu.cn

Abstract. ICEBERG is proposed by Standaert *et al.* in FSE 2004 for re-configurable hardware implementations. ICEBERG is a fast involutional SPN block cipher and all its components are involutional and allow very efficient combinations of encryption/decryption. ICEBERG uses 64-bit block size and 128-bit key and the round number is 16. In this paper, we firstly find the best linear approximation of 6-round ICEBERG. We find that 2^{122} of ICEBERG keys are weak for linear cryptanalysis, and the linear deviation can be strengthened more heavily than the linear characteristic by the multi-path effect(Linear Hull). And we discover a 6-round linear hull consisting of 7 linear characteristics with a linear deviation of $2^{-29.99}$. Then we give a linear attack against 7-round ICEBERG for the weak keys.

Keywords: Linear Cryptanalysis, ICEBERG, Linear Hull, Weak Keys.

1 Introduction

RFID systems and sensor networks have been aggressively deployed in a variety of applications, but their further pervasive usage is mainly limited by lots of security and privacy concerns. As RFID tags and sensor networks are low cost with limited resources, the present cryptographic primitives cannot be feasible. So the security primitives suitable for these light-weight environments must be designed. Recently, several light-weight block ciphers have been proposed such as PRESENT [1], mCRYPTON [2], HIGHT [3], SEA [4] and KTANTAN [5] etc. In general, a block cipher based on SP-network structure has the different encryption and decryption process like AES [6], which will increase the hardware costs. Although the block cipher based on the Feistel structure does not have such disadvantage, its slow avalanche effect requires the large round number to guarantee the security. In this way, how to design an involutional block cipher based on SP-network structure has become an important object in the field of light-weight block cipher.

At FSE 2004, Standaert *et al.* proposed a fast involutional block cipher with SP-network structure optimized for reconfigurable hardware implementations, named as ICEBERG [7]. ICEBERG uses 64-bit text blocks and 128-bit keys and the round number is 16. Specially, all components are involutional and allow very efficient combinations of encryption/decryption.

M.D. Ryan, B. Smyth, and G. Wang (Eds.): ISPEC 2012, LNCS 7232, pp. 381–392, 2012.
© Springer-Verlag Berlin Heidelberg 2012

In their paper, they give some security evaluations of ICEBERG. The designers point out that the upper-bound of the differential characteristic for full round ICEBERG is 2^{-160}, and the input-output correlation of the best linear characteristic is smaller than 2^{-64}. These evaluations are very loose, and do not show how many rounds are vulnerable to attack.

In this paper, we will give the concrete linear cryptanalysis for reduced-round ICEBERG. Firstly, we identify the best linear characteristics for 6-round ICE-BERG by analyzing the property of linear layer of ICEBERG, then we present the linear cryptanalysis results on 7-round ICEBERG, but unluckily, the success rate is low. Further more, we give a detailed analysis towards the rate of weak keys in linear cryptanalysis. We can recover 2^{122} key values in the whole key space with 2^{63} plaintext-ciphertext pairs in $2^{90.19}$ 7-round encryptions, the success rate is 26.1%; when using the whole codebook, the success rate can reach 95.7%. We list the results in Table 1.

The paper is organized as follows. Section 2 introduces the ICEBERG algorithm. In Section 3, we discuss the feature of linear transformation of ICEBERG and identify the best 6-round linear approximation. Then Section 4 and Section 5 present both the 7-round linear attack results and the 7-round attack by linear hull under weak key. Section 6 concludes this paper.

Table 1. Results of linear cryptanalysis on 7-round ICEBERG

Type	Time Complexity	Data Complexity	Success rate	ratio of weak keys
LC	$2^{91.19}$	2^{64}	0.6%	1
LC under weak keys	$2^{90.19}$	2^{63}	26.1%	2^{-6}
LC under weak keys	$2^{91.19}$	2^{64}	95.7%	2^{-6}

LC: Linear Cryptanalysis

2   Description of ICEBERG

ICEBERG is a block cipher with SP-network structure. It operates on 64-bit block and uses a 128-bit key. It is an involutional iterative block cipher based on the repetition of 16 identical key-dependent round functions. The round function ρ_K can be expressed as:

$$\rho_K : \mathbb{Z}_2^{64} \rightarrow \mathbb{Z}_2^{64} : \rho_K \equiv \epsilon_K \circ \gamma,$$

where γ is the non-linear layer and ϵ_K is the linear layer.

It is an involutional cipher since its encryption is only different from its decryption in the key schedule. Because the key schedule has little relationship with our analysis, we will not describe it here.

2.1   Non-linear Layer γ

Function γ is composed of non-linear substitution layers $S0$ and $S1$ and bit permutation layer $P8$. Fig. 1 depicts the non-linear layer γ. Each substitution layer consists of 16 identical S-boxes in parallel. The bit permutation layer consists of eight identical bit permutations $P8$. The γ layer can be expressed as:

$$\gamma : \mathbb{Z}_2^{64} \to \mathbb{Z}_2^{64} : \gamma \equiv S0 \circ P8 \circ S1 \circ P8 \circ S0.$$

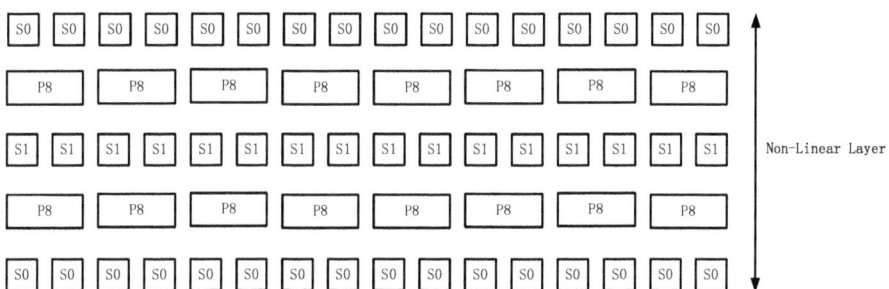

Fig. 1. The Non-Linear Layer γ

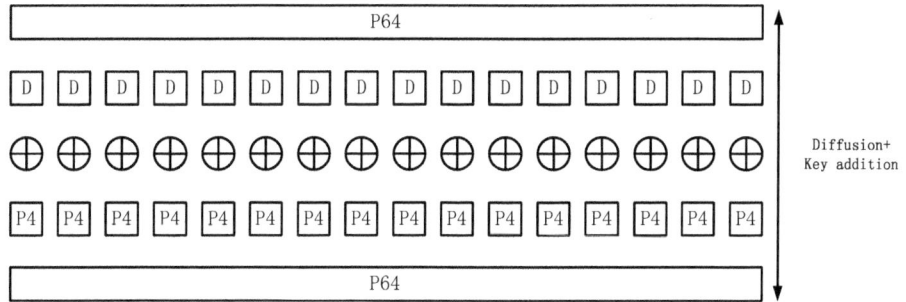

Fig. 2. The Linear Layer ϵ_K

The γ layer can be viewed as one layer consisting of the application of eight identical 8×8 S-boxes listed in Table 2.

2.2   Linear Layer ϵ_K

Fig. 2 depicts the linear layer ϵ_K. The ϵ_K can be described as:

$$\epsilon_K : \mathbb{Z}_2^{64} \to \mathbb{Z}_2^{64} : \epsilon_K \equiv P64 \circ P4 \circ \sigma_K \circ M \circ P64.$$

Table 2. The 8×8 S-box

	00	01	02	03	04	05	06	07	08	09	0a	0b	0c	0d	0e	0f
00	24	c1	38	30	e7	57	df	20	3e	99	1a	34	ca	d6	52	fd
10	40	6c	d3	3d	4a	59	f8	77	fb	61	0a	56	b9	d2	fc	f1
20	07	f5	93	cd	00	b6	62	a7	63	fe	44	bd	5f	92	6b	68
30	03	4e	a2	97	0b	60	83	a3	02	e5	45	67	f4	13	08	8b
40	10	ce	be	b4	2a	3a	96	84	c8	9f	14	c0	c4	6f	31	d9
50	ab	ae	0e	64	7c	da	1b	05	a8	15	a5	90	94	85	71	2c
60	35	19	26	28	53	e2	7f	3b	2f	a9	cc	2e	11	76	ed	4d
70	87	5e	c2	c7	80	b0	6d	17	b2	ff	e4	b7	54	9d	b8	66
80	74	9c	db	36	47	5d	de	70	d5	91	aa	3f	c9	d8	f3	f2
90	5b	89	2d	22	5c	e1	46	33	e6	09	bc	e8	81	7d	e9	49
a0	e0	b1	32	37	ea	5a	f6	27	58	69	8a	50	ba	dd	51	f9
b0	75	a1	78	d0	43	f7	25	7b	7e	1c	ac	d4	9a	2b	42	e3
c0	4b	01	72	d7	4c	fa	eb	73	48	8c	0c	f0	6a	23	41	ec
d0	b3	ef	1d	12	bb	88	0d	c3	8d	4f	55	82	ee	ad	86	06
e0	a0	95	65	bf	7a	39	98	04	9b	9e	a4	c6	cf	6e	dc	d1
f0	cb	1f	8f	8e	3c	21	a6	b5	16	af	c5	18	1e	0f	29	79

Table 3. The $P64$ Permutation

0	1	2	3	4	5	6	7	8	9	10	11	12	13	14	15
0	12	23	25	38	42	53	59	22	9	26	32	1	47	51	61

16	17	18	19	20	21	22	23	24	25	26	27	28	29	30	31
24	37	18	41	55	58	8	2	16	3	10	27	33	46	48	62

32	33	34	35	36	37	38	39	40	41	42	43	44	45	46	47
11	28	60	49	36	17	4	43	50	19	5	39	56	45	29	13

48	49	50	51	52	53	54	55	56	57	58	59	60	61	62	63
30	35	40	14	57	6	54	20	44	52	21	7	34	15	31	63

It consists of the 64-bit permutation layer $P64$, the parallel binary matrix multiplications M, the key addition layer σ_K, the parallel 4-bit permutation layer and the identical 64-bit permutation as in Fig. 2. $P64$ and $P4$ are listed in Table 3 and Table 4, respectively. The matrix multiplication M is based on the parallel application of a simple involutional matrix multiplication. Let $V \in \mathbb{Z}_2^{4 \times 4}$ be a binary involutional matrix (i.e. such that $V^2 = I_n$):

$$V = \begin{bmatrix} 0 & 1 & 1 & 1 \\ 1 & 0 & 1 & 1 \\ 1 & 1 & 0 & 1 \\ 1 & 1 & 1 & 0 \end{bmatrix}.$$

M is then defined as:

$$M : \mathbb{Z}_{2^4}^{16} \to \mathbb{Z}_{2^4}^{16} : x \to y = M(x) \Leftrightarrow y_i = V \cdot x_i \qquad 0 \le i \le 15.$$

Table 4. The $P4$ Permutation

Then the diffusion box D is defined as performing multiplication by V.

The encryption process for R rounds is defined as follows:

$$\sigma_{RK_0^R} \circ \gamma \circ (\bigcirc_{r=1}^{R-1} \rho_{RK_1^r}) \circ \sigma_{RK_1^0}$$

where σ_K is the key addition layer.

3   Linear Cryptanalysis of 6-Round ICEBERG

Linear cryptanalysis(LC) is a known-plaintext or a ciphertext-only attack, introduced by Matsui in 1993 [8]. The principle of linear cryptanalysis is that there is a linear approximation between text bits and key bits in the encryption algorithm, holding with a probability much further away from $1/2$, so it can be a distinguisher between a given cipher and a random permutation. The effectiveness of a linear relation is measured by a parameter called bias, denoted as ε, which is the absolute value of the difference between the parity of the linear relation and $1/2$. The higher the bias, the more attractive the linear relation is, since they demand less plaintext-ciphertext pairs. In this section, we give the best linear approximation of 6-round ICEBERG we found.

3.1   Linear Characteristic of 6-Round ICEBERG

The way to search the best linear characteristic of an iterated SPN block cipher depends on two components. The linear distribution of the active S-box in the non-linear layer determines the bias of the inner round while the linear layer determines the number of active S-boxes. So the higher bias of the active S-box and the fewer active S-boxes in one round, the better the linear approximation is. According to the linear distribution, we can see the bias at most is 2^{-2}, if we do not control the number of active S-boxes carefully, after the linear layer, the number of active S-boxes will be enlarged heavily. Therefore, we will focus on the linear approximation with fewer active S-boxes which is determined by the linear layer of ICEBERG.

Linear Layer $P64$-$DP4$-$P64$

To achieve hardware efficiency, the linear layer of light-weight block cipher is always designed to be a permutation which can be implemented by wire-crossing, sometimes to be involutional. However, permutations make diffusion slow. As we see, 3 rounds for PRESENT are needed to reach full diffusion when a bit-flip occurred in the input influences all output bits while at least 5 rounds for

PUFFIN [9]. It is believed that the fewer rounds required to achieve full diffusion the more resistant the cipher should be. Unlike other light-weight block cipher, besides two same permutations on 64 bit named $P64$ is emplaced at the beginning and end of the linear layer of ICEBERG, there are 16 permutations on 4 bit named $P4$ and 16 diffusion boxes named D in the middle. The diffusion box D, which makes each output bit equal to the exclusive-or among the three input bits, results in only 2 rounds being required to reach full diffusion. The diffusion pattern is depicted in Fig. 3. $P4$ and D can be regarded as a whole, named $DP4$ depicted in Table 5. Now we give the following three properties of the linear layer of ICEBERG in view of linear cryptanalysis.

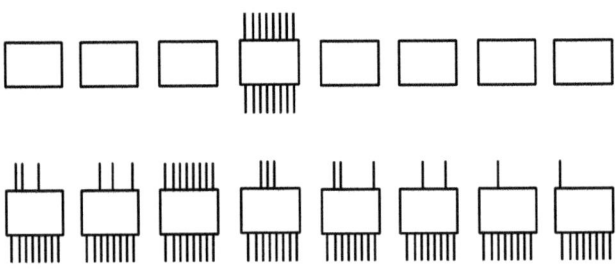

Fig. 3. Diffusion of Difference Activating S5 over 2 Rounds of ICEBERG

Table 5. The $DP4$ Linear-Layer

0	1	2	3	4	5	6	7	8	9	10	11	12	13	14	15
0	13	14	3	7	10	9	4	11	6	5	8	12	1	2	15

P1. According to Table 3, the four input bits of each $DP4$ must come from four different S-boxes; moreover, as $P64$ is involutional, the four output bits must go into four different S-boxes.

P2. Each two bits in each S-box must go into different bytes after $P64$, also in different nibbles of $DP4$.

P3. $DP4$ makes one active bit on one end to three active bits on the other end or two active bits to two active bits.

Because of the above three properties, the number of active S-boxes for two rounds at least is four, and there are three primary patterns ($1 \rightarrow 3$, $2 \rightarrow 2$, $3 \rightarrow 1$) and two auxiliary patterns ($2 \rightarrow 3$, $3 \rightarrow 2$) for the two-round differential characteristic as depicted in Fig. 4. For each pattern, we take the diffusion box $DP4$ as the origin to begin our analysis.

☐ *Pattern*($1 \rightarrow 3$): It implies there should be $m(1 \leqslant m \leqslant 8)$ active $DP4(s)$ with $1 \rightarrow 3$ (1 nonzero input mask bit to 3 nonzero output mask bits), and after passing the bottom $P64$, the $3m$ nonzero output mask bits of $DP4s$

should be into three active S-boxes, each of which has m nonzero input mask bits. Whilst the m nonzero input mask bits should be into the same one active S-box by passing through the top $P64$ in reverse order. To sustain this condition, we need to search m-$DP4$s whose three output mask bits will be located in the same three bytes after $P64$. Meanwhile, deduced by the reversed $P64$, the m input mask bits should be just right located in the same one byte. The pattern is depicted in Fig. 4(a).

☐ *Pattern*$(2 \rightarrow 2)$: It implies there should be $m(1 \leqslant m \leqslant 8)$ active $DP4(s)$ with $2 \rightarrow 2$ (2 nonzero input mask bits to 2 nonzero output mask bits), and after bottom $P64$, the $2m$ nonzero output mask bits of $DP4$s should be into two active S-boxes, each of which has m nonzero input mask bits. While the m nonzero input mask bits should be into two active S-boxes after passing the top $P64$ in reverse order. To satisfy this condition, we need to search m-$DP4$s whose two nonzero output mask bits are located in the same two bytes after $P64$. Meanwhile, deduced by the reversed $P64$, the $2m$ nonzero input mask bits should be just right located in the same two bytes. The pattern is depicted in Fig. 4(b).

☐ *Pattern*$(3 \rightarrow 1)$: Since $DP4(x) = DP4^{-1}(x)$, $P64(x) = P64^{-1}(x)$, *Pattern* $(3 \rightarrow 1)$ is *Pattern*$(1 \rightarrow 3)$ in reverse order. It is depicted in Fig. 4(c).

☐ *Pattern*$(2 \rightarrow 3)$: From the above analysis, we can deduce $2 \leqslant m \leqslant 6$. It is depicted in Fig. 4(d).

☐ *Pattern*$(3 \rightarrow 2)$: It is the reversal of *Pattern*$(2 \rightarrow 3)$, depicted in Fig. 4(e).

Table 6 gives $|\Gamma_i|$ and one example in Γ_i for each pattern. It should be noticed that the pattern is not an intact two-round linear approximation, it begins with the output mask(s) of the active S-box(es) in this round and ends at the input mask(s) of the active S-box(es) in the latter round.

3.2 6-Round Linear Characteristic

Resort to the above five patterns, eight 6-round best linear approximation patterns can be deduced as follows,

- $1 \rightarrow 3 \rightarrow 1 \rightarrow 3 \rightarrow 1 \rightarrow 3$,
- $3 \rightarrow 1 \rightarrow 3 \rightarrow 1 \rightarrow 3 \rightarrow 1$,
- $1 \rightarrow 3 \rightarrow 1 \rightarrow 3 \rightarrow 2 \rightarrow 2$,
- $2 \rightarrow 2 \rightarrow 3 \rightarrow 1 \rightarrow 3 \rightarrow 1$,
- $2 \rightarrow 2 \rightarrow 2 \rightarrow 2 \rightarrow 3 \rightarrow 1$,
- $1 \rightarrow 3 \rightarrow 2 \rightarrow 2 \rightarrow 2 \rightarrow 2$,
- $1 \rightarrow 3 \rightarrow 2 \rightarrow 2 \rightarrow 3 \rightarrow 1$,
- $2 \rightarrow 2 \rightarrow 2 \rightarrow 2 \rightarrow 2 \rightarrow 2$.

Table 6. Γ_i for each pattern

Pattern	i	$\|\Gamma_i\|$	OM	IM	DP4s
$1 \to 3$	1	64	$(0,1_x)$	$(0,1_x),(2,80_x),(3,2_x)$	$(0,1_x,d_x)$
	2	13	$(5,84_x)$	$(5,84_x),(6,28_x),(7,28_x)$	$(1,2_x,e_x),(3,2_x,e_x)$
	3	1	$(5,c4_x)$	$(5,c4_x),(6,29_x),(7,68_x)$	$(1,2_x,e_x),(3,2_x,e_x),(7,2_x,e_x)$
$2 \to 2$	1	96	$(0,1_x),(1,10_x)$	$(0,1_x),(1,10_x)$	$(0,3_x,3_x)$
	2	27	$(0,5_x),(1,11_x)$	$(0,5_x),(1,11_x)$	$(0,3_x,3_x),(5,c_x,c_x)$
	3	12	$(6,a8_x),(7,2c_x)$	$(6,a8_x),(7,2c_x)$	$(1,c_x,c_x),(3,c_x,c_x),(5,3_x,3_x)$
	4	5	$(6,a9_x),(7,6c_x)$	$(6,a9_x),(7,6c_x)$	$(1,c_x,c_x),(3,c_x,c_x),$ $(5,3_x,3_x),(7,c_x,c_x)$
	5	1	$(6,ab_x),(7,7c_x)$	$(6,ab_x),(7,7c_x)$	$(1,c_x,c_x),(3,c_x,c_x),$ $(5,3_x,3_x),(7,c_x,c_x),(8,c_x,c_x)$
$3 \to 1$	1	64	$(0,1_x),(2,80_x),(3,2_x)$	$(0,1_x)$	$(0,d_x,1_x)$
	2	13	$(5,84_x),(6,28_x),(7,28_x)$	$(5,84_x)$	$(1,e_x,2_x),(3,e_x,2_x)$
	3	1	$(5,c4_x),(6,29_x),(7,68_x)$	$(5,c4_x)$	$(1,e_x,2_x),(3,e_x,2_x),(7,e_x,2_x)$
$2 \to 3$	2	218	$(1,12_x),(3,6_x)$	$(0,1_x),(2,c0_x),(4,1_x)$	$(0,a_x,5_x),(2,6_x,9_x)$
	3	119	$(2,c4_x),(3,2_x)$	$(2,c4_x),(3,7_x),(4,21_x)$	$(0,c_x,c_x),(2,1_x,d_x),(4,4_x,7_x)$
	4	51	$(1,1c_x),(3,1c_x)$	$(1,1e_x),(2,c0_x),(3,1e_x)$	$(0,2_x,e_x),(2,4_x,7_x)$ $(6,c_x,c_x),(8,3_x,3_x)$
	5	17	$(1,3c_x),(3,3c_x)$	$(1,3e_x),(2,c0_x),(3,3e_x)$	$(0,2_x,e_x),(2,4_x,7_x)$ $(6,c_x,c_x),(8,3_x,3_x),(11,c_x,c_x)$
	6	3	$(6,eb_x),(7,7c_x)$	$(0,40_x),(6,eb_x),(7,7e_x)$	$(1,c_x,c_x),(3,c_x,c_x),(5,3_x,3_x)$ $(7,c_x,c_x),(8,c_x,c_x),(13,4_x,7_x)$
$3 \to 2$	2	218	$(0,1_x),(2,c0_x),(4,1_x)$	$(1,12_x),(3,6_x)$	$(0,5_x,a_x),(2,9_x,6_x)$
	3	119	$(2,c4_x),(3,7_x),(4,21_x)$	$(2,c4_x),(3,2_x)$	$(0,c_x,c_x),(2,d_x,1_x),(4,7_x,4_x)$
	4	51	$(1,1e_x),(2,c0_x),(3,1e_x)$	$(1,1c_x),(3,1c_x)$	$(0,e_x,2_x),(2,7_x,4_x)$ $(6,c_x,c_x),(8,3_x,3_x)$
	5	17	$(1,3e_x),(2,c0_x),(3,3e_x)$	$(1,3c_x),(3,3c_x)$	$(0,e_x,2_x),(2,7_x,4_x)$ $(6,c_x,c_x),(8,3_x,3_x),(11,c_x,c_x)$
	6	3	$(0,40_x),(6,eb_x),(7,7e_x)$	$(6,eb_x),(7,7c_x)$	$(1,c_x,c_x),(3,c_x,c_x),(5,3_x,3_x)$ $(7,c_x,c_x),(8,c_x,c_x),(13,7_x,4_x)$

OM means the output mask of the active S-box in this round;
IM means the input mask of the active S-box in the next round;
The tuple (a,b) means the input mask or output mask of S_a is b;
The triple (a,b,c) means the input mask on the a-th $DP4$ is b while its output mask is c.

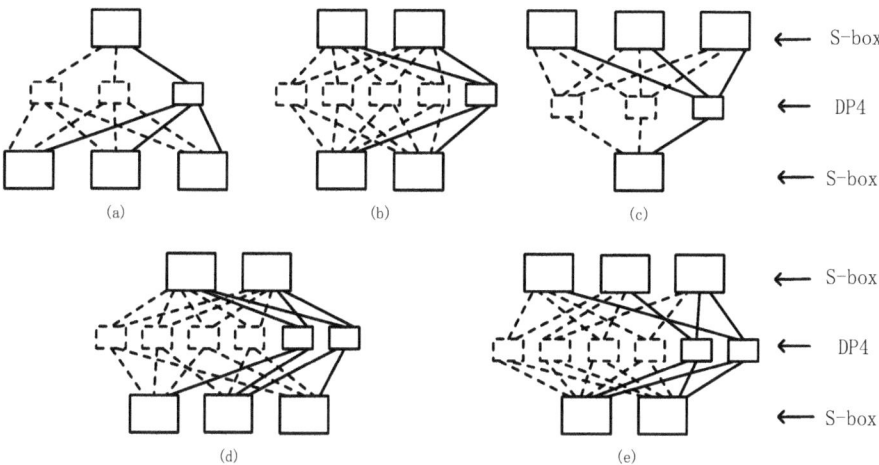

Fig. 4. Patterns for linear layer $P64$-$DP4$-$P64$

By further analysis of these 8 patterns, we obtain the best linear approxima-tion for 6-round of ICEBERG in pattern $1 \rightarrow 3 \rightarrow 1 \rightarrow 3 \rightarrow 1 \rightarrow 3$, with bias $2^{-31.06}$, which is depicted in Table 7. Since ICEBERG is involutional, there is a trail in $3 \rightarrow 1 \rightarrow 3 \rightarrow 1 \rightarrow 3 \rightarrow 1$ with the same highest bias and the opposite order.

4   Linear Attacks against 7-Round ICEBERG

Using the 6-round linear approximation $(00004000 \; 00000000_x)$ $\rightarrow$ $(00070083 \; 00000420_x)$ with probability of $2^{-31.06}$, we present a linear attack to the 7-round ICEBERG. Firstly, we choose 2^{64} plaintext pairs. According to the input mask in round 7 $(00070083 \; 00000420_x)$, we know there are four active S-boxes, which result in 32 subkey bits in round 7 needing to recover. The time complexity of this step is $2^{64+32-2} = 2^{94}$ one-round encryptions, equals to $2^{91.19}$ 7-round encryptions. The success rate is computed with the method in [12] as follows,

$$Ps = \Phi(2\sqrt{N}|p - 1/2| - \Phi^{-1}(1 - 2^{-\alpha-1}))$$
$$= \Phi(2\sqrt{2^{64}} \cdot 2^{-31.06} - \Phi^{-1}(1 - 2^{-32-1}))$$
$$= 0.6\%.$$

The remaining 96 master key bits can be recovered by exhaustive search.

5   Linear Attacks under Weak Keys against 7-Round ICEBERG

Since the bias of the best 6-round linear approximation is quite low, the suc-cess rate of the attack is very small. So in this section, we consider the linear

Table 7. 6-Round Best Linear Approximation We Found

Round		Output Mask	Bias ε_r
		$S_5=40_x$	
R_1	S-box	$S_5=40_x$	$2^{-3.42}$
R_1	LT	$S_5=40_x$, $S_6=1_x$, $S_7=40_x$	
R_2	S-box	$S_5=40_x$, $S_6=1_x$, $S_7=40_x$	$2^{-8.83}$
R_2	LT	$S_5=40_x$	
R_3	S-box	$S_5=40_x$	$2^{-3.42}$
R_3	LT	$S_5=40_x$, $S_6=1_x$, $S_7=40_x$	
R_4	S-box	$S_5=40_x$, $S_6=1_x$, $S_7=40_x$	$2^{-8.83}$
R_4	LT	$S_5=40_x$	
R_5	S-box	$S_5=40_x$	$2^{-3.42}$
R_5	LT	$S_5=40_x$, $S_6=1_x$, $S_7=40_x$	
R_6	S-box	$S_5=40_x$, $S_6=6_x$, $S_7=40_x$	$2^{-8.14}$
R_6	LT	$S_0=20_x$, $S_1=4_x$, $S_4=83_x$, $S_6=7_x$	

hull attack under weak keys. The concept of linear hull was first announced by Nyberg [10], and Keliher et al successfully exploited this method to attack the Q cipher, then M. Q. Wang et al practice it to attack the PRESENT cipher later. A linear hull is a collection of all linear relations with a and b as input and output masks, denoted ALH(a, b). Since it is infeasible to compute the bias of the linear expression aX+bY(X,k)=0 over the secret key, researchers have adopted the average potential over all independent and uniform random sub-keys. However, in 2009, Murphy proved that Nyberg's results can only be used to give a lower bound on the data complexity and will be no use on real linear cryptanalysis [11]. In fact, the linear hull has this kind of positive effect in linear cryptanalysis for some keys instead of the whole key space. So the linear hull can be used to improve the traditional linear cryptanalysis for some weak keys. We continue using the best linear approximation's input and output mask as the linear hull's input and output mask. Table 8 shows the distribution rank of the bias of each linear trail. As we see in the table, the top 7 linear trails are with relative higher biases than others. We detailed their biases in Table 9.

Table 8. Bias Rank of the linear trails

Bias(log_2)	[-32,-31)	[-33,-32)	[-34,-33)	[-35,-34)	[-36,-35)	[-37,-36)	[-38,-37)	[-39,-38)	
Trails	1	0	6	1	2	11	13	16	
Bias(log_2)	[-40,-39)	[-41,-40)	[-42,-41)	[-43,-42)	[-44,-43)	[-45,-44)	[-46,-45)	...	#Total
Trails	36	56	79	120	134	250	295	...	14033

Assuming that the subkeys are independent from each other. So if we define the relation of the key of the 7 linear trails as $K_0, K_1...K_6$, we can see, if $K_0 = 0, K_1 = K_2 = ... = K_6 = 1$ or $K_0 = 1, K_1 = K_2 = ... = K_6 = 0$, the multi-path

Table 9. 6-Round Linear Hull

Input Mask	Output Mask	Bias ε_r
$(00004000\ 00000000_x)$	$(00070083\ 00000420_x)$	$+2^{-31.06}$
$(00004000\ 00000000_x)$	$(00070083\ 00000420_x)$	$-2^{-33.46}$
$(00004000\ 00000000_x)$	$(00070083\ 00000420_x)$	$-2^{-33.46}$
$(00004000\ 00000000_x)$	$(00070083\ 00000420_x)$	$-2^{-33.55}$
$(00004000\ 00000000_x)$	$(00070083\ 00000420_x)$	$-2^{-33.55}$
$(00004000\ 00000000_x)$	$(00070083\ 00000420_x)$	$-2^{-33.55}$
$(00004000\ 00000000_x)$	$(00070083\ 00000420_x)$	$-2^{-33.55}$

effect should be maximum, which is the sum of all the biases of the 7 linear trails, equals to $\pm2^{-22.99}$. So the rate of weak keys in the whole key space should be $2^{-7} + 2^{-7} = 2^{-6}$, which can work for 2^{122} key values. Under the weak keys, we can recover the 32 subkey bits in the last round of 7-round ICEBERG, if we use 2^{63} known plaintexts, the success rate will be

$$Ps = \Phi(2\sqrt{N}|p - 1/2| - \Phi^{-1}(1 - 2^{-\alpha-1}))$$
$$= \Phi(2\sqrt{2^{63}} \cdot 2^{-29.99} - \Phi^{-1}(1 - 2^{-32-1}))$$
$$= 26.1\%.$$

If we use 2^{64} known plaintexts, the success rate is 95.7%. And the time complexity will be $2^{64+32-2} = 2^{94}$ one round encryptions, equals to $2^{91.19}$ 7-round encryptions.

6   Summary

In this paper, we analyze the property of the linear layer of ICEBERG and identify the best 6-round linear approximation with bias of $2^{-31.06}$. Then we present the first linear analysis of 7-round ICEBERG under weak keys. Our attack requires $2^{90.19}$ 7-round encryptions and 2^{63} known plaintexts, the success rate is 26.1%; when using the whole codebook, the success rate can reach 95.7%.

Acknowledgments. We would like to thank anonymous reviewers for their very important comments. This author was supported by National Natural Science Foundation of China (No.61133013, No.61070244 and No.60931160442), Tsinghua University Initiative Scientific Research Program (No.2009THZ01002 and No.20111080970), Outstanding Young Scientists Foundation Grant of Shandong Province (No.BS2009DX030).

References

1. Bogdanov, A.A., Knudsen, L.R., Leander, G., Paar, C., Poschmann, A., Robshaw, M., Seurin, Y., Vikkelsoe, C.: PRESENT: An Ultra-Lightweight Block Cipher. In: Paillier, P., Verbauwhede, I. (eds.) CHES 2007. LNCS, vol. 4727, pp. 450–466. Springer, Heidelberg (2007)

2. Lim, C.H., Korkishko, T.: mCrypton – A Lightweight Block Cipher for Security of Low-Cost RFID Tags and Sensors. In: Song, J.-S., Kwon, T., Yung, M. (eds.) WISA 2005. LNCS, vol. 3786, pp. 243–258. Springer, Heidelberg (2006)
3. Hong, D., Sung, J., Hong, S.H., Lim, J.-I., Lee, S.-J., Koo, B.-S., Lee, C.-H., Chang, D., Lee, J., Jeong, K., Kim, H., Kim, J.-S., Chee, S.: HIGHT: A New Block Cipher Suitable for Low-Resource Device. In: Goubin, L., Matsui, M. (eds.) CHES 2006. LNCS, vol. 4249, pp. 46–59. Springer, Heidelberg (2006)
4. Standaert, F.-X., Piret, G., Gershenfeld, N., Quisquater, J.-J.: SEA: A Scalable Encryption Algorithm for Small Embedded Applications. In: Domingo-Ferrer, J., Posegga, J., Schreckling, D. (eds.) CARDIS 2006. LNCS, vol. 3928, pp. 222–236. Springer, Heidelberg (2006)
5. De Cannière, C., Dunkelman, O., Knežević, M.: KATAN and KTANTAN — A Family of Small and Efficient Hardware-Oriented Block Ciphers. In: Clavier, C., Gaj, K. (eds.) CHES 2009. LNCS, vol. 5747, pp. 272–288. Springer, Heidelberg (2009)
6. Joan, D., Vincent, R.: The Design of Rijndael: AES - The Advanced Encryption Standard. Springer, Heidelberg (2002)
7. Standaert, F.-X., Piret, G., Rouvroy, G., Quisquater, J.-J., Legat, J.-D.: ICE-BERG: An Involutional Cipher Efficient for Block Encryption in Reconfigurable Hardware. In: Roy, B., Meier, W. (eds.) FSE 2004. LNCS, vol. 3017, pp. 279–299. Springer, Heidelberg (2004)
8. Matsui, M.: Linear Cryptanalysis Method for DES Cipher. In: Helleseth, T. (ed.) EUROCRYPT 1993. LNCS, vol. 765, pp. 386–397. Springer, Heidelberg (1994)
9. Huiju, C., Howard, M.H., Cheng, W.: PUFFIN: A Novel Compact Block Cipher Targeted to Embedded Digital Systems. Digital System Design Architectures (DSD 2008), pp. 383–390 (2008)
10. Nyberg, K.: Linear Approximation of Block Ciphers. In: De Santis, A. (ed.) EUROCRYPT 1994. LNCS, vol. 950, pp. 439–444. Springer, Heidelberg (1995)
11. Murphy, S.: The Effectiveness of the Linear Hull Effect. Technical Report, RHUL-MA-2009-19 (2009), http://www.isg.rhul.ac.uk/ssean/LinearHull.pdf
12. Selçuk, A.A., Biçak, A.: On Probability of Success in Linear and Differential Cryptanalysis. In: Cimato, S., Galdi, C., Persiano, G. (eds.) SCN 2002. LNCS, vol. 2576, pp. 174–185. Springer, Heidelberg (2003)

Overcoming Significant Noise: Correlation-Template-Induction Attack*

An Wang[1], Man Chen[2], Zongyue Wang[2], and Yaoling Ding[3]

[1] Institute for Advanced Study, Tsinghua University, Beijing 100084, China
wangan1@tsinghua.edu.cn
[2] Key Laboratory of Cryptologic Technology and Information Security,
Ministry of Education, Shandong University, Jinan 250100, China
[3] Department of Computer Science and Technology, Tsinghua University,
Beijing 100084, China

Abstract. Due to low Signal to Noise Ratio (SNR) in general experimental environments, previous attack methods such as correlation power analysis (CPA) do not always screen out the correct key value. Sometimes the success rate of the attack is so slight that we have to find other ways to make certain of the prosperity. In this paper, rather than adopting the traditional means of singling out a single key value, we suggest a way of setting up a threshold for the attack. Accordingly, we propose a feasible method to filter the inherently enlarging candidate key space, which is called *correlation-template-induction attack*. The method contains three steps: First, we apply a variation of CPA and get a set of candidate key values. Then, we filter the candidate key space with template attack, which is easy to implement and requires encryptions of just a few input data to screen out the correct key. Next, to achieve optimal of our attack, we mix the concept of induction together with our attack. The experimental results given in this article on an AES smart card implementation guarantee the effectiveness of our method.

Keywords: power analysis attack, correlation power analysis, template attack, correlation-template-induction attack.

1 Introduction

Side-channel attacks, especially power analysis attacks, are of great threaten to cryptographic devices, and thus gain attentions from different classes of people ranging from cipher designers to hardware engineers. Power analysis attacks contain different sorts of attacks: differential power analysis (DPA) attacks, template attacks, collision attacks, correlation power analysis (CPA) attacks, etc. DPA was first introduced by Kocher et al. in 1999 [7]. Later, the correlation factor between power consumption samples and a specific power model, such as

---

* Supported by the National Natural Science Foundation of China (Grant No. 61133013 and 60931160442) and the Tsinghua University Initiative Scientific Research Program (No.2009THZ01002, No.20111080970).

M.D. Ryan, B. Smyth, and G. Wang (Eds.): ISPEC 2012, LNCS 7232, pp. 393–404, 2012.

the Hamming weight model, of the handled data was taken into account. The so-called CPA was explicitly proposed in 2004 by Brier et al. [5]. Subsequent studies apply CPA to practical environments [10,11,12], and even to other aspects of side-channel attacks [8]. Collision attack was proposed in 2003 [14] and was further studied in [3,4,8,13]. It detects collisions among the intermediate values of the algorithm to recover the key. Template attack [1,6] consists of a preprocessing template construction stage to give a standard description of the device's characters, and a matching template stage to recover the key. Owing to its high efficiency, template attack is widely used.

Efficient as power analysis attacks are, there are some drawbacks when faced with the real world situations. Whenever an attacker records the power consumptions of the target cryptographic device, noise always exists and somehow makes the consumptions remarkable deviate from their real values. Take the execution of CPA to AES as an example. If the success rate of a single key-byte is 90%, the probability of recovering the entire key value for 16 key-bytes will be only 18.5%! Bogdanov et al. pointed out that one can widen the judgement scale to attacks like CPA to reduce the possibility of miss-judgement of key values [2]. But their method can only be achieved under the condition that no mistake occurs in collision attack stage. The widening of the discriminant criteria's value range, thus enlarging the candidate key space apparently, requires large amounts of searching efforts to get the unique correct key value. So we have to deal with the problem that how to reduce the size of the candidate key space so that we can search less times.

Template attack is easy to implement and is very efficient, while CPA has a uniform key value distribution. Thus, in this paper, we put forward the *correlation-template-induction attack* by combining CPA and template attack, making the most of each method's advantages. In the real world situations where significant noise exists, this is a feasible method, tolerant of certain noise, to filter the candidate key space. On one hand, using our method, one can obtain the correct key with a high probability. On the other hand, the efficiency of the method is greatly improved by analyzing the selection of the parameters we use in the attacks.

2   Preliminary

2.1   Correlation Power Analysis

In CPA [5], the attacker has to first choose an intermediate value of the cryptographic algorithm he is interested in, which is determined by the plaintext and a part of the key value. Second, the attacker records the power consumptions of the intermediate values together with the input data to the device during the many times of the encryption operations. Till now, the attacker has got all he needs to process CPA. Next, he can calculate the correlation factor for each possible key value, and pick up the most significant one to elicit the correct key.

Let $\mathcal{T}$ be the set of power traces T^i that are acquired (**AcquireTraces**) during the execution of a known algorithm using a set $\mathcal{P}$ of known texts P^i

(**ChooseInputs**) for the particular time when the intermediate values are processed. N is the number of known texts. $\mathcal{F}^k$ denotes the set of Hamming weights of the intermediate values computed(**ComputeIntermediates**) by the algorithm with part key value k and with input $\mathcal{P}$. ρ_k is the Pearson correlation coefficient calculated by $\mathcal{T}$, $\mathcal{F}^k$(**Correlation**). That is,

$$\textbf{Correlations}(\mathcal{F}^k, \mathcal{T}) = \frac{N \sum F_j^k T^j - \sum F_j^k \sum T^j}{\sqrt{N \sum (F_j^k)^2 - (\sum F_j^k)^2} \sqrt{N \sum (T^j)^2 - (\sum T^j)^2}}.$$

where F_j^k is the jth element in $\mathcal{F}^k$, $j = 1, 2, \ldots, N$. The formula $\underset{i \in \{0,\ldots,255\}}{\arg \max} \rho_i$ outputs the key value correlated with the biggest correlation coefficient. With an 8-bit micro-controller, CPA can be expressed as follows.

Algorithm 1. Correlation power analysis for recovering a key byte

1: $\mathcal{P} = (P^1, P^2, \ldots, P^N) \leftarrow$ **ChooseInputs**()
2: $\mathcal{T} = (T^1, T^2, \ldots, T^N) \leftarrow$ **AcquireTraces**($\mathcal{P}$)
3: **for** k from 0 to 255
4:    $\mathcal{F}^k \leftarrow$ **ComputeIntermediates**($k, \mathcal{P}$)
5:    $\rho_k \leftarrow$ **Correlation**($\mathcal{F}^k, \mathcal{T}$)
6: **end for**
7: $k = \underset{i \in \{0,\ldots,255\}}{\arg \max} \rho_i$
8: **return** k as a key candidate

When the SNR is high enough, Algorithm 1 works quite well (see Figure 1). In Figure 1, Correlation is the correlation coefficient; Samples mean the sample points of the power consumption trace; Key-byte shows different guesses for the key byte. Obviously, the correlation coefficient is most significant when the key value is 30. However, when the SNR is low, noise often influences the result of attack. Therefore, the output of $\underset{i \in \{0,\ldots,255\}}{\arg \max} \rho_i$ does not always single out the correct key value (especially when the maximum correlation coefficient of some particular model is small). Figure 2 expresses an example where this case occurs (a particular sample point is chosen to illustrate the error). To get the correct key value with a high probability, that $\underset{i \in \{0,\ldots,255\}}{\arg \max} \rho_i$ outputs more key values can be a feasible way.

2.2   Template Attack

Template attack [6,1] can basically be divided into two stages: the template construction stage and the matching template stage. Like CPA, template attack first chooses the special value which depends only on the plaintext and a part of the key. Here, we take Hamming weight of the intermediate value $F = f(k, P)$ as the special value to elaborate template attack (other power consumption models are also utility identically).

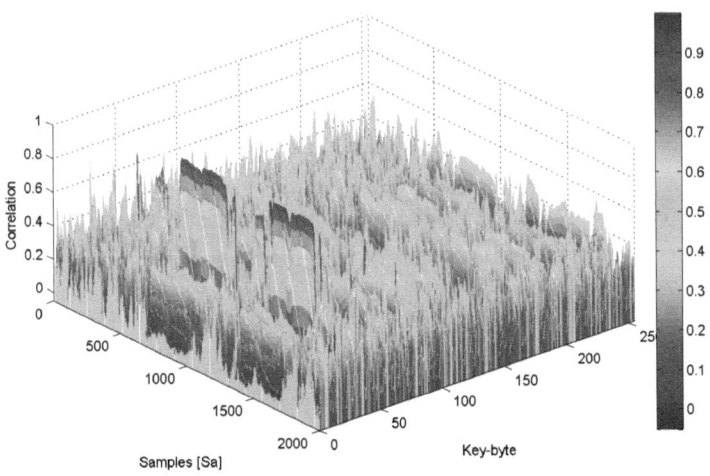

Fig. 1. CPA with high SNR (the correct key is 30)

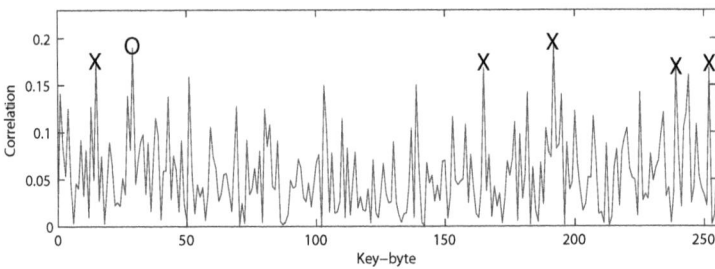

Fig. 2. CPA with low SNR (the circle corresponds to the correct key 30, and the crosses correspond to some wrong keys)

Let **ChooseInputs** and **AcquireTraces** have the same meanings as the definitions in Section 2.1 except that the traces are acquired when processing $f(k, P)$ with different plaintext P. **GetCharacter** exploits the differences between the power consumption traces of diverse Hamming weights and outputs a multivariate normal distribution for each Hamming weight value, i.e. Hamming weight $i \sim N(m_i, C_i)$ [9]. n denotes the dimension of the multivariate normal distribution. **Record** records the multivariate normal distributions for later usage. **ChooseInput** randomly outputs a value for the template attack. **AcquireTrace** obtains the power consumption trace of $f(k, P)$. Given the power consumption trace T and the multivariate normal distribution (m, C), the similarity between them can be judged [6] by

$$\textbf{MatchTemplate}(T, (m, C)) = \frac{\exp(-\frac{1}{2} \cdot (T - m)' \cdot C^{-1} \cdot (T - m))}{\sqrt{(2 \cdot \pi)^n \cdot det(C)}}.$$

The formula $\underset{i\in\{0,...,8\}}{\arg\max}\ Similarity_i$ outputs Hamming weight value whose multivariate normal distribution the trace matches best. **ComputeKey** computes the key candidates which lead to the given Hamming weight. With an 8-bit micro-controller, the template attack can be expressed as follows.

Algorithm 2. Template attack for getting the key-byte candidates

Template construction stage (for a device under control):
1: $\mathcal{P}^i = (P_1^i, P_2^i, \ldots, P_L^i) \leftarrow$ **ChooseInputs**()
2: [Such that $F_j^i = f(k, P_j^i)$ has the Hamming weight i for the key byte k in the device, $i = 0, 1, \ldots, 8,\ j = 1, 2, \ldots, L$]
3: $\mathcal{T}^i = (T_1^i, T_2^i, \ldots, T_L^i) \leftarrow$ **AcquireTraces**($\mathcal{P}$)
4: **for** i from 0 to 8
5:    $(m_i, C_i) \leftarrow$ **GetCharater**($\mathcal{T}^0, \mathcal{T}^1, \ldots, \mathcal{T}^8$)
6: **end for**
7: **Record**($(m_0, C_0), (m_1, C_1), \ldots, (m_8, C_8)$)

Matching template stage (for the target device):
1: $P \leftarrow$ **ChooseInput**()
2: $T \leftarrow$ **AcquireTrace**(P)
3: **for** i from 0 to 8
4:    $Similarity_i = $ **MatchTemplate**($T, (m_i, C_i)$)
5: **end for**
6: $HW = \underset{i\in\{0,...,8\}}{\arg\max}\ Similarity_i$
7: $\mathcal{S} \leftarrow \phi$
8: **for** each F_j^i such that $HW(F_j^i) = HW$ **do**
9:    $k \leftarrow$ **ComputeKey**(F_j^i, P)
10:    $\mathcal{S} \leftarrow \mathcal{S} \bigcup \{k\}$
11: **end for**
12: **return** $\mathcal{S}$ as the key-byte candidates

With high SNR, Algorithm 2 works quite well (see Figure 3(a) where the voltage can be distinguished easily). When confronted with low SNR however, the noise will cause deflection of the power consumption trace, and thus, the attack may single out the wrong key value. Figure 3(b) is an example. However, if one widens the output range of the term $\underset{i\in\{0,...,8\}}{\arg\max}\ Similarity_i$, the probability of erroneously filtering out the correct key value will be significantly reduced. Yet, the candidate key space will be increased apparently.

3   Correlation-Template-Induction Attack

In this section, we describe our strategy of attack. Due to the low Signal to Noise Ratio, previous attack methods don't always obtain the correct key value. Waddle and Wagner stated in their article [15] that an attack suggesting two likely subkeys is more helpful than an attack suggesting none. Following this sort

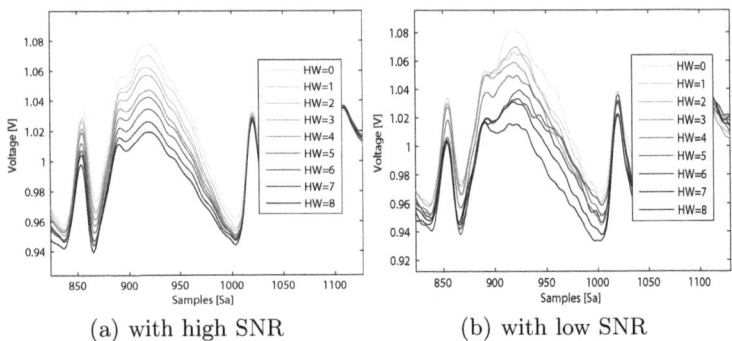

(a) with high SNR   (b) with low SNR

Fig. 3. Different power consumptions based on different Hamming weights

of concept, the attacker can enlarge the set of the candidate key values. However, this enlarging makes the attacker searches more times to get the unique correct key. In this paper, we use a second filtering step to get rid of some candidate keys.

3.1   Our Attack Model

Instead of concentrating on the maximum correlation coefficient, we relax the restriction to several largest correlation coefficients. Since each of the correlation coefficients provides a key value, the enlarged candidate key space of CPA is acquired. The more largest correlation coefficients we use, the higher success rate of recovering key we get. To balance the success rate and the complexity, we set a percentage threshold $\mathfrak{T}_{CPA}$. That means key values related to correlation coefficients bigger than the certain percentage $\mathfrak{T}_{CPA}$ of the maximum one are survived. The symbol $\mathfrak{T}_{CPA}$ is directly bound up with the Signal to Noise Ratio and has to be set to different values accordingly. This variation of CPA is listed in Algorithm 3 and can be called by **ModifiedCPA**. Similarly, we employ a threshold $\mathfrak{T}_{TA}$ in template attack to increase the success rate. We say the key value survived when the key responds to Hamming weight within $\mathfrak{T}_{TA}$ of the Hamming weight calculated from experimental results. $\mathfrak{T}_{TA}$ judges the influence of the noise to **MatchTemplate**. This variation of template attack, **ModifiedTemplateAttack**, is listed below as Algorithm 4.

Algorithm 5 lists our method in which $\#\mathcal{S}$ denotes the size of $\mathcal{S}$. First, we call **ModifiedCPA** to get the key-byte candidates. Then, **ModifiedTemplateAttack** obtains another set of possible key values. The intersection of the two sets dramatically decreases the number of the candidates. Identically, by adopting the easy-implementing **ModifiedTemplateAttack** and intersecting the sets a few times can we get a small candidate key space.

Step 6 to step 11 of Algorithm 5 illustrates the concept of *induction attack*. When $\#\mathcal{S}$ is smaller than some threshold $\mathfrak{T}_{CTI}$, to match the candidate key with the key in the device, every candidate key value in $\mathcal{S}$ is used as an input. That

Algorithm 3. Modified correlation power analysis for getting the key-byte candidates

1: $\mathcal{P} = (P^1, P^2, \ldots, P^N) \leftarrow$ **ChooseInputs**()
2: $\mathcal{T} = (T^1, T^2, \ldots, T^N) \leftarrow$ **AcquireTraces**($\mathcal{P}$)
3: **for** k from 0 to 255
4:    $\mathcal{F}^k \leftarrow$ **ComputeIntermediates**($k, \mathcal{P}$)
5:    $\rho_k \leftarrow$ **Correlation**($\mathcal{F}^k, \mathcal{T}$)
6: **end for**
7: $\rho = max(\rho_i)$, $i = 0, 1, 2, \ldots, 255$
8: $\mathcal{S} \leftarrow \phi$
9: **for** each ρ_k s.t. $\rho_k > \rho \cdot \mathfrak{T}_{CPA}$ **do**
10:   $\mathcal{S} \leftarrow \mathcal{S} \bigcup \{k\}$
11: **end for**
12: **return** $\mathcal{S}$ as the key-byte candidates

Algorithm 4. Modified template attack for getting the key-byte candidates

Template construction stage is the same as algorithm 2.
Matching template stage:
1: $P \leftarrow$ **ChooseInput**()
2: $T \leftarrow$ **AcquireTrace**(P)
3: **for** i from 0 to 8
4:    $Similarity_i =$ **MatchTemplate**($T, (m_i, C_i)$)
5: **end for**
6: $HW = \underset{i \in \{0, \ldots, 8\}}{\arg \max} Similarity_i$
7: $\mathcal{S} \leftarrow \phi$
8: **for** each F^i such that $HW - \mathfrak{T}_{TA} \leq HW(F^i) \leq HW + \mathfrak{T}_{TA}$ **do**
9:    $k \leftarrow$ **ComputeKey**(F^i, P)
10:   $\mathcal{S} \leftarrow \mathcal{S} \bigcup \{k\}$
11: **end for**
12: **return** $\mathcal{S}$ as the key-byte candidates

Algorithm 5. Correlation-template-induction attack for getting the key-byte candidates

1: $\mathcal{S} \leftarrow$ **ModifiedCPA**()
2: **while** $\#\mathcal{S} > \mathfrak{T}_{CTI}$ **do**
3:    $\mathcal{S}' \leftarrow$ **ModifiedTemplateAttack**()
4:    $\mathcal{S} \leftarrow \mathcal{S} \cap \mathcal{S}'$
5: **end while**
6: **for** each $k \in \mathcal{S}$ **do**
7:    $P \leftarrow$ **ChooseInput**($\mathcal{S}$)
8:    $T \leftarrow$ **AcquireTrace**(P)
9:    $D \leftarrow$ **LeastSquares**($T, (m_0, C_0)$)
10:   **if** $D > \mathfrak{T}_{LS}$ **then** $\mathcal{S} \leftarrow \mathcal{S} \setminus \{k\}$
11: **end for**
12: **return** $\mathcal{S}$ as the key-byte candidates

means, instead of choosing randomly, we select from the key-byte candidates
ChooseInput($\mathcal{S}$). $\mathfrak{T}_{CTI}$ is up to the efficiency rate between **ModifiedTemplateAttack** and induction attack. **LeastSquares** is adopted to see wether the
deflection from (m_0, C_0) is 0 or not. If the selected key value equals the correct
key, the intermediate value should be zero and $D \leq \mathfrak{T}_{LS}$ should be met. The
term $D \leq \mathfrak{T}_{LS}$ singles out the most likely key-byte candidates. $\mathfrak{T}_{LS}$ judges the
influence of the noise to **LeastSquares**.

3.2 Efficiency Analysis

CPA requires a number of power consumption traces and it has to calculate the
correlation coefficient for each guessed key value k. Assuming the guessed key is
of m bits, CPA needs to call **Correlation** 2^m times.

One template attack requires just one trace to get rid of some wrong key
values. The template construction stage is a pre-processing phase. Thus, its
runtime can be neglected in template attack. In the matching template stage,
it requires to **MatchTemplate** for each one of the Hamming weight. Suppose
the guessed key is of m bits, leading to $m + 1$ different Hamming weights. That
means one template attack needs to call **MatchTemplate** $m + 1$ times. That's
to say, since **Correlation** and **MatchTemplate** have equivalent efficiency, the
complexity of a single template attack is far less than that of CPA.

We discuss the efficiency of our method in two cases: $\mathfrak{T}_{CTI} = 1$ or $\mathfrak{T}_{CTI} >$
1. Suppose $\mathfrak{T}_{CTI} = 1$, thus skipping induction attack steps. If the total key
value is separated into t bytes and the success rate of one CPA for a single
key-byte value is α, the success rate for the entire key is α^t. In general, this
rate is not that practicable and we have to manipulate CPA a second or more
times to enhance the success ratio. Our method insures $\mathcal{S}$ includes the correct
key value inherently with the extremely high probability. The aforementioned
calculation requirements of CPA and template attack suggest that template
attack is outclassed by CPA in runtime, i.e. $\mathcal{C}_{CPA+nTA} < 2\mathcal{C}_{CPA}$ (Although
template attack is executed for n times, in almost all cases, n is so small that
this inequality always holds). Therefore, we conclude our method outstrips CPA.

Suppose $\mathfrak{T}_{CTI} > 1$. It is obvious that **MatchTemplate** is more complex
while induction attack has to traversal all candidate key values. Therefore, when
the size of candidate key space is less than $\mathfrak{T}_{CTI} > 1$, With just a few possible
key-byte values, $\mathcal{C}_{IA} < \mathcal{C}_{TA}$, and induction attack gets less keys with higher
possibility than template attack does. In fact, the success rate of executing CPA
twice is far less than that of executing correlation-template-induction attack
(Please refer to Table 2). Therefore, we can conclude that correlation-template-
induction attack is superior to CPA both in efficiency and success rate.

Besides, we find there are some ways of accelerating our method in practice.
That is, instead of choosing random inputs to the device in template attack, we
choose some special values related to the candidate key values we have screened
out. Here, attack on the output of the first AES AddRoundKey on an 8-bit micro-
controller, i.e. $HW(P \oplus k)$ is stated as an example. Since the key value in the
micro-controller is an unknown constant, the XOR operation depends entirely on

the input to the device. That means the output of the XOR operation is a random variable. Let $\mathcal{P}^i$ donate the set of plaintext-bytes having Hamming weight i when it traversals from 0 to 255, then Table 1 shows its size $\#\mathcal{P}^i$. We can see that with a random input, one gets Hamming weight 0 with probability $\frac{1}{256}$, gets Hamming weight 1 with probability $\frac{8}{256}$, etc. If we set $\mathfrak{T}_{TA}$ to 1 (By analyzing Figure 3(b), the Hamming weight bias in our device is ± 1 in almost all cases), $\#\mathcal{S}'$ is the size of key-byte candidates we can get from the **ModifiedTemplateAttack**. With only one random input, algorithm 4 can screen out

$$E(\#\mathcal{S}') = \frac{9 \cdot 1 + 37 \cdot 8 + 92 \cdot 28 + \cdots + 9 \cdot 1}{256} \approx 139.65$$

candidate key values on average from 256 key-byte values. However, if one chooses plaintext-byte from the candidate key space directly, assuming s is the number of the key-byte candidates we get from **ModifiedCPA**, with probability $\frac{1}{s}$ he chooses the correct key value, then he can screen out only 9 members from 256 key-byte values for $\mathcal{S}'$. Since those 9 members are not always all key-byte candidates from **ModifiedCPA**, after the intersection step, $\#\mathcal{S}$ can be even smaller than 9.

Table 1. The relation between Hamming weight of intermediate and number of candidate key-bytes when $\mathfrak{T}_{TA} = 0/1$ in **ModifiedTemplateAttack**

HW	0	1	2	3	4	5	6	7	8
$\#\mathcal{P}^i$	1	8	28	56	70	56	28	8	1
$\#\mathcal{S}'$	9	37	92	154	182	154	92	37	9

4   Experimental Results

We employed AT89S52 chip for setting up experiment platform of software. Under the configuration of bandwidth 350 MHz and sampling rate 1 GS/s, an oscilloscope named Agilent 54641A was used for a practical attack. The codes of AES algorithm written by assembly language were programmed into the microcontroller, in which 30 (0x1E) was chosen as a correct key-byte which we tried to attack.

We executed our correlation-template-induction attack to recover the correct key-byte of AES. First, aiming at Hamming weight of the S-box's output corresponding to the key-byte, modified CPA aforementioned was executed, and 256 correlation coefficients were acquired. The threshold $\mathfrak{T}_{CPA}$ was set to 50%, and 42 key-bytes survived. Subsequently, we employed modified template attack for getting Hamming weight of S-box's input. The threshold $\mathfrak{T}_{TA}$ was set to 1, and 154 key-bytes survived. Figure 4 shows the result of modified CPA. Particularly, we rearranged the horizontal axis by Hamming weight of the corresponding intermediate which was focused on by template attack. In Figure 4, the lateral shadow covers 42 survived key-byte values from modified CPA, and the longitudinal shadow covers 154 survived key-byte values from modified template attack. Thus, the 26 key-byte values in the overlapped shadow survived.

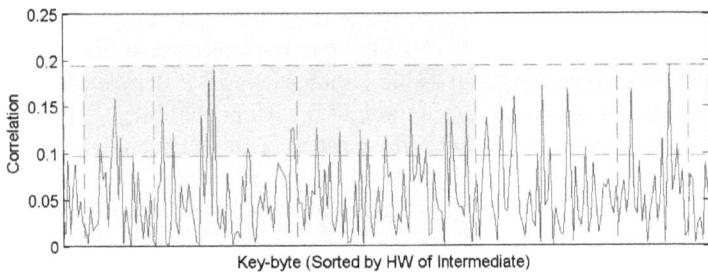

Fig. 4. The correlation coefficients correspond to 256 cases of key-byte. The 26 key-bytes in the overlapped shadow survived after the first modified template attack.

Afterwards, we executed 3 modified template attacks which reduced the size of the survived key-byte candidates space to 14, 8, 3 respectively. The results are described in Figure 5(a,b,c). Because the threshold $\mathfrak{T}_{CTI}$ was set to 5 in our experiment, step 6-11 of Algorithm 5 were triggered, in which the three survived key-byte values were chosen as the plaintext bytes for the induction attack. In induction attack, the acquired traces were compared with the predetermined template, which is described in Figure 5(d). Obviously, the trace corresponding to key-byte 30 is close to the template of Hamming weight 0. Therefore, this key was recovered correctly.

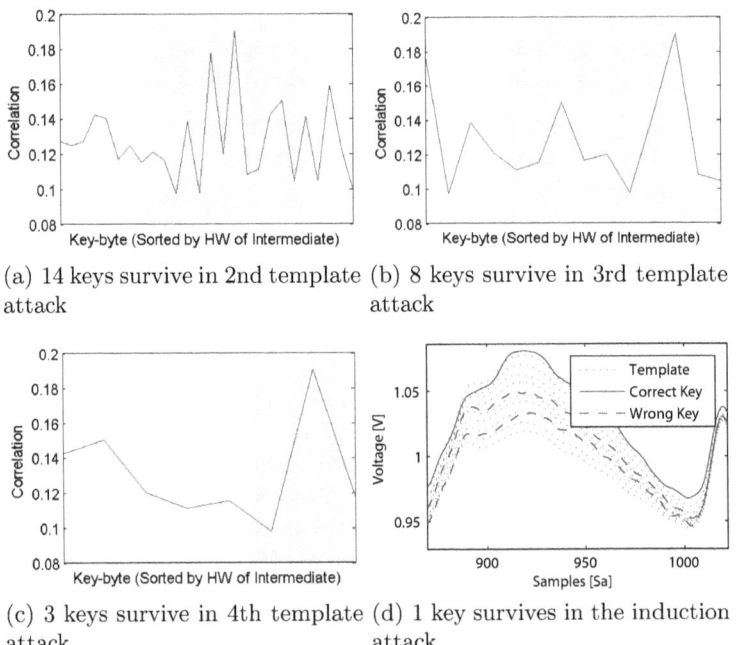

(a) 14 keys survive in 2nd template attack

(b) 8 keys survive in 3rd template attack

(c) 3 keys survive in 4th template attack

(d) 1 key survives in the induction attack

Fig. 5. Results of three template attacks and one induction attack

Table 2. Comparison of complexity and success rate between four methods

	CPA[5]	CPA+CPA[5]	CPA+TA (modified)	C-T-I attack
Precomputation	0	0	$9\mathcal{C}_{cons}$	$9\mathcal{C}_{cons}$
Traces required	$100n$	$200n$	$106n$	$107n$
Key recovery stage	$256\mathcal{C}_{corr}$	$512\mathcal{C}_{corr}$	$256\mathcal{C}_{corr} + 54\mathcal{C}_{match}$	$256\mathcal{C}_{corr} + 39\mathcal{C}_{match}$
Success rate (byte)	90%	99%	99.30%	99.40%
Success rate (all)	18.53%	85.15%	89.37%	90.82%

Table 2 shows the complexity and success rate between CPA, CPA twice, and two our methods (skipping and not skipping induction attack). Every trace for computation of key recovery is from the average of n traces under low SNR environment ($n = 10000$ in our experiment). The symbols $\mathcal{C}_{corr}, \mathcal{C}_{cons}$, and $\mathcal{C}_{match}$ stand for the complexity of computing a correlation coefficient, constructing a template, and matching a template respectively. Under the same environments, it's obvious that the complexity of our methods is much higher than the traditional methods. Meanwhile, based on the accuracy of our device and the chosen parameters, we estimate that the success rate of CPA, modified CPA, modified template attack, induction attack are 90%, 99.9%, 99.9%, 99.9% respectively in our experiment environment. So we have the success rate of attacks aiming at a single key-byte and all 16 key-bytes. As is shown, the success rate of our method is higher than the traditional methods.

5   Conclusion

Power analysis techniques are of great concern because a very large number of vulnerable products are deployed. The attacks proposed before are easy to manipulate, but sometimes they don't succeed in obtaining the correct key value as the result of the influence of the significant noise. In this article, we have presented a technique to enhance the attacks by enlarging the candidate key space. We also find some way to optimize our means. The validity of our method is certified by the experimental results presented in Section 4.

As a matter of fact, the method in our article is not the optimal scheme. More side-channel techniques mix together can achieve higher success rate with higher efficiency. We are looking forward for more perfect proposals.

References

1. Agrawal, D., Rao, J.R., Rohatgi, P.: Multi-channel Attacks. In: Walter, C.D., Koç, Ç.K., Paar, C. (eds.) CHES 2003. LNCS, vol. 2779, pp. 2–16. Springer, Heidelberg (2003)
2. Bogdanov, A., Kizhvatov, I.: Beyond the Limits of DPA: Combined Side-Channel Collision Attacks. Cryptology ePrint Achieve, Report 2010/590, to appear in IEEE Transactions on Computers (2010), http://eprint.iacr.org/

3. Bogdanov, A.: Improved Side-channel Collision Attacks on AES. In: Adams, C., Miri, A., Wiener, M. (eds.) SAC 2007. LNCS, vol. 4876, pp. 84–95. Springer, Heidelberg (2007)
4. Bogdanov, A.: Multiple-Differential Side-Channel Collision Attacks on AES. In: Oswald, E., Rohatgi, P. (eds.) CHES 2008. LNCS, vol. 5154, pp. 30–44. Springer, Heidelberg (2008)
5. Brier, E., Clavier, C., Olivier, F.: Correlation Power Analysis with a Leakage Model. In: Joye, M., Quisquater, J.-J. (eds.) CHES 2004. LNCS, vol. 3156, pp. 16–29. Springer, Heidelberg (2004)
6. Chair, S., Rao, J.R., Rohatgi, P.: Template Attacks. In: Kaliski Jr., B.S., Koç, Ç.K., Paar, C. (eds.) CHES 2002. LNCS, vol. 2523, pp. 13–28. Springer, Heidelberg (2003)
7. Kocher, P., Jaffe, J., Jun, B.: Differential Power Analysis. In: Wiener, M. (ed.) CRYPTO 1999. LNCS, vol. 1666, pp. 388–397. Springer, Heidelberg (1999)
8. Moradi, A., Mischke, O., Eisenbarth, T.: Correlation-enhanced Power Analysis Collision Attack. In: Mangard, S., Standaert, F.-X. (eds.) CHES 2010. LNCS, vol. 6225, pp. 125–139. Springer, Heidelberg (2010)
9. Mangard, S., Oswald, E., Popp, T.: Power Analysis Attacks: Revealing the Secrets of Smart Cards. Springer, Heidelberg (2007)
10. Oswald, E., Mangard, S., Herbst, C., Tillich, S.: Practical Second-Order DPA Attacks for Masked Smart Card Implementations of Block Ciphers. In: Pointcheval, D. (ed.) CT-RSA 2006. LNCS, vol. 3860, pp. 192–207. Springer, Heidelberg (2006)
11. Oswald, E., Parr, C.: Breaking Mifare DESFire MF3ICD40: Power Analysis and Templates in the Real World. In: Preneel, B., Takagi, T. (eds.) CHES 2011. LNCS, vol. 6917, pp. 207–222. Springer, Heidelberg (2011)
12. Plos, T.: Susceptibility of UHF RFID Tags to Electromagnetic Analysis. In: Malkin, T. (ed.) CT-RSA 2008. LNCS, vol. 4964, pp. 288–300. Springer, Heidelberg (2008)
13. Schramm, K., Leander, G., Felke, P., Parr, C.: A Collision-Attack on AES Combining Side Channel- and Differential- Attack. In: Joye, M., Quisquater, J.-J. (eds.) CHES 2004. LNCS, vol. 3156, pp. 163-175. Springer, Heidelberg (2004)
14. Schramm, K., Wollinger, T.J., Paar, C.: A New Class of Collision Attacks and Its Application to DES. In: Johansson, T. (ed.) FSE 2003. LNCS, vol. 2887, pp. 206–222. Springer, Heidelberg (2003)
15. Waddle, J., Wagner, D.: Towards Efficient Second-Order Power Analysis. In: Joye, M., Quisquater, J.-J. (eds.) CHES 2004. LNCS, vol. 3156, pp. 1–15. Springer, Heidelberg (2004)

Author Index

GPSR Compliance

*The European Union's (EU) General Product Safety Regulation (GPSR)
is a set of rules that requires consumer products to be safe and our
obligations to ensure this.*

*If you have any concerns about our products, you can contact us on
ProductSafety@springernature.com*

In case Publisher is established outside the EU, the EU authorized
representative is:

Springer Nature Customer Service Center GmbH
Europaplatz 3
69115 Heidelberg, Germany

Batch number: 09473985

Printed by Printforce, the Netherlands

Lecture Notes in Computer Science

The LNCS series reports state-of-the-art results in computer science research, development, and education, at a high level and in both printed and electronic form. Enjoying tight cooperation with the R&D community, with numerous individuals, as well as with prestigious organizations and societies, LNCS has grown into the most comprehensive computer science research forum available.

The scope of LNCS, including its subseries LNAI and LNBI, spans the whole range of computer science and information technology including interdisciplinary topics in a variety of application fields. The type of material published traditionally includes

- proceedings (published in time for the respective conference)
- post-proceedings (consisting of thoroughly revised final full papers)
- research monographs (which may be based on outstanding PhD work, research projects, technical reports, etc.)

More recently, several color-cover sublines have been added featuring, beyond a collection of papers, various added-value components; these sublines include

- tutorials (textbook-like monographs or collections of lectures given at advanced courses)
- state-of-the-art surveys (offering complete and mediated coverage of a topic)
- hot topics (introducing emergent topics to the broader community)

In parallel to the printed book, each new volume is published electronically in LNCS Online.

Detailed information on LNCS can be found at
www.springer.com/lncs

Proposals for publication should be sent to

LNCS Editorial, Tiergartenstr. 17, 69121 Heidelberg, Germany

E-mail: lncs@springer.com

ISSN 0302-9743

ISBN 978-3-642-29100-5

Lecture Notes in Computer Science

LNCS   LNAI   LNBI